GENDER-RELATED
DIFFERENCES

GENDER-RELATED DIFFERENCES

ORIGINS AND OUTCOMES

KATHARINE BLICK HOYENGA
Western Illinois University

KERMIT T. HOYENGA
Western Illinois University

ALLYN AND BACON
Boston   London   Toronto   Sydney   Tokyo   Singapore

Editor-in-Chief, Social Sciences: Susan Badger
Senior Editorial Assistant: Dana Hayes
Production Administrator: Annette Joseph
Production Coordinator: Susan Freese
Editorial-Production Service: TKM Productions
Manufacturing Buyer: Louise Richardson
Cover Administrator: Linda K. Dickinson
Cover Designer: Suzanne Harbison

Copyright © 1993 by Allyn and Bacon
A Division of Simon & Schuster, Inc.
160 Gould Street
Needham Heights, Massachusetts 02194

Library of Congress Cataloging-in-Publication Data
Hoyenga, Katharine Blick.
   Gender-related differences : origins and outcomes / Katharine
Blick Hoyenga, Kermit T. Hoyenga.
      p.   cm.
   Includes bibliographical references and index.
   ISBN 0-205-14084-X
   1. Sex differences (Psychology).   2. Sex differences.   I. Hoyenga,
Kermit T.   II. Title.
BF692.2.H686   1993   92-33898
155.3′3 — dc20   CIP

Printed in the United States of America
10 9 8 7 6 5 4 3 2   98 97 96 95 94

"Objectivity" is not meant here to stand for "disinterested contemplation" (which is a rank absurdity) but for an ability to have one's pros and cons within one's command and to use them or not, as one chooses.
    —Friedrich Wilhelm Nietzsche, *The Genealogy of Morals*
    (1956, p. 255)

Contents

PREFACE   xiii

UNIT ONE
THE STUDY OF GENDER-RELATED DIFFERENCES   1

CHAPTER 1   EPISTEMOLOGY OF GENDER KNOWLEDGE   5

Overview of This Book   6

Concepts and Realities   6
Definitions of Gender   6   Assumptions and Realities   9

Pathological Gender Assumptions   11
*"If It's Good for the Goose . . ."   11   "If It's Feminine, It's Inferior"   12
Sex Differences Are Always Small   12   If It Exists, It Must Be Due to Culture
and Environment   12   If It's Biological, It Must Be Immutable   13   Which
Contributes Most: Nature or Nurture?   14   Sex Roles Are Entirely Cultural/
Experiential   16   If It Depends on Culture or a Situation, It Cannot Be Biological
(Or If It's Biological, It Must Be Cross-Culturally Universal)   16   If We Differ
from One Another, It Cannot Be Biological   16   If It's Biological, It Must Be
Proximal   17   If It's Biological, It Must Be Present at Birth (Or If It's Present
at Birth, It Must Be Biological)   17   Biological Data Require Higher Standards of
Evidence   18   The Assumption of Biological Determinism   18*

Paradigms of Sex Differences   19
*Explanations and Theories   19   Epigenetic Development: A Model for Sex
Differences   20*

Summary   22
Endnotes   22

CHAPTER 2   MEASURING ROLES AND DIFFERENCES   24

Measuring Gender-Related Differences   24
*Predictions and Methodology   25   Types of Variables   27   The Statistics of
Gender-Related Differences   32   Meta-Analysis   36   The Concept of
Covariance   37   Sources of Bias in Measuring Gender-Related Differences   38*

Measuring Sex Roles   41
*The History of Sex-Role Scales   41   Scales That Measure Sex Roles   43
Validity of Scales   45*

Summary   49
Endnotes   50

CHAPTER 3   THE EVOLUTION OF SEX   51

Introduction   51

Evolution, Selection Pressures, and Genes   52
  Genes versus Traits   52   Evolution and Genes   59   Genetic Variability   64

The Advantages of Sexual Reproduction   69
  The Benefits of Asexual Reproduction: The Costs of Sex   69   Sexual Reproduction and Variability   70

Summary   74
  Endnotes   75

CHAPTER 4   THE EVOLUTION OF SEX DIFFERENCES   76

Introduction   76

Natural Selection, Sex, and Reproductive Roles   77
  Sex Differences in Reproductive Roles   77   Sex Ratios: Parental Investments and Reproductive Roles   79   Social Traits   80

Sexual Selection   83
  Two Types of Sexual Selection   83   Sexual Selection and Sexual Dimorphism   84 The Genetics of Female Choice   86   Mating Systems   87

Evolutionary Characteristics of Sexually Dimorphic Species   89
  High Predation   89   Large Sex Differences in Reproductive Roles   89 Social Living   89   High Intersexual Competition for Limited Resources   90 Low Sex Ratios among Mating and among Older Adults   90   Sex Differences in Variability of Reproductive Success   90

Facts and Speculations about Humans   91
  What Were Our Ancestors Like?   91   K versus r Selection Strategies   91

Summary   92
  Endnotes   93

UNIT TWO
BIOLOGICAL COVARIATES   95

CHAPTER 5   THE GENETICS OF GENDER   97

Introduction   97

Sexually Dimorphic Evolution: Sex Chromosomes and Hormones   98
  Sex-Linked Genes   98   Sex-Limited Genes   99   Evolution of Sex Linkage and Sex Limitation   99

Gender Differences in Gene Activity   100
  Recombination Frequency   100   Genomic, or Parental, Imprinting   102 X-Inactivation   103

Sex-Determining Genes   105
  Y-Linked Genes 105   Sex Hormone Genes 107

Exploring Sex Linkage   108
  *Family History Studies 108   Genetic Probes 110   Sex Chromosome
  Abnormalities 111   Limitations of Sex Linkage Research 116*

Sex Chromosome Maps   117
  Y Linkage   117   X Linkage 119

Summary   123
  Endnotes 123

CHAPTER 6 HOW DO HORMONES AFFECT OUR BRAINS?   124

Introduction   124

Basic Ideas about Hormones   125
  *Three Continua of Hormone Effects 125   Effects on Organs Other than the
  Brain   127   Techniques of Study 128*

How Can Sex Hormones Affect Your Brain Cells?   130
  *Overview of Brain Studies 130   Genomic versus Nongenomic Membrane
  Function 133   Outcomes of Functions for Neurons 137*

Principles of Hormone Effects   140
  *The Principles 140   The Active Hormone for Masculinization and
  Defeminization 140   Variability across Species 141   Variability within a
  Species 146   Environmental Modifiers 148   Timing Effects 149   Nonlinear
  Effects 150*

Summary   151
  Endnotes 152

CHAPTER 7 SEX DIFFERENCES IN PERINATAL HORMONES   153

Introduction   154

Basic Terms and Concepts of Perinatal Hormone Effects   154
  *Effects of Hormones on Development 154   Basic Developmental Processes 154
  The Sex Hormones of Fetal Differentiation 156   Perinatal Hormones Affect
  Behavior 158*

Sex Differences in Perinatal Hormone Levels   160
  Perinatal Hormone Levels 160   Perinatal Levels of Brain Receptors and Enzymes 160

Sex Differences in the Brain   161
  SDN-POA versus SNB 161   Other Sexually Dimorphic Brain Areas 163

Human Perinatal Hormone Syndromes 167
  *Variations in Androgen Levels 168   Exogenous Hormones 169   Normal Variations
  in Perinatal Hormone Levels 170*

Summary   174
  Endnotes 174

CHAPTER 8   SEX DIFFERENCES IN POSTPUBERTAL HORMONES   176

Introduction   176

Postpubertal Sex Hormones: Control and Effects   177
Puberty 177   Gonadotropic Hormones and the Gonads 177   Nongonadal Sources of Sex Hormones 178   Hormone Levels 178   Hormone Receptors and Enzyme Levels in the Adult Brain 179   Examples of Postpubertal Hormone Effects on the Structure and Function of the Brain 180

Hormone Cycles   181
Circadian Cycles 182   Estrous Cycles 183   Menstrual Cycles 184   The Premenstrual Syndrome (The Late Luteal Phase Dysphoric Disorder) 191   Monthly Hormone Cycles in Males 195   Annual Cycles 196

Special Periods of Life   196
Pregnancy 197   Age and Menopause 198   Exogenous Hormones 201

Summary   202
Endnotes 203

**UNIT THREE
ENVIRONMENTAL COVARIATES   205**

**CHAPTER 9   LEARNING AND DEVELOPMENT:
CONCEPTS AND THEORIES   207**

Introduction   208

Learning Processes   208
Operational Definitions of Three Learning Paradigms 209   Cognitive Explanations 212 Evolution of Learning 213

Theories of How Gender-Related Differences Developed   216
All Theories Are Now Cognitive 216   Freud and Psychoanalytic Theory 216 Kohlberg and Cognitive-Developmental Theory 218   Bandura's Social-Cognitive Theory 219   Evolutionary Concepts of Parental Care 220

Basic Developmental Processes   223
Processes that Change with Development 224   Processes Occurring Throughout Development 229   Huston's Concepts of Sex Typing 232   Predictability and Stability 232

Summary   235
Endnotes 236

**CHAPTER 10   CULTURAL INFLUENCES ON GENDER-RELATED
DIFFERENCES   237**

Introduction   237

Concepts and Tensions in Current Anthropology   238
Historical 238   Current: Humanistic versus Scientific Paradigms 239

Evolution of Social Behavior and Culture   240
  *Wrangham's Theory of Primate Social Structures 241   Hunting and Kin Groups 243
  Evolution of Culture among Humans 247*
Culture and Child Socialization   250
  Types of Parental Care 250   Sexually Dimorphic Developmental Environments 253
Cultural Variability among Adults   255
  *Jobs and Tasks 255   Traits 256   Status of Women 259   Possible Reasons for
  Gender-Related Role Assignments and Evaluations 262*
Summary   263
  Endnotes 264

CHAPTER 11 STEREOTYPES AND SEX TYPING   265

Introduction   265
Gender Categories   266
  *Categorization Processes 266   Content of Gender Categories 269   Maintenance
  and Change 274   Individual Differences in Stereotyping 276*
When Stereotypes Become Prejudices   277
  *Definitions and Processes 278   Changes Over Time? 280   Some Examples of
  the Effects of Prejudice 282*
The Development of Stereotypes   286
  *Processes of Acquisition 286   Stereotypes in Mass Media 288   Children's
  Stereotypes 290*
Summary   295
  Endnotes 295

CHAPTER 12 GENDERED ENVIRONMENTS   297

Introduction   297
Home Environment   298
  *Basic Background Information 298   Types of Parenting 299   Parental
  Behaviors: Objective Data 301   Parents of Sex-Atypical Children 302   Parents
  as Models: Sexual Division of Child-Rearing Labors 303   Parents as Models:
  Sexual Division of Household Labor 305   Gendered Toys 307*
School Environment   308
  *Observational Studies of Teachers' Behaviors 308   Peer Interactions 313
  Peers versus Teachers 317*
Dimorphic Effects   317
  *Competition 318   Task Preferences and Peer versus Adult Orientation 320
  Social Comparison Processes 320*
Work Environment   322
  *Income Differentials 322   Job Segregation 324   Why Are Jobs
  Segregated? 325*

Summary   332
  Endnotes 332

UNIT FOUR
SEX AND STATUS   335

CHAPTER 13   PROSOCIAL VERSUS EGOISTIC DOMINANCE:
MURDER VERSUS DEPRESSION?   337

Introduction   338

The Concept of Personality   338
  Measuring Personality Traits 338   Meta-Analytic Studies 341   Prosocial versus
  Egoistic Dominance 346

Homicides   351
  Gender-Related Differences in Homicides 351   Developmental Covariates 356
  Biological Covariates 357

Depression   360
  Sex Differences 360   Sex Differences in Stress 362   Biological Covariates 367

Summary   368
  Endnotes 370

CHAPTER 14   DEVELOPMENTAL RATE: SEXUAL MOTIVES AND
SPATIAL VISUALIZATION   371

Introduction   371

Background   372
  Sex Differences in Task Performances 372   Developmental Rate Covariates 374
  Evolutionary Theories 375

Sex and Mating   378
  Human Mating Preferences 378   Sex Differences in Sexual Motives 382
  Hormones and Sexual Activity 386   Sexual Preferences in Humans 387

Spatial Tasks   389
  Sex Differences 389   The Structure of Spatial Performances 391
  Developmental and Situational Covariates 393   Biological Covariates 396

Summary   399
  Endnotes 400

REFERENCES   401

INDEX   469

Gender-Related Differences: Origins and Outcomes examines the origins of gender differences from as many perspectives as possible, believing that all provide useful information. The book is feminist as defined by Pollis (1988): It contains "a core set of assumptions regarding the [desirability of] the elimination of women's secondary status in society" (p. 87). Thus, the most desirable outcome is the elimination of sexual inequities.

PERSONAL EPISTEMOLOGIES AND SCIENTIFIC SCHEMA

This book explores the principles and concepts relevant to gender-related differences. The term **gender-related differences** is used because one male differs from another and one female from another as much as the mythical average female differs from the average male. The basic principles are discussed: how genes, sex hormones, developmental history, and current cultural and interpersonal environments can all be origins of the final outcome of sex differences.

The way that any person, scientist or reader, conceptualizes a given set of gender-related differences, measured in a specific group of human or nonhuman organisms, depends on her personal epistemology, or knowledge schema. Our epistemology uses the framework of evolutionary theory. This approach is unacceptable to many social scientists (Barlow, 1991; also see Chapter 1), and we think that the reasons for the opposition are personally and politically valid (most human endeavors, including science, involve politics). We also think that these reasons are a reaction to the *misuses* of evolutionary theory. In fact, we strongly believe that any use of evolutionary theory to justify social exclusion or social stratification is a misuse of that theory and thus should be vigorously opposed.

In this regard, presentation of data from studies done with nonhuman animals is absolutely necessary. Only data from nonhumans can provide the necessary context for evolutionary ideas. The fact that most organisms with sexual reproduction also have gender-related differences in appearances and behaviors allows students to view human sex differences in a different light. Also, for ethical reasons, only research done with nonhumans can use the most powerful experimental designs (active manipulation of variables and random assignment of subjects to groups) to explore the influences of biological and developmental variables. Thus, the research on nonhumans provides the information needed to interpret intelligently the less well controlled data coming from human research.

In view of the need to understand all the processes that may be able to affect sex differences, we present ideas, concepts, and data from as many points of view as possible, including molecular genetics, hormone physiology, neural function, biomedical research, child development, personality theory and research, cross-cultural research, sociology, and cultural and physical anthropology. No specific background is required; all basic terms and concepts are defined and described for the reader. However, the reader is expected to be an upper-division undergraduate or graduate student to have enough background to provide the appropriate context for learning this material.

In attempting to ensure that the knowledge of other fields is presented fairly, we literally immersed ourselves in each field before writing about how it approaches gender issues. We also tried to read many different opinions of people in the same field to get some feel for the diversity and controversy. When no resolution seemed possible — and this was often the case — we tried to describe the differing viewpoints as accurately as possible.

Our view of these knowledge fields is a hierarchical one, similar to that of Colleen Clements (1985, 1989), a medical ethicist. She describes knowledge fields by using the simile of a spring whose coils expand as you move up a hierarchy. At the lowest level (in this book, at least) is molecular genetics; cultural systems of groups of people are found at the highest level.[1] Research can be done at each level, independently of every other level. However, more understanding is created when the links between levels are examined; Clements says that finding cross-level linkages is one of the few ways we can verify our scientific ideas and concepts.

Although we have an evolutionary schema and we see that as providing ways of exploring linkages, we also think that the knowledge of each discipline is valuable in and of itself. Our focus as psychologists is on the person, believing that the individual is more than just a combination (however complex) of all the different social groups into which he can be categorized (by himself or by some scientist). Thus, we are ultimately concerned with the individual level of the hierarchy. An individual actively chooses group relationships, either by choosing with which groups to identify or by choosing personal actions within some group of which that person is a part, by choice or not (e.g., family and gender groups). The individual actively affects others' behaviors, just as those others affect his behavior.

ORGANIZATION

The book is organized into four units of interrelated chapters. Each unit, except the last, has four chapters. The first unit describes the epistemology and science of gender research and gender-related knowledge. This includes one chapter that describes how sex evolved and one that describes how sex differences evolved. Unit One is required for all reading plans.

The other units and chapters are somewhat more independent of each other and could be used separately. Unit Two describes the biological covariates of gender-related differences. Within Unit Two, Chapter 5 describes how gender affects genetic activities, and Chapters 6 through 8 describe the hormonal covariates of gender-related differences. Unit Three looks at the ways in which environments can create gender-related differences. Chapter 9 describes developmental processes, Chapter 10 describes the effects of culture, Chapter 11 describes stereotypes, and Chapter 12 looks at how the environments of males and females systematically differ from each other, from birth to death. Unit Four has only two chapters. Certain gender-related differences were selected to examine in greater detail to serve as examples of how principles and data from both Units Two and Three can be combined to look at the origins and outcomes of factors connected to gender-related differences.

Each chapter begins with a brief outline, a quotation, and an "incident" description that will hopefully intrigue readers as well as introduce them to some of the major topics of that chapter. The incidents are sometimes drawn from research, sometimes from newspapers. For example, Chapter 1 begins with a very brief questionnaire as its incident. After the incident, each chapter has from one to three paragraphs describing that chapter's goals and themes, including how the quote and the incident are related to those goals and themes. An introduction to the chapter then follows, describing its topics and organization. The introduction to Chapter 1, however, describes the organization of the entire book.

DOCUMENTATION

The extensive documentation in this book reflects our belief that we — scientists and students — can understand something only if it is placed in context. For example, knowing that all our chromosomes, not just our sex chromosomes, carry gender labels (parent of origin) means nothing without some sort of context. We also had to use multiple primary references when we could find no usable reviews in an area. Many areas either lacked reviews or else the reviews contained only hotly disputed conclusions or erroneous data. We emphasized meta-analytic reviews wherever possible, as providing a somewhat more objective overview of an area. Other types of reviews were used only if we independently read and verified the descriptions of the key studies. If we found the review to be in error, we cited the individual studies themselves and not the review.

If a valid review was lacking, we looked for consensus. If almost all studies of a given relationship seemed to produce similar results, we simply described one or two of the best or most recent as examples. Such agreement was rare, however. In most instances, different studies provided disparate results, which then prompted us to use evolutionary schema to select those that would be discussed. In this case, we tried to indicate the lack of agreement, as well. Only if results could be replicated — hopefully several times by different teams of researchers — was a controversial area discussed at all. The replication is indicated by including multiple citations for a given statement. These multiple citations are a signal not only of some discrepancy but also of the fact that whatever relationship is being described can be reliably found in the research and so needs to be taken seriously. We also included multiple citations whenever we found cross-cultural research on a given relationship as a useful antidote for cultural myopia.

Readers will find that some atypical formats in source citations have been adopted in this text. In some cases, we cited all sources that documented the topic sentence of a given paragraph right after that sentence. If necessary, we then used individual authors' names to identify their work throughout the paragraph. Where a very long list of references was needed to document a point, the list appears as an endnote. (Other endnotes contain relevant but not essential material.) Because of the controversial nature of much of this book's material, multiple references to document a point are necessary. It is our belief that student readers should concentrate not on who did what but on the fact that several different groups of people were able to find similar results, which is, in fact, the purpose of the multiple citations. Finally, we also made extensive use of tables to present details of information and the associated documentation; most of these tables can be found in the accompanying Instructor's Manual.

We have also employed a somewhat unique method of citing references at the end of the book. The pages on which each source is cited are indicated in boldface type at the end of the entry. We have done the same in our other books and have found it useful in our own reading to be able to look up discussions of specific research results.

The documentation in this text benefits students in several ways. The readers have access to primary source material either in the text itself or in the associated Instructor's Manual and can thus easily pursue their interests in that area, perhaps culminating in an independent paper or project. Students can also see that careful and extensive documentation is a necessary part of scientific argument, just as much as logical, careful, persuasive reasoning is a part of the literary or humanistic approach to understanding the world.

STYLE

Because of linguistic awkwardness, but with great regret, unless discussing effects and processes limited to one gender, any nonhuman animal is referred to as *it*. For humans, we usually used plural pronouns, but in places where pronouns were very common and could not easily be pluralized, we alternated genders from paragraph to paragraph.

As the text documents (see Chapter 2), the gender of the researcher is not infrequently relevant to the direction of the results or to the size of the gender-related difference. Because of this, in areas in which researchers' genders are probably relevant, their genders were indicated in the text by the use of appropriate pronouns. We hope that this will also serve to remind readers that gender of subject is not the only relevant gender-linked variable. Gender of researcher and, presumably, gender of reader affect attitudes and hence behavioral, memory, and interpretive biases.

Two other stylistic conventions should be noted. First, the word *real* is often used with quotation marks around it to remind the reader that what is "real" can vary from situation to situation and from person to person. Second, abbreviations are commonly used throughout the text but are explained at the first occurrence within each chapter.

ACKNOWLEDGMENTS

In closing, we would like to acknowledge the following individuals who reviewed our manuscript at various stages: David Buss, University of Michigan; Jacqueline Eccles, University of Michigan; Claire Etaugh, Bradley University; Kathryn Hood, Pennsylvania State University; Janice M. Juraska, University of Illinois; Diane Ruble, New York University; and Nancy Russo, Arizona State University.

ENDNOTE

1. *Higher* and *lower* in this context do not reflect value judgments or any kind of moral or scientific evaluation. Calling a level *higher* means only that it involves interactions among systems, each of which at a *lower* level is another interacting collection of even lower subsystems. Cells are collections of organelles, which are themselves collections of molecules; organs are collections of cells; individual organisms are collections of organs; social systems are collections of individuals; and so on. The levels are interconnected, so a change to a system at any level affects systems at all other levels.

UNIT ONE

THE STUDY OF GENDER-RELATED DIFFERENCES

This unit provides the background and context for interpreting gender-related differences. **Gender-related differences** refer to any characteristicistics that occur in different frequencies, likelihoods, or degrees in one gender when compared to the other. These differences usually occur only in a few *specific* situations. The term also refers to differences in the *same* characteristics as they appear within each gender. In fact, gender-related differences are often larger when measured within each gender than when each gender is separately measured and then compared to the other. Men and women usually differ more from other people of the same gender than the average woman differs from the average man. Since the definition of **gender-related traits** is situation specific, there can be no "transcendent" sex differences. This means that no difference between the sexes transcends situational characteristics, appearing regardless of the setting, the measurement technique being used, or the past histories of the people being measured.

The four chapters in Unit One provide the background information necessary for understanding the material of the other units. The unit includes a discussion of how gender-related knowledge is constructed and a description of how gender and gender-related differences originated in our evolutionary history. This is consistent with the book's focus on how gender knowledge is created and how research concerned with describing and documenting the role of each type of origin (hormones, culture) is to be evaluated.

The first two chapters of Unit One describe the knowledge structure of gender-related differences research and theory. Chapter 1 looks at the epistemology of gender research, and Chapter 2 looks at the measurement of gender-related differences and sex roles. Thus, Chapter 1 covers myths and biases, and Chapter 2 examines questions of research design and interpretation.

The next two chapters apply evolutionary theory to gender. It is a mistake to view evolutionary theory as a theory of psychology (or a theory of culture) (Barkow, 1991). However, as Barkow also pointed out, any theory of psychology (or culture) that could not have evolved is also mistaken. By analogy, any psychological theory of memory that posits nerve cells doing things that no nerve cell has ever been observed to do would have to be mistaken. In other words, a psychological theory can be of value (see Chapter 2) in predicting and explaining behavior even if it says absolutely nothing about evolution. However, that theory is unlikely to be correct if it attempts to explain human behavior by hypothesizing certain **mechanisms** (motives, perceptions, cognitive structures) that could not be reasonably seen as having been selected for by past evolutionary pressures.

Since evolutionary theory is not, in itself, a theory of culture or learning or hormone effects, special theories are needed to describe those mechanisms. These special theories are therefore theories about either **proximate mechanisms** (see Chapter 1) or else about **processes** that can produce sex differences. These topics are covered in Units Two and Three. Nevertheless, the mechanisms and processes must be consistent with the evolutionary theory presented in this unit.

Evolutionary theory is increasingly being used to inform and guide psychological research and theory. Although others would disagree (e.g., Charlesworth, 1986a), Ghiselin (1986) said that "psychology, like many other fields, is now in the midst of a Darwinian renaissance" (p. 21). The theory has been applied to personality (Buss, 1984a); human developmental research (Ghiselin, 1986; Charlesworth, 1986a); human sexuality (Buss, 1985, 1986, 1987a, 1988, 1989b; Symons, 1979); impression management and self-esteem (Barkow, 1991); and sex differences (Daly & Wilson, 1983). Furthermore, consistent with evolutionary ideas, human motivational and personality traits have been found to have important genetic as well as environmental/learning components (see Chapters 9 and 14).

> One of the major features of the evolutionary theory is its colligative power, the power to pull and bind together a vast array of diverse phenomena into a plausible account of their origins, interrelationships, and functions. This colligative power can perhaps best be depicted as a network of many empirical facts and concepts . . . that help us organize our present knowledge and stimulate the search for new knowledge. . . . As for predicting the future of evolutionary theory . . . , my guess is that . . . it will be used to seek leads to understanding present functions of behavior, to identify the determinants of behavior during ontogeny, and to establish the correlates and economics of individual reproductive success. (Charlesworth, 1986b, pp. 20, 30)

Evolutionary theory is as much a theory of environmental as of genetic influences. "The organism takes an active role in its interactions with the environment. . . . Selection of behavioral innovations in new environments would bring new [evolutionary] selection pressure into play" (Ghiselin, 1986, p. 13). As you will see in Chapter 3, evolutionary selection pressures are always specific to a given environment. The relevant environment includes: number and types of peers; amount and availability of food supplies; type and availability of potential mates; types of developmental environments, including types of mothering; and so on. The genes are being selected for or against by the environment: A gene that is of "good" quality in one kind of environment might be of "poor" quality in another environment. For example, there are genetic predispositions to obesity in humans as well as non-humans. One explanation of why these genes are so relatively common in today's humans is that those genes once conferred upon their bearers an increased ability to survive during times of famine (Hoyenga & Hoyenga, 1984). So the same genes that were "good" in times of famine are now "bad" in times of plenteous food supplies, producing a tendency toward obesity and obesity-related diseases.

Finally, the authors do not see the use of evolutionary theory as being incompatible with feminist goals. In fact, the authors view evolutionary theory as saying little about the *desirability* or moral value of current social conditions. In this case, evolutionary theory per se is not in opposition to certain feminists' visions of what would be a more desirable world. (In fact, the authors often agree with many of them.) The authors also do not see evolutionary theory as saying that change, if deemed desirable, is impossible. After all, evolution gave all of us brains that are open to experiences (see Chapters 9 and 10) and therefore to changes induced by exposure to different socialization practices and social expectations. If we change our gender stereotypes, gender-related differences should also change. Evolution is a theory about how we came to be what we are; it is not a theory of who we ought to be.

CHAPTER 1

EPISTEMOLOGY OF GENDER KNOWLEDGE

OVERVIEW OF THIS BOOK
CONCEPTS AND REALITIES
PATHOLOGICAL GENDER ASSUMPTIONS
PARADIGMS OF SEX DIFFERENCES
SUMMARY

It is astonishing what havoc is wrought in psychology by admitting at the outset apparently innocent suppositions that nevertheless contain a flaw.
—William James (1890, p. 224)

Please answer the following questions:

1. *Are you a male or a female?*
2. *Are you very masculine or very feminine?*
3. *What about you makes you feel masculine?*
4. *What about you makes you feel feminine?*

Your answers to these questions indicate your gender identity, your gender-role identity, and your ideas about gender stereotypes. Why you may have answered the questions the way you did is the core focus of this book. Perhaps you answered the third and fourth questions with facts about your appearance, demeanor, and style of dress. Maybe you included some personality characteristics, hobbies, interests, or abilities that you think of as particularly masculine or feminine. But you probably answered the first question without even thinking about it. Can you imagine what it would actually be like to experience some difficulty answering that question?

Although people with **testicular feminization** or **androgen insensitivity** have the chromosomes, internal body organs, and hormones of a male, from the outside they look completely female (see Chapter 7). Because of this, they are usually reared as and regard themselves as being females. Since they are infertile, they often come to clinics for diagnosis and treatment of that problem. Restak (1979) described the quandary faced by any physician who attempts to treat their infertility: "To all outward appearances they [people with testicular feminization] are perfectly normal women. And therein lies the problem. They're not women at all, but men. . . . The diagnosis of testicular feminization can be counted upon to set off an emotional powder keg. What is at stake is no less than the patient's sexual identity. In a sense, she is not a *she* at all but a *he*" (p. 88, emphasis added). Do you think the physician is correct in calling that person a *he* instead of a *she?* Why or why not?

5

OVERVIEW OF THIS BOOK

Although this book is devoted to gender and gender-related differences, the emphasis is not on a list of differences. Instead, it examines and evaluates the *nature* of their possible origins. The text describes the various processes that can create gender-related differences, how the processes work, and how their effects can be evaluated and documented. Both feminist and traditional research are incorporated by using a hierarchical model of knowledge fields that is structured by evolutionary theory. The whole body of research must be integrated in order to understand why we differ from one another and why our similarities are even more important than our differences. Because of the variability within as well as between the genders, nothing in this text contains any justification — social or biological — for sexual prejudice. Prejudice should always be viewed as an invalid outcome.

Unit One introduces the major concepts and techniques that are part of the gender literature. The second and third units describe, respectively, the biolological and environmental processes that can create gender-related differences. **Biological** means *some physiologically measurable structure or process occurring inside the organism's skin,* whereas **environmental** means *some person or people or series of events occurring outside the organism's skin.* Making this distinction is a useful fiction for purposes of organization, but the distinction has no basis in reality since the two processes are in continuous interaction.[1] In Units Two and Three, the emphasis is on origins and possible outcomes. How can biological and environmental events create sex differences — through what processes and mechanisms? How can we investigate their roles? What are some of the implications of their operations? Unit Four describes certain selected gender-related differences, specifically relating them to the concepts, processes, and possibilities described in Units Two and Three. The discussion illus-trates how biology and environment are combined in continuous interactions to produce certain outcomes — certain selected types of gender-related differences.

CONCEPTS AND REALITIES

The quandary of gender labeling described at the beginning of this chapter can occur only if defining gender according to chromosomes is deemed to be more "real" than any other way of defining gender. In fact, no such emphasis on any biological factor is ever warranted. The reasons for this will become clear.

Definitions of Gender

Gender researchers sometimes use the word sex to refer to biological aspects of masculinity/ femininity and use the word gender to refer to psychological aspects (Atkinson, 1987; Deaux, 1985; Prince, 1985). However, the use of two separate terms for gender and sex establishes an arbitrary and undesirable dichotomy. We are the products of both our biologies and our past and present environments, simultaneously and inseparably; we are bodies as well as minds at one and the same time. Some problems created by using this dichotomy are described later in this chapter. In view of this, the terms **gender-related differences, sex differences, sexually dimorphic,** and **gender differences** are used interchangeably and without any implication as to what the causes might be. In all cases, the terms mean gender-related differences. For example, **sex hormones** refer to hormones that have different levels in males than in females and for which levels also differ from one man to another and from one woman to another.

Definitions of terms describing specific identities and roles. The terms feminine and masculine are used to identify categories of gender-related differences and gender-related characteristics. **Feminine** refers to any trait that is either experimentally seen more often in, to a greater extent in, or (very rarely) only in females as opposed to males. When combined with "stereotypical," it refers to any trait that is culturally believed to be associated more often with females than with males in some particular culture or subculture.

To be **feminized** means to have some feminine trait increased or made more frequent or more salient. In most cultures, breast development and being nurturant to babies are both viewed as being feminine. Anyone, woman or man, could be feminized by becoming more nurturant. A woman would also be described as being feminized after breast augmentation surgery. If some feminine trait is inhibited or lost, the organism is said to be **defeminized.**

The definitions of **masculine** are parallel to those given for feminine: a gender-related difference occurring more often in males, or a culturally defined masculine trait or role. Being **masculinized** means having some masculine characteristics emphasized or increased. A man or woman might be masculinized by successful assertiveness training or by developing muscles through weight lifting. Conversely, being **demasculinized** means losing some masculine characteristics. Males would be demasculinized by losing some chest hair after being surgically castrated for treatment of prostate cancer, and both sexes would be demasculinized by becoming less assertive or aggressive.

Biological gender definitions. **Biological gender** refers to designations based on measuring any one of the typical biological differences found between males and females. Almost every biological aspect of gender is a continuum rather than a typology (a pair of opposite types). In other words, people do not come in just two, discretely different biological "flavors." People in the middle of one of the biological continua include those, for example, who have levels of masculine sex hormones that are below those typical of males but above

those typical of females. Other people are born with external sex organs that are too small to be normal penises but too large to be normal clitorises.

As presented in Table 1.1, biological gender definitions include hormones, chromosomes, gonads, and anatomy. **Chromosomal gender** is based on the sex chromosomes. **Gonadal gender** refers to the internal sex glands, or **gonads.** These two types of gonads secrete different amounts of the various sex hormones, which lead to the organism's **hormonal gender.** Males have relatively more of the masculine sex hormones, or **androgens,** in their blood, and females have relatively more of the feminine sex hormones, the **estrogens** and **progestins** (see Chapters 7 and 8).

Hormonal gender normally leads to the internal and external anatomical aspects of gender. The sex hormones present before birth cause the appropriate masculine or feminine organs to develop. The male fetus's testes secrete the androgens that cause the masculine internal organs and genitals to develop and the feminine organs to atrophy or disappear. The absence of masculine sex hormones in the normal female fetus allows feminine internal organs and genitals to develop. The feminine hormones found in both male and female fetuses come largely from their mothers' ovaries or from the placenta.

In a normal fetus, all these biological definitions of gender are congruent, all being male/masculine or all being female/feminine. But there are various types of gender abnormalities in which these definitions are incongruent. For example, in people with the testicular feminization syndrome described in the introduction to this chapter, the chromosomes, gonads, and hormones are masculine, but the external sex organs are feminine, and there are no internal sexual organs.

Psychological gender definitions. **Psychological gender** refers to measuring how people interact with other people or with things in their

TABLE 1.1 *Biological and Psychological Definitions of* Gender

	Biological[a] Gender Definitions	
	Masculine[b]	*Feminine[c]*
Chromosomal gender (mammals)	XY	XX
Gonadal gender	Testes	Ovaries
Hormonal gender	Relatively more androgens (prenatally, neonatally, and postpubertally)	Relatively more estrogens and progestins (during the period between puberty and menopause)
Gender of internal sexual organs	Vsas deferens, ejaculatory duct, etc.	Uterus, fallopian tubes, etc.
Gender of external	Penis and scrotal sac	Clitoris, labia, and outer part of vagina
	Psychological[d] Gender Definitions	
	Masculine	*Feminine*
Gender of rearing	"Male" on birth announce-ment and birth certificate	"Female" on birth announcement and birth certificate
Gender identity	"I am a male"	"I am a female"
Gender-role identity	"I am masculine"	"I am feminine"
Gender stereotypes:	Beliefs about masculine and feminine traits and jobs and interests	Beliefs about masculine and feminine traits and jobs and interests

[a]Some physiologically measurable structure or process occurring inside the organism's skin
[b]A trait that occurs more often in males than in females
[c]A trait that occurs more often in females than in males
[d]Based on the organism's interactions with some person or people or series of events occurring outside the organism's skin

environments, including paper-and-pencil tests (social and nonsocial environments). Any reliably measured behavioral difference between the sexes could become a psychological gender definition.

In normal newborns, the gender of external organs is inspected and used to specify the psychological definitions. *Female* or *male* is placed on the birth certificate and on the birth announcements. This designation determines whether an infant is reared as a male or as a female, resulting in the **gender of rearing** and in all the cultural/environmental/stereotypical aspects of gender-related characteristics. Any systematic sex difference in how people are treated can be described as creating a **gendered environment** (see Chapters 11 and 12).

In most people, the gender of rearing leads to their gender identity and their gender-role identity. **Gender-role identity** refers to the answers given to the second question. In other words, gender-role identity designates the degree to which a person describes herself as being masculine and feminine, or how masculine and feminine a person feels. It is possible that gender-role identity and gender identity may reflect the same construct. But whether there is any important difference between the two is not only theoretically important but can be experimentally tested (see Chapter 2).

According to sociological concepts, roles are "the regulation of behaviors by participants in social interaction by rules or social norms attaching to the status relationships" (Sherif, 1982, p. 392). A role

> is not a set of expectations but of relations, the culture providing the base for the role by defining who should or should not be assigned or allowed to enter a specific role in a specific social circle and what duties and rights are 'normally' needed in order that the function of the role (again culturally defined) be carried forth. (Lopata & Thorne, 1978, p. 720)

The term **gender** (or **sexual**) **stereotypes** is used to describe the sociological/anthropological/cultural aspects of masculine versus feminine roles (Eagly, 1983; Huston, 1983; Spence & Helmreich, 1980). Gender roles are those expected of, prescribed for, or proscribed (prohibited) for a given sex in a given society (e.g., worker, housewife, father). The contents of the gender roles for a given culture are the gender or sexual stereotypes (see Chapter 11).

However, an individual's own personal sexual stereotypes may differ from those endorsed by the majority of the people in his culture. There can also be a mismatch between a person's behaviors and the roles stereotypically and culturally prescribed for that gender. A person's knowledge of any such discrepancy can affect how that person presents and evaluates himself (von Baeyer, Sherk, & Zanna, 1981; Zanna & Pack, 1975). For example, in most cultures males are "supposed to be" muscular and assertive, so a shy, skinny male may feel hesitant

about joining groups, feeling himself to be somehow out of place.

Assumptions and Realities

To be an informed and critical reader, you have to be able to evaluate some of the most common assumptions made by the researchers and theorists. The epistemology of a science — the science of knowing about that field — determines what its research will reveal. The epistemology of gender determines how gender knowledge will be constructed. It determines what gender researchers will deem capable of being studied, which research techniques will be used, how the resulting data will be described, and how the descriptions of those data will be organized, summarized, interpreted, and applied.

The relative nature of social reality.   One person's beliefs can affect many people's mutual social realities. Our beliefs affect how we perceive other people currently around us, how we respond to them, what we will remember about them, and how we will react to similar people on other occasions.[2] In one study, subjects who were either strongly opposed to or strongly in favor of capital punishment (the death penalty) were both exposed to the same material that presented evidence in favor of opposing sides of the issue (Lord, Ross, & Lepper, 1979). Reading the *same* material produced shifts of opinion in *opposite* directions: The pro group became even more in favor of and the anti group became even more in opposition to capital punishment than before.

Our beliefs can actually create our realities. For example, suppose that many people believe that a rise in interest rates will cause stock market prices to drop precipitously. If interest rates then do rise, a lot of people will rush to sell their stocks before the prices fall. The frenzied sell-off is actually what causes the market to fall, dramatically creating a self-fulfilling prophecy.

Gender stereotypes also similarly create our social realities (Morawski, 1985; Unger, 1983; also see Chapter 11). For example, a man who perceives himself to have a very masculine gender-role identity may see women as generally being very feminine. When he interacts with a woman, he might see her acting very much like he expected. Not only will his beliefs distort his perceptions and memories of her but he will also tend to reward (smile at, listen to) her when she acts stereotypically feminine, and he will tend to punish (ignore) her when she displays masculine characteristics. Therefore, the way he treats her will tend to make her act more feminine when she is with him—at least as long as she wants him to smile at her!

Because of our gender-stereotypic assumptions and because of the possibility of creating a reality that conforms to those assumptions, a third cause of sex differences—one other than biological and environmental—has to be entertained. Stereotypes may cause us to behave in sexually dimorphic ways. Even if stereotypes do not directly create sex differences, the stereotypic assumptions of others may sometimes impel us to act out their stereotypic beliefs.

This is as true of researchers and theorists as for anyone else. What they think to be true determines how their data will be gathered, interpreted, and applied to their social and economic realities. Many people no longer assume that there is some absolute social reality, but assume instead that there are multiple and relative and malleable realities. If people interactively create their own social realities, they will have to accept the fact that their own models and research may actually be *creating* (and not just discovering) the version of social reality seen in their research data (Belle, 1985).

The effects of implicit beliefs on research. Researchers have long understood the potential ill effects that personal beliefs may have on their research, as illustrated by the quote from William James at the beginning of this chapter. Jensen (1989) described several "pathologies of

propaganda and prejudice. These are not easily

detected, treated, or prevented. . . . Propaganda refers to a pattern of selective presentation or marshaling of evidence for a preestablished point of view; ignoring or minimizing disconfirming data; and 'accentuating the positive and eliminating the negative' in the discussing of and argument from the data gathered. (p. 149)

Salespeople but not scientists should be good propagandists.

Scientific prejudice is the passive equivalent of scientific propaganda. It involves the acceptance of argument and data for a preestablished or favored point of view that would never be acceptable for a contrary opinion. It demands more of alternative ideas than is demanded of one's favorite ideas. It plays the game of science on an uneven field that favors one's own view. (p. 149)

A very interesting example of these biases occurred in anthropology. A great controversy surrounded Derek Freeman's publication of a book criticizing Margaret Mead's anthropological research in Samoa (Caton, 1984; Clements, 1989; Ember, 1985; Freeman, 1983, 1985a, 1985b). Although most anthropologists no longer believed that Mead's techniques and conclusions were valid, they expressed great outrage that Freeman would actually publish such a criticism. Ember (1985) described Freeman's book as saying to other anthropologists: "'You're wrong, I'm right; you're no good, I'm great'" (p. 910). One journal that published several very critical reviews of Freeman's book also published a so-called reply that was printed over Freeman's name but actually written by one of its editors. According to Clements, the public nature of the Mead critique threatened some very cherished assumptions of the cultural anthropologists, and so they misread and misinterpreted what Freeman had said, seeing methodological errors where there were in fact none to be seen.[3]

Mednick (1989) identified three cherished beliefs in sex differences research: fear of success, androgyny,[4] and the "feminine voice" in moral development. She concluded that, despite their popularity with researchers and theorists, there was little evidence in favor of any of these constructs. She argued that using such constructs, despite the lack of evidence, "deters rather than advances the goals of feminist psychology" (p. 1118).

PATHOLOGICAL GENDER ASSUMPTIONS

Koch, one of the major historians and philosophers of the science of psychology, described some of the effects of untested research beliefs in his essay entitled "The Nature and Limits of Psychological Knowledge." He listed several symptoms of what he called the "pathology of knowledge." One of those pathologies involved "making a set of arbitrary and strong simplifying assumptions, . . . proposing an 'as if' model observing that set of restrictions, and then gratefully falling prey to total amnesia for those restrictions" (Koch, 1981, p. 258).

Pathological assumptions are those made prior to research or theorizing that are not explicitly stated and so cannot be tested or evaluated. An assumption that eventually turns out to be untrue may have systematically distorted all the research guided by it. The distortion of science and knowledge is what is pathological. Thus, pathologies have nothing necessarily to do with the truth or falsity of any such simplifying assumptions; instead, pathologies have to do with the effects that unexamined assumptions may be having on the scientific literature. Researchers and theorists (and textbook authors) are usually unaware of their particular pathological assumptions. The "amnesia" described by Koch is quite real. Only someone who is not making the same assumption can detect those assumptions in another's writing and theorizing.

In this book, the term **biological bias** refers to the possibility that biological factors may be part of the processes that can create gender-related differences. There may be biological biases for and against certain sexually dimorphic behaviors but there is no **biological determinism:** biological factors would not and do not ever, all by themselves, account for any gender-related difference. This terminology is used to discourage making some of the kinds of assumptions that Koch would call "pathological." A concept that should be used to replace arguments about the relative importance of culture versus biology is introduced at the end of this chapter.

The next section describes some of the usually unstated and therefore untested assumptions that provide the scaffolding for current gender-related differences research. It is very important for you to identify and question any such pathological assumptions you may have so that you can more clearly perceive what is being said—and what is not being said.

"If It's Good for the Goose . . ."

Researchers sometimes assume that if they can explain why someone differs from other people of the same gender, they can thereby explain sex differences in that same behavior (Stewart & Lykes, 1985). This is not necessarily true; not all similar-looking effects have similar causes. Some instances of obesity in humans can be attributed to genetic factors, others to overeating (Hoyenga & Hoyenga, 1984). Because of this, it would not be wise to assume that just because one person is fatter than another for genetic reasons, any other overweight person is fat solely because of her genes. Apparently similar traits in two distinct people may have different causes: the reasons that one man differs from another may be different from the reasons that that man differs from a given woman. In fact, gender often affects how one characteristic is related to another. The sexes may also react quite differently to the same situation, such as competitive situations (see Chapter 12). What is "good for the goose" is not necessarily also "good for the gander," at least when it comes to explaining the behaviors of both.

Another very important example comes from the hormone literature. Gender may affect the way that changes in some hormone levels are related to changes in some behavior. Even if aggression is related to a person's level of masculine sex hormones, if females are more sensitive to masculine sex hormones than males are, any sex difference in aggression could *not* be attributed to, or explained by, sex differences in hormone levels. That is, suppose a typical female is more sensitive to an androgen than is a typical male. Then higher than normal levels of androgens in females (though still in the female-typical range of androgens) might have effects on females' aggression equivalent to the effects that the much higher androgen levels found in males have on males' aggression. High-androgen females might be just as aggressive as high-androgen males despite the males actually having the higher absolute levels of androgens.

"If It's Feminine, It's Inferior"

Another assumption affects how gender differences are interpreted. Many feminine characteristics, such as dependency or being "childlike," share somewhat pejorative social connotations (Belle, 1985; Sampson, 1977). At the very least, the masculine counterpart seems to have more favorable connotations (e.g., independent, mature). But why should independence and isolation (ignoring others) be more socially desirable than dependency and fusion (being sensitive to others)? It may be that it is impossible for the human brain to contemplate differences between groups and *not* to assume that those differences reflect degrees of desirability as well. But until it has been demonstrated to be impossible, we should at least try to separate the concepts and resist assuming that *different* somehow means that one is inferior to the other in some way.

Sex Differences Are Always Small

The main goal of feminist research is to encourage the elimination of the secondary status of women in our society (Pollis, 1988). According to some feminists, the best way to accomplish this goal is to emphasize the small size of gender differences.

However, as Eagly pointed out (private communication, 1987), the size of the average sex difference in personality traits is about equal to the size of the average effect of various experimental manipulations. Sex differences in aggression are about the same size as are the differences in aggression created by exposing different groups to environments that either do or do not encourage aggression. So, gender differences are about as important as many of the other variables that psychologists know about.

In areas other than cognitive skills and personality traits, sex differences can be very large (Huston, 1983). For example, most obese people and most people with eating disorders are female (Hoyenga & Hoyenga, 1984). Similarly, **self-medicators** are people who eat sweets or chocolate whenever they feel nervous about something: 92 percent are women (Schuman, Gitlin, & Fairbanks, 1987).

If It Exists, It Must Be Due to Culture and Environment

Gender research has frequently suffered from pathological assumptions regarding biological biases. Unger and Denmark (1975) said, "Feminist leanings would tend to make one seek for environmental etiologies [causes]" (p. 605). Similarly, Longino and Doell (1983/1987) stated, "Feminists . . . have identified sexist bias in the . . . search for physiological rather than environmental explanations" of gender differences. One criterion suggested for feminist research involves assuming that "there are no significant differences between women and men not attributable to differences in socialization, current reinforcement, and social expectations" (Kahn & Jean, 1983, p. 662). This has led to a flood of "hundreds of articles . . . in an attempt to demonstrate that psychological sex roles are a more important determinant of behavior than is biological sex" (Myers & Gonda, 1982a, p. 521). Only recently have other feminists described some of the possible fallacies involved in these assumptions.

Because of this history, the authors will discuss pathological biological assumptions more thoroughly than pathological psychological assumptions. Biology is not necessarily incompatible with feminism. In fact, the psychological pathologies just described probably constitute much more of a threat to many feminist goals.

Clements (1989) pointed out some of the reasons why these assumptions about biology were originally made. Some theorists related evolutionary theory to the eugenics movement, which was also linked to Nazi war crimes. Thus, she said that any consideration of evolutionary and biological ideas seemed to be antithetical to the goals of social equality and freedom, making "biological determinism . . . a dangerous political perspective" (p. 73).

The eminent John Maynard Smith (1985) also described why social scientists were frequently opposed to extending evolutionary theory to humans' behaviors. Implying that biology was relevant to human behavior

> offended academic anthropologists and sociologists, who resented the threatened takeover [of their science by biology], and also the radical left, who saw in the implied 'biological determinism' a renewed attempt to justify racial, economic and sexual inequality by a claim that the status quo is justified because it is natural, and rooted in our genes. . . . Such 'biological determinism' is seen as scientifically unjustified (which, of course, it is), and socially pessimistic, since it implies that the world's present ills are incurable. (p. 48)

Barlow (1991) described the same types of responses to evolutionary theory, but with regard to U.S. rather than English scientists.

If any sex differences were directly related to chromosomes or sex hormones, they could be described as being "normal" and "real" (as opposed to "artificially" induced by culture) and could be used by the people (men) in power

to support their own political and social aims (Eagly, 1983; Morawski, 1985). Among others, Longino and Doell (1983/1987) and Shields (1985) have documented how biological explanations were used against women. Sex differences in scores on certain trait measures were interpreted as biological and thus supposedly justified the restriction of women to certain roles that were usually less prestigious than those assigned to males.

However, biological data can only be used politically when it is being misinterpreted. Nevertheless, misinterpretations were sometimes encouraged not only by some of the evolutionary theorists themselves but also by some of the most widely read popularizers of the day. The social science researchers were often right in concluding that the popularizers were wrong—but for the wrong reasons. Because of not being trained in biology, physiology, and genetics themselves, the social science researchers failed to recognize just why the popularizers were wrong. These popularizers made errors of interpretation, overgeneralized well beyond the plausible boundaries of the actual scientific data, and—in not a few cases—made pathological assumptions of their own concerning the role of biology for behavior in general and for sex differences in particular. The social science researchers, in opposing these invalid claims, either inadvertently perpetuated the pathological assumptions made by the popularizers themselves, or they made opposing pathological assumptions of their own.

Biological biases do not inevitably lead to social inequities. As Longino and Doell (1983/1987) pointed out, evidence of biological biases can serve social/political aims only if certain additional assumptions are made, many of which will now be described.

If It's Biological, It Must Be Immutable

Biological biases can be used to justify social/cultural decisions only if we assume that they are immutable, and that any attempt to modify or reverse their influence would inevitably be harmful. Why do people tend to assume that *biological* means *inevitable?*

The term *biological* is often equated with *genetic,* even though learning and stress can have just as biological an effect as genes can. For example, simply exposing a female rat (who was made sexually excitable by giving her some sex hormones) to a male rat changes the biochemistry of the female rat's brain (Vathy & Etgen, 1989). Exposing a young rat to a stressful rearing environment durably affects the structure of its brain (Sirevaag, Black, & Greenough, 1991). The correct meaning of *biological* has to be inferred from the context in which it is being used. In the epistemology of gender, *biological* often refers to sex chromosomes and to the effects of sex hormones. This is correct but incomplete. In a more general sense, *biological* reflects the effects not only of the organism's genes but also the influences of its prenatal and postnatal environments on its biologically measurable characteristics.

Contrary to the assumption of immutability, biological differences can be reversed, modified, or even eliminated even if the biology is genetic. For example, not every identical twin will develop schizophrenia after his twin did, even though both twins have the same genes and schizophrenia does have a strong genetic basis (Hoyenga & Hoyenga, 1988). The influence of genes may be indirect. People's genes affect which environments they choose to develop in (friends, hobbies), and then those environments affect which behaviors they develop. Genes may also affect how a person reacts to a given developmental environment: people with different genes will develop differently even in identical environments (see Chapter 9).

The first way to reverse or eliminate a bias due to sex chromosomes or prenatal sex hormone levels is to manipulate the relevant biology. In some lower animals, females can be

behaviorally defeminized and masculinized by giving them high levels of androgens during the critical period in which their brains develop (see Chapters 6 and 7). Theoretically, the same could be done with humans.[5]

Second, the environmental variables that also affect any sex difference can be manipulated to override any biological biases. Even though the structure and function of cells in the brain can be altered by the sex hormones present during a critical early period of the organism's life (see Chapter 5), experiences can have similar effects on the structures and functions of brain cells (Hoyenga & Hoyenga, 1984, 1988). In other words, systematic sex differences in developmental environments (because of parental treatments and social stereotypes) can have just as durable and anatomical an effect as do biological variables, and thus could either increase or oppose the effects of those biological variables.

Developmental theorists such as Freud and Kohlberg (see Chapter 9) have explicitly assumed that the developmental environment can have durable effects on behavior. Since the brain is responsible for behaviors, these developmental variables must therefore have equally durable effects on brain anatomy. As genetic researchers have pointed out:

> If the genome [set of genes] impresses itself on the psyche largely by influencing the character, selection, and impact of experiences during development . . . then intervention is not precluded even for highly heritable traits, but should be the more effective when tailored to each specific child's talents and inclinations. (Bouchard, Lykken, McGue, Segal, & Tellegen, 1990)

Which Contributes Most: Nature or Nurture?

"The culture/nature dichotomy structures public policy, institutional and individual social practices, the organization of the disciplines (the social versus the natural sciences), indeed the very way we see the world around us" (Harding, 1986/1987, p. 300). Thus, researchers frequently ask how much *nature* (sex chromosomes and hormones) influences a given sex difference, compared to how much *nurture* (culture, current environment, and developmental experiences) influences that same difference. Just asking the question involves making several potentially pathological assumptions.

Why the question may be pathological. First, the nature/nurture question dichotomizes the issue and so ignores the fact that culture and biology always combine interactively to affect behaviors. "Thinking in terms of nature versus nurture is nowhere more mischievous than in the study of sex differences. . . . The quest for 'real' sex differences . . . is a quest for immutable human nature, and it implicitly resurrects the false dichotomy of nature versus nurture" (Daly & Wilson, 1983, p. 266). "And why do people have such great difficulty admitting that nature and nurture are inseparable, even though they can be analyzed separately?" (Barlow, 1991, p. 286).

Second, asking the nature/nurture question frequently confuses what causes a given behavior to appear in a certain individual at a given time with what causes groups of people to differ from one another. The first question cannot be answered (see below). With regard to the second question, to decide if individual differences in aggressiveness among the people in some group could be related to differences in their hormones, we would look at hormone levels in both the very aggressive and in the not very aggressive people. Do people with high levels of aggression tend also to have higher levels of hormones? How strong is the relationship? We could do the same in evaluating the role of socialization to see how much individual differences in nurturance can be explained by differences in socialization. Do those people who were rewarded by their parents for taking care of younger children tend also to be

the most nurturant and least aggressive as adults?

Why the question cannot be answered. Any question involving a dichotomy is ultimately unanswerable (Hoyenga & Hoyenga, 1979, 1984, pp. 238–240). Scientists *can* determine the extent to which genetic and environmental factors are important to the development of individual differences in behavior among a given group of organisms. But even to do that researchers would have to have complete control over which genes each animal got as well as its rearing environment. This can be approximated in carefully controlled laboratory conditions with animals that have been selectively bred for so many generations that the exact genetic differences between them are known. But because of the controlled and artificial conditions and species, the results cannot be generalized to conditions and species that are normally found outside the laboratory, to gene patterns that were not possessed by any of those organisms, or to environments that were not experienced by any of them.

Under other, very restricted conditions, researchers can find out if heredity or environment *could* have an impact on the trait of interest.[6] Inbred laboratory animals or identical human twins can be used to demonstrate the role of environment. Since these organisms share identical genes, all differences between them have to be attributed to differences other than in their genes. Since they have identical genes, only environmental differences between them could be used to explain why they act differently from each other.[7] Organisms raised in rigidly controlled laboratory conditions can be used to demonstrate the role of genetics. Since they share identical environments, all differences between them have to be attributed to differences other than in their developmental or current environments.

In either case, scientists *cannot* generalize to gene patterns not studied or to environments not measured or controlled. An environment may have a certain effect on a certain behavior only in the presence of a certain gene. Organisms may "inherit" environments, much as they inherit genes. For example, we often live close to where our parents did (West, King, & Arberg, 1988). In other words, research can establish that certain genes or certain environmental events can affect the behavior in question. *Research techniques do not enable scientists to pit a given gene against a given environment and say which is more important for a certain behavior either for any specific organism (similar behavior can have different causes) or for any conditions other than those used in the original study.*

Sex Roles Are Entirely Cultural/Experiential

The desire to avoid the implications of biological determinism has led researchers to assume that people's scores on scales measuring psychological masculinity and femininity (see Chapter 2) reflect only their past experiences and culture, not their biology. Researchers assume that if they can show that subjects' scores predict any sexually dimorphic behaviors, they will have demonstrated that biology cannot explain why the sexes differ in that behavior (Baumrind, 1982). There have been a few attempts to test the assumption that scores on sex-role scales reflect only socialization and not biology (Baucom, Besch, & Callahan, 1985; Dabbs & Ruback, 1988; Daitzman & Zuckerman, 1980). Although the studies have not produced entirely consistent results, they have been able to demonstrate that people with different hormone levels also tend to get different scale scores.

If It Depends on Culture or a Situation, It Cannot Be Biological (Or If It's Biological, It Must Be Cross-Culturally Universal)

Another line of reasoning is very closely related to the one just discussed. Suppose some aspect of subjects' behaviors is directly related to some aspect of their current environment. For example, suppose that working women have higher motivation to achieve than do women who do not work outside the home. If something like this were true, researchers have sometimes assumed that the mere existence of this association is proof that biology is not involved. Similarly, researchers have looked for trans-culturally universal sex differences. Finding none, these researchers have then concluded that biology has little or no influence on any gender-related differences.

These types of assumptions are hard to resist. "For example, changes in an aggression research laboratory script [instructions given to the subjects] can create or wipe out 'sex differences,' suggesting that they are culturally and not biologically determined" (Macaulay, 1985, p. 192). "Because we know that sex differences in performance on some spatial ability tasks . . . disappear with practice . . . or reinforcement . . . , it seems reasonable to assume that these differences are largely culturally determined" (Nielsen, 1990, pp. 123–124).

Contrary to these assumptions, establishing that either biology or environment affects a certain behavior in a certain group of people does not allow researchers to conclude anything about any other set of factors. Many factors could work together in very complex fashions. Most important, demonstrating that one factor has some sort of influence does not demonstrate the absence of any influence from any other factor (see Chapter 2). For example, the presence of certain levels of sex hormones prenatally can affect how the organism responds to an environmental variable. High levels of masculine hormones during the prenatal period of life alters how a sheep's endocrine systems respond to changes in the amount of daylight present during seasonal changes (Wood et al., 1991).

If We Differ from One Another, It Cannot Be Biological

Another frequent assumption is that although the variability within each class of psychologically distinguished sets of characteristics is often clearly recognized, biological variables are often assumed to have little or no variability. For example, "a variable with this much variability would seem to be an unlikely candidate for one with much biological basis" (Unger, 1979, p. 1086). In another version of this argument, biological factors are seen to be so potent that small differences between people could not possibly reflect biological influences. For example, Mosley and Stan (1984) described Sherman as believing that gender-related differences in cognitive behavior are "too small to implicate a major [?] biological mechanism" (p. 170).

Biological factors do not have less variability than environments do, and biological effects are not always potent. Individuals of the same sex will have different hormone levels not only after puberty but also before birth (Hoyenga & Hoyenga, 1979, 1988; see Chapters 7 and 8). In any one person, hormone levels also vary according to the time of day, the stage of the weekly and monthly hormone cycles, the season of the year, the person's current stress level, and the person's recent past experiences (including winning a tennis match).

If It's Biological, It Must Be Proximal

Talking about biological factors seems to imply to most people that biology is the proximal (immediate and direct) cause of any sex differences related to biology. However, one series of experiments convincingly demonstrated how biology could exert distal rather than direct influences. Moore (Moore, 1985; Moore & Power, 1986; Moore & Rogers, 1984) discovered that if a rat fetus had masculine sex hormones present in its body, after birth that baby rat's urine would have a certain odor. Having that odor caused its mother to groom its genitals more often than the genitals of babies lacking that odor (which would usually be females). The more genital grooming that occurred, the more that particular rat displayed masculine types of sexual behaviors as an adult.

Thus, sexual behaviors are affected distally by biology (the scent of the rat pup's urine). In turn, sex differences in odors caused the proximal environmental differences (maternal grooming) that ultimately led to the sex differences in sexual behaviors seen in adult rats.

Recent research has added yet another wrinkle (Clark & Galef, 1989). Male rat pups may get more genital stimulation from their mothers because they are slower to urinate in response to that stimulation than are female pups. Male pups "make" their mothers stimulate them more by being slower to urinate on being stimulated. And thus, the causal chain of events continues.

If It's Biological, It Must Be Present at Birth (Or If It's Present at Birth, It Must Be Biological)

Many people assume that any difference that appears at birth (**congenital** traits) must be biological (they usually mean genetic) and any difference that shows up later in life must *not* be genetic. Both conclusions are in error. Some congenital and sexually dimorphic traits occur not because of direct and indirect effects of genes (e.g., prenatal levels of sex hormones, sex chromosomes) but because of the impact that some prenatal environmental events have on the fetus. One example is prenatal stress. Some influence from stressed mothers is transmitted to the fetus presumably because some of the hormones associated with maternal stress can cross the placental barrier (Hoyenga & Hoyenga, 1984). If male fetuses were more vulnerable to the effects of stress than were female fetuses, stressing pregnant women could produce systematic sex differences in the behaviors of their offspring.

Sex differences that do not appear until later in life are usually assumed to be the product of stereotypes and socialization. However, many genetically affected traits, including rate of growth, Huntington's disease, Alzheimer's disease, diabetes, and mental disorders, have no visible signs at birth. Moreover, many sex differences appear only after puberty, since having an adult level of sex hormones is what causes them to appear; this includes breast and muscle development in humans. Puberty may enhance human sex differences not only because those adolescents are, for the first time, experiencing the phenomenological (conscious) effects of adult levels of sex hormones. Only after puberty do they get to know what having adult levels of sex hormones really feels like, inside their own heads and bodies.

Biological Data Require Higher Standards of Evidence

This was described earlier as being the pathology of science that Jensen (1989) called "prejudice." As Sherman (1978) pointed out, since biological data have so often been used against women, requiring a higher standard of evidence for that data than for research demonstrating the role of environment might seem only prudent.

The authors would like to argue not for lowering the standards for biological evidence but for requiring environmental evidence to achieve the same high standards. Environmental data can also have untoward consequences if subsequently proven false. For example, if a researcher recommends a given child-rearing practice based on her developmental research, and it later turns out that the children subjected to that practice become severely handicapped in some way, that person would have done as much damage as those who misused bioligical data. Given the assumption that the environment is even more potent than genes and hormones, perhaps scientists ought to be even more careful with environmental data!

Furthermore, standards are sometimes applied unevenly. There is no such thing as a perfect experiment; errors and other interpretations are always possible. Thus, all one can reasonably look for in either the biological or the environmental area is whether the data achieve some **preponderance of evidence** criterion. Do most of the data suggest a similar conclusion? Can logical, valid reasons for the discrepancies be found? Do different researchers, with different expectancies, get the same kind of data? Does the research with nonhumans confirm the conclusions reached from human research with regard to how the various mechanisms work, and on what? Or vice versa?

The Assumption of Biological Determinism

One pathological biological assumption — that of **biological determinism** — deserves special attention, as illustrated by several previous quotations. Making many of the assumptions just described usually means that the theorist/ researcher is also assuming biological determinism (e.g., Baumrind, 1991). This is the idea that the presence of any biological influence or bias affecting any gender-related difference always, inescapably, leads to an unchangeable, irrevocable sex difference in that area. (The pathologies of assuming that biological influences are unstoppable and unchangeable have already been discussed.) Biological determinism is usually also understood as meaning that biological contributions to sex differences are both necessary and sufficient causes for the sex differences with which they are associated.

Two aspects of causation apply to this assumption. First, the concept of a necessary and sufficient cause in behavioral theorizing and the epistemology of psychology has gone the way of the phlogiston in chemistry and physics. Most of the behaviorally relevant causes of anything are neither necessary nor sufficient. For example, smoking undeniably causes lung cancer. But smoking is not necessary, since nonsmokers do (though rarely) get the kind of lung cancer caused by smoking, and smoking is not sufficient since most smokers will die of something else before they get lung cancer. Instead of being necessary and sufficient, smoking changes the probability of getting lung cancer.

In just the same way, biological factors like

sex chromosomes or sex hormones may change the probability of certain behaviors. Neither are ever necessary or sufficient causes of any behaviors. Environments can have effects on behavior similar to those of hormones even in the absence of the hormones, so hormones are not necessary. Hormones are not sufficient either, because a given level of hormones may lead to a given behavior if and only if the organism is in a certain kind of environment. Biological factors affect only probabilities, just as do past experiences and socialization.

Second, the best defense against an improper use of the idea of biological determinism is education. Knowledge about pathological assumptions can allow a person to "fight fire with fire," to be able to state just how and why the biological data are being improperly interpreted and applied whenever they are used to justify social decisions. Anderson (1986) provided an excellent example of this. In recent popularizations of sociobiological theory, it had been claimed that human males differ strikingly from nonhuman primate males. Humans prefer the youngest postpubertal females as sexual partners, but nonhuman primate males prefer older females who have already given birth. Anderson used evolutionary theory and her own data to show how the popularizations both ignored relevant data and misapplied the theory itself.

Biological determinism as a concept shares much with the concept of a unicorn—frequently discussed but mythical. All behavioral differences between men and women are importantly affected by learning and by cultural experiences. Pure biological determinism for any behavioral or psychological trait, including one's identity as a biological male or female, is a myth.

PARADIGMS OF SEX DIFFERENCES

In this section the basic epistemology of causal models or paradigms is discussed. The details

of and documentation for the various aspects of the paradigms are covered in later units.

Explanations and Theories

A **theory** is a system of interrelated statements from which empirical phenomena can be deduced. The theory of gravity is a set of statements about how objects exert attractive forces (somewhat like magnetism) on each other, and from this system of statements you can deduce if you release your hold on your coffee cup, it will drop to the floor. A **theory of behavior** is any system of statements or beliefs from which behavioral predictions can be made.

Theories are judged according to several criteria. A theory is valid as long as it successfully predicts the behavior that is actually observed in the laboratory or in the world outside the laboratory. A theory should also be able to summarize past observations and so serve as a convenient way of remembering that past data. Furthermore, the theory—to the extent that it successfully predicts and summarizes a wide variety of behavioral observations and data—is also one explanation of those observations and data. The theory says why those behaviors occurred when and the way in which they did. A theory can be compared to other theories based on these criteria: better theories do a better job of predicting and summarizing.

Thus, better theories are more useful than theories that do not meet these criteria as well. Better theories provide a better "handle" on the world; they enable us to better comprehend, predict, control, and change our own behaviors as well as the behaviors of others when we deem it desirable to do so. Science progresses by fits and starts, each change representing a change in explanatory paradigms. Researchers think they understand something and then someone else challenges their assumptions. The line of research may then be abandoned or its data may be reconceptualized and incorporated into a new theory. The only real test of scientific models, and of progress, is the degree to which the current models let us, researchers and students alike, accurately predict, understand, and make desirable changes in the world.

Everyone has theories. Anytime we explain a behavior, either something we have done or something someone else has done, we are using a theory. Dweck and Leggett (1988) have described some of the ways in which having different kinds of personal theories can affect us. A scientific theory will most likely differ from a personal theory we have been using all our lives only by being "better": explaining and predicting more phenomena.

Psychology has moved away from the search for a general theory of behavior. Current psychologists formulate mini-theories that attempt to explain only a limited array of behavioral phenomena as opposed to all behaviors. Thus, there are theories specific to cognitive development and other theories that attempt to combine cognitive and social development. There are theories of certain types of achievement strivings and theories of aggression. Eventually, a **meta-theory** — a theory of how and why and when the various smaller theories might be applied — may be developed that provides a broader scope for prediction and understanding.

Epigenetic Development: A Model for Sex Differences

Evolutionary ideas can be used as a meta-theory for sex differences. As a model, it "provides a guide and prevents certain kinds of errors, raises suspicions of certain explanations or observations, suggests lines of research to be followed, and provides a sound criterion for recognizing significant observations on natural phenomena" (Lloyd, 1979, as cited by Symons, 1989, p. 136). Evolution works largely on developmental processes: how and where the organism develops importantly affects the behavioral traits of the adult and thus which genes will be selected for. This also means that

the selected genes are **open to instruction,** meaning that their activity can be modified by the environment outside the organism's skin. Genes' activities can be modified by the developmental environment and also by the adult's environment.

The concept of epigenetic development.   The **epigenetic development** of any behavioral characteristic means that both genes and environments, acting together at all times, determine the structure and function of brain cells and thus the behavior of the organism. *Epigenetic* is used in the sense of probabilistic (as opposed to predetermined) theories (Miller, 1988). "Experience plays a crucial role in inducing, guiding, altering, and sustaining the developmental trajectory of the organism" (Miller, 1988, p. 416). Genes, along with experiences, guide development throughout the organism's life. The implications of these statements will become clearer to you throughout this text.[8]

Epigenesis occurs because only a few genes are active in each cell of one's body. The other genes are inactive, having no effects on those cells. Which genes are active is determined by the environment of the cell; since muscle and liver cells have different environments (being in muscles versus livers, respectively), they have different genes active in them. During development, which genes are active, and when, is determined by the environments of the fetal cells. Which genes are active, and when, in turn determines what type of organ a group of fetal cells will **differentiate** (develop) into: liver or muscle.

The environment of a cell is affected not only by what other kinds of cells are around it but also by the external environment of the organism. For example, stress affects the biochemistry of the organism's brain, which is the environment of its nerve cells, both before and after birth. The hormones secreted by the organism's gonads also become part of its cells' environments.

Since development is epigenetic, this means

that genes cannot be separated from environment since they are both part of the same process. Starting out with certain genes because of evolution may mean that some cells in the organism will have their genes "turned on" (as in turning on a light switch) in response to certain environments. Conversely, having a different current environment means that different genes will be currently active. For example, learning changes the activity of genes in certain parts of the brain (Hoyenga & Hoyenga, 1988). Having the genes for schizophrenia means that the organism will be more responsive to certain pathological environments; developing schizophrenia requires both the environment and the genes.

Epigenesis and hierarchical meta-theories.   The authors use a hierarchical meta-theory similar to those used by others (Clements, 1985, 1989; Goodman, 1991; Hinde, 1989). Phenomena are classified into levels, such as the biochemical level, the organ level, the level of individuals, the level of groups, and the level of culture. Each level can be visualized as a different plane of existence. Clements uses the image of a coil with expanding rings, each ring corresponding to a given level. On each level (each ring of the coil), phenomena can be studied and theories and explanations can be made without reference to any other level of observation or theory. The behavior of individuals can be studied without referring to either the activities of their internal organ systems (the ring/level below it) or the cultural belief systems (the ring/level above it). However, the most complete (and hence useful) explanations will come from theories that explicitly describe how levels are interrelated — how organ function is related to individual survival and how individual traits are differentially expressed in varied kinds of cultural environments.

Evolution and epigenesis are superordinate constructs. Other high-level constructs occupy subordinate positions. describing interactions that occur only within a given level or only across two levels. In contrast, the theory of evolution is relevant to all the levels. It explains what causes gene frequencies to change across generations and why sex hormones came to control — directly or indirectly — the activity of certain genes at the level of the cell (Unit Two). The learning theories are also related to evolution: they describe how developmental environments may have come, across generations, to affect our adult behaviors at the level of individuals. Evolution can also explain how our capacity to establish rules and customs might have created the capacity for the cultural level (Unit Three).

Use of the appropriate high-level theory (culture or learning) depends on which variables are currently being investigated. However, the concepts of evolution and epigenesis are overarching: the genes are selected by evolution because of their "openness" to "instructions" from certain kinds of environments. This serves as a reminder that not only are mental and brain events just different versions of the same process but genes and environments are also always part of one process. Evolutionary theory provides one way of understanding those processes.

Systematic versus individual variables.   Subordinate theories must be broken down into at least two components. One component reflects the systematic differences between men and women; the other refers to an individual's own personal level of any biological or environmental variable:

Gender differences in biology =
Individual + Systematic

and:

Gender differences in environment =
Individual + Systematic

Systematic variables refer to certain levels, or certain ranges of levels, of the variables that differ nearly universally between men and women *and* that have similar effects on the behaviors of most people within each gender group. For any systematic variable, most women differ from most men. Sex chromosomes are one systematic variable: most women possess two X chromosomes, whereas men have one X and one Y chromosome.

Individual variables are those on which individuals within a gender group differ. Each of us had our own parents, our own ordinal birth position (e.g., first, last, or only), and our own unique family setting. Sex chromosomes can also be seen as an individual variable. There are many different X and Y chromosomes that we could inherit, and who we are depends on which specific two we *did* inherit.

Some of the more important variables have both systematic and individual components. For example, adult men have a higher level of masculine sex hormones than adult women do (systematic), but some men consistently have more than other men do (individual). Any way in which the environment or the biology of men and women differ systematically—such as in exposure to sexual stereotypes and in levels of sex hormones present—affects the *systematic* terms of those equations. Individual differences, such as a person's precise level of sex hormones at a particular moment and his uniquely individual past experiences, belong to the *individual* terms of those equations.

SUMMARY

There are both biological and psychological definitions of gender, but the actual gender-related differences that do appear and that can be measured reflect the epigenetic influence of both kinds of concepts, developmentally as well as currently. Because researchers and theorists have made some of the possibly erroneous biological and environmental assumptions described here, these assumptions have created our experimental realities.

Theories provide us with ways to predict, explain, understand, control, and change behaviors, including gender-related differences.

Theories explain by postulating various relationships among variables such as evolutionary history, hormones, environments, and behaviors. As long as the concept of epigenetic development is kept in mind, we can apply learning, cultural, or biological theories to data and thus learn about how these factors can affect sex differences.

Pathologies can be avoided by not giving surplus meaning to the terms used in research on gender-related differences. Scientists must use careful and differentiating definitions and must critically examine and then either discard or formalize and test their assumptions. Gender differences are always the product of an environmental/biological interaction, and they reflect systematic as well as individual differences in both environmental and biological variables. The paradigm of epigenetic development describes this interaction and also guards against the tendency to make many of the pathological assumptions described in this chapter. Also, as many feminists have pointed out, there is no such thing as a totally unbiased or error-free research project. Data, interpretation, theory, criticism, and then still more data are what lead to progress.

ENDNOTES

1. Here, *interaction* means the strong form in which each influences the other, at all times, as opposed to the weaker, statistical form of interaction, which is explored with analyses of variance (see Chapter 2).

2. Our nonsocial realities—our perceptions of brightness and whether we see something as we walk by it—are also affected by our beliefs and expectancies, but the social environment is more important for gender epistemology.

3. Many other such stories could be told about scientists in all disciplines; the Mead-Freeman story was chosen for two reasons: most students have heard of Mead's research, and the opposition to Freeman was largely fueled by an opposition to biolological determinism (which will be covered later in this chapter).

4. **Androgyny** means displaying an equal number of masculine and feminine traits, or displaying masculine traits as often as feminine traits.

5. Perhaps this is being done inadvertently because of the effects of various drugs taken by women during their pregnancies and the effects of prenatal stress on their developing fetuses (see Chapter 7).

6. However, even this does not enable researchers to establish that heredity or environment actually had an impact for any given organism.

7. Even identical twins may have nonidentical biologies; for example, they may have had different prenatal developments because of differing uterine positions or birth conditions.

8. In other words, expect to acquire this new concept slowly, using it to integrate new information as you read. Then use the new information to increase your understanding of epigenesis.

CHAPTER 2

MEASURING ROLES
AND DIFFERENCES

MEASURING GENDER-RELATED DIFFERENCES
MEASURING SEX ROLES
SUMMARY

> *What has occurred in the area of sex-role research is a rash of new scales and a bevy of eager researchers who wish to relate androgyny to everything and anything.*
> —J. Worell (1978, p. 780)

Viney (1989) suggested that the appropriate mascot for psychology might be the twelve-eyed toad, as opposed to the cyclops. He was describing and defending William James's views of the science of psychology, suggesting that pluralism (having twelve eyes, from a poster done by the Polish artist Roman Cieslewicz) was better for progress than striving for a constraining, distorting unity (having only one eye). Viney believed that looking at any problem from multiple viewpoints, using many different kinds of methodology, is a sign of strength, not weakness—something with which Peplau and Conrad (1989) would agree: "Feminists are correct in encouraging the use of a rich variety of methods and in challenging the claim of any method to superior status. But we should also reject the claim that some methods are necessarily more feminist than others" (p. 395).

This chapter described how gender-related differences and sex roles were and are being measured. The first section covers the measurement of gender-related differences: kinds of research, types of variables, statistical differences, and sources of bias. Given the existence of bias, the twelve-eyed toad is an appropriate symbol for research: the use of a multiplicity of paradigms will decrease the impacts of the biases. The second section covers the measurement of sex roles. It describes concepts, types of scales, and problems of validity. As you will see, the use of sex-role scales has run into difficulties, as the quotation from Worell given above indicates.

MEASURING GENDER-RELATED DIFFERENCES

Since the nature of scientific theories affect how and what is measured and how the results are interpreted, this section points out some of the goals guiding this research. It includes a discussion of traditional versus feminist research methods and goals and is followed by a suggested integration.

Predictions and Methodology

Many scientific disciplines can supply data and explanations relevant to gender-related differences. In the biological area, data and theories from genetics, evolutionary research, medicine, sociobiology, neurophysiology, endocrinology, and psychobiology are relevant. Anthropologists, sociologists, and developmental and social psychologists can describe how acculturation and culturally specific sexual stereotypes are all relevant to the origins of sex differences.

Traditional methods and goals.   Two goals of **traditional** types of research are (1) to provide a model for individual differences research and theorizing and (2) to develop more adequate and comprehensive theories of sex and gender. Researchers need a theory to define what gender-related differences mean, how they develop, why they occur, how they can be changed, what variables need to be studied, and how those variables should be measured.

The methods and philosophy of traditional research originated with logical positivism and include a belief in the value of deterministic predictions. **Determinism,** as it is currently used in science, is the belief that whatever we choose to do at any given time, the choice would be completely predictable given a complete knowledge of our past behaviors and choices.[1] If we know enough about the current situation, past history, biology, personality, and perceptions of any individual, and if we know which theory to use, we could predict all future behaviors of that individual. Theories that provided the predictions are then seen as being possible explanations for those behaviors. Note, however, that "Truth" is not really part of this model: explanations can be better or worse, but not either True or False.

Predictions are derived from a theory according to either a deductive or inductive reasoning process. **Deductive reasoning** is the type found in logical syllogisms (arguments with premises and a conclusion). If a prediction is made by this process, the conclusion will be valid as long as the premises hold true and the argument is logically valid.[2] In contrast, in **inductive reasoning,** a conclusion is reached solely on the basis of generalizing from past experiences. Since certain events have always occurred in certain situations, those events will also occur in the current, similar situation. Since the arrival of morning has always meant that the sun has come up, we could correctly inductively conclude that the sun is very likely to come up tomorrow morning also.

When researchers follow the traditional model, they do **nomothetic** research. Only a few traits or characteristics are measured at any given time, and these traits are measured in a large number of people. Distinctions between or among different types of individuals are emphasized, as contrasted to emphasizing the unique aspects of each type or person (Belle, 1985). Thus, males are contrasted with females.

Feminist research goals and methods.   The epistemology of traditional research methods and philosophy can be contrasted with that of the various feminist approaches. Feminist scientific criticism and research started with critiques of existing research and paradigms as being male-biased. Feminists then attempted to redress the imbalance of knowledge by explicitly studying women. Finally, the feminist theories reconceptualized the whole scientific and social/cultural set of systems. Gender is seen as one principle by which human societies are organized, but the structure is "man-made" (Wylie, 1991, p. 40). "Gender is, in its various forms, a fundamental structuring principle which cannot be ignored or reduced to other . . . factors" (p. 41).

In this process, three types of feminist goals for gender-related differences research have been identified (Hare-Mustin & Maracek, 1988; Kahn & Jean, 1983; Kimball, 1986; Wylie, 1991). The following discussion is based on a synthesis of their ideas. Each of the three approaches reflects how the data being gathered on women will — or will not — be integrated into research done with male subjects. Each paradigm agrees with the goal of eliminating sex differences in social status; however, each differs in how best to accomplish this goal.

First, the **integration and elimination goal** "suggests that the study of women should be infused as rapidly as possible into each area of traditional psychology, and that when this is done there will be no need for a separate field of the psychology of women" (Kahn & Jean, 1983, p. 661). Researchers with this goal tend to assume that all sex differences are small and completely "attributable to differences in socialization, current reinforcement, and social expectations" (p. 662). Hare-Mustin and Maracek (1988) described this approach as having what they call a **beta bias:** "the inclination to ignore or minimize differences" (p. 458). Researchers choosing this goal often have as secondary goals the validation of (or failure to validate) sex differences found by other researchers, and the desirability of emphasizing the similarities between women and men. The traditional methods of research just described would be employed, but the development of new methods would also be encouraged.

The second **goal of integration following equality** also desires to incorporate sex differences and feminist research into the mainstream research. In this case, however, the goal of integration is seen as being desirable only after prejudice against females and femininity has been eliminated. People taking this position also often assume that most, if not all, gender differences and gender stereotypes come from the inferior status of women relative to men. "All ideas about difference are social constructs" (Hare-Mustin & Maracek, 1988, p. 457). "Arguing for no differences between women and men . . . draws attention from women's special needs and from differences in power and resources between women and men" (p. 460). Because of this, gender differences research must always attempt to control the confounding effects of sex differences in power and status. Once the effects of power differences in the real world are identified, the imbalance of power can be corrected and most gender differences will vanish.

The third **goal of continued separation and self-definition** would be achieved by studying women separately from men, focusing on research that directly involves only women, such as pregnancy, menstruation, menopause, and lactation. This approach identifies gender differences as originating from factors other than power and status differentials. Hare-Mustin and Maracek (1988) described this approach as having an **alpha bias,** or tendencies toward an "exaggeration of differences" (p. 457). People with this goal see that the major problem for women has been that whatever is judged as being female or feminine has also often been judged as being inferior to being male and having masculine characteristics. The research goals would be to understand women and to recognize the strengths of females and the values of femininity.

Idiographic research is favored by the continued separation model. Idiographic techniques emphasize studying a few individuals in depth, by interviewing them at length, instead o studying just one or two aspects of many people.[3] Having knowledge of many of the traits and past events of several individuals would give researchers the opportunity to discover the unique structures of those individuals' personalities.

Postmodernism critiques of science take an even more radical point of view, which states that none of the three approaches just described have any special claim to validity (Hare-Mustin & Maracek, 1988; Wylie, 1991). Researchers with this viewpoint insist that no methods or criteria for establishing knowledge can be formulated independently of particular (and therefore biased) sociopolitical standpoints. Women's experiences and perspectives are just one of the standpoints that have been obscured by traditional scientific methods. No one set of rules for gathering knowledge can be allowed "privilege" or special status, relative to any other. However, there then seems to be no reason, other than personal preference, for choosing among the alternative points of view held by the various social groups, including women and minority groups.

Integration of traditional and feminist goals: probabilistic predictions.

If idiographic techniques are going to be emphasized, the deterministic predictions described as being the goal of traditional research may not be scientifically possible. However, deterministic predictions may not be possible with traditional methods either. For instance, in the field of physics (which seems to represent the quintessence of deductive reasoning and prediction), deterministic predictions cannot be made in some areas. As an example, physicists can predict where a majority of a particular group of particles may go, but they cannot predict with any certainty that a particular particle will go to any particular place.

Perhaps probabilistic predictions may be all one can hope for in the social sciences, whether the paradigm is traditional or one of the feminist types. Researchers may never be able to accurately predict any more than what a specific proportion of what kinds of people will do what kinds of things in certain kinds of situations. If an unbiased coin is flipped 100 times, a person can predict quite accurately that, for about 50 of those flips, heads will come out on top. For any given flip, a person cannot deterministically predict whether heads or tails will come up, just as one may never be able to predict with complete accuracy the next behavior of any given individual. Similarly, no one can specifically know which people will do what. One cannot accurately predict a given person's behavior just from a knowledge of that person's hormone levels, and making social decisions solely on the basis of gender (hormone levels, rearing histories) is therefore never warranted.

The authors would still retain the criterion that a useful theory/explanation and scientific paradigm is one that can be successfully employed to predict and explain past experiences and research and to create changes in people and social conditions. Nevertheless, the definition of *useful* is likely to vary across situations and historical periods. This would be true not only for scientific theories but also for evolutionary pressures (see Chapters 3 and 10).

In addition to probabilistic predictions, other ideas must be considered. The tendency to reorganize perceptions according to biases and expectations is a basic function of brains and their sensory systems (see Chapters 9 and 11). Scientists should investigate how people construct their social realities, as will be described shortly, and how this construction affects the outcomes of experiments. How powerful is this process? What are its limits? For example, researchers would have to recognize that evolutionary theory can be interpreted in a male-biased fashion, but it does not actually work that way (see Chapters 1, 3, and 4). At all moments in evolutionary history, the "interests" of both sexes were involved in evolution, since it takes two sexes to create viable offspring. A pluralism of viewpoints and explanations is to be encouraged, as described in the introduction, since the interplay among them can strengthen (as well as obfuscate) the accumulation and integration of ideas and knowledge.

Types of Variables

Much of research can be conceptualized as measuring the relationships between independent and dependent variables. An **independent variable** is not only assumed to be related to the occurrence of the dependent variable but it is also assumed to *precede* the dependent variable. The time order is what defines variables as being independent or dependent (Kerlinger, 1986): whichever variable occurs first is the independent variable. The **dependent**

variable occurs *after* the independent variable in any given experiment. A dependent variable in most psychological experiments is a score on some sort of scale or measuring instrument that reflects a personal characteristic.

Any given experiment will often have one or more independent variables as well as one or more dependent variables. Each independent variable should have at least two (to be a valid experiment) or more levels or values in each experiment. Dependent or independent variables can have just a few **(categorical)** or many different **(continuous)** levels or scores, depending on what is being measured and how.

In most of the relevant research, gender is at least one of the independent variables (it occurred first, at conception), and the dependent variable is some measurable trait or characteristic of women and men. Any measure of sexually dimorphic behaviors or traits could be a dependent variable. If you do some research and find out that men are taller, on the average, than women, height is the dependent variable. If you measure height in inches or centimeters (or using any continuous scale), the dependent variable is also *continuous.* Male versus female would be the two levels of the one *categorical* and *independent* variable of gender.

Independent variables occur first in real time. As just described, an independent variable is one that occurs before the dependent variable develops or occurs. "Real time" should be contrasted with "experimental time," or the order in which the variables were actually measured. **Real time** refers to when the subject developed that value of that variable, as opposed to when that variable was actually measured.

Since which variable occurs *first* in real time determines which is the independent and which is the dependent variable, this affects how researchers interpret their experiments. For example, suppose that one variable was a score on some scale that measured sexual stereotypes and also suppose that the other variable was

gender identity. Both variables are measured at the same time. But suppose we assumed that gender identity actually had occurred first because we think that people acquire their knowledge of gender stereotypes after they develop their gender identities.[4] The subject's gender identity would be viewed as the independent variable, and her stereotype score would be the dependent variable. We might conclude that people's knowledge of their identities are what caused them to learn the stereotypes. But suppose that we instead assumed that the stereotype score came first. Then we might conclude that learning about cultural stereotypes would be what caused a person to acquire his or her gender identity. One of the developmental theories described in Chapter 9 makes this latter assumption.

Sometimes researchers do not know the real time order of the variables, and so some research does not have an independent variable. In fact, if one is unsure which variable actually came first, one would probably be better off in viewing the research as having only dependent variables. In this case, no variable is assumed to have preceded any of the other variables. If the variables in a particular study were the weight and height of adult subjects, since neither variable can be assumed to precede the other in the subjects' developmental histories, both are dependent variables. The fact that all subjects may be weighed before they have their heights measured is irrelevant since the subjects have their weights and heights simultaneously present at all times. Researchers can still study how the two variables are related to each other and might also find out that the person's gender affects the nature of the relationship.

Types of independent variables. In terms of the design and interpretation of research, there are two important types of independent variables (Kerlinger, 1986). In the **active (or manipulated) independent variable,** the experimenter actively changes or produces the variable level, making a decision for each subject as to which level of the independent variable that particular subject gets. If the amount of practice on some task is the active and categorical independent variable (performance would presumably be the dependent variable), the experimenter is able to assign to each subject the number of practice trials that that particular subject will get. If the assignment is randomly done, the experimenter may flip a coin or consult a table of random numbers to decide which of two or more different levels of practice the subject will get. Random assignment maximizes the power of an experiment.

For the **passive** (or **measured**) **independent variable,** the experimenter is not able to decide which subject gets which level of the variable. A passive or measured (also called an **organismic variable**) is some trait that each subject already possesses, such as an IQ (a score on some test that measures an intelligence quotient). The experimenter cannot actively manipulate this kind of independent variable (the experimenter does not change a subject's IQ). Researchers can sometimes ensure that the passive variable is, in fact, an independent variable by doing **longitudinal research** in which one variable is measured well before the time that the other variable could have occurred or developed. For example, people's IQs can be measured in childhood and their occupational choices can be measured many years later.

One common passive independent variable in human sex-related differences research is gender. Gender is an independent variable because even though gender and behaviors may be measured at the same time, subjects' genders are assumed to have been assigned (by having XX or XY chromosomes) before their behaviors were learned. However, gender would be only a relatively more distal cause of any behaviors: sex differences in genes, hormones, rearing, cultural stereotypes, and social power are all possible proximal causes.

In addition, an active independent variable

can be **randomly assigned,** but a passive independent variable obviously cannot be. If random assignment is used, the experimenter not only actively decides which subject will get which level of each independent variable but the decision is made randomly. If an independent variable has two levels (e.g., drug versus no drug), the experimenter will use some randomizing procedure to determine which drug level the current subject will get. Having an independent variable be both active and randomly assigned further increases the validity of an experiment, as will be described shortly.

All independent and dependent variables must be concretely defined before they can be used in research. Specifying one's variables this way operationalizes them. An **operational definition** is a complete description as to how some variable was manipulated or measured. For example, suppose that the independent variable was manipulated and involved placing different groups of subjects into different situations. The operational definition of each situation used must include sufficient detail so that some future researcher could exactly duplicate those situations to exactly duplicate the variable.

Operationalization of measured variables (independent or dependent) would include specifying (1) the type of measuring instrument used; (2) where that instrument came from (its source); (3) the validity and reliability (which will be described shortly) of that instrument; (4) the exact conditions under which the measurement was made; and (5) (with human subjects) the instructions the subjects were given when being tested.

Explanatory variables.   Other variables are introduced by researchers in their theories (explanations) of research results. If the relationship between independent and dependent variables that the experimenter observed could be completely and totally equated to how these variables were operationalized, nothing would be explained. There would be no premise upon which to predict similar relationships in future experiments. To add information and predictive power, an explanation (a theory) must be added. **Explanatory variables** are therefore identified and studied as commonalities across *sets* of behaviors. Explanatory variables are also commonly called **intervening variables.** For example, depriving a rat of food may cause either faster running or faster eating, depending on the situation. Hunger is assumed to be caused by the independent variable of food deprivation. In turn, hunger is assumed to cause both the dependent variables — the increased running and the increased eating. Thus, hunger is used to explain why food deprivation causes both running and eating.

A **theoretical definition** is what gives meaning to an explanatory variable. Such a definition gives the explanatory variable characteristics that have not yet been directly observed or measured in any experiment. For example, the operational definition of IQ would be the test used to measure the subjects' IQs. A theoretical definition might add what theorists think is the pattern of skills and abilities possessed by a person with some particular IQ score. A score at or above a certain value could be said to identify a genius, and a person who is a genius might also be assumed to have many characteristics that have not yet been directly measured, such as the ability to create new devices or to write like Shakespeare.

For example, a gender schema has been given a theoretical definition (Bem, 1985; Markus, 1977). **Gender schemata** are cognitive structures theoretically possessed by people who get certain patterns of scores on a paper-and-pencil test, such as the Bem Sex Role Inventory **(BSRI).** A **schema** is a cognitive structure that affects how the person possessing it processes (perceives, remembers, evaluates) certain types of information. It is an explanatory variable, since in its theoretical definition it was given properties that have not yet been discovered — properties that can be speculated about and described in a theory. One such property would hypothetically affect the schematic person's

processing of information. Words that were directly related to stereotypic masculinity and femininity, such as *aggressive* or *nurturant,* can be hypothesized to be salient or attention getting for schematic people.

If schematic people are particularly sensitive to gender-relevant information, as opposed to gender-irrelevant information, this could be verified in several ways. For example, gender-relevant words might be better remembered than gender-irrelevant words, but only by schematic subjects. Schematic people should also respond faster than nonschematic people do to gender-related trait words when asked to indicate whether each trait was or was not characteristic of themselves. Since these predicted relationships were discovered in actual research (Bem, 1985), this supports the theory. By correctly predicting the relationships discovered in subsequent research, gender schema theory provides one useful explanation for the outcome of the experiments.

Possible types of relationships. Figure 2.1 depicts some of the relationships likely to be found in gender research. It is extremely important for you to realize that a very large number of different types of relationships could be used to explain the data of any one study (see documentation in Hoyenga & Hoyenga, 1993). Simply assuming that what was observed in a given experiment was a certain type of relationship — without considering the other types that could have also led to the same data — is to commit a pathological assumption. These different possibilities might be used in different theories to explain the relationships that some experimenter actually observed between independent and dependent variables. For example, supposed an experimenter observed that a given hormone level (or a given environmental event) and a given behavior tended to covary (change at the same time; covariation will be discussed shortly). Maybe a person's androgen level increased (or the person got insulted) at about the same time he

FIGURE 2.1   *Linear versus Nonlinear Relationships*
This figure illustrates various types of linear and nonlinear relationships. Part A: Linear, negative relationship. Part B: Linear, positive relationship. Part C: Nonlinear, monotonic, positively accelerated relationship. Part D: Nonlinear, monotonic, negatively accelerated relationship. Part E: Nonlinear, curvilinear or nonmonotonic (inverted U-shaped) relationship. C_n = scores on some dependent variable; A_n = scores on some independent variable or a second dependent variable.

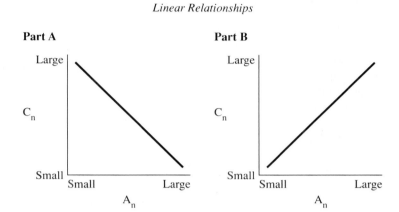

Linear Relationships

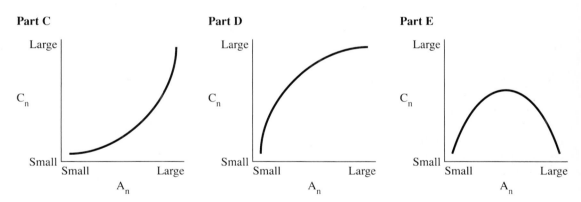

Nonlinear Relationships

stopped being passive and started aggressively attacking someone else. If this is what was observed, what are some of the possible explanations?

In this case, it is not certain which variable—if any—was the independent variable. Perhaps there was a **common prior cause:** maybe having been insulted caused both the attack and the increase in hormones. Perhaps the

relationship was **indirect:** maybe having experienced a rise in hormones made the person more obnoxious and that got him insulted, and the insult then led to the attack. For example, the mother rats' genital grooming of their male pups (see Chapter 1) was only indirectly related to their adult sexual behaviors. The resulting increase in male sexual types of behavior occurred because of the increased grooming, not directly because of their high prenatal hormone levels. Or perhaps there was a **reversed relationship:** maybe acting aggressively caused the person's hormone levels to increase. The experimenter might have done longitudinal research, for example, in which one variable was measured long before the second one (dependent variable) was measured. But if the independent variable is not manipulated, the relationship observed by the experimenter could still be **spurious.** Changes in the dependent variable could have been due to a third variable not measured or observed or manipulated.

Even if the independent variable is manipulated, one must still consider the possibility of other relationships. Unless the independent variable had been randomly assigned, spurious relationships are still possible: subjects who had differing levels of the independent variable might also differ on some third variable more directly related to the dependent variable. In addition to that possibility, a **simplex interactive relationship** could be present. A given outcome may occur if and only if, for example, a given hormone level was also present. Maybe the effect that being insulted has on aggression depends on what the person's hormone levels are at the time of the insult; maybe only people with high hormone levels can be violently angered by being insulted.

In the area of gender-related differences, even more complex relationships are likely to be found. In **complex interactive relationships,** two or more independent variables influence each other, as well as both having some influence on the dependent variable. Maybe being insulted and angry and having high hormone levels mutually increase each other, as well as both increasing the likelihood of aggression. Even more complex relationships can also occur, as where links among variables cycle into and out of relationships, or where a given relationship being observed at one time means that same relationship will not occur the next time it is studied (Hoyenga & Hoyenga, 1993).

It is important to remember that there are many possible theoretical relationships underlying (explaining) each type of observed relationship. This is true even in experiments in which the independent variable is actively manipulated and its levels randomly assigned to different subjects. The use of any less powerful experimental design means that there are even more explanations available that must be considered.

The Statistics of Gender-Related Differences

This section describes how to interpret the various statistical types of sex differences. More complex types of relationships require correspondingly more complex experiments and statistics to handle them.

Validity and reliability.   Traditional research can be evaluated according to several criteria:

1. The dependent variable must be demonstrated to be both valid and reliable.
2. The way subjects are selected from the relevant population or group, and the type of independent variable used, determine the degree to which the experimental conclusions are externally and internally valid, respectively.[5]
3. Results should be analyzed with standardized procedures to determine whether the results are reliable (repeatable), as opposed to reflecting variations in the dependent variable that are only spuriously or randomly related to the independent variable.

First, experimenters need to demonstrate that the scores on a measuring instrument or scale are a reliable and valid index of either the dependent variable or one of the passively measured independent variables. One kind of **reliability** means that if experimenters repeated their measurements on the same group of people on two separate occasions, any given person would tend to get the same score relative to other people's scores on both occasions. High-scoring people get relatively high scores the next time around, and low-scoring people also tend to repeat their relatively low performances.

The **validity** of any way of measuring a dependent variable refers to the degree to which a measuring technique is measuring what the experimenter thought and hoped it was. If a thermometer was used to measure height, one would have a very invalid (though reasonably reliable) measuring instrument. One validity problem is particularly important for gender-related differences research: is the technique or measurement method measuring the same trait in males as it is in females? Quite often this is not the case.

Internal validity (or **conclusion validity**) is concerned with the degree to which experimenters can confidently conclude that measured variations in the dependent variable are directly related to the differences that the experimenters had either measured (passive) or created (active) in the independent variable. This validity reflects the extent to which an experimenter can eliminate or control the influences of possible **confounding variables** (spurious relationships) or the various other alternative relationships or explanations.

The most reliable and powerful way of eliminating the influence of confounding variables or possible alternative relationships— and therefore of maximizing internal validity— is to do two things: (1) Have an actively manipulated independent variable and (2) randomly assign each of the two or more levels of that variable to two or more separate groups of experimental subjects. For example, an independent variable of hormone level could actively be manipulated by injecting male hormones into some randomly selected nonhuman subjects and injecting a control substance into other subjects. The subjects in each group (hormone versus control or comparison group) receive their respective level of the independent variable (injections of either some or no hormones) before any dependent variable (such as aggression) is measured.

In human sex differences research, since gender is a passive independent variable and since both developmental environments and hormone levels are usually measured rather than actively manipulated, biological and psychological aspects of gender are always confounded with each other and with status and power differences. Relative to females, males are not only more masculine but they have male chromosomes, more male sex hormones, less female sex hormones, different developmental histories, and more social power and status (Eagly, 1983). Since ethical considerations preclude active manipulations of most hormonal and developmental variables for human subjects, researchers can seldom use the most powerful designs. This means that the more powerful nonhuman research must be considered in its proper context. These facts also necessitate an even greater attention to sources of biases whenever gender-related differences in humans are being explored.

External validity is the degree to which experimenters can generalize their results to types of subjects that they did not actually test. Can the researcher correctly conclude that similar manipulations would affect other people the same way they affected her subjects? External validity describes the limitations to the researcher's ability to generalize results obtained with, for example, undergraduate college students in standardized and controlled laboratory conditions, to men and women in situations outside the researcher's laboratory.[6] There are also limitations to the ability to generalize from one species to another, or from nonhumans to humans.

Which internal validity problems occur in gender differences research depend on the variable being measured. For some behaviors, laboratory research is less likely to see significant gender differences than is research that tests subjects outside the laboratory (Deaux, 1984; Unger, 1981). On the other hand, when subjects' stereotypes are being measured, subjects are more likely to treat people in a stereotyped fashion in a laboratory than in a "real-world" situation. Only the artificial laboratory situation eliminates all information other than gender, forcing subjects to use gender stereotypes if they are to make any judgments at all.

External and internal validity are often in direct conflict with each other, especially in gender-related differences research. The internal validity of research with human subjects is impaired because the most important independent variable — gender — cannot be actively manipulated and randomly assigned. Thus, experimenters are especially likely to do research in a laboratory situation in which other possible confounding variables can be rigorously controlled. But by doing so, not only is the external validity of the conclusions decreased but experimenters are probably even less likely to see significant gender differences in some of the dependent variables.

This also illustrates the trade-off that must be considered when the preponderance of evidence criterion (see Chapter 1) is used to interpret a body of research. Although research done with nonhuman subjects often uses a more powerful design than that commonly employed with humans, it is less relevant to (lower external validity with regard to) conclusions about humans. Data from humans have greater external validity (for any conclusions about humans) but less internal validity. Thus, a truly informed conclusion must intelligently combine data from both sources.

The third criterion for evaluating research is **conclusion** or **experimental reliability.** This type of reliability is measured by the extent to which one can assume that if the experiment were repeated, the same pattern of results would be obtained. This form of reliability is conceptually similar to (though not identical to) the reliability of the measurement method. Suppose you observed that women tended to be taller than men. Maybe the difference you observed was an accident because by chance most of your subjects came from a motel that, at the time, was housing a team of professional female basketball players and several professional male horse jockeys. Any difference found between two groups must be carefully evaluated to determine the likelihood that chance factors alone could account for the observed difference, including what types of subjects happened to have been measured.

Conclusion or experimental reliability can be measured with various statistical analysis techniques. One would compute the size of the difference between the average of males and the average of females: by how much do males differ from females, on the average? One would then compare the size of the difference to how much males differ from each other and how much females differ from each other, on the average. By so doing, one can estimate the likelihood that a difference of such a size could have occurred by chance factors alone. Several statistical techniques will do just that.

Even very unlikely outcomes — such as choosing the one motel with female basketball players and male jockeys or winning a state lottery — will sometimes occur just by chance alone. If the statistical analyses suggest that chance alone could explain why the female subjects were taller than the males, one would have to conclude that the sex difference observed was probably not "real." It was just the result of chance variations due to biased selections of subjects (try another motel!).

Psychology journals generally require that a difference reach a certain arbitrarily chosen statistical confidence or **significance level** before it can be regarded as experimentally reliable and therefore worth publishing and communicating to other people. This level is set such that the observed differences would have occurred by chance factors alone in only 5 out of 100 times if the experiment had been repeated. This is generally stated as $p < .05$. If the probability is $p \leq .001$, only in 1 time out of 1,000 times that the experimenter was conducted would a difference that large have occurred because of chance factors alone (which seems to be pretty good odds).

Gender difference in averages.   The genders can differ because one tends to have more than the other of something, such as weight or height. To find out whether men differ significantly from women in height, one could measure people's height with a reliable and valid measuring stick. After gathering the data, one would then add together all the heights of the male subjects and divide by the number of men measured to get the average or **mean** height of men. The same would be done for women. Comparing the mean of some men to the mean of some women would indicate just how different the sexes are from each other in height.

Even though one can conclude that males significantly differ from females along some particular trait dimension, that difference in and of itself is essentially meaningless. There are at least two reasons for this. First, gender differences are often small, especially compared to the variability of that trait within each gender. Often, far larger differences exist among men alone, and among women alone, compared to the size of the sex difference in most personality and cognitive traits (Deaux, 1984; Eagly, 1978, 1987; Eagly & Carli, 1981; Frodi, Macaulay, & Thomas, 1977; Hall, 1978). In fact, in the personality and cognitive areas, gender differences usually account for less than 5 percent of the total variability in people. Because of this, *significant* does not necessary mean *important*. Basing any decisions as to public policy, practices, and expectancies on any such small gender difference would be a grave mistake that could cost society some of its best people. It would also lead to a lot of misery in the group being unfairly discriminated against because a small difference was mistakenly thought to be important.

Second, one needs to know more about the test before the sex difference can be interpreted. Just knowing the scores on some trait that reveals statistically significant gender differences does not mean that one knows what that difference means. Sometimes getting a given score does not mean the same thing in women as it does in men, as will be described below.

Gender differences in variability.   Gender differences in variability may be more socially important than are gender differences in average scores. Sex differences in **variability** mean that men differ more from each other, on the average, than women do from each other — or vice versa.[7] In the early days of psychology, researchers claimed that even though average IQ scores did not significantly differ between males and females, the "fact" that men were so much more variable than women "explained" why men were so much more often creative geniuses than women were (Shields, 1987). Any such gender differences in variability can mean one of two things. If males were more variable in IQ scores, maybe more males than females were retarded *and* also more males had IQ scores in the range above the genius level. Alternatively, only one of those two statements could be true and would account for the gender difference in variability by itself.

Gender differences in the meanings of scores and traits.   Gender differences in some characteristic are meaningful only if it is known that the measurement method is both reliable and valid. But what if validity is sexually dimorphic (Locksley & Colten, 1979)? One example comes from the area of gender-role identity (O'Heron & Orlofsky, 1990). In this research, both men and women were asked to rate themselves on overall masculinity and femininity. Of most interest here, the relationships between gender-role identity and the other scale scores that were seen for males were not seen for females. Only in males was gender-role identity associated with scores on certain other sex-role scales (discussed later in this chapter). Also, only in males did having a low gender-role identity score mean having higher scores on depression and anxiety scales and a social maladjustment scale. Gender-role identity scores took on different meanings in male and female subjects.

To examine that type of sex difference, correlation coefficients can be calculated separately for males and for females, as was done above. A **correlation** is a statistic that measures the degree to which individuals' scores on two different scales are related to each other. A correlation of 0 (zero) means that, across individuals, one trait is not related to the other trait. The two traits vary in level separately and orthogonally (or independently) from each other, across individuals. A correlation of $+1.0$ (a *perfect positive correlation*) means that if one person's score on one scale is high, that person's score on the other scale would also be relatively high. Weight and height are positively correlated since taller people also tend to weigh more than do shorter people. The correlation is not a perfect positive one because some short people are obese and some tall people are very emaciated. This correlation would therefore be somewhere between 0 and $+1$.

A *negative correlation* means that high scores on one scale tend to be associated with low scores on the other scale. Suppose that before each trip you filled the gas tank in your car. At the end of each trip, the amount of gas remaining in your tank would be negatively correlated with the distance driven: across different trips, the further you went on each, the less gas you would have left. This correlation would not be a perfect negative one (-1.0) since the speed at which you drive and the number of hills you encountered will affect your vehicle's gas mileage.

Gender differences in relationships can also be measured and identified in research having more than one independent variable. Suppose a person's gender was used as one independent variable and that same person's **socioeconomic status (SES)** (high, medium, or low, as judged by income and job) was used as a second independent variable (note that both are passive). If weight were the dependent variable, one would be assuming that the person's gender and SES came first and therefore preceded his or her degree of obesity. If gender affected the

relationship between SES and the probability of being obese, that could be demonstrated by a statistically **significant interaction** between gender and SES. In the United States, among lower SES subjects, more females than males are obese, but among high SES subjects, more females than males are underweight (Hoyenga & Hoyenga, 1984).

These gender differences are the most theoretically, practically, and socially important types. In the above example, the different implication of SES for the sexes suggests very interesting gender differences in the impact of culture on diets and dieting behaviors. A fat male company executive may be quite erroneously regarded as being more competent than a fat female company executive. Some executives might subscribe to the myth that a really competent women should be able to be a successful dieter.

More complex relationships require specialized techniques. For example, **multiple regression techniques** are used to explore how several independent variables might be related to dependent variables when the independent variables are related to each other. **Factor analyses** are used to find out what variables are related to what other variables. One can factor analyze subjects' responses to items on a personality test to see how many factors (variables) there are, and which questions are part of (related to) which factors. To be an intelligent consumer of information, all one needs to keep in mind is that these other kinds of relationships might be possible, even when the researchers themselves did not look for them.

Meta-Analysis

Meta-analysis is a relatively objective way of reviewing existing research that can sometimes show reliable sex differences when the more informal, narrative methods of reviewing a field would not (Mann et al., 1990). To do a *meta-analytic review,* one would identify all relevant studies (doing a computer search among all published articles would be one way to start). Once the relevant studies have been identified (e.g., all the studies that investigated sex differences in the performance of some task), they would be read and evaluated. If the studies met certain reasonable a priori criteria, they would be included in the review. For example, a study must include enough data for the right kinds of statistics to be calculated.

The next step is to calculate an effect size for each study from its data. An **effect size** indicates the relative importance of gender to the range of variation associated with the trait in that particular experiment. In the reviews presented later in this book, the authors use the weighted effect size called *d* (Hedges & Becker, 1986). This *d* is the ratio of the average difference between the sexes divided by the variability averaged over both sexes.[8]

According to a convention, a *d* of .2 is called *small,* a *d* of .5 is *medium,* and a *d* of .8 or over is *large* (Cohen, 1977). However, as pointed out by Rosenthal and Rubin (1982; Rosenthal, 1984), a small effect size can still have important social and personal consequences. Even a small effect can determine how many males versus how many females will qualify for a given job or a given school, when qualifications are based on having a scale score above some specified value. Even if a sex difference accounted for only 4 percent of the total variability in test scores, 60 percent of the higher-scoring versus 40 percent of the lower-scoring gender would qualify for any job requiring above-average scores. The more people competing for a given job, the greater the impact of even a small effect size.

The meta-analytic reviewer can also calculate effect size homogeneity across studies. If effect sizes prove to be homogeneous (or similar to each other), the reviewer can conclude that the sex difference is of the same magnitude across all the different kinds of subjects and experimental procedures. If the effect sizes are not homogeneous, this suggests that different experiments, using different subjects

and/or different procedures, found importantly different relationships. The researcher then often divides the studies, perhaps by age of subject. The homogeneity analysis can be done on each set of studies to see if subject age can be related to the differences in effect sizes.

The Concept of Covariance

The rest of this section is probably the most important to your understanding of sex differences. Now that you know the types of relationships and some statistical techniques for demonstrating various types of gender differences, how can they be applied to an understanding of the origins of sex differences?

Definition of covariance. Covariance can occur only if at least two variables[9] are being investigated. One variable is either manipulated or measured, and a second variable, the possible **covariate,** is measured at the same or some later time.[10] If changes in the second variable are associated with different values (manipulated or measured changes) of the first variable, the two covary.[11] **Covary** literally means that variation in the value of one variable depends on what value the other variable takes; the variation in one is related to (or "covaries" with) changes in the second variable.

Strength of conclusions. Suppose that a researcher found covariance between a behavioral trait and some environmental variable. How confident should the person be in concluding that the covariation is, in fact, important? Describing how the strength of conclusions vary according to the experiment's design is essentially a problem of internal validity. Because of the use of different experimental designs, some conclusions are inherently stronger and less likely to be in error. The conclusions can be strengthened if the independent variable is manipulated rather than just measured. The strongest conclusions can be reached if the covariate or independent variable is manipulated and if each subject is randomnly assigned to one value of that variable.

Range of variation also affects what conclusions can be made about covariance. **Range of variation** refers to how much variability in one variable is linked to changes in the other. Suppose two or more sets of characters (measurable behavioral traits or morphological characteristics) are compared to see how they covaried with a given set of manipulations of the organisms' developmental environments (e.g., some animals raised in social isolation and others raised in the company of peers). A character with a narrow range of variation would change only slightly when the developmental environment was changed, and a character with a wide range would change markedly. Although a statistically significant covariation could occur in both cases, the wide range of variation in a variable would mark its covariate as being more important to it than if that variable changed only slightly in response to differing developmental environments.

What conclusions of covariance do not mean. The design and the measured range of variation are important to the strength of one's conclusions. Even more important are the limitations of those conclusions.

1. *Do not conclude that similar appearing variations in similar appearing behaviors have covariates similar to the ones observed.* Since many animals must be sacrificed in animal shelters, one could observe a covariation between an injection and the later occurrence of death. However, one could not therefore conclude that an animal that was found dead in its cage one day must have received a lethal injection from someone. There are many different ways to die. Even if covariation between hormone level increases and increases in aggressiveness were observed, one could never legitimately conclude that a given aggressive behavior was caused by high hormone levels in that organism; there are many different things that can lead to aggression.

2. *Do not conclude that what was discovered has any implications for conclusions about variables that were not measured or manipulated.* If it was observed that perinatal sex hormone levels affect learning scores in adult animals, one could not legitimately conclude that developmental environments are therefore unimportant. The developmental environments could be even more important (create a wider range of variation) than do perinatal hormone levels. Or if one found that parental practices affected problem-solving styles in their children, one could not conclude anything about how perinatal hormones might also affect those problem-solving styles.

Even if a researcher discovered that a given covariant accounted for all of the observed variations in some behavior in a group of subjects (something that is very unlikely to happen), that does not mean that an unmeasured variable is therefore irrelevant. If the variable was manipulated so that it took on different values than it had had in the original group, one might still find that changes in the variable were associated with changes in that behavior. Furthermore, maybe the environmental variable that was manipulated (or measured) was related to the behavior because the environment affected hormone levels, and, in turn, the hormone levels affected the behaviors observed.

3. *Do not uncritically apply research results to oneself or to any one other person.* Suppose that some person was convinced that prenatal hormone levels covaried with spatial abilities. Also suppose that this person had always felt that he was poor in the kinds of math that were related to spatial abilities. Does that mean that he personally had the "wrong" hormone levels? No. After all, maybe the person's hormone levels were fine but his early school environment did not allow him to develop an aptitude for mathematics. Even if he had the "wrong" hormone levels, that does not mean that he is forever burdened with being poor in math. Since the current environment is also an important covariant of mathematics learning, with proper practice and instructions, the person's scores on math aptitude tests could markedly improve.

Sources of Bias in Measuring Gender-Related Differences

There are at least eight sources of systematic biases. Each affects the number and type of gender differences that are likely to be seen in the research literature.

Gender of experimenters and subjects.

Many scientists tend to use only male subjects (Borrill & Reid, 1986; Carlson & Carlson, 1960; Signorella, Vegega, & Mitchell, 1981; Vannicelli & Nash, 1984). For example, in the 1963 issues of the *Journal of Personality and Social Psychology,* only 20 percent of all research articles included both sexes; in 1983, only 10 percent did so (Lykes & Stewart, 1986). Many researchers using both sexes did not report whether they had tested for sex differences in their variables.

The bias against studying females is found in research using nonhuman as well as human subjects. Karen Berkley (1992) surveyed 100 articles recently published in the area of neurosciences. Of those articles, 45 percent failed to state the sex of the subject being used, and of those that stated the sex of subject, 57 percent used only male subjects. Of the articles stating the sex of their subjects, only 17 percent used females.

Researchers have given several reasons for the preference for male subjects. In the case of nonhuman subjects, experimenters will frequently say they study males because the periodic changes of hormones in females make their behavior too variable. The greater variability in females might overwhelm any effect of an independent variable such as training. Researchers using human subjects are likely to plead courtesy by way of explanation: females just should not be manipulated and have their privacy invaded by male researchers. Besides, female humans also have hormone changes. (As Chapters 7 and 8 will show, this assumption about hormones is invalid.)

This bias decreases the number of sex differences found in the data—no sex difference is found if at least two sexes aren't tested! Such bias may be diminishing over time as the number of female scientists increases. As the references cited in the paragraph above pointed

out, female scientists are more likely to test for sex differences in their data than are male scientists.

The subjects' gender often seems to determine how the dependent variable will be measured and what type of independent variable will be used (Fine, 1985; McKenna & Kessler, 1977). A common independent variable in aggression research is anger. However, more male than female subjects are exposed to anger-arousing conditions. If measuring the dependent variable requires subjects either to receive and/or give painful shocks to another human, males also tend to be used more often. If the research involves female subjects, some questionnaire that supposedly measures strength of aggressive impulses is usually the dependent variable, instead of actual aggressive behaviors. Gender differences cannot be consistently explored, evaluated, and explained if males and females are systematically exposed to different kinds of variables.

The gender of experimenter is often related to the type of gender difference seen in the study (Eagly & Carli, 1981; Rumenik, Capasso, & Hendrick, 1977; Vannicelli & Nash, 1984). For example, male researchers are more likely than female researchers to find that females are more influenceable than males, whereas female researchers are more likely than male researchers to find that female subjects are more sensitive to facial expressions and nonverbal cues than male subjects (Eagly, 1983). Reasons why this occurs can be best explained in the context of the bias to be described later: experimenter bias.

Publication biases and spurious versus "real" differences.

Suppose a researcher is exploring gender differences in the degree to which some characteristic is displayed. Because journals require the .05 significant level for publication, an unknown number of experiments that found no significant gender difference could have been done but never published. In addition to the one study that did get published because its author found a significant gender difference. Maybe the experimenters who found nonsignificant gender differences submitted their findings to a journal but the editors rejected the manuscripts. Even more likely, the scientists themselves never even submitted their research because they supposedly hadn't found anything. This is also called the **file drawer problem.** There is no way to know how many experiments that found no sex differences are sitting in the file drawers of their experimenters, unpublished and thereby lost to science.

Meta-analytic reviews try to estimate the magnitude of this bias, but of course these reviewers cannot be certain of how many *file drawer* studies there are. Because of this bias, the numbers and sizes of gender differences are overestimated by the published literature. Different kinds of statistics, with different kinds of assumptions, may help to alleviate this particular bias (e.g., see any good description of Baysian reasoning, as in Berger & Berry, 1988).

Social desirability and measurement. This type of bias affects both internal and external validity. Is the laboratory measurement procedure sufficiently like a "real-world" set of conditions that the results of the experiment are externally valid (generalizable or applicable) to people outside the laboratory setting? This problem exists because subjects' biases affect their scores on the dependent variable (Atkinson, 1987), which threatens both external as well as internal validity.

Subjects' scores on scales in which they are rating either themselves or their attitudes toward other people do not always accurately reflect the subjects' feelings or true characteristics. Sometimes subjects may lie. Perhaps an experimenter has inadvertently angered them and so they lie in retaliation. Perhaps subjects really do not know the truth about themselves (Hoyenga & Hoyenga, 1984) and so they create stories about themselves. Even more likely, subjects may consciously or unconsciously distort their responses to make themselves look good

to themselves and/or to others, including the experimenter. This is called **social desirability bias.**

If there are gender differences in the social desirability of some trait, that would create sex differences in subjects' answers. For example, most people in Western cultures feel that it is more socially desirable for a man than for a women to be aggressive. So, men and women in Western cultures may significantly differ in the degree to which they claim that *being aggressive* is one of their characteristics just because of the sex difference in the desirability of *aggressiveness*. A sex difference in social desirability can also reverse an actual sex difference, making it seem as though it did not actually exist. To make themselves look good, males may claim less of a trait and females more of a trait than they actually possess, thereby obscuring any sex difference.

Gender-related differences research may have been systematically measuring gender differences in social desirability. Using the concepts just previously defined, these two independent variables (sex differences in frequency of claiming to possess a trait and sex differences in trait desirability) are often completely confounded in much personality research. Furthermore, if subjects' concerns about the social desirability of their answers led to a systematic bias in those answers, that bias could eventually change the realities of those subjects.

Sampling biases. Most knowledge about human sex differences comes from studies using college students as subjects (Atkinson, 1987). Sears (1986) found that 85 percent of the articles recently published in a major social psychology journal used college students, mostly freshman in introductory psychology courses. These subjects were either volunteer participants receiving extra-credit points toward their course grades or were required to participate as part of their coursework in an introductory psychology course. These subjects are obviously not a random sample of people in the United States; they are not even a random sample of college students.

Studying only introductory psychology students means that most knowledge concerning sex differences in personality traits and social behaviors is (externally) valid only for introductory psychology students. It cannot be uncritically assumed that the research conclusions could be validly applied to older or younger subjects, subjects with less education or lower IQ scores, subjects in ethnic groups less commonly represented by introductory psychology students, and subjects tested in situations other than the psychological research laboratory. Often, it is even unknown if the sex differences found in the types of people we have not studied would be larger or smaller than those among college freshman, or whether more or fewer gender differences in those other populations would be found.

Knowledge about gender differences in other species is also limited by sampling biases. Because rats are such available (inexpensive) subjects, more is known about hormone covariates of sex differences in rats than in other species (see Chapters 7 and 8). This limits conclusions, especially since informed evolutionary reasoning requires data from a wide variety of species.

Experimenter bias and relative realities.   What one expects to see often determines what one, in fact, does see (Deaux, 1984; Jones, 1986; Skrypnek & Snyder, 1982; Snyder, 1984; Unger, 1983; see Chapter 1). If experimenters think that a man should be more aggressive than a woman, they may expect to see, and so actually think they *do* see, more aggression in the male than in the female subjects because of unconscious biases. This **experimenter bias** may even affect nonhuman subjects.

Expectations create reality not only because of biases in perceptions (one tends to see what one expects to see) but also because of biased selections of subjects and methods, and biases

in terms of how we behave toward the subjects (Rosenthal, 1963, 1966; Sherwood & Nataupsky, 1968). If experimenters expect a female to be friendlier than a male and if they do not use any controls for experimenter bias, the female will actually turn out to be friendlier. But this may occur only because the experimenters were (inadvertently) friendlier toward the female than toward the male subjects.

Controlling against experimenter bias is an important methodological issue in the gender-related differences and stereotypes literature. To the greatest extent possible, different researchers with different expectations and beliefs should study the same variables, measured in similar ways, in the same types of subjects. Different types of subjects should also be systematically studied, and variables should be studied in as many different situations as possible, especially outside the experimental laboratory.

MEASURING SEX ROLES

The degree to which a person possesses masculine and feminine traits is usually measured by paper-and-pencil sex-role tests. A person's **sex role** is described as her score(s) on a test that attempts to measure the degree to which that person possesses masculine and/or feminine traits and characteristics. Various sex-role scales conceptualize masculinity and femininity as inherent in the sexes or as conforming to stereotypes. There is still debate over whether any of these scales validly measure any useful conceptualization of a sex role (Carrigan, Connell, & Lee, 1985; Draper, 1987, p. 75; Sherif, 1982; Spence, 1991).

The History of Sex-Role Scales

One controversy has been whether sex differences (inherent) cause sex roles or whether sex roles (stereotypes) cause sex differences. Because of this controversy, the history of sex-role scales has been dominated by arguments over the relative importance of biology versus environment.

Sex differences before 1973.   According to Morawski (1985), up to the early 1900s, when researchers studied gender differences, they usually assumed that the differences were biologically caused. However, since the gender differences found were almost always very small, they were frequently not replicated. Because of this muddled state of affairs, in the early 1900s "there ensued a quiet transition from the study of sex differences to the exploration of 'masculinity' and 'femininity'" (Morawski, 1985, p. 204). In other words, researchers and theorists stopped looking at sex differences in favor of measuring something they called sex roles. Whereas the study of all other types of individual differences (personality, IQ scores) continued into the present time, the "study of sex differences was abandoned almost totally for nearly 30 years" (McGuinness, 1987, p. 2).

Starting around 1930, the sexes were observed to rate themselves differently on the various traits and behaviors that appeared as items on sex-role scales, and this was attributed to their biology. Thus, if subjects were given a large number of questions about themselves, any consistent sex differences found in the answers would be assumed to reflect, at least indirectly, biological factors. Sex roles measured this way were also thought to reflect mental health (Constantinople, 1973). A woman who displayed supposedly masculine traits — such as independence and assertiveness, for example — was said to need curative therapy. After all, since sex differences were based on biology, and sex roles were based on sex differences, a person with an so-called improper sex role was denying his or her biology.

Sex-role researchers of this time also assumed that each sex-role trait could be characterized by a single, **bipolar** dimension. One end of a bipolar dimension would reflect masculinity, such as being very independent, and the other end of the dimension would reflect femininity, such as being very dependent. The dimension had femininity at one end; at the other end, not being feminine was equated with being very masculine. The subjects' sex-role scores were calculated by summing up the number of items answered in the so-called masculine fashion.[12] Conversely, the fewer feminine items the subjects endorsed, the less masculine and the more feminine the subjects were assumed to be. All subjects could be identified as falling somewhere along one dimension, with **M** (masculinity) at one end and **F** (femininity) at the other.

Because of these assumptions, these early sex-role researchers also assumed that both M and F could be adequately measured by items that were selected on the basis of sex differences.[13]   For example, since males were more likely than females to say that they preferred showers to tub baths, that item was included on one early sex-role scale. Preferring showers was said to reflect masculinity. Because gender differences were used to select the items for these scales, researchers were simply assuming that sex differences could be equated to sex roles.

Events of 1973 and 1974.   Events occurring in 1973 and 1974 produced a dramatic change, for at least two major reasons. First, in 1973, Constantinople published her review that cataloged the inadequacies of the older scales and theories. Second, two new and different kinds of sex-role scales were published. In 1974, Bem published her **BSRI** (Bem Sex Role Inventory); shortly after, Spence published her **PAQ** (Personality Attributes Questionnaire) scale (Spence, Helmreich, & Stapp, 1974).

Other reasons for change came from important social developments. One was the rising influence of the women's rights movement. Another was the 1974 publication of Maccoby and Jacklin's extensive review of sex differences, extending Maccoby's earlier review (1966). These two reviewers concluded that there were only four reliable sex differences:

men were more aggressive, women got higher scores on tests of verbal ability, and men got higher scores on both tests of spatial and of mathematical ability. Thus, once again, sex differences research—as opposed to sex-role research—was discouraged.

Starting at this time, an increasing proportion of social scientists were women. The increase in women helped to divert the emphasis from masculinity and biological causes to femininity and cultural (sex role) causes of sex differences (Unger, 1983). Starting in 1930, a growing number of U.S. behavioral scientists believed either that all human behavior was either entirely determined by social and environmental factors (McGuinness, 1987) or else that the effect of biological variables was trivially small (Costa & McCrae, 1987). This trend was associated with the rise of humanism and the increasing activity and activism of the social scientists. The humanism movement was part of the reason for the opposition to Freeman's book on Mead described earlier.

After 1973: Changes in the concept of sex roles. Not so coincidentially, the new scales contained separate and independent scales for M and F, which were now seen as being **orthogonal** and as **unipolar.** It was thought that there were separate, independent M and F dimensions, each being unipolar, or varying from high to low levels of a given traits, such as high versus low levels of aggression. Since M and F were separate traits and separate dimensions, they could therefore be present in the same individual. This created the possibility of new types of sex roles. The sex role of **androgyny** described individuals who possessed an equal number of both feminine and masculine stereotypic traits.

The items for these new sex-role scales were not collected on the basis of sex differences. Instead, scale items were selected by a criterion group of subjects who judged each potential scale item or personality trait as belonging either to the cultural stereotype of masculinity

or to that of femininity. Sex roles were now assumed to be based on environmental/social/stereotypic factors and to reflect little if any biological influence.

Scales That Measure Sex Roles

Since 1973 and 1974, the most commonly used sex-role scales contain lists of personality trait names such as nurturant and assertive. Each subject whose sex roles are being measured is asked to rate the degree to which a given trait or characteristic is typical of herself or himself. Subjects often rated themselves on dimensions labeled *very characteristic of me* at one end (1) and *very uncharacteristic of me* at the other end (7). These ratings (numbers) are then summed or averaged across similar types of traits—one average for masculine and another for feminine traits. Finally, the summed scores are converted into sex-role scale scores for each individual. If a subject said *4* for *nurturant* and *6* for *eager to sooth hurt feelings,* since these are both feminine items, the subject's feminine score average for these two items would be 5.0.

People are often categorized according to whether their M and F scores fall above or below the median scores[14] for the group as a whole, as in Table 2.1. People whose M and F scores both fall above the group's medians are categorized as **androgynous.** People with M and F scores below the medians on both scales used to be called androgynous but are now usually called **undifferentiated.** Subjects with higher than median levels of M but lower than median levels of F are said to have a **masculine** sex role, and subjects with higher than median levels of F as well as low levels of M are said to have a **feminine** sex role. Subjects can also be categorized as having **sex-typed** or **opposite-sex-typed** sex roles.

Sex-role scales can be categorized according to how the items for that scale were selected. These categories are based on (1) the criteria used during scale development to select their items and (2) the types of instructions the

TABLE 2.1 *Sex-Role Categories*
Various sex-role categorizations are possible when masculinity scores (M), femininity scores (F), and gender identity are used to classify people. A four-category system would ignore gender identity. The labels in parentheses are those used in such a four-category system.

Gender	High M & F	High M, Low F	Low M, High F	Low M & F
Male	Androgynous	Sex typed (masculine)	Opposite sex typed (feminine)	Undifferentiated
Female	Androgynous	Opposite sex typed (masculine)	Sex typed (feminine)	Undifferentiated

researchers gave to subjects during this item selection phase, all of which affected which kinds of items were included (Heerboth & Ramaniah, 1985; Myers & Gonda, 1982b; Ramaniah & Hoffman, 1984). Since different sex-role scales contain different items, results coming from the use of a given scale should not be generalized to (are not externally valid with regard to scores on) scales found in a different category.

1. *Scales based on gender differences.* This category includes scales that used gender differences as the major basis for item selection. It includes almost all of the scales developed and used prior to 1973, some of which have been modified since their original introduction. For example, the Adjective Check List was modified by Heilbrun (1976) to include separate and independent masculinity (M) and femininity (F) scales. The California Psychological Inventory was also made into separate MCS (M) and FMN (F) scales by Baucom (1976, 1980).

Some tests developed after 1974 also used sex differences in self-endorsement as a selection criterion. For example, Fagot (1977a; Fagot & Littman, 1976) used gender differences in children's play behaviors to select items for her sex-role scale. Any behavior found to occur more often in boys than in girls became an item on the M scale. Similarly, any behavior found to occur more often in girls became part of the F scale. The sex roles of other children could be measured by the frequency with which they displayed these M and F behaviors.

2. *Gender-role identity scales.* In gender-role identity scales, subjects usually rate themselves on the two traits of *masculine* and *feminine*. Storms (1979) measured the gender-role identities of his subjects by asking them such questions as: How masculine is your personality? and How feminine do you act, appear, and come across to others? Sex-role scales appearing in other categories have also frequently been said to measure gender-role identities (e.g., Sinnott et al., 1980; Bem, 1978; Baucom, Besch, & Callahan, 1985). However, as defined here, sex-role scale scores and gender-role identity scores do *not* measure the same constructs (O'Heron & Orlofsky, 1990).

3. *Gender stereotype scales.* Gender stereotype scales contain personality trait names selected according to cultural stereotypes about the traits and behaviors of either the **"typical"** or the **"ideal"** man and woman. Although the difference between the ideal and typical stereotypes can have an important effect on which items get selected for a sex-role scale (Heerboth & Ramanaiah, 1985; Myers & Gonda, 1982b; Stoppard & Kalin, 1978), individuals' scores on these two types of scales are often very highly and positively correlated with each other.

The Broverman scale was the first to explicitly employ the typical gender stereotypes. Broverman's Sex Role Stereotype Questionnaire consists of items generated by asking approximately 100 men and women enrolled in three undergraduate psychology classes to think of all the "characteristics, attributes, and behaviors" on which they believed men and women differed (Broverman et al., 1972;

Rosenkrantz et al., 1968). Other subjects rated the degree to which each item characterized an adult man or woman.

The Sex Role Behavior Scale combined ideal and typical stereotypes (Orlofsky, 1981; Orlofsky, Cohen, & Ramsden, 1985; Orlofsky, Ramsden, & Cohen, 1982). This test included not only personality traits but also preferences and motives. Items were selected on the basis of subjects judging that a characteristic, although being desirable for either gender, was significantly more typical (stereotypical) of one than of the other gender.

Items on the PAQ and the Extended Personality Attributes Questionnaire (EPAQ) were selected using procedures similar to those just described (Helmreich, Spence, & Holahan, 1979; Spence, 1979; Spence & Helmreich, 1979, 1980; Spence, Helmreich, & Holahan, 1979; Spence, Helmreich, & Stapp, 1974, 1975). The PAQ has three scales; some items were taken from the Sex Role Stereotype Questionnaire, and others were selected according to criteria similar to those used in the Sex Role Behavior Scale. Later, Spence and her colleagues added other scales that contained stereotypic but *undesirable* personality traits to create the EPAQ. These scales were originally validated, at least in part, by demonstrating sex differences in self-endorsements of M and F traits.

Other scales emphasize the ideal gender stereotypes. The PRF ANDRO Scale contains items taken from another personality test called the Personality Research Form (Berzins, Welling, & Wetter, 1978). Bem described the BSRI items as being favorable personality characteristics (Bem, 1974, 1975, 1978, 1979, 1985). Items were selected on the basis of being judged to be more desirable in U.S. society for a man than for a woman to have (M), or as being more desirable for a women than for a man (F). The original BSRI scale had 20 M and 20 F terms, as well as 20 neutral terms. Because factor analyses suggested that more than just the three factors (or types of variables: M, F, and neutral) were involved in the scale, the BSRI was shortened. Subsequently, Bem (1985) recommended that the shortened scale not be used.

Spence recently suggested that the ways in which both the BSRI and the PAQ are used should be changed. Spence no longer describes scores on her PAQ as measuring generalized or global sex roles. Instead, she suggested that both of these scales

measure positive and negative aspects of the personality traits of instrumentality and expressiveness (Spence, 1985, 1991; Spence & Helmreich, 1979, 1980; Spence & Sawin, 1985). **Instrumentality** refers to certain traits that make it easier for a person to work with objects and tasks, such as independence and self-sufficiency. **Expressiveness** refers to traits that involve the expression of emotions, such as crying easily and having empathy for others.

Bem's usage of the BSRI has also changed. Bem now uses the BSRI to measure gender schema (Bem, 1981a, 1982, 1985; Crane & Markus, 1982; Markus, 1977; Markus, Crane, Bernstein, & Siladi, 1982). The gender schema concept, as previously described, is a cognitive structure that creates a generalized readiness to process information on the basis of sex-linked associations.

4. *Idiosyncratic scales.* A person's sex role can be measured by the degree to which that person identifies various unique and possibly idiosyncratic traits as applying to himself. The person would have previously identified these traits as being part of his own unique definitions of M and F (Baldwin et al., 1986).

Validity of Scales

This section describes some of the factors that may impair the external and internal validity of self-report sex-role scales.

Conceptual heterogeneity. It is instructive to read the introductions to a large number of research papers, all using one of the common measures of sex roles, to see what the various authors claim is being measured. For example, the BSRI and the PAQ have been used to measure: degree of sex typing, sex-role orientation, sex-role attributes, gender stereotypes, sex role, masculine and feminine personality traits, sex-role identity, sex-role preferences and behaviors, and self-concept (see documentation in Hoyenga & Hoyenga, 1993).

Scores on these same tests have also been used to explain a wide variety of behavioral phenomena. Some of these explanations have led to potentially confusing circular analyses. For example, instances of prejudice and stereotyping are explained by relating them to the sex-role expectancies shared by the people within a given culture. Sex-differences in motives, preferences, emotional responses, personality characteristics, task performances and skills, and mental and physical health are often said to be caused by sex roles. In turn, sex roles themselves are explained by describing a culture's sexual stereotypes and how child-rearing practices are affected by those stereotypes, causing children to acquire sex roles. Thus, sex roles are both the cause and the effect.

Relationships among the various types of sex-role measures.   The sex-role scales are often used as though they all measured the same traits or characteristics. However, the correlations among scales are usually small and often not significantly different from zero (Hoyenga & Hoyenga, 1993). The two most highly correlated scales are the BSRI and the PAQ, but much of this overlap comes from the seven items that appear on both scales (e.g., Spence, 1991). If people are classified into either the four or eight different sex-role categories shown in Table 2.1, the different scales do not agree on which individuals should be placed in which category more than 50 percent of the time (Cunningham & Antill, 1980; Gayton, et al., 1977; Herron, Goodman, & Herron, 1983; Kelly, Furman, & Young, 1978; Small, Erdwins, & Gross, 1979).

One study combined M and F scores from five different sex-role scales to yield summed M and F scores of high reliability. Furthermore, the pattern of correlations calculated among the scales also provided impressive evidence for at least some validity of the sex-role concept (Marsh, Antill, & Cunningham, 1987). Evidently, some aspect of people's beliefs and values about themselves and how those beliefs and values are related to the culture's sexual stereotypes is being tapped by all the sex-role scales.

Self-ratings and self-concepts.   Personality theorists point out that unless researchers in-

clude some measure of how important the trait is to the people rating themselves, self-descriptions will include much more than just each person's self-concept (Kihlstrom & Cantor, 1984; Markus, 1977, 1983). A better measure of sex roles might have scores derived only from the traits that each subject endorses and that are very important to that subject's self-concept. For example, you might think of yourself as liking showers more than tub baths, but you might also see that as having very little importance to your life or to your image of yourself.

Since current sex-role scales include no measure of importance, these scales probably measure more than just self-concepts. Scale scores will have been contaminated to an unknown degree with unanticipated dimensions, traits, and characteristics, including but not limited to social desirability biases. "We may be tapping only habitual social scripts . . . without recognizing the highly individual ways in which gender may signify something of important in an individual life" (Carlson, 1985).

Do conscious and consensual stereotypes cause sex roles?   The validity of currently popular sex-role scales depends on the extent to which these scales measure some conscious (overtly expressible, can be verbalized) and consensual (public and shared) experiences of cultural sexual stereotypes. Use of these sex-role scales to explain sex differences in behavior also assumes that cultural sexual stereotypes set up powerful norms for behavior. Suppose that the individual's perceptions of the cultural stereotypes are what caused that person's sex role to develop the way it did. If so, if sex differences are caused largely by sex roles, and sex roles are entirely due to cultural stereotypes, then, at the very least, a person's perceptions of cultural stereotypes should be related to that specific person's sex-role self-concept.

The overlap between stereotype ratings and self-concepts may not be as great as would be predicted by the discussion above. The way subjects rate men and women in general or masculinity and femininity typically differs from the way subjects rate themselves on the same scale (Broverman et al., 1972; Myers & Gonda, 1982b; Spence et al., 1975). Subjects' ideas of their own M and F may not include the traits commonly found on sex-role scales (Jones, Sensenig, & Haley, 1974; Myers & Gonda, 1982b; Smith & Midlarsky, 1985). When subjects are asked to describe examples of masculine and feminine behaviors that they have actually displayed, describing an aggressive act does not mean that later they will rate themselves highly on a sex-role trait of aggression (Signorella & Frieze, 1989).

Rather than validly measuring any conceptualization of a sex role, items on these scales may simply reflect the social segregation of women and men into different kinds of roles and occupations (Eagly & Steffen, 1984; Eagly & Wood, 1985; Locksley & Colten, 1979). More men than women are employed, and employed people are rated as being more M than unemployed people are, regardless of gender. This means that men may be rated as being more *independent* or *assertive* than women, simply because men are more often employed outside the home. The opposite traits *(dependent, passive)* may not really be part of some F stereotype, but could be part of the cultural stereotype of a person who is not employed outside the home.

Finally, sex-role traits may be neither conscious nor consensual. Spence and Sawin (1985) had subjects chosen from the community rate both their own M and F on a scale of 0 to 10. Two people responded with 0 to both scales, but the other 81 subjects' answers were all in the upper half of the gender-appropriate and the lower half of the gender-inappropriate scale. When the subjects were asked to describe their own manhood or womanhood, one of the most frequent responses was: "Don't know." Spence (1985) said the subjects seemed to lose "track of masculinity and femininity" and could only describe aspects of themselves that they personally valued. They did not seem to be consciously aware of what was feminine and what was masculine about themselves. Spence (1985) summarized her data by saying that "personal senses of masculinity or femininity appear to be phenomenologically real *though their meanings remain unarticulated,* and [the subjects' sex roles seem] to be relatively independent of any given class of masculine or feminine behaviors (p. 79, emphasis added).

So, sex roles may be preconscious (not easily articulated), idiosyncratic, and intensely personal. How well we perceive ourselves to fit the stereotypes and how masculine and how feminine we perceive ourselves to be may involve characteristics unique to each of us that are not readily available to our own conscious awareness. If all this were true, only idiosyncratic types of scale could validly measure such a sex role.

Item selection: number and favorability of traits. In selecting items for many current sex-role scales, only favorable traits were included because the scale developers did not want their subjects' self-reports contaminated by differences in the social desirability of M compared to F. This decision reflected the assumption (often unvoiced) that M and F were unitary traits. Hence, any items reflecting M or F would be relevant and any set of such items would adequately measure a subject's sex role. Also, only M and F traits that could be independent of each other were selected (see Chapter 13) so that M and F could be viewed as separate, independent dimensions.

Contrary to these assumptions, one's self-concept probably involves multiple, superordinate and subordinate, as well as situation-dependent selves (Kihlstrom & Cantor, 1984; Markus, 1977). This means that who you are depends, in part, on where you are. Also, when factor analyzed, the BSRI can be broken down into three or even four independent, unipolar personality factors (Chapter 11) (Kimlicka, Wakefield, & Friedman, 1980; Pedhazur & Tetenbaum, 1979). On the other hand, the

PAQ (the original 24-item sale) has just the two factors: instrumentality and expressiveness (Helmreich, Spence, & Wilhelm, 1981). Other sex-role scales have been explicitly designed to be multidimensional based on the assumption that sex roles were complex (Bernard, 1981, 1984; Kelly et al., 1977; Orlofsky, 1981; Orlofsky, Ramsden, & Cohen, 1983; Spence, Helmreich, & Holahan, 1979).

Contrary to the assumption of the independence of M and F traits, some research has found that some aspects of M and F are negatively correlated and so could be opposite ends of the same dimension. Stereotypical masculinity by itself, or gender-role identity, is seen as the bipolar opposite of stereotypical femininity (Deaux & Lewis, 1984; Major, Carnevale, & Deaux, 1981; Storms, 1979). The BSRI has also been used in a bipolar fashion (Bem, 1982; Russell & Sines, 1978; Sines & Russell, 1978; Spence, 1985, 1991). When Bem uses the BSRI to measure gender schematic processing, she uses it as a bipolar scale. Bem (1982) says that sex-typed people are schematics who sort gender information "on the basis of some particular dimension" (p. 1192).

As Markus (1983) pointed out, self-knowledge or self-concept is multidimensional. We do not see ourselves as unchanging, unidimensional, or cardboard figures but as complex, multifaceted creatures. Therefore, how we perceive ourselves to fit the stereotypes probably involves multiple and idiosyncratic dimensions, some of which are unipolar and some bipolar.

Sex-role scales and behaviors.   To demonstrate that a scale measures sex roles, the developers had to demonstrate that their tests had validity. They ususlly used the test validity design that Fisk (1971) called an **a priori related process.** The test developer assumes that a particular response (e.g., endorsement of a culturally stereotypic trait) will occur in the test situation only if certain past experiences had taken place (e.g., particular sex-role socializa-

tion experiences). These past experiences determine both a subject's scores and her behaviors. For sex-role scales, the relevant a priori process is the person's own sex role.

Some sex-role scales may be valid only for certain kinds of people. With regard to the BSRI, Bem stated that the relevant a priori processes may be activated only in sex-typed people (Bem, 1981a, 1981b, p. 1192). Since the BSRI measures gender schemas, and only some people have these schemas, the BSRI taps "different things for different people" (Bem, 1981b, p. 369). For nonsex-typed people (androgynous males and females, masculine females, and feminine males), the BSRI measures instrumentality and expressiveness, not masculinity or femininity. But "when sex-typed individuals [women who are F but not M; men who are M but not F] so describe themselves, however, it is precisely the masculine/feminine connotations of the items on the BSRI to which they are responding" (p. 370). Some high-scoring females may be in some sense consciously, willfully, and deliberately feminine — or they may just be expressive.

Bem originally validated the BSRI as a measure of sex roles by relating BSRI scores to the types of behaviors predicted by her theory of androgyny. Sex-typed people were predicted to behave more consistently from situation to situation than would androgynous people because only sex-typed people's behaviors were thought to be importantly determined by their internalized sex role — something that is present in all situations. Androgynous people were viewed as being more flexible, more free to respond to the specific requirements of a particular, unique situation. Androgyny has, in fact, been consistently related to behavioral flexibility just as predicted by the theory (Bem, 1975, 1978; Taylor & Hall, 1982).

Androgynous people who are not trapped by sex roles should be able to develop higher levels of self-esteem. In fact, androgyny is correlated with self-esteem, but the correlation is largely with M items; the endorsement of F items adds little to a researcher's ability to predict a subject's self-esteem score. Even the relationship between masculinity and self-esteem may be spurious since the scales share several items in common (Whitley, 1983). In other words, people may get similar scores on M scales and on self-esteem scales because people tend to answer simple items in consistent ways from one scale to another.

Other validity studies have fared even less well. Archer (1989a, 1989b, 1990; Archer & Rhodes, 1989) found that self-ratings on sex-role trait scales are not strongly related to self-ratings on sex-role attitude scales and sex-role behavior scales. However, when BSRI scores are used as measures of gender schema, they may be better able to predict behaviors (e.g., Bem, 1985; Frable, 1989; Matteo, 1988). Finally, being masculine may be more important to a man's self-esteem and mental health than either sex role is to a woman's self-esteem and mental health (O'Heron & Orlofsky, 1990).

Other researchers have questioned whether self-ratings measure personality traits (Locksley & Colten, 1979). For example, Myers and Gonda (1982a) found that self-ratings on the BSRI *aggressive* item did not correspond to what subjects said about how often they actually behaved aggressively. Aggressive people did not, with any consistency, rate themselves as being aggressive on the BSRI. Signorella and Frieze (1989) got similar results.

The validity data for sex-role scales has to be regarded as problematical. "To assume that scales labeled masculine and feminine are reliable and valid measures of sex roles, sex-role identity, sex-role orientation, sex-role beliefs and behaviors is . . . untenable" (Gilbert, 1985, p. 165). "The sex role literature does not consistently distinguish between the expectations that are made of people and what they in fact do" (Carrigan, Connell, & Lee, 1985, p. 578). Despite this, thousands of research projects have been done with these scales, and such a massive effect cannot be ignored.

In the rest of this book, the authors we will

be taking the point of view that items on sex-role scales reflect cultural sexual stereotypes. As Chapter 11 will document, these stereotypes do exist, there is considerable consensus about their contents among the people of a given culture, and they do affect each and every person. However, whether personal endorsements of culturally defined, sexually stereotypical traits, resulting in scores on a sex-role scale, measure anything like a sex-role concept is problematical. It is not yet proven that scores on these scales go beyond instrumentality and expressiveness to predict a broad range of gender-related attitudes, behaviors, and expectancies (Spence, 1991). When research using these scales, particularly the PAQ and the BSRI, is discussed in this book, it is viewed as measuring self-reported tendencies toward instrumentality and expressiveness (following Spence's suggestions). The authors will also indicate which scale was used, to discourage a pathological assumption that a sex role had been measured—which is yet to be proven or even adequately defined.

SUMMARY

The research measuring gender-related differences has produced dissatisfying results for a number of reasons. The most important type of difference concerns how gender affects the interpretation of test scores, and this possibility has been relatively ignored. For ethical reasons, the most powerful experimental designs—those involving random assignment and active manipulation of independent variables—cannot often be used with human subjects. Because of the various systematic biases, the number and extent of sex differences cannot be reliably estimated from the literature. Also, because only a few types of subjects have been sampled, the external validity of any sex differences can be questioned. A more pluralistic idea of research may be important to pursue, attempting to fit the results of disparate methodologies into a complete picture of gender-related differences across cultures and across species.

The sex-role concept has been used to refer to a variety of constructs and measured in a correspondingly wide variety of scale types. But these scales may not validly or reliably measure sex roles according to any current definition. Regardless of how they are caused, both sex differences and sexual stereotypes do exist and can be measured. To measure gender-related differences adequately, one needs a variety of researchers—having different theories, approaches, and expectations—gathering data using several different types of design and measurement techniques. To assess the impact of stereotypes, one must measure an individual's knowledge of stereotypes—whether or not the knowledge is conscious—and then relate that knowledge to a specific person's interpersonal behaviors and evaluations of himself and others.

ENDNOTES

1. Hence, *biological determinism* indicates that, because of biology, we are not free to make our own gender-related choices (see Chapter 1).

2. For example, the following is a logically valid argument and conclusion: All wolves are bad; this animal is a wolf, therefore this animal is bad. On the other hand, the following is a deductively invalid argument: some murderers should be executed; John is a murderer, therefore John should be executed.

3. Connell & Radican, 1987; Jones, Sensenig, & Haley, 1974; Kihlstrom & Cantor, 1984; Myers & Gonda, 1982a; Nyborg, 1987; Smith & Midlarsky, 1985; Spence & Sawin, 1985; Wallston & Grady, 1985.

4. In fact, we usually assume that gender stereotypes are acquired by a lifetime of exposure to a culture that includes the stereotypic beliefs that certain traits are appropriate only for women and others are appropriate only for men.

5. Although the term *valid* is used for both criteria 1 and 2, note that the use of that term has somewhat different implications when it is used to refer to the dependent variable as opposed to the research outcomes. If both forms of validity are high, the researcher can be confident in the value (usefulness in predicting behavior) of his or her conclusions and explanations.

6. As Chapter 1 already pointed out, one cannot legitimately generalize results obtained with male subjects to conclusions regarding female subjects.

7. To look for gender differences in variability, one would measure something, say weight or height, in a group of men and a group of women. One would calculate the mean score for each sex separately, and then calculate the **average variability** in each gender by subtracting each subject's score from the average for that gender. Last, one would add up all the differences and divide by the number of subjects of that gender to measure the average variability in each gender. A **standard deviation** or a measure of **variance** is calculated in similar ways and also describe the average score variability within a group.

8. For those of you with a more statistical background, this effect size is measured in standard deviation units and so reflects how the difference between men and women is related to the weighted average standard deviations for men and women. Thus, $d = .5$ means that the sex difference is equal to half a standard deviation for both sexes combined. The weighted effect size is corrected for the size of the sample from which the estimate came.

9. Remember that the word **variable** should be taken literally: A variable has to have two or more different values. Thus, *gender* is a variable because it can take on at least two different values: male or female. *Female* is not a variable because it has only the one value.

10. In the terminology introduced earlier, the first variable is an independent variable, and the possible covariate is a dependent variable.

11. Note that although covariation can be measured by simply using a correlation coefficient, an analysis of variance or a *t* test can also establish significant covariation. In more complex research, multiple regression and multivariate analyses of variance can establish a significant covariation between one or more independent and dependent variables.

12. The subjects would say that they possessed the masculine side of each item's dimension, such as "very independent."

13. However, some scales also used items selected because of differences between what homosexual versus heterosexual males said or did.

14. The **median scores** are calculated for scale for each particular group of subjects that takes the test; to do this, all of the subjects' scores on each of the two scales separately are arranged in rank order, from highest to lowest, and the scale score above which half the people fall is the median.

CHAPTER 3

THE EVOLUTION OF SEX

INTRODUCTION
EVOLUTION, SELECTION PRESSURES, AND GENES
THE ADVANTAGES OF SEXUAL REPRODUCTION
SUMMARY

Why Sex?
Reproduction is the process in which one cell turns into two, and
sex that in which two cells fuse to form one. Darwin has taught us
to expect organisms to have properties that endure successful sur-
vival and reproduction. Why, then, should they bother with sex,
which interrupts reproduction? . . . I regard [this question] as the
most interesting in current evolutionary biology.
    —John Maynard Smith (1988, p. 165)

Lively (1987) examined some New Zealand snails that can reproduce sexually or asexually. He measured the number of males present in many different sites as a way of estimating the relative frequency of sexual versus asexual reproduction in each locale (only sexual species have males). He also counted the number of microparasites found per snail per site. The more microparasites that snails in a given site had, the more often they reproduced sexually (the more males they had).

This chapter describes the basic aspects of evolutionary theory, which are then used in all other chapters. These concepts are also need-ed to explain why sex may have evolved. Why don't we just reproduce asexually, like some sponges do? We could start a bud off our trunk, have it develop, and then have it drop off to be our new child. Think of all the

problems that would eliminate! It may turn out that sex, or sexual reproduction, is due to microparasites—sort of a germ theory of sex.

INTRODUCTION

This chapter is divided into two major halves. The first half describes what evolutionary theory is (and, by implication, what it is not). The second half describes why we may have come to have sex in the first place. Sexual reproduction implies having (at least) two dif-ferent sexes. The evolution of sex differences— how evolutionary selection pressures created two sexes who are different from each other—is described in Chapter 4.

Evolutionary theories started with Darwin. They are a family of models that are evolu-tionary because of common ideas about selec-tion pressures and gene frequencies. Since evolution has to work at the level of the gene (the only biological aspect of one's parental heritage), a description of the gene's "purposes" in certain evolutionary situations is presented. Obviously, no gene has a consciousness, nor do the authors wish to anthropomorphize either genes or evolution. In evolution, the organism's intentions are not necessarily relevant. For example, having sexual activity does not imply either the presence or absence of any conscious desire to have offspring; however, the gene can "live" for another generation only if its current host successfully reproduces.

In all this, no value judgments are ever implied. Reproductive success means just that — having lots of viable offspring — and has no implications for the social, moral, or political value of any individual or group. As Maynard Smith (1988) pointed out, people seem to need both myths and science, but only myths have value judgments and symbolic meanings. Science, including the science of evolution, is to be taken literally and used only to guide the development of theories at other levels (see Chapter 1). Any attempt to derive symbolic (as opposed to scientific) meaning out of evolutionary ideas moves it from the realm of science to that of myth. And, as Maynard Smith quoted Bernard Shaw, "Darwinism is a rotten myth" (p. 21).

EVOLUTION, SELECTION PRESSURES, AND GENES

In some sense, our minds and bodies are simply what our genes used to survive and to reproduce themselves. Evolutionary principles, theories, and predictions are all concerned with how the frequency of a gene changes over generations because of the effects it has had on organisms' survival and reproduction. Although this basic principle of evolution is simple to state, its implications are both profound and complex.

Any gene will increase in frequency to the degree to which it improves an organism's survival and reproduction, relative to the effects that other organisms' genes have on those individuals' ability to compete with the first organism. Any gene that improves survival or reproduction will appear in more of the animals of the next generation than will the genes that were less beneficial. The more a gene facilitates survival and/or reproduction, compared to the effects of the competitors' genes, the more likely that gene is to be passed on to future generations.

Thus, **evolutionary selection pressures** refer to systematic changes in gene frequencies. **Gene frequencies** are the proportions of organisms that possess that particular gene in any given generation and in any given population. Genes that favor survival will increase in frequency; a greater proportion of the organisms of the next generation will have that gene, compared to the proportion of the current generation. Conversely, any gene that impairs survival or reproduction is less likely to be passed on to offspring; its bearer is less likely to be able to reproduce. Any such gene will decrease in frequency over future generations.

Both the increases and the decreases in gene frequencies are always *relative*. First, they are relative to what the other genes also present in the same organism are doing. A gene that would improve survival in the presence of certain genes might actually impair survival in the presence of different genes. In Maynard Smith's (1988) words, to increase in frequency over generations, a gene must be a "good mixer." Second, the changes in gene frequency are also relative to the environment. A given gene/trait that is beneficial to organisms in one type of environment may actually be a hindrance in a different environment.

Genes versus Traits

Understanding evolution requires some basic facts about genes. It is especially important to understand why genetic variability is required for evolution, including for the evolution of sex.

Chromosomes, genes, and proteins. Every one of our body cells contains the same genes on the same chromosomes.[1] Unless we are part of a pair of identical twins, no one else will ever have exactly the same genes that we do.

All organisms above the level of insects (and even many insects) are **diploid,** meaning that their chromosomes come in pairs.[2] Humans have 23 pairs of chromosomes (making a total of 46 chromosomes). Of those pairs, 22 pairs are called **autosomes.** The twenty-third pair is the pair of **sex chromosomes:** genetically normal male mammals have one X and one Y, and females have two Xs. Thus, the sex chromosomes are therefore matched, being of the same type (or **homologous**) for female mammals, and are unmatched (or **heterologous**) for male mammals.[3] One member of each of our 23 chromosome pairs came from our fathers **(paternal chromosome)** and one from our mothers **(maternal chromosome).** A pic-

ture, or **karyotype,** of all human chromosome pairs sorted by size is presented in Figure 3.1. Each chromosome, depending on its size, carries thousands of genes. The total set of chromosomes is an individual's **genome** or **genotype.**

The gene is the unit of heredity. Each gene is associated with a specific gene product, a molecule of **RNA (ribonucleic acid).** In turn, many (but not all) of these large molecules of RNA are used as templates or schematics, specifying how a particular protein[4] is to be manufactured or assembled from amino acid building blocks. A gene carries all the information a cell needs to manufacture a molecule of RNA, and, eventually, in most cases, a protein molecule. As shown in Figure 3.2, Part A, each chromosome is a molecule of **DNA (deoxyribonucleic acid).**

Each DNA molecule contains a double strand of **nucleotide** chains,[5] the double helix

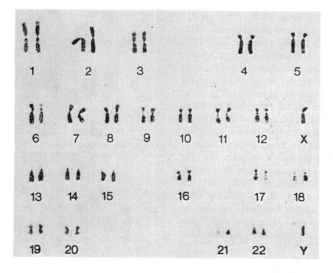

FIGURE 3.1 *XY Karotype*
A karyotype displays the pairs of chromosomes by arranging them according to size and physical appearance. The number under each chromosome pair "names" it by identifying to which autosome the pair corresponds. The X and Y chromosomes appear in the last column, in the second and fourth rows, respectively. Note the size of the X compared to the Y chromosome.

Source: From "A Cytogenetic Survey of an Institution for the Mentally Retarded: I. Chromosome Abnormalities" by P. A. Jacobs, J. S. Matsuura, M. Mayer, and I. M. Newlands, 1978, *Clinical Genetics, 13,* p. 42. Copyright © 1978 Munksgaard International Publishers Ltd., Copenhagen, Denmark. Reprinted by permission.

FIGURE 3.2   *Structure of a DNA Molecule*

Part A: A DNA molecule is constructed from phosphate, sugar, and nucleic acids. Part B: The double-helix form of the two strands of the DNA molecule. The two strands are opposite in polarity, or are complementary to each other, meaning—for example—that every guanine found on one strand is associated with a cytosine on the other. For the replication of DNA or the production of RNA, the two strands are separated at the dotted lines. PA = phosphoric acid; S = sugar; A = adenine; T = thymine; G = guanine; C = cytosine.

Part A

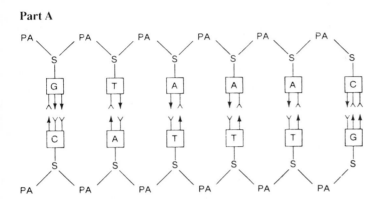

Part B

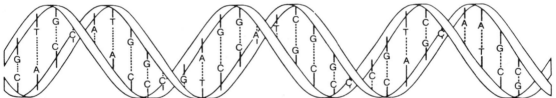

Source: From *Psychobiology,* by K. B. Hoyenga and K. T. Hoyenga. Copyright © 1988 by Wadsworth, Inc. Reprinted by permission of Brooks/Cole Publishing Company, Pacific Grove, CA 93950.

discovered by Watson, Crick, Wilkins, and Franklin. The two strands are held together by the bonds that form between the complementary organic nitrogen bases: adenine with thymine and guanine with cytosine, as can be seen in Part A and Part B of Figure 3.2. The double strands, with their connecting links, are twisted in a helical fashion, resembling the twisted ladder seen in Part B.

These two strands of a DNA molecule separate whenever the bonds between the com-

plementary bases are broken by enzymes. One time this happens is during cell division and growth. As part of the process by which each cell can divide and become two "daughter" cells, each separate strand of each of that cell's DNA molecules serves as a template for the formation of a **complementary** strand. Adenine is inserted in the complementary strand for every thymine in the original strand, for example. In Figure 3.1, each chromosome appears doubled because each strand of DNA had just formed this complementary or mirror image copy of itself. Shortly after this has happened, the strands will separate, and each daughter cell will get one copy of each strand so that each daughter cell will have one complete copy of each of the original cell's chromosome pairs.

The DNA strands also separate when RNA is synthesized. After the two DNA strands separate, one (the coding strand) is "read" by appropriate enzymes. **Reading** the DNA means that its message is translated into a molecule of RNA. This RNA is very similar to the other, noncoding strand of the DNA molecule. However, in RNA, uracil is substituted for the DNA's thymine. At any given time, only part of a chromosome or DNA molecule is read; a **gene** is thus *the part of a coding DNA strand that is read as a unit.*

The genetic message can be described as a sequence of codons. Each **codon** is a set of three nucleotide bases in a DNA or RNA molecule, and the three bases function together as a coding unit (or "word"). The DNA codons are read by specific enzymes acting like decoders, which translate the DNA message into messenger RNA molecules. Some codons tell these enzymes where to start reading the genetic DNA message (thus specifying where a gene begins), and other codons specify where to stop reading. In most cases, each codon specifies a single amino acid.

The resulting RNA is one of three types: **transfer RNA (tRNA), ribosomal RNA,** and **messenger RNA.** Each specific type of tRNA "recognizes" (attaches to) a specific amino acid and carries that amino acid to where the proteins are being manufactured, in the **ribosomes:**[6] tRNA molecules are sort of a cellular version of a trucking firm. The ribosomal RNA becomes part of the ribosomes' structure. The messenger RNA is the template or code for the protein that is to be manufactured. One or more ribosomes move along a strand of the messenger RNA. As illustrated in Figure 3.3, a ribosome identifies the amino acid specified by each messenger RNA codon and removes the correct amino acid from its specific tRNA (the transporting truck). Then the ribosome attaches the amino acid to the end of the growing chain of acids. When the ribosome reaches the *stop* codon, the chain is completed and released into the cell as a protein molecule.

The proteins are then the next step in the causal chain between a gene and its outcomes. The proteins may become part of the **structure** of the cell in which they were manufactured. Cells with different genes active in them will thus have different structures—different cellular anatomies—the microanatomy of a liver versus a brain cell. The protein may also become an **enzyme,** controlling various metabolic reactions. By these means, genes control the function of cells. The protein may also be released from the cell and travel elsewhere in the body to affect other cells. Because of this, the genes active in one cell can come to affect cellular structure and function in other parts of the body.

Although all body cells have the same genes (with exceptions; see endnote 1), different types of cells can have completely different types of proteins. Since development is epigenetic (see Chapter 1), the environment of the developing fetal cell determines which genes will be turned on, which will be turned off, and when. When these events occur during fetal development, they sometimes have irreversible effects. For example, once a fetal cell starts to **differentiate** as a nerve cell, afterwards it will never be able to activate the relevant genes and so have the proteins appropriate for a liver cell. "Liver" genes are permanently "turned off" **(inactivated)** in nerve cells. Only a few genes are active in any fully differentiated cell. More genes are active in brain cells than in other cells, which means that more of our genome is devoted to our brains than to any of our other organs.

Some organisms, like bacteria, have all their DNA read, but most of the DNA of higher animals is never translated into RNA. Maybe only 5 to 10 percent of human DNA is ever decoded or used. Though the largest human

FIGURE 3.3   *Manufacture of a Protein Molecule*
According to molecular genetics, genetic information flows from DNA to messenger RNA
to protein. Each gene is a relatively short segment of a long DNA molecule—a segment that
acts as a coding unit. The DNA code that is part of a gene is expressed in two steps. First,
the sequence of nucleotide bases in the coding strand of the DNA double helix is transcribed
onto a single, complementary strand of messenger RNA (except that thymine is replaced by
the closely related uracil [U]). Second, the messenger RNA is translated into protein. The complementary molecules of transfer RNA add amino acids one by one to the growing peptide
chain as the ribosome moves along the messenger RNA strand. Each of the 20 amino acids
found in proteins is specified by a codon, which is a sequence of three RNA bases. A = adenine;
C = cytosine; G = guanine.

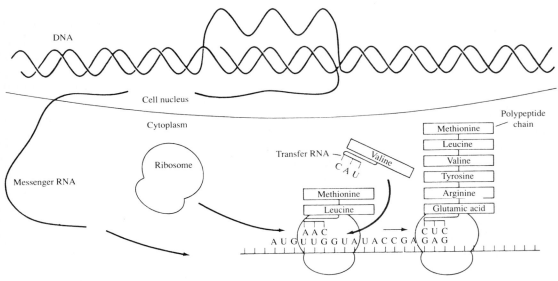

Source: © Scientific American Inc., George V. Kelvin. From Francisco J. Ayala, "The Mechanisms of
Evolution," *Scientific American 239* (1978): 56–69. Reprinted by permission.

chromosome has enough bases to serve as
codons for 200,000 proteins all by itself, so
much of the DNA is unused that the human
probably has only about 100,000 functional
genes on all its chromosomes taken together
(Brennan, 1986). The percent of coding DNA
found in other animals varies from 10 to 50
percent.

Phenotype versus genotype. As described
above, the genotype or genome is the collection
of genes a diploid organism has on each of its

pairs of chromosomes. The **phenotype** refers
to the physical appearance, functions, and
behaviors of an entire organism (or sometimes
of a cell, depending on the level of discussion).
The organism's (or cell's) genotype is never
directly related, in any one-to-one fashion, with
its phenotype, for the following reasons:

1. According to epigenesis, phenotypes depend on
environments (developmental histories, learning,
culture) as well as genes. Organisms could have differing phenotypes, despite having identical genes, if
they experienced different environments. And two

organisms with different genes could have identical phenotypes, if the environment did not activate those divergent genes.

2. Phenotypic traits often depend on multiple genes rather than being the direct product of a single gene; the latter is called a **major gene effect.** Genes can combine additively or in a more complex fashion. For example, in **epistasis,** one gene pair, or set of pairs, affects the activity of a totally different set. If some aspect of the phenotype depends on epistatic interactions among genes, these effects are **nonadditive** (their effects do not simply add together) and will depend on the organism having a certain specific pattern or set of genes.

3. One gene almost always affects many different phenotypic traits, which is called **pleiotropism.** For example, the single gene that is the probable cause of cystic fibrosis in humans has multiple effects on the sufferer's phenotype: thick mucus, susceptibility to infections, malfunctioning pancreas, and excess salt in the sweat.

4. Since most animals are diploid, having two members of each chromosome, that means that the genes carried by each homologous chromosomes are also doubled or paired. The paired genes can either be the same, specifying the same RNA and/or protein, or be different from each other. This is directly related to the evolutionary reason for sex and the sexes. The phenotype will depend on how many of the gene pairs are the same versus being different, and on how the different the two paired genes are.

Heterozygous versus homozygous. Loci are the actual physical locations ("addresses") of the genes along the DNA strands. Similar to homologous chromosomes, **homologous** genes are those found on the same loci on both members of the homologous chromosome pair. For example, the two genes, each one of which is located at the very tip of each of the chromosome pair called *21,* are homologous because each has the same locus. If the homologous genes are genetically the same, having the same sequence of bases and so the same codon sequence, the organism is **homozygous** at that locus. Two homozygous genes code for exactly the same RNA molecule and therefore exactly

the same protein. If the homologous genes are different, the organism is **heterozygous** at that locus.

The set of genes that occupy the same genetic locus on a given chromosome pair in various members of the same species are called **alleles.** For example, if one person had two different genes, each on the very tip of one of her chromosome 21 pair, the genes would be alleles of each other. This would make that person heterozygous for that locus. **Polymorphic** genes (or loci) are those having more than one allele in a population, such as the genes for eye colors in humans. Although any one person could have only two alleles (unless that person had more than just the usual two of that chromosome), different members of that species could have the other alleles. Individuals can be heterozygous only if the genes at that locus are polymorphic.

Most species are polymorphic at an average of from 10 to 70 percent of all their gene loci (Nei, 1988). The average proportion of loci expected to be heterozygotic, in the sense of coding for different proteins in any given individual, ranges across species from just above 0 to 50 percent. However, when heterozygosity is judged at the nucleotide level (a different sequence of bases can end up coding for the same protein), almost all genes are polymorphic (Nei, 1988; O'Brien et al., 1983). The average human genome may be heterozygous for about 10 million nucleotide sites (out of 3.5×10^9 total nucleotides).

Silent or swamped mutants. The phenotypic implications of being heterozygous depend on just what the two homologous genes are like. In many cases, one gene will have had one or more of its bases altered or **mutated** into a form that cannot be read (translated into RNA). For the organism that is heterozygous because one locus contains a mutated gene, the product of only the one nonmutated or normal gene will be manufactured. In effect, the mutant gene is "silent." Having a nonfunctional mutant gene plus a functional gene (heterozygous) will mean that cells in which that gene is active will have half as much of the protein product as will the cells of organisms that are homozygous for the nonmutant gene. However, the net effect on cellular functions of there being one silent gene in a heterozygous pair may be slight and even barely detectable (Kacser & Burns, 1981).

Only organisms that are homozygous for a silent gene would have a phenotype strongly affected by that gene. The homozygous organism with two mutant genes would have no functional genes of that type, and so it would have none of the protein product normally associated with that genetic locus. This lack could appear in the phenotype in a variety of ways, such as mental retardation resulting from the lack of an important enzyme (e.g., the retardation due to phenylketonuria, or PKU, in humans).

In other cases, the mutant gene is read, but the protein product of one gene "swamps" the effects of the heterozygous gene. Maybe a mutated gene codes for a nonfunctional or malfunctioning protein, or maybe the protein product of the mutated gene is not quite as functional or effective. The effect of the swamped gene is not usually detectable in the phenotype (though it might well be detectable by sensitive biochemical analyses). For example, a gene coding for black coat color in a cat may swamp the effects of other homologous coat-color genes. A heterozygous cat with one black gene and one brown gene will look the same as a homozygous cat with two black genes. A gene coding for blue-colored eyes in a human will be swamped by the product of the homologous but heterozygous gene coding for brown-colored eyes.[7]

Gregor Johann Mendel—the father of genetics—described the silent or swamped mutant gene as being **recessive,** and the other gene as being **dominant.** These terms do not reflect what is currently known about the molecular basis of genes (Mendel certainly knew nothing about DNA!), but they do often adequately describe the phenotypic outcomes of heterozygosity versus homozygosity. Although the terms are used in this book, recessive can mean several things: the gene may be unreadable; its products may not be functional; or its product simply may not be as effective in affecting the phenotype as is the protein product of the dominant gene.

Active mutated genes.   Other things can happen when the mutant gene is actually read and translated into functional protein products. The enzymatic product of the mutant gene may function differently than does the product of the nonmutated gene. Or maybe the mutant gene product functions up to some point in the chemical reaction it is supposed to control, but then it changes the whole reaction in some way. The two protein products may also combine to have quantitatively, or even qualitatively, different kinds of enzymatic effects than the protein products of each gene alone.

Although the phenotype of the organism with the heterozygous locus does not always reflect its heterozygosity, some heterozygosity does have phenotypic effects. For example, people heterozygous for the genes causing a high cholesterol level do have higher than normal levels, but not as high as someone who is homozygous for the disease-creating gene. The homozygous, recessive person will have very dangerously high cholesterol levels, whereas the heterozygote's levels will only be moderately elevated (Kadowaki et al., 1988).

Sometimes heterozygosity can produce heterosis. In **heterosis,** the heterozygote's phenotype is quite different from that of either of the homozygous phenotypes. Under some conditions, having both protein products present (being a heterozygote) may facilitate survival and reproduction above the levels characteristic of either homozygous phenotype.[8] Heterosis is another type of nonadditive interaction among genes.

Heterosis is similar (though not identical) to the idea of **hybrid vigor** (Crow, 1987). Hybrids often have greater fertility and vitality than do either of their inbreed parent strains. However, this is most often due to a dominant gene from one parent preventing what would otherwise be a deleterious homozygosity. If only one strain were used as parents and so provided all the genes, the offspring would be homozygous at most or all loci. Inbred organisms are homozygous at most loci. These organisms often have impaired fertility and vitality.[9] They may also have reduced learning skills.

Thus, hybrid vigor does not necessarily reflect heterosis. Nonetheless, the genes controlling one's immune system may exhibit heterosis (Tanaka & Nei, 1989). As will be described shortly, heterosis may be one of the major reasons for the evolution of sex.

Evolution and Genes

In summary, evolution works on gene frequencies: a *gene frequency* is the proportion of organisms in some population that have that specific gene in their genotype. Now that you know what a gene is, the following will describe how gene frequencies can be changed by evolutionary selection pressures.

Basic principles. **Selection pressures** refer to the ways in which a gene's effects on the survival and reproduction probabilities of one generation will affect gene frequencies in some future generation. The current survival and reproductive successes of individuals in a given species tell us about current selection pressures. However, they do not tell us about past selection pressures, unless the current environment is identical to the past environment. To know about past selection pressures in humans, we need to know in what types of environments our ancestors lived, loved, and died. Current patterns of survival and reproduction also do not tell us about how our traits and dispositions might have evolved (or how they may have been related to past selection pressures). The only possible exception would be where the current

environment is identical to the past environment, which is most emphatically not the case with humans or many other currently living species.[10]

Humans are a good example of how selection pressures have shifted over historical and prehistorical times (Crow, 1958, 1989; Luna & Moral, 1990). Starvation and disease have been and still are the major causes of death in less technologically developed cultures. Furthermore, the amount of sexual activity was and is directly related to the number of births. In contrast, more technologically advanced cultures have birth control, and the major causes of death are the diseases of civilization — heart disease and cancer. The major selection pressures working on technologically advanced humans are therefore the diseases of civilization and variations in the desire to have children (since the existence of birth control can eliminate reproduction in the absence of this desire).

The **selection environment** is a complex as well as important concept. The environment, of course, includes things like climate, availability of sexual partners, food availability, competitors of other species, and predators. The environment also includes the other organisms of the same species that compete for food and sexual partners. These other organisms usually not only have different genes but they have learned to do different things. An organism is not only subjected to the selection pressures from all these aspects of its environment but it also actively changes its environment. An organism's ability to compete successfully and thus to pass on its genes to the next generation depends on all these factors.

Adapted traits are those whose genes have increased in frequency because of being subjected to some evolutionary pressures in previously experienced selection environments. *Adapted* does *not* mean any of the following:

1. The trait is only (or even mostly) affected by genes; instead, the developmental environment could be the major factor, the gene merely creating the possibility of the organism acquiring an

adaptive response when exposed to a given, typical environment.

2. Selection is currently in operation; it may not be.
3. The trait is "desirable" or inevitable; it was simply expedient at some point in the past.

The *origin* versus the *maintenance* of adapted traits may reflect quite different selection pressures. A trait may have evolved because it facilitated survival, for example, but may be maintained because it facilitates reproduction. Finally, the possibilities of pleiotropy should always be kept in mind: adapted genes may have been selected because of their influence on some trait other than the one an experimenter is currently measuring.

Proximate versus ultimate causes.   A single phenomenon can have a multitude of explanations. If there is an evolutionary explanation for a given trait, there will also be an equally correct cultural/developmental/learning/environmental/motivational explanation. The evolutionary explanation is the **ultimate cause,** whereas the environmental/motivational explanation is the equally valid and potent **proximal cause.**

Evolution may have selected for a given gene because it made certain kinds of behavioral traits somewhat more likely to occur in the typical environments encountered by members of that species. If those traits promoted survival and reproduction, the frequency of that gene (or genes) would have tended to increase, as long as individuals in the species still continued to encounter similar environments. Under these circumstances, and subject to stringent mathematical and field testings (as will be described shortly), the trait might be said to have an evolutionary explanation.

But that analysis says absolutely nothing about why the organism may do what it does. In other words, a knowledge of selection pressures does not, in and of itself, lead to a knowledge of **mechanisms.** Mechanisms may be structural (e.g., developing bigger horns to facilitate self-defense), perceptual (better

eyesight to see predators at a distance), motivational (reasons to have sex or to strive for high status), or cognitive (being better able to learn where the likely locations of food and mates are). A complete evolutionary theory of psychology will include a description of both selection pressures and mechanisms (Crawford, 1989; Symons, 1989; Tooby & Cosmides, 1989). It will specify past selection pressures, which genes changed in frequency, and how those genes affect development. It will also describe how the genes ultimately affect the physiology, behaviors, and motives of the adult developing in various environments.

Reproductive fitness is always relative.   Evolutionary theory has been described as a view of life in which everything is at war with everything else. If you and your mate have short, relatively unfertile lives (say, having only two children), the relative frequency of your genes may still not decrease in future generations. If you and your equally short-lived and relatively infertile mate are competing only with other similar pairs in your own particular environmental **niche** (locale), your genes are as likely to be passed on (relatively speaking) as are anyone else's.

However, suppose that other mated pairs in your niche lived much longer and had a dozen children, as opposed to your two. Further suppose that the subsequent dramatic increase in population put a strain on resources. There no longer was enough food and shelter to go around, and disease killed about 50 percent of the children of any one generation. Under these circumstances, your genes, especially the ones responsible for your short life and relative infertility, are very likely to decrease dramatically in frequency in future generations.

Maynard Smith used these facts when he proposed the idea of an **Evolutionarily Stable Strategy (ESS)** (Maynard Smith, 1974, 1978, 1982, 1984, 1988). Animals are viewed as strategists (metaphorically speaking), making choices among behaviors according to potential risks and possibilities for increasing survival and reproduction. The value of certain options will depend on what everyone else around you—the competition—is also doing. A strategy is stable if its reproductive value is greater or equal to the value of all the other strategies that could be employed by any potential competitor.[11]

The male bluegill sunfish is a good example of a strategist (Dominey, 1980). Large males build nests and defend territories from other males—territories good enough to attract females to spawn and mate with them. That is a good strategy for a large male. Small males are "sneaks" or female pretenders: they look and act like females, attempting to enter the other male's nest when a female does, so that the sneak's sperm will fertilize many of her eggs. If you are small male who cannot compete for territories with the much larger males, that is a good strategy for you.

Strategies can vary within and across individuals. An individual may "choose" (metaphorically speaking) a certain strategy when small, and another strategy when its full size has been achieved. An individual may switch strategies if and when the environment changes. Or an individual may use a given strategy, different from those used by other individuals of the same sex, age, and species, for its entire life. The "choice" may be solely genetic or it could be environmentally induced by activation of relevant genes. The developmental environment of the human child may affect his adult reproductive strategy (see Chapter 9).

An ESS is often a mix of strategies maintained across generations in a population because the mix produces a stable set of costs and benefits to the population. For example, if all sunfish tried to become female-impersonating sneaks, that would not be stable, because no one would be building the nests the female requires for spawning. At any one time, the more sneaks there are, the more reproductively successful a territorial male will be, making that a more frequent "choice" for future males, and

vice versa. Only the mix of strategies—a certain number of territorial males and a certain number of sneaks—will be stable.

Concepts of reproductive success.   To measure the selection pressures working on any current population, it is necessary to measure the reproduction of most or all the individuals of a given sex (or, better yet, both sexes) in that population. Suppose there is a significant positive correlation between a certain trait (e.g., dominance ranking) and the number of offspring (e.g., dominant males father more children). That constitutes good evidence that evolutionary selection pressures are working in favor of dominance, and could have done the same in the past.

For several reasons, however, lifetime reproductive success, rather than just success in any given breeding season, should be measured. A developing organism may "choose" to defer reproduction until that individual achieves full adult size. A male that waited until he was full-sized and so had at least some chance to attain dominance and greater reproductive success might sire many more offspring over his lifetime than would the male who competed too soon, got injured, and so did not survive past even one mating season.

The question then becomes one of whether the reproductive success of the offspring should also be included in measures of the parent's reproductive success. If you had many offspring, but they were all sterile, should you be viewed as having great reproductive success? Theorists such as Kirkpatrick, Lande, and Arnold (Arnold, 1983; Kirkpatrick, 1985; Lande & Arnold, 1985) claim that only the original parent's progeny should be counted. They say that counting the offsprings' progeny confounds selection (number of original progeny) with inheritance (ability to pass on your fertility to your offspring). An organism that had a large number of sterile offspring would be reproductively successful, but since her fertility was not heritable (she reproduced but the offspring did not), the relevant gene frequencies would decrease.

On the other hand, counting the progenies' progeny may sometimes be theoretically useful. One example comes from work on the variations in the sex ratios of offspring (Charnov, Los-den Hartogh, Jones, & van den Assem, 1981; Finnell, 1988; Trivers & Willard, 1973). The **sex ratio** is the number of male compared to the number of female offspring. The sex ratio often covaries with the expected reproductive success of male versus female offspring, or with the parents' successes in producing grandchildren.

Clutton-Brock impressively related the sex ratio of the female red deer's offspring to her position on the females' *(hinds)* dominance hierarchy (Clutton-Brock, 1985; Clutton-Brock, Albon, & Guinness, 1986). The red deer (similar to American elk) on the island of Rhum, northwest of Scotland, were extensively studied for 12 years. Since red deer live only 10 to 12 years, and since individuals can be identified, the entire reproductive output of nearly every deer on the island—and their offspring—was measured.

The reproductive success of offspring depends on their gender. The red deer stag can maintain a harem of from 10 to 20 hinds, but some males never get a harem and so never reproduce. Within a harem, the females establish a fairly rigid dominance hierarchy. Dominant hinds have sons who will survive and sire a tremendous number of progeny, but mothers of low rank tend to have sons who die prematurely or who are not be able to compete with other males for a harem. Although daughters will have only slightly more reproductive success if they come from dominant as opposed to subordinate mothers, daughters will always have less reproductive success than will the most reproductively fit males. Females can get pregnant only a limited number of times, which is at most once per season; a stag can have up to 20 offspring a season. Still, all daughters have

more success than do the completely non-reproductive sons of subordinate mothers.

Relationships between a female's dominance, her reproductive success, and the sex ratio of her offspring are illustrated in Figure 3.4. If you compare Parts A and B, you will see that the rank at which hinds deviated from the population mean sex ratio (averaged over all mothers) of 55 percent males was .625, which is very close to the rank at which the lifetime reproductive success of sons exceeded that of daughters (rank = .56). This confirms the predictions made by evolutionary theory and also demonstrates how the theory can be tested.

Several species in addition to red deer show variations in offsprings' sex ratios according to the mother's dominance (Finnell, 1988). This can be most succinctly explained by saying that reproductive fitness includes not only the number of progeny but also some indication of the likely reproductive success of those particular progeny. As Hartung (1985) has done for humans, computer testing of various math models can determine for how many generations we have to count progeny to have useful measures of the fitness of a parent in the current generation. If his results provide any guide, two or three generations may be enough.

Testing evolutionary theory. The theories concerning selection pressures can be tested, even in humans. However, there are "good" as well as "bad" attempts to apply evolutionary theory[12] to humans. The two can be distinguished by the fact that, among other things, the bad attempts are more general and vague, more exciting, more controversial, and less scientific (less testable) (Kitcher, 1982, 1985).

Appropriate attempts to test evolutionary ideas involve both mathematical modeling and field/experimental testing, preferably in that order (Arnold, 1983; Arnold & Wade, 1984a, 1984b). Mathematical modeling is necessary to determine whether the ideas are reasonable or

Part A

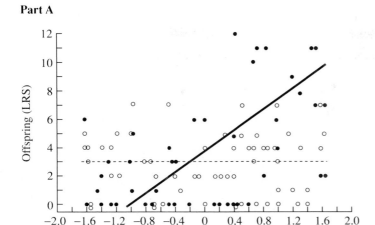

Part B

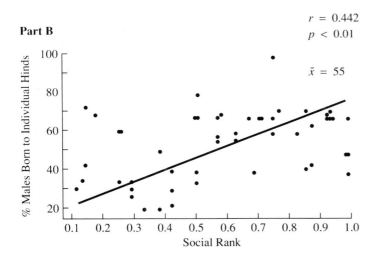

$r = 0.442$
$p < 0.01$

$\bar{x} = 55$

FIGURE 3.4   *Important Illustration of How Evolutionary Theory Can Be Tested*
Part A: Lifetime reproductive success (LRS) of sons and daughters of red deer hinds in relation to their mother's social rank (filled circles represent males; open circles represent females). Part B: Percentage of male offspring born to different hinds plotted against the mother's dominance rank.

Sources: Part A: From "Great Expectations: Dominance, Breeding Success and Offspring Sex Ratios in Red Deer" by T. H. Clutton-Brock, S. D. Albon, and F. E. Guinness, 1986, *Animal Behaviour, 34,* p. 468. Copyright 1986 by Academic Press, Inc. (London) Ltd. Reprinted by permission. Part B: Reprinted by permission from *Nature* vol. 308, pp. 358–360; Copyright © 1984 Macmillan Magazines Limited.

feasible. Most evolutionary theories involve so many different variables (types of genes, environments, organisms, mating systems, etc.) that one person, unaided, sometimes cannot decide whether all the variables in a given theory would interact in expected, understandable, and feasible ways. Thus, the theorist formulates a set of equations embodying his ideas, hypotheses, and explanations. Various values for the major ideas/terms in the equations are then evaluated in a computer simulation of how evolution would operate if the ideas contained in those equations were correct. Is the outcome of the computer simulation reasonable and stable and in accordance with evolutionary theory? Are the values that were inserted into the equations reasonable? Or does getting a reasonable outcome require unreasonable values for some of the variables (such as having to have three sexes)? If so, the theory needs more work![13]

The next step is to take the theory, as embodied in the set of equations, to see if what *could* work is actually in operation for some particular species. Genetic research can be done with existing species, assessing, for example, the genetic basis for various theoretically adapted traits or the degree to which sex differences in appearance and behaviors are related to genetic activity (epigenesis). Fossil records can also be evaluated: just what were the living conditions at the time the first anatomically modern humans evolved (200,000 to 100,000 years ago)? Behaviors of currently living species can also be studied: the membership of a socially living group can be manipulated to see how dominance relationships and reproductive success are related, for example. Traits and predispositions that are hypothesized to have been adaptive in the original environment can be tested to see if they exist in current organisms.

Genetic Variability

For evolutionary selection pressures to work, members of a species that occupy a given environmental niche must have different genes. If every member had exactly the same genes and they were all homozygous, there would be no genetic variability from which selection pressures could select. Both sexual and asexual organisms have variability. Although each asexual **(parthenogenic)** offspring is a genetically identical clone of its mother, different mothers have different genes, and evolution can select among them. This section describes how genetic variability is created and maintained. The last part of this chapter describes how genetic variability is related to the evolutionary reasons for sex.

Mutations.   **Mutations** are heritable changes in gene structure. Darwin thought that these

changes were the sources of variability most important to evolution.

Mutations can occur in any cell, although only those occurring in egg and sperm cells are passed on to offspring. Because of exposure to mutagens such as X-rays, radioactivity, cosmic rays, certain chemicals, and extremes of temperature, at least one base in a DNA molecule is altered or mutated. One base may be substituted for another, a base may be deleted, or a completely new base may be inserted. Although all cells have repair mechanisms, some damage is not recognized by these mechanisms and so is not repaired, leading to a change in the DNA's base sequence or code. Aging might be the accumulation of many DNA mutations in many body cells (Bernstein, Hopf, & Michod, 1988).

Most heritable mutations impair survival and reproduction. Since mutations usually act like recessive (silent or swamped) genes, the heterozygote is seldom much affected. Selection against the gene would therefore occur mostly in homozygotes: if the gene is lethal in a homozygous state, the death of homozygote organisms will decrease that gene's frequency in the population. On the other hand, some mutations would be of benefit and would be selected for, increasing in frequency and spreading throughout the population. By their spread, the favorable mutations would change the whole species's characteristics (Williams, 1988). This is the process of evolution as visualized by Darwin.

Mutations are frequent enough to be an important source of variability (Kondrashov, 1988; Nei, 1988). Perhaps there is one mutation per 10,000 to 1,000,000 **gametes** (sperm and egg cells) produced. Assuming that the human genome has around 100,000 functional genes and that the average ejaculation from a male produces 360,000,000 sperm, about 63 percent of those sperm would carry one or more new mutations on at least one gene. We all probably carry 5 to 8 lethal mutated recessive genes in our genome (Brennan, 1986). Each offspring may carry at least one, and maybe two or three DNA sequences not found in either parent (Neel, 1984).

Two kinds of recombination: both create variability. **Meiosis,** which occurs only in sexually reproducing organisms, is a process of cellular division that produces **haploid** (the chromosomes are not paired) cells for gametes. Meiosis increases genetic variability because it causes various kinds of gene mixing, or **recombination.** There are two kinds of meiotic recombination. First, each offspring gets a set of chromosomes different from the set possessed by either parent: the **independent assortment of chromosomes.** Haploid gametes, one from a male and one from a female, fuse to form a new, diploid organism with a new combination of chromosomes. Second, genes also get mixed between homologous chromosomes because of **crossovers** that occur during meiosis. The two kinds of recombination will now be described in more detail.

Independent assortment during meiosis. To understand how independent assortment creates genetic variability, it is useful to contrast mitosis with meiosis. **Mitosis** is the process a cell goes through to reproduce itself. During mitosis, as illustrated in Figure 3.5, each pair of DNA strands separates from each other. Each separate strand serves as a template for the formation of a complementary strand that will be identical to its original mate. Thus, the original genome is faithfully and reliably replicated for each daughter (barring unrepaired mutations).

In contrast, during meiosis, the cell goes through two separate divisions to produce gametes. In humans, each of the 23 chromosome pairs is duplicated, just as during mitosis. Then the pairs separate such that each of the four daughter cells gets only one from each of the original 23 pairs. After each of the two meiotic divisions that occur in mammalian females, one cell is discarded as a **polar body.** Thus, only one daughter cell, or **egg,** is

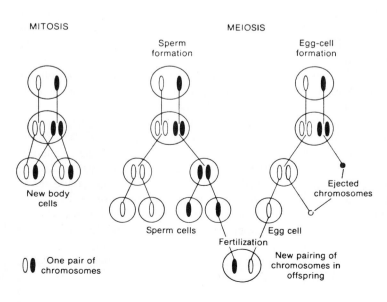

MITOSIS

MEIOSIS

Sperm formation

Egg-cell formation

New body cells

Sperm cells

Fertilization

Egg cell

Ejected chromosomes

New pairing of chromosomes in offspring

One pair of chromosomes

FIGURE 3.5   *Comparison of Mitosis and Meiosis*
Mitosis and meiosis have different effects on a pair of chromosomes (although only one pair is illustrated here, it is important to remember that humans have 22 pairs of autosomes and 1 pair of sex chromosomes). Mitosis produces diploid cells (all chromosomes are paired), whereas meiosis produces haploid cells (only one member of each chromosome pair is present).

Source: From *Psychobiology,* by K. B. Hoyenga and K. T. Hoyenga. Copyright © 1988 by Wadsworth, Inc. Reprinted by permission of Brooks/Cole Publishing Company, Pacific Grove, CA 93950.

eventually produced from every original cell. In males, four daughter cells, or **sperm,** are produced from the two meiotic divisions of every potential sperm cell.

Each daughter cell (sperm or egg) gets a *randomly* selected member of each one of the 23 pairs. This is the independent assortment type of recombination. Eventually each new **zygote,** produced by the fusion of a sperm with an egg, will have received one member of each pair of its chromosomes from its mother and the second member from its father. No other child of the same parents will receive exactly the same set of chromosomes from either parent (unless the children are identical twins). Recombination reshuffles gene patterns in each generation of a sexually reproducing species.

Crossover: changing genes within chromosomes.   The second type of recombination changes gene patterns by shuffling genes within a given chromosome. When the zygote just described grows up and reproduces, or when its germ cells undergo meiosis, the chromosomes it got from its father will be paired with the homologous chromosomes it got from its mother. At one stage in meiosis, when the homologous paternal and maternal chromosomes are paired, the single strands within each chromosome commonly break and rejoin, sometimes causing damage. Specialized DNA repair mechanisms can use the information on the homologous chromosome to repair some damage (damage to both strands, for example). Still, about half the time that such repair occurs, parts of the strands adjacent to the damage are exchanged between the homologous paternal and maternal chromosomes (Brooks, 1988).

In crossover, parallel segments break off the two chromosomes and each is rejoined to the other chromosome, as illustrated in Figure 3.6. Crossover probably occurs once for each pair of homologous chromosomes during each meiosis. Thus, crossover can create a chromosome with a gene pattern not seen in the parent

from whom that chromosome originally came. As long as the breakage occurs between genes rather than inside a gene (not unlikely, considering how much of human DNA is never used and so is not inside any gene), this process creates new gene patterns. Since crossover is so common during meiosis, it is probably a major mechanism for creating and maintaining variability.

The frequency of crossover varies not only between but also within species, and its frequency is under genetic control (Burt & Bell, 1987; Brooks, 1988). Domesticated animals have more crossovers than do comparable wild animals, with the highest rates of crossovers seen in domesticated dogs, cats, and birds. Crossovers can also occur during mitosis in body cells, but they probably do not do so to any great extent. One exception is the immune system, where great variability is essential and may be the reason for sex, as will be described shortly.

Integrations of viruses into genomes.   Many viruses, called **retroviruses,** insert their genetic code into the DNA of their host's cells. The virus invades the cell and uses the cell's own enzymes to translate the viral RNA into DNA. Then it embeds itself in the host cell's own DNA. Given the appropriate signal, the viral segment independently duplicates itself, often using the DNA duplication machinery of the host cell to do so. As long as the viruses remain buried in the genome, the host's immune system cannot attack them.

Much of a human's noncoding DNA could represent the residue of past viral DNA invasions. Some of these viral residues are called retroviruslike elements because they no longer reproduce and so no longer can create infectious viruses (Mager & Henthorn, 1984). One particular viral DNA sequence was found to be repeated 800 to 1,000 times in the human genome, being absolutely identical in the 25 unrelated humans that were tested. In some cases, the viruses embedded in the genome are

FIGURE 3.6   *Crossover Creates New Chromosomes*
The new chromosomes created by crossover events have new combinations of genes. *M* refers
to the two strands of each chromosome of maternal origin, *P* refers to those of paternal origin.
The depicted chromosomes are in one of the parents; the offspring receives one of the two
new chromosomes shown in Part C.

Part A

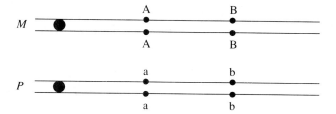

Original chromosome pair: each strand is
double due to replication prior to meiosis;
this shows two heterozygous loci (Aa and
Bb).

Part B

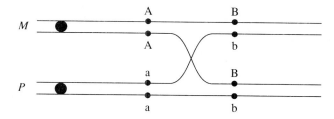

The crossover event: the resulting four
different strands will go to different
gametes (or perhaps to a polar body in a
female—see Figure 3.5).

Part C

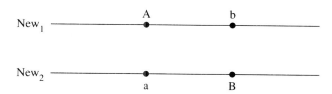

Two new strands created: each of the new
strands will appear in one of the four
gametes (or polar bodies); offspring that
receive either of these two strands will
have a gene combination that that
particular parent did not have.

translatable and still potentially infectious
(Rabson et al., 1983; Steele et al., 1984). In still
other cases, the viral sequences may still be
translated but not into a virus. Regardless, incorporation of viral DNA can increase genetic
variability.

Viral DNA sequences can mutate during the
evolution of their host. Sometimes the mutated
product of these sequences may have acquired
functional roles, as in the human placenta
(Rabson et al., 1983). Some human pathologies
might represent the effects of these viral sequences, including psychosis (T. J. Crow,
1987). In such pathologies, illness could be acquired either by infection or by inheriting the
viral gene from an already infected parent.

Highly adapative traits versus maintenance of variability.   One implication of the discussion up to this point might be that evolution should have changed gene frequencies until everyone in the current population ended up with the "best" genotype, measured solely in terms of reproductive fitness, for the environment in which they all evolved. If true, there should be little or no variability left in the adaption-producing genes in that population. In fact, in the past, if researchers found little or no variability in the genes for some trait in some population, the trait was said to have been strongly selected for. It was also assumed that most current species were adapted and thus largely homozygous for almost all their genes. In this view, evolution works until there is no genetic variability left to work with.

In contrast, researchers now realize that genetic variability is actively maintained even in "adapted" species. There are high levels of heterozygosity in both species and in individuals within most current species. There are several reasons for this:

1. As long as different groups of individuals systematically occupy somewhat different environmental niches, the species as a whole remains genetically polymorphic (Bell, 1987). Different groups would be subjected to slightly different evolutionary pressures because they occupy different environments.

2. Many mutations and recombinations are neutral, not affecting adaptations. In humans, the gene for freckles could be a neutral trait. These genetic polymorphisms would be passively maintained and would remain available for future selection if the environment did change in such a way that, say, having freckles became useful.

3. Variability would also be maintained if both environments and genes had similar effects on a given trait and on reproductive success (Price, Kirkpatrick, & Arnold, 1988). For example, food availability and genes both affect a bird's breeding date and her reproductive success. Well-fed birds breed earlier, and birds that breed earlier, either because of heredity or nutrition, have more eggs and more offspring.

Therefore, early breeding birds will have more eggs and their genes will increase in frequency. But only some of these birds will be genetic early breeders; others will simply be well fed. The combination of effects maintains the polymorphism.

4. Conflicts and variations among selection pressures can also maintain polymorphisms. Maybe the optimum phenotype for feeding and survival is somewhat different from the optimal phenotype for reproduction. In the case of red deer, the same genes that are associated with a high probability that a female will survive to adulthood are also associated with a reduction in adult fertility (Pemberton et al., 1991). Thus, one set of environmental conditions (low competition, warm spring weather) selects for one set of alleles, and another set of conditions (high competition, cold springs) would favor the opposite alleles. If so, there are a number of different reproduction strategies from which an organism could "choose." In these cases, the genes for all strategies have to remain in the population.

5. Perhaps heterozygosity itself was maintained by evolution. The homozygous condition for either gene may confer less reproductive fitness than the heterozygous state. Some data cited above showed that heterosis can sometimes increase reproduction and survival.

6. Finally, because of competition, **frequency-dependent selection** can maintain variability. This refers to the fact that the relative frequency of a phenotype in the population affects the selection pressures working on it. For example, some reproduction strategies are stable only if a small minority of males employ those strategies. The more males that employ those strategies, the less success each individual male will have. If females prefer unusual to common males, this will be another frequency-dependent selection mechanism, maintaining variability (Knoppien, 1985; Salceda & Anderson, 1988; Santos, Tarrio, Zapata, & Alvarez, 1986).

Predators can have similar effects. Perhaps predators are more likely to find the familiar/common phenotype among their prey. Perhaps the predator does not even see the unusual individual since it does not look or act like what the predator is looking for or expects to see. This is particularly likely if the prey is camouflaged and relatively sparsely distributed over a large territory (Jones & Harvey, 1987). This will, of course, be of benefit only as long as the phenotype remains rare. In all these examples of frequency-dependent selection pressures, heterozygosity would be maintained by matings between common and rare individuals.

THE ADVANTAGES OF SEXUAL REPRODUCTION

Why aren't we all females? Why are there two sexes? The answer is variability — but not in the way you might expect. This section will look first at the disadvantages of sex, closely following Lewis's (1987) description, and then describe the advantages of sex. It is easier to appreciate how much of an evolutionary advantage sex has given us if we appreciate the price we had to pay to get it.

The Benefits of Asexual Reproduction: The Costs of Sex

Although many current organisms can reproduce asexually, only a few multicellular organisms are completely asexual. Except for the rotifer, completely asexual species have had a short (evolutionarily speaking) life span.

Most other species have some form of sex. Some are **hermaphrodites,** being able to act like both a male (producing sperm) and a female (producing eggs) (Herre, Leigh, & Fischer, 1987). Some hermaphroditic organisms have male and female functions simultaneously present. For example, each member of a pair of one type of coral reef fish takes its turn in egg laying and in producing sperm. Other hermaphrodites make a permanent switch. The bluehead wrasse fish changes from female to male as it increases in size with age; its ovaries degenerate and are replaced with testes. The **parthenogenes** alternate between sexual and asexual forms of reproduction (Lewis, 1987). Some species have sexual and asexual reproduction at different parts of their life cycle, such as some protozoa. Many invertebrates and plants can reproduce sexually or asexually at

any point in their life cycle. What are the costs of all this sex?

1. *Cost of recombination.* What if an organism already evolved to be perfectly suited for its own little niche of the world? Just when evolution has selected for a set of genes enabling a group of organisms to be perfectly fit for their environment, then they change all their genes around by reproducing sexually. None of their offspring will have the same combination of genes that the parents found to be so useful.

This is one of the major costs of sex. Because of this cost, many current species have genes that can control and thus limit the amount of crossing-over that occurs during meiosis. These genes limit recombination and make offspring more similar to their parents and hence more adapted to their parents' environments.

2. *Cellular-mechanical costs of sex.* Mitosis is relatively quick; meiosis takes much, much longer. Bacteria take only 20 minutes for mitosis, but cellular exchange (genetic recombination) between two different bacteria takes 90 minutes. In other organisms, meiosis can take three to four hours; human males require 7,500 hours to produce new sperm. Much energy is being consumed during this whole time.

The costs do not end there. Sexual reproduction requires that the gametes find each other and then that they fuse to form a new organism. Both processes increase the time required for the new organism to begin growing and developing.

3. *Fertilization.* The necessity for a sexually reproducing individual to be fertilized by an individual of the other sex carries with it at least two costs. First, personal risks include injury from other organisms of one's own species ("jealousy" from like-sexed organisms; vigorous rejection from the chosen mate) and the exchange of disease and parasites. The current AIDS epidemic makes this cost seem even more real. Second, one cannot reproduce if an appropriate mate cannot be found. This is a big problem for any member of a species that is very sparsely distributed over its environmental niche. The problem would be especially acute if the organism were a sparsely distributed, immobile plant.

4. *Cost of genome dilution.* An asexual female has all of her genes present in each of her offspring, whereas the sexual female contributes only 50 percent

of her genes to each offspring. In effect, genes coming from the male's sperm dilute the sexual female's genes by 50 percent in each offspring. Considering this from the point of view of the reproducing female, what does the sexual female get from the male that repays her for the loss of 50 percent of her genes in each of her offspring?

At the level of the gamete, the male (the sperm) typically offers little. Male meiosis results in four sperm, each containing a genome and only enough food reserve for each sperm cell to live until it can "find" an egg. In the female, meiosis produces one egg with considerable energy reserves (taking the cytoplasm from the rejected polar bodies discussed earlier) to enable the zygote to live until fed by the parent (e.g., after hatching or through the placenta). A female thus produces one gamete for each four gametes produced by a male, or one gamete where an asexually reproducing female could have produced four. This discrepancy in gamete production dramatically reduces the sexual female's reproductive potential. The costs can be reduced if male gametes have more energy (are larger and so help to feed the resulting zygote), if the male feeds the female before mating with her, or if the male helps to feed the resulting offspring.

5. *Sex takes two sexes.* The final cost of sex can be found in the fact that it takes two sexes. Males might have to compete to attract the attention of females, as happens in mountain sheep. Such competition can be lethal. Human males can be seen as engaging in many dangerous activities (risk taking) to attract females' attentions (Daly & Wilson, 1983). Females might also choose to mate only with male birds that have huge, colorful tails that make them very visible to predators and hamper their attempts to flee those predators.

The species also has to maintain two sexes—individuals with often differing needs and evolutionary functions and hence different selection pressures. This means that selection will not be able to maximize the fitness of each sex for the specific evolutionary roles of each, since each sex has to share almost all of its genes with the other. The only exception to complete sharing is the Y chromosome in mammalian males, and this is very small, carrying few functional genes. This increases the **genetic load** of the species. Each sex must carry almost all the genes that are required only by the other, such as those for gonads and vaginas and penises.

Sexual Reproduction and Variability

The core of most hypotheses attempting to explain the evolutionary advantage(s) of sex involves genetic variability. In past decades (see Bremermann, 1987; Stearns, 1987a, 1987b), the theories concerning sex were a relatively straightforward extension of the ideas presented up to this point and could be phrased in the form of the following logical argument:

1. Evolution works by means of genetic variability.
2. Sexual reproduction increases variability.
3. Therefore, sexual reproduction increases the rate of evolution, which gives sexually reproducing species a competitive edge in the "war of all against all," relative to asexual species.

Problems with this argument gradually began to surface. Since sexual reproduction has such extensive costs for an individual, there must be even more extensive benefits for the individual, not just the species. If this were not the case, the disadvantages of sex would mean that a mutation leading to asexual reproduction would allow that individual and its asexual relatives to take over, outcompeting its sexual relatives, and so becoming the surviving strain. So why wouldn't everybody become asexual once sexual generations and evolutionary pressures had "fitted" them to their environmental niches—especially when asexual organisms inherently reproduce so much more quickly?

The answer to the newly reformulated question is variability, but variability in the offspring of a single parent that provides a significant benefit to that parent's reproductive fitness. If sexual reproduction is advantageous to the individual parent, asexual clones cannot "take over" a species: this makes sex an ESS.

DNA repair theories of sex. These theories of sex concentrate on the DNA replication step of cellular reproduction (Bernstein et al., 1984, 1985). Sexual reproduction involves an exchange of chromosomes among diploid individuals. Because of the exchange, the new organism's cells would have the information needed for the repair of one of its chromosomes available in the homologous chromosome coming from its other parent. For example, mutations are a particular problem for organisms if both strands of a DNA molecule are damaged. In this case, only information from the homologous chromosome — a chromosome that came from a different organism — could be used to reverse the damage.

Most current theorists seem to think that DNA repair could be one of the evolutionary forces maintaining sexual reproduction (Bremermann, 1987; Stearns, 1987a, 1987b). Damage caused by mutations is relatively common. Bacteria shift from asexual to a type of sexual reproduction whenever their environment suddenly changes, which usually means that genes previously inactivated will now need to be activated. But those genes could have mutated, and a mutation would not have been detected or repaired if it had occurred in one of the inactivated genes. So when the environment changes, bacteria tend to exchange genetic material (a form of sexual reproduction) to repair previously **repressed** (inactivated) and mutated but now necessary genes.

On the other hand, if DNA repair is so important, how have the very ancient, asexual rotifers done so well without it? And why are asexual rather than sexual species concentrated in regions of the earth (at the poles and at high elevations) where radiation and therefore mutations should be most common? In fact, asexual organisms seem to concentrate in extreme environments of all types (e.g., cold, hot, etc.). Mutation is also more common in cellular organisms than in organisms that lack the cytoplasm to buffer them from mutagens in the environment (Hamilton, Axelrod, & Tanese, 1990). Therefore, DNA repair is probably not the whole answer to why we have sex.

Variability theories: Tangled Bank theories. Some explanations relate environmental variability to genetic variability (Bell, 1987; Bierzychudek, 1987). According to

Stearns (1987a, 1987b), Ghiselin may have first formulated this idea, which was then developed further by Williams, Maynard Smith, and Bell (see Stearns, 1987a). The **Tangled Bank** refers to the complexity, and thus to the variations from one point to another, of an environment in which sex would be adaptive.

Organisms inhabit particular niches in their environments, each niche varying from others in the availability of food, shelter, water supplies, types of predators, and so on. Niches vary from continent to continent, from pond to pond, and from one part to another within the same pond. Any sexually reproducing parent that was hypothetically perfectly fitted to its particular environmental niche would have offspring that, because of genetic recombination, would be less fit for that niche than were the parents. However, sexually reproduced offspring might fit some other niche. Asexual offspring, being clones of their parent, would not be likely to fit any niche that differed in any important way from that of their parent. The asexual offspring would have to stay close to their parent, competing directly with it, or die. Therefore, only sexually reproducing species can take advantage of an environment that varies from one place to another.

Furthermore, genetic variability created by sexual reproduction and recombination can also be of benefit within a given niche. If there are many organisms of the same species within a given niche, there will be fierce competition for resources. This competition will be intense for asexual offspring; since all are genetically identical, all will have identical requirements and traits. But sexually reproduced offspring will differ from each other, perhaps including differences in requirements and in traits that will reduce competition. Once again, sexual reproduction provides a competitive advantage.

Variability theories: the Red Queen theory. **Red Queen** theories emphasize changes in environments over time, as opposed to the changes in space emphasized by the Tangled

Bank theories (Bell, 1987; Bierzychudek, 1987; Bremermann, 1987). According to Stearns (1987a), Levin first proposed this idea. Variants were later proposed by Jaenike, Hamilton, Rice, and Bremermann. Haldane should also receive credit, since he suggested in 1949 (see Clarke, 1979) that parasites could maintain polymorphisms in their hosts. This idea was later extended to sexual reproduction. The name refers to what the Red Queen told Alice in Wonderland: "Now here, you see, it takes all the running you can do to keep in the same place" (Maynard Smith, 1988).

Seger and Hamilton (1988) described one version of this theory, which was further developed by Hamilton, Axelrod, and Tanese (1990; Hamilton, 1990). Hamilton and his colleagues also did the computer modeling necessary to show that this theory could account for sexual reproduction even in species having as low a reproductive rate as humans do. Since the authors think this is probably the major evolutionary reason for sex (and hence for this book), more time will be spent on this theory than on the others so that you can understand it and appreciate its implications. The present description of the Red Queen theory will follow that of Bremermann (1987) and of Hamilton and colleagues (see above).

The major evolutionary force providing an advantage for sexual reproduction is exerted by **micropredators** or parasites. Micropredators, such as bacteria and viruses, have a much shorter life span, and so also have a much faster rate of evolution than do larger organisms. For example, bacteria such as *Escherichia coli* can have three generations per hour. A swine influenza virus can mutate into a different variant within a seven-day period of infection of a given host (Kilbourne, Easterday, & McGregor, 1988).

Mutations that can circumvent a host's (prey) internal defense mechanisms can arise very rapidly in these micropredators, and will then propagate among the parasites currently occupying (infecting) the host organism. "Anti-parasite adaptations are in constant obsolescence" (Hamilton et al., 1990, p. 3566). Sexual reproduction is the host organisms' answer, restoring something like a "balance of power" to the "coevolutionary arms race" (Stearns, 1987a, p. 24). "If this asymmetry [in the time needed for evolution] allows parasites to evolve improved methods of attack much faster than their hosts can evolve improved methods of defense, then the hosts' best defense may be one based on genotypic diversity, which, if recombined each generation, can present to the parasites what amounts to a continually moving target" (Seger & Hamilton, 1988, p. 176).

Because recombination mechanisms ensure genotypic variability among offspring, some offspring will be more unusual (atypical) than others. The rare phenotype will often have an advantage during an epidemic. If one's defense mechanisms are different, they may also turn out to be more effective than those of one's susceptible (and so short-lived) brothers and sisters.

Examples of Red Queen defenses. Describing several examples of research consistent with Red Queen arguments will make the theory clearer. One type of grass can reproduce both sexually and asexually. During some experiments, some plots of grass were attacked by aphids, but the asexual clones suffered more damage than did the sexual offspring (Stearns, 1987a). A rust fungus was released in Chile to control bramble bushes. The parthenogenic bramble has been checked, but the sexually reproducing bramble is still going strong (Hamilton et al., 1990). The research done on snails by Lively (1987), which was described at the beginning of this chapter, is another example.

The last example comes from a potential ecological disaster: the cheetahs (O'Brien et al., 1983, 1985). A zoo in Oregon lost 18 of its 42 cheetahs to feline infectious peritonitis despite extensive medical treatments. Why were cheetahs so susceptible? If a virus is successful in a given organism, it will also be successful in all genetic clones of that organism. Since most sexually reproducing species have genetically variable offspring, the offspring vary in the defense they can mount against the same invader. Current cheetahs, both in the wild and in zoos, are highly inbred and have become essentially homozygous at almost all loci. Thus, any microparasite that can successfully attack one cheetah, can attack nearly all of them. In fact, 90 percent of the cheetahs became severely ill from the peritonitis, although only about 10 percent of the domestic cats equally exposed to the same infection even become ill.

Restoring the balance of power in the coevolutionary arms race. Microparasites are in continual "escalation." In any long-lived species (relative to microparasites' life span), the parasites within the body of any one individual are evolving. The parasites (viruses, bacteria, etc.) not immediately killed will reproduce, mutate, and eventually only those most resistant to the host's defenses will remain. Often, the resistant parasites will have acquired a type of camouflage in which they "fool" the immune responses into treating them just like a normal part of the host's body. The retroviruses' habit of inserting themselves into their host's genome is an ultimate expression of this trait.

Microparasites acquire camouflage by carrying new proteins, created by their mutations, in the walls of their cells. These proteins, or **antigens,** are indistinguishable from the antigens carried in the walls of the host's cells. Therefore, the host's defense mechanisms do not recognize the microparasites as being foreign and the host's immune cells do not attack the parasite. Host and parasite will often achieve a sort of standoff. The host's defense systems will "learn" how to attack that type of parasite, but the parasite's acquired camouflage makes the attack less likely to occur.

The relevant antigens are coded by genes in the immune regions of the host's genome. If the offspring of a host were all genetic clones of

their parent, carrying the same antigens, the microparasites of their parent could successfully invade, impair, and even kill all of them. If the microparasites became camouflaged by mutation in the parent, and if the offspring are genetic clones of the parent, the microparasites will also be completely camouflaged in the offspring. Since the offsprings' immune system has not yet had a change to learn how to attack that type of parasite, and the camouflage removes the opportunity for learning, the parasite would often be lethal for the offspring. Among humans, inbreeding, which decreases heterozygosity and thus the advantages of sex, is associated with a "high rate of postnatal mortality including multiple family deaths" (Bittles et al., 1991, p. 799). But with recombination, the sexually reproduced offspring of heterozygotes will have antigens that differ from those of either parent and from those of every other sibling. Any microparasites passed on from the parent would be recognized as foreign in the offsprings' bodies and therefore destroyed before they killed the offspring.

Sexual reproduction and variability in the immune regions of the genome in mammals. This process (or stalemate between hosts and microparasites) reaches its ultimate form in mammals. They have relatively long lives and have relatively prolonged and intimate contact with their offspring (through pregnancy and nursing). All mammals might sexually reproduce because variability is so important to them. In mammals, the longer the age to maturity (and hence the longer the offspring remain in close physical contact with their mother and her diseases), the more crossovers occur during meiosis (Burt & Bell, 1987).

The immune regions of the mammalian genome are more variable than any other region. This variability is generated during both meiosis and mitosis (Tonegawa, 1985). The immune region genes, including those of the **major histocompatibility complex (MHC),** may be the only ones to engage in regular crossover during mitosis.[14] The genes associated with the immune system are reshuffled, creating new protein products, during the initial mitotic growth of the immune system cells before birth. Because of this diversity, some cells should be able to respond to any possible invader. If the organism is infected after birth, the kinds of cells that can attack a given invader proliferate rapidly (learning). Extensive mutations also occur then, producing further variants of immune cells, one of which may attack the invader even more effectively.

Sexual reproduction increases variability in the immune regions. If a locus in the immune region is heterozygous, both alleles can be expressed and both protein products can be manufactured. Independent assortment (sexual reproduction) can increase heterozygosity if mating regularly occurs among males and females that have different alleles. In addition, mammals' MHC region is very susceptible to crossover during meiosis (Tanaka & Nei, 1989). Both facts mean that fantastic levels of variety in immune products are created within a given sexually reproducing organism and from parent to offspring.

MHC heterozygosity is actively maintained in animals by mechanisms related to sexual reproduction. For example, mice tend to prefer sexual partners whose MHC genes differ from their own. Since 1976, this preference has been studied by researchers at the Sloan-Kettering Cancer Center in New York (Beauchamp et al., 1988; Yamazaki et al., 1976, 1988), as well as by other researchers (Egid & Brown, 1989; Egid & Lenington, 1985). Mice apparently distinguish among the genotypes of potential sexual partners by means of their odors. Males learn to avoid the odors with which they were reared (genetically similar siblings and their mothers), thus learning to prefer mates with MHC genotypes different from their own. Since female mice show similar preferences, MHC heterozygosity is actively maintained in mice by both sexes' choices of sexual partners.

Selective abortions of fetuses with MHC genotypes similar to those of the mother might also increase MHC heterozygosity (Stearns, 1987b). Human couples that have had recurrent but unexplained abortions may be inadvertently illustrating this. In several instances, the couple had immune genes very similar to each other (Faulk, McIntyre, & Coulam, 1988; Hauck & Ober, 1991; Stearns, 1987b; Unenoyama, 1988). In some cases, foreign antigen (protein) injections (from some other man) were given to mothers who had had several previous spontaneous abortions. These mothers were then able to carry their pregnancies to term. Couples that share many MHC genes also tend to have fewer children (Ober et al., 1988). Are babies that are too similar in immune characteristics to their mother selectively aborted to maintain variability?

SUMMARY

Evolutionary selection pressures work at the level of the gene, a region of a DNA molecule or chromosome that is read as a unit. This unit is read into molecules of RNA, most of which are eventually translated into molecules of structural or enzymatic proteins. Most animals are diploid, having homologously paired chromosomes. Of each chromosome pair, one came from the sexually reproduced organism's father and one from its mother. Because of dominance, heterosis, epistasis, and polygenic traits, the genotype is never related directly to the phenotype. Genetic variability is created by mutation, by independent crossovers during meiosis, and by insertion of viral genes. Variability is maintained by frequency-dependent selection pressures, gene-environment interactions, heterosis, evolutionarily neutral mutations, and traits that are affected in similar ways by both environments and genes.

The duplication of chromosomes, along with meiosis and recombination, seems to be the core evolutionary reason for sex. DNA repair is made possible by having a pair of chromosomes, one member of each pair having come from different organisms. The variability of sexually reproduced offspring also enables them to capitalize on variable environments. Finally, just as predicted by the Red Queen Theory, the variability in the immune regions are increased by sexual reproduction (because of both independent assortment and crossovers), enabling animals to better resist attacks of micropredators and macropredators. More specifically, the rapid evolutionary rate of micropredators means that the increase in genetic variability created by sexual reproduction is necessary for the survival of an individual's offspring.

ENDNOTES

1. At least, this is true unless we are genetic mosaics (Chapter 5) or unless we are discussing the genes of the immune system, as will be discussed in Chapter 4.

2. **Haploid** organisms have only a single one of each of their chromosomes; **tetraploid** organisms have four of each chromosomes; and so on.

3. Among other species, the males have the matched and the females the unmatched pair of sex chromosomes.

4. A protein is simply a complex organic molecule that consists of chains of amino acids. Amino acids contain oxygen, nitrogen, and carbon and are the building blocks of proteins. Amino acids are strung together on a chain, each one attached to the previous amino acid molecule to build a protein molecule.

5. Each **nucleotide** contains sugar (deoxyribose), an inorganic phosphate, and one of the following four molecules **(organic nitrogen bases)**: adenine, guanine, cytosine, or thymine.

6. **Ribosomes** are the organelles found in the cytoplasm of the cell—outside the nucleus—that synthesize proteins.

7. Thus, two brown-eyed people can have a blue-eyed baby if they were both heterozygous.

8. Some people, such as Crow (1987), refer to this use of heterosis as **overdominance**, meaning that the evolutionary fitness of the heterozygote is greater than that of either type of homozygote at that locus.

9. Bekoff, 1988; Deckard, Wilson, & Schlesinger, 1989;

Harvey & Read, 1988; Jensen, 1983; Mitton & Grant, 1984; O'Brien et al., 1985; O'Brien et al., 1983; Ralls, Brugger, & Ballou, 1979; Wildt et al., 1987.

10. You may want to reread this paragraph several times until you are sure what can—and what cannot—be logically inferred. This is the most frequent source of error in the popularizations of evolutionary theory.

11. In technical terms, an ESS is one that cannot be invaded by any mutant; specifically, a mutant with a different strategy would not be able to invade or reproduce more frequently than others in the population because of having a superior competitive strategy.

12. The authors accept the theory of evolution much as they accept the theory of gravity and Einstein's theory of relativity (it's good enough to get people to the moon!). However, some people get the impression thast the theory of evolution should be doubted because, after all, even evolutionary theorists sometimes disagree. This impression arises primarily because people doing evolutionary research describe it as though they were testing evolutionary theory. This is a convenient shorthand fiction for them that confuses few people sophisticated in that research, but it can confuse less sophisticated people. In fact, current evolutionary theorists are testing specific applications of evolutionary theory to particular behaviors in specific species found in certain environments. Does aggression in certain male primates living in a semi-natural zoo environment actually increase dominance rankings which, in turn, increase the number of offspring an aggressive, dominant male will have? If the answer to this question is no (as it is quite likely to be), one of the least likely reasons is that the evolutionary theory is wrong.

Much more likely—especially in view of the tremendous preponderance of evidence supporting evolutionary theory from every species so far tested—is that that particular hypothesis (the specific application of the theory to that situation) was in some way flawed. Maybe the researchers improperly interpreted evolutionary theory in applying it to that species. Maybe the way of measuring aggression and dominance was improper. Maybe the way of measuring offspring number was inappropriate to the hypothesis and to the theory. Maybe for this species dominance is no longer important, perhaps because they now live in a zoo instead of the jungle or savannah.

13. This is analogous to the fact that laboratory research establishes whether a given relationship could ever exist, but only research done outside the laboratory can establish that the relationship exists for people in their everyday lives.

14. However, the DNA breaks and crossovers that occur during mitosis in some body cells may turn them into tumors (Yunis & Soreng, 1984).

CHAPTER 4

THE EVOLUTION OF
SEX DIFFERENCES

INTRODUCTION
NATURAL SELECTION, SEX, AND REPRODUCTIVE ROLES
SEXUAL SELECTION
EVOLUTIONARY CHARACTERISTICS OF SEXUALLY DIMORPHIC SPECIES
FACTS AND SPECULATIONS ABOUT HUMANS
SUMMARY

Theodosius Dobzhansky once entitled a lecture, "Nothing in Biology Makes Sense Except in the Light of Evolution."
—M. Daly and M. Wilson (1983, p. iii)

In the authors' hometown in the spring of 1988 a man lost his life. One evening, he and his wife noticed that a fire had broken out in their house trailer. They immediately grabbed their kids and got out. But then, for some reason, the man became confused and thought that one or more of his children were still inside. He went back in—and perished from smoke inhalation.

Can evolutionary theory explain why a man would risk his life to save his children? Possible answers to that question have also been applied to the sex differences in parental and social behaviors among mammals. Why should the two sexes differ in any way other than what is required for sexual reproduction? Males might have testes and penises and females might have ovaries and vaginas, but why have *other* differences evolved? Why are males often the larger sex, at least in mammals? Why might females have longer life expectancies? These questions are addressed in this chapter.

INTRODUCTION

This chapter describes the evolution of sex differences. According to Darwin (1871), there are two different kinds of evolutionary selection pressures. Both can produce sex differences. The greater the extent to which either (or both) selection pressure is sexually dimorphic—differing in its impact on the two sexes—then to that extent, sex differences would be expected to evolve.

There are two selection pressures. The first, **natural selection,** refers to the likelihood that the organism will survive long enough to have opportunities to reproduce, the likelihood that it will be fertile, and the likelihood that it will be able to carry out its role in the rearing of its offspring. The organism's role in mating and the rearing of its offspring is its **reproductive role.** The first section describes sex differences in natural selection pressures. The second selection pressure is **sexual selection.** This describes the ability of an organism to gain the cooperation of a reproductively competent mate. Sex differences in sexual selection pressure are covered in the second half of the chapter.

Both sexual and natural selection ultimately affect, and so can be measured by, lifetime reproductive fitness or success. Even though both pressures affect reproduction, researchers and theorists have found it to be very useful to retain the concept of two pressures since, for many species, the pressures are in conflict. Conflict implies that at least two types of pressures do exist.

NATURAL SELECTION, SEX, AND REPRODUCTIVE ROLES

One very consistent way in which the two sexes differ is in reproductive roles. If natural selection operates so as to increase the fitness of each sex to its own particular role in reproduction, then, to that extent, the two sexes will experience different natural selection pressures. The greater the sex differences in selection pressures for the members of any given species, the more dimorphic the two sexes of that species will become.

Sex Differences in Reproductive Roles

One reason that the sexes differ in reproductive roles and thus in selection pressures is that they differentially "invest" in their common offspring, as will now be described. Differential investments lead to sex differences in natural selection pressures.

Trivers and parental investment.   Trivers's theory of parental investment (1972, 1974) describes sex differences in the costs and benefits of various types of reproductive roles. Trivers (1972) defined **parental investment** as "any investment by the parent in an individual offspring that increases the offspring's chance of surviving (and hence reproductive success) at the cost of the parent's ability to invest in

other offspring" (p. 139). The cost of parental investment is measured by the negative effect it has on later reproductive success. For example, male offspring might "cost" more than females, if the mother is less likely to breed the season following the birth of a male than in the season following the birth of a female. Males might "cost" more by requiring more food, for example, because of being larger than females.

Parental investments also provide benefits. To some point, the more a parent invests in the offspring, the more likely that offspring is to survive and reproduce. In Trivers's model, in any given season of breeding, a parent invests just enough to maximize his or her own net lifetime reproductive success (LRS). Of course, offspring almost inevitably "want" more investment than parents are willing to provide (because of increasing costs to the parent), so parent-offspring conflict occurs (see Chapter 9).

The greater the discrepancy in the amount each sex invests in parenting, the greater the sex difference in natural selection pressures. Each gender will be subjected to somewhat different types and amounts of selection pressures because of the differences in types and amounts of parental investment. Because of the evolutionary processes that led to two sexes and hence sexual reproduction (Stearns, 1987a), the gametes of males and females became very different in size. The female of most sexually reproducing animals has invested more than the male just in the production of the gametes, because eggs are so much larger than sperm. If only the female rears the offspring, only females will be subjected to pressures selecting for gene characteristics that increase the ability to rear offspring successfully. Only the female might evolve whatever ability or skill is required to retrieve offspring that stray from the nest, for example.

From these discrepancies between the sexes in parental investments, Trivers's theory would predict that females would often be a limiting resource for males: since females invest more, males should have to compete for access to females. If the two sexes differ in maximal parental investment per season, the sex that invests the least will have to compete for access to the sex that invests the most. The sex that invests the most will be the more selective sex, more selective in its choices among prospective mates.

Typical sex differences in parental investments. Female parental care and male competition for females is true of many species, especially polygynous[1] species. (Mating systems, including polygyny and monogamy, will be discussed at greater length in a later section of this chapter.) Among polygynous species, each male competes with other males for reproductive access to several females. For example, in the polygynous red-winged blackbird, paternity tests have shown that more than 20 percent of a male's reproductive success comes from fertilizing females who are nesting on some *other* male's territory. The males who were most successful at fertilizing all the females on their own territory were also the most successful at fertilizing other males' mates (Gibbs et al., 1990). The male of this species has the bright red spot on his wing that the female lacks, and the male also provides very little parental care.

In other birds, males and females form monogamous bonds and share roughly equally in the parental duties once the eggs hatch. As predicted by parental investment theory, the sexes in these species tend to be very similar to each other. In the United States, robins are monogamous, and it is also very hard for humans (though presumably not for the robins themselves) to distinguish a female robin from a male robin.

But the fact that females carry the eggs internally changes the sexual mix of costs and benefits, even in monogamous birds. For most (but not all) females, mating with multiple males would not increase their reproductive success: a female can lay only so many eggs per

season, and just one male can fertilize all of them. Since males invest much less in their sperm than females do in their internally developing eggs, the more females a male can fertilize, up to a point, the more reproductive success the male can have.

For example, bank swallows are monogamous but males pursue a mixed reproductive strategy (Beecher & Beecher, 1979). After pair-bonding, and when his female is likely to be fertile, the male "guards" her. Every time she leaves the nest, he follows, trying to defend his mate from the sexual attentions of other males that may also be pursuing her whenever she leaves the nest. The guarding male may try to bump another pursuing male or he may enter into a vigorous face-to-face fight. On some occasions, when many other males are about, he may force his mate back into their nest or may knock her to the ground. When his mate is no longer fertile, he will join the other males in pursuing other fertile females. As long as his mate stays with the eggs, his "investment" is safe. The same mix of pair-bonding with opportunistic matings would not be as adaptive for her, and so she does not as often actively pursue other mates.

The sexual disparity in parental investment can be even more extreme in mammals than in polygynous birds (Gittelman & Thompson, 1988; see Chapter 9). In some mammals, the male invests only his gametes, and the female is left in sole charge of the offspring after being impregnated. She must maintain them during pregnancy, give birth to them, feed them during their helpless period, and train them to assume their adult roles. Since only female mammals lactate, only females can feed offspring. This sexual discrepancy in parental investments will create sex differences even among monogamous mammals. For example, even in cultures with monogamous marriage systems, some theorists have claimed that human males will engage in mate guarding, motivated by (using the mechanism of) sexual jealousy (Daly & Wilson, 1983).

Atypical reproductive roles. If these evolutionary pressures just described were the only ones operating, males would be expected to have harems or to wander from female to female, leaving parental care solely to the females. Because of male competition, males would evolve characteristics such as bright coloration and/or larger size. But there are exceptions that prove parental investment theory, such as phalaropes and pygmy marmosets.

Phalaropes are shorebirds that pair-bond (monogamous). Once the female lays the eggs, the male is solely responsible for parental care. In this species, the parental investments are probably larger in the male. And in phalaropes, females compete for males, and females are larger and more brightly colored than are the males (Daly & Wilson, 1983).

In the primate known as the pygmy marmoset, the male has an extensive parental role and so an extensive paternal investment (Wamboldt, Gelhard, & Insel, private communication). These animals live in large family groups. Until the infants are over three weeks of age, the mothers carry them. After that age, although the feeding, protection, and grooming are done mostly by the females, males perform most of the infant carrying. As predicted by the similarity in parental investments, males and females are also very similar to each other in size, appearance, and behaviors; either may be the larger sex (Ralls, 1976, 1977).

Increased paternal investment. If it takes two sexes to rear the offspring successfully, because one parent alone could not adequately feed and/or defend the offspring, this reduces the cost of genome dilution (costs of sex), reduces the sexual disparity in parental investments, and reduces gender-related differences. The more important paternal care is, for whatever reason (see documentation in Hoyenga & Hoyenga, 1993), the fewer sex differences in natural selection pressures would exist to create sex differences in either appearances or behavioral dispositions.

Sex Ratios: Parental Investments and Reproductive Roles

As described earlier, systematic variation in the ratio of male to female offspring might be better explained if evolutionary theories took into account the variations in the reproductive fitness of offspring. Sex ratios are also related to sex differences in parental investments and in reproductive roles.

Red deer. As predicted by Trivers and Willard (1973), dominant female deer are more reproductively successful (more grandchildren) when they have relatively more male than female offspring. Subdominant females are more successful when they have relatively more female offspring (see Figure 3.4 in Chapter 3). Red deer also invest more in sons than in daughters — 33 percent of the mothers with sons fail to breed in the following year, compared to 18 percent of the mothers of daughters (Clutton-Brock, 1985). This extra investment in males would be much more beneficial for dominant than for subdominant hinds. Males contribute little by way of parental care, but males compete vigorously for females because they can reproduce only as long as they can successfully defend their harem against other male challengers. Males weigh about twice as much as females do and have developed elaborate antlers. Differential parental investment in daughters versus sons, and by fathers as opposed to mothers, has led to large sex differences and biased sex ratios.

Primate females. Researchers have studied both naturally living as well as zoo-maintained primates. Females have hereditary dominance ranks in both conditions, not only within but also across groups (Bernstein & Ehardt, 1985; Chapais, 1988a, 1988b; Chapais & Larose, 1988; Johnson, 1987; Rhine, Cox, & Costello, 1989). Under some conditions, dominant females, and females in dominant groups, are more reproductively successful. The son of a dominant female is also more likely to live, or more likely to join a dominant group himself and so have more reproductive success. The reproductive successes of daughters of high- versus low-ranking females do not differ. Under these conditions, high-ranking females not only produce more offspring but they have more sons than do low-ranking females (Aureli et al. 1990; Meikle, Tilford, & Vessey, 1984; Paul & Kuester, 1987; Van Schaik et al., 1989).

Under other conditions, a dominant female primate may maximize her reproductive success by having more daughters than sons (Silk, 1983; Small & Hrdy, 1986). In one group of caged but socially living macaque monkeys, Silk found that dominant females had greater reproductive success than did subordinates, but maternal rank affected daughters' survival more than sons' survival. The daughters of subordinate mothers usually died before two years of age.[1] Female offspring are frequently attacked in these crowded cage conditions, and subdominant mothers are less able to defend them. Sons of subordinate and dominant females are equally likely to survive. Given all this, one could then use evolutionary theory to predict the results: dominant females had daughters and sons equally frequently, whereas low-ranking females had more sons.

Thus, what sex offspring parents should have depends on who they are and what the competition is. In general, mortality in females is more sensitive to crowding (and competition) than is mortality in males (Rhine, Wasser, & Norton, 1988). Under conditions in which raising a female offspring creates a greater cost to a female's future reproduction than raising a male (Gomendio et al., 1990; Van Schaik et al., 1989), sons would be produced, unless the daughters had correspondingly greater reproductive success.

Mechanisms. A female mammal could affect the gender of her fetus by varying her genital tract chemistry and so biasing for or against X- versus Y-carrying sperm. Or her physiology could have selective spontaneous abortions based on the products of Y chromosome genes. After birth, she could select by a failure to feed, by abandonment, or by actually killing the offspring of the "wrong" sex. Primate females could also regulate the sex ratio by changing the time in the menstrual cycle that fertilization occurs (Paul & Kuester, 1987).

Humans may also show variations in sex ratios of their children (Clutton-Brock & Iason, 1986; James, 1987a, 1987b). Having sexual activity more frequently increases the likelihood that sex will occur close to the time of ovulation. This seems to increase the proportion of females born. Males are more likely to be born if sexual activity occurs some time before or some time after the actual moment of ovulation. Sex ratios in humans may also be sensitive to the hormone levels of their parents at the time of conception. Finally, more socially dominant couples may have relatively more males, though James thinks that the relevant aspect of dominance may be within a given social group rather that something like socioeconomic status per se. Thus, royalty tends to have more sons, but personal servants tend to have more daughters. Dominance may be related to sex ratios because dominance affects hormone levels (see Chapter 13).

Social Traits

Much of what is unique to humans, including our brain's learning capacity, may be the result of selection pressures supplied by social living conditions (Cheney, Seyfarth, & Smuts, 1986; Jolly, 1985; Lewin, 1987; Lovejoy, 1981; Trivers, 1971). The cues coming from others' behaviors (facial expressions, odors, sounds) can be so very subtle, complex, variable, and rich that a large brain may represent a significantly important and necessary adaptation to living with many others of our own kind. Even the one nonprimate that has such a large brain — the dolphin — also has a complex social system (Booth, 1988). Since females and males often have differing social and reproductive roles within a social group, social types of selection pressures would also be expected to differentially affect the sexes. This section covers the natural selection pressures specifically related to social interactions, emphasizing where sex differences in selection pressures would be expected.

Inclusive fitness.   Hamilton (1963, 1964) introduced the idea of **inclusive fitness,** also called **kin selection.** A gene may increase its chances of being passed on from one generation to another not only by increasing the total reproductive success of a particular bearer but also by increasing the probability that another organism that carries the same gene will survive and reproduce. Under most conditions, organisms sharing your genes are also likely to be your relatives. Acts that increase the survival and reproduction of fellow gene bearers could be called **kin aiding.**

Inclusive fitness includes not only your own personal reproductive success but also the success of relatives who carry many of your genes and thus are likely to carry the gene leading to kin aiding. The tendency to aid relatives would be increased by natural selection pressures because that tendency increased the probability of the relevant, "kin-aiding" gene surviving from one generation to the next.

More precisely, the likelihood that an altruistic act will increase a relative's reproduction is multiplied by the probability that the organism and its relative share the particular gene associated with altruistic act. The probability is usually measured by the degree of kinship, with parents and full siblings being the closest possible relatives of each other (other than identical twins). The more closely related you are to another individual, and the more a given action of yours will benefit that individual's chances of having children, then, to that degree, aiding that individual will increase *your* inclusive fitness. *Inclusive fitness is the sum of fitness from personal reproductive success plus the reproductive success of relatives to which you have contributed by behaving altruistically, weighted by the degree of relationship (probability of sharing the kin-aiding gene).*

Another way to look at this extremely important concept is to analyze its costs and benefits. A gene that promotes altruistic acts toward relatives will be passed on if and only if its benefits are greater than its costs. Costs refer to the risks incurred by the altruistic act, such as the risks the father described at the beginning of this chapter incurred by running back into the burning trailer. Benefits are represented by the product of the degree of relationship multiplied by the increase in reproductive fitness of the recipient. Rescuing one's baby would certainly be a benefit! Conversely, if an act of harm decreases another organism's reproductive potential, that act will decrease your own inclusive fitness to the degree that the harmed individual is related to you. Harmful acts should preferentially be directed toward nonrelated individuals.

In some cases, relatives not only share some of your genes but are also your most vigorous competitors. Under those conditions, relatives may be the target for spitefulness rather than altruism (Motro, 1988). Predicting whether relatives will be the targets of helpful or spiteful acts means that all the factors involved have to be considered: number of genes shared, costs to you in terms of helping them when they are your competition, and the degree to which you benefit their reproduction.

Daly and Wilson (1983) described an excellent example of sex differences in inclusive fitness. The ground squirrels studied by Paul Sherman usually live in colonies of related females and unrelated males. They sometimes give an alarm call when a potential predator is spotted. Calling has risks, since the predator's attention is attracted to the caller. Calling would increase the inclusive fitness of females more than males since only females are living near any relatives. It is not surprising that females are more likely to give an alarm call, and females with living relatives are more likely to give such calls than females who lack nearby relatives. Thus, the nature of the social grouping—whose relatives are most likely to be nearby—will affect the degree to which there are sex differences in social selection pressures.

Cooperation and reciprocity. Inclusive fitness cannot explain all altruism, particularly among humans (Harpending, Rogers, & Draper, 1987). We are frequently altruistic toward unrelated strangers! We adopt unrelated babies and invest considerably in pets that are not even of our same species. We humans also have a complex social system of reciprocity in which we expect "favors" to be returned. These altruistic actions frequently benefit both parties and are even necessary to most social interactions.

Kin selection describes cooperative and even altruistic social interactions that take place among kin. **Reciprocal altruism,** or **cooperation,** refers to acts performed at some cost to the self with the expectation of a future reward (reciprocation of the favor). Cooperative acts can take place among either relatives or nonrelatives. Kin selection might have been the first evolutionary step toward reciprocal altruism (Maynard Smith, 1988).

Several models for the evolution of cooperation have been described (Hamilton, 1964; Michod, 1982; Trivers, 1971). If one gains (measured in the currency of reproduction) more than one loses by being cooperative, "cooperation-promoting" genes should increase as long as those conditions hold. Receptivity to social influence might be the mechanism selected for (Simon, 1990). Under social living conditions, receptivity or social sensitivity would lead to altruism and cooperation. With regard to this mechanism, three meta-analytic reviews of the psychological literature have concluded that female humans are consistently (but only slightly) more receptive to social influence than males are (Cooper, 1979; Eagly & Carli, 1981; Becker, 1988, in historical order).

Since the benefits of altruistic acts nearly always occur only after some delay, only certain species should display such behaviors. The species would be long lived, so the delay would be tolerable. The species would live in long-term social groups, where reciprocating and delayed altruism could have had a chance to develop. The species would live in groups whose members are very mutually interdependent; the individual could not survive without the group. There would be extensive parental care. The species would be likely to have only loose (as opposed to rigid) dominance hierarchies. Members of the social group would have to have some mechanism that would allow them to detect and thus to eject cheaters, or those who receive benefit but do not reciprocate (Nunney, 1985). Finally, members of the species would often aid one another in fights.

In humans, reciprocal altruism would involve very complex social situations and cues. Cheaters would have to be identified and punished. Complex emotional systems may have evolved to regulate such a system, including guilt (over cheating), trust and friendship (offered to proven noncheaters), a sense of injustice and a dislike of inequities, and gratitude (a promise of future reciprocation). Perhaps some of this required complexity became part of the selection pressure leading to our large brains (Pagel & Harvey, 1988).

Recognition of individuals. Inclusive fitness could not have evolved without the ability to recognize one's kin. The ability to recognize specific individuals is also implied by reciprocal altruism and mate selection. How do animals recognize each other?

The importance of kin recognition can be illustrated by describing the society of naturally living macaque monkeys and certain types of baboons. Each social group contains several family groups, or **matrilinies,** each consisting of several generations of related females. Females typically remain throughout their lifetimes in the group into which they were born, whereas the males emigrate, eventually joining a different group.[2] Recognition of individuals plays an important part in the interactions among members of a macaque social group (Bernstein & Ehardt, 1985, 1986a, 1986b; Cheney, Seyfarth, & Smuts, 1986; Ehardt & Bernstein, 1986). For example, males defend kin only if they recognize the attacker as subordinate to themselves. Females come to the aid of kin when they are attacked, regardless of who is doing the attacking. (A more detailed analysis of dominance and aiding relationships in chimpanzee and monkey societies is presented in Chapter 13.)

Hepper (1986) listed some mechanisms by which animals could recognize one another and thus differentiate between relatives and non-relatives. In some cases, where the only organisms one meets during the day are kin, such as is the case for nestling birds, the animals can simply behave altruistically toward everyone. Other species use an animal's presence on a given home range or territory as a cue indicating kinship. If the animal is on one's range, it "must" be kin. Other organisms use specific cues to recognize specific individuals, including appearance, sounds made, and odors. In some cases, since kin share genes, this may mean that kin will also share specific gene-produced cues, including odors. In other cases, sharing an environment, including the type of diet, can also lead to cue commonality — what one eats determines how one smells.

Some of these principles, as well as sex differences, are illustrated in a study done with macaque monkeys (Wu et al., 1980). Young monkeys prefer to interact with an unfamiliar relative rather than an unfamiliar nonrelative. The young monkeys, especially the females, seemed to discriminate relatives from non-relatives based on sight, even though — as just described — the young monkeys had never seen any of the test monkeys.[3]

SEXUAL SELECTION

Darwin (1871) noted that sometimes organisms possess traits that seemed counter-adaptive —

traits that actually impair rather than facilitate survival and reproduction. The classic example is the long, flowing bright tail of the male peacock, which slows him down and makes him much more visible to predators. Natural selection pressures do not seem able to explain such tails. Darwin proposed a second evolutionary selection pressure: sexual selection. According to Triver's (1972) parental investment theory, the gender most subjected to sexual selection pressures should be the one that invests the least amount in the offspring.

Two Types of Sexual Selection

Darwin (1871) described two types of sexual selection pressures. One is called **intrasexual competition.** Members of one sex — usually males — compete with each other for access to the other sex. For example, male bighorn sheep engage in long battles for access to sexually receptive females. In the second type of sexual selection, **sexual choice,** members of one sex — usually females — actively choose with whom they will mate. Female peacocks prefer and preferentially mate with the most dramatically colored males. Partner preferences are not important to the first type of sexual selection, but are crucially important to the second.

These two forms of sexual selection can be hard to distinguish in practice. Some males may engage in dominance battles with each other, and then females will also actively choose the dominant male, (e.g., vervet monkeys [Keddy, 1986]). Among the dragonflies found in eastern North America, male body size is influenced by both pressures (Moore, 1990). Larger males are more successful in contests with other males when fighting to gain access to females, but then the females themselves seem to prefer moderately sized males, rather than either very large or very small males. The actual sizes of males is thus a compromise between the two effects.

Sexual selection: competition. In some species, careful tests have documented the fact that males compete with one another but females do not actively select among the competing males. Among elephant seals, males form dominance hierarchies at the breeding site and only the top-ranking males mate. In one year, the five highest-ranked males sired 85 percent of the offspring (Daly & Wilson, 1983). The outcome of the competition among males determines a male's reproductive success (Ralls, 1977).

Some species of birds provide especially good examples of male competition (Alatalo, Lundberg, & Glynn, 1986; Searcy & Yasukawa, 1983). Male pied flycatchers and red-winged blackbirds arrive on breeding territories before females do. Some males can successfully claim and defend multiple nesting sites. Although the males are larger and much more brightly colored than the females, these male attributes seem irrelevant to females. Instead, females select a territory based on its quality as a nesting site; in the process, they mate with whichever male "goes with" that site. Among blackbirds, being larger, having the bright red mark on the wing, and being aggressive all help a male claim and defend a desirable territory, and so these traits were a product of competition selection rather than female choice.

Any gene associated with some trait or characteristic that gives the male an "edge" in his competition would increase in frequency over future generations. Traits relevant to male competition would often impair reproductive success if they were present in females, since females do not have to engage in similar competitions. Thus, evolutionary pressures would act so (and a cost/benefit analysis would suggest) that such traits would come to be expressed only in, or at least to a greater extent in, males than in females.

Sexual selection: choice.   In the past 15 to 20 years, sexual choice has been increasingly studied. The consensus is that this strong evolutionary force affects most species. It often affects the male more than the female, since the female usually does the choosing because she has the greater parental investment.

There are exceptions, however. In Mormon crickets (Gwynne, 1981), males invest more than females do because they feed the females large amounts before mating, and so females compete for males. Sexual selection is exerted by males on the female crickets: the males will actively reject any female who is not sufficiently large. In some katydids, males also feed females before mating, and when the relative amount of male investment is increased (as when food is made scarce), females begin to compete for males (Gwynne & Simmons, 1990).

The choice of females among males is often relative rather than absolute. Instead of a tail of a given color, females may prefer the brightest among any set of possible tails. Under these conditions, males will develop brighter and brighter tails, as only those in each generation with the brightest tails will be able to pass on their genes. Female choice should itself be genetically based, as should the male trait being selected for by the females.

Sexual Selection and Sexual Dimorphism

This discussion is based on the work initially done by Darwin (1871), which was then added to by Lande, Arnold, Wade, and Kirkpatrick (Arnold, 1983; Arnold & Wade, 1984a, 1984b; Kirkpatrick, 1982, 1985; Kirkpatrick & Ryan, 1991; Lande, 1980; Lande & Arnold, 1985). Sexual selection can create gender-related differences in appearance and behaviors. These sex differences will tend to evolve as long as:

1. The sexes differ in degree of selection pressure exerted on each of them, such as in the amount of competition, or in the degree of "choosiness" (selectivity in the opposite sex).
2. The sexes differ in the direction of the selection pressure, as when the males and females look for different attributes in a potential mating partner.
3. The character selected for in one sex would impair the reproductive fitness of the other sex, meaning that the cost/benefit ratio was sexually dimorphic.

Sex differences either in the degree or in the type of sexual selection pressure could lead to sex differences. Natural selection may restrict the sexually selected trait's appearance to only one sex. Although the trait could impair the survival and/or the reproduction of both sexes (costs), the trait might improve only one sex's ability to attract mates because of sexual choice (benefit). The net effect is that if females do the choosing, females are exposed only to natural selection pressures. Males will be affected by both sexual and natural selection pressures, often working in conflict with each other.

Two examples of increased dimorphism. Male widowbirds claim territories, and females prefer males with long tails. Andersson (1982) proved that tail length was important to females by counting the number of active nests on a male's territory, both before and after manipulating their tail length. In one group of males, the tail was left untouched as a control for time. In the second control group, the tail was cut, and then the cut end glued back on, as a control for cutting and gluing. In a third group, the tail was cut to a length of about 14 centimeters. In the fourth and last group, tails taken from the group-3 males were glued onto the ends of the group-4 males' tails, making them about 25 centimeters longer. The elongated tail males had nearly twice as many nests, on the average, as did the other groups. Thus, males with longer tails have greater reproductive success. Probably because of this, male widowbirds have a tail that is half a meter long, whereas the tail of the female is only about seven centimeters long.

Burley's work with zebra finches demonstrates the effect of sexual choice in monogamous species (1981, 1986, 1988; Harvey, 1986). Females prefer males with novel coloring to those with more typical coloring, and the male is much more colorful than the female. Burley manipulated the "attractiveness" of these birds by giving them colored leg bands. She then tested for sexual preferences of both sexes (which bird of the opposite sex, wearing which color of band, the test bird preferred to perch next to). She found that males could be made attractive to females by giving them red bands to wear; males were made unattractive by light green bands. Females were made attractive to males by giving them black bands to wear; females were made unattractive by giving them light blue bands. In this case there could be no doubt about what the basis for choice was: the bands were obviously artificially added by the experimenter.

Some of the other results of Burley's experimenters demonstrated the degree to which sexual selection can produce effects quite contrary to those of natural selection. Attractive males (made so because of wearing a red leg band) had more offspring per year than did unattractive males. Attractive males and females not only had greater lifetime reproductive success, they actually lived longer as well! Burley speculated that the mates of the attractive birds might have done most of the work, thus reducing the stress levels on the attractive birds. Furthermore, if a pair differed in attractiveness, there were more offspring of the attractive partner's sex. Some fathers were seen dropping young at some distance away from the nest, so selective infanticide might have been used to change the sex ratio.

Sexual selection in opposition to natural selection. The tails of male peacocks and male widowbirds are excellent examples of sexual selection working in opposition to natural selection, as are the tails of male guppies (Breden & Stoner, 1987). Female guppies often prefer males with bright tails—but so do guppy predators. In Trinidad, guppy populations live in waters with few predatory fish and males have bright tails. In laboratory tests, these particular females prefer to mate with bright-tailed males. But among guppies living in waters with many predators, males have dull tails and females show no preference for bright as opposed to dull tails. After all, in the area with many predators, a bright-preferring female would not have offspring because there would not be any uneaten males left with which to mate. Thus, bright males and bright-preferring females became extinct.

In general, if sexual selection is operating in opposition to natural selection, and if sexual selection affects males to a greater degree or more often than it affects females, then, on the average, males will be less "fit." Males would have shorter life spans, for example. This is true for some of the species already discussed: several species of blackbirds, red deer, houseflies; most fish; and many mammals, including humans (Clutton-Brock, 1985; Daly & Wilson, 1988b; Searcy & Yasukawa, 1983; Trivers, 1972).

Characteristics limited to reproductive periods. Natural selection, working in opposition to the selection created by female choice, often limits the effect of extreme traits on a male's fitness by limiting the time in which he must display that trait. Many traits produced by female choice or male competition, such as horns and bright colors, appear only after puberty. Other traits appear only during breeding seasons. Some hoofed males shed their horns after breeding season, and male widowbirds shed their tails.

The Genetics of Female Choice

Why do females have preferences in the first place?

Direct benefit to the female's reproduction. In some cases, a female may select a certain male because his traits or genes directly improve the female's reproductive success (Kirkpatrick & Ryan, 1991). She may select the male who defends her or provides food for her and her offspring. The male's genes could have pleiotropic effects, producing the selected-for trait in him (which may not be advantageous to his long-term survival) and also increasing the

female's survival and fertility. Sometimes the genes selected by females are those indicating that the male will carry out his parental role more effectively than other males would (Dahlgren, 1990; Hill, 1991; Hoelzer, 1989). The gene may code for some signal displayed only by males that have the signaling genes and that are also in a position to be "good fathers."

Sometimes traits selected by females might be good for both sexes. For example, female pheasants select males on the basis of the length of their spurs. Males with longer spurs not only live longer but their offspring are also more likely to survive (Schantz et al., 1989).

Sexy son theory. Weatherhead and Robertson (1979) suggested that females would be willing to accept even poor quality but attractive males as long as the female's sons would also be attractive. Thus, their "sexy sons" would have considerable reproductive success during their short but sexually active lives. By picking sexy males, females can have sexy sons and thus lots of grandchildren. In some math modeling, the sexy son principle did not work out (Kirkpatrick, 1985; Maynard Smith, 1985a; Rice, 1988). Still, the idea may work if the math models explicitly incorporate the number of grandchildren in their measure of reproductive fitness. Certainly some aspects of the behavior of Burley's finches seem to fit sexy son ideas.

Good genes theories. These theories focus on the idea that females are looking for traits in males that somehow "reveal" the quality of his genes to her. Some of these theories are called **handicapping theories** because only males that are in good condition (because of having good genes) and that have the gene for the trait will be able to survive despite possessing and displaying some "handicapping" trait. Zahavi (1975) suggested that the extreme trait is a kind of "blessing in disguise:" since such a trait is obviously a handicap to survival, a male that does survive must be in all other respects superbly fit. By picking such handicapped males, females ensure that they are getting the best-quality mate and therefore the best-quality genes for their offspring. In some math modeling, the handicap principle did not work out (Kirkpatrick, 1985; Maynard Smith, 1985a; Rice, 1988).

There are other versions of the good genes idea (Andersson, 1986; Heywood, 1989; Pomiankowski, 1987; Tomlinson, 1988). For example, Hamilton and Zuk (1982) suggested that females may choose traits that indicate the male's health. Sometimes a signal, such as being brightly colored, would be able to be displayed only by males who are in good condition; under these circumstances, the term **honest advertising model** seems appropriate (Hill, 1990). In species that are subjected to heavy infestations of parasites, bright coloration in males might be a signal of being genetically resistant to parasites. Only bright males would be free of parasites — though these bright males would also be more visible to predators. Under these conditions, females' choice of bright males would evolve because their mutual offspring would also be resistant to parasites. There is evidence for such a process (Milinski & Bakker, 1990; Pomiankowski, 1989; Ward, 1988).

Female choice depends on both genes and developmental experiences. In some cases, the genes associated with female choice have been identified. For example, a single dominant gene controls mate choice in ladybirds (Majerus et al., 1986). In the presence of the gene, the ladybird prefers dark males; in its absence, the ladybird has no preference. In natural populations, both types of females are present and so both types of male, dark and light, will reproduce. But in this species, males and females look alike, both being dark or light with equal probability. Either the selected-for male trait does not impair reproduction or else evolution has not yet had time to restrict the dark coloration to males alone.

Sexual choices are also sensitive to developmental experiences. As mentioned earlier, the preference a male mouse has for a female with MHC genes different from his own is based on developmental experiences (Yamazaki et al., 1988). In other cases, males and females make sexual choices based on the degree to which the potential mate resembles the individuals with whom they were reared (Bateson, 1982; Beauchamp et al., 1988; Kruijt, Bossema, & Lammers, 1982; Lenington, Egid, & Williams, 1988; Murphy, 1980).

Mating Systems

The mating system of the species determines how sexual and natural selection can affect sex differences. Different **mating systems,** or different ways of "allocating" mates to individuals, allow different levels of opportunity for sex differences in selection pressures to operate. Some of the effects of monogamy versus polygyny have already been mentioned.

Types of mating systems. The following description of mating systems was taken from Emlen and Oring (1977, p. 217). **Monogamy** refers to a mating system in which each sex has only one mate. Monogamy may be seasonal or for a lifetime. Long-term mate fidelity may have evolved in certain species because it maximizes their reproductive success. Monogamy occurs in more than 90 percent of birds but is rare among mammals. In view of the disparity between male and female parental investments, monogamy would be expected to occur only whenever either sex could not reliably increase his or her reproductive success just by increasing his or her number of mates. Thus, monogamy might develop if the offspring required considerable paternal care and if neither parent could take care of more than one set of offspring at a time. Or monogamy could occur if the opposite sex was so widely dispersed over the environment that more than one mate cannot be found during a breeding season. Another possibility is that the genes for altruism, when selected for, might simultaneously increase the frequency of genes that promote monogamy (Peck & Feldman, 1988).

Polygyny occurs whenever males are likely to mate with multiple females. Some males attract multiple mates by defending very attractive and/or large territories, as do the red-winged blackbird and the flycatcher. Other males monopolize females (e.g., a few male elephant seals monopolize dozens of females). Dominance polygyny seems to characterize some primates, such as the female vervet monkeys who prefer dominant males. Even in some monogamous species such as bank swallows, males are more polygynous than females.

In **polyandry,** a female mates with multiple males. It occurs in fewer than 1 percent of species and then only in birds where the male can incubate the egg. Its rarity is not surprising, given the relative investments of the sexes in sperm and eggs. The phalaropes (mentioned earlier) use a polyandrous mating system and the male is solely responsible for the eggs.

Sexual selection, dimorphism, and mating systems.   The degree to which the sexes in any species will differ from each other depends, in part, on the mating system being employed. The mating system sets limits on sex differences in parental investment and in sexual selection (Emlen & Oring, 1977; Jarman, 1983; Leutenegger, 1978, 1982; Leutenegger & Kelly, 1977; Ralls, 1976, 1977). Sexual selection is expected to be more potent in polygyny and polyandry than in monogamy. If sexual choice is a potent evolutionary force, only a few males (polygynous systems) or a few females (polyandrous systems) would be expected to be attractive enough to the opposite sex to be able to mate. Thus, polygamous species should be the most sexually dimorphic, in both body size and in other characteristics as well.

Sexual selection occurs to a more limited extent in monogamous species. But even in some monogamous, nondimorphic species, sexual selection may be occurring (Majerus,

O'Donald, Kearns, & Ireland, 1986; O'Donald, 1980). This is especially likely if the selected-for trait did not affect the female's reproductive success. This means that whatever traits the females "like" in males will also appear in the females — unless those traits are actively selected against by natural selection. Also, remember the monogamous, sexually selecting zebra finches studied by Burley. These finches are quite sexually dimorphic, the male being much brighter than the female.

In any mating system, the effects of sex differences in parental investments can be easily confounded with the effects of sexual selection. Mating systems usually have either high or low levels of both types of selection pressures, making it difficult for researchers to disentangle their effects. This makes it difficult to determine whether sexual selection by itself, or whether the natural selection operating because of the sex differences in reproductive roles, contributed to any sex differences observed. Probably the safest conclusion is that both pressures worked together.

Social/mating systems do covary with the sexual anatomy of primates, including the size of the testes and penis (controlling for body sizes) (Diamond, 1986; Harcourt et al., 1981; Short, 1979). The size of the testes is directly related to how many males normally live in a typical breeding group. The more sexually competing males there are, the relatively larger the testes are. Female ovaries do not vary in relative size among species. Overall, relative testes' size seems to reflect relative frequency of sexual activity, which in turn reflects the amount of male competition. Although the data are far from perfect, humans seem to have had a largely polygynous breeding system in the past. The human testes is smaller than that of chimpanzees, perhaps reflecting less polygyny in human's evolutionary history. The penis of human males is rather dramatically larger than that of a gorilla, an orangutan, or a common chimpanzee, perhaps because of sexual selection.

EVOLUTIONARY CHARACTERISTICS OF SEXUALLY DIMORPHIC SPECIES

This section is organized around a list of characteristics that should appear more often in sexually dimorphic than in less dimorphic species. Because of a past history of certain sex differences in sexual and/or natural selection pressures, certain dimorphisms should have evolved. In this discussion, dimorphisms include any gender-related difference in appearance, physiology, or behavior. The characteristics will first be described in the context of natural and sexual selection pressures. The following section relates those characteristics to human evolutionary history.

1. High Predation

Species that were subjected to high levels of predation might have become dimorphic, for three reasons. The first two reflect natural selection pressures. First, as was argued before, having many predators, including microparasites, might encourage the evolution of sex because sexual reproduction increases the difference between parent and offspring. Second, in some species the cost associated with finding a mate can be very high. If there were many predators about, leaving cover to find a mate could be very risky. Leaving cover would produce a benefit commensurate with the risk only if one was sure that an organism of the opposite sex was one's target. Making the sexes distinguishably different (at least to the species involved), especially at a distance, would curtail the risk associated with predation. Thus, the sexes might look very different, make different sounds, and/or emit different odors.

The third reason is related to sex differences in sexual selection. High levels of predation would tend to limit the effects of sexual selection. Females' preference for a maladaptive trait in males could cause that trait to increase only up to a point. However, if the selected-for trait was at all maladaptive, natural selec-

tion would work to limit the trait's expression to males (or the sex being subjected to sexual selection). This would create sex differences for that species (e.g., only peacock males have long tails).

2. Large Sex Differences in Reproductive Roles

Species in which males and females display different traits and behaviors during the reproductive process should become dimorphic because of both selection pressures. Trivers has pointed out that a disparity between male and female investments creates an opportunity for sexual selection. The resulting sexual selection can create (though it does not always do so) sex differences. Male competition should lead males to develop weapons of offense and bluff, and traits such as horns and red shoulders (red-winged blackbirds) that aid them in their competition. Female choice can lead males to develop extreme forms of whatever it is that females find to be attractive, including large bright tails.

Natural selection also operates so as to maximize the fitness of both sexes for their own particular reproductive roles. In general, if the sexes have very similar reproductive roles, there are few sex differences. If the sexes have very different reproductive roles, as in the elephant seal, the sexes also look and act very differently.

3. Social Living

Social living conditions create new possibilities for evolutionary selection pressures. Social living creates new opportunities for polygyny or polyandry, both of which usually lead to sex differences in sexual selection pressures and in parental investments.

Inclusive fitness, kin recognition, and cooperation, all of which occur more commonly in socially living species, have already been discussed. Sex differences in the kin structure of any social group could also create sex differences in evolutionary pressures. If the social group consists of female relatives (mothers, sisters, daughters, granddaughters) and unrelated males, social living could well exert different kinds of evolutionary pressures on the sexes. Sex differences are very common (though not necessarily large) among social behaviors in most mammals.

4. High Intersexual Competition for Limited Resources

Up to this point, very little has been said about intersexual competition, or competition between the sexes for limited resources. Natural selection pressures would act so as to reduce the competition between males and females. Math modeling has established that this pressure can create sex differences (Slatkin, 1984).

The authors might mention what, in some form at least, might represent the ultimate sex difference developed to reduce this competition. Males in several species, especially those competing for very limited resources, often die shortly after mating (Daly & Wilson, 1983). This obviously reduces the competition between the sexes for food. Furthermore, Darwin (1871) noted that some birds restricted to very geographically restricted locales (e.g., islands) developed such sexually dimorphic beaks that males and females actually ate different kinds of food.

5. Low Sex Ratios among Mating and among Older Adults

Uneven sex ratios in a species represent the end result of sexual selection pressures. If sexual selection is going on in a species, particularly a polygynous species, only a few males get to mate each season. If the number of mating males was compared to the number of mating females, the ratio would be very small. A low sex ratio (few males) among mating adults implies not only polygyny but sexual selection. Such a low sex ratio is also frequently asso-

ciated with (and therefore a sign of) relatively small paternal investment and very sexually dimorphic reproductive roles. For all these reasons, species with small sex ratios among mating adults would be expected to be sexually dimorphic.

With regard to the sex ratio among older adults, sexual selection can reduce the male life span relative to that of the female. If only males are affected by sexual selection, only males will be adversely affected by the selected-for trait and only males will die prematurely because of that trait. Male competition also carries with it high levels of risk, as does extensive competition combined with extensive sexual activity (e.g., male elephant seals not infrequently die after a particularly successful mating season) (Daly & Wilson, 1983).

Lowered sex ratios among the elderly can also reflect the ultimate effects of sex differences in natural selection pressures. If females supply most of the parental care, and since the limited reproductive capacity of females (only so many offspring per year are possible) is what limits the species, offspring survival will depend more on mothers than fathers. Thus, species' survival will depend more on maintaining adequate numbers of females than males; theoretically, one male would be enough. Clutton-Brock (1985) pointed out that during one season of starvation, the population of 6,000 reindeer on an island in the Bering Sea declined to just 42. Only one of those was a male. The greater the proportion of females surviving such a tragedy, the faster the population can recover.

6. Sex Differences in Variability of Reproductive Success

Another way to measure sexual selection is to compare the variability in the reproductive success of the two sexes. If males have more variability, this could be due to sexual selection. For example, in red deer, the range in offspring per year per hind is 0 to 1; the range for stags is 0 to 10 (Clutton-Brock, 1985). If there are sex differences in the variability of lifetime reproductive success, evolutionary pressures are currently at work on the species, including sexual selection pressures.

FACTS AND SPECULATIONS ABOUT HUMANS

What about humans? Models verified on one species must be independently tested on human populations. The types of tests available are very limited; for example, breeding studies cannot be done.

There are two extensively studied peoples being used today as models for what our ancestors might have been like: the warlike Yanomano Indians of the Amazon and the more peaceful !Kung of the Kalahari Desert (Harpending, Rogers, & Draper, 1987; Chagnon, 1988a; Lewin, 1988). The !Kung do not have as strongly differentiated sex roles as the Yanomano do.

What Were Our Ancestors Like?

We know our ancestors were socially living, at least since the end of the Pleistocene (10,000 years ago); they gathered, hunted, and grew crops (although not necessarily all at the same time). The fossil record tells us that the physical sexual dimorphism characteristic of us today was present at the end of the Pleistocene, perhaps when agriculture became more widespread. We know little about their mating system, although most human cultures to date have been characterized as mildly to very polygynous (Daly & Wilson, 1983). This would include the polygyny produced by pre- and extramarital sex, and death or divorce with subsequent remarriage.

Humans in the far distant past may have been subjected to significant numbers of predator attacks, but that is not true of our most recent ancestors. In earlier times, deaths most commonly occurred because of infections, aggression, and starvation (see Chapter 13). At least some of our ancestor populations must have experienced high levels of competition for limited food resources. Perhaps the current sex differences in obesity (more women) and starvation resistance (women more than men) are vestiges of this history (Hoyenga & Hoyenga, 1984). Small sex ratios are evident among our elderly because women do live longer than men, on the average, in nearly every modern human society (Daly & Wilson, 1983).

We are a socially living species, and probably have been throughout at least our modern evolutionary history. And we frequently show sex differences in social traits (see Chapters 9 and 13). However, sex differences in reproductive roles vary extensively from one culture (social group) to the next. But in all cultures, females are assigned the primary responsibility for young children, probably because only females lactate (see Chapters 10 and 11).

Some data suggest that males in most current cultures have significantly greater variability in reproductive success than females do. Daly and Wilson (1983) pointed out that among the !Kung, the male variance is 9.27 and the female variance is 6.52 (the mean for males and females has to be equal—think about it!). The more strongly polygynous Yanomano have a much greater sex difference in the variability of reproduction. Among the Zavante in Brazil, the male variance was three times the female variance.

K versus r Selection Strategies

Another way to compare humans to other species is to examine the two modal types of reproduction strategies defined in Table 4.1 (Daly & Wilson, 1983, p. 201). Species differ from one another in the extent to which they follow K versus r strategies as they are defined in that table, and individuals within species may also differ. Across species, human reproductive strategies are the most K-like. For example, we have extensive parental investment in our offspring, a requirement that might in fact have led the monogamy seen in many current

TABLE 4.1   *Some of the Reproductive and Life-Historical Differences between* r-*strategies and* K-*strategies*

r-strategist	K-strategist
Many offspring	Fewer offspring
Low parental investment in each offspring	High parental investment in each offspring
High infant mortality (mitigated during population explosions)	Lower infant mortality
Short life	Long life
Rapid development	Slow development
Early reproduction	Delayed reproduction
Small body size	Large body size
Variability in numbers, so that population seldom approaches K	Relatively stable population size, at or near K
Recolonization of vacated areas and hence periodic local superabundance of resources	Consistent occupation of suitable habitat, so that resources more consistently exploited
Intraspecific competition often lax	Intraspecific competition generally keen
Mortality often catastrophic, relatively nonselective, and independent of population density	Mortality steadier, more selective, and dependent upon population density
High productivity (maximization of r)	High efficiency (maximization of K)

Source: Modified from E. R. Pianka, 1970, *American Naturalist, 104,* pp. 592–597. Copyright 1970 by The University of Chicago Press. Used by permission.

as well as subsistence-level primitive societies. We have also been described as having females that employ relatively more of a *K*-type of strategy and males that employ relatively more of an *r*-type of strategy (see Chapter 14).

SUMMARY

Both kinds of selection pressures can produce sex differences. Natural selection is concerned with survival and with carrying out one's reproductive role. It can produce sex differences because of sex differences in: (1) parental investments, female mammals usually investing more than males do; (2) reproductive roles; and (3) inclusive fitness. Social traits, including altruism and cooperation, can evolve under

certain conditions, and sometimes the selection pressures can be sexually dimorphic because of sex differences in reproductive roles and because of the kinship structures of social groups.

Sexual selection takes two forms: competition and sexual choice. Both forms usually affect males more than females, perhaps because of the typical difference in parental investments as hypothesized by Trivers. Both forms act to create sex differences, although the sex difference is most likely to appear if the trait is more disadvantageous to one sex or offers no compensating advantages to that sex (e.g., males getting lots of females in "compensation" for their short lives).

One or more of the following characteristics

should typify any sexually dimorphic species: high predation, large sex differences in reproductive roles, social living, sex differences in variability of reproductive success, high intrasexual competition for limited resources, and low sex ratios (few males) among mating and elderly adults. We might never know how evolution affected humans because we may never know exactly what pressures affected our ancestors, but we can test possibilities, either with indirect tests in human populations or with more direct tests in nonhuman animals. These tests can make us either more or less confident in applying certain evolutionary ideas to humans.

ENDNOTES

1. Less than 20 percent survived, compared to the 65 percent survival of the daughters of dominants.

2. Emigration may be one mechanism that animals use to avoid inbreeding (Clutton-Brock, 1989). Inbreeding leads to homozygosity, and, as described earlier, that can have undesirable consequences in terms of survival and reproduction.

3. Frederickson and Sackett (1984) stated that they attempted to replicate this research and failed. However, as the authors noted, and as Holmes (1988) also pointed out, when only the conditions that are nearly equivalent across the two studies are compared, the results were nearly identical. The monkeys could recognize kin, and the females did so more than the males; in fact, the recognition was significant only in females.

UNIT TWO

BIOLOGICAL COVARIATES

This unit discusses biological covariates and Unit Three discusses environmental covariates of gender-related differences in traits and characteristics. Each unit has four chapters. However, you should keep in mind that although the two types of covariates can be experimentally separated, they should not be conceptually separated. That is, we can manipulate or measure events inside the organism, such as its breeding history or its hormone levels, or we can manipulate or measure events outside the organism, such as its developmental history or its current environment. Despite the fact that we can manipulate or measure those things separately, lifetime development is epigenetic. This means that both influences are always working, and have always worked, concurrently, inseparably, and inextricably combined.

The strength of any conclusions made about the possibility of biological covariates for any given gender-related difference would depend on the design of the experiment used to explore them (see Chapter 2). If an independent variable, the putative biological covariate, was actively manipulated, and its two or more different levels were randomly assigned to subjects, we could be fairly confident in concluding that the trait in question had biological covariates. Very little research done with human subjects can use this strong design (see Chapter 2). Also, you should remember that establishing that a biological covariate exists says nothing about the strength or importance of any possible environmental covariates. Finally, no matter what you read in this unit, remember that biological determinism is a myth (see Chapter 1).

Chapter 5 describes the interactions between an organism's gender and the activity of its genes. However, it is important to consider what is *not* covered in Chapter 5. Basic genetic concepts were covered in the first part of Chapter 3 so that you could understand the principles of evolution. How the organism's hormonal gender (see Chapter 1) changes the activities of genes in various cells of its body is covered in Chapters 6 through 8.

What Chapter 5 *does* cover are the sex differences found at the level of genes. You might think that this would refer only to the sex chromosomes, the X and Y chromosomes of most animals. The X and Y will be covered, but they are only a small part of how the organism's gender interacts with its genes. For example, whether a gene came from your mother or your father (parental gender) is often important in determining its effects on you. Also described in Chapter 5 is how genetic gender causes gonadal gender — the sex-determining gene was discovered in 1991.

Chapters 6 through 8 describe hormonal covariates of gender-related differences. Chapter 6 covers basic principles of how our sex hormones affect our brains and thus our thoughts and behaviors. Hormones can affect brain cells not only by turning genes on and off within those cells but also by mechanisms similar to those used by brain cells to talk to each other.

Chapter 7 and 8 cover the two periods in organisms' lives when the sexes have consistently different levels of sex hormones. One of those stages—the **perinatal** period—starts before birth (prenatal) and continues for a period of time after birth (neonatal). The second period starts after puberty. However, sex differences in sex hormone levels during the second period not only depend on the age of the organism (whether the human female is menopausal or not, for example) but also on the day of the month and the time of the day.

CHAPTER 5

THE GENETICS OF GENDER

INTRODUCTION
SEXUALLY DIMORPHIC EVOLUTION: SEX CHROMOSOMES AND HORMONES
GENDER DIFFERENCES IN GENE ACTIVITY
SEX-DETERMINING GENES
EXPLORING SEX LINKAGE
SEX CHROMOSOME MAPS
SUMMARY

> *No one really knows what makes a male a male or a female a female.*
> —Gina Kolata (1986, p. 1076)

During my first years of teaching, I gave a guest lecture on sex chromosomes to an introductory psychology class. I had discussed some implications of certain anomalies of the sex chromosomes, including the anomaly called Turner's syndrome in which a person has only one sex chromosome—an X. I had described their physical appearance, their social characteristics, and their cognitive deficits. One girl came to me after class and said, "I think I am a Turner's girl." One look and I knew she was right. "No one ever told me I was, but I fit everything you said. Everything except that part about being poor at math. That's my favorite college subject, and my major is accountancy."

I never forgot that lesson—and neither should you. People with various chromosome anomalies are expected to be just as different from each other as people with normal chromosomes. Nevertheless, studying people with sex chromosome anomalies can give us information

about the roles of the X and Y chromosomes—what makes males male and females female.

INTRODUCTION

There are three ways in which the gender of a parent affects the genes that that parent gives to offspring. The three types of **gendered inheritance** are as follows:

1. Only a male (at least in mammals) can give the male-causing chromosome, the Y chromosome, to his offspring, making them males as well. If, instead of the Y, the male contributes his X chromosome, the offspring will be female. The mother can contribute either of her two Xs to a male or female child.

2. **Mitochondria** (the energy factories of cells) also have DNA, and the mitochondria of a zygote come only from the egg, or from the mother. Although this particular type of gendered inheritance will not be discussed in this chapter, several human diseases have been linked to mitochondrial inheritance, the most common of which is a deafness induced by the

use of certain antibiotics (Hu, et al., 1991). This form of inheritance is also one part of what is called **maternal inheritance** (discussed further in Chapter 9) since it involves all the ways an offspring is influenced by a parent, including a human child being socialized into the culture (Kirkpatrick & Lande, 1989; Stamps, 1991).

3. Female and male parents have different meiotic events. Some genes are "labeled" according to the gender of parent from which they came and then differentially affect the offspring. Cross-over frequencies in certain chromosomes during meiosis also sometimes depend on the gender of the parent creating the germ cells.

The chapter focuses on the implications of the first type of gendered inheritance. The question of just how genes cause a male to be a male is examined. At one level of analysis, the question is easy to answer: in mammals Y chromosomes cause testes to form. Looking across species, one realizes that the real question is actually a great deal more dificult to answer. In some species, such as birds, it is the female that has the two unmatched sex chromosomes. The sex with the unmatched sex chromosomes is **heterogametic** (male mammals with their XY and female birds with their ZW). And then there is the platyfish. The species has three sex chromosomes, although each individual fish normally has only two of them: WY, WX, and XX are females, whereas XY and YY are males (Kallman & Borkoski, 1978).

The first section of this chapter describes how sexually dimorphic evolutionary selection pressures might have changed gene frequencies and how these changes might have affected gender-related differences. The second section looks at the evidence for sex differences in gene activity that are *not* related to sex hormones, which is relevant to the second type of gendered inheritance described above. Next, the kinds of research that can be used to explore the question of what traits might be affected by genes found on the sex chromosomes are described. The chapter concludes with tentative maps of human X and Y chromosomes.

SEXUALLY DIMORPHIC EVOLUTION: SEX CHROMOSOMES AND HORMONES

Chapters 3 and 4 described why and how evolutionary selection pressures created sex (sexual reproduction) and sex differences. This section concentrates on how the genes themselves were changed by the evolutionary selection pressures so as to create sex and sex differences. Most of the discussion is limited to mammals.

Sex-Linked Genes

A **sex-linked gene** in mammals is one located on either the X or Y chromosome. These genes would be called, respectively, **X-linked** and **Y-linked** genes. An X- or Y-linked trait is one whose phenotypic expression was affected by an X- or Y-linked gene. Sex-linked genes are responsible for sex as well as some sex differences.

Any gene found *only* on the Y chromosome would appear, and so could be expressed, only in males. Consequently, if a trait were affected by a Y-linked gene, the trait would appear only in the male phenotype. Y-linked traits are not quite as uncommon as they once were thought to be; however, most of these Y-linked genes have copies of themselves on either the X chromosome or on one of the autosomes (Maxson, 1990; Maxson & Roubertoux, 1990). In this case, males could have more copies of the gene than females do, because of the Y chromosome, and so males could express the corresponding trait more often, or more completely, than females.

X-linked genes also have sexually dimorphic effects. Suppose a female were homozygous for some X-linked gene (identical alleles on both her Xs). If both homologous X-linked genes were fully expressed (which is usually not true, as described later), the female with the two homologous genes would have more gene product in her body cells than would the male with only the one X. If the female were heterozygous at that genetic locus, she could have both

X-linked gene products present — something the male could never have.

In fact, X-linked traits can be called *dominant* or *recessive* only according to how they are expressed in females, because only females can have paired X-linked genes. For a female to express a recessive X-linked trait, she must be homozygous at that locus. On the other hand, a male will express *any* X-linked gene, dominant or recessive, since he has only the one X. Males have no homologous genes to oppose any recessive gene's effects.

Any X-linked gene is expressed in a sexually dimorphic fashion. Any dominant, X-linked gene is expressed in twice as many females as males, because females have twice as many chances to inherit it (having two instead of just the one X chromosome). On the other hand, males are more likely to express recessive X-linked genes. For example, if the proportion of the people in some population who have that gene is p, then the proportion of males who will have the gene and express the trait is also p. The proportion of females who will express the trait is lower, since the female will have had to inherit two X chromosomes, both having the same X-linked recessive gene on them ($p \times p = p^2$).

Sex-Limited Genes

Sex-limited genes are located on autosomes whose activity depends on the organism's sex, thereby creating sex differences. Most sex-limited genes have their activity regulated by the level of sex hormones present in the body. This is a classic example of an epigenetic effect. A certain amount of a specific sex hormone coming into the cell from the bloodstream may be required to turn a given gene on. Or maybe the degree or duration of gene activity is regulated in some continuous fashion by sex hormone levels. Another possibility is that the effect of the gene's product is moderated by hormone levels. (Sex limitation is discussed more fully in Chapters 6, 7, and 8.)

Evolution of Sex Linkage and Sex Limitation

Suppose that some trait is under sexual selection pressure because females prefer males with more extreme levels of that trait. For example, suppose female birds prefer longer-tailed males. To begin with, both sexes will experience tail lengthening (Lande, 1980). The genes involved are autosomal and so will appear fairly rapidly (a few thousand to several thousand generations) in both sexes. If the female is subjected to some counterselective natural selection pressure, such as from predators, and since long tails are of no benefit to her, evolution will capitalize on any mutational or recombinational event that would limit the trait's expression to males. This type of control evolves very slowly, perhaps taking millions of generations (Lande, 1980). A trait can become dimorphic through either sex linkage or sex limitation, as long as it has a different cost/benefit ratio for the two sexes.

Sexual dimorphism by means of sex linkage may occur in at least two ways. First, if a mutation or a recombinational event created a new gene on the X or the Y, any trait affected by the product of that gene would be sexually dimorphic, as described above. If such a sex-linked gene were especially advantageous to the survival and reproduction of the sex in which it appeared most often, the frequency of that gene could increase over generations.

Second, consider the previous example where females preferred the longer-tailed males and so the frequency of autosomal long-tailed genes increased. Then, if during some male meiosis a crossover event caused the trait to be transferred to a Y chromosome, the male offspring would benefit from having the large tail and the female offspring would also benefit from not having the large tail. This male's progeny should outreproduce the competition, and the Y-linked gene would increase in frequency.

Crossover may also create sex linkage of any trait that is more beneficial to the reproductive role to one sex than to the other because of natural selection pressures. A trait could be of more benefit to females and also have a greater cost to males. For example, sensitivity to the social cues used by other animals to signal distress may benefit females' ability to raise offspring and to interact in female kin groups, but it could hinder a male's competition with other male primates (see Chapter 13).

Both natural and sexual selection could use similar mutational or recombinational events to bring an autosomal gene under the control of sex hormone levels, making it sex limited. For instance, a gene might be moved to a location that was activated only if a high enough level of some sex hormone were present. The intensity of both natural and sexual selection pressures would again be a function of the sex difference in cost/benefit ratios.

Some of these genetic events might have involved proviruses. As one example, some autosomal genes regulating growth might have been brought under the control of sex hormones by the insertion of a provirus (Sluyser et al., 1988). This makes sense since abnormal activity in some growth genes (**oncogenes**) have also been related to the development of certain tumors and the rate of certain kinds of tumor growth can be increased by sex hormones. Provirus genes have been frequently found to be associated with oncogenes. As another example, one provirus became incorporated into the mouse genome at some distant point in the mouse's evolutionary history. This caused the expression of a particular immune gene, located in the MHC, to come under the control of androgen levels in the body (Stavenhagen & Robins, 1988).

GENDER DIFFERENCES IN GENE ACTIVITY

The gendered-inheritance effects discussed in this section do not fit well into classic genetic or Mendelian theory (e.g., the theory of genes and traits described by Gregor Mendel in the nineteenth century). Nevertheless, they are striking, systematic, widespread, and important both to evolutionary processes and to gender-related differences.

Recombination Frequency

In this section, recombination will be used to refer only to crossover, not to independent assortment. Recombination rates are under genetic control since high rates can be selected for or against in breeding studies (Brooks, 1988). Certain areas on the chromosomes, called **hotspots,** are areas in which breakage and crossover is particularly likely to occur during meiosis. These hot spots are probably noncoding regions of the DNA where chromosome breakage would not damage a gene. The frequency of these recombinational events is sexually dimorphic; however, the direction of the sex difference depends on species and on whether autosomes or sex chromosomes are being considered.

Autosomal recombination: mostly higher in females. "There is a very widespread sex difference in the underlying genetic system which has gone nearly completely unnoticed in our recent efforts to understand sexual selection and the evolution of sex. . . . In almost every species studied, the sexes differ in rates of crossing over" (Trivers, 1988, p. 270). Why?

Sex differences in the frequency of crossover events during meiosis are nearly universal (Hayman, Moore, & Evans, 1988; Sharp & Hayman, 1988; Shiroishi et al., 1990; Trivers, 1988; Zhuchenko et al., 1988). Autosomal crossovers may be present in the meiosis of one sex and totally absent in the meiosis of the other sex. For example, crossovers occur only in female and not in male fruit flies; on the other hand, crossovers do not occur in female butterflies and moths, only in males. The sexes may also differ in rate of crossover events. Female mice have more crossovers of more gene groups during meiosis than do males, but crossovers are much higher in male tomato and arabidopsis plants than in females, and crossovers are also more common in male than in female marsupials (Australian pouched animals).

Although "recombination is typically greater in females than in males, there are numerous exceptions" (Trivers, 1988, p. 274). According to Trivers, greater recombination in females has been demonstrated in most mammals (including humans, mice, and horses), the majority of insects, chickens, some protozoa, a mollusc, some worms, some newts, and some plants. In mammals, the rate of autosomal recombination is about 30 percent higher in females than in males. Some exceptions — where recombination is greater in males — include a marsupial, some other newts, butterflies and moths, a salamander, sea lice, and other plants (Bennett, Hayman, & Hope, 1986; Callan & Perry, 1977; Hayman et al., 1988; Trivers, 1988; Zhuchenko et al., 1988).

Recombination in sex chromosomes: higher in male humans.

One sex chromosome region has a very high rate of recombination in male mammals: at least once during every meiosis. The genes that often cross over between the X and Y during male meiosis are called the **pseudoautosomal genes** in humans, chimpanzees, and mice.

Since pseudoautosomal crossovers are so frequent, some genes that are found on the X in one generation will move to the Y chromosome in the next. Overall, these genes show patterns of parent-offspring inheritance more typical of autosomes than of sex chromosomes, which led to them being called pseudoautosomal genes. The pseudoautosomal region is found on the tip of the short arm (the upper part in most diagrams and pictures) of the X and Y chromosomes. The pseudoautosomal area is less likely to cross over from one X to the other during a female meiosis, compared to the frequency of X to Y crossovers (or vice versa) during male meiosis. In fact, the rate of recombination between X and Y may be 10 to 20 times the greater than that occurring between the homologous areas of two Xs (Rouyer et al., 1986; Weissenbach et al., 1987).

As might be expected, homologous X- and Y-linked pseudoautosomal genes are often alleles of each other. In other words, in the pseudoautosomal areas, genes found at a given locus on the Y often have homologous genes, or alleles, found in the comparable X-linked locus. One pseudoautosomal gene, the *MIC2 gene,* found on both the X and Y, codes for the cell protein antigen called *12E7*. This protein is found on the walls of all cells.

Other regions of the human X and Y also show great similarities to each other, as well as interesting differences from the X and Y chromosomes found in other primates (Cooke, Brown, & Rappold, 1984; Page et al., 1984). This suggests that regions of the X and Y *other than* the pseudoautosomal region are also prone to crossovers, though much less frequently than the pseudoautosomal region. Some of these crossovers occurred relatively recently in human evolution, some time after we had diverged from the ancestors of other living primates.

Possible explanations.

One reason for limiting crossovers to one sex is genetic damage. Although having hot spots should limit crossovers to areas between genes, sometimes genetic damage will occur. Limiting crossovers to just one gender, or having just one gender experience frequent crossover events, may reflect the need to protect against that damage. If one chromosome of each pair came from a parent that had less frequent crossover events, and therefore less chance of damage, this would give the developing organism at least one functional gene. Species might have therefore developed differences in crossover frequency.

Recombination may be higher in the sex chromosomes of males because both Xs are active during female meiosis but males inactivate their only X at that time. Inactive chromosomes have more crossovers.

Trivers pointed out that although there are

many exceptions, the heterogametic sex usually has the lowest autosonomal recombination rates. He suggested that the only exceptions to this rule occur in species with either (or both) of two characteristics: (1) substantial paternal investment (including mating costs) and (2) low levels of sexual selection. Species with low levels of sexual selection would be much less affected by having males' favorable gene patterns being broken up by recombination; such males are not being chosen for their unique "beauty." Thus, such species would be more likely to be exceptions to the heterogametic rule, meaning that males would have more recombinational events than females would. Species with low levels of sexual selection are also likely to have substantial paternal investments in offspring. Species with one or both of these characteristics often have more frequent crossover events in males even when males are the heterogametic sex.

Females' greater rate of autosomal recombination might also be related to sex differences in parental investments. The more extensive contact a parent has with offspring, the more likely the parent is to pass on to the offspring the microparasites that have evolved inside the parent. This would make it even more important for the offspring to be immunologically different from that particular parent. In mammals, the maternal-offspring contact is particularly intimate because the fetus develops internally and is later fed with the mother's milk. In mice, for example, females' greater rate of recombination during meiosis extends to the immune region of the genome (Loh & Baltimore, 1984; Shiroishi et al., 1990). The longer the offspring remain in close contact with their mothers, the more important it would be for mothers and offspring to be immunologically different. Burt and Bell (1987) found that the longer offspring remained dependent on their mothers, the more meiotic crossovers occurred in that species.

The time required for gamete formation may also be relevant. Recombination rate de-creases whenever gametes are being formed more rapidly. If crossovers occurred, this would greatly slow the process of gamete formation (Trivers, 1988). Female meiosis occurs before birth, and the female is born with her life's supply of eggs. The male must continually engage in meiosis to remain fertile, and having to engage in high levels of recombination may slow down the rate of sperm formation enough to impair his reproductive fitness. So maybe females do the recombination because they have more "time to spare" than males do.

Genomic, or Parental, Imprinting

Some genes are "labeled" according to the parent from which they came (Chakraborty, 1989; Hall, 1990; Marx, 1988a; Sapienza, 1990; Sapienza et al., 1987; Solter, 1988; Swain, Stewart, & Leder, 1987). In the resulting offspring, the genes coming from one parent can be either more or less active than the homologous genes coming from the parent of the other sex. This process is called **parental,** or **genomic, imprinting.**

Description of processes. During the meiosis occurring in each parent, many autosomal genes are somehow marked[1] to indicate the parent of origin. Genomic imprinting is usually reversed in every meiosis. Thus, before a gene is passed on, it might be relabeled to reflect the sex of the person in whom the genes are currently found. For example, during her creation of egg cells, a female will remove the "male" label from her paternal chromosomes (the ones she got from her father) and attach a "female" label to them. In some pathological cases, however, the original imprint may prove to be irreversible and will be transmitted from parent to child to grandchild, unchanged.

Most molecular genetics research on parental imprinting has been done with mice. Whether paternal or maternal genes are the more active in an offspring varies from strain to strain and from organ to organ. For example, one study tested five strains of mice. One strain showed no differential activity between the maternal and paternal genes in offspring, one showed greater activity in maternal chromosomes, and three showed greater activity in paternal chromosomes (Sapienza et al., 1987).

Implications and outcomes of parental imprinting. One of the implications of this sex difference is that mammals require both a mother and a father; parthenogenesis is not possible. A mouse embryo can be manipulated to have either two sets of maternal or two sets of paternal chromosomes, as well as the normal maternal-paternal combination. Only embryos with one paternal and one maternal set develop normally. The paternal chromosomes are most important for the development of extraembryonic tissue (e.g., placenta), and maternal genes are more important for the embryo proper (Hall, 1990; M. Hoffman, 1991a; Solter, 1988; Swain et al., 1987). In other cases, paternal genes have more of an effect on the development of the skeleton and muscles, whereas maternally derived genes have more of an effect on the brain. In contrast, parthenogenesis commonly occurs in some birds, such as the turkey; both sets of chromosomes can be of maternal origin in them.

Some human genetic diseases show differential transmission from fathers as opposed to mothers, depending on which parent passed the relevant gene on to the offspring (Hall, 1990). If this is so, your chances of getting some diseases may depend on whether your mother or your father gave you the gene! These diseases include certain kinds of cancer and diabetes, the infantile form of muscular dystrophy (M. Hoffman, 1991a; Sapienza, 1990; Swain et al., 1987), maybe manic-depressive disorder (T.J. Crow, 1988; J.F. Crow, 1989; Kupfer, Carpenter, & Frank, 1988; Rice et al., 1984; this disorder is discussed again later in this chapter), and perhaps some types of retardation (see the last section of this chapter).

Two other examples, Prader-Willi syndrome

and Huntington's disease, are discussed here so you can see how the parent of origin can affect the offspring. Two genetic diseases, Prader-Willi and Angelman syndromes, may represent the effects of different parental imprinting of the same gene on chromosome 15 (Sapienza, 1990). Prader-Willi sufferers are extremely obese, retarded, and short. They frequently got both their copies of chromosome 15 from their mothers. Angelman's people suffer from excessive laughter, jerky movement, and retardation. Their only copy of the relevant gene on chromosome 15 came from their fathers. The gene for Huntington's disease is autosomal and dominant. People with this disease have a slow death, with mental and physical dysfunctions usually appearing by age 40 or so. The early-onset form of the gene (onset as early as age 2) is evidently created during the male meiosis, since most of the people who develop the disease early are born to affected fathers (Farrer & Conneally, 1985; M. Hoffman, 1991a; Myers et al., 1983; Ridley et al., 1988; Sapienza, 1990; Solter, 1988).

Several suggestions have been made about why genomic imprinting might have evolved (Chakraborty, 1989; Hall, 1990). Imprinting can further increase variability, or it could be an epigenetic effect of the evolution of placentas. Imprinting also means that sexual reproduction is an ESS in mammals; they cannot be invaded by a mutant parthenogen, since imprinting makes parthenogenesis impossible. Imprinting might reflect a more flexible way of structuring epigenetic developmental processes. Any, all, or none of the possibilities may be true.

X-Inactivation

Early in fetal development, one of the two X chromosomes present in every female mammal is turned off or inactivated. This is called **X-inactivation.** All daughter cells of the zygote that differentiate from (are descendants of) one of those original fetal cells will have the same X inactivated. In some species, such as marsupials (e.g., pouched animals such as kangaroos and opossums), the paternal X may be preferentially inactivated in all females' cells (another gendered-inheritance effect: Charlesworth, 1991; Rastan et al., 1980). But in most mammalian females, whether the maternal or paternal X has been inactivated varies from one cell to the next.

The inactivated X is visible, in appropriately stained body cells, as a dark mass at the edge of the cell's nucleus. The dark stain, characteristic of inactive chromosomal material, is called a **Barr body.** Although all female cells (with the exception of germ cells undergoing meiosis) have one X inactivated, in only a few of those cells will the inactive X be visible as a Barr body. The Barr body was the basis for the Olympic committee's test for an athlete's sex, to prevent males from competing as females; Olympic committees now test for the presence of a Y chromosome.

Description.   X-inactivation occurs early in the fetal development of all female mammals (Berg, 1979; Gartler & Riggs, 1983; Grant & Chapman, 1988; Jablonka & Lamb, 1988; Lyon, 1972; Migeon, 1979; Wrigley & Graves, 1988). Lyon first described this process in 1961, and most of her ideas were confirmed by subsequent research. Although in humans, inactivation of paternal or maternal Xs usually occurs independently and randomly in each of the early zygote's cells, an abnormal gene can affect the randomness of the process. If the X is abnormal, maybe because a piece of an autosome crossed over and attached to it, few cells in the adult will have the abnormal X active. Either the abnormal X is preferentially inactivated, or else the cells that have the abnormal X active preferentially die off during development.

The inactivation of the human X is not complete (Buckle et al., 1985; Craig, Levy, & Fraser, 1987; Goodfellow et al., 1987). Genes on the pseudoautosomal region remain active on both X chromosomes. Because both sexes have all the pseudoautosomal genes active, both sexes have equal levels of the pseudoautosomal gene products. Some X-linked genes *not* in the pseudoautosomal region also escape inactivation, such as the *STS* gene which codes for an enzyme called steroid sulfatase (its absence leads to the severe skin lesions of *congenital ichthyosis*). Since the STS gene is only partially inactivated in humans, human females have two at least partially functioning copies of that gene. Men, on the other hand, have only one (the Y-linked STS gene is nonfunctional). Thus, females have higher levels of steroid sulfatase in their bodies than males do—a fact that has unknown implications, except by way of being an instructive example.

Meiosis changes X-inactivation. When the human female's eggs are being formed during her fetal development, the second X is reactivated. Evidently two Xs are needed for normal female meiosis. In fact, although ovaries develop normally in fetal females with just one X, egg cells do not develop, which means the fetus's ovaries will usually degenerate before birth. On the other hand, throughout the male's adult life, his only X is at least partially inactivated during sperm formation (Jablonka & Lamb, 1988; Lifschytz & Lindsley, 1972).

Implications for sex differences.   Because of X-inactivation, mammalian females are functional **mosaics,** having different genes active in different body cells. Some implications of this can literally be seen in the coat colors of female mice and cats. In cats, for example, the orange color comes from an X-linked gene. Suppose that a female had the orange gene on only one of her Xs. The result would be a calico (or tortoiseshell) cat, with splotches of orange mixed with splotches of other colors. Wherever you see orange on a calico cat, you see where the X with the orange gene is active. The splotches of other colors are skin areas where the X *without* the orange gene is active. Throughout their bodies, all female mammals, including humans, have patches of tissue with one X active adjacent to patches that have the other X active.

Color perception is partially X linked. Genes coding for the ability to see green and red are X linked in humans and at least some other primates[2] (Jacobs & Neitz, 1985; Mollon, Bowmaker, & Jacobs, 1984). Therefore, a mutant color gene, incapable of normal functioning, will more often affect the color perception of men than women since men do not have a second X that could provide them with a normal product (8 percent of men versus about 0.5 percent of women are color blind). These color-blind people are unable to distinguish red from green (seeing both as yellow). To be red-green blind, a woman would have to have inherited two mutant genes, one on each of her Xs.

Women with one mutant gene would be expected to have "splotchy" visual **retinas** (the light-sensitive part of the eye). These heterozygous females would have color-blind retinal areas intermixed with color-normal areas, depending on where in the retina each X had been inactivated (Born, Grutzner, & Hemminger, 1976). This patchiness can be of benefit. In squirrel monkeys, some females but not males have **trichromatic** vision (three-color vision, similar to our normal color vision). The other females and all males are color blind, unable to distinguish red from green (Jacobs & Neitz, 1985; Mollon et al., 1984). In this primate, some X chromosomes have a redlike gene and other Xs have a greenlike gene; the two genes may be alleles of the same locus. Only the heterozygous females that have a different X, and so a different type of X-linked color gene active in different parts of their retinas, will have trichromatic vision. This may be the first step toward the evolution of a fully trichromatic color vision for this species.

It is interesting that there are different red genes present on various human X chromosomes (Neitz & Jacobs, 1986). A female who inherited both types of X would have each active in different parts of her retina. Would she be tetrachromatic, able to see four colors rather than the three? Is color vision evolving further in human primates?

Aging processes interact with those of X-inactivation in females. An inactivated X-linked gene can become reactivated during aging (Brown & Rastan, 1988; Wareham et al., 1987). This may be part of age-related deteriorations in cellular functions.

Because of X-inactivation, females are usually less affected by even a dominant X-linked mutant gene than are males. On the other hand, heterozygous (sometimes called carrier) females may sometimes show detectable signs of a recessive disease, and some can even express the disease completely (e.g., see Gomez et al., 1977, described in Hoyenga & Hoyenga, 1993). Because of X-inactivation, female twins will differ more from each other than do male twins, at least to the extent that phenotypically important X-linked genes are heterozygous in them.

Most theorists regard X-inactivation as a **dosage-compensation mechanism.** Since females have two and males only one X, if there were no X-inactivation, females would have a "double dose" of all X-linked gene products. Since multiple copies of genes and chromosomes are usually deleterious (e.g., the effects of trisomy 21 in Down's syndrome), X-inactivation prevents any deleterious effects.

SEX-DETERMINING GENES

The most basic question for this section of the chapter is how genes control gender. The sex-determining gene is Y linked, but other important genes are X linked and autosomal.

Y-Linked Genes

Inheriting a Y chromosome from your father almost always means you will develop as a male (see exceptions below). Nettie Stevens (1861–1912) was the first person to observe that sex chromosomes determine gender (Booth, 1989). If the organism has a Y chromosome, the primitive gonads present in the fetal mammal will differentiate as testes. In the absence of a Y, the primitive gonads will turn into ovaries.

TDF and XX males.   Some humans and mice lack Y chromosomes and yet still develop testes (XX males) (Andersson, Page, & de la Chapelle, 1986; de la Chapelle, 1981, 1986, 1987; Eicher & Washburn, 1986; Kolata, 1986; Page, Brown, & de la Chapelle, 1987; Roberts, 1988). Some people with a Y chromosome develop ovaries (XY females). Why?

Researchers thought that if they could identify the factor responsible for testes in XX animals, that same factor would also have to be present in XY males and be coded for by a Y-linked gene. The gene might have mutated in XY females. If so, this factor/gene would have been proved to be responsible for one important aspect of maleness: testes. The searched-for factor was called the **testes-determining factor (TDF)**. The gene coding for this hypothesized factor was called the **sex-determining gene (SXD gene).**

With sophisticated genetic techniques at their disposal, researchers studied XX animals with testes, including human XX males. Some XX males had inherited an unusual X chromosome from their fathers. Genes very close to the pseudoautosomal region had broken off the Y chromosome and crossed over, attaching themselves to the X. Thus, the XX males have part of what is normally on a Y attached to their paternal X, and this gene (or genes) leads to the fetal development of testes. XX male mice are also created by an abnormal crossover during the meiosis of their male parent.

The relevant area for sex determination (SXD) was found to be close to the pseudoautosomal region. "Scientists in Britain confidently announced yesterday [May 9] that they had ended the 30-year search for the gene that switches mammalian development from its usual destination—the female—to the male" (Cherfas, 1991). The product of this gene also seems to regulate the activity of other genes.

It is expressed only in males, and then only in fetal gonads during the time they are differentiating into testes. Two XY women were found that had a mutation in that gene that was not present in their fathers' chromosomes. Thus, a new mutation which happens to inactivate that specific gene will mean that tests will not form. Most convincingly, when the gene was inserted in XX mouse embryos, some of them developed as completely normal-looking males! The SXD product is still unknown, but that gene seems to be necessary for testes and hence maleness.

H-Y antigen.   **H-Y antigen** is a protein found on the surface of all cells of normal male mammals (Meck, 1984; Stewart, 1986). It was discovered in tissue grafting studies. Inbred, highly homozygous females were found to reject tissue from brothers but not from sisters, although brothers accepted tissue from sisters. This led to the search for a male-specific, cell-wall or cell-surface protein that could have caused the rejection of the male tissue by their otherwise genetically identical sisters. The search led to H-Y antigen. Researchers have now established that the Y-linked H-Y antigen genes are located well away from the SXD gene and may be close to—or identical with—the genes regulating spermatogenesis (Burgoyne, Levy, & McLaren, 1986; Eicher & Washburn, 1986; E. Simpson et al., 1987; Stewart, 1986).

Y-linked genes, growth rate, and gonads. Growth rate may be linked to sexual differentiation. Mittwoch (1986, 1988, 1989, 1990) suggested that certain Y-linked genes in mammals, including the SDX gene, enhance fetal growth rates. She suggested that gonads with fast-growing cells differentiate into testes, whereas gonads with slower-growing cells differentiate into ovaries. Gonads in XY fetuses grow faster than those in XX fetuses, even before they start to differentiate into tests or ovaries.

Mittwoch also pointed out that the left and right gonads do not grow at the same rate. Since she claimed that faster-growing gonads preferentially turn into testes, this led to some interesting explanations of various sexual phenomena. In humans, the left fetal gonad grows more slowly than does the right. Some people are true **hermaphrodites,** having both a testicle and an ovary. In true hermaphrodites, the left, slower-growing gonad is almost always the one that turns into an ovary, whereas the right, faster-growing gonad becomes a testis. Furthermore, Mittwoch pointed out that testes are larger in Caucasian than in Oriental men and that XX males are more common in Caucasians, whereas XY females are more common in Japan. Interestingly, in Mongolian gerbils, the fetuses in the right portion ("horn") of the mother's uterus are more likely to be males than are those found in the left horn (Clark & Galef, 1990).

Sex Hormone Genes

Once testes have developed under the influence of TDF, most of the rest of gender-dimorphic development is controlled by sex hormones. This section describes what is known about the genes that control sex hormone level and activity.

Enzymes.   The sex hormones are all synthesized from cholesterol under the control of various enzymes. Since these enzymes control the rate at which various phases of hormone synthesis are carried out, they also control the amount and type of sex hormones to be found in the bloodstream and in various cells of the body. The location and nature of some of these enzyme-coding genes is unknown. Most of the known genes are autosomal, although at least some are sex linked.

These enzymes are found in specific locations throughout the body. Since sex hormones are biochemically similar to each other, they can be transformed into each other.[4] The degree to which a body cell is exposed to a certain hormone can be regulated by controlling

the levels of **synthesizing enzymes** in that cell.

Hormone receptors.   If a cell is to respond in a specific way (see Chapter 6) to a certain hormone, the cell must have a specific protein, called a **receptor protein,** present. Each sex hormone has its own unique receptor protein. The control over which cells are affected by which hormone is exerted by controlling which type of hormone receptor is to be found in each cell (Strähle et al., 1989).

The receptor for testosterone is coded for by an X-linked gene both in humans and mice (Lubahn et al., 1988; Meyer, Migeon, & Migeon, 1975). The gene has at least two alleles, only one of which codes for a functioning **androgen receptor.** In the absence of a normal androgen receptor, any androgen found in an organism of either gender will not have its typical or expected effects on body cells, brains, or behaviors, either before birth or after puberty.

Since the androgen receptor gene is X linked, females as well as males have androgen receptors. Androgen receptors allow a female's body tissue to respond to androgen after puberty, producing the increase in pubic and axillary hair and the increase in acne that human females experience at puberty. A heterozygous female with one androgen-insensitive gene and one normal androgen-receptor gene would be expected to pass the problem on to half her sons. She herself would show little if any phenotypic effect. However, just as is the case with the other X-linked genes, half her body tissues have androgen receptors and half do not (as was shown in mice: Takeda et al., 1987). A female homozygous for the mutant gene will have scanty or absent pubic and axillary hair.

In the absence of a functional androgen receptor, an XY person will develop testes (the TDF is present) but the rest of that person's development will be feminine, resulting in a female phenotype. Such XY people have complete **androgen insensitivity.**[5] Usually the syndrome is not recognized at birth unless the abdomen is examined and the undescended testes discovered. These people are often reared as females and not identified until puberty or later, when lack of menstruation or infertility may bring them into some clinic. Once recognized, their testes are usually removed because of the danger of cancer.

EXPLORING SEX LINKAGE

Both X- and Y-linked traits affect other gender-related differences in addition to gonads. Three kinds of research can be used to explore sex linkage: (1) family history studies, (2) genetic probes, and (3) studies of people with sex chromosome anomalies. This research has produced the maps of Y- and X-linked genes presented at the end of this section.

Family History Studies

Although family history studies are the oldest type of research, this technique is still being used today. In **family history research,** generations of family members are examined for the presence versus the absence of some phenotypic trait. Adoptive family trees can be compared with those of genetically related family members. If a trait "breeds true," or if parents pass the trait on to their offspring in ways predictable from classic genetic theory, the trait may have some genetic basis. The results are often presented as a type of genealogy tree, as in Figure 5.1—a sort of "who gave what to whom" picture. That figure is a pedigree of one family with an X-linked disease, color blindness. None of the first-generation male's offspring were affected, but three of his daughters passed the gene on to their sons who were then color blind as well.

Family history studies have become very sophisticated. Researchers recognize that genomic imprinting can affect the family history of a trait and that a pseudoautosomal gene will often have the family tree characteristics

FIGURE 5.1 *Pedigree of an X-linked Disease*
The X-linked disease shown in this pedigree is color blindness. The person whose family history was explored is indicated by the circle with the 3 inside (for third generation). Males are represented by squares; females are represented by circles; people with the trait are represented by filled symbols. Note that the trait is passed on to the third generation by four unaffected (heterozygous) females of the second generation.

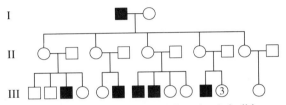

Source: From *Principles of Human Genetics,* 3rd edition, by Curt Stern. Copyright © 1973 by W. H. Freeman and Company. Reprinted by permission.

of an autosomal gene. Another interesting possibility to keep in mind is that adoptive parents may put more effort into influencing their children's development than do natural parents, trying to make their adoptive children more similar to themselves (Bouchard, 1984).

Patterns of sex-linked heritability. Mothers will give their sons and daughters one of each their Xs with equal frequency, just as mothers do with their autosomes. Thus, mother-offspring inheritance patterns are not as informative for sex linkage as are father-offspring patterns. A father gives his X to all his daughters and his Y to all his sons. If a trait is Y linked, then barring abnormal meiotic crossovers, a father exhibiting that trait will pass it on to all of his sons but to none of his daughters. Obviously, the TDF is one such trait.

The inheritance of X-linked traits is considerably more complex. If the gene acts like a recessive but is phenotypically visible in a male, none of that male's sons will receive that trait but all of his daughters will carry that X.

If, by chance, the other X that the daughter received from her mother also carried the same recessive gene (a rare event), the daughter would express that trait as fully as would a son. Even if the daughter's maternal X had the normal allele, X-inactivation can lead to phenotypically detectable effects or even to the full expression of the trait. Thus, the degree to which the father and daughter will have similar levels of any X-linked trait depends on what gene is carried by the daughter's maternal X and on the daughter's X-inactivation patterns.

Variations in how active a gene is also affect parent-offspring similarities. Maybe the relevant gene leads to the trait phenotype in only some of the people having that gene. **Penetrance** is the proportion of people with the gene who have any signs of the trait. Traits also vary in **expressivity,** meaning that some people will show slight and others dramatic phenotypic effects of having the same gene. Both the penetrance and the expressivity of genes vary because of the effects of other genes (epistasis), gene-environment interactions (epigenetic development), genomic imprinting, and X-inactivation.

Recombination frequency and linkage analysis. Another family history type of technique maps genes associated with various inborn defects. The mapping technique, or **linkage analysis,** uses crossovers to trace genes in certain family trees. Suppose that the genetic loci of several genes were known (at least two are needed) and each gene was associated with a specific, measurable aspect of a person's phenotype. Color blindness is used as an example, since the genes are located on the X chromosomes. Another possible X-linked gene makes a person more likely to develop **manic-depressive disorder,** a mental disorder in which the person has periods of relatively normal mood, alternating with periods of mania and periods of depression. This is also called **bipolar affective disorder.** Any family we used for this hypothetical an-

alysis would have to be one in which some members were color blind and some members had bipolar affective disorder.

If the two traits of interest were on *separate* chromosomes, whether they occurred together or separately in any family member's phenotype should be random. The randomness occurs because of the independent assortment of paternal and maternal chromosomes during meiosis. In other words, if the two traits were on separate chromosomes, random assortment during meiosis would ensure that all four kinds of family members (ones that have both traits, ones that have just one trait, ones that have just the other trait, or ones that have neither trait) would all be equally likely to occur in the family history tree.

On the other hand, suppose—just as one possible example—the two traits were on the *same* chromosome. In this case, a majority of all the family members would have only one of the following three possible types of trait combinations:

1. Most people in the family would be positive for both traits, or
2. Most family members would be negative for both traits, or
3. Most family members would have one trait but not the other.

Which of the three possibilities would be the case for any particular family would depend on which genes were present on the "family" chromosome. In other words, blood relatives, having inherited the family chromosome, would all tend to share the same trait combinations because of sharing the same chromosome.

However, there would be at least some members of the family that would not have the family chromosome (whatever it was). For example, a few family members might have only one of the traits despite the fact that the family chromosome originally had both traits on it. A person who do not have the family chromosome would have had to been the recipient of some crossover event to separate the two traits. A crossover would have occurred during the meiosis of one of the person's two parents, which ended up separating the two traits originally located on the same chromosome. This crossover would have put those traits on separate chromosomes, at least for that person. The further apart the genetic loci of the two traits on the chromosome, the more *exceptions* there would be, or the more family members there would be who do not have the family chromosome.

The number of exceptions to be found in any family tree would depend on the distance between the two genes on that chromosome. Crossovers are less likely to occur in a small than in a much larger area. The smaller the distance between the color blindness and bipolar loci, for example, the fewer crossovers would be expected and so the fewer exceptions there would be. Two traits coded for by genes located close together on the same chromosome are said to be **genetically linked.** The degree of the linkage reflects the absolute genetic distance between the genes for the traits: the closer the two genes are physically to each other, the greater the linkage. The degree of linkage is experimentally measured (roughly) in family history studies by the frequency of exceptions[6] called the **recombination frequency.**

If the various alleles of the two trait genes were, in fact, located on the same chromosome, there are two other types of genetic linkage possible. For example, other families would, by chance (reflecting past recombinational events), possess a chromosome that had one trait but not the other. In such families, the two traits would **assort in opposition.** A family memnber who got the family chromosome, and thus who had one trait, would not be likely to have the other trait (again, with exceptions). To repeat, the smaller the distance between the physical loci of the two traits, the fewer recombinations expected and the fewer exceptions there would be.

Genetic Probes

Even more sophisticated techniques are available to the researcher interested in sex-linked genes and traits.

Description.   A sample of chromosomes from a person can be subjected to specialized enzymes, each of which will break a DNA molecule at a particular sequence of somewhere between four to six nucleotide bases.[7] The resulting human DNA fragments can be analyzed in various ways, including the use of probes from a library of human genes. These probes have been developed and maintained for researchers. A probe specifically recognizes (by attaching to) a particular DNA nucleotide base sequence. If the probes are radioactively labeled, the DNA fragments to which they become attached can also be identified by their acquired radioactivity. Researchers know to what locus(i) on what chromosome(s) many of these probes attach. Some loci are known genes, but others are not.

An example.   Some probes respond specifically to X- and Y-linked loci. Several research projects done by Mendlewicz and his colleagues illustrate how the sex linkage of an early onset form (occurring before age 30) of manic-depressive disorder was analyzed through family history studies and with linkage/probe research. One study examined the risk of disease in relatives of people with manic-depressive disorder, looking for X linkage by looking at the probabilities (risk ratios) that given pairs of relatives would share an X chromosome (e.g., father-daughter = 1.0; father-son = 0) (Risch, Baron, & Mendlewicz, 1986). Since the risk ratios presented in Table 5.1 matched the predictions, a few cases of manic-depressive disorder may reflect the influence of a dominant, X-linked gene.

Another study combined family history/linkage studies with genetic probe studies to look at the rare, X-linked form of the disorder

TABLE 5.1 *Risk Ratios by Sex of Proband (Male/Female) for Early Onset Cases* (New York Data)*

Relative	Prediction	Observed (BP + UP)
Father	0:1	$\dfrac{3/30}{8/61} = 0.76†$
Son	0:1	$\dfrac{0/5}{9/20} = 0.00$
Mother	2:1	$\dfrac{19/38}{15/61} = 2.00$
Daughter	2:1	$\dfrac{2/4}{5/13} = 1.30$
Brother	2:1	$\dfrac{19/58}{13/76} = 1.92$
Sister	2:3	$\dfrac{10/35}{24/56} = 0.67$

Source: Reprinted with permission from *Journal of Psychiat. Res., 20* (4), Neil Risch, Miron Baron, and Julien Mendlewicz, Assessing the role of X-linked inheritance in bipolar-related major affective disorder, Copyright 1986, Pergamon Press plc.

*Early onset defined as onset before 30 for probands, sibs and offspring; onset before 40 for parents.

BP = bipolar; UP = unipolar, or depressed only.

†In all three cases of affected fathers of male probands, the mother was also affected.

(Mendlewicz et al., 1987). The X-linked trait used to explore possible linkage to the bipolar gene was a gene for a blood coagulation factor that has two alleles. In one family history, a second-generation female was heterozygous for the blood factor and also had the bipolar disorder. She passed it on to both her daughters and to one of her two sons. Since a second son who did not get the disorder was also the only child who was homozygous for the *a* allele for the blood coagulation factor, presumably the mother's X chromosome with the *A* blood allele was also the X that also had the manic-depressive gene on it. Eleven such family pedigrees were examined and the results indicated that the two genes were close to each other (linked) on the X.

Sex Chromosome Abnormalities

Another way to explore the possible sex linkage of traits is to study people with various kinds of sex chromosome anomalies. We have already seen how the study of XX males helped lead to the identification of the SXD gene.

Logic of research. The logic of this research is essentially one of dosage effects. The more copies of the Y chromosome a man has, the more active Y genes and the more Y-gene products he will have. If the dosage level of a gene product does have some phenotypic effects, a man with more than one Y chromosome should also have more of any trait affected by a Y-linked gene.

X-inactivation complicates the logic of X linkage. Only one X remains active in any body cell, and so all the other Xs a person may have would be inactivated. Thus, dosage effects would be expected only for genes that are not inactivated. This would include some or all the genes in the pseudoautosomal region. In these cases, XXX females and XXY males might have more gene products than do XX females and XY males, respectively.

Types of abnormalities. The incidence of various types of abnormalities depends on a number of factors, including parental age and the viability of the fetus (Boué, Boué, & Lazar, 1975; Carothers et al., 1978; Hook et al., 1983, 1984; Selvin & Garfinkel, 1976; Yamamoto et al., 1975). Live-born babies have the fewest abnormalities, followed by fetuses from therapeutic abortions and prenatally screened fetuses. Spontaneously aborted fetuses have the most abnormalities. In fact, about 50 to 70 percent of spontaneous abortions may have some abnormality, one which may often have been the cause of the abortion.

Older parents are more likely to have fetuses with **polysomies:** more than two of some chromosome, including more than two sex chromosomes. (A person with three instead of the normal pair of any chromosome would have a **trisomy,** a person with four chromosomes would have a tetrasomy, and so on.) Polysomies occur during the last phase of gamete formation. Since this phase is delayed in females until just before ovulation, perhaps the effect of maternal age occurs because age causes some deterioration in the egg cells, since they have to be held in the ovaries from before birth to the time of ovulation. Increasing paternal age also increases risks for some chromosome abnormalities. Parental age is not related to the risk of having a child with only one sex chromosome — or indeed to any form of **monosomy** (having one instead of the normal pair).

Number of sex chromosomes, per se, has some general effects on human phenotype and development (Barlow, 1973; Ratcliffe, 1981). Having extra chromosomes, especially ones carrying much inactive genetic material (the inactivated X of normal females, most of the Y chromosome), slows mitosis. This would slow some fetal developmental processes, leading to lower birth weight and to fewer ridges on the fingertips, both of which are seen in babies with abnormal sex chromosomes. Intelligence also tends to be below normal, although extra Xs seem to have a more deleterious effect than do extra Ys. Height is increased by having one extra sex chromosome; an extra Y chromosome increases height more than does an extra X. The level of immunoglobulins (part of the immune system) in the blood is also systematically related (though in a complex fashion) to the number of extra sex chromosomes present.

Klinefelter syndrome is the most frequent sex chromosome disorder in males, occurring in slightly over 1 out of 1,000 male births. Klinefelter men have at least one extra X chromosome and thus are *47,XXY* (normal male: *46,XY*; normal female: *46,XX*). According to Leonard and colleagues (1979), any man with two or more Xs and at least one Y can be classified as Klinefelter. The extra Xs could have come from either their fathers or their mothers (Hassold et al., 1991).

A person with one extra Y chromosome would be described as *47,XYY*. Such males occur in just under 1 per 1,000 male births. The authors also include in this classification males with more than two Ys, although they are rare. The XYY may not be related to maternal age (Carothers et al., 1978), which is not surprising since the extra Y had to come from the father.

Monosomy X, or **Turner's syndrome,** is *45,X0*, having only one sex chromosome present, an X. This abnormality is also unrelated to maternal age. When both live-born and aborted Turner's syndrome babies were examined, their one X had usually come from their mothers (Hassold, Benham, & Leppert, 1988). However, the Turner fetuses with paternal Xs had significantly younger mothers than did the fetuses with maternal Xs. Over 95 percent of Turner fetuses are aborted before birth, showing that sex chromosome monosomy has more severe effects than does trisomy. Most live-born Turner's syndrome individuals are mosaic, with some body cells having either a second X or a Y; very few nonmosaic Turner fetuses survive until birth.

A few women with more than two Xs have been found.[7] Some may resemble Down's syndrome individuals in facial features. In general, the more Xs these women have, the more phenotypic abnormalities they have, and the lower their IQs. The extra X (or Xs) usually came from their mothers (Hassold et al., 1991). Although trisomy X women tend to be taller than XX women, women with four or more X chromosomes are shorter than XX women, probably as an indirect consequence of the slowed fetal development rate.

Physical appearance and physiology. Physical appearance and physiology are probably the most obvious aspects of the various sex chromosome abnormalities (Hoyenga & Hoyenga, 1993). Height, fertility, life span, brain electrical activity, and sex hormone levels are all affected by sex chromosome abnormalities. The types of brain activity seen in XXY and XYY men are similar to those recorded in children. **Lateralization of brain function** refers to the fact that right-handed people normally use their left hemispheres more than their right hemispheres for verbal tasks; the reverse is true for some nonverbal tasks. XXY, XYY, and X0 people all have unusual patterns of brain organization. The interest in the effects of sex chromosome anomalies on brain organization largely stems from the sex differences that have been discovered in humans (see Chapters 7 and 13).

Some anomalies are associated with a distinctive appearance. Some besides the XXY produce a Klinefelter-like phenotype. Many XX and XXYY males have Klinefelter characteristics (de la Chapelle, 1981; Sorensen et al., 1978; Varrela, Alvesalo, & Vinkka, 1984), except that XX males are shorter than either XY or XXY males. Turner females usually have a webbed neck, a shieldlike chest, and are very short. The physical appearance of Turner's syndrome females seems to be due to a loss of chromosome material from both ends of the missing X, which would include the region normally left inactivated in XX females (Wyss et al., 1982). Despite the X-inactivation in normal females, the loss means that Turner females still have fewer genes active than do XX females, accounting for some of the abnormalities.

Development. Developmental abnormalities, particularly in cognitive development, are commonly reported in X0, XXY, XXX, and XYY individuals. Several teams of researchers each carried out a massive screening of all or nearly all babies born in a certain place within a certain time (see documentation in Hoyenga & Hoyenga, 1993). Babies with the chromosome abnormalities were identified and have so far been studied for 10 to 17 years. These children were compared either with their own unaffected siblings or with chromosomally normally children born at the same time. The parents were, in most cases, told at least something about the chromosome findings of their children.

Learning disorders. These children more often had difficulties in school than did the comparison children. Dyslexia was more common in XXY boys than in their comparisons, and speech impairments were common in X0 and XXY children. Over 90 percent of the XXX females had relatively severe school problems. Spatial visualization was particularly impaired in both XXX and in X0 females. XXY boys had the most problems in rapidly retrieving verbal material from memory.

Again, genotype cannot be equated with phenotype. One XYY boy was hyperactive and had a learning disorder, but his identical twin brother had neither trait (Hier, Atkins, & Perlo, 1980). Decker and Bender (1988) compared XXY to XY learning-disordered boys and found that although the cause of the disorder was obviously different in the two groups, the phenotypic effects of the two were indistinguishable. So, chromosomally normal people can express the same phenotypic traits as do the chromosomally abnormal people.

Intelligence and achievements. Extra sex chromosomes, especially Xs, are associated with lowered IQ scores. However, both XXY and XYY males may be deficient in ways not measured by typical IQ tests (Owen, 1979). Theilgaard (1972) tested one Klinefelter male with an above normal IQ of 118 who nevertheless gave the following answer when asked to find similarities between air and water: "It's to walk in and to swim in." Many of the XXY men tested seemed to have difficulties in expressing themselves — difficulties that were not adequately measured by the IQ tests.

Sex chromosome anomalies are not incompatible with high IQs or high levels of achievements. One study (Porter et al., 1988) tested adult Klinefelter males living in the community. Although their average IQ was lower than normal, especially on the verbal tests, these XXY males "were, in general, as well educated, as likely to be employed, and of socioeconomic status equal to that of other men in the community" (p. 246). One XXY male was a chemical engineer and another an insurance broker. Another Klinefelter male, identified in a screening of 1,280 male (and 981 female) college students (Nanko, 1983), had an IQ of more than 140—the maximum score on the test he took!

Turner's syndrome females show an interesting pattern of specific cognitive deficits, some of which may be related to their unusual brain organization (Ebbin, Howell, & Wilson, 1980; McCauley et al., 1987; Pennington et al., 1985; Waber, 1979). Although the organization is atypical, it is not true that one (or the other) side of the Turner's syndrome brain is subnormal. Turner females are especially likely to show deficits in the ability to visualize objects in three-dimensional space and in some memory tasks. They may also have some difficulty in inferring what emotion is being revealed by what set of facial expressions.

Turner deficits may reflect either the direct effects of monosomy on brain organization or the lack of sex hormones (Buchsbaum & Henkin, 1980; Pennington et al., 1985; Reske-Nielsen, Christensen, & Nielsen, 1982). The gonads in Turner females start degenerating before their birth. By puberty, most Turner's syndrome females have only streaks of tissue for gonads and are infertile. Thus, they have very low levels of all sex hormones both before birth and after puberty.

Frequency in prisons. The most controversial aspect of chromosome abnormalities is the increased likelihood of XYY and XXY men showing up in prisons or in high-security mental institutions, compared to their frequency at birth. XXX women also show up in prisons in greater than expected numbers (Hook, 1979). As shown in Table 5.2, there is little doubt that XXY and XYY men do appear at greater than expected numbers in these places.

The reason for this concentration is still unclear. Most of the XXY and XYY criminal offenses are against property. When possible confounding factors such as IQ were controlled, the sole reason for Klinefelter's increased prison appearances turned out to be reduced IQ: a Klinefelter man does not commit more crimes—he is just easier to catch (Witkin et al., 1976; Owen, 1979). These analyses still left some of the more frequent appearances of the XYY male unaccounted for, but the investigators pointed to deficits in intelligence that could not be measured by the IQ tests being used (Witkins et al., 1976; Owen, 1979). Perhaps the same traits that affect these other aspects of intelligence also affect something related to the tendencies to commit certain kinds of criminal acts.

Emotional/social characteristics. People with extra Xs seem to be somewhat emotionally and socially immature. XXX women may also be more likely to develop schizophrenia (Pennington, Puck, & Robinson, 1980; Tennes et al., 1975; Tsuang, 1974). XXX babies may be placid and somewhat unresponsive, and XXX children are developmentally delayed in walking, talking, and in social skills. XX males do not suffer from Klinefelter-type social/emotional problems, although they seem to suffer somewhat from "emotional immaturity," according to one interviewer (Sorensen et al., 1979).

Turner's syndrome individuals have been variously described as either completely normal, outgoing, and socially skilled, or as being socially isolated, withdrawn, and depressed (Chen, Faigenbaum, Weiss, 1981; McCauley et al., 1987; Downey et al., 1989; McCauley, Sybert, & Ehrhardt, 1986; Nielsen & Stradiot, 1987). Turner women seem somewhat better adjusted in some countries other than the United States, especially where an extensive social/emotional support group exists for Turner's syndrome people. Older Turner women may be less likely to have an emotional

TABLE 5.2   *Frequency of XXY and XYY Men in Various Penal Settings*
XXY and XYY men are more often found in penal settings than would be expected on the basis of their frequency in male births. This table shows the rate (per 1,000) at which XXY and XYY men are found in various mental and penal settings, such as prisons, homes for juvenile delinquents, and hospitals for the criminally insane. The expected frequencies (frequencies at birth) for XYY men = 00.9, and for XXY men = 01.2.

Mental-Penal	Penal	Mental
Studies done up to 1972		
XYY 19.2 (24)	03.9 (16)	03.0 (10)
XXY 11.2 (24)	02.7 (15)	04.5 (10)
Studies done from 1972 to 1977		
XYY 18.4 (12)	06.1 (8)	02.8 (8)
XXY 05.1 (10)	07.5 (7)	04.5 (8)
Combined (data taken from Hook, 1979)		
XYY 20.0	04.4	02.9
XXY 09.8	03.8	04.5
Japanese male juvenile delinquents (Nanko, Saito, & Makino, 1979)		
XYY	3.6 (1371)*	
XXY	2.9 (1371)*	
Summary of previous studies of delinquents (Nanko, Saito, & Makino, 1979)		
XYY	04.8 (21)	
XYY	02.9 (19)	

Note: The number in parentheses refers to the number of studies contributing to that observed frequency except for the numbers marked with an *. In that case, the number refers to the number of male juvenile delinquents tested by the authors.

disorder than do their comparisons, but they may also have poorer overall psychological health and poor social relationships. The best conclusion is that the environment has a major impact on the social/emotional adjustment of Turner's syndrome females.

XXY males may be at a somewhat increased risk for some emotional and social problems (Bancroft, Axworthy, & Ratcliffe, 1982; Nielsen, Pelsen, & Sorensen, 1988; Ratcliffe et al., 1982; Salbenblatt et al., 1981; Schiavi et al., 1984; Theilgaard, 1986, 1990). In developmental studies, the mothers of XXY boys, much more frequently than the mothers of control boys, commented about their sons' timidity and lack of assertiveness. These boys also tended to be socially isolated and to be less

interested in girls, sex, and dating than were control boys. Adult XXY males are less sexually active, more submissive, and express aggression in only disguised forms, compared to XY males. But many XXY males are indistinguishable from XY males in emotional/social characteristics. The somewhat maladjusted XXY males may benefit from supplemental hormone treatment to completely normalize their somewhat low (though in the normal male range) androgen levels.

The characteristic most frequently associated with the XYY genotype is poor control over strong emotional impulses. One study identified XYY males in a general screening of all males (Noel et al., 1974). After an interview, the interviewer (blind to the genotype) was able to accurately distinguish the 7 XYY males from the 28 control males matched for age, socio-economic status, and education, largely on the basis of traits like impulse control. Some XYY males showed a relative lack of control, being described as having "ready outbursts of emotion" (p. 392). Other XYY males, especially the ones with the higher IQs, were hypercontrolled and rigid. Another study found that 4 of 14 XYY boys identified at birth, compared to 2 of the 110 control boys, were referred for psychiatric treatment (Ratcliffe & Field, 1982; Ratcliffe, Murray, & Teague, 1986; Ratcliffe, Jenkins, & Teague, 1990). All four XYY males had frequent, intense temper tantrums, sometimes to the extent of physically frightening their mothers.

Because of the effect of the extra Y on height, "chromosome determinations were carried out in all men in the top 15 percent of the height distribution" (Schiavi et al., 1984; Theilgaard, 1986a, 1986b, 1990). Twelve XYY men were compared to two control groups, one matched for socioeconomic status, height, and age, and one matched on those characteristics plus IQ. XYY males showed an earlier onset of sexual interest, a heightened sexual interest, and more sexual partners, compared to their controls. Based on an interview, the XYY male was not more aggressive, except towards his wife, where one male was said to differ "markedly" from his control. However, 5 of the 12 XYY and none of the 24 control men had a record of criminal convictions (though 8 men in the control groups for XXY men did have convictions). XYY men had higher average testosterone levels than did their controls[9] and XXY men who committed crimes also had higher testosterone levels than the XXY men who did not commit crimes. The XYY criminals described their acts usually as being quite impulsive.

A gene on the Y chromosome might affect control over strong emotional impulses. Having a higher IQ would decrease the effects of an extra Y on impulse control, and environ-mental factors would also be expected to be critically important. For example, XYY male criminals tend to be younger than XY criminals (Price, cited in Ratcliffe & Field, 1982). Probably only a small proportion of XYY males would ever have these problems, and age and experience also improves impulse control, which would therefore eliminate many of the problems that a few XYY males have.

Limitations of Sex Linkage Research

None of this research is immune from the kinds of biases described in Chapter 2. For example, Nanko, Saito, and Mankino (1979) surveyed all studies involving XYY juvenile delinquents and discovered that as the sample size increased (number of males studied increased), the fewer XYY males were found (ratio of XYY to XY males decreased). Nanko and colleagues suggested, quite plausibly, that when the sample size was small, only the researchers who actually found XYY males reported their data. This bias would artificially elevate the frequency of XYY males found in the small sample size studies. Nevertheless, when Nanko and his colleagues corrected for this bias, they still concluded that XYY males were found at much greater frequency among juvenile delinquents than among male newborns.

Sampling and testing biases are also common. Most of what researchers know about chromosomally abnormal people (with the important exception of the developmental studies) depends on the characteristics of people who selected themselves for study in one way or another: infertility, commission of a crime, psychiatric diagnoses, retardation, and so on. Researchers do not yet know to what extent results concerning selectively sampled people will be found to be representative of people in general with that genotype. In the developmental studies, the frequent testing and examinations and the knowledge of their parents may cause these people to systematically differ from people with the same chromosome anomalies who had not been frequently tested and examined and who had been born to unaware parents. One major problem with work in the area of the emotional and social characteristics is the lack of standardized assessment procedures. Except for diagnoses of various types of psychiatric disorders, different investigators often either use different kinds of assessment procedures or else just describe an interviewer's impressions.

By their very nature, these research projects can study only major gene effects. Only traits that are strongly affected by a particular sex-linked gene can be analyzed. Most of the traits of interest to psychologists reflect the cumulative and interactive inputs of many genes. This includes most aspects of emotional responses, social behaviors, cognitive processes, and aggression or impulse control. Thus, although there could be genes on the X and Y that have some role to play in the epigenetic development of such traits, that will be very difficult to demonstrate with these kinds of studies.

SEX CHROMOSOME MAPS

This section summarizes much of the chapter's information with maps of the X and Y chromosomes. The maps should be regarded as similar to the ones in any road atlas—subject to changes without notice. Still, looking at a map helps us realize just what the ultimate goal of much of this research is.

Y Linkage

Only a few Y-linked genes or traits are well verified. Nevertheless, several potential Y-linked traits have been identified in mice, and the same may be true of other mammals as well (Carlier et al., 1990; Maxson, 1990; Maxson & Roubertoux, 1990; Yamazaki et al., 1990). This includes effects on sperm physiology, sex ratio, body weight, testosterone levels, sensitivity to testosterone, immune responses, and several

behavioral traits including exploration, aggression, sexual activity, infanticide, and aggression. Interestingly enough, Y-linked traits in mice also often appear in female mice but to a lesser extent. Thus, copies of the Y-linked genes may also be found on the autosomes or on the X. Despite this, the Y chromosome is, in fact, very small, and much of it in mammals is never transcribed into mRNA.

Why is it so small? The human X and Y chromosomes have evolved such that the X is now three times larger than the Y in humans. Over 300 diseases and genes have been localized to the X, but only 7 DNA sequences—and not all of those active—were identified as of 1985 as being Y-linked (Goodfellow, Davies, & Ropers, 1985). Most of the Y, especially on the *long arm (q),* is inactive. In fact, 1 in 3,000 normal females has this region of the Y present in their genotype (presumably because of a paternal meiotic crossover event) with no discernable phenotypic effects (Goodfellow, Darling, & Wolfe, 1985).

Charlesworth (1978) suggested that the small size of the Y is due to the infrequency of crossovers with the X (except in the pseudo-autosomal region). In the absence of crossovers and independent assortment (all males get the one Y their father has), most of the Y is reproduced asexually rather than sexually. Asexual reproduction allows deleterious mutations to accumulate on the species' chromosomes. The number of mutations per Y chromosome will randomly vary among members of the population, but suppose that something happens to those few animals with no mutations: all Y chromosomes left in the population will have at least some. Since recombination is not occurring, a nonmutated Y cannot be randomly regenerated. And the next time something happens to the few animals carrying just one or two mutations on their Y chromosomes, the whole process repeats.

Mutation is not the only way that the Y could accumulate deleterious genes. Since the

Y chromosome has no homologue, it cannot be repaired after damage the way autosomes can be, or the way that Xs can be repaired during female meiosis. The Y can also be successfully invaded by viruses that insert several copies of the DNA nucleotide bases coding for their genome somewhere into the Y chromosome. Up to 30 percent of the Y chromosome of mice may be taken up by copies of one virus alone (Eicher & Washburn, 1986). The human Y may also contain considerable viral material; one has been identified (Silver et al., 1987).

Over time, the number of deleterious genes (mutations and insertions) on the Y will steadily accumulate. One defense is to decrease the size of the Y by moving (random crossover and subsequent natural selection) critical genes to the X or an autosome. As another defense, most of the Y is permanently inactivated, leaving only the essential male-determining genes. There may also be some selection pressures working to keep the Y from becoming too small. Burgoyne (cited by Koenig et al., 1985) has suggested that if the Y gets too small, it will not be able to pair up properly with the X during male meiosis, leading to chromosome trisomies. This pressure might tend to preserve inactive, viral genes, used just to increase the size of the Y.

Possible genes and likely traits: a map of the human Y.   A tentative map of the human Y chromosome appears in Figure 5.2. There is very little polymorphism in the human Y,

FIGURE 5.2   *Y Chromosome*
This is a tentative map of some known and possible Y-linked genes. A vertical line indicates the possible range of locations that a gene, or set of genes, could occupy along the Y. The centromere divides the short arm (*p*) from the long arm (*q*).

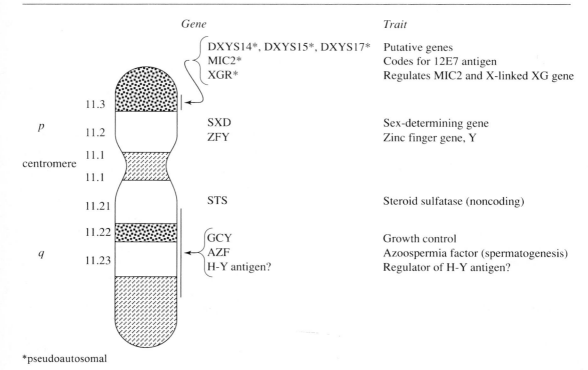

Gene	*Trait*
DXYS14*, DXYS15*, DXYS17*	Putative genes
MIC2*	Codes for 12E7 antigen
XGR*	Regulates MIC2 and X-linked XG gene
SXD	Sex-determining gene
ZFY	Zinc finger gene, Y
STS	Steroid sulfatase (noncoding)
GCY	Growth control
AZF	Azoospermia factor (spermatogenesis)
H-Y antigen?	Regulator of H-Y antigen?

*pseudoautosomal

meaning that most males share the same Y-linked genes (Malaspina et al., 1990). The **centromere** is a part of the chromosome to which the spindles that form during mitosis and meiosis attach; the spindles keep the paired chromosomes in alignment. Many of loci not labeled in Figure 5.2 can still be studied. Researchers can use Y-specific DNA probes that have a specific genetic locus but have not yet been related to any known gene, protein, or disease.

The *short arm (p)* of the human Y contains many of the genes that were discussed. This region may also contain a gene tentatively called *XGR,* which controls both the activity of the X-linked XG gene (codes for the Xg red blood antigen). The human Y does not have a functional STS gene: the gene found on the Y is never translated into RNA or proteins. The SXD gene is found just below the pseudoautosomal region. If crossovers during male meiosis occur here, an affected offspring can lose part of a normal X, have it replaced with SXD from his father's Y, and develop into an XX male.

The *long arm (q)* of the Y contains genes that promote growth (height) and genes that are necessary for spermatogenesis. The other sequences so far identified as being part of the long arm of the Y either have not yet been recognized as a gene or they are inactive (never read) genes.

X Linkage

The X chromosome is much larger than the Y and has been related to far more genes and diseases. X chromosomes are subject to some crossovers during female meiosis, so geneticists can use linkage types of family history studies to establish X linkage.

Possible genes and likely traits: a map of the human X.   Figure 5.3 presents a map of the X chromosome, summarizing much of what was said about X linkage. The X's pseudo-

autosomal region corresponds to the one on the Y and contains the same genes.

Some of the other diseases that have been used as examples can also be found on this map of the X. Duchenne and Becker motor dystrophy are alleles of a gene located in the short arm (*p*) in a region subject to frequent breakage, crossovers, and mutations (Darras & Francke, 1987; Goodfellow, Davies, & Ropers, 1985). Genes coding for color vision (red and green) and the gene that may be responsible for some rare cases of manic-depressive disorder have been placed on the long arm (*q*). The androgen receptor gene is located either just above or just below the centromere.

Several immune deficiency syndromes are X linked. One disease, the Lesch-Nyhan syndrome, is associated with various mutations of the HPRT gene locus. Affected males have retarded growth, motor disorders, mental retardation, and compulsively mutilate themselves. Mutations of the MPRT locus seem to occur much more often in the meiosis of males than of females (Francke et al., 1976). Affected males can die of either a measles virus infection or from infection with the mononucleosis virus (the Epstein-Barr virus) (Purtilo et al., 1977; Sullivan et al., 1980). The X linkage of these genes may explain why XXY males have frequent immunological problems (Ratcliffe, 1982).

Two X-linked enzymes control the level of some of the brain's **transmitter substances** (chemical substances that neurons secrete on to each other so that one can "talk" to another) (Kochersperger et al., 1986; Sims et al., 1989). These two enzymes are **monoamine oxidases (MAOs),** which control the level of **serotonin,** among other transmitters (serotonin levels are abnormally low in the XYY genotype). The genes may be located close to the HPRT locus or to a locus responsible for Norrie disease,[10] which has been mapped to the region of Xp11.3–11.2.

There are several forms of X-linked mental retardation. Of the 124 to 162 possible or

FIGURE 5.3 *X Chromosome*
This is a tentative map of some known and possible X-linked genes. The disease associated with the mutant gene (if any) is indicated in parentheses. Also see the caption of Figure 5.2.

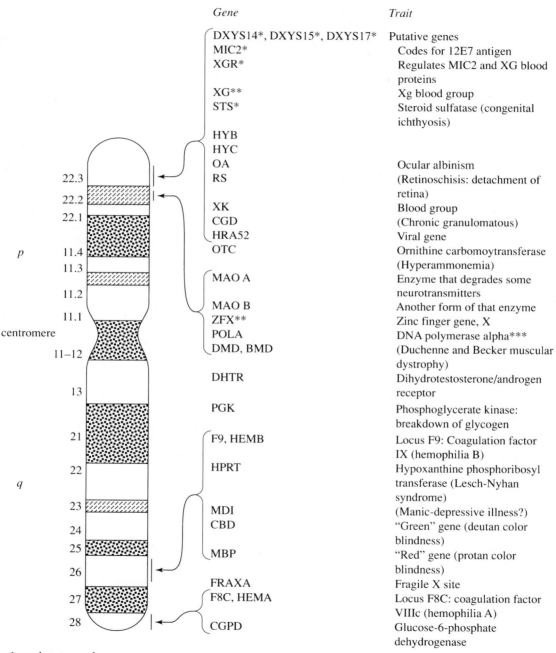

Gene	Trait
DXYS14*, DXYS15*, DXYS17*	Putative genes
MIC2*	Codes for 12E7 antigen
XGR*	Regulates MIC2 and XG blood proteins
XG**	Xg blood group
STS*	Steroid sulfatase (congenital ichthyosis)
HYB	
HYC	
OA	Ocular albinism
RS	(Retinoschisis: detachment of retina)
XK	Blood group
CGD	(Chronic granulomatous)
HRA52	Viral gene
OTC	Ornithine carbomoytransferase (Hyperammonemia)
MAO A	Enzyme that degrades some neurotransmitters
MAO B	Another form of that enzyme
ZFX**	Zinc finger gene, X
POLA	DNA polymerase alpha***
DMD, BMD	(Duchenne and Becker muscular dystrophy)
DHTR	Dihydrotestosterone/androgen receptor
PGK	Phosphoglycerate kinase: breakdown of glycogen
F9, HEMB	Locus F9: Coagulation factor IX (hemophilia B)
HPRT	Hypoxanthine phosphoribosyl transferase (Lesch-Nyhan syndrome)
MDI	(Manic-depressive illness?)
CBD	"Green" gene (deutan color blindness)
MBP	"Red" gene (protan color blindness)
FRAXA	Fragile X site
F8C, HEMA	Locus F8C: coagulation factor VIIIc (hemophilia A)
CGPD	Glucose-6-phosphate dehydrogenase

*pseudoautosomal

**not inactivated

***used in DNA replication and repair

120

probable X-linked diseases, one-fourth of them can lead to mental retardation. More recently, a total of 89 different X-linked disorders have been identified that involve retardation either as a primary or secondary component (Neri et al., 1991). One of those involves the HPRT site; another the Norrie site. However, the most common X-linked retardation is the fragile X syndrome. In fact, fragile X is the most common inherited form of retardation (Chudley & Hagerman, 1987; Fryns, 1984; M. Hoffman, 1991b; Nussbaum & Ledbetter, 1986; Sutherland, 1985). It affects nearly 1 in 2,000 males. Unlike Down's syndrome, fragile X can be passed on from one generation to the next.

The fragile X mutation.   A fragile site is a genetic locus that is especially likely to break. Such a site is detected in cultures of cells from some person, usually after the cells are exposed to chemicals, such as caffeine, which increase breakage. A fragile site appears as a constriction or gap in a chromosome that was stained while the cell was undergoing meiosis or mitosis. The locus of the fragile X has recently been identified at Xq27.3, below the loci for color blindness (Oberlé et al., 1991).

Most of the males (80 percent) that inherit the fragile X show X chromosome breakage in cell cultures. More than half of these are retarded (IQs ranging from 30 to 65). These males also rend to be larger at birth, have larger than normal testes, have prominent foreheads, have smaller than normal cerebellar parts of their brains, and have large, malformed ears. Fragile X boys show signs of both hyperactivity and autism (Barnes, 1989; Borghgraef et al., 1987; Curfs et al., 1989). In fact, about 10 to 15 percent of autistic males have fragile X. Their intellectual performances typically decline with age. They may be particularly likely to have arithmetic deficits. However, fragile X males may have better than normal levels of memory (as is sometimes true of autistic people, as well), but their ability to remember in what order two or more things were presented is often severely impaired.

Heterozygous females sometimes also show some phenotypic effects of having at least one fragile X (Barnes, 1989; Nussbaum & Ledbetter, 1986; Cohen et al., 1989; Grigsby et al., 1990; Reiss et al., 1988). They are sometimes mildly retarded, they usually show X breakage in cell cultures, and they may be susceptible to schizophrenia and affective disorders as well as autism. They also tend to be socially withdrawn, shy, and learning disabled, particularly in math. But 50 to 60 percent of females carrying a fragile X will show no phenotypic signs and will also seldom show X breakage in cultures. Even the 10 percent of the female carriers who do have X breakage in cell cultures often will still show no signs of the disorder. The older the female gets, the fewer intellectual deficits she will report. An older female may remember having had problems when younger, but she will say she found "a way to work around them."

This disorder has no simple genetic explanation. Some male carriers are not affected despite having only one X, and some female carriers are affected despite being heterozygotic. The unaffected male carriers do not show X breakage in normal cell cultures but they can and do pass the fragile X on to grandchildren, who will then often be retarded. X-inactivation in females may be part of the explanation for why some female carriers are affected. Differential rates of mutation/crossover in male versus female meiosis may also explain some of these unusual characteristics.

The pedigree of a fragile X family presented in Figure 5.4, although hypothetical, is representative and is based on extensive research data (Nussbaum & Ledbetter, 1986). All mothers of fragile X males are fragile X carriers. This means that a mutation that occurred during a mother's meiosis, creating the fragile site, does not cause retardation in her son (Sutherland, 1985). The pedigree shows that the risk of retardation increases as a

FIGURE 5.4 *Artificial Pedigree of Fragile X*
This illustrates the differential inheritance of retardation (Part A) and of fragile X itself (Part B). I, II, III, and IV refer to successive generations in the same family.

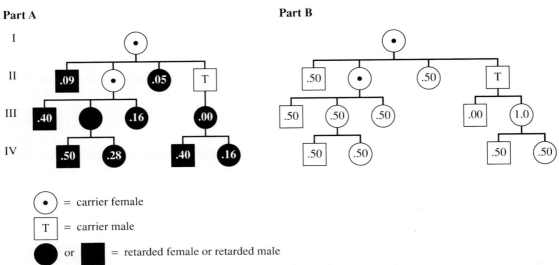

= carrier female

T = carrier male

● or ■ = retarded female or retarded male

Embedded numbers = probability of retardation (Part A) or probability of inheriting the fragile X (Part B).

Source: Part A reproduced, with permission, from the Annual Review of Genetics, volume 20, © 1986 by Annual Reviews Inc.

function of the number of subsequent female meiotic events through which that particular X chromosome goes. If the original carrier (generation I) passes the fragile X on to an unaffected daughter, the risks of retardation to that daughter's offspring also depend on gender. If an affected daughter has children, the risk to her children also depends on their gender. The daughters of unaffected but transmitting males (only a male meiosis) have essentially no risk of retardation. But after the X passes through another female meiosis (in the daughter of a transmitting male), the risk to that daughter's offspring increases from 9 to 40 percent for males and from 5 to 16 percent for females.

Contrast all these risks of retardation to the risk for inheriting the fragile X itself as presented in Part B of Figure 5.4. The difference in offspring risk after male versus female meiosis suggests that parental imprinting affects the activity of the fragile X locus (Laird, 1988, 1991; Laird, Lamb, & Thorne, 1990; Schaap, 1989). Male meiosis somehow erases the imprint. In fact, of the three affected males that have had daughters, in none of the sex daughters is there much sign of X breakage in cell cultures (Laird, 1991). Something that happens during female meiosis, perhaps associated with reactivation of the previously inactivated X, may make that site increasingly more fragile. This would lead to more crossover events until the risks of retardation match the risks of getting that particular, very fragile X.

Two implications of X linkage for gender-related differences. One implication of X linkage is that since there are many forms of X-linked mental retardation, males are affected more often than females. In fact, it was not until the early 1970s that X linkage was used to explain the 25 percent higher frequency of males among retarded and institutionalized populations. The frequency of all forms of X-linked retardation are estimated at 1 per 600 male births (Nussbaum & Ledbetter, 1986), with about half of those being fragile X retardation (Neri et al., 1991). Second, since there are many X-linked recessive diseases, and any such disease affects more males than females, this could explain some of the greater life expectancy of females in developed countries.

SUMMARY

Gender-related genetic differences are the end result of sex differences in evolutionary pressures. Because of evolution, some genes became sex linked and others became sex limited. The selection pressures exerted by microparasites on mammalian females, which have such extensive and intimate contact with their offspring, may have led not only to sex but also to some of the other forms of gendered inheritances. Some genes are subject to parental imprinting, the sexes systematically differ in the crossover frequency of some genes, and X-inactivation affects sex differences in X-linked traits.

The sex-determining genes are X linked, Y linked, and autosomal. A critically important gene is located just below the pseudoautosomal region found at the tip of the Y chromosome; testes do not form without that gene. H-Y antigen may be related to spermatogenesis. The only sex hormone gene that is sex linked is the X-linked, androgen-receptor gene.

Family history studies can, for example, contrast father-daughter versus father-son similarities, or they can look for linkage by examining recombination frequencies (the fre-

quencies of exceptions). Genetic probes can also be used to explore sex linkage of traits and genes. People with sex chromosome abnormalities represent another opportunity to explore sex linkage—an opportunity that has yet been inadequately explored.

By integrating the results of all these types of research, plus others, geneticists are steadily expanding the maps of the X and Y chromosomes. The Y is much smaller but is critical for testes and spermatogenesis. The X chromosome is associated with a great many diseases and genes, including color blindness, hemophilia, various forms of muscular dystrophy, perhaps some cases of manic-depressive disorder, immune disorders, and several forms of retardation. X-linked disorders affect males more often than or more severely than females.

ENDNOTES

1. The label may involve DNA methylation, in which small molecules are chemically linked or attached to a DNA molecule.

2. Genes coding for the ability to see blue are autosomal.

3. Berta et al., 1990; Gubbay et al., 1990; Jäger, Anvret, Hall, & Scherer, 1990; Koopman et al., 1990, 1991; McLaren, 1990; Page et al., 1990; Sinclair et al., 1990).

4. Progestins can be transformed into some androgens and, in turn, some androgens can be transformed into some estrogens as long as the correct enzymes are present in that cell.

5. These people were also mentioned in Chapter 1, including in the introduction to that chapter.

6. Family members who do not have the family chromosome because of some recombinatorial event in one of their two parent's meiosis.

7. These enzymes have come from bacteria and are normally used by them to attack viruses.

8. Archidiacono et al., 1979; Berg et al., 1988; Fryns et al., 1983; Funderburk, Valente, & Klisak, 1981; Gardner, 1979; Nielsen et al., 1977.

9. XYY men with convictions did not have higher levels than did the XYY men without convictions, however.

10. Norrie disease is a rare neurological disorder characterized by congenital blindness and often a loss of hearing as well as retardation.

CHAPTER 6

HOW DO HORMONES AFFECT OUR BRAINS?

INTRODUCTION
BASIC IDEAS ABOUT HORMONES
HOW CAN SEX HORMONES AFFECT YOUR BRAIN CELLS?
PRINCIPLES OF HORMONE EFFECTS
SUMMARY

> *Over the last 15 years [from 1979], sex differences within the brain have moved from being a subject of speculation . . . to being a focus of intense research and widespread interest.*
> —Timothy DeVoogd (1984, p. 171)

A team of researchers at the University of Illinois (Montemayor, Clark, Lynn, & Roy, 1990; Roy, Lynn, & Clark, 1985) has demonstrated that the activity of brain cells affects how those cells will respond to estrogen. McEwen (1991a, 1991b) has pointed out that our brain cells affect each other in ways similar to how our sex hormones affect our brain cells, with similar types of outcomes.

The quote and the research results just described indicate why this is one of the most exciting areas of research today. Because of differences in hormone levels, the sexes do have different brains, in species ranging from songbirds to humans. This is not surprising, given the sex differences in evolutionary history described in Chapter 4. This history would have created tendencies for certain traits and characteristics to become sex limited in their expression. This chapter describes how sex hormones can create sex differences in brain structure, activity, and function.

Since nerve cells and sex hormones have such similar effects on other nerve cells, and since neural activity also controls the rate at which our gonads secrete those hormones, are our thoughts affecting our gonads? Can this then affect our subsequent thoughts and feelings? Can what we think (the electrical activity of our nerve cells; see Chapter 1) impact the degree to which our hormones can have an effect on us? The mind/brain and the gonads are in constant and intimate interaction. This chapter describes how that interaction occurs.

INTRODUCTION

This chapter emphasizes basic mechanisms and principles of sex hormone effects on brain cells. These mechanisms and principles characterize the effects that hormones have during both the perinatal (prenatal and neonatal) and post-pubertal periods of life. The next two chapters in this unit will describe the sex differences in hormone levels that occur during the perinatal period (Chapter 7) and then again after puberty (Chapter 8), along with some outcomes and possible implications of those differences.

The present chapter starts by describing three continua of hormone effects, or three dimensions on which hormone effects can be categorized. It then goes on to describe some effects of sex hormones on organs other than the brain and how the effects of sex hormones can be studied. The core of the chapter is presented in the next two sections. The first describes the two mechanisms by which sex hormones can affect individual cells, including brain cells. The second lists and describes the basic principles of hormone effects — principles that apply regardless of when those hormone effects occur during development, including how masculine sex hormones masculinize and defeminize males' brains and behaviors.

BASIC IDEAS ABOUT HORMONES

Sex hormones are secreted by the gonads and the adrenal glands. The secretion occurs both during the perinatal period (though only testes and adrenals may be active then) and again after puberty. The output from the ovaries greatly decreases at menopause in human females and at reproductive senescence in non-human females. Once secreted, sex hormones circulate in the bloodstream, reaching all organs, including the brain.

Three Continua of Hormone Effects

The hormones bathing your brain at the present moment are having effects on its activity and even on its structure. The hormones you experienced during your perinatal period have also affected your brain. One way to describe those effects is to categorize them along each of three dimensions or continua of types of hormonal influences.

The concept of three continua replaces an earlier idea in which perinatal versus postpubertal hormones were viewed as having not only

quantitatively but qualitatively different kinds of effects: **organizational** versus **activational** effects. This distinction was introduced in 1959 by Phoenix and his colleagues (Baum, 1990). Organizational or perinatal hormones were thought to have relatively permanent and irreversible effects on the brain's anatomy and thus on the adult organism's behaviors. Activational effects occurred in adult organisms, changing whenever the adult's hormone levels changed, and were characterized as leading to only temporary and reversible changes in the brain's activity and the adult's behaviors.

However, research results have often not been entirely consistent with this dichotomy of hormone effects, as other reviewers have also noted (Arnold & Breedlove, 1985; vom Saal & Finch, 1988; McEwen, 1991b; Williams, 1987). As one example, Williams and Blaustein (1988) showed that both postpubertal and perinatal sex hormones could have temporary and reversible effects on rats' sexual behaviors. For these and other reasons described below, a dichotomy between perinatal and postpubertal hormone effects no longer seems warranted.

The reversibility continuum.   Hormone effects differ along a dimension of **reversibility**. Suppose that changing an organism's hormone levels caused a given outcome. For example, the seasonal increase in testosterone (T) leads to the development of antlers in male deer and elk, and the pubertal increase in feminine sex hormones leads to the development of breasts in female humans. A *reversible* effect or outcome is one in which if the hormone is restored to its original level, the outcome could decrease or disappear. On the other hand, if hormone levels are changed but the outcome does not change, the effect is *nonreversible* or *irreversible.* To continue the example given above, once breasts form in female humans, they represent relatively irreversible hormone effects. The same is true of penises in male animals, which form during the perinatal period. Once those structures have appeared, changing the person's hormone levels will not change those aspects of the individual's anatomy. On the other hand, antlers represent reversible effects, since they drop off when the levels of T drop at the end of every breeding season.

There are three important points to make about this dimension. The first is that most hormone effects would be classified as falling somewhere along the middle of the continuum. That is, the amount of change in the outcome that occurs for a given change in hormone levels can vary all the way from a complete change to the way it was before, to a moderate change, to no change at all. The most common hormone effects are those that change moderately when hormone levels are changed.

Second, hormone levels can be manipulated directly or indirectly. A direct change could be accomplished by giving the organism an injection or a pill or by removing the organism's gonads. Hormones can also be manipulated indirectly by changing the organism's environment. As will be described in this chapter, hormones often change when environments change.

Third, and probably most important, one must distinguish between the irreversibility of effects measured at the behavioral level from those measured at some anatomical or biochemical level. Even with regard to durable effects on the brain's anatomy, one should not refer to any biological determinism of behaviors. Here, the concept of **level of reversibility** becomes critically important. Not only can environmental manipulations have behavioral as well as anatomical effects similar to those of hormone manipulations but the brain anatomical connections formed before birth are only one part of the cause of the complex behaviors of most interest to psychologists. Although the effects measured at the level of brain *anatomy* may not be reversible, the effects measured at the *behavioral* level may be reversed by altering the organism's experiences (which presumably also change some part of the brain's anatomy but maybe not the same part).

Sometimes postpubertal hormones can have relatively irreversible effects, and sometimes perinatal hormone effects can be reversed. For example, giving a female rat small doses of T shortly after her birth can permanently defeminize her or decrease the likelihood of her displaying normal female types of sexual behavior as an adult. If, however, these hormone-treated females as adults are given extensive sexual experiences, their sexual behaviors become much more typically feminine (Hendricks, Lehman, & Oswalt, 1982). Conversely, postpubertal hormone manipulations can have durable or even permanent effects on both the brain and behavior (vom Saal & Finch, 1988). Furthermore, once a hormone manipulation has a certain kind of effect on the organism, it can certainly remember what happened—and the memory can have very durable effects on brain anatomy and behavior.

The continuum of critical/sensitive period effects. Some traits are more sensitive to hormone effects at certain times in life than at others. At one period of an organism's life, a given dose of a sex hormone may have a particular effect on that organism's brain and behavior. At any other periods of life, before or after the critical/sensitive one, higher and more prolonged doses of hormones may be required to see the same effects.

This sensitivity is also best viewed as a continuum. There are variations in the degree to which an organism is sensitive to hormone effects, and in the degree to which higher hormone doses given at other times can have effects on that organism's brain and behavior similar to those of lower doses given at the critical time. These effects vary not only with age but also with sex, species, and behavior. As Moore (1991) has pointed out, reproductive strategies (see Chapter 4) may predict species differences in sensitive periods as well as reversibility. In species in which male reproductive strategies are "chosen" early in life and are permanent, the sensitive period might be perinatal.

In other species, a male can shift from one strategy to the next, depending on conditions. In such species, sensitive periods might start later in life, perhaps at puberty or even later.

Feminizing effects can be also separated from demasculinizing effects. Not only may the two have different critical periods but they may have different hormone sensitivities and involve different biochemical/anatomical changes. Because of this, an experimenter can vary the timing of any hormone manipulations so as to produce a rat that acts very feminine and very masculine.

The structural versus functional continuum. Sex hormones can affect both the **structure** (interconnections among nerve cells, anatomy of cells and organs) and the **function** (electrical activity and biochemistry) of the brain. Structural versus functional effects are also on a continuum, with all degrees of both types of effects occurring during *both* the perinatal and the postpubertal periods of life. For example, functional types of effects occur during both periods (Williams & Blaustein, 1988). In functional effects, sex hormones change the biochemistry and the electrical activity of brain cells. However, the electrical activity may affect the anatomy (structure) of the developing brain just because the brain's anatomy is sensitive to hormones as well as the environment at that time (epigenetic development).

Contrary to the earlier idea of a dichotomy of hormone effects, postpubertal hormones can also alter the brain's anatomy. For example, the parts of the rat's brain which control sexual and reproductive behaviors have their anatomy changed when postpubertal sex hormone levels are altered (Olmos et al., 1987, 1989). In one part of the brain, the number of connections between brain cells increases and decreases as hormone levels wax and wane during each female's sexual cycle. Having been a mother means that certain kinds of connections appear in another part of the rat's brain (Hatton & Ellisman, 1982). These connections do not appear in male brains or in brains of females who have not had babies, but they are seen in females who have been mothers, regardless of how long it was since they had given birth. A pregnancy also causes long-term (lifetime?) effects on the hormone levels in a human female, increasing the levels of an estrogen and decreasing levels of two androgens (Musey et al., 1987). Also, human females who have had an early puberty have higher estrogen levels, perhaps throughout their reproductive lives, than do women who have had a later puberty (MacMahon et al., 1982). These effects of pregnancy and puberty timing presumably reflect durable changes in brain structure or function.

Effects on Organs Other than the Brain

The liver, kidney, and adrenal are also hormone-sensitive organs.[1] In other words, there are not only male and female gonads and brains but also male and female livers, kidneys, and adrenal glands. Some of the perinatal effects seem to be permanent, structural as well as functional, and probably limited to certain periods of development. Other perinatal effects can be reversed by appropriate postpubertal hormone treatments. In many cases, since the products of these organs can affect brain activity as well as sex hormone levels, some hormone effects on behavior can be indirect, secondary to the effects that hormones had on organs other than the brain. Two such organs will be described: gonads and adrenals.

Gonads. Perinatal hormone levels affect the adult gonads' structure and function (Vanderstichele et al., 1987; Varma & Bloch, 1987; Vomachka, 1987). For example, human females exposed prenatally to DES (an artificial estrogen) have higher T levels than normal after puberty. Because the ovary has androgen receptors, perinatal androgen can permanently affect it (Lyon & Glenister, 1980). Since the adult gonad is affected by perinatal sex hormones, the only way to equate adult gonadal hormone levels across groups exposed to different perinatal hormones is to remove each adult's gonads before testing and give each of them equivalent replacement hormone injections.

Adrenals. The adrenal glands (at least the outside portion of them, the **adrenal cortex**[2]) also secrete sex hormones. Furthermore, the adrenal cortex is altered by changes in both postpubertal and perinatal sex hormone levels (Aguilar, Bellido, & Aguilar, 1987; Eguchi et al., 1976; Purvis, Calandra, & Hansson, 1977). For example, removing the gonads of an adult female monkey increases her levels of **cortisol**, which is a stress hormone secreted by the adrenal cortex (Kaplan et al., 1986). Therefore, even if adults of both sexes have their gonads removed, they cannot be assumed to have the same hormone levels.

Techniques of Study

Two types of techniques are used to study the effects of sex hormone levels on brain anatomy and behavior, each with several subtypes. Each type tries to establish the degree to which behavior is sensitive to changes in hormone levels. The different types and subtypes will produce conclusions of differing internal and external validity (see Chapter 2).

Hormone sensitivity. When hormone level is an independent variable in some experiment, **hormone sensitivity** is measured as the amount of change seen in some dependent variable (often a given behavior) for a given change in hormone level. The hormone sensitivity is a way of quantifying the degree of hormone-behavior covariation. The changes in hormone levels can be either manipulated or measured.

If a behavior is sensitive to hormonal changes, the effects can be described in terms of a species-specific, gender-related characteristic. If a hormone treatment increases the like-

lihood, frequency, or intensity of a masculine characteristic, such as increasing body size, the treatment is described as **masculinizing.** A treatment that decreases body size would be **demasculinizing. Feminizing** treatments increase the frequency, intensity, or likelihood of feminine behaviors such as lactation, and **defeminizing** treatments decrease those same behaviors.

Type I: Active manipulations of hormone levels. To study the effects of sex hormones, researchers can **gonadectomize**[3] animals during various developmental periods or as adults. Animals gonadectomized shortly after birth are then compared to sham-operated or **intact controls** at some later point in their lives. The control animals are usually subjected to similar neonatal surgeries to control for the effects of stress; however, their gonads are left in place throughout the potentially sensitive period being investigated. After that period, the controls may also be gonadectomized. Then, both groups of animals are often given equivalent doses of replacement hormones[4] before being tested. When adults are gonadectomized, the experimental animals would have their gonads removed and the controls would be subjected to a sham surgery. After a period of time, animals from both groups would be tested.

Most of the research done on experimental animals combines gonadectomies with hormone injections. **Exogenous** hormones come from sources outside the animal, such as the syringe of an experimenter. Hormone injections can be given in addition to or instead of castrations at various developmental periods. Control animals are usually given sham injections of some hopefully inert fluid. The two groups are then compared to see what effects the hormone injections had. For example, if testicular hormones are normally what causes males' brains to be masculinized and defeminized relative to females, neonastally castrated males who are given a sufficiently large androgen injection right after their surgery should be similar to their gonadally intact controls when both are tested as adults.

As just implied, most research on the perinatal effects of hormones in rodents starts shortly after the animals' birth. At this time, they are given hormone injections and/or gonadectomized. Then they are tested as adults. The use of prenatal treatments would require giving hormone injections to pregnant female animals, which often interferes with their pregnancies. Furthermore, the neonatal period for the rodent brain is very similar to the prenatal period for the brains of other mammals in terms of its responses to sex hormone manipulations.

Exogenous prenatal hormones are a major source of information regarding the perinatal effects of hormones on humans. For many years (and, in the case of some hormones, continuing today), sex hormones were given to women with various pregnancy problems. The hope was that these treatments would be of benefit (they were not; see Chapter 7). The net effect is that there are many people alive today who as fetuses were exposed to abnormal levels of exogenous sex hormones. These people can be studied and compared to various control groups.

Hormone levels have also been manipulated in adult humans. Humans have been gonadectomized for treatment of cancer, among other conditions. In some cases, the people were given replacement hormones after their cancer regressed. In other cases, people have been given hormones for treatment of problems like sexual inadequacy or for birth control. People have also obtained some anabolic steroids (androgens) from illicit sources.

Type II: Hormone level as a measured independent variable. Researchers can measure hormone levels in many different organisms and attempt to relate (correlate) differences in hormone levels with differences in behaviors. To do correlational research with **endogenous** (naturally occurring) hormone changes, re-

searchers measure hormones and behaviors either across time or across individuals. The researchers are doing **intraindividual studies** if they measure changes in hormone levels from one time to another in several individuals, relating the hormone changes observed to the behavioral changes also seen in the same individuals at about the same time. If researchers measure both hormonal and behavioral differences among several individuals all at about the same time, relating individual differences in hormone levels to individual differences in behaviors, they are doing **interindividual studies.** Both intraindividual and interindividual types of research have been carried out with human as well as nonhuman subjects. However, for ethical reasons, proportionately more of the hormone research done with humans uses these types of designs rather than the manipulated hormone designs.

Intra- versus interindividual studies are relevant to different kinds of questions about hormone-behavior relationships. An intraindividual study might ask the following type of question: do the changes in hormone levels that occur during the menstrual cycle in women lead to any changes in their behaviors? An interindividual study might ask this kind of question: do the men who have the highest levels of T in their group also have the highest levels of aggression in that group? Interindividual hormone techniques have also been used to assess perinatal hormone effects, especially in humans. Some babies, sometimes because of various inborn defects, have abnormally high or abnormally low levels of perinatal sex hormones. Can any effect of this be detected by comparing them with various control groups who have presumably had more normal perinatal levels of sex hormones?

Questions of validity. As described in Chapter 2, experiments with manipulated independent variables have inherently greater internal validity, compared to those with measured independent variables, such as the inter- and intra-individual studies. For example, with a measured hormone level, it is not certain that the hormone led to the behavior. Maybe the change in behavior changed the hormone level.

However, there are several aspects of studies involving manipulated hormone levels that can impair their external validity. First, hormone levels must be manipulated only within ranges of levels normally observed in that species (**physiological** as opposed to **pharmacological,** or very high levels) if conclusions are to be generalized to naturally occurring hormone variations. Second, even if all organisms have been gonadectomized and given equivalent hormone injections, their hormone levels still may not be identical. The adrenals also secrete sex hormones, the rate at which their livers break down the sex hormones may differ, and, as will be described, their diets may also cause their hormone levels to differ.

Third, as will be described in the last section of this chapter, the *pattern* or *timing* of hormone changes is often critically important to their effects. Only if the manipulations of hormone levels mimic naturally occurring rates of increase and times in between peaks, for example, can conclusions be freely generalized to effects of naturally occurring variations. However, the effects of timing also imply that for intraindividual and interindividual types of hormone studies to have any internal or external validity, hormone levels must be measured often enough to determine each individual's pattern of changes. Nevertheless, despite the fact that an individual's hormone levels do vary over time and with changes in her environment, individual differences in hormone levels are still relatively stable over time (reliable differences; see Chapter 2) (Apter, Reinilä, & Vihko, 1989; Apter & Vihko, 1990; Couwenbergs, Knussmann, & Christiansen, 1986; Dabbs, 1990b; Dai et al., 1981; MacMahon et al., 1982; vom Saal & Finch, 1988). This fact increases the internal validity of these studies.

HOW CAN SEX HORMONES AFFECT YOUR BRAIN CELLS?

Hormones can affect cells, including brain cells, in one of two different ways. **Genomic functions** refer to sex hormones' effects on the activity of genes within any cell, including a nerve cell. Turning a gene off or on in a cell means that the hormones will eventually affect the cell's structure and/or function (see Chapter 3). **Nongenomic membrane functions** are the effects that sex hormones have directly on the **membrane** (outer wall) of any cell, including nerve cells — effects that do not involve changes in the activity of any of the genes within that cell. These two functions can affect cellular growth, the cells' biochemistries, or their electrical activity, or simultaneously have all these effects.

Overview of Brain Studies

To understand what hormones can do (and have already done) to the nerve cells, or **neurons,** in your brain, you must first understand something about what it is that neurons do and how they do it. A picture of a neuron is presented in Figure 6.1. Because of what neural interconnections do, and by means of specialized neurons, such as those in the nose that are sensitive to odors, neurons receive, translate, and encode information in the world around us. The resulting information is sent through their axons to and around the brain. For example, your eye receives, processes, and encodes visual information, and your optic nerve sends that information to the rest of your brain for further processing. Some neurons also respond to changes in internal states — changes in moods and motives — and so change what other neurons are doing. Neurons remember what has happened to us in the past by what type of interconnections they form with which other specific neurons.

FIGURE 6.1   *Basic Parts of a Neuron*

A neuron has three basic parts: **dendrites, cell body** (contains the nucleus, which contains the chromosomes), and **axon.** The axon may be myelinated, or covered with a fatty wrapping, which speeds up the rate at which the axon carries information from one point to the next. One neuron "talks" to another across specialized gaps between nerve cells called **synapses.** The three kinds of synapses illustrated here are **axo-dendritic, axo-somatic,** and **axo-axonic.**

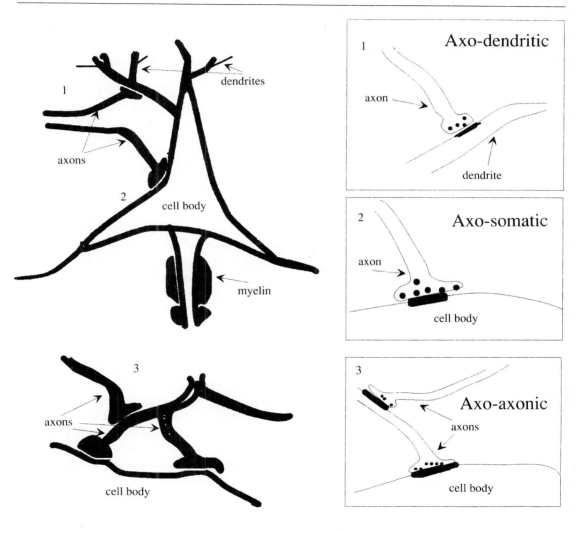

Action potentials.   The membrane of a neuron is much like a miniature battery, being negatively charged on the inside and positively charged on the outside. If the inside is connected to the outside, electrical current will flow, just as cur-rent will flow between the negative and positive poles of a battery when connected to each other. This batterylike membrane charge is called a **membrane potential.**

The **action potential** is a reversal of this

normal membrane potential. A tiny part of the cell's membrane temporarily becomes positively charged on the inside and negatively charged on the outside because of a temporary connection or "short circuit" being made between inside and outside. If one thinks of the axon of a neuron as being a long, thin cylinder, the action potential would be a reversal of the membrane charge that formed a small ring around that cylinder. The reversal of potential, or the action potential, is generated on the initial segment of the cell's axon. At any given moment, the likelihood of an action potential is based on the summation of all the information a neuron is receiving on its cell body and dendrites (see Figure 6.1). From the initial segment, the action potential travels down the axon to the presynaptic terminal. If the axon is myelinated, the action potential travels faster, jumping from one node of Ranvier to the next. A **node of Ranvier** is a small ring around a myelinated axon that has no myelin (fatty) covering; a full action potential can be generated only at such a node in a myelinated axon.

Neurons use these action potentials to carry information from one place to another in the brain. Which neurons are active (having action potentials) and the way in which the action potentials in a given neuron are distributed in time communicate information to other neurons in the brain. *Everything we think and experience is some higher-order function of these patterns of electrical activity in the neurons of our brains.*

Synaptic potentials.   Neurons communicate with one another by means of synaptic potentials. Synaptic potentials occur at **synapses,** which are areas in which two or more neurons come in close, functional contact with each other. As Figure 6.1 shows, there are three kinds of synapses, defined by their locations. The activity in axo-dendritic and axo-somatic synapses summate to affect the likelihood of an action potential in the initial segment. The axo-axonic synapses regulate activity at a

synapse. Since the membranes of these adjacent neurons are not in actual physical contact even at synapses, there are small gaps, or **synaptic clefts,** between the two cells. The changes in the electrical activity that occur in the neuron membranes on either side of the cleft are the **synaptic potentials.**

The mechanisms of synaptic activity are similar to those of sex hormone effects. The **presynaptic cell** has a synaptic membrane specialized for the release of chemical substances. The chemicals released by the presynaptic membrane are **transmitter substances.** The second cell's membrane, the **postsynaptic membrane,** is specialized to respond to the transmitter substances released by the presynaptic cell.

Transmitter substances are stored in special places, or **vesicles,** just inside the specialized membrane of the presynaptic cell. (The vesicles are the small circles in Figure 6.1.) When that part of the presynaptic membrane is invaded by an action potential (which is now called a **presynaptic potential**), its membrane potential temporarily reverses. Because of that reversal, some transmitter substance molecules are released into the synaptic cleft. These molecules diffuse[5] across the cleft, eventually coming in contact with the posysynaptic membrane.

Specialized receptors in the postsynaptic membrane are specific protein molecules that recognize (by binding or attaching themselves to) specific transmitter molecules. Once a molecule of receptor protein binds to one or more molecules of transmitter substance, certain changes occur in the postsynaptic cell. After the changes begin, the transmitter molecule may break off the receptor molecule. Then it either combines with another receptor, is broken down by some enzyme found in the synaptic cleft, or is pumped back into the presynaptic cell for reuse.

The changes that occur in the postsynaptic cell are specific to the type of receptor and the type of cell. In some cases, the potential of the postsynaptic cell is changed (the **postsynaptic potential**), being either excited or inhibited.

Levels of certain enzymes within the postsynaptic cell can also be changed. Eventually, even the activity of the postsynaptic cell's genes may be affected.

The anatomy of sex hormone effects.   Figures 6.2 and 6.3 depict some of the brain structures whose anatomy, electrical activity, and transmitter substance biochemistry are sensitive to sex hormone levels, either perinatally and/or postpubertally. One of these structures is shown in Figure 6.2 and again in more detail in Figure 6.3. This is the **hypothalamus,** a collection of **nuclei** (neuron groups). It regulates the "master gland of the body," the **pituitary,** and various motivated behaviors. Within the hypothalamus, the **preoptic area (POA),** part of the preoptic area called the **sexually dimorphic nucleus of the preoptic area (SDN-POA),** the **ventromedial (VMH)** area, and the **anterior hypothalamus** are all involved in controlling sexual behaviors and sexual hormone levels. In rats, increased POA activity is associated with an increase in masculine sexual behavior and a decrease in feminine sexual behavior, or **lordosis.** POA lesions abolish masculine sexual behavior in many species. In female rats, POA lesions disrupt the sexual cycle and their maternal behaviors. The VMH area in rats controls lordosis, and VMH lesions in primates prevent ovulation. The positive feedback and cyclic gonadotropin release are related to the sexual cycle and ovulation, both of which will be discussed shortly.

The hypothalamus is interconnected with the parts of the brain collectively called the limbic system, which is also illustrated in Figure 6.2. The **limbic system** controls emotional reactions and behaviors. For example, the **amygdala** is involved in the control of sex hormone levels and masculine sexual behaviors. Other parts of the limbic system include the **septal** area, or **septum.** The **caudate** is part of the motor system of the brain, but it is also active during cognitive and emotional processes. The **hippocampus** is involved in stress responses as

well as the formation of memories and the processing of spatial information (see Chapter 13). The **reticular activating system** is a general term, referring to many different areas in the center of the brain all the way from the brainstem to well within the brain itself. Much of the reticular system seems to be involved in arousal and attention. The system also includes areas controlling sleep and certain reflex movements.

Genomic versus Nongenomic Membrane Function

In genomic functions, the activity of a cell's genes are altered. Genomic hormone functions usually require minutes to hours before they affect a sensitive cell's activity.[6] Nongenomic effects can occur within seconds and do not involve any direct changes in genetic activities.

Genomic effects.   One way in which sex hormones can affect neural anatomy and function is described by the so-called classic model of genomic effects (see Hoyenga & Hoyenga, 1993; Parikh et al., 1987; Walters, 1985). First, the hormone circulating in the bloodstream must enter the cell. The hormone in the blood may be **free** or it may be **bound to** (attached to) some blood protein, such as *albumin,* from which it breaks off before entering the cell. The method by which the hormone enters the cell is unknown. A molecule of sex hormone may simply diffuse across the cell's wall since membranes are at lest somewhat permeable to sex hormones (Carlson, Gruber, & Thompson, 1983). Another possibility is that some blood protein, or some protein in the membrane, may act like a transporter and actively carry the sex hormone molecule into the cell.

Next, the sex hormone molecule binds to a specific receptor protein found within that cell. Analogous to transmitter receptors, each type of sex hormone has its own specific receptor protein. Unless present in very large quantities, a sex hormone does not bind appreciably to a

Part A

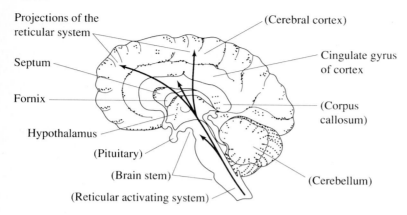

Projections of the reticular system

Septum

Fornix

Hypothalamus

(Pituitary)

(Brain stem)

(Reticular activating system)

(Cerebral cortex)

Cingulate gyrus of cortex

(Corpus callosum)

(Cerebellum)

Part B

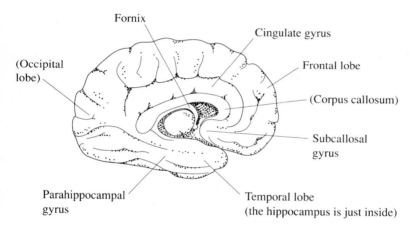

Fornix

Cingulate gyrus

(Occipital lobe)

Frontal lobe

(Corpus callosum)

Subcallosal gyrus

Parahippocampal gyrus

Temporal lobe (the hippocampus is just inside)

Part C

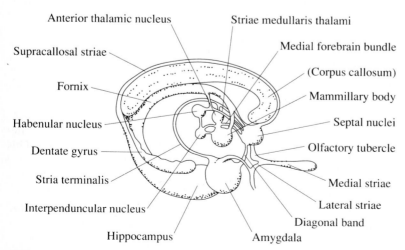

Anterior thalamic nucleus

Supracallosal striae

Fornix

Habenular nucleus

Dentate gyrus

Stria terminalis

Interpenduncular nucleus

Hippocampus

Striae medullaris thalami

Medial forebrain bundle

(Corpus callosum)

Mammillary body

Septal nuclei

Olfactory tubercle

Medial striae

Lateral striae

Diagonal band

Amygdala

FIGURE 6.2 *The Reticular Activating System and the Limbic System*
The reticular activating system and the limbic system are both shown in midsagittal (Parts A and B) and in cutaway (Part C) views. All the structures *not* in parentheses are part of the limbic system. (A midsaggital section is done by cutting the brain into two mirror-image halves along a vertical plane, from the front to the back of the head.)

Source: From *Psychobiology: The neuron and behavior* by K. B. Hoyenga and K. T. Hoyenga. Copyright © 1988 by Wadsworth, Inc. Reprinted by permission of Brooks/Cole Publishing Company, Pacific Grove, CA 93950.

FIGURE 6.3 *The Hypothalamus*
The various component structures of the hypothalamus are shown. This composite is from various studies in humans and in experimental animals. Current understanding of the physiologic roles of these structures is also indicated.

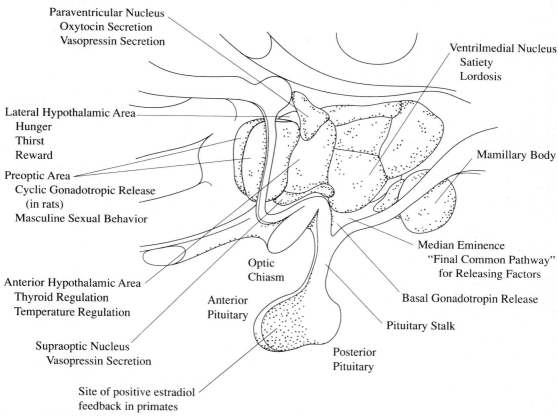

Source: Modified with permission. D. T. Krieger and J. C. Hughes (eds.), *Neuroendocrinology.* HP Publishing Company, publishers of *Hospital Practice.* Illustration by Carol Donner.

receptor specific to some other hormone. Estrogen (E) receptor proteins (and presumably the others as well) are in a state of dynamic flux across the cytoplasm[7] and nucleus of the cell. Both proteins that are bound and those that are unbound to hormone molecules are found throughout the cell, but mostly in the nucleus (Parikh et al., 1987; Walters, 1985). Only receptor proteins that are bound to hormone molecules and that are located in the nucleus can affect the activity of genes in that nucleus.

To affect a gene's activity, the hormone-receptor complex must bind to the DNA. This binding affects the activity of specific genes, probably ones adjacent to the site on the DNA to which the hormone-receptor complex attached itself. A gene that was turned off (repressed) can be turned on again by sex hormones so that the RNA coded by that DNA starts to be manufactured. Eventually, the RNA will be translated by the cellular machinery into the relevant proteins. Alternatively, a gene may be repressed by a hormone-receptor complex. Some perinatal as well as postpubertal effects of exogenous sex hormones can be blocked if a drug that prevents gene activation and/or RNA synthesis is administered along with the hormone (Etgen, 1987; Meisel & Pfaff, 1984; Renner et al., 1984; Salaman & Birkett, 1974).

The sex hormone-receptor binding places on the cell's DNA may be clustered among the DNA binding sites for other substances that also control genetic activity. In view of the juxtaposition of binding sites, it is not surprising to find that the effects of progesterone (P), for example, interact with the effects of other genetic-controlling factors (Edwards et al., 1991; Schüle et al., 1988).

At least in part, the state of the DNA in a cell determines whether that cell's genetic activity can be regulated by (is sensitive to) sex hormones. In cells that are not sensitive to hormones, certain proteins completely mask the DNA sites to which hormones and their receptors would normally bind (Whalen & Olsen, 1978). In these cells, even if hormones were present, they would not affect the activity of that cell's genes. In other cells, the DNA binding sites might be unmasked for one gender (because of perinatal hormone or other epigenetic effects?) but not for the other. In the unmasked cells, hormones change genetic activity. The integration of proviral genes into various parts of the genomes may have been one evolutionary mechanism for conferring hormone sensitivity onto genes (see Chapters 3 and 5).

New proteins and new species of RNA molecules are produced when sensitive cells are exposed to sex hormones. This includes the proteins that act like receptors for other hormones (De Kloet, Voorhuis, & Elands, 1985; Kaye, 1983; O'Malley, Schwartz, & Schrader, 1976;

Spranger, Fahrenbach, & Bethea, 1991). Not only does E increase the levels of the P receptor protein, P can increase the number of E receptors. These effects occur only in certain brain areas (Romano, Krust, & Pfaff, 1989; Samama & Aron, 1989). Other genes regulated by sex hormones include those coding for the brain's **endorphins,** or the endogenous morphinelike substances normally found in the brain (Adams et al., 1991; Romano et al., 1990). In rats, these regulatory activities have been directly linked to sexual behaviors. Some gene activity may be permanently altered by perinatal hormone levels. This is apparently the case for the growth hormone gene in rats, whose activity may be durably increased by perinatal exposure to sex hormones (Maiter, Koenig, & Kaplan, 1991). One estrogen-induced protein may become part of the system that neurons use to secrete transmitter substances onto one another (Mobbs et al., 1988).

Nongenomic membrane functions.   Baulieu (1978) was one of the first to suggest that hormones could affect neurons without changing the activity of their genes. In fact, some sex hormone effects on behavior are *not* blocked by protein synthesis inhibitors (Shivers et al., 1980). Instead, the effects are blocked by drugs that suppress the **electrical activity** (action potentials or synaptic potentials) of neurons (Rothfeld et al., 1986).

Towle and Sze (1983) suggested that specialized hormone receptors existed not only inside hormone-sensitive cells but also in those cells' membranes. Thus, some of the nongenomic membrane functions are very similar to synaptic potentials. The hormone combines with a specialized receptor protein in the membrane of the cell, and the combination rapidly changes that cell's activity, analogous to the postsynaptic effects previously described (McEwen, 1991a, 1991b; Nabekura et al., 1986; Oomura, Minami, & Nabekura, 1986; Rosner, 1990). A P receptor localized to neuron membranes has been identified (Ke & Ramirez, 1990). The P receptor has been found in the membranes of cells located in the cerebral cortex, cerebellum, and hypothalamus (see Figure 6.2), among other places.

Sex hormones change the electrical activity of cells in some parts of the brain that lack classic hormone receptors. Cells in these areas may also have membrane receptors. As just mentioned, this includes the **cerebellum,** which coordinates motor activity and motor learning (S. S. Smith, 1989; Smith, Waterhouse, & Woodward, 1987a, 1987b). Tiny amounts of E and P affect cerebellar neural activity even when dropped directly onto its cells. E has also affected cerebellar cells within 5 to 10 minutes after the hormone was injected into the bloodstream.

Hormones can directly affect both enzymes and membranes in the absence of any kind of receptor. Earlier (Hoyenga & Hoyenga, 1979), the authors called these the *nonspecific* effects of hormones. Since these effects can occur even in cells that lack either internal or membrane receptors, these effects could potentially occur in any cell in the brain. In view of the fact that P affects cellular metabolism in the uterus by affecting how mRNA is translated into proteins (Loosfelt et al., 1981), similar processes could occur in neurons. Sex hormones may directly diffuse into a membrane and remain there, changing its anatomy and thus its operation (Carlson et al., 1983). Sex hormones can affect the microanatomy of the membranes of nerve or uterine cells within seconds after being applied in very tiny quantities to the outside of the cell (Garcia-Segura, Baeten, & Naftolin, 1985; Garcia-Segura et al., 1987; Rambo & Szego, 1983). Sex hormones also affect membrane excitability (Bauer & Bauer, 1990; Erulkar & Wetzel, 1989). These latter effects may or may not require membrane receptors.

Outcomes of Functions for Neurons

The outcomes of both the genomic and the nongenomic membrane functions for neurons

include (1) growth, (2) biochemical changes, and (3) changes in electrical activity.

Sex hormones affect cellular growth. Sex hormones can be described as helping to make life and death decisions for developing neurons. Perinatal organisms have more neurons in most parts of their brain than do adults; in some areas of the brain, as many as 50 percent of the cells present at some time before birth will be lost during the perinatal period.[8] Some cell loss is controlled by sex hormones (Menzies, Drysdale, & Waite, 1982; Nordeen, Nordeen, & Arnold, 1987).

Not only can neurons taken from prenatal animals' brains survive (when cultured in an appropriate medium) but they can grow and establish new connections. Hormones affect both their growth and their connections (Toran-Allerand, 1980, 1984; Toran-Allerand, Ellis, & Pfenninger, 1988). Although E increases cellular growth, T does so only if E is also present in the culture; in the absence of E, T has no effect. Cells taken from adult organisms do not respond to E, meaning that the relevant genes were permanently turned off when the development of this part of the brain was completed. Other researchers have confirmed these growth-promoting effects of sex hormones (Arimatsu & Hatanaka, 1986; Uchibori & Kawashima, 1985a, 1985b). Prenatal neurons using the transmitter substance *dopamine*[9] may be especially sensitive to the growth-promoting properties of E and T (Engele, Pilgrim, & Reisert, 1989; Reisert, Engele, & Pilgrim, 1989; Reisert et al., 1987). Thus, some of the growth in the intact, developing organism probably depends on the joint effects of postnatal environments and perinatal hormone levels (Juraska, 1991; Juraska, Fitch, & Washburne, 1989).

Not only will fetal neurons grow in culture, they will grow when transplanted into the adult brains or bodies of recipient animals (Hoyenga & Hoyenga, 1988). Cells from the adult host brains develop new processes (but not new cells), some of which grow into and make synaptic contacts with the implanted cells. This type of growth can also be sensitive to E (Nishizuka & Arai, 1982).

Even the growth of new neural processes that occurs after brain damage in the adult is affected by sex hormones. After experimental lesions of certain parts of the brain, non-damaged neurons adjacent to the damaged area often start growing new axons or dendrites. These new processes can extend into and make functional synapses with neurons that have lost their normal presynaptic inputs because of the damage. Sex hormones affect this growth process as well (Hoyenga & Hoyenga, 1988; Loy & Milner, 1980; Milner & Loy, 1982; Morse, Scheff, & DeKosky, 1986; Yu, 1988).

Hormone changes occurring after puberty also affect neural growth processes. In certain cells of the female rat's brain — cells that control hormone secretion and sexual behaviors — synapses are formed and then die, over and over again, every week as her hormones change (Olmos et al., 1989). However, in some cases, adult female rats may be more sensitive to the growth-promoting effects of E than are adult males (Miyakawa & Arai, 1987). As described earlier, once synapses had formed because of the hormonal changes associated with motherhood and lactation, they remained for the rest of the female rat's life (Hatton & Ellisman, 1982).

Sex hormones affect the biochemistry of neurons. If different organisms are exposed to different levels of perinatal sex hormones, they grow up to have different levels of certain brain proteins and different rates of protein synthesis (Angelbeck & DuBrul, 1983; Litteria, 1977a, 1977b, 1980a, 1980b; Litteria & Thorner, 1974, 1975, 1976). This suggests that certain genes are permanently turned off or on by perinatal sex hormones. Manipulating perinatal sex hormone levels also changes perinatal protein levels, protein synthesis, and RNA levels in the brain (Adcock & Greenstein,

1986; Litteria & Popoff, 1984; Stanley, Borthwick, & Fink, 1986; Stanley & Fink, 1986; Ventanas et al., 1986). These changes may be the mechanisms by which hormones affect the interconnections made by the developing neurons.

Perinatal hormone levels can also alter how postpubertal hormone levels affect the biochemistry of neurons. For example, Whalen and Olsen (1978) found that E did not bind as well to the DNA taken from male hypothalamic neurons as it did to female DNA. More reently, the DNA of hypothalamic cells in adult female rats was discovered to have a greater capacity for binding E than does the DNA of males (Brown et al., 1988). Because of this, cells in males might be less sensitive to genomic effects than would be the comparable female cells (Nordeen & Yahr, 1983), all because of the sex differences in perinatal hormone levels.

Sex hormones affect electrical activity.   One type of research recorded the effects of sex hormones on the electrical activities of cells, which were located either in neuron cultures or in slices taken from the brain. Therefore, the activity being recorded could not be influenced by any cells in any other brain area: the hormone had to be having a direct effect on the cells being studied.[10]

This research on neuron cultures and slices led to some important and exciting information. Since hormones have a direct effect on nerve cells, hormones can be affecting an organism's perceptions, feelings, and motives. Work at this level allows researchers to see how sex hormones may be affecting the brain's codes — our very thoughts. In some cases, whether the cells were excited or inhibited by sex hormones depended not only on the hormone but also the gender of the animal from whom the brain slice was taken. Since the changes in activity took place within one to two minutes, genomic functions are presumably ruled out.

Sex hormones also indirectly affect electrical

activity by controlling the levels or activities of transmitter substances, which control neurons' ability to communicate (Harlan, 1988; Heritage et al., 1980; McEwen, 1988, 1991a, 1991b; Romano et al., 1988; Romano et al., 1989). In some cases, the genes controlling the rate of transmitter manufacture are sensitive to sex hormones. In one interesting example of this, Simerly (1989) explored how both perinatal and postpubertal hormones affect the rate of dopamine synthesis in rat brains by controlling the activity of the relevant gene. Perinatal hormones decreased the number of cells in the adult that had this gene active, either by controlling which cells died perinatally or by permanently inactivating that gene in the affected cells. The presence of any postpubertal hormone tended to turn off that same gene in any of the remaining adult cells that had such a gene active at all.

Sex hormones also change neural activity by regulating the sensitivity of postsynaptic neurons to transmitter substances. E may often be indirectly excitatory. For example, E increases the responses of cerebellum cells to an excitatory transmitter substance, **glutamate** (S. S. Smith, 1989; Smith et al., 1987a). By way of comparison, the effects of E are even larger than those of **norepinephrine,** the excitement or arousal transmitter substance. Similarly, E inhibits the responses of cortical cells to inhibitory transmitter **(adenosine),** thus leading to an increase in activity in this case as well (Phillis & O'Regan, 1988). E also reverses the inhibitory effect that dopamine has on pituitary cells (Dufy et al., 1979). Some of these changes in sensitivity are presumably genomic because of the time required. Although dopamine usually excites cells in the caudate nucleus (Figure 6.2), between 5 and 10 hours after an injection of E, dopamine developed inhibitory effects (Demotes-Mainard, Arnauld, & Vincent, 1990).

Conversely, P often has inhibitory effects. It increases the inhibitory effects of the transmitter **GABA** (gamma-aminobutyric acid) on cells in the cerebellum, brainstem, and hippocampus (Canonaco et al., 1989; Majewska et al., 1986; Smith et al., 1987a, 1987b). GABA is one of the major inhibitory transmitter substances of the brain, and anti-anxiety drugs have the same kinds of effects on GABA reactions as does P. P directly increases the effect of GABA at its receptor and may also increase the levels of GABA receptors. P also decreases the reactions of cerebellum cells to the excitatory transmitter glutamate (Smith et al., 1987b).

These reactions may explain the calming effects that high doses of P have (Canonaco et al., 1989; Rodriguez-Sierra, Hagley, & Henricks, 1986; Rodriguez-Sierra et al., 1984). In both rats and humans, P inhibits aggression and anxiety and can reduce the effects of conflict or stress. Normal female and neonatally castrated male rats may be more responsive to the anti-anxiety effects of P than are normal males and females given neonatal androgen injections.

Although a description of when hormones were having what type of effect was given in the above discussion, the authors deliberately did not dichotomize the perinatal and postpubertal periods. Sex hormones affect electrical activity and, in turn, the amount and pattern of electrical activity can modify the brain's "wiring diagram" at any age (Balazs et al., 1987; Galli & Maffei, 1988; Lipton, 1986; Shatz & Stryker, 1988). For example, electrical activity can affect the survival of neurons in a culture. Some neurons in perinatal rats are electrically active, and this activity can affect their growth and their ability to form proper synaptic connections with other neurons. Thus, if sex hormones do affect the electrical activity even of perinatal neurons, that could then affect growth and formation of synapses, perinatally as well as postpubertally. By regulating electrical activity, perinatal hormones may similarly affect which transmitter substance a given neuron will use in the adult brain (Schotzinger & Landis, 1988; Walicke, Campenot, & Patterson, 1977).

Sex-linked effects. Some sex differences in the brain may be sex linked rather than sex limited. This would be the case for any possible dosage effects of genes on the X chromosome which, directly or indirectly, affect transmitter levels (see Chapter 5). Furthermore, some sex differences in the fetal development of brain cells do not depend on perinatal sex hormone levels. These aspects of fetal development may be under the direct control of genes located on one of the sex chromosomes (Kolbinger et al., 1991).

PRINCIPLES OF HORMONE EFFECTS

The cellular effects of hormones can be genomic or nongenomic, and the outcomes of these cellular effects can involve growth, electrical activity, or biochemistry. In turn, the outcomes affect behaviors in ways that can be summarized by a list of principles. Since gender research and theorizing are active, developing areas of knowledge, both amendments and deletions will undoubtedly be necessary in the future.

The Principles

First, the principles will be listed. The next subsections will supply some of the details, documentation, and possible implications.

1. Testosterone (T) is the masculinizing and defeminizing hormone at the gonadal level. However, depending on species, behavior, organ, and age, either T or one of its metabolites may be the effective hormone at the cellular level. In other words, in some species, the ultimate effects of the T coming from the males' testes may occur only *after* the cells being affected convert the T into some hormonal metabolite.
2. Because of epigenetic development and differences in evolutionary selection pressures, species differ with regard to which behaviors are most sensitive to (will covary with) which hormones at which points in development. In general, only those aspects of brain and behavior that show consistent sex differences will covary with

hormone levels. Even then, if testing conditions are changed such that sex differences are no longer seen, hormone sensitivity will also change.
3. Because of epigenetic development, the effects of hormones on anatomy and behavior will depend on an organism's genes even within a species. This creates variability in behavioral outcomes across strains, across areas of the brain, and across behaviors.
4. The environment modifies hormone effects. Not only can the environment affect hormone levels at any time of life, the past environment and the current test conditions can affect the degree to which consistent hormone-behavior relationships are seen.
5. Hormone effects often depend critically on timing. This includes considering which period during the life span those hormones are present. It also includes the pattern, over time, of variations in hormone levels. For example, hormones are normally secreted in multiple hourly pulses, and pulsatile hormone treatments can have different kinds of effects than do treatments involving equivalent levels of hormones that do not change during the test.
6. Hormones often have nonlinear effects on the brain and behavior.

A description of each of these principles is now given in more detail so that you can better appreciate just how hormones can affect behaviors. Further examples will be presented in Chapters 7 and 8 when the sex differences found in both perinatal and in postpubertal sex hormone levels are described. What you should concentrate on here, rather than the detail of specific experiments and their results, is understanding the principles. Try to remember at least one example of each to make its operation seem more concrete to you.

The Active Hormone for Masculinization and Defeminization

With regard to masculinization and defeminization, both during the perinatal period and after puberty, there are two major metabolites of T. T can be converted into either E and/or **dihydrotestosterone (DHT).** Depending on species, organ system, and age (critical period), these other two hormones may actually exert the masculinizing and defeminizing effects on the brains and bodies of males. That is, T is secreted by the males' testes. This T is absorbed by the cells of the various organs of the body. T may be used as is, or the cells may convert T into E (by an **aromatizing enzyme**) or into DHT (by a **reducing enzyme**). Then the converted hormone may attach to a hormone receptor, move to the nucleus, and there affect the genetic activity of the cell. Thus, the hormone that enters a cell may not be the hormone that binds to an internal receptor and exerts genomic effects.

The major point is that just because the T secreted from the males' testes is responsible for their being masculinized and defeminized, that does not mean that, at the cellular level, T is the active hormone. Some organ systems may be masculinized by E, and other systems by DHT. In some species, T exerts its masculinizing and defeminizing effects on brain structure and behavior only after first being **aromatized** or converted into E inside the neurons being affected. Some examples will be given of the differential effects of T, E, and DHT, and the implications for sex differences, in the rest of this unit.

Variability across Species

Several reviews have attempted to relate hormone sensitivities to the mating and social systems of a species. For example, only in some species do the annual changes in hormone levels covary with the annual changes in mating behaviors (Crews, 1984).

Reproductive behaviors.   The degree to which males display parental behaviors may affect the evolution of hormone-sensitive parental behaviors (Brown, 1985). In other words, if only females display parenting behaviors, those behaviors would tend to become sex limited in their expression. Also, if only females display

parenting behaviors, females will have greater parental investment and so will be more sexually selective than males. This means that sex differences in sexual selection pressures will act to limit the selected-for traits to males.

Although there are exceptions, in many species in which both sexes have prominent parental roles, both E and T injections given to adults of either sex will often evoke parental behaviors. If only the female has a prominent parental role (the male's role is over once the female is impregnated), only E and not T injections will evoke parental behaviors. Furthermore, in paternal species of birds, **prolactin** (the milk-production pituitary hormone) stimulates the male to respond to eggs and young (by sitting and feeding, respectively). In nonpaternal species, prolactin does not affect the male.

The social and mating systems of the animals are related to hormone sensitivities as well as sexual dimorphisms (Adkins-Regan, 1981; Baum, 1979; Baum, Stockman, & Lundell, 1985; Hart, 1974). For example, the relative development of the brain, in addition to the complexity of the social system, may affect the hormone sensitivity of various kinds of aggressive behaviors. In species with more complex brains, and in species living in larger social groups, aggression is less sensitive to hormone changes. Instead, in these species, aggression is relatively more sensitive to the environment (Hart, 1974).

There are large species differences in the degree to which aromatization is required for the masculinizing and defeminizing effects of T. This is often tested by using injections of the androgen DHT, which cannot be converted into E, to see if DHT injections will elicit masculine sexual behaviors in either sex. In some mammals, but never in animals such as lizards and newts, the aromatization of T to E is often required for the social and courtship behaviors in the adult male. In many mammals, if both sexes display the behavior being tested, neurons in males will often be aromatizing T to E so that the same behavior can be stimulated by the same hormone — E — in both sexes. On the other hand, DHT injections can increase masculine sexual behaviors in adult hamsters, guinea pigs, mice, rhesus monkeys, and in some strains of rats (Adkins-Regan, 1981; Butera & Czaja, 1984, 1985; Olsen & Whalen, 1984). In other strains of rats, DHT does not lead to sexual behavior, but neither do physiologically relevant levels of E; only T itself will work (McGinnis & Dreifuss, 1989). Female monkeys, but not female rats, are strongly masculinized and defeminized by perinatal DHT treatments (Pomerantz, Goy, & Roy, 1986).

First example of species variability: song control nuclei in finches versus canaries. The brain areas that control singing and learning song patterns have been identified in several species of birds (DeVoogd, 1984; DeVoogd, Brenowitz, & Arnbold, 1988; Nordeen & Nordeen, 1990; Nottebohm & Arnold, 1976). The degree of the sex difference in the gross sizes of the song control areas, and in their neural interconnections, covaries with adult sex differences in singing behavior. For example, adult female canaries and zebra finches do not sing and their song centers are much smaller than those of males. As expected, there are few sex differences in the anatomy of wrens since the adults of both sexes sing. However, the differences in the sizes of song control areas between two same-sex adults of the same species may or may not covary with their singing behaviors.

Adult female canaries can be made to sing by injections of androgens, but this is not true of adult female finches. Juvenile changes in sex hormone levels have relatively more irreversible effects on the song control centers and on singing in finches than in canaries (Alvarez-Buylla, Kirn, & Nottebohm, 1990; Konishi & Akutagawa, 1988; Nordeen & Nordeen, 1988, 1990; Nordeen, Nordeen, & Arnold, 1986, 1987; Pohl-Apel, 1985). In finches, E (either

from experimental injections or from the aromatization of T in normal males) increases the number of androgen receptors during the juvenile period. E also regulates the growth of cells in the song control areas. Among the early E-treated females, the size of the song control area in adults is correlated with the female's singing: bigger song control areas mean more singing. In fact, during the period of time that the juvenile male finch is learning to sing, new neurons are being generated. These neurons are then incorporated into his song control nuclei, giving him bigger nuclei as an adult than are seen in the female finch.

In canaries, the size of the song control areas in the female can be increased by *adult* hormone treatments (Brenowitz & Arnold, 1990; Burd & Nottebohm, 1985; DeVoogd & Nottebohm, 1981; Goldman & Nottebohm, 1983; Nordeen & Nordeen, 1990; Nottebohm, 1980, 1989; Nottebohm, Nottebohm, & Crane, 1986). A female canary can be made to sing as an adult because adult hormone treatments can increase the size of her song control areas. Hormones increase the number of synapses and neural processes, making her cells grow larger, more complex, and with more interconnections.

Most astonishingly, new neurons[11] appear every year in canaries of both sexes (Alvarez-Buyela, Theelen, & Nottebohm, 1988; Bottjer & Dignan, 1988; Burd & Nottebohm, 1985; Nordeen & Nordeen, 1990; Nottebohm, 1985, 1991; Nottebohm, Nottebohm, & Crane, 1986). The new neurons appear in late summer, after courtship is over, when the males are learning new songs to be sung the following breeding season. The new neurons make functional connections between various song control areas, as well as interconnecting neurons within an area. These new neurons may make it possible for the male to learn his new songs, as he does every year. They may also make it possible for the female to learn to recognize the new songs even though she, without hormone treatments, will not sing them.

However, the singing and the anatomy of

song control areas are under the joint control of hormones and experiences. If the female canary is deafened before the hormone treatment begins, she will not learn to sing. She will also not generate many new neurons in her song control areas. The survival of new cells may require the joint effects of hormones and auditory stimulation.

Hormones, brain anatomy, and behavior have been carefully interrelated in these birds. These data also illustrate the variability between species, since only female canaries and not finches respond to adult hormone treatment with brain growth and singing. This example is even more important when one considers that singing is a learned behavior in these species. Hormones affect the capacity for learning, or the organism's ability to respond to its environment by learning to sing new song patterns.

Second example: positive feedback. Positive feedback is another example of a very important species difference in the effects of both perinatal and postpubertal hormone levels. Both examples document the hazard of uncritically generalizing from rats to humans. To understand the species difference, you must understand the positive feedback system, which includes part of the brain, the "master gland" of the body, and the gonads.

Figure 6.4 shows the hypothalamus and the pituitary. These two structures cooperatively control many internal glands, including the adrenal glands and the gonads. Certain hypothalamic cells secrete **releasing factors** into the blood vessels of the **pituitary stock,** the structure connecting the hypothalamus to the pituitary. The releasing factors cause specific pituitary cells to release hormones into the body's bloodstream. The bloodstream carries the pituitary hormones to their **target organs,** often stimulating the release of hormones. For example, the **corticotropin releasing factor (CRF)** from the hypothalamus stimulates the release of **adrenocorticotropic hormone**[12] **(ACTH)** from the pituitary. In turn, ACTH

stimulates the release of various adrenal steroids, including **cortisol,** from the target organ, the adrenal cortex. The hormones from the target organ also flow throughout the body, affecting many other organs, including the brain.

The target organ's hormones usually inhibit the hypothalamus. This creates a **negative feedback loop,** which is much like the relationship that a room's thermostat creates between the room's temperature and the output of heat from some furnace that heats the room. A rise in room temperature (target organ hormone levels; e.g., cortisol from the adrenal gland) is sensed by the thermostat (hypothalamus). The hypothalamus/thermostat then turns off the furnace (the release of CRF is inhibited, which decreases the pituitary's release of ACTH, which slows the adrenal's release of cortisol). When the room temperature (cortisol) drops, the thermostat turns the furnace back on (with less cortisol to inhibit them, the hypothalamus and thus the pituitary are turned back on, and once again they stimulate the adrenals' release of cortisol). Thus, the CRF from the hypothalamus stimulates the pituitary, and the pituitary's ACTH stimulates the adrenal cortex. In turn, the cortisol from the adrenal cortex inhibits the hypothalamus, which is the negative feedback part of the loop.

The **gonadotropic releasing hormone (GnRH)** causes certain pituitary cells to release either one of two hormones into the bloodstream: **luteinizing hormone (LH)** or **follicle stimulating hormone (FSH).** LH and FSH stimulate the gonads, as illustrated in Figure 6.4. In turn, the T, E, and P released from the gonads act back on the hypothalamus (and also directly back on the pituitary) to inhibit the release of GnRH, LH, and FSH. This is the negative feedback loop for the gonads.

Ovulation in females requires **positive feedback.** If E reaches a sufficiently high level, the feedback switches from negative to positive. During positive feedback, E no longer inhibits the hypothalamus and pituitary but actually

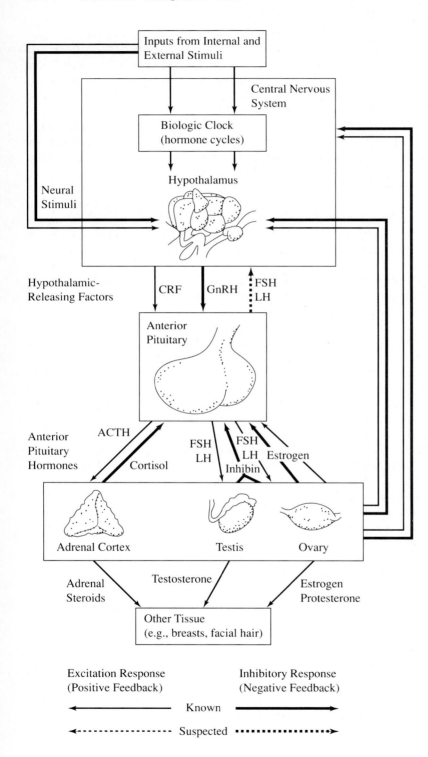

FIGURE 6.4 *Positive and Negative Feedback in the Neuroendocrine System*
Both types of feedback are suggested in the schema, indicating the relationships among its components: the central nervous system, hypothalamus, anterior pituitary, and target glands and tissues. Hormone secretion is regulated by a balance of stimulatory (fine lines, positive feedback) and inhibitory (thick lines, negative feedback) effects. FSH = folicle stimulating hormone; GnRH = gonadotropic releasing hormones; LH = luteinizing hormone; ACTH = adrenocorticotropic hormone; CRF = corticotropin releasing factor.

Source: Modified with permission. D. T. Krieger and J. C. Hughes (eds.), *Neuroendocrinology*. HP Publishing Company, publishers of *Hospital Practice*. Illustration by Albert Miller.

stimulates both organs. FSH and LH levels therefore increase markedly, and the increase in LH leads to **ovulation,** or the release of one or more eggs from the female's ovaries. Positive feedback occurs only if: (1) the brain is capable of responding to high E levels with an increase in FSH and LH; and (2) the E level is above a threshold, or high enough to trigger the positive instead of the negative feedback.

Normally, only females ovulate and so only females display positive feedback. However, whether the *ability* to display positive feedback is sexually dimorphic depends on the species. The brain of the normal adult male rat is incapable of positive feedback (very high levels of E do not increase LH or FSH in his body). On the other hand, the brain of the normal adult male primate—including the human—is quite capable of this response.

This species difference in response to postpubertal hormones comes about because of differing effects of perinatal hormones. Perinatal E or T injections given to female mice or rats will change the structure of the hypothalamus, permanently rendering them incapable of positive feedback. Conversely, if a male is neonatally castrated, his hypothalamus will be capable of positive feedback (Corbier, 1985; Hutter & Gibson, 1988). Two facts about rats are important: (1) exposure to perinatal T or E permanently impairs the ability of the hypothalamus to respond to high levels of E with a surge of GnRH (no positive feedback) and (2) in the rodent, the hypothalamus is critically necessary for positive feedback.

Both male and female primate brains are capable of positive feedback. Under certain conditions, adult primate males, including the human, can show the positive-feedback surge of LH in response to an injection of E, even if those males had been exposed to normal male levels of perinatal T (Barbarino, De Marinis, & Mancini, 1983; Karsch, Dierschke, & Knobil, 1973). If adult male primates (but not males of

lower species) are given an ovarian transplant, they can have menstrual cycles and even ovulate (Norman & Spies, 1986).[13]

Primate males may be capable of positive feedback because the feedback loops through the pituitary are more important than are the loops through the hypothalamus. This is the reverse of what is true for rodents. The **preoptic area** (see Figure 6.3) controls the positive feedback in rats (and nonprimates), whereas in primates, basal (negative feedback) and surge release (positive feedback) of GnRH are largely controlled by the pituitary itself (Karsch, 1987). Pituitaries—unlike hypothalami—do not have a gender (are not sexually dimorphic) (Chappel, 1985; Pau et al., 1988; Ramirez, Feder, & Sawyer, 1984). Thus, the primate preoptic area is not necessary for positive feedback; instead, their pituitaries control positive feedback, with some "priming" from the VMH.

Although they are capable of it, primate males do not normally show positive feedback. They must be either castrated or given a series of E injections before they can show an increase in LH in response to a single, large E injection. Some hormone coming from the testes other than T evidently inhibits the positive feedback loop. This may be a hormone called **inhibin** (Dubey, Zeleznik, & Plant, 1987; Westfahl et al., 1984). Castration would, of course, remove inhibin, and E pretreatments might suppress the secretion of inhibin. As shown in Figure 6.4, inhibin is also secreted by the ovary. Inhibin specifically controls FSH, and not LH, so that the two hormones are under somewhat separate negative control systems (Rivier, Rivier, & Vale, 1986; McLachlan et al., 1989; Tsonis et al., 1988).

Thus, species differences in responses to perinatal and postpubertal hormones are to be expected. Female finches and canaries respond differently to adult androgen injections. Rodents and primates have different systems for controlling positive feedback, leading to differences in responses to postpubertal and to perinatal hormone manipulations. In both species, the structure of the hypothalamus is permanently altered by the presence of perinatal T (or one of its metabolites). Since positive feedback in the rodent depends on its hypothalamus, perinatal T renders the normal adult male brain permanently incapable of responding to high levels of E with a surge of LH. In the primate, the positive feedback is controlled by the pituitary, so the normal adult male *can* experience an ovulatory surge of LH.

Variability within a Species

Different members of a species, because of having different genes, will have different hormone sensitivities. This demonstrates that many hormone effects are sex limited, changing the activities of various genes. Before a given organism can display a given sex-limited trait, it must have the relevant gene.

The genetics of hormone sensitivities. Table 6.1 presents some examples of the genetics of sex-limited behaviors, including **infanticide** (Svare & Mann, 1981). Few virgin female mice kill young, but 30 percent of the males of one strain of mice, versus 80 percent of the males of another strain, do so. Castrating the adult males of either strain inhibited pup killing, and T injections increased the behavior to normal levels. Adult T injections also increased the number of females who would kill young. However, perinatal injections of T suppressed adult infanticide.

These data can be placed in an evolutionary context. The strain whose males have the lowest adult levels of T do the most pup killing. Presumably they also have low perinatal levels of T, accounting for their higher pup-killing tendencies. But they are also very sensitive to postpubertal T, such that even their own low postpubertal levels can maximally stimulate their pup killing. On the other hand, the males with higher levels of postpubertal T can block

pregnancies in fertilized females, evidently by emitting odors that cause females to abort. However, males with low levels of T cannot block pregnancies. Maybe their high levels of pup killing are an evolutionarily stable reproductive strategy. Since they cannot "kill" the offspring of other males before the birth of those offspring, males with low T kill them after birth instead.[14]

Types of hormones and types of behaviors. Another example of variability within a species is how the different kinds of hormones covary with the different kinds of aggression. Mice have two separate brain circuits controlling aggression—one more sensitive to postpubertal E than to T (the E-pathway) and one more sensitive to postpubertal T than to E (the T-pathway). Perinatal E exposure increases the brain's ability to respond to changes in adult hormone levels, but only for the E-pathway. Conversely, perinatal T exposure increases the adult hormone sensitivity only of the T-pathway (Simon & Whalen, 1987). These two pathways control slightly different kinds of aggression.

Sexual behaviors in rats also show complex hormone sensitivities that vary according to strain, type of hormone (E, T, or DHT), and type of sexual behavior (masculine mounting, feminine sexual behavior or lordosis, and feminine invitational behavior) (Dunlap & Sridaran, 1988; Gladue, 1984; Hart, 1979; Södersten et al., 1986; Turkenburg et al., 1988). Probably it would be safest to conclude that variability is the rule and that DHT, T, and E all cooperate in the perinatal and postpubertal hormonal control of sexual behaviors. For example, T increases the brain's ability to aromatize T into E in adult as well as developing male rats; thus, changes in T will change the brain's E levels. E also increases the number of androgen receptors in the brain (MacLusky et al., 1988).

TABLE 6.1 *Examples of the Genetics of Hormone Sensitivity*

Effect	Species/Sex	References
Genetic Control of Hormone Level		
Estimated heritabilities: E = .47 to .76 Free T = .34 to .43 DHT = .02 to .12 T/DHT = .42 T = .03 to .26	Human males	Meikle, Bishop, Stringham, & West, 1987; Meikle, Stanish, Taylor, Edwards, & Bishop, 1982
Adrenal androgen levels are also heritable	Human males	Rotter, Wong, Lifrak, & Parker, 1985
Interindividual variability greater than intraindividual heritability	Human males	Couwenbergs, Knussman, & Christiansen, 1986
Adrenal and testicular T levels are related: $r = +.595$	Human males	Parker & Lifrak, 1981
Consistent strain differences in E levels	Sheep females	Wheeler, Baird, Land, & Scaramuzzi, 1977
Genetic Control of Sexual Dimorphism		
Degree of sexual dimorphism in tyrosine hydroxylase activity in substantia nigra, corpus striatum (greater in males) varied with strain	Mouse	Vadász, Baker, Fink, & Reis, 1985
Male rats have higher perinatal androgen levels (and greater sex differences in levels) than do male hamsters	Hamsters versus rats	Vomachka & Lisk, 1986
Genetic Control of Perinatal Hormone Effects		
Effects of perinatal T on aggression depend on strain	Mice females	Vale, Ray, & Vale, 1972; Michard-Vanheée, 1988
Effects of perinatal T on feminine sexual behavior depend on strain tested	Mice females	Vale, Ray, & Vale, 1973
Genetic Control of Postpubertal Hormone Effects		
Sensitivity of feminine sexual behavior to E injections varies with strain	Guinea pig females	Goy & Jakaway, 1959
Sensitivity of masculine sexual behavior to castration and later hormone injections varies with strain	Mice males	Clemens et al., 1988; McGill & Manning, 1976; Wee, Weaver, & Clemens, 1988
Sensitivity of aggression to injection of P varies with strain	Mice females	Svare, 1988

T = testosterone; DHT = dihydrotestosterone; E = estradiol; P = progesterone

Environmental Modifiers

Environmental events can either mimic or reverse the effects of hormones (see documentation in Hoyenga & Hoyenga, 1993). The environmental setting can also affect the degree of hormone sensitivity that any behavior will display. For example, Chapter 1 described how perinatal sex hormones affected male rats' adult sexual behavior by affecting both the scent of their urine and how long they took to respond to their mother licking their external genitals. Licking then directly affected their adult sexual behaviors.

Intrauterine position. Variations in fetuses' positions within a mother's uterus can affect some of their sexually dimorphic adult behaviors (see Hoyenga & Hoyenga, 1993). This obviously is relevant only when more than one fetus can be in the same uterus, or, in the case of many species, when more than one sex can be found in a given horn of the uterus. Whether a fetus is between two males or between two females affects the perinatal hormone levels to which that fetus is exposed. Although females are often masculinized and defeminized by intrauterine proximity to males, intrauterine position may also affect behaviors other than gender-related behaviors.

Prenatal stress. Prenatal stress advances the normal surge of T in neonatal male mice by 24 hours and increases the level of T found in females. It also leads to the feminization and demasculinization of several kinds of gender-related behaviors in males and to the masculinization and defeminization of females (see Hoyenga & Hoyenga, 1993). The pregnant female is usually stressed by being exposed, on several different days of her pregnancy, to a combination of restraint, heat, and bright lights. Giving the mother a drug that blocks the effects of one of the major stress hormones[15] also blocks the effects of stress on her offspring. The mother's stress hormones cross the placenta and can affect the fetal development of her offspring. However, since prenatal hormones do not seem to affect the sexual anatomies of prenatally stressed fetuses (vom Saal et al., 1990), stress may have developmental effects separate from its effects on hormone levels.

The evolutionary implications of prenatal stress may be found in the ways in which it affects adult organisms' responses to stress as well as their reproductive behaviors. That is, using the model of epigenetic development, prenatal stress would lead to the development of different reproductive strategies. These strategies might be ones that would be more appropriate for the extremely stressful environment in which that organism might have to mature and reproduce. In fact, prenatally stressed offspring do, as adults, have different responses to stress (see Hoyenga & Hoyenga, 1993; Fride et al., 1986).

Prenatal stress, the size of the sexually dimorphic part of the preoptic hypothalamus (SDN-POA), and adult hormone levels were all found to be interrelated in one study (Anderson et al., 1986). The males who were sexually inactive as adults had lower T levels than did the sexually active males. The correlation between adult T levels and masculine sexual behavior was $+.80$ for prenatally stressed males and $+.60$ for control males. The correlation between the size of the SDN-POA and adult masculine sexual activity was $+.77$ for stressed males and $+.90$ for control males, and the correlation between size of the SDN-POA and adult T level was $+.87$ for stressed males and $+.60$ for control males.

Prenatal stress also affects human offspring (Joffe et al., 1985; Oakley, 1985; Ramsey, Abell, & Baker, 1986; Reeb et al., 1987; Stott, 1971; Van den Bergh et al., 1989). A mother's anxiety can increase the motor activity of her fetus, and mothers with either very high or very low levels of anxiety tend to have babies who are less physiologically and behaviorally healthy than do mothers with moderate anxiety levels.

The mother who is stressed by lack of social support or by exposure to quarreling families can also affect her offspring. The best documented outcome is a decrease in birth weight, itself a major risk factor for later problems in the child. Stott (1971) demonstrated that social stress can also lead to mental and physical problems, at least in certain susceptible children.

Situational determinants of hormone levels.

How exercise affects T levels depends on physical condition, gender, duration of exercise (short term versus endurance), and type of exercise (running versus swimming) (see Hoyenga & Hoyenga, 1993). Active muscles use T, and exercise increases the rate at which gonads product T. In females (except when they are swimming), production rate keeps pace with rate of use. But for males and longer duration exercise, production rate falls behind rate of use (because males have greater use due to greater muscle volume?) and so T levels can fall. Moreover, physical conditioning can increase the basal levels of T in females but decrease them in males, especially if the conditioning is particularly strenuous.

These relationships should affect how one interprets hormone-behavior covariations. Sometimes a covariation occurs because a hormone causes the behavior, and sometimes the behavior causes the hormone. Or maybe the same situation that causes the behavior also, separately, causes the gonad to change the rate at which it produces sex hormones. Even more likely, the relationship between experience and hormone may be cyclical or reciprocal (see Hoyenga & Hoyenga, 1993).

Prior experience modifies hormone-behavior relationships.

In some cases, if the organism has prior experience with the behavior being measured, this can decrease the sensitivity of that behavior to later hormone manipulations (see Hoyenga & Hoyenga, 1993). If this proves to be true of humans, adults would respond only slowly and indirectly to hormone changes because of their extensive past experiences. In other cases, a behavior changed when a hormone did only if the animals had been given a special prior experience. Experience with competition may affect the degree to which aggression will later covary with T levels.

Situational modifiers of hormone-behavior relationships.

Castration or hormone injections may lead to certain behaviors only in certain situations (see Hoyenga & Hoyenga, 1993). Evolutionary theory would predict this, since sex differences evolve in response to specific pressures coming from specific environmental features. This means that it makes little sense to say that, for example, T always increases aggression in both sexes of all species. Some forms of aggression are not controlled by T. Only the kinds elicited by certain situations such as intermale competitions will be sensitive to current T levels, and then only in those types of testing situations.

The way in which the hormone changes of the menstrual cycle affect feminine sexual behaviors in female primates depends critically on the social conditions of the test. Hormone changes lead to changes in sexual behaviors only for female primates living in larger social groupings; there is little hormone-behavior covariation if the primates are housed just as male-female pairs. You ought to think about this in terms of epigenetic development and monogamous versus multimale/multifemale mating systems. Are primates prepared, evolutionarily speaking, to form both types of mating systems, depending on current conditions?

Timing Effects

Hormones often have different effects depending on when and how their levels are changed. The effects of hormone timing will be divided into two sections: life-cycle timing, and short-term timing within the testing situation itself.

Sensitive period effects. One sensitive period for hormone effects is the perinatal period. Even within this period, different behaviors (different parts of the brain) have different sensitive periods. Furthermore, variability both within and between species is to be expected. For example, some behaviors in the rhesus macaque are masculinized by prenatal T treatments from days 40 through 64 of gestation, and other behaviors are masculinized by T treatments from days 115 through 139 (Goy, Bercovitch, & McBrair, 1988). Similarly, in rats, different behaviors are affected by prenatal versus neonatal treatments with T (Hoepfner & Ward, 1988; Sachs & Thomas, 1985). Feminine sexual behavior in rats may be more suppressed by neonatal than by prenatal treatments, whereas masculine sexual behavior may be more facilitated by prenatal than by neonatal treatments in rats. In ferrets, just the reverse pattern of sensitive periods may be true (Yahr, 1988).

The period right after birth might be another sensitive period. For example, in rats, the first hour or so after birth may be a time when the size of the SDN-POA and also adult sexual behaviors are especially sensitive to hormone levels (Corbier, 1985; Corbier, Roffi, & Rhoda, 1983; Roffi et al., 1987; also see Chapter 7). The first few days after birth may also be important for primates (Epple, Alveario, & St. Andre, 1987; Pomerantz, Goy, & Roy, 1986).

Puberty may be a second sensitive period for both rats and primates (less information is known concerning other species). Whether hormones are present during the time of puberty, and which hormones are present, has durable effects on the adult animal's behaviors. This includes sexual behaviors, parental behaviors, partner preferences, and activity in an open field (fear? curiosity?) (Brand & Slob, 1988; De Jonge et al., 1988; Gibber & Goy, 1985; vom Saal & Finch, 1988).

Short-term timing. Sometimes the sensitivity of a given behavior to a given hormone depends on the time of day the hormone is given (Yahr, 1988) or the way in which the hormone levels change over hours and days (Jones, McEwen, & Pfaff, 1988; Takahashi, 1990; Williams, 1987). Michael, Zumpe, and Bonsall (1984) also found that how much T *varied* over the day was more important to the sexual activities of male rhesus monkeys displayed than were their *average* levels of T. The more that daytime and nighttime T levels differed from each other, the less sexual behavior the male displayed.

Sex hormones, gonadotropic hormones, and GnRh are all secreted episodically, in pulses. In primates, gonadotropin pulse amplitude increases just before puberty (Bercu et al., 1983). In human females, the pulses of LH occur every one to three hours, with the number of pulses per hour and their size varying over the course of the menstrual cycle (Frohman, 1980; Sollenberger et al., 1990). In human females who have stopped menstruating, treatment with a surge of GnRH every 60 minutes can more effectively restore fertility than can treatments that are spaced 120 minutes apart (Filicori et al., 1989). Injections of T that cause irregular changes in T levels over days will increase the sexual behaviors of castrated adult male rats more than will injections of the same amount of hormone delivered in a more constant fashion (Taylor, Bardgett, & Weiss, 1990). However, constant hormone levels are more effective for restoring normal levels of aggression in these castrated males than are irregularly varying levels.

Nonlinear Effects

Until recently, it was assumed that within the physiological range of sex hormones, there was a critical threshold for any given behavior. If an organism's sex hormones fell below that critical threshold, the organism would be deficient in hormone-sensitive behaviors. On the other hand, if hormone levels were any where above the critical threshold levels, further increases in hormones were assumed to have no effect on behavior. Thus, giving a male higher than threshold levels of T was not supposed to give him higher than normal levels of sexual behaviors.

Recently, however, researchers have begun to question these assumptions. Sexual behavior might not always be directly related to hormone levels because sexual behavior is sensitive to timing and patterning effects (see section above). Researchers are also now finding evidence that, at least in some situations, variations of T within the normal range can affect masculine sexual behavior in male rats and humans (Hart, 1983; Malmnäs, 1977; O'Carroll & Bancroft, 1984; Taylor, Weiss, & Rupich, 1985). For example, Albert and his colleagues (Albert et al., 1990) found that as T levels were increased in castrated adult rats, at least up to the highest physiological level, their aggression also increased. However, increasing T levels above those normally seen in any adult male rat did not increase aggression any further. Pharmacological hormone levels might have qualitatively as well as quantitatively different effects. Also, maybe the ways of measuring sexual behavior are inadequate to pick up the subtle, but evolutionarily very important, effects of varying T levels on masculine sexual behavior (Hart, 1983).

In multimale/multifemale mating systems, where the dominant male does *not* perform most of the copulations, most of the males' reproductive competition with each other is postreproductive. After copulating, male rats plant seminal plugs in the vaginal tracts of females. These plugs make it harder for the sperm of a later-copulating male to reach the female's eggs. Higher levels of T might lead to better plugs and/or to greater efficiency in displacing the plugs left by previous males. Even in primates, including the human, mating systems might affect how much sperm is released per ejaculation; if the mating system were polygynous, an increased sperm production rate would help the male compete with other males for reproductive success (Harvey & May, 1989).

Dosage effects of perinatal hormone levels have also been examined (Feder, 1984; Gorski, 1985). The higher the dose of E or T given to a neonatal female rat, the more masculinized and defeminized the female is when tested as an adult. However, the effects of phamacological doses of T on the perinatal development of the male are less clear. Sometimes there is no apparent effect on his behaviors, but most frequently he seems feminized and demasculinized (Sachs & Thomas, 1985), suggesting nonlinear effects. In some cases, perinatal hormone effects are nonlinear at the molecular level as well as at the behavioral level. Low E doses increase the response of certain brain neurons (some of the ones that use dopamine as a transmitter substance) to amphetamines, whereas high doses inhibit the response (Ramirez & Dluzen, 1987). Since the effects of hormones on transmitter responses can be curvilinear, nonlinear effects of sex hormones on behavior might similarly be expected.

SUMMARY

Testes masculinize and defeminize during both the perinatal and postpubertal periods. However, there are many subtleties underlying that deceptively simple fact. Perinatal masculinization and defeminization are separate processes; one can occur in the absence of the other. Hormone sensitivities, the degree to which variations in some behavior are associated with changes of hormone levels, vary according to the three dimensions of hormone effects. Sensitivity may have more or less of a critical/sensitive period, sensitivity may lead to permanent or only to more temporary effects, and sensitivity involves either or both the structure and the function of many organs of the body, including the genitals and the brain.

Hormone sensitivity can be studied by actively manipulating the independent variable (hormone level) and randomly assigning the various subjects to the different hormone level groups, or by correlating hormone levels with behavioral levels. The active manipulation can involve either gonadectomies or hormone injections (or both). For ethical reasons, most of the active manipulation/random assignment studies have involved nonhuman subjects. Thus, the human research is subject to more internal validity problems, including the fact that not only do hormones affect our experiences, but our experiences affect our hormones. On the other hand, hormone manipulation studies sometimes have external validity problems.

Hormones affect neurons either by influencing their genetic activity or by nongenomic effects on their membranes. Sex hormones affect neurons' growth, survival, biochemistry, electrical activity, and responses to transmitter substances. All of these occur during both the perinatal and postpubertal periods.

Six principles were described: (1) T, or one of its metabolites—E or DHT—defeminizes and masculinizes the brains and bodies of males both during the perinatal periods and after puberty; (2) species differ in hormone sensitivities; (3) individuals within species differ in hormone sensitivities; (4) the environment modifies hormone-behavior covariations; (5) hormone effects often depend critically on timing; and (6) hormones often have nonlinear effects.

The emphasis should be on variability across species and among individuals within a species. Because of the variability and because environment modifies hormone-behavior relationships, biological determinism is an inappropriate way to describe hormone effects. Evolutionary concepts—and the concept of epigenetic development, which emphasizes the role of the environment in the organism's lifetime developmental processes—provide much more useful descriptions of hormone sensitivities.

ENDNOTES

1. Bardin & Catterall, 1981; Dieringer, Lamartiniere, & Lucifer, 1980; Jean-Faucher et al., 1987; Lui & Lucier, 1980; Mooradian, Morley, & Korenman, 1987; Pak, Tsim, & Cheng, 1984, 1985; Tsim, Pak, & Cheng, 1985.

2. The word *cortex* means the outside portion of something. The adrenal cortex is the outside portion of the adrenal gland (just as the cortex of the brain is on the outside of the brain).

3. **Gonadectomize** means to remove the gonads from. It will be used synonymously with **castration.** **Ovariectomy** means specifically to gonadectomize (or castrate) a female, whereas **orchidectomy** means to gonadectomize a male. Removing the gonads from an animal any time after birth is relatively untraumatic and is done under anesthetic.

4. However, for reasons just described, equivalent hormone doses do not guarantee equivalent blood levels of those hormones.

5. Diffusion occurs because of osmotic forces or osmosis—the movement of molecules of a substance in a solution from a region of high concentration to a region of low concentration.

6. However, the effects of hormones on oncogenes may occur much more rapidly (Spelsberg et al., 1989).

7. **Cytoplasm** refers to the substances found inside the membrane and outside the nucleus of any cell.

8. Bayer, Yackel, & Puri, 1982; Cowan, Fawcett, O'Leary, & Stanfield, 1984; Finlay & Slattery, 1983; Hoyenga & Hoyenga, 1988; Nowakowski, 1987; Oppenheim, 1981; Rakic, 1985a, 1985, 1988; Seress, 1985.

9. Dopamine is a transmitter found, among other places, in the **limbic system,** or in the emotional-controlling areas of the brain.

10. Heart cells: de Beer & Keizer, 1982; electrical activity in neurons: Dufy et al., 1979; Moss & Dudley, 1984; Nabekura et al., 1986; Oomura et al., 1986; Schiess, Joëls, & Shinnick-Gallagher, 1988; Sibbald, Sirett, & Hubbard, 1987; Teyler et al., 1980.

11. Although it was thought for many years that after birth no new cells appeared in the brains of higher animals, exceptions are now being discovered. The formation of new neurons have been discovered in the cortex and hippocampus of adult rodents (Bayer, 1985; Kaplan, 1985). Kaplan has argued that new neurons may also form in the adult primate brain, but Rakic (1985b) has disagreed.

12. Adrenocorticotropic hormone: *tropic* means going toward; *adreno* refers to the adrenal gland; *cortico* refers to the cortex, or outside portion of the adrenal gland. Literally, the name of the hormone means: the hormone that goes toward the cortex of the adrenal gland.

13. Before primate males can have babies, an artificial uterus must be developed. To put it another way, if an artificial uterus is developed, and if ovarian transplant donors could be found, someday males may be able to have babies.

14. Females will often copulate with multiple males while pregnant; that copulation inhibits the tendency of those males to kill her offspring when born, regardless of strain. This would be females' responses to both those male strategies.

15. These stress hormones are the endorphins; naltrexone blocks the effects of endorphins on behavior and so is frequently used to explore the possible effects of endorphins.

CHAPTER 7

SEX DIFFERENCES
IN PERINATAL HORMONES

INTRODUCTION
BASIC TERMS AND CONCEPTS OF PERINATAL HORMONE EFFECTS
SEX DIFFERENCES IN PERINATAL HORMONE LEVELS
SEX DIFFERENCES IN THE BRAIN
HUMAN PERINATAL HORMONE SYNDROMES
SUMMARY

> *For the human, it is conceivable that effects of steroid hormones on behavior and mood may be even more widespread than for nonhuman species, partly* because *of some consequences associated with a high degree of neocortical development. Emergent properties of neocortical activity such as consciousness . . . may provide an even richer substrate for hormone-behavior interactions than is the case for nonhuman species.*
> —H. H. Feder (1984, p. 191)

In the September 4, 1979, issue of the National Enquirer, *the headline on page 3 read, "The Village Where 38 Girls Turned into Boys." One part of the article said that "the mothers of the village thought they had given birth to little girls—so imagine their confusions and trauma when their children turned into boys." These children were XY and had testes, but were born looking like girls because their bodies were relatively insensitive to their own androgens. Nevertheless, the very large pubertal surge of androgens that they all experienced masculinized their appearance—including an enlargement of their penises—and most of them changed their gender and their gender-role* identity from female and feminine to male and masculine. Was their ability to make this shift in any way related to their prenatal androgen levels? Could they change identities at puberty because they already had "masculine" brains?

During the perinatal period, testes are more active than ovaries. Testicular hormones such as testosterone (T), or one of the metabolites of T, masculinize and defeminize the brains and bodies of males. Perhaps paradoxically, the great development of the neocortex (cerebral cortex) in humans may have produced an increased—though also increasingly elusive—sensitivity to hormonal influences. Our very sense of our own gender identity and gender-role identity may be subtly influenced. This chapter describes sex differences in perinatal hormones, emphasizing humans wherever possible.

INTRODUCTION

Baum (1990) eloquently described the history of research that explored how sex differences in the brain were related to the sex differences in perinatal hormone levels. As he pointed out, prior to this research, the basic assumption was that there were no important sex differences to be found in the brains of any mammals. The first report of microscopic sex differences in a mammalian brain was by Dorner and Staudt in 1969 (see references in Baum, 1990). Since organisms' behaviors are durably affected by what hormones are present during their fetal development, as discovered by Young and colleagues in 1959 (see references in Baum, 1990), that also suggests that fetal hormones do change the brain.

These early findings led to the research described in this chapter. First, the basic concepts, techniques, and terminology of hormone effects on the brain are described. The sex differences in perinatal hormone levels and effects are then described. T and its metabolites lead to sex differences in the brain, including the sexually dimorphic nucleus of the preoptic area (SDN-POA) described in Chapter 6. Finally, some possible outcomes of variations in perinatal hormone levels for humans are described.

BASIC TERMS AND CONCEPTS OF PERINATAL HORMONE EFFECTS

As Moore (1985) pointed out, "It is to be hoped that in future research there will be less emphasis on documenting sex differences and their origin in perinatal hormones and greater em-phasis on studies of exactly how hormones have contributed to the development of the be-havior" (p. 44). Since research has not yet fulfilled this hope, you will have to actively create ideas and hypotheses for yourselves, based on the cellular effects and principles described in the last chapter. Although cellular and behavioral levels of hormonal effects have not yet been connected, researchers now know what to look for. Maybe some of you will find the links that are needed.

Effects of Hormones on Development

As Table 7.1 describes, of the five phases of biological gender development, phases 2 through 4 depend on perinatal hormone levels. Males are normally masculinized and defem-inized by the hormones coming from their testes. The fifth phase will be discussed in Chapter 8.

Prior to the first developmental phase, males and females develop identically. In the first gender-differentiated phase, chromosomal gender determines how gonads differentiate (see Chapter 5). In that phase, as in the phases con-trolled by sex hormone levels, the inherent developmental process is feminine. At each phase, something has to be added to get mas-culinization and defeminization.

Basic Developmental Processes

Prior to the third month, both sexes develop **Wolffian structures** and **Muellerian structures.** During the second phase, if androgens are pres-ent, the Wolffian structures differentiate into vas deferens, seminal vesicles, and an ejac-ulatory duct. Testes also secrete another hor-mone, the **Muellerian inhibiting hormone (MIH).** MIH makes the Muellerian structures degenerate in fetal males. Not only do fetal females not have testes, their ovaries are relatively inactive, and so females do not have

TABLE 7.1   *Five Phases of Biological Gender Development in Humans*

Phase	Causal Agent	Effects in Males	Effects in Females
1. Gonadal	Y chromosome	Testes	Ovaries
2. Internal sexual organs	Androgens and MIS*	Wolffian structures develop into ejaculatory duct, etc.; Muellerian structures degenerate	Wolffian structures degenerate; Muellerian structures develop into uterus, fallopian tubes, etc.
3. External sexual organs	Androgens	Scrotal sacs and penis	Labia and clitoris
4. Brain	Androgens	Masculine organization	Feminine organization
5. Puberty	Male and female sex hormones	Muscles, body hair, pubic and axillary hair	Subcutaneous fat, breasts, pubic and axillary hair

*Muellerian inhibitory substance

the male-typical androgen level. Because of this, the Wolffian structures in females degenerate. Since the lack of testes means that females lack MIH as well, a female's Muellerian structures develop into a uterus, Fallopian tubes, and the upper portion of a vagina.

Phases 3 through 5 all depend solely on the level of androgens present. Starting around the fifth fetal month, the third phase begins. The presence of male-typical levels of androgens cause a penis and scrotal sacs to develop in fetal males. The fourth phase occurs before, during, and after this phase: the presence of androgens leads the fetus to develop a masculinized and defeminized brain. The lack of male-typical levels of androgens means that a female does not develop masculine structures. Instead, she develops a vagina, a clitoris, labia, and a female brain during the second through the fourth phases.

Some developing fetuses experience one or more abnormalities during these developmental processes. Going over these abnormalities

will help you understand the nature and implications of the causal developmental processes just described. For example, in fetuses that suffer from Turner's syndrome (see Chapter 5), their ovaries first develop (they have no Y) and then degenerate (because they lack the second X). Despite the lack of functional ovaries, Turner's syndrome people develop normal female internal and external sex organs, proving that the normal female development of these organs depends on the absence of masculine levels of androgens.

Abnormalities of the androgen receptor (see Chapter 5) have their greatest effects on a fetus with a Y chromosome. Such fetuses develop normal testes and so have normal masculine levels of androgens during both fetal development as well as after puberty. Since the androgens have no effect (or only a greatly reduced effect) on any part of the body, the external sex organs, brain, and puberty are all feminized. This person will have neither male nor female internal organs. Since androgens are rendered impotent by the lack of receptor, the Wolffian structures degenerate. Since MIH is still present and acting normally, the Muellerian structures also degenerate.

The Sex Hormones of Fetal Differentiation

The fetal testes are responsible for much of the sex hormones secreted. Testes secrete mostly androgens, but also some feminine sex hormones. Although T is the major androgen secreted by fetal testes, T is converted into other sex hormones by enzymes found in body cells, including many brain cells (Hutchison & Steimer, 1984). In adult rats and fetal humans, most dihydrotestosterone (DHT) is formed from T by cells outside the testes, but in perinatal rats and adult humans, significant levels of DHT are secreted by the testes themselves (Miller, 1988; Preslock, 1980). The adrenal glands of both sexes also secrete androgens and estrogens (E). The fetal ovaries may be somewhat active in producing E, though perhaps only enough to affect the development of the ovaries themselves.

The placenta and the mother's gonads are additional sources of hormones affecting the fetus. The placenta converts some androgens into estrogens such as estradiol and it also secretes progesterone (P). Hormones from the mother also cross over and circulate in the bloodstream of the fetus. In fact, although in primates and many other mammals the placenta is the major source of P during pregnancy, for rats during the last half of pregnancy, the mother's ovaries are the major source (vom Saal & Finch, 1988). In the human, the primary sources of E are the fetal and maternal adrenal glands.

Testosterone, estradiol, and the aromatization hypothesis. The **aromatization hypothesis** says that the defeminizing and masculinizing

actions of T on the brain, both perinatally and postpubertally, occur only after brain cells aromatize the T into E. Thus, E would be the hormone most critically important for masculinzing brain development (Naftolin & MacLusky, 1984). If so, in some species, males' brains may be masculinized and defeminized by a feminine hormone.

Several lines of evidence support the aromatization hypothesis (Hutchison & Steimer, 1984; Jost, 1983). (1) Neonatal injections of E can defeminize and masculinize the brains and behaviors of female rodents in much the same way as neonatal injections of T. (2) Injections of E can restore sexual behaviors in castrated adult male rodents in much the same way as T in injections. (3) Androgens that cannot be aromatized into E cannot masculinize or defeminize behavior either perinatally or postpubertally. (4) Many nerve cells have the aromatizing enzyme that converts T into E. (5) When drugs that specifically block only the effect of E are given to neonatal male rats, these rats' behaviors are demasculinized and feminized in much the same way as after neonatal castrations. (6) Genetically male mice with androgen insensitivity have mostly masculinized and defeminized brains, presumably because the T aromatized into E still affected the brain even without androgen receptors.

However, as the rest of this chapter will document, E is not the only masculinizing and defeminizing hormone (Feder, 1984). Depending on species, part of the body, type of behavior, and stage of development, nonaromatizable androgens such as DHT, and sometimes even T itself, may be involved. For example, during the perinatal period of humans, T itself causes the development of the Wolffian structures, whereas DHT is probably critical to the development of external male sexual organs (Jost, 1983).

Progesterone. P is also present in rather high levels perinatally in both sexes. P is usually not said to be either consistently masculinizing or demasculinizing in its actions. However, it can affect brain anatomy and development and also adult behaviors when administered during the perinatal period, probably because it interacts with E and T. For example, P can oppose both the masculinizing and defeminizing effects of either T or E when either hormone is injected into perinatal rats (Beyer & Feder, 1987). Perinatal P can also increase the rate at which cells in the cortex of the neonatal rat grow new branches on their basal dendrites (Menzies, Drysdale, & Waite, 1982). Both neonatal non-human subjects and human fetuses have been exposed to various artificial progestins; these exposures sometimes have masculinizing and sometimes feminizing effects on the offsprings' behaviors, as will be described.

A hypothesis: estradiol is a general growth hormone and sexual specificity for perinatal brain effects is conferred by enzyme and receptor levels. Several theorists have suggested that E has growth functions in the perinatal and adult brain quite apart from any possible masculinizing and defeminizing effects (Döhler, 1986; Döhler et al., 1984; Toran-Allerand, 1980, 1984). In view of the growth-promoting effects of E already described, perhaps it acts as a general "tonic" for brain growth during the perinatal period.[1] Normal feminine development would also require normal feminine levels of perinatal E.

According to this hypothesis, sex differences in fetal development depend not only on hormone levels but also on the location of receptors and enzymes. Some parts of the brain in both sexes have the aromatizing enzymes present. These enzymes would be able to convert the T coming from the male testes to E, thus producing male-specific effects. Such areas would also have to have E receptors. Other sex-specific areas might have reducing enzymes and androgen receptors present. In other words, regulating which cells had which receptor and

enzyme genes active would determine the area-specific concentrations of sex hormones and thus could create sex differences.

Other brain areas, with or without E receptors, might be sensitive to the growth-promoting effects of perinatal E in both genders. For example, there are high levels of E receptors in the cortex of both sexes during the perinatal period, but the cerebral cortex of adults has only very low levels (MacLusky et al., 1976). When neonatal male rats were injected with either E or T, only E caused the pituitary to grow (Aguilar, Bellido, & Aguilar, 1987). Very high levels of E given to neonatal rats caused the cortex to mature faster (Heim & Timiras, 1963), and neonatal injections of E increased the rate at which some axons in the brain became myelinated (Curry & Heim, 1966). Furthermore, E has its greatest growth effect on the neurons in the cortex that interconnect with cells outside that particular area of the cortex. Rather than accelerate growth per se, neonatal E may speed up the normal neural maturation processes (Muñoz-Cueto, Garcia-Segura, & Ruiz-Marcos, 1990).

Variations in E activity across individuals and across species are consistent with this hypothesis. Although mutations of the androgen receptor are relatively commonly found, there are no mutant E receptors in living animals, suggesting that E effects are necessary for life to begin (Wilson & Agrawal, 1979). E levels are particularly high in mammalian fetuses as opposed to nonmammals. Mammals have relatively more fetal brain development as well as more aromatizing activity in their fetal brains than in their adult brains. In species whose brains grow throughout life, such as fishes and reptiles, aromatase activity also remains high throughout life (Callard, 1983).

Rats can also be treated perinatally with **tamoxifen,** which blocks the effect of E. Tamoxifen can feminize and demasculinize perinatal male rats, just as would be predicted by the aromatization hypothesis (by blocking the masculinizing and defeminizing effects of E). Tamoxifen also affects females, suggesting that some E is required for normal female brain development (Hancke & Döhler, 1984; Hines et al., 1987; Döhler, 1986; Döhler et al., 1984). Perinatally tamoxifen-treated females are both defeminized and demasculinized: all forms of secual behavior are suppressed. Similarly, if the rat mother's ovary is removed during her pregnancy (the pregnancy is then maintained by daily P injections), her female offspring are somewhat feminized. So the E coming from the other *is* important to normal female development, as was also suggested by other research (Weisz & Ward, 1980; Weizenbaum, Adler, & Ganjam, 1979; Witcher & Clemens, 1987). As will be described, the SDN-POA, which is normally larger in males, is even smaller in tamoxifen-treated than in normal females.

Is perinatal E active?   Most of perinatal E is attached to specific blood proteins (Rosner, 1990; Toran-Allerand, 1984; Westphal, 1986). The protein present in the bloodstream and brains of perinatal rodents is called **alpha-fetoprotein (AFP)** (Westphal, 1986). Adults have this hormone only in very small amounts, but in perinatal rats, there is a very high level of AFP to bind to the E molecules coming from their mothers. A similar protein is found in the bloodstreams of perinatal and adult humans: **sex hormone-binding globulin (SHBG)** (Rosner, 1990). Although SHBG binds more tightly to T than to E, the reverse is true of AFP. The hormones bound to both SHBG and to AFP are usually assumed to be inactive, not usable by cells. If so, AFP would protect the female brain from the masculinizing and defeminizing effects of E. Are both present simply to provide a "reserve" of hormones for use? This would also mean that the E present perinatally in the bloodstreams of both sexes would be inactive and therefore largely irrelevant to their brains' developments.

However, both AFP and SHBG might have roles to play in addition to (or instead of) the reserve function (Rosner, 1990). SHBG does bind to cells' membranes, and then hormones bind to SHBG. After this, the activity of the cells are altered. Is SHBG a temporary membrane-type of hormone receptor? SHBG may also play a role in transporting the hormones to the interior of cells, although there is as yet no direct evidence of this. The same might be true of AFP. In fact, AFP is found inside brain cells even though they do not manufacture it (see Toran-Allerand's references). This suggests that AFP is actually carrying the E into the fetal cells.

Another possibility is that SHBG and AFP may bind to the E that comes from the placenta or the maternal bloodstream, "storing it up," so that the neonatal brain is still being exposed to E even after birth. Since rodents have such short gestation periods and are born with brains still very sensitive to sex hormones, perhaps AFP evolved as a mechanism to ensure adequate E exposure even after birth for females who lack the active testes of their brothers.

Some evidence does suggest that AFP may facilitate a growth effect of E. If AFP is destroyed in perinatal rats, there are "gross neurological changes in 64% of the animals, including external hydrocephaly [water on the brain], equilibrium [inner ear] disturbances, and high excitatory states" (Mizejewski, Vonnegut, & Simon, 1980, p. 275). AFP is most densely located in brain areas that are not masculinized and defeminized, suggesting that AFP is associated with the generalized growth effect of E rather than its sexually dimorphic effects. Congenitally low levels of AFP lead to severe neurological defects.

Perinatal Hormones Affect Behavior

The behaviors most often used to index the effects of perinatal hormones on the brain are the masculine and feminine sexual behaviors displayed by mammals below the primate level. **Masculine sexual behaviors** include mounting, intromission, and ejaculation; **feminine sexual behaviors** include lordosis and feminine sexual invitation behaviors. **Lordosis** is the posture that nonprimate females assume when sexually interested, which makes it easier for males to mount them. Lordosis and mounting remain sexually dimorphic even when both genders are castrated as adults and given equivalent doses of postpubertal hormones.

Christensen and Gorski (1978) exposed neonatal female rats to E, T, or cholesterol (control) by inserting small gelatin capsules directly into a brain area. The capsules slowly released their hormone contents into the surrounding brain areas. This procedure eliminated any possible effects that perinatal hormone treatments might have on any part of the body other than the brain. The capsules were implanted on either the second or fifth day after birth into either the preoptic area, the interior hypothalamic area, the ventromedial hypothalamus (VMH), or the reticular formation (another control condition) (see Figure 6.2 in Chapter 6).

After puberty, the females were first castrated, given various prolonged hormone treatments, and then their sexual behaviors were tested. Feminine behaviors were tested by pairing the neonatally treated females with a stud male after the females had been given prolonged treatment with either E or E plus P. The same neonatally treated females, both after adult E treatment and then after a subsequent adult T treatment, had their masculine sexual behaviors tested. They were paired with test females brought into **heat** (maximum sexual receptivity) by hormone injections. Neither the cholesterol implants nor the implants made outside the VMH or preoptic areas had any effects on any adult sexual behaviors.

There were two major types of findings. First, neonatal preoptic implants increased masculine sexual behaviors. Giving a female a preoptic implant of either T or E increased adult mounting and intromissionlike behavior (intromission without a penis), compared to the untreated control females. In fact, there were no significant differences between the effects of T and E, which supports the aromatization hypothesis. Furthermore, both E and T injections induced mounting in these neonatally treated females when they were tested as adults. Masculine behavior was most strongly increased by day 2 implants, but was also somewhat increased by day 5 implants.

Second, feminine sexual behaviors were affected in different ways by preoptic versus VMH implants. Normal females show some lordosis in response to adult injections of E alone, but their lordosis was increased if a series of E injections was followed by a P injection. Neonatal implants of either E or T into the preoptic area increased the likelihood that the female would display lordosis in response to postpubertal injections of E alone, without P injections. This makes these neonatally treated females more like males in this regard. On the other hand, VMH implants of either E or T decreased the likelihood that the female would display lordosis in response to the combined E plus P treatment. Thus, the VMH normally controls lordosis and is usually defeminized in males by their neonatal T (probably after being converted into E). Feminine behaviors were affected only by day 2 and not by day 5 implants, suggesting that sensitivity to masculinization might last longer than sensitivity to defeminization (Timing Effects).

Another study demonstrated the role of sex hormones in an even more dramatic fashion. The preoptic areas of male neonatal rats were removed and implanted into the preoptic areas of neonatal female littermates (Arendash & Gorski, 1982). The preoptic areas would already have been masculinized by the males' perinatal T. After they reached adulthood, the sexual behaviors of the brain-transplant recipient female rats were tested. Their mounting behaviors were increased relative to the females given a sham surgery, but their lordosis behaviors were also increased! The increase in mounting was attributed to the females having been given a masculinized preoptic area. The increase in lordosis was related to the increased size of the preoptic area in the transplant recipients. The increased number of preoptic neurons would increase the total number of E receptors, which could explain the enhanced lordosis. Since the transplanted females had more E receptors, they responded more to the adult E injections.

SEX DIFFERENCES IN PERINATAL HORMONE LEVELS

In this and the following sections, discussion is limited to the three species about which there is the most information (rats) or which are most relevant to the present text (nonhuman primates and humans). As previously described, perinatal hormone effects depend on the levels of hormone-binding proteins also found in the blood. In humans, males have more SHBG than females do, but there are no sex differences in AFP levels in perinatal rats (see documentation in Hoyenga & Hoyenga, 1993). **Free E or T levels** refer to hormones not bound to either SHBG or AFP.

Perinatal Hormone Levels

There are consistent gender-related differences in perinatal hormone levels in rats, primates, and humans (see Hoyenga & Hoyenga, 1993). During some of the periods in which the brain is being formed (prenatal + neonatal for rats, midgestation for primates, and second/third trimesters for humans), males have significantly more T in their blood than do females. During at least part of those critical periods, all males have levels higher than those seen in any females. There is extensive variability seen within each gender, as well as strain differences in the degree of sex dimorphism: not all females are equally different from all males. The other sex hormones are less likely to be sexually dimorphic.

There is a neonatal surge of hormones in all three species (see Hoyenga & Hoyenga, 1993). In male rats, the surge affects the masculinization and defeminization of sexual behaviors (e.g., see Timing Effects in Chapter 6; Corbier, Roffi, & Rhoda, 1983; Roffi et al., 1987). The neonatal surge of T is larger in males than in females in all three species. However, since SHBG levels are also high in male newborn humans, males may not be exposed to such dramatically high free T levels as was first thought,[2] though they still have higher free T levels than do female neonates. The neonatal surge of E is not sexually dimorphic. Although the surge of P has sometimes been reported to be higher in female than in male rats, it is higher in male than in female humans.

Perinatal Levls of Brain Receptors and Enzymes

Most studies have measured what researchers call **cytosolic receptors.** In view of what is now known about the cellular effects of hormones, this is best interpreted as being an index of receptors that are not currently bound to sex hormone molecules. These studies thus measure cells' capacity to bind hormones and therefore their ability to experience genomic effects. Since both female and male brains can respond to perinatal E or T, sex differences in cystosolic receptors would not be expected and are rarely found (see Hoyenga & Hoyenga, 1993). More occupied, or nuclear, E and A (androgen) receptors are found in males than in females, because males have higher T levels. This T is then converted into E, which binds to and occupies E receptors.

If some brain cells in males are normally masculinized and defeminized by E, the cells must have the enzymes necessary to convert T to E, as well as the relevant receptors. Fetal brains do have aromatizing enzymes in some areas critical for sexual and emotional behaviors, such as the preoptic area and the hypothalamus (see Hoyenga & Hoyenga, 1993).

Although the perinatal cerebral cortex does not seem to have much aromatizing activity in rats, both the cerebral cortex and the hippocampus of the neonatal primate do have aromatizing activity present. Thus, these areas, which are so important to cognitive processes, may be exposed to more E in primate males than in females. This could lead to sex differences in cortical and hippocampal anatomy and thus to sex differences in various cognitive processes (see Chapter 13). The presence of aromatizing enzyme in the hypothalamus and limbic areas and in the **association cortex** are worthy of special note.[3] The high levels of aromatizing enzyme and E receptors suggest that wherever the E comes from (aromatization from testicular T; secretion by maternal ovaries or placenta), it is important to the development of the primate brain, especially the cerebral cortex.

Curiously, there are no E receptors in adult cortex even though they are present in the perinatal cortex of both primates and rats (see Hoyenga & Hoyenga, 1993). In rats, the peak in cortical E receptors occurs at the same time as does the neonatal surge in sex hormones so that a dramatic rise in E receptors occurs right after birth. Females not only have higher levels but the difference between the right and left sides of the brain is opposite in the two sexes (more on the left side in males and more on the right in females: see documentation in Hoyenga & Hoyenga, 1993).

If some areas are to be masculinized and defeminized by DHT, their neurons must have both reducing enzymes and A receptors. Primate brains do have significant amounts of reducing enzymes, and the enzyme levels are higher in prenatal than in neonatal or adult brains (Hoyenga & Hoyenga, 1993). The level is particularly high in the corpus callosum, which interconnects the left and right sides of the cerebral cortex. Significant levels of reducing enzymes are also found all over the fetal human brain, and there are lower levels in females than in males.

Perinatal A receptors are more widespread in primate than in rat brains. Although rats have more E than A receptors, primates usually have equal levels of both receptors, except in the cortex where A receptors are relatively more numerous. The peak levels of A receptors occur at different developmental times in primate cortex (Hoyenga & Hoyenga, 1993) and hypothalamus. Figure 7.1 shows that A receptor levels in prenatal primate cortex depend jointly on gender and side of the brain. One thing to be noted is that although only males have consistent right-left differences, the females are very variable—some females have A receptor patterns very similar to those of males.

P receptors are found in the limbic system, hypothalamus, and cortex of perinatal rat brains (see Hoyenga & Hoyenga, 1993). Although cytosolic P receptors are higher in males, nuclear receptors are higher in females. The adult cortex has few P receptors, so those found in neonatal cortex might have some special significance.

SEX DIFFERENCES IN THE BRAIN

Despite years of controversy, sex differences in brain structures have been conclusively demonstrated, including in the human brain. Some of them are due to postpubertal hormones. The sex differences attributable to perinatal hormone differences often show differing types of hormone sensitivities across brain areas. To provide an example, the authors will contrast the developmental processes responsible for two sexually dimorphic areas of the CNS—the SDN-POA and the SNB (an area in the spinal cord). Sexually dimorphic areas in the human brain will also be discussed.

SDN-POA versus SNB

Two CNS areas that are sexually dimorphic in most species are the **sexually dimorphic nucleus of the preoptic area (SDN-POA)** and the **spinal**

FIGURE 7.1 *Lateralization of Cortical Androgen Receptors*

Androgen receptor levels in the frontal and temporal lobes of the fetal rhesus monkey cerebral cortex are described here. The dashed lines connect right- and left-side values in the individual subjects. Open bars are the means (averages) of the various side-gender groups.

Frontal Lobe Androgen Receptor

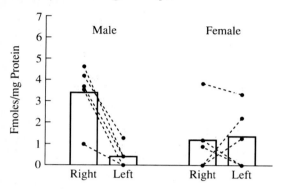

Temporal Lobe Androgen Receptor

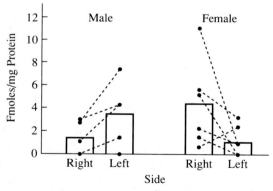

Source: From "Androgen Receptors Are Differentially Distributed between Right and Left Cerebral Hemispheres of the Fetal Male Rhesus Monkey" by Samuel A. Sholl and Kil L. Kim, 1990, *Brain Research, 516,* p. 123. Copyright 1990 by Elsevier Science Publishers. Reprinted by permission.

nucleus of the bulbocaverosus muscle (SNB) in the spine. Although the SDN-POA is masculinized by E (at least in rats), the SNB is masculinized by DHT.

Gorski and colleagues discovered the SDN-POA in 1978, and he described the history and context of the discovery in a review published ind 1984. There is a dramatic sex difference in the medial preoptic area of rats. The preoptic area in general controls hormone feedback loops and sexual and aggressive behaviors (Bermond, 1982; Edwards & Einhorn, 1986; Gorski, 1984; Hennessey, Wallen, & Edwards, 1986). One small part of that area with a dense collection of nerve cells is five times larger in the male rat than in the female: the male's area has more cells in it. In fact, brains can be "sexed" just by looking at this area. Gorski called this the SDN-POA.

The SDN-POA is involved in positive feedback and sexual activity (Preslock & McCann, 1987). Experimental damage to the SDN-POA produces a "marked and significant reduction of masculine sexual behavior (. . . mounting)" in female rats which had been induced to show high levels of male sexual behavior before the damage by means of chronic treatment with T (Turkenburg et al., 1988). Genetically obese male rats not only have impaired masculine sexual performances and motivations, but they have smaller than normal SDN-POAs (Young, Fleming, & Matsumoto, 1986). However, the sexual behaviors of hormonally normal male or female rats do not seem to be much affected by damage to the SDN-POA (Arendash & Gorski, 1983). The biochemistry of the rat's SDN-POA is also sexually dimorphic (Hammer, 1985, 1988; Jacobson, Arnold, & Gorski, 1987; Watson, Hoffman, & Wiegand, 1986).

The rat is not the only species in which the male SDN-POA is larger. In both quails and humans, at least some parts of the SDN-POA are larger in males (Allen et al., 1989; Swaab & Fliers, 1985; Swaab & Hofman, 1988; Ciglietti-Panzica et al., 1986). Dimorphisms in the preoptic area have also been discovered in gerbils, ferrets, guinea pigs, hamsters, mice, and primates (Ayoub, Greenough, & Juraska, 1983; Byne & Bleier, 1987; Commins & Yahr, 1984a, 1984b; Tobet, Zahniser, & Baum, 1986), but they are not always the same as those found in the rat. For example, contrary to what is seen in rats, part of the preoptic area of guinea pigs is twice as large in females as in males, whereas another part is 10 times larger in males. Also, the dimorphisms in guinea pigs, gerbils, and ferrets seem far more sensitive to postpubertal sex hormones than is true for rats.

Perinatal injections of either T or E can masculinize the rat SDN-POA. Across several different studies, pregnant rats were given various hormone injections and/or neonatal rats were castrated and/or given hormone injections (Döhler et al., 1984; Gorski, 1984; Rhees, Shryne, & Gorski, 1990a, 1990b; Tartelin & Gorski, 1988). As Figure 7.2 shows, males that had been neonatally castrated had smaller SDN-POAs than did normal males. Females given either perinatal E or T injections had larger SDN-POAs than did the untreated females. In fact, if females had been given either T or E both prenatally and neonatally, the size of their SDN-POA equaled the size of that structure in the normal male. As Figure 7.2 also shows, the androgen-insensitive (or TFM) male rat had a male-sized SDN-POA. Perinatal treatment with an E antagonist (blocking the normal effect of E) decreased the size of the SDN-POA in both sexes relative to untreated controls (Döhler et al., 1984, 1986). Therefore, perinatal aromatization of T to E normally leads to SDN-POA growth in males, and normal female levels of E must be present during the perinatal period for normal female function and anatomy.

The sex difference in the rat SDN-POA size does not appear until the day of birth (Gorski, 1984; Jacobson, Davis, & Gorski, 1985; Rhees et al., 1990a). This area of the brain cannot be identified until 20 days after the start of the pregnancy. After that, the size of the SDN-POA increases in both sexes, although the increase is much more dramatic in males. The critical period for the effect of E begins by day 18 of gestation and ends rather abruptly on day 5 after birth. Some parts of SDN-POA nerve cells grow much more in male than in female rats during the first 10 days after birth (Hammer & Jacobson, 1984). The SDN-POA of the adult rat is the end product of the growth and selective death of nerve cells in this area.

In contrast to the SDN-POA, the SNB is masculinized by DHT (Breedlove, 1984; Forger & Breedlove, 1986; Sengelaub & Arnold, 1986; Sengelaub et al., 1989; Sengelaub et al., 1989; Rand & Breedlove, 1988). In rats and humans, the bulbocavernosus muscle is present only in males and is attached to the penis. In rats, the part of the spinal cord that contains the cell bodies of the neurons (the SNB) controlling those particular muscles is very small in females compared to males. The comparable nucleus in humans and dogs, the **Onuf's nucleus,** is also larger in males than in females. In all species, the area in males contains more nerve cells than does the comparable area in females.

Both the SNB and the bulbocavernosus muscle are sensitive to peripubertal and postpubertal DHT or T, but not to E. The perinatal androgens in males prevent the disintegration of the bulbocavernosus muscle; this muscle degenerates in females shortly after their birth. If the muscle remains, the nerve cells that control the muscle also remain. The perinatal androgens prevent cell death, and male rats without androgen receptors develop like normal females. In contrast, postpubertal androgens act directly on the nerve cells themselves, increasing the number of interconnections either in castrated males or in normal females.

Other Sexually Dimorphic
Brain Areas

The SDN-POA and SNB are not the only sexually dimorphic areas of the brain. Table 7.2

FIGURE 7.2 *Hormonal Control of the SDN-POA*

This is a schematic illustration of how the perinatal hormonal environment influences the volume of the sexually dimorphic nucleus of the preoptic area (SDN-POA) when the volume is expressed as a percentage of that of control males from several independent experiments. Female rats received either: (1) a single injection of 1.25 mg TP (testosterone propinate; a long-lasting form of testosterone) on day 4 (TP D-4); (2) daily injections of TP for a prolonged period (from day 16 of gestation through postnatal day 10: PROL TP); (3) a single injection of EB (estradiol benzoate, a long-lasting form of estradiol) on postnatal day 2 (EB D-2); or (4) a prolonged treatment with DES (diethylstilbestrol: PROL DES). Male rats were gonadectomized on day 1 of postnatal life (GX D-1). Some of them were then injected with 100 micrograms of TP on day 2 (TP D-2). Some animals with TFM (testicular feminizing mutation) were also studied. Striped, dotted, and open bars are significantly different from each other.

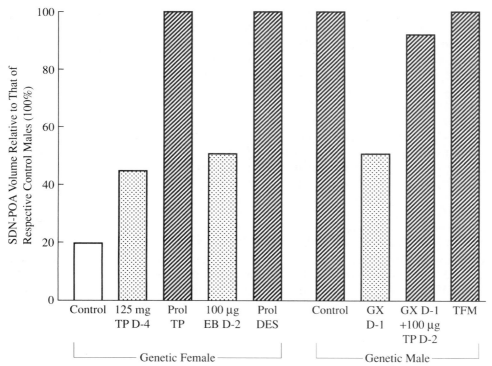

Source: From "Sex Differences in the Brain: The Relationship between Structure and Function" by G. J. De Vries, J. P. C. De Bruin, H. B. M. Uylings, and M. A. Corner, 1984, *Progress in Brain Research, 61,* p. 134. Copyright 1984 by Elsevier Science Publishers. Reprinted by permission.

describes some of the sex differences that have been found in the human brain. Overall, the structures that connect the two halves of the brain are often larger in females. As yet, very little is known about how they may develop. For example, Allen and colleagues (1991) reported that although the sex difference in the shape of the corpus callosum was significant

TABLE 7.2 *Sex Differences in Human Brains*

Structure	Description of Sex Differences	References
Suprachiasmatic nucleus	Shape is spherical in males and elongated in females	Hofman & Swaab, 1991
Region of the bed nucleus of the stria terminalis (controls aggressive and sexual behaviors and sex hormone levels)	2.47 times larger in males	Allen & Gorski, 1990
Preoptic-anterior hypothalamic area; an area suggested to be analogous to the SDN-POA in rats	2.5 times larger in males, with 2.2 times as many cells; dimorphism begins to appear between 2 and 4 years of age	Hofman & Swaab, 1991; Swaab & Hofman, 1988; Swaab & Fliers, 1985
INAH-1 (in preoptic-anterior hypothalamic area: the SDN-POA described just above	1.2 times larger in males (difference reduced from above study because this study matched the ages of the males and females?)	Allen, Hines, Shryne, & Gorski, 1989
INAH-1 (also in preoptic-anterior hypothalamic area)	No significant sex difference	LeVay, 1991
INAH-2 (see above)	Larger in males but only because size apparently decreases after menopause in women	Allen et al., 1989; LeVay, 1991
INAH-3 (see above)	2 to 2.8 times larger in the male brain	Allen et al., 1989; LeVay, 1991
Onuf's nucleus in the spinal cord (controls perineal muscles)	Has about 20% more motorneurons in males	Forger & Breedlove, 1986
Massa intermedia (a structure connecting the two halves of the cerebral cortex)	53.3% larger in females; is more often present in females (78%) than in males (68%)	Allen & Gorski, 1991
Anterior commissure (another structure connecting the two halves)	12% larger in females	Allen & Gorski, 1991
Frontal cortex	Greater neuronal density in females	Haug, Kühl, Meeke, Saas, & Wasner, 1984
Temporal cortex	Differences in electrical activity evoked by auditory stimulation suggests a different "functional organization . . . for the sexes"	Baumann et al., 1991

(continued)

TABLE 7.2 *continued*

Structure	Description of Sex Differences	References
Corpus callosum	Absolute size greater in males; relative size often greater in females; shape depends on gender, with females having a larger or more bulbous posterior (splenial) region; shape also depends on handedness, but more in males than in females; left-handed males have larger sizes, especially in posterior region; among women, those with larger splenums get higher scores on tests of verbal fluency	See documentation in Hoyenga & Hoyenga, 1993
Cortical organization/ localization of function	When localization of language functions was tested in brain surgery patients, the areas that, when stimulated, blocked speech showed sex differences (e.g., females were more likely to have language areas in the frontal lobes)	Ojemann, 1991; Ojemann, Ojemann, Lettich, & Berger, 1989; also see Hoyenga & Hoyenga, 1993
Aging effects	Men show greater loss of brain weight and corpus callosum size with age; women show less atrophy of cells	Gur et al., 1991; Witelson, 1991
Relationship of brain size to IQ	In both sexes, subjects with higher IQs (≥ 130) had larger brains (measured with an imaging device and corrected for body size) than did those with lower IQs (< 100); however, differences in brain size between higher and lower IQ subjects were much more dramatic in males than in females	Willerman, Schultz, Rutledge, & Bigler, 1991

only for adults, the magnitude of the sex difference was larger for children than for adults. However, the smaller number of children's brains studied meant that the even larger sex difference in children failed to reach statistical significance. The sex difference in the human SDN-POA becomes visible only between the ages of 2 and 4 (Swaab & Hofman, 1988). Thus, the sex differences in perinatal hormone activities described earlier, as well as sex differences in experiences after birth (see Chapter 9), could play a role. More information about the role of perinatal hormones will come when researchers have a chance to examine the brain of people who have been exposed to gender-atypical levels of perinatal sex hormones.

HUMAN PERINATAL HORMONE SYNDROMES

Human fetuses have been exposed to various abnormal sex hormone levels. In reviewing the effects of this, the authors emphasize mechanisms and research designs. Since subjects are usually not randomly assigned to perinatal hormone groups, there are many ways that the abnormal group's behaviors can be interpreted other than direct covariation with perinatal hormone levels. In some cases, the affected people were studied without comparing them to any control group. This is a problem particularly when qualitative impressions were formed on the basis of interviews, as opposed to using well-validated behavioral tests.

Even when matched comparison (control or contrast) groups are used, it is not certain that all relevant or important variables other than perinatal hormone levels have been matched. The most common matching is by age, sex, and socioeconomic group. Some matched comparison group subjects are unrelated to the hormonally abnormal subjects and some are the same-sex siblings closest to the hormonally abnormal subjects in age. Using siblings for comparison purposes matches the two groups

on more variables than does using an unrelated comparison group. For example, people who seek medical help for their hormonally abnormal offspring often tend to have a higher socioeconomic status than would a randomly selected group of comparison families.

The sibling comparison groups also have their problems. Siblings might also have the genes causing the disorder, but in them the genes are not so fully expressed and so their presence is undetected. Therefore, siblings might have been subjected to some lesser degree of abnormality in hormone levels. A similar problem can occur in exogenous hormone studies, where the abnormal hormone levels came from medications supplied by the pregnant woman's doctor. Whatever problem the woman had that led to her getting the medication might also have been present, perhaps to some lesser degree, in the earlier or later pregnancies involving the siblings.

In human research, the nature of the relationship remains unknown. In some cases, the people with abnormal perinatal hormone levels also look different and so might elicit different reactions from the people around them during their childhoods. If so, any significant differences in behaviors reported between abnormal perinatal hormone people and some comparison group could reflect differences in developmental experiences rather than any direct effect of perinatal hormones on the brain.

The following data should be reviewed as you read later chapters. The best approach is to look for consistencies. Despite the problems with experimental design and interpretation, do any consistencies occur across studies? Do these consistencies relate in any meaningful way to data from the much better controlled laboratory research done with nonhuman animals? For example, rough and tumble play behaviors are commonly reported to be affected by perinatal hormone levels in humans, and research in nonhumans has led to similar outcomes

(Hoyenga & Hoyenga, 1988). The evidence must be interpreted using the preponderance of evidence criterion (see Chapter 1) since no one study can ever be perfectly internally or externally valid.

Variations in Androgen Levels

Children of both sexes have been exposed to levels of androgens abnormal for their gender, usually because of some genetic problems (see documentation in Hoyenga & Hoyenga, 1993; also see the review done by Reinisch, Ziemba-Davis, & Sanders, 1991). It is interesting to note that primate research has not been able to establish that exposing male fetuses to higher than normal male levels of T has any measurable effects on their adult behaviors (Resko, Buhl, & Phoenix, 1987). In rat research, higher than normal T levels are usually demasculinizing and feminizing (see Chapter 6).

Androgen insensitivity: absent or abnormal androgen receptors. People suffering from the **androgen insensitivity syndromes** do not have a normal androgen receptor gene on their X chromosome(s) (see Chapters 5 and 6). Genetic males with this syndrome respond to perinatal T and so are born with the external appearance of normal females. They are almost always reared as females. The most frequently cited effect of androgen insensitivity was that those reared as females had a verbal IQ score higher than their performance score, whereas the reverse was found true of the three reared as males[4] (see Hoyenga & Hoyenga, 1993). The best designed study compared androgen insensitivity females to both male and female controls (Imperato-McGinley et al., 1991). There are consistent sex differences in at least some forms of **spatial ability** (see Chapter 13), with males tending to get higher average scores on some tests designed to measure the ability to visualize and manipulate imaginary objects in

three-dimensional space. Androgen-insensitive females had the lowest spatial scores.

Partial androgen insensitivity: absent or abnormal enzymes. In some people, one of the enzymes necessary to convert cholesterol into T is defective or missing so that androgen secretion by the fetal testes is abnormally low. In the more common versions of this disorder, the person has normal levels of testicular androgen (both perinatally and postpubertally) and normal androgen receptors, but has abnormalities in the enzymes that convert T into its androgenic metabolites. These people have one of several possible deficiencies in 5-alpha-reductase (converts T to DHT) (Imperato-McGinley & Gautier, 1986; Imperato-McGinley et al., 1980).

Genetic males are markedly affected by this problem. Wolffian organ development depends on T, and external genital development depends on the ability of genital fetal tissues to convert T into DHT. Genetic males with 5-alpha-reductase deficiency have normal internal male accessory organs but have genitals varying from normal female to partially masculinized, with the latter being more common. At puberty, when the testicular secretion of DHT increases and there is a prolonged secretion of T, the genitals begin to masculinize. The testicles may also descend into the scrotal sacs. The penis may reach functional size, allowing adequate sexual relationships. However, ejaculation occurs from the urethra, which is still located in the peritoneal area rather than at the tip of the penis. Spermatogenesis may also occur. On the other hand, development of the prostate gland, acne, normal male facial and body hair, and temporal recession of the hairline (male pattern baldness) remain deficient, suggesting that these are controlled by DHT rather than by T.

The most interesting people are the genetic males who were reared as females but who later switched their identities, as described in the introduction to this chapter. More than 38 cases from the Dominican Republic have been described, and other cases have been reported from Dallas, Turkey, and New Guinea (see Hoyenga & Hoyenga, 1993). Some researchers have claimed that detailed investigations into these subjects' lives has shown that, although being reared as normal females, they spontaneously changed their identity at puberty as they began to be physically masculinized.

The extent to which these people had normal female rearing prior to puberty has been a matter of some controversy (Herdt & Davidson, 1988; Imperato-McGinley, Peterson, & Gautier, 1976; Imperato-McGinley et al., 1980; Money, 1976; see references in Hoyenga & Hoyenga, 1993). In the Dominican Republic, because of inbreeding, the disorder is common and can be recognized at birth. The recognized boys are labeled as *guevedoces* (penis at 12) or as *machihembra* (man-woman). In Sambia, most midwives claim that they can recognize such a male at birth, and he is then reared as a *Turnim-man* (a male who looks like a female but who is nevertheless expected to masculinize at puberty). In these cases, the gender of rearing is ambiguous. The parents do not really believe that the child is either completely male or female, and the ambiguity of gender rearing may make the gender switch possible. Nevertheless, one male was born in southern Italy, reared unambiguously as a female (there was no family history of this disorder), and still spontaneously changed gender identity at puberty.

Adrenogenital syndrome. People with the **adrenogenital syndrome** have abnormally high levels of androgens both prenatally and — unless recognized and corrected by giving the person regular doses of cortisol — throughout life. Genetic females would obviously be more affected than would be genetic males. In fact, adrenogenital males would go unrecognized were it not for the illnesses that some suffer because of their adrenal deficiencies.

Genetic females with the syndrome are born with somewhat masculinized external genitals.

The surge of androgens from the fetal adrenals occurs too late in development to affect the internal organs, so the woman has normal ovaries, fallopian tubes, and uterus. Her vagina may not be open, and her clitoris may be enlarged. There are two forms of this disorder, both with masculinized external genitals: simple virilizing and salt wasting. The adrenal deficit is less severe in the simple virilizing form, but in the salt wasting form there are cortisol deficiencies as well as deficiencies in a hormone that regulates salt levels. Most of these women have been reared as females, but a few, unidentified until later in life, have been reared as males. The most interesting research involves adrenogenital people whose problems were recognized and corrected with replacement adrenal hormones shortly after birth. This limits the hormone abnormality to the perinatal period. The females' external genitals were also surgically corrected shortly after birth, and they were given a functional vagina at puberty.

Adrenogenital females have often been found to have been somewhat masculinized, but adrenogenital males (genetic males) have at least occasionally been reported to be somewhat feminized (see Hoyenga & Hoyenga, 1993). Here, as elsewhere, the preponderance of evidence criterion demands that these data be viewed in the context of data from other syndromes and from research done with nonhumans. Also, the most recent data from Dittman and his colleagues (1990a, 1990b) have ruled out several of the possible alternative interpretations of the syndrome's effects on females that were described earlier. This leaves the masculinizing effects of prenatal androgens as a possible explanation for their increased preferences for having a career versus getting married, and their lesser interest in having children.

Exogenous Hormones

Researchers have also studied the offspring of women who took exogenous sex hormones during their pregnancies because of certain problems. It turns out that supplemental sex hormones very seldom had any favorable effects, and instead had many highly undesirable side effects. For example, **DES** (diethylstilbestrol), an artificial estrogen, was given to between two and three million pregnant women in the United States during the 1940s. The DES-exposed offspring had an increased risk of reproductive cancers (both males and females), structural abnormalities of the reproductive system, and decreased fertility (Barnes et al., 1980; Bibbo et al., 1978; Cousins et al., 1980; Vessey et al., 1983).

Many of these sex hormones were artificial (like DES) and had effects on the body different from those of the natural hormones. Some female offspring were masculinized by progestins, including being born with an enlarged clitoris[5] (see Hoyenga & Hoyenga, 1993). Since the same masculinization of social and aggressive behaviors were reported in progestin-masculinized females both with and without external masculinization of genitals, differential rearing may not account for all the masculinization effects. In view of the inconsistency of results from one study to the next, DES may not exert any consistent masculinizing or defeminizing effects.

However, there was one randomized, double-blind study of the effects of prenatal DES that implied that DES may feminize emotional reactions. In the early 1950s, a controlled trial of the value of DES supplementation in pregnancies was carried out. Women were assigned randomly to DES and placebo groups, and neither the attending physicians nor the women themselves knew which drug had been used during the pregnancy. Many years later, the offspring of these two groups of mothers, still blind as to the drug to which they had been exposed, were investigated by sending questionnaires to their family physicians (Vessey et al., 1983). Compared to placebo-exposed people, not only did the DES women have more physical abnormalities of their cervix but both the

DES men and women also had a significantly higher level of both depression and anxiety. These emotional disorders are more commonly found in women than in men (see Chapter 13). Overall, psychological problems occurred twice as often in the DES as in the control group. At least one other study found similar effects of DES exposure (Katz et al., 1987).

Some female and male offspring have been feminized by E and by P (the natural hormone) (see Hoyenga & Hoyenga, 1993). Exposure to higher than normal levels of P may decrease T levels in the developing human male, as it does in male mice, leading to demasculinization and feminization of adult sexual behaviors (Pointis et al., 1987). One older study, done by Yalom, Green and Fisk in 1973, compared three groups of males. Since untreated, diabetic pregnant women have abnormally low levels of E, they are sometimes treated with supplementary E. The three groups of males (hormone-exposed offspring of diabetic women, offspring of non-diabetic women, and nonhormone-exposed offspring of diabetic women) represented three levels of exposure to perinatal E. Many behaviors were inversely related to perinatal E levels, including aggressiveness and spatial performances. The two diabetic groups differed the most from each other, with the offspring of the control women scoring in between those two groups. Thus, diabetes per se could not account for this pattern of results. However, male offspring born to diabetic mothers may have decreased testicular functioning, as was found in rats (Bender, King, & Lin, 1988).

Normal Variations in Perinatal Hormone Levels

So far, there are little data concerning the effects of normal individual differences in prenatal hormone levels on developmental processes and behaviors in humans. Finegan, Bartleman, Zacher, and Mervyn (1989, as cited by Lytton & Romney, 1991) did find that high prenatal levels of T in fetal boys (assessed through amniocentesis) were associated with masculinized play (block building, more common in boys; see Chapters 11 and 12) at age 4.

More data are available on neonatal hormone levels because one team of researchers has been relating individual differences in neonatal hormone levels to the development of gender-related behaviors (Jacklin, Maccoby, & Doering, 1983; Jacklin et al., 1984; Jacklin, Wilcox, & Maccoby, 1988; Maccoby et al., 1979; Marcus et al., 1985). In three separate groups of infants (a total of 135 males and 121 females), T, E, P, androstenedione, and estrone levels were measured in the umbilical cord right after the infant's birth. On the day after, the mother was asked for her permission to include the infant in a longitudinal study, and in most cases, permission was granted.

The level of hormones at birth might be important to development for two reasons. First, individual differences in sex hormone levels at birth might be an index of individual differences in the levels present during the various prenatal sensitive periods: people could be consistently high or consistently low at both times. For example, Klinefelter's people have low T levels both as adults as well as right after birth, and individual differences in hormone levels are reliable, at least during adulthood (see Chapter 6). Second, since the human is exposed to a surge of hormones after birth (though usually somewhat after the time these researchers measured hormone levels; see Chapter 6), the neonatal period may be another sensitive period. Neonatal hormone levels could also reflect individual differences in the amplitude of the postnatal surge and provide some clues as to the functions and effects of that surge.

Gender and birth order effects. The first study of the ongoing series described above examined the effects of gender and birth order on the level of sex hormones present in the umbilical cord. The only hormone for which there was a significant sex difference was T, with males having the higher levels. However, there

was also an interaction of sex with birth order for T. First-born males had higher levels of T than did later-born males, but birth order did not affect T levels in newborn females. For both sexes, first-borns had higher E and P levels than did later-born infants. The effect of birth order depended on spacing; the closer a younger infant was, in time, to the birth of an older sibling, the lower was that younger infant's hormone levels, particularly for males. With a gap of five years or more between siblings, sex hormone levels returned to the first-born level. The reasons for a birth order effect are unclear, but may be related to changes in the mother's uterus that affect the placenta. The mother's hormone levels during pregnancy may also change because of prior pregnancies (vom Saal & Finch, 1988; see Chapter 6).

Some behavioral correlates of neonatal hormone levels. The first behavior assessed by the research team described above was timidity. Timidity was assessed in children from 6 to 18 months of age by measuring their reactions to novel toys in both the laboratory and the home. Timid children did not move toward the toy but stayed with their mothers and often cried. Girls were significantly more timid than boys in two of the three samples. However, neonatal sex hormones were correlated with timidity scores only in males, not in females. In males, neonatal P and T were negatively correlated with timidity ($r = .70$ and $-.30$, respectively) and were positively correlated with E ($r = +.50$). Thus, males who had had high E, but low P and T, were the most timid.

During the first three years of their lives, the children's neonatal sex hormone levels were also related to their muscular strength. Boys were stronger than girls across all ages tested, and, in one sample but in both sexes, higher neonatal androstenedione levels were associated with lower strength scores. Neonatal P had opposite effects on the sexes in all three samples. Boys with high neonatal P had higher strength scores, whereas girls with high neonatal P had lower strength scores. Remember that there were no sex differences in neonatal P levels, so the reversed correlations were unexpected and as yet unexplained.

These children's moods were also assessed during the first two years of their lives by mailing diaries to the mothers on one or more occasions. Each mother was to use the diary to describe her child's moods over one 24-hour period, at 15-minute intervals. Proportional mood scores were calculated (proportion of waking hours in which the child experienced a certain mood) and related to neonatal hormone levels. Boys were more often reported to be happy/excited, whereas girls were more often reported to be quiet/calm. Neonatal hormones tended not to be related to mood scores in girls, but in boys, small but significant and positive correlations were found between the proportion of happy/excited moods and neonatal levels of androstenedione, estrone, and P. The same three hormones were negatively correlated with boys' quiet/calm mood scores.

Finally, at 6 years of age, the children were given a battery of cognitive tests. There were no sex differences in scores, and—in this case—hormones were more strongly related to behavior in girls than in boys. Higher levels of T and androstenedione were associated with lower scores on tests of spatial ability.

Implications. First, these results suggest that behavioral characteristics such as strength, mood, timidity, and scores on spatial tests might be hormone sensitive. Second, by themselves, these results do not divulge anything about what the nature of that sensitivity might be. The relationships between hormones and behaviors could be either direct or indirect; if they were indirect, that would mean that the hormone-behavior connections were being mediated by some other, more important variable such as neonatal stress and distress. The relationships could be linear or curvilinear. If the relationships were linear, it would then have to be explained why they are sometimes inverted across the sexes, as in the case of P and strength. Third, these studies illustrate the kind of research that can be done to explore normal hormone-behavior relationships in humans.

Perinatal T, Brain Organization, and the Immune System

Prior to his death in 1984, Norman Geschwind, along with colleagues, proposed that the level of perinatal T to which the developing human embryo was exposed permanently affected not only brain organization but also the activity of the immune system. His hypothesis, along with relevant evidence, is described here. The importance of his hypotheses is not in its "correctness"; in fact, it is likely to be superseded by an even more useful theory. Instead, it is important because it attempted to integrate large quantities of information across several fields of research, and because it has led researchers to pay attention to astonishing relationships that might otherwise have been ignored. It has also provided a focus for research, both for supporting research and for research that has failed to support the proposed ideas.

The theory. The theory described here has been presented in several places (Galaburda et al., 1987; Geschwind & Galaburda, 1985a, 1985b, 1985c; Schachter, Ransil, & Geschwind, 1987; Sherman, Galaburda, & Geschwind, 1985). In its original form, the theory stated that the presence of perinatal T slowed the fetal development of the left side of the cortex relative to the growth rate of the right side. This difference in the rate of fetal development affected **lateralization** of brain function, or the degree to which left and right sides of the brain carried out different functions. Thus, it would affect handedness (less right-handedness in males) and speech development (more speech disorders in males). Later data (1987 references) suggested that prenatal influences other than T levels (e.g., genes, growth gradients) may determine which side of the brain is smaller.

According to the revised theory, prenatal T promotes the growth of the smaller side, whichever side — left or right — that is.

Because of this, it would perhaps be best to rephrase (from the original) the first of the two hypotheses that will be discussed: *Prenatal T might affect organization of functions within the brain, including some of the functions that have in the past been assumed to be lateralized, and so T also affects certain abilities and skills.* The sexes also might differ in sensitivity to T. Having had high versus low perinatal T might cause men to differ from each other in certain systematic ways. The same might be true for high versus low women, but the sex difference in perinatal T might *not* lead to similar relationships when women were compared to men. Perinatal differences in T levels might affect the brain organization of males more than of females because males have the higher T levels and so more room for variation. On the other hand, if brain organization is in any way related to ability and skills, and females were more sensitive to T than were males, an extremely high level of T for either sex might be associated with a somewhat unusual pattern of abilities and skills equally often in both sexes.

Second, Geschwind predicted that *sex hormones affect the immune system and hence immune diseases such as allergies; therefore, higher levels of perinatal T, compared to others of the same gender, would mean a greater frequency of immune diseases.* Sex hormones do affect the immune system (see documentation in Hoyenga & Hoyenga, 1993). Although the sex hormones have a variety of effects on how the immune system responds to stress and foreign antigens (proteins in viruses and bacteria), certain types of immune function are more inhibited by T than by E. Because of this, postpubertal animals with lower T levels have more active immune systems. This means that females have more active immune systems than males do and so are more resistant to viral and bacterial diseases. Females are also more vulnerable to autoimmune disorders, where the immune system attacks the organism's own body. For example, human females are much more likely than human males to suffer from autoimmune diseases such as systemic lupus erythematosus,[6] allergies, and the various forms of arthritis. Similarly, males with arthritis have lower T levels than do males without arthritis (Cutolo et al., 1988), and T has been successfully used to treat arthritis in men (Cutolo et al., 1991).

According to the hypothesis, the immune-inhibiting effects of T, when they occur in the prenatal period, would have very different types of effects from those just described. During the prenatal period, the immune system is being instructed as to which proteins belong to the body and therefore which proteins will later be attacked as "foreign." The inhibitory effect of T means that this instructional process will not be as complete in high T as opposed to low T males. Therefore, high neonatal T males, when compared to low T males (but *not* when compared to females) are predicted to suffer more frequently from the autoimmune disorders.

Supporting evidence. Neonatal T levels do seem to affect brain organization, and the sexes do seem to have somewhat different organizations of brain functions (see Hoyenga & Hoyenga, 1993). The right-left differences in brain androgen receptor levels found in the primate brain, as illustrated in Figure 7.1, provide one example. Also, a right-hand preference can be demonstrated in human fetuses (ultrasound pictures of thumb sucking) as early as 15 weeks (Hepper, Shahdullah, & White, 1990).

One impressive study investigated sex differences in the effects of the stimulations that are normally carried out in the conscious human patient who is undergoing brain surgery (Ojemann et al., 1989). Electrical stimulation of the brain was used to block normal function. The researchers found that certain areas of the cortex, when stimulated, blocked the patient's ability to speak. Which areas, when stimulated, had this effect varied not only with gender but also with IQ level. For example, only among the people with lower IQ scores were males found to be more likely than females to have language functions stored in the parietal parts of their brains.

Some interesting associations among hair color, learning disabilities, handedness, life expectancies, immune disorders, levels of verbal and mathematical abilities, and myopia (near-sightedness) have been also discovered (see Hoyenga & Hoyenga, 1993). However, some of the predicted effects are not consistently seen. This is particularly true with regard to the predicted individual differences in autoimmune diseases. One possible explanation of the lack of consistency is random experimental error. Since all of the associations among traits and characteristics predicted by the theory tend to be weak, differing T levels probably have different effects, depending on when in the prenatal period the levels are elevated for each individual. Whether a person gets a learning disorder or becomes a mathematical genius or has frequent allergies might depend on the timing of his T surges. That, in turn, might reflect factors such as the mother's age, her stress levels, and the infant's genes and perinatal experiences.

and defeminization of males depends on species, age, and the part of the body being affected. It might be either T itself, or one of its metabolites, DHT and E. In humans, DHT masculinizes the external genitals. Deficiencies in the reducing enzyme can allow people to change their gender identity at puberty. E may promote growth, particularly in the cerebral cortex and hippocampus.

In view of the widespread appearance of hormone receptors in the primate perinatal brain, hormones probably have pervasive though subtle effects on humans' behaviors as well. Adrenogenital females tend to be somewhat masculinized, and androgen insensitive females to be somewhat feminized. DES may not have consistent effects on gender-related differences, with the possible exception of feminizing susceptibility to depression and anxiety. Neonatal hormone levels also covary with some behaviors, though the nature of the relationships needs to be explored. However, the effects of prenatal stress described in the last chapter should remind us that the environment inside (e.g., hormone levels) and outside the organism are in continuous, intimate interaction, starting even before birth.

SUMMARY

Testicular T is the ultimate cause of the masculinization and defeminization of males' bodies and brains during the perinatal period. Thus, sex differences in T ultimately lead to sex differences in the anatomy and function of the brain. The parts of the brain so affected include the SDN-POA in both humans and non-humans. Structures in the limbic system of the brain are also frequently sensitive to perinatal hormone levels in honhumans; in view of the similar sex differences found in the human brain, the same might be true of humans as well.

The proximal cause for the masculinization

ENDNOTES

1. In the rest of the discussion of this hypothesis, unless a specific reference is cited, please see Döhler (1986), Döhler et al. (1984), and Toran-Allerand (1980, 1984) for the supporting research.

2. On the other hand, don't forget that the exact roles played by SHBG have not yet been established; the high levels of this protein to be found in the male newborn human may have an important active role to play, rather than just to "protect" him from the effects of such a high T level.

3. The **association cortex** is involved in stimulus-processing functions even more elaborate than those carried out in the primary sensory parts of the cortex such as the visual and the auditory cortices.

4. These latter males at birth were seen to have abdominal lumps which turned out to be testes; during this period of history, some doctors thought that any baby with testes should be reared as a male.

5. In this case, the masculinizing effects are probably due to the artificial progestin being converted into an androgen in the body of the fetus.

6. Lupus is a disease in which the immune system attacks various organs of the body. About 80 percent of the sufferers are females, and the disease is always disabling, very frequently fatal, and much more common than AIDS.

CHAPTER 8

SEX DIFFERENCES IN POSTPUBERTAL HORMONES

INTRODUCTION
POSTPUBERTAL SEX HORMONES: CONTROL AND EFFECTS
HORMONE CYCLES
SPECIAL PERIODS OF LIFE
SUMMARY

> *What is needed to brighten this empirical picture is some hard*
> *thinking from biological, interactive and psychological perspectives,*
> *about the way an individual's experience and actions are influenced*
> *by biological and social contexts.*
> —M. B. Parlee (1982b, p. 94)

In 1923, the Board of Education in Great Britain said that "the periodic disturbances, to which girls and women are constitutionally subject, condemn many of them to a recurring, if temporarily, diminution of general mental efficiency. Moreover, it is during the most important years of school life that these disturbances are most intensive and pervasive, and whenever one of them coincides with some emergency, for example, an examination, girls are heavily handicapped as compared with boys" (as quoted by Richardson, 1991, p. 318). More recently, Dabbs, Hopper, and Jurkovic (1990) reported that testosterone levels in men were "related to drug and alcohol abuse, antisocial and generally intemperate behavior, and affective disorder" (p. 1263).

As illustrated by the conclusions cited above, researchers first concentrated only on the possible hormonal covariates of behaviors in women. Researchers were assuming that only women had significant changes in hormone levels from day to day in adult life and that only women were sensitive to their hormonal changes. Later research established not only that men's hormone levels did change but that men were also sensitive to their hormones. Today, as the quote from Parlee indicates, researchers recognize that the environment has overwhelmingly important effects on an individual's sensitivity to postpubertal hormonal changes and that there are important individual differences in sensitivities. Thus, only a very few women are handicapped by "periodic disturbances," and the relationship between T and behaviors in males found by Dabbs and his colleagues was moderated by their socioeconomic status (SES).

INTRODUCTION

This chapter describes gender-related differences in sex-hormone levels after puberty. The discussion begins by describing how the postpubertal hormone cycles are controlled and how those hormones are able to affect the brain. The effects that postpubertal hormones have on the brain and behavior after puberty often depend on what levels of which hormones were present perinatally. The chapter then goes on to describe the hormone cycles, which vary from 1-day cycles to 365-day cycles. Special periods in life with regard to hormone levels include pregnancy, the effects of aging, and the impact of exogenous hormones.

Enough information about several important issues is given so that you can make better informed personal and social decisions. To what degree can the premenstrual syndrome in women be traced to their sex hormones? What kinds of hormone cycles do males have? How much do hormones decline with age, and how might this affect us?

POSTPUBERTAL SEX HORMONES: CONTROL AND EFFECTS

Between the neonatal period and puberty, both sexes have only very low hormone levels. At puberty, testes begin functioning again, and the ovaries begin to function. The adrenal cortex also enlarges at puberty, increasing its output of steroids, including the sex hormones.

Puberty

When puberty occurs, the pituitary, hypothalamus, and gonads begin their adult patterns of "conversation." Each "talks" to the other and so controls its activity. Not only do sex differences in hormone levels appear again at puberty but puberty itself is a gender-dimorphic event. Females of many species, including the human, experience the increase of hormones before males do (Gupta et al., 1975; Stanhope & Brook, 1988; Savin-Williams & Weisfeld, 1989; Marx, 1988b). When boys and girls who lacked the normal levels of hypothalamic hormones, including gonadotropic releasing hormones (GnRH), were studied, researchers found that larger doses of GnRH

were required in boys "to make equivalent progress through puberty" (Stanhope & Brook, 1988, p. 303). In other words, the female pituitary responds to GnRH at lower levels of that hormone than is true of males. The sex difference in puberty timing may be related to how long it takes the brain to increase the pituitary's GnRH sensitivity to the levels necessary for female and then for male puberty, respectively. However, in humans, males become fertile at an earlier age than females do (age 11 versus age 15): females have several anovulatory (infertile) menstrual cycles before they begin to ovulate.

Puberty itself is in the brain. It occurs because of changes occurring within the brain—changes that can occur even in the absence of gonads. In fact, even before **menarche** (the age at which menstruation begins), girls start to have monthly cycles in the pituitary's secretion of hormones (Hansen, Hoffman, & Ross, 1975).

Gonadotropic Hormones and the Gonads

The hypothalamus, pituitary, uterus, and the gonads mutually influence each other. In the human female, the luteinizing hormone (LH) increases the secretion of estradiol (E), progesterone (P), and testosterone (T) by the ovaries (Schnatz, 1985). Much of the T is aromatized within the gonad itself into E before being released. The ovaries also secrete other androgens such as **androstenedione,** but not dihydrotestosterone (DHT) (Longcope, 1986). **Prolactin,** another pituitary hormone, either stimulates or inhibits the ovaries, depending on the prolactin level and menstrual cycle stage (Kalison, Warshaw, & Gibori, 1985). In turn, E and P affect the tissue that lines the uterus. The uterus itself is an active organ, even in nonpregnant women. **Prostaglandins** are fat-related substances secreted by the ovaries and the uterus, and sex hormones increase the uterus's secretion of prostaglandins. Prostaglandins help to regulate ovulation and the release of P from the ovaries.

In the human male, LH controls T secretion and follicle stimulating hormone (FSH) controls **spermatogenesis** (formation of sperm). Testicular leydig cells secrete T into the bloodstream under LH influence. Sertoli cells control spermatogenesis under the control of FSH.

Both sexes have two other hormones. **Inhibin** is secreted by ovaries and by testes; it inhibits the release of FSH in both sexes. **Activin** is formed from inhibin (Lee et al., 1989). Activin also comes from the testes and has effects generally opposite to those of inhibin. Both probably also have nonreproductive functions, since they affect the adrenal, kidney, bone marrow, spinal cord, placenta, brain, and pituitary.

Nongonadal Sources of Sex Hormones

Organs other than the gonads contribute to sex hormone levels and thus to postpubertal sex differences.

The adrenal cortex. As has already been pointed out, the adrenal is a major source of sex hormones in adults of both sexes. In human females, the ovary and the adrenal cortex contribute about equally to T and to levels of androstenedione, but the other androgens found in females (such as DHT) come almost exclusively from the adrenals (Abraham, 1974; Longcope, 1986). The adrenal is a much less important source of androgens for the male because of their testes. Much of the P in rats also comes from their adrenal glands (Ogle & Kitay, 1977). Furthermore, in rats—and possibly in other species as well—the adrenal's secretion of P stimulates the testes to release T (Feek, Tuzi, & Edwards, 1989).

Fat tissue. Fat tissue converts androstenedione into *estrone,* an estrogen. This conversion accounts for about half of males' estrogens. Since estrone is carcinogenic, this explains why overweight people of both sexes have an increased risk for some forms of cancer.

Blood proteins. One protein found in the blood, **albumin,** binds only weakly to sex hormones, so that any hormone bound to it is thought to be active. The amount of sex hormone-binding globulin (SHBG) in the blood regulates free and hence active hormone levels, though SHBG may have some roles of its own to play (see Chapter 6). Males have less SHBG in their blood than females do, and so males have 20 times as much free T as females do (Grumbach, 1980; Rosner, 1990). Since SHBG binds to T more strongly than it does to E, the amount of SHBG present in the blood is more importantly related to free T than to free E levels. Furthermore, E increases, whereas T tends to decrease SHBG levels in adult humans.

Hormone Levels

Radioimmunoassay procedures are, to date, the most accurate way to measure blood or brain levels of sex hormones. First, hormones are radioactively labeled.[1] Then the movement of the radioactive substance in the brain is traced. Alternatively, the amount of radioactivity in a given quantity of blood can be measured, or the amount of radioactivity in a given amount of saliva can be measured, as an index of the amount of free hormone in the blood (serum) (Vittek et al., 1985). One review summarized several radioimmunoassays of total blood levels of sex hormones (free + bound) (Overpeck et al., 1978). Other research (Perachio et al., 1977; Saksena & Lau, 1979; Södersten & Eneroth, 1981; vom Saal & Finch, 1988; Wood, 1982; Zumoff et al., 1990) also contributed data to the following discussion of sexually dimorphic hormone levels.

There are several important facts to be kept in mind:

1. There are large individual differences within each sex for all three types of sex hormones. Hormone levels dramatically vary from one person to the next, and from one moment to the next even within a given person.

2. There is often considerable overlap between the sexes in blood levels of some hormones. For example, both males and females have more T than E in their blood, except for certain parts of the female's reproductive cycle. In some species, such as rats and mice, androgen levels in pregnancy increase to male-typical levels. Therefore, with exceptions, sex differences in hormones should *not* be viewed as dichotomous.

3. Not only the size but even the direction of sex differences vary according to the subjects' age and which stages of the various hormone cycles (daily, monthly, yearly) they were in at the time of the measurement.

4. Since the gonads are not the only source of sex hormones, sex differences can either be decreased or increased by the activities of cells in other organs.

The sexes overlap in levels of some hormones. In adult humans, the sexes overlap in E, P, and androstenedione levels. Measured in picograms per milliliter of blood, females' levels of E levels have a range that starts somewhere between 35 and 50, and goes up to somewhere between 193 and 400, depending on the menstrual cycle stage. E levels vary both from time to time and from female to female. The E range in males is from 19 to 56, overlapping with the lower part of the female range. The sexes have similar levels of P during part of the menstrual cycle (200 to 500), but P levels may reach up to 14,000 after females ovulate. After menopause, the range of E in females is from 10 to 34, and P levels are only about 88. After about age 50, males have more E and P than females do. Females' androstenedione levels can be as low as 1,000 or as high as 2,100, varying with the menstrual cycle stage and from one woman to the next. Males' range is from 1,082 to 1,260.

Nonoverlapping levels of T. Sex differences in T levels follow a somewhat different pattern. Females in the part of the menstrual cycle with the lowest T levels display levels ranging from 200 to 400; in the highest T part of the cycle, T levels range from 285 to 440. In comparison,

the T range of males is from 5,140 to 6,460. Thus, after puberty, there is no overlap in T levels between normal human males and females. After menopause, the range in females is from 198 to 262, which means that the sex difference in T levels does not show as important effects of age/menopause as does the sex difference in E and P. When cerebrospinal fluid concentrations of sex hormones are measured, again males have much more T present than do females: 111 versus 14.

Hormone Receptors and Enzyme Levels in the Adult Brain

As in the perinatal brain, the presence of various enzymes and receptors control which cells of the postpubertal brain are able to respond to which of the sex hormones. Of course, any nonspecific hormone effects (see Chapter 6) are potentially able to affect any neuron. Sensitivity to adult hormonal changes is, in part, a function of perinatal hormone levels: perinatal androgens tend to increase adult sensitivity to androgens, for example (Hoyenga & Hoyenga, 1988). In the following discussion, except where noted, the references can be found in Hoyenga & Hoyenga (1988).

E activities. Just as predicted by the aromatization hypothesis, the adult male brain, in both primates and rats, has high levels of aromatase activity. Aromatizing enzyme is found in the male hypothalamus, preoptic area, and amygdala. In primates of both sexes, some parts of the brain respond to E but not to T. These areas lack both aromatase activity and androgen receptors. In other parts of the male primate brain, including the hippocampus, thalamus, and part of the cortex, T affects the brain directly since there are androgen receptors but no E receptors or aromatase activities.

Sex differences in adult aromatizing activity depend on the species. In rats, greater levels of aromatizing activity are found in males in certain areas of the hypothalamus but not in the amygdala. In the primate, the pattern of aromatase activity across brain areas is very similar in male and females. But aromatization may be more important to the sexual behavior of the primate female than of the male since both T and E very effectively stimulate her feminine sexual behavior but E cannot facilitate his masculine sexual behaviors. In the primate adult and in rat neonates and adults, T increases aromatizing activity.

E receptors are found in similar parts of the brain across many different kinds of species, including insectivores, rodents, and primates (Stumpf & Sar, 1978). In general, the hypothalamus and structures of the limbic system are the most likely to have E receptors, suggesting that sexual, motivational, and emotional parts of the brain may be the most sensitive to E. Sex differences can be seen at the level of the cell (more E receptors in females in certain specific cells) but not at the level of gross brain areas.

Androgen activities.   Reducing enzymes convert T into DHT. In primates, the fetal brain seems to contain more reducing enzymes than does the adult brain (Michael, Bonsall, & Rees, 1987; Jenkins & Hall, 1977). Perhaps reflecting this lack in the adult male primate brain, DHT combined with E more effectively stimulates adult masculine sexual behavior in the male rat than in the male primate.

A (androgen) receptors, found mostly where the E receptors are, show more species differences. The A receptors unique to primates (rats do not have them) are found in the brain areas that control motor and sensory functions,[2] including the reticular formation, amygdala, and parts of the spinal cord. Since sex differences in A receptor levels are seldom reported (Handa et al., 1986, 1988), the adult female brain retains the capacity to respond to T just as the male brain can respond to E. The adult male human cerebral cortex (only males were studied) also has A receptors (Sarrieu et al., 1990).[3]

P activities.   In the primate, P receptors are found only in the hypothalamus and preoptic area, whereas in the rat, P receptors are also found in the cortex, amygdala, and midbrain (Garris et al., 1983; MacLusky et al., 1980; Rees, Bonsall, & Michael, 1985). P receptors are found in fewer places than are E receptors, possibly reflecting a more restricted influence of P than of E. P may have less effect on primates than on rodents, and P may have less effect on primates than does E.

Examples of Postpubertal Hormone Effects on the Structure and Function of the Brain

Table 8.1 briefly describes a few examples of how postpubertal hormones can affect neural anatomy and our perceptions. Since hormones affect how nerve cells respond to stimuli in the world outside us, our perceptions of certain events could be subtly biased by our own current hormone levels. For example, Dabbs has done extensive work on how variations in T levels are related to humans' behaviors, which are an indirect index of how T affects the brain. He and his coworkers have discovered that although there is reasonable evidence of covariance, the degree of relationship between hormone and behavior depends on the situation and on what is being measured.[4] Hormone-behavior relationships among men may be weakened by social controls (social rules). Hormones also seem more likely to be related to behavioral reactions to certain types of situations (environmental stimuli) (e.g., threat, occupational decisions) than to scores on paper and pencil personality tests.

The levels of several transmitter substances are also regulated, directly or indirectly, by postpubertal sex hormones (Hoyenga & Hoyenga, 1988). One example is the control that sex hormones have over monoamine oxidase (MAO) levels. MAO is an X-linked enzyme (see Chapter 5) that degrades or breaks down the transmitter substances called **biogenic**

TABLE 8.1   *Hormone Effects on the Brain*
Some examples of how postpubertal hormones affect neural anatomy and the brain's responses to stimulus information coming from the environment outside the organism, including temperature, touch, and taste (all using rat subjects).

Neural Change	Effects of Hormones	References
Cerebellar neuron responses to sensations of movement: neural responses to spontaneous movements were recorded in awake females	E increased the activity whereas P decreased the activity	Smith, Woodward, & Chapin, 1989
Responses to stimulation of the vagina in hypothalamic and midbrain neurons	Cells excited by the external stimuli also respond to E	Haskins & Moss, 1983
Responses of neurons to touching the flank of the female rat	Receptive field (area on skin to which neuron will respond) increased or enlarged by E	Bereiter & Barker, 1980; Bereiter, Stanford & Barker, 1980; Kow & Pfaff, 1973/1974, 1982; Rose, 1986; Sakuma & Pfaff, 1980
Ventromedial hypothalamic neurons sensitive to glucose also respond to NE	E did not affect glucose responses but it did change how these cells responded to NE, from an inhibitory to an excitatory or mixed response	Kow & Pfaff, 1985
Number of synapses in lateral septum	E increased the number, but only in females	Miyakawa & Arai, 1987
Number of synapses in the arcuate	E increased the number, but only in females	Rodriguez-Sierra & Clough, 1987

P = progesterone; E = estradiol; NE = norepinephrine, a neurotransmitter; the septum is part of the limbic system; the arcuate helps to control the pituitary; the ventromedial hypothalamus controls sexual responses, hormone levels, and eating.

amines. Biogenic amines include **dopamine (DA)** and **serotonin (5-HT),** as well as **norepinephrine (NE),** and are used by neurons throughout the limbic system and reticular system. Any substance that inhibits MAO, which includes some of the drugs used to treat depression as well as sex hormones, increases the levels of those transmitters in the brain. **Acetylcholine (ACh),** a generally excitatory transmitter, is also regulated by sex hormones. For example, the death of neurons that secrete

ACh is one of the main causes of the memory problems of Alzheimer's disease, and E treatments have been shown to improve Alzheimer's symptoms in some postmenopausal women (Fillit et al., 1986).

HORMONE CYCLES

Although most of you have heard of the menstrual cycle (and have learned some myths about it), many of you are probably unaware that there are other cycles in females as well, and few of you probably know that males also have cycles that affect their hormone levels and behavioral biases. Because of this, political statements that argue about what the "place" of women "ought" to be because of their hormone cycles are neglecting the fact of, and effects of, the cycles that males also have. In fact, hormone levels are constantly changing in all of us. Since the pituitary releases GnRH in pulses, hormone levels change from minute to minute. But this section will describe the longer hormone cycles—those that last for periods ranging from 24 hours to 365 days. Cycles are an inherent part of brain function.

Circadian Cycles

Circadian cycles describe the hormone changes that regularly recur during each 24-hour period. Normally, the amount of daylight per 24 hours and the daily pattern of the organism's sleep and activity periods affect the timing of the circadian hormone cycles. Organisms, including humans, who are allowed to "free run" by being placed somewhere away from all timing cues (as in an underground isolation chamber in constant light) still show circadian hormone cycles. The "free run" period is typically somewhat longer than 24 hours.

Circadian patterns of hormone changes. Young human males going through puberty tend to have larger circadian T cycles than older males do. The magnitude of the cycle in rats also varies with age, strain, and season (Boyor et al., 1975; Wong et al., 1983). Seasonal and age-related changes in human circadian cycles will be discussed later in this chapter.

Figure 8.1 displays some circadian T cycles from male rats, rhesus monkeys, and humans. The cycle in the male rat is quite dramatic: the highest T levels occur at night when the rat is most active, but T levels also tend to fall throughout most of the night. There are large individual differences, especially in the daylight

T levels. If the day/night cycle is artificially reversed (night becomes day), the rat's hormone cycles also reverse.

As Figure 8.1 also shows, the circadian T cycle in the male human is much less dramatic. The highest T levels typically occur at night. In fact, T levels tend to increase throughout the night, contrary to what was observed in rats. When T levels in saliva were measured (as an index of free T), at 7:00 A.M. levels were 1,350 ng/ml, which declined to 750 ng/ml by 10:00 P.M. (Dabbs, 1990). Nighttime peaks in T concentration tend to occur 30 to 10 minutes prior to a period of REM sleep (rapid eye movement, or dreaming sleep) (Roffwarg et al., 1982).

In male rhesus monkeys, there is a rise in T levels at the beginning of the lights-off period (sleep time). Thus, T levels are higher at 9:00 P.M. than at 9:00 A.M. (Chambers, Resko, & Phoenix, 1982). After castration, the circadian T rhythm is reversed, now peaking at 10:00 A.M.

The circadian rhythm of cortisol levels matches the androgen pattern seen in castrated males, probably because both reflect hormone secretion by the adrenal cortex. Cortisol (secreted by the adrenal cortex) is higher during the day than during the night in both human and nonhuman primates (Guignard et al., 1980; Michael, Setchell, & Plant, 1974; Miyatake et al., 1980). Although both T and cortisol tend to increase during the night, the increase in cortisol is more dramatic, and the levels stay comparably higher until evening. Overall, daytime cortisol levels are higher than nighttime levels.

Females also have circadian cycles. The circadian T rhythm in female rhesus monkeys resembles that seen in castrated males, and castration of the female has little effect. Since the ovary is not involved, circadian androgen rhythms in either intact or castrated females presumably reflect circadian changes in adrenal activity. In human females, free T levels are 80 percent higher in the morning than in the evening (Dabbs & de la Rue, 1991) and may also reflect circadian patterns of adrenal secretion.

Behavioral correlates of circadian hormone cycles. Circadian changes in T covary with changes in sexual behaviors. In human females, orgasm may be most likely to occur when sexual activity takes place after midday (Palmer, Udry, & Morris, 1982). However, as you might imagine, the other factors affecting humans' sexual behavior—the working day and weekends versus weekdays—exert much more powerful effects on sexual activities than does time of day.

Human males show some reliable circadian variations. Positive moods are most likely, and negative moods least likely, at midday and late afternoon compared to mornings (Taub & Berger, 1974). Cognitive task performances decrease from morning to afternoon (Klaiber et al., 1982). Whether these circadian cycles in humans depend on sex hormone levels remains to be determined, although Klaiber and his colleagues found that androgen injections would prevent the afternoon decline in performances.

Sexual behaviors have a diurnal rhythm in nonhumans as well. Male rats' maximum sensitivity to T (the ability of T injections to increase mounting) occurs during the time of day when their surges of T are most likely to happen (Södersten, Eneroth, & Ekberg, 1980). In rhesus monkey males, the males having the highest number of ejaculations during the day had the smallest circadian change in T levels (Michael, Zumpe, & Bonsall, 1984). Furthermore, rhesus male sexual activity is greater at 9:00 A.M. (after the nocturnal increase of T) than at 9:00 P.M. (Chambers et al., 1982).

Estrous Cycles

In animals below the primate level, females have estrous instead of menstrual cycles. In some species, females may have some vaginal secretions during certain stages of their cycle, such as the vaginal blood seen in the sexually receptive bitch just before she becomes sexually receptive. However, these females do not have menstruation, or the marked sloughing of the walls of the uterus, and so they have estrous rather than menstrual cycles. Cats, dogs, horses, and rats all have estrous cycles.

Estrous cycles, hormones, and sexual behavior. The rat's estrous cycle lasts from four to five days. Both hormone levels and sexual interest vary across days, with peak sexual interest occurring after first E and then P reaches its peak (Hoyenga & Hoyenga, 1993). T and androstenedione levels also show cyclical changes, following the E pattern (Dupon & Kim, 1973; Södersten & Eneroth, 1981).

Other animals, such as the domestic bitch, have seasonal as well as estrous cycles (Wildt et al., 1979). The bitch has several months of sexual inactivity, followed by a single estrous period with a prolonged proestrus-estrus stage. Over a 28-day period, estrus[5] occurred in most bitches just before ovulation and just after the LH peak. Estrus continued for several days after her ovulation.

Estrous cycles in brain activity. The activity of preoptic brain cells in female rats covaries with their estrous cycle (Sibbald, Sirett, & Hubbard, 1987). Brain slices were used in order to isolate the preoptic cells from all other neural, hormonal, or sensory input. Slices from the preoptic region were taken under anesthesia from the brains of female rats during the various estrous cycle stages and from the brains of males.

The brain slices taken from metestrus and proestrus females were the ones most likely to have spontaneously active nerve cells. Active neurons were less likely to be found in estrus or diestrus females or in males. Thus, active cells were most likely to be found in the low hormone parts of the cycle, probably because prolonged exposure to E (e.g., the periods of time after the high hormone parts of the cycle) increases neural excitability, just as it increases sexual activity. Castration decreased the likelihood of finding active cells in females, and

FIGURE 8.1 *Circadian Testosterone Rhythms* This figure illustrates circadian changes in blood levels of testosterone (T) in males of three species: rat, rhesus monkey, and human. In rats, which are nocturnal, T levels fall throughout most of the night. In the diurnal primates, T levels tend to increase at night, at least in intact males.

Sources: Part A: Keating, R. J., and Tcholakian, R. K. (1979). In vivo patterns of circulating steroids in adult male rats. I. Variations in testosterone during 24- and 48-hour standard and reverse light/ dark cycles. *Endocrinology, 104* (1), 185. © The Endocrine Society. Reprinted by permission. Part B: From "Diurnal Variations of Serum Testosterone Levels in Intact and Gonadectomized Male and Female Rhesus Monkeys" by A. A. Perachio, M. Alexander, L. D. Marr, and D. C. Collins, January 1977, *Steroids, 29,* p. 26. Copyright 1977 by Butterworth-Heinemann. Reprinted with permission of the copyright holder, Butterworth-Heinemann. Part C: *Acta Endocrinol* (Copenh) 1980; 94: 536–45. Reproduced with the permission of Acta Endocrinologica.

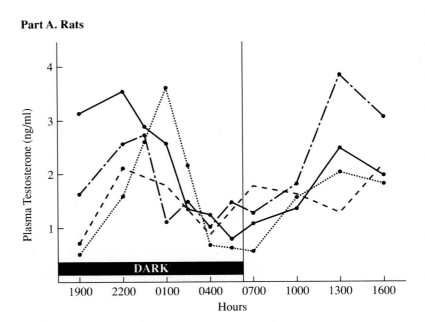

Part A. Rats

E injections made prior to the brain surgery increased neural activity.

Menstrual Cycles

Female humans, and females of some of the higher primates, have true menstrual cycles; of all the other animals, only the elephant shrew and the bat do (Finn, 1986, 1987).

Evolution and the possible functions of the menstrual cycle. In menstruating species, the wall of the uterus develops more completely in each sexual cycle in preparation for the

FIGURE 8.1   *(continued)*

Part B. Monkeys

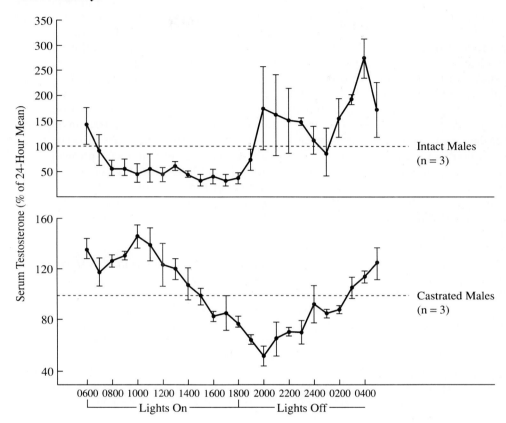

Part C. Humans

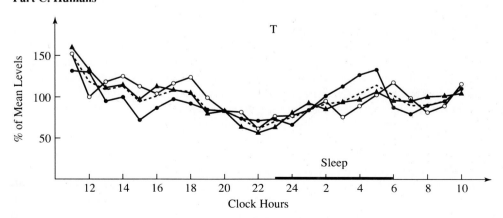

implantation of the fertilized egg (Finn, 1986, 1987). Right after ovulation, some of the cells lining the uterine wall specialize and increase in number, making the wall much thicker. Once the uterine cells differentiate so completely, they cannot revert to their previous undifferentiated form when fertilization does not occur. In this case, they must degenerate and fall away from the wall. The greater uterine development of these species allows a fertilized egg to burrow further into the wall during the very first days of fetal development, which may protect it from the mother's immune system.

Another relatively unique feature of the human menstrual cycle is that ovulation is hidden. We humans do not have clearly perceptible, salient signals serving as cues to our times of ovulation. Some other primate females have colored swellings of the external sexual organs, which are reliable signals that ovulation has occurred. Furthermore, the odors of female primates — the female **pheromones** — change markedly with menstrual cycle stages. Because of the pheromones, a male can distinguish sexually receptive from unreceptive females solely by how their vaginal secretions smell.

Looking across primate species, the ones with the polygynous or promiscuous mating systems have prominent cues to ovulation, whereas monogamous females tend to keep their ovulations hidden (Harvey & May, 1989). For example, the golden lion tamarind has a monogamous mating system, concealed ovulation, and is continuously sexually active across her sexual cycle (Stribley, French, & Inglett, 1987). Thus, hidden ovulation may be an adaptation to monogamy. If human males do not know when their females are receptive, they may show more mate guarding (be less likely to leave their mate unattended) than males whose females have clear ovulatory signals. Conversely, in those species with multimale mating systems, the signs of ovulation may act to encourage male competition, and the female may then copulate with more than one male. If copulation acts to inhibit future infanticide by those males, this may be a very useful strategy for females.

Continuous receptivity may also be an adaptation to monogamy. If the female remains continuously sexually receptive, such as in the human and the golden tamarind, the pair-bond may be strengthened by the possibility of having sexual activity at any time. This may also act to decrease male aggression toward the female. Interestingly enough, when male and female rhesus monkeys are housed in opposite-sexed pairs, copulation occurs throughout the menstrual cycle. But in social groups, males tend to copulate with a given female only around her time of ovulation (see Chapter 5). Apparently, rhesus macaques can adjust to either promiscuous or monogamous mating systems.

Description of the human menstrual cycle. During the menstrual cycle, one or more egg cells and their **follicles** (sacs in the ovary that hold egg cells) systematically change their rate of hormone secretion. This, in turn, affects the pituitary's secretion of GnRH and causes the menstrual cycle. The major hormonal events are illustrated in Figure 8.2 (Schnatz, 1985).

Figure 8.3 shows gametogenesis during the life cycles of males and females. By the sixth fetal month, each ovary contains nearly 7 million egg cells. But at birth, only about 400,000 eggs are left in each ovary, one in each primordial (undeveloped) follicle. Each woman can anticipate only about 400 ovulations in the course of a normal reproductive life span. In each ovulation, one (rarely more than one) egg is released; several others degenerate. At any time throughout the menstrual cycle, regardless of stage, several follicles begin the primary growth process. This growth process goes on continuously from before birth until after menopause. By menopause, there are very few if any eggs left.

At the end of the luteal phase when E and P levels are falling, FSH starts to increase. Several follicles that have grown enough by that

FIGURE 8.2   *Human Menstrual Cycle*

This figure summarizes the hormonal events of a normal ovulatory cycle in human females. Hormone levels are presented as a percent of maximum secretion. The stages of the cycle are M = menstrual, F = follicular, O = ovulatory, L = luteal, P = premenstrual (sometimes also called the late luteal stage).

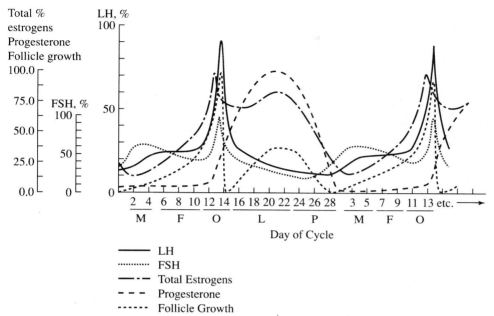

time to respond to FSH enter the second stage growth process. They also increase their secretion of E. Both the follicle's cells and the egg cell itself secrete hormones. Because of this, rising E levels characterize the **follicular stage,** as can be seen in Figure 8.2. Under E's influence, the cells lining the uterus undergo some development and differentiation. Since E decreases body temperature, body temperatures decrease steadily throughout this phase.

Once E levels reach and maintain the critical level for positive feedback long enough (300–500 pg/ml of E for 36–48 hours: Ferin, 1980; Schnatz, 1985), an LH surge is triggered, marking the **ovulatory phase.** A smaller surge

in FSH also occurs at this time. The secondary follicle that is large enough by this time will be ovulated; all other developing eggs and follicles degenerate (which is the fate of 99.9 percent of all follicles and eggs). The one ovulated egg, or oocyte, starts to complete the first meiotic division at the time of the LH surge (see Figure 8.3). The cilia in the fallopian tubes "suck" the egg into the tubes and then guide the egg into the uterus. The human egg may live for only six hours after ovulation if not fertilized.

Because the follicle is ruptured by ovulation, the secretion of E declines. However, under the influence of LH, the other developed follicles undergo some structural changes resulting in an

FIGURE 8.3   *Gametogenesis*
Gametogenesis is the formation of sperm and egg cells. It occurs at different parts of the life cycle in males and females.

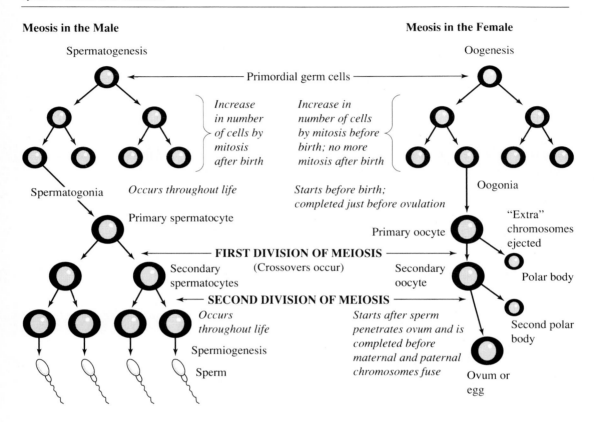

Meosis in the Male

Spermatogenesis

Primordial germ cells

Increase in number of cells by mitosis after birth

Increase in number of cells by mitosis before birth; no more mitosis after birth

Spermatogonia

Occurs throughout life

Primary spermatocyte

FIRST DIVISION OF MEIOSIS
(Crossovers occur)

Secondary spermatocytes

SECOND DIVISION OF MEIOSIS

Occurs throughout life

Spermiogenesis

Sperm

Meosis in the Female

Oogenesis

Starts before birth; completed just before ovulation

Oogonia

Primary oocyte

"Extra" chromosomes ejected

Polar body

Secondary oocyte

Starts after sperm penetrates ovum and is completed before maternal and paternal chromosomes fuse

Second polar body

Ovum or egg

increased secretion of P beginning during the ovulatory phase. Because of negative feedback, GnRH is inhibited and the release of FSH and LH from the pituitary is also inhibited.

After ovulation, LH turns the ruptured follicle into a gland called the **corpus luteum** (literally, body yellow). The corpus luteum secretes both E and P, leading to the high levels of both hormones, especially P, seen in the **luteal phase.** The P and the continued exposure to E leads to further proliferation of the cells lining the uterus. If fertilization occurs, the fertilized egg will burrow into the wall of the uterus. It will begin to secrete **human chorionic gonado-**

tropin, which keeps the corpus luteum active for about eight weeks, or until the placenta can develop enough to supply the P needed to maintain the pregnancy.

Since P increases body temperature, body temperatures increase throughout the luteal phase. If a woman measured her temperature every morning before getting up, a break in the steady pattern of falling daily temperatures by an increase in temperature would indicate that ovulation had just occurred.[6] If ovulation had not occurred, there would be no corpus luteum. Because of this, there is much less P and E in the luteal phase of an **anovulatory** cycle, compared to a cycle in which ovulation had occurred. Shifts in body temperature are also not as marked in anovulatory cycles.

Without fertilization, the **premenstrual phase** begins. Without chorionic gonadotropin, the corpus luteum regresses ("dies") after about 10 to 14 days of activity. As the corpus luteum regresses, its hormone output declines. Because of the decline in E and P, the uterine wall cells can no longer be maintained. Eventually the cells slough off and are discharged through the vagina, along with some blood from broken blood vessels, beginning the **menstrual phase**. At the end of menstruation, the cycle starts all over.

Some correlates of the menstrual cycle.   Table 8.2 presents one behavioral correlate of post-pubertal hormone changes: changes in food intake associated with the menstrual cycle in both humans and other primates. (Some other possible covariates are covered later in this chapter and in Unit Four). However, eating is directly related to natural and sexual selection pressures. Furthermore, finding food is more related to the female than to the male reproductive role in mammals (see Chapter 4); therefore, sex limitation of food intake is not surprising.

If a covariation between some behavior such as eating (or any other behavior) and the hormone changes of the menstrual cycle can be demonstrated, the behavior could be sensitive to sex hormone levels. On the other hand, the change in behavior could have preceded rather than followed the hormone change. Even if the behavior occurred after the hormone change,

TABLE 8.2   *Hormones and Food Intake*
Food intake as an example of behavioral covariates of changes in postpubertal hormone levels in humans, with nonhuman primate data on food intake to corroborate the human data.

Hormonal Covariates	References
Food Intake	
Food intake highest in luteal and lowest in ovulatory phase of menstrual cycle in human, monkey, and baboon females	Bielert & Busse, 1983; Cohen, Sherwin, & Fleming, 1987; Gong, Garrell, & Calloway, 1989; Kemnitz, 1981; Kemnitz et al., 1989; Lissner et al., 1988; Lyons et al., 1989; Rosenblatt et al., 1980
Some women have premenstrual food cravings, especially for sweets or chocolate; only women with premenstrual depression showed an improvement in mood after eating a high-carbohydrate meal during the premenstrual period	Bancroft, Cook & Williamson, 1988; Bowen & Gruenberg, 1990; Cohen, Sherwin, & Fleming, 1987; Smith & Sauder, 1969; Tomelleri & Grunewald, 1987; Wurtman, 1990
Monkey and human females with longer than average menstrual cycles tend to eat more than those with shorter cycles	Kemnitz, 1981; Weizenbaum et al., 1980
Physiology	
Birth control pills can increase or decrease weight and body fat, depending on ratio of P to E in the pills; P increases appetite and E increases nausea	Amatayakul, Silvasomboon, & Thanangkul, 1980; Berger & Talwar, 1978; Hall et al., 1980

E = estradiol; P = progesterone

the conditions that led to the behavior could have first affected hormone levels (at some unknown latency) and then have affected behaviors. The covariation could also be indirect. Women acquire attitudes toward their menstrual cycles from their culture, and anticipation of menstruation may evoke the attitude that can then evoke some behavioral problem, such as anxiety or depression. Alternatively, women with menstrual problems may be more likely to acquire the cultural attitudes, and this could also account for any association between attitudes and hormone changes (see Chapter 2 and Hoyenga & Hoyenga, 1993, for other possibilities).

T levels in human females undergo cyclical changes, paralleling the changes in E. Females who have abnormally high levels of T throughout their cycles tend to have more body hair, more acne, and longer follicular but shorter luteal phases (Paulson et al., 1977; Schmidt & Spone, 1985; Smith et al., 1979). High T levels in females can also cause infertility (Steinberger et al., 1979). Under some conditions, a woman's T levels may covary with her sexual responses (Hoyenga & Hoyenga, 1993; see Chapter 14).

Moods in women may also vary with the menstrual cycle. Tension, depression, and anger in normal women may slightly increase premenstrually, and feelings of vigor or energy may decline (Hampson, 1990b). For most women, the mood changes associated with going from weekdays to weekends are much larger than any changes associated with the menstrual cycle (Mansfield, Hood, & Henderson, 1989; McFarlane, Martin, & Williams, 1988; Rossi & Rossi, 1980). The changes in a woman may also affect the man she lives with, who in turn responds to her so as to increase or decrease the effects of the hormone changes themselves (e.g., Mansfield et al., 1989). Some of the mood changes undoubtedly affect the changes in food intakes (documented in Table 8.2). Even more dramatic changes in moods are seen in the women who suffer from the premenstrual syndrome.

Some carefully controlled studies using a large number of subjects have found changes in cognitive performances correlated with menstrual cycle stages (Barnes, 1988; Becker et al., 1982; Hampson, 1990a, 1990b; Klaiber et al., 1982; Sommer, 1973; Wuttke et al., 1975; see Chapter 13). The changes are often so small as to be statistically insignificant in less well-controlled studies, or in studies using fewer subjects. These changes are also small enough to be socially unimportant and personally irrelevant to almost all women. However, these changes are theoretically important because they document the covariation of hormone changes with characteristics in which gender-related differences are found.

Effects of experiences. Not only may the hormone changes affect the moods, attitudes, and performances of females but real-world experiences also affect hormones (see Chapter 6). Females' sexual activities may affect their menstrual cycles (Cutler, Garcia, & Krieger, 1979; Quadagno et al., 1981; Veith et al., 1983). Women with regular weekly sexual intercourse may have 29-day cycles, whereas women with less frequent intercourse may have significantly shorter or longer cycles. Sleeping with men (with or without sexual activity) may increase ovulation frequency, though just spending time with males in a social setting does not affect females' menstrual cycling.

Pheromones secreted by the axillary sweat glands may account for some of these effects. Female volunteers had extracts of male sweat rubbed onto their upper lips and left in place for six hours, three times a week. The treated women had less variability in their menstrual cycles compared to their pretreatment cycles, and also as compared to women given a control treatment (Cutler et al., 1985).

Exposure to other women also affects the menstrual cycle. McClintock (1971) first observed that women who live together tend to menstruate together. Women who live in the same house tend to, over time, synchronize their cycles such that their phases occur on the same days. This synchrony may reflect the influence of pheromones secreted from female sweat glands (Russell, Switz, & Thompson, 1980). Not all women will show the same degree of synchronization (Jarett, 1984; Matteo, 1987; Quadagno et al., 1981). Women who are sensitive to others' feelings and emotions, and women who feel emotionally close to each other, may be particularly likely to synchronize. On the other hand, women who live with sexual partners may be less likely to synchronize with coworkers, compared to women without live-in sexual partners. Anxious and stressed women are less likely to become synchronized.

Stress can have other dramatic effects on the cycle (Cutler et al., 1987; Jarett, 1984; Matteo, 1987; Rowell, 1970). Being anxious or having unpleasant things happen to you can disrupt the cycle, even in female baboons. Stress is particularly likely to prolong the follicular phase, and it also suppresses ovulation. Exposure to deaths of loved ones, failures, or even having a dramatic success or getting married can affect menstrual cycle timing. Women may also tend to synchronize their menstruations with the onset of the full moon.

The Premenstrual Syndrome
(The Late Luteal Phase Dysphoric Disorder)

In the **premenstrual syndrome (PMS)** (also called the **Late Luteal Phase Dysphoric or Affective Disorder** by the American Psychological Association), severe mood changes are linked to menstrual cycle stages. Most typically, unpleasant moods either occur more frequently or increase in intensity during the premenstrual (late luteal) phase; moods return to normal somewhere after the onset of menstruation. According to some recent reviews (Halbreich, Alt, & Paul, 1988; Logue & Moos, 1986; Sack et al.,

1987), 40 percent or more of women experience some **perimenstrual** symptoms (symptoms occurring just before and after menstruation). For some 2 to 10 percent, the symptoms are severe and even disabling. In a recent study of university women who were unaware that PMS was being investigated, only 4.6 percent would have been diagnosed as having PMS (Rivera-Tovar & Frank, 1990).

Before going on, it is important to realize how socially and politically sensitive research and theories are in this area. First, there is a fear that PMS data will be used to exclude all women from certain sensitive (and often important and well-paid) jobs. Second, PMS data may make women seem to be somehow inferior to men since only women suffer from this particular problem. To guard against these possibilities, the best weapons are an understanding of the pathological assumptions (see Chapter 1) and remembering that men also have relatively large hormone cycles.

Effects of experiences on the PMS.   Whatever the best explanation of PMS turns out to be, perimenstrual symptoms are as susceptible to modification by experiences and life events as are any of the other aspects of the menstrual cycle (see documentation in Hoyenga & Hoyenga, 1993). The likelihood of a women claiming that she has perimenstrual symptoms varies with her sociocultural grouping. More Catholics than Protestants have PMS, and although PMS is more common in women who work outside the home, it may be rarest of all in highly achieving women executive types. Highly instrumental women (Bem Sex Role Inventory, or BSRI) who prefer a contemporary role for women, and highly expressive women who prefer the traditional woman's role, both report more distress than do expressive contemporaries and instrumental traditionals. Women also report more symptoms if they are first told that PMS is prevalent than if they had been told that PMS is very rare.

Although perimenstrual negative moods are usually explained by the woman as being due to her hormonal changes, positive moods that occur in the same period are attributed to having had pleasant things happen! However, even in women with relatively severe PMS, the occurrence of stressful events accounted for more of the changes in mood scores over days (10 percent) than did the phase of the cycle (7 percent) (Beck, Gevirtz, & Mortola, 1990). Nevertheless, in individual women, there was no relationship between the severity of symptoms reported during that cycle and the amount of daily stress that that woman also experienced during that particular cycle.

In Ruble's study (1977) of undergraduate women, all the women were 6 or 7 days premenstrual, and all were told that through "new scientific techniques" it was possible to accurately predict the onset of menstruation. They were further told either that their own periods were due in a week to 10 days or that their own periods were due immediately. The women who thought they were immediately premenstrual rated themselves as experiencing more pain, more water retention, and more changes in eating than did those women who believed themselves to be in the luteal phase. If women simply *believed* they were premenstrual, they experienced many of the commonly reported perimenstrual symptoms.

Because of these expectancies, the way PMS is measured is critically important to whether a women who reports problems will be experimentally confirmed as having PMS. More women are diagnosed as having PMS in retrospective than in prospective studies of perimenstrual symptoms (Endicott & Halbreich, 1988; Englander-Golden, Whitmore, & Dienstbier, 1978; Gise et al., 1990; Hamilton & Alagna, 1988; Parlee, 1982a; Rubinow et al., 1984). For example, if women are simply asked to report the symptoms they experienced during their last premenstrual period, they are at least 50 percent more likely to be diagnosed as having PMS than are women who rate their

symptoms every day for one or two months before being diagnosed.

The American Psychological Association definition of Late Luteal Phase Dysphoric Disorder requires that a change in symptoms occur only in conjunction with the premenstrual period, and that the change be confirmed by having the woman keep records of her daily moods for at least two cycles. Women are diagnosed as having PMS only if their symptoms significantly worsen during the perimenstrual period and only if the increases in symptoms are limited to the perimenstrual period. Given these conditions, only about 20 percent of women who come into clinics with PMS complaints would be diagnosed as actually having PMS.

However, these data should not be interpreted as meaning that most women who complain of having PMS are having problems "only in their heads." Some reasons for this statement are as follows:

1. Baboon females also have some perimenstrual behavior changes (Hausfater & Skoblick, 1985).

2. The more severe the woman's problems are, the more likely that the diagnosis of PMS will be confirmed by a prospective study using daily symptom ratings (Endicott & Halbreich, 1982).

3. There is extensive variability between and within women (van den Akker & Steptoe, 1985). Different women have different kinds of symptoms at comparable stages of the cycle, and the same women can report experiencing both positive and negative changes during the same stage. Thus, by averaging symptoms over women, researchers may be missing many of the details of the actual hormone-related changes.

4. Women with and without PMS (confirmed by prospective diary ratings) responded differently to a carbon dioxide "challenge" (Harrison et al., 1989). Breathing carbon dioxide can elicit panic attacks in people prone to such attacks. The control women felt anxious after the challenge, but only the PMS women experienced a complete panic attack. The panic attacks could be elicited either in the follicular as well as in the late luteal phases. PMS women may be biochemically different.

5. Sometimes observers see daily changes in symptoms associated with the menstrual cycle phases, even when the women themselves do not report the changes (Hamilton & Alagna, 1988).

6. Some of the women who claim they do *not* have PMS would, in fact, be diagnosed as having PMS after they made prospective, daily ratings of their moods (Morse et al., 1988). Many of the women who claim to have PMS that could not be prospectively confirmed are, in fact, subject to large mood swings. Figure 8.4 shows changes in self-rated depression over the menstrual cycle in three women: one with a prospectively confirmed diagnosis of PMS (top), one who said she did not have PMS and whose belief was confirmed with her daily ratings (middle), and one who did not have PMS even though she said she did (bottom). The woman at the bottom did have tremendous mood swings, even though these swings were not tied to specific menstrual events. The reason the woman might be confused is easy to see: sometimes she *does* experience a perimenstrual decline in mood, and so she labels herself as having PMS.

7. Most important, saying that cultural/experiential causes rule out hormonal causes is making one of the pathological assumptions (see Chapter 1). Just because an expectancy can produce a pain does not mean that hormones cannot also produce a pain. Expectancies can come to produce pains because of conditioning. If a woman frequently experiences menstruation and pain at the same time, the belief that menstruation is coming soon may elicit pain and tension as conditioned responses. In short, recognizing that experiences, cultural conditioning, and expectancies can modify perimenstrual symptoms does not rule out a direct or indirect hormonal contribution.

PMS symptoms, possible causes, and possible treatments. PMS consists of several syndromes or subtypes (DeJong et al., 1985; Halbreich & Endicott, 1985; Halbreich, Endicott, & Nee, 1983; Haskett et al., 1980; Rosen, Moghadam, & Endicott, 1988). Both mental and physical symptoms are reported. The most common physical symptoms reported are swelling, painful breasts, weight gain, and general aches and pains. Emotional symptoms most commonly include irritability, depression, tension, mood swings, restlessness, anxiety,

concentration difficulties, and fatigue. Different symptoms, including emotional versus physical symptoms, and irritability versus depression, may have different causes and patterns of change over time. In women who experience premenstrual depression, the depression may be called atypical, hostile, or anxious. The atypical subtype, compared to the two other subtypes, experiences more perimenstrual physical symptoms.

All three subtypes of PMS may be more likely to occur in women who clinically suffer from an **affective disorder** (depression and manic-depressive disorders). One study found that 78 percent of women with PMS had also experienced at least one episode of clinical levels of depression at some point during their lives (Pearlstein et al., 1990). However, these women were *not* more likely than other women to have an anxiety type of emotional problem, such as a phobia. Thus, whatever makes a woman vulnerable to depression apparently also increases her vulnerability to PMS.

When hormone changes during the premenstrual period have been investigated, the amount and ratio of E to P, the rate of hormone decline, and the amount of endogenous opioids have all been found to be only inconsistently related to symptoms (Facchinetti et al., 1987; Halbreich et al., 1988; Parlee, 1982b; Ruble et al., 1980; Sack et al., 1987). However, there are other ways of asking the question of how changes in sex hormones might be related to mood swings. Halbreich, Endicott, Goldstein, and Nee (1986) measured not only absolute levels and ratios of E and P but also how long a time might elapse between when a certain hormone level occurs and when moods might begin to change. For many reasons, an immediate effect of hormones might not be expected (see Chapter 6). Genomic effects take time to start, and if structural changes are involved in the syndrome, these will also take time. Thus, hormone effects might be similar to the effects that antidepressant drugs have on depressive symptoms, which take from 7 to 10

FIGURE 8.4 *Depression and the Menstrual Cycle*
This figure presents daily morning self-ratings of depression made by three women. PMS +:
a woman with premenstrual syndrome; a control woman; and PMS −: a depressed woman
without PMS.

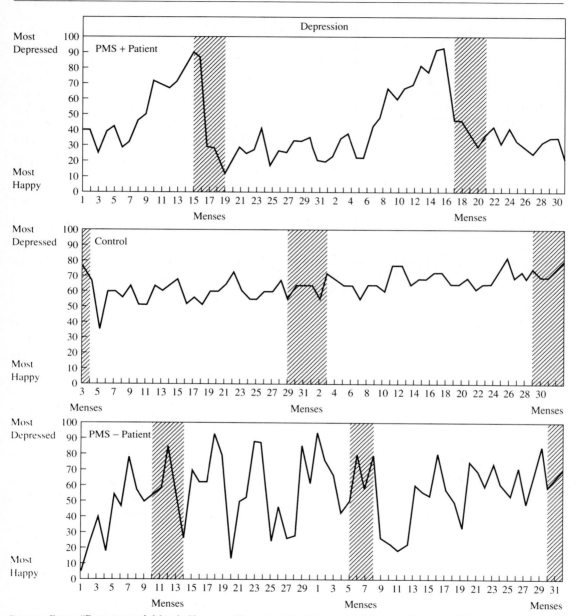

Source: From "Premenstrual Mood Changes: Characteristic Patterns in Women with and without
Premenstrual Syndrome" by D. R. Rubinow, P. Roy-Byrne, M. C. Hoban, G. N. Grover, N. Stambler,
and R. M. Post, 1986, *Journal of Affective Disorders, 10,* p. 87. Copyright 1986 by Elsevier Science
Publishers. Reprinted by permission.

days to begin to appear (Hoyenga & Hoyenga, 1988).

Figure 8.5 shows how the size of the correlation between hormone level and symptom varied according to the number of days allowed to occur between the time of hormonal measurement and the time of the behavioral rating. The correlations between P levels and daily symptoms ratings peaked with a five- to six-day lag between the two events, showing that a given level of P is most likely to affect moods

FIGURE 8.5 *Correlations between Symptoms and Hormone Levels*
This figure illustrates how correlations between plasma levels of progesterone with daily ratings of symptoms (bloatedness, breast pain, irritability, mood swings, loss of sexual interest) change as a function of the number of days allowed to elapse between hormone measurement and behavioral rating. This allows the time lag between hormonal change and behavioral covariate to be assessed. Seventeen patients were tested; a correlation $\geq .41$ was significant at the .005 level.

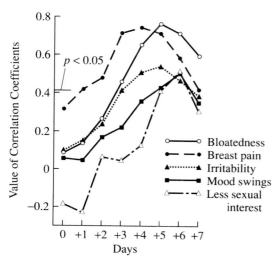

Source: From "Premenstrual Changes and Changes in Gonadal Hormones" by U. Halbreich, J. Endicott, S. Goldstein, and J. Nee, 1986, *Acta Psychiatr. Scand.*, *74*, 581. Copyright © 1986 Munksgaard International Publishers Ltd., Copenhagen, Denmark.

five to six days after that level first appeared. The rate at which P declined during the premenstrual period best predicted the severity of symptoms, an impression confirmed (though not significantly) by other data as well (e.g., Rubinow et al., 1988).

Sex hormones, calcium supplements, anti-inflammatory drugs, antidepressants, and anti-anxiety drugs have all been explored as possible treatments for PMS (Adler, 1990; Alvir & Thys-Jacobs, 1991; Dennerstein et al., 1985; Magos, Brincat, & Studd, 1986; Maxson, 1988; Shapiro, 1988). Drugs that shut down the ovary can lead to dramatic improvements but are seen as "last resort" forms of therapy. Sleep deprivation, exposure to bright lights, and muscle relaxation techniques may also be of benefit. Simple changes, such as eliminating refined sugars from the diet, may also be helpful. Cognitive forms of psychotherapy may help a woman with PMS control her reactions to negative events.

In summary, the PMS is real but is probably rarer than previously thought. Its greatest relevance to us (unless we or someone close to us suffers from it) is that it exemplifies hormone-behavior covariation. Thus, it can indicate which traits might be hormone sensitive.

Monthly Hormone Cycles in Males

Very little effort has gone into identifying male rhythms other than the circadian (discussed above) and the annual cycle (to be discussed below). Despite this lack of attention, there clearly seems to be weekly and monthly cycles in males. For example, in early research, Richter (1968) documented monthly cycles in male mental patients. Some men showed dramatic and monthly changes in mental symptoms, activity levels, body temperature, and even incidents of fevers.

Later, Doering, Kraemer, Brodie, and Hamburg (1975) confirmed the existence of monthly cycles. They discovered rhythmic changes in T levels, with periods ranging from 8 to 30 days in length. The amount by which T levels changed during that period ranged, over different males, from a 9 percent change to a 28 percent change (compared to each subject's own average T level).

Annual Cycles

Annual cycles have been documented in human, rat, and lower primate males.[7] Females also have annual cycles (Haus et al., 1980; Kauppila et al., 1987; Ronkainen, Pakarinen, & Kauppila, 1986; Touitou et al., 1983).

The nature of the annual cycles. In nonhuman primates, T increases during the annual breeding season, a characteristic the male primate shares with the males of many nonprimate species. Mating behavior and aggression among males also increase. In human males, T reaches a peak somewhere between July and November, with younger men having earlier seasonal peaks. The lowest level occurs six months earlier, between February and June. The annual cycle would probably be reversed for men living in the southern hemisphere. The T levels increase from around 660 to 710 ng/100 ml of blood at the trough, to 725 to 800 ng/100 ml at the peak. The circadian rhythm also undergoes monthly changes: the time of the day that T levels peak varies continuously from month to month, in an annual cycle of its own. The peak during November is at 2:00 P.M.; the peak during May is at 8:00 A.M.

Annual cycles in women have been found in prolactin and cortisol levels, as well in ovarian activity. Cortisol peaks in the spring, whereas prolactin levels are highest during the winter. The circadian change in prolactin (increasing overnight) is much larger in winter than in summer. Prolactin rhythms are also much larger in winter than in summer. Prolactin rhythms are also much larger in women than in men. Ovarian activity tends to be somewhat suppressed during the winter.

Possible correlates. There is no direct relationship between the annual changes of T and any behavioral changes in nonhuman males.[8] Even castrated males show the annual cycle of aggression, but males isolated from all contact with females do not have annual T changes. Furthermore, the correlations among T levels and behavior depend on the time during the day the T levels are measured: the T levels measured at 8:00 A.M. are more strongly related to behaviors than are the T levels measured at 8:00 P.M. The latency of these effects (time between T measurement and time of correlated behavioral change) is from three to four weeks.

Researchers have looked for possible correlates of the annual T cycle in human males (Michael & Zumpe, 1983; Reinberg & Lagoguey, 1978; Reinberg et al., 1978; Roenneberg & Aschoff, 1990a, 1990b; Smolensky et al., 1981). Small annual rhythms in several behaviors have been identified, including sexual intercourse, masturbation, new cases of sexually transmitted diseases, reported rapes, sales of contraceptives, and conceptions. The annual peak in these cyclical behaviors generally occurs somewhere between May and November, which includes the time of increasing as well as the time of peak T levels. The annual rhythm in human conceptions is particularly intriguing. Roenneberg and Aschoff (1990a, 1990b) have looked at 3,000 years of monthly birthrates spanning 166 regions of the globe. They concluded that the seasonal pattern is based on biological factors and that both temperature and the number of daylight hours affect the timing and patterning of the seasonal changes.

SPECIAL PERIODS OF LIFE

The sexes also differ from each other because of the fact that hormones undergo changes during special periods of life, such as pregnancy and menopause. Humans also voluntarily ingest sex hormones. This means that we can experience a change in hormones for reasons other than a cyclical process, and sex differences in hormone levels will vary tremendously, depending on what is happening to each male and female.

Pregnancy

One possible source of data concerning hormone sensitivity are the hormonal and behavioral changes associated with pregnancy.

The sex hormones of pregnancy.   The sex hormones increase during pregnancy in all species (Dawood & Saxena, 1977; Mishell et al., 1973; Motohashi et al., 1979; Weizenbaum, Adler, & Ganjam, 1979; vom Saal & Finch, 1988). Rats have more P than primates do, and, among the primates, human females have more E and P than do baboons, chimpanzees, or rhesus monkeys (Hobson et al., 1976; Diczfalusy, 1977; Motohashi et al., 1979; Ogle & Kitay, 1977). In rats and mice, but not hamsters, androgen levels increase to male-typical levels (vom Saal & Finch, 1988).

Hormones decline precipitously right after birth. Even without breastfeeding, it may be six weeks or more before a woman's hormone cycles, ovaries, and uterus return to pre-pregnancy activities. With breastfeeding, it may take much longer for hormone cycling to return in human females. Breastfeeding increases blood levels of prolactin, which tends to suppress ovulation (Konner & Worthman, 1980). Mothers who feed their babies often during the day have a greater suppression (are less likely to ovulate), and the suppression lasts longer, than is true for the mothers who feed their babies less often.

Possible correlates of pregnancy changes in hormones.   Pregnancy is time of low risk for severe psychiatric disorders (e.g., O'Hara, 1986). Pregnant women also report feelings of elation, tranquility, and sleepiness. Pregnancy may also lead to periods of mild depressions

in many women, especially if they are receiving little support from their husbands. Nausea is common and normal; in fact, its absence may be a sign of future problems (Hoyenga & Hoyenga, 1979). The nausea comes from the rise in E (see Table 8.2).

Most women do not experience any severe problems after birth. One study examined postpartum moods in both the mother and the father and found that the time was "emotionally unique" but "not a period marked by depression" (Quadagno et al., 1986, p. 1018). When the changes in moods from the prepartum to postpartum periods were analyzed, the husbands and wives both felt more nervous, worried, helpless, and anxious, as well as enthusiastic and happy during the postpartum period. Women were more likely than their husbands to feel more miserable and tearful as well as more enthusiastic and less self-confident. Cultural attitudes, a feeling of pessimism in late pregnancy, the number of other stressful events also occurring around that time, the amount of social support, and the quality of the marriage are all important to how a postpartum women feels (Boyce, Hickie, & Parker, 1991; Condon & Watson, 1987; Magnus, 1980; O'Hara, 1986; Stemp, Turner, & Noh, 1986).

Nevertheless, carefully done studies have documented a real increased risk of psychosis during the six months after childbirth (Davidson & Robertson, 1985; Martin et al., 1989; McNeil, 1986; Nott, 1982; Robinson & Stewart, 1986; Schöpf et al., 1985). About 10 percent of women may experience some severe emotional problem starting sometime during this period. Maybe about a third of these women will have no other severe problem at any other period in their lives. Generally the affective disorders, such as clinical depressions, if they are going to occur, show up in the first three weeks; schizophrenia tends to show up later. Furthermore, the prognosis is much better for the affective disorders than for schizophrenia: 50 percent of schizophrenics become chronically impaired, and each future childbirth leads to a successive worsening of the symptoms.

Most women with affective disorders recover, though many will have further episodes, both during later pregnancies and between pregnancies (Davidson & Robertson, 1985; Martin et al., 1989; McNeil, 1986; Noll, 1982; Robinson & Stewart, 1986; Schöpf et al., 1985). The study done by Martin and colleagues (1989) compared women with clinical levels of postpartum depression with matched controls. There were fewer stressful events during the pregnancies of the to-be-depressed women than in their controls. Thus, although feeling depressed after giving birth is very sensitive to stress and to levels of social support, the appearance of clinical levels of depression, diagnosed by an interview rather than by scores on some paper-and-pencil test, seems to reflect some other set of processes.[9] The women who become depressed again in periods other than postpartum ones are likely to have a family history of similar disorders, suggesting some genetic susceptibility. For example, women who have PMS may also be more likely to experience postpartum depression (Pearlstein et al., 1990).

The postpartum time may also be a period of increased vulnerability for males. Affective disorders may be more likely to appear at this time in genetically predisposed husbands as well as wives (Davenport & Adland, 1982). Furthermore, males suffer from symptoms so often that a cluster of symptoms, or **couvade syndrome,** has been identified in some husbands of women who are about to give birth (Bogren, 1983, 1984). Men can gain weight and experience toothaches, loss of appetite, and diffuse aches and pains.

In summary, the postpartum period can be a period of stress and increased vulnerability for both husband and wife, as well as being a time of great joy. The rapid postpartum decline of hormones in a woman may increase her vulnerability, but the large changes in lifestyle experienced particularly by first-time mothers also

play a role (O'Hara, Rehm, & Campbell, 1983). Fatigue from lack of sleep and feelings of social isolation because of having to stay home to care for a new baby could increase feelings of depression.

Age and Menopause

Our hormones decline as we age. The changes may be more abrupt in females but a menopauselike syndrome can be seen in human males as well. Menopause as such may occur only in humans, but monkey and rat females also experience a decline in ovarian function with age, which is termed **reproductive senescence** (Hodgen et al., 1977; Short et al., 1990; vom Saal & Finch, 1988; Wise et al., 1989).

The physiology of age and menopause. Aging occurs in both the brain and gonads (Huang et al., 1978; Marx, 1988b; Matsumoto et al., 1984; vom Saal & Finch, 1988; Wise et al., 1989). Young mice who are castrated and then given ovaries taken from elderly and no longer fertile female mice can still have babies despite the age of their "new" ovaries. But elderly, nonreproductive mice who are castrated and given young, replacement ovaries still cannot have babies. If aged female rats whose ovaries are no longer functioning are given implants of hypothalamic tissue taken from newborn rats, their ovaries are rejuvenated. Constant exposure to E can accelerate the aging of both the cyclic brain centers and the ovaries; E deprivation slows this aging. Living in social isolation can also hasten reproductive senescence in female rats (LeFevre & McClintock, 1991). During the last decade of reproductive life, women lose eggs from their ovaries at an accelerated rate such that by menopause, there are virtually no follicles left (Richardson, Senikas, & Nelson, 1987).

Hormonal changes in human females gradually occur over the last decade before cyclic ovarian activity and ovulation finally ceases (Steger & Peluso, 1987; vom Saal & Finch,

1988). This may make them unique among primate females. The length of the follicular phase and E levels both decrease. Cycles become more irregular as well as shorter, and ovulation occurs in fewer cycles. In the absence of ovulation and corpora lutea, there is only low P. The ovary loses its ability to aromatize androgens into estrogens. Instead of E, the postmenopausal ovary secretes mainly T, androstenedione, and estrone, with some women having rather large amounts secreted and others virtually none (Longcope, 1986; Longcope, Hunter, & Franz, 1980). The rest of the estrone present in menopausal women comes from conversion of androstenedione by fat cells. The output of steroids from the adrenal cortex also declines with age in both sexes (Vermeulen, 1983; vom Saal & Finch, 1988).

Aging males, in species ranging from rodents to nonhuman primates to humans, have declining T levels (see documentation in Hoyenga & Hoyenga, 1993). Dabbs (1990a), in a large study, found that T levels declined from a mean of 864 ng/100 ml of blood at age 32, to 602 ng/100 ml of blood at age 44. The age-related decline is most pronounced in free T (the T not bound to SHBG). SHBG levels themselves only slightly change with age (both increases and decreases have been seen). Thus, some studies do not detect any change in T output, but only an change in SHBG levels (Sparrow, Bosse, & Rowe, 1980), which will affect the amount of free T available. Aging also dampens the amplitude of the circadian T rhythm largely because fewer T surges occur at night in older men.

Estrogen levels may actually increase with age in human males (Bartsch & Voigt, 1984). This is particularly true of males with higher levels of body fat, since fat can convert some androgens into some estrogens (Sparrow et al., 1980).

Age-related changes in sexual behaviors.   Sexual behavior also declines with age in rodents, monkeys, and human males. However, the de-cline in T is not directly related to the decline in sex.[10] T injections will not restore the sexual activity of these older males to levels typical of younger males. On the other side of the coin, regular sexual activity may maintain youthful levels of T in older men (Bartsch & Voigt, 1984).

Some researchers have suggested that some older males may have problems similar to those of menopausal women. Hormone treatments have also been tried. For example, not only hormones but transmitter substances in the brain decline with age. For the substances whose level is hormone-sensitive, T injections may increase their levels to those typical of younger animals (Goudsmit, Fliers, & Swaab, 1988). Double-blind placebo studies have reported that androgen treatments of human males between the ages of 45 and 60 can lead to a decrease in neuroticism, an increase in extroversion (being sociable), and an increase in masculine self-image (see documentation in Hoyenga & Hoyenga, 1993). The cognitive performances of aging males may also sometimes be improved with androgen treatments (Kaiser et al., 1978).

Fetherstone and Hepworth (1985) reviewed the so-called male menopause literature and pointed out that "a significant number [of men] do experience psychological and social difficulties at some point in middle age" (p. 235). Sexual difficulties are frequently reported but are more often due to cultural and lifestyle changes than to hormonal changes.

The menopause in human females is only rarely associated with a decline in sexual interest or arousability, which makes the human female unique in the animal kingdom. In one study, only 50 percent of menopausal women experienced any decline in sexual interests, although nearly 20 percent reported a significant decrease (Bachmann et al., 1985). In a review of the literature, vom Saal and Finch (1989) concluded that the ability to be sexually aroused is changed very little, but intercourse can become painful because of atrophy of the vagina or osteoporosis (loss of bone). Results may also depend on how sexual interest is measured. When vaginal contractions were used to measure sexual arousal, menopausal women were less aroused by an erotic film than were younger, cycling women, but there was no difference between the two groups in sexual responses to private fantasies (Davidson, 1985).

Other aspects of menopause in human females. The most commonly reported menopausal symptom is **hot flashes** or **hot flushes.** They are reported by 60 to 70 percent of menopausal women (Casper, Yen, & Wilkes, 1979; Hagen et al., 1982; Hammer et al., 1984; Hunter, 1990; Meldrum et al., 1980). During such periods, women sweat profusely, feel very hot, and become flushed. The hot flash is associated with an LH surge; increased adrenal activity may also occur during flashes. Hot flashes can be eliminated by taking replacement estrogens.

Many symptoms covary with hot flash frequency (Casper, Yen, & Wilkes, 1979; Hagen et al., 1982; Hammar et al., 1984; Hunter, 1990; Meldrum et al., 1980). About 30 percent of women with recurring episodes of depression may have even more frequent periods of depression after menopause. Longitudinal studies do see a small increase in depressive symptoms in some women at this time. The frequency of depressed moods is positively related to the frequency of the hot flashes and to the level of prolactin, but depression is also related to a woman's feelings about her loss of fertility. Women with hot flushes, compared to those without, more often experience tingling sensations, insomnia, nervousness, fatigue, muscle and joint aches (arthritislike symptoms), dizziness, headaches, and heart palpitations. Although Hunter (1990) did not find depression to be correlated with these physical symptoms, she did see a postmenopausal increase in depression.

Many women have some degree of **osteoporosis,** or loss of bone calcium (Cauley et al., 1990; Culliton, 1987; Lee, 1991; Riis, Thomsen, & Christiansen, 1987; vom Saal & Finch, 1988). Older men can also suffer from osteoporosis. This loss makes breakage more likely and can lead to the so-called dowager's hump. Once one of a woman's bones, such as a hip bone, does break from a fall because of her osteoporosis, her health can decline very rapidly. This can lead to death: 12 percent of hip fracture patients die. Calcium supplements, intake of estrogens and progestins, and exercise can all delay the loss of bone. Cigarette smoking, alcohol consumption, and low activity levels seem to increase the rate of osteoporosis.

As was true for the premenopausal syndrome and postpartum psychosis, the woman's culture, beliefs, expectancies, and life circumstances decisively affect her menopausal experiences (Flint, 1982; Greene & Cooke, 1980; Hällström & Samuelsson, 1985; Hunter, 1990; Kaufert, 1982; Polit & LaRocco, 1980; Utian, 1987). Women are more likely to report symptoms if they are less educated, not working, and in poorer physical health. If either her culture or she personally has a negative stereotype of the postmenopausal woman, she will be more adversely affected. Women with problems postmenopausally are likely to have had similar problems premenopausally. Having severe and/or frequent life stresses (death, illnesses, retirement) also increases menopausal symptoms.

Hormone therapy is the most commonly used medical treatment. Therapy might consist of oral E (or E-impregnated patches applied to the skin), E plus P in sequence, or E plus T. There are risks, including an increase in uterine cancer and a possible link between E replacement therapy and breast cancer.[11] Combining E with P may decrease the risk of uterine cancer to levels barely above those of menopausal women who do not use replacement hormones, but it may increase the risk of breask cancer. The incidence of stroke may be especially high if the menopausal women who take E also smoke. On the other hand, the use of estrogen after either natural or surgical menopause[12] seems to decrease the risk of a heart attack and increase life expectancy (Bush et al., 1983; Henderson, Paganini-Hill, & Ross, 1991; Ingemar et al., 1990; Kalin & Zumoff, 1990).

Both physiological and psychological symptoms respond to the hormonal replacement therapy. Some studies were done with menopausal women and some with women whose ovaries had to be surgically removed. The hormones worked on most of the physical symptoms, including hot flushes, vaginal dryness, and osteoporosis. In double-blind, cross-over, placebo control studies, E (with or without P or T) decreases overall distress, anxiety, and depression, and increases energy level, feelings of well-being, and appetite, as well as scores on certain cognitive tasks, especially those measuring more complex abilities (Barnes, 1988; Fedor-Freybergh, 1977; Gerdes, Sonnendecker, & Polakow, 1982; Montgomery et al., 1987; Sherwin, 1988a, 1988b, 1988c; Sherwin & Gelfand, 1985). Some of these effects may represent pharmacological rather than physiological effects of T and E.

Probably a good way to view the desirability of hormone therapy during and after menopause would be for each woman to perform a risk/benefit analysis and make her own own decision. All treatments for all illnesses have risks and side effects as well as potential benefits. Even our own body produces hormones that have a mixture of good and bad effects on us. The estrone created from androstenedione by fat cells is a good example. This conversion occurs in both sexes, and in both sexes it increases the risk for at least some forms of cancer. On the other hand, the fat-created estrone may limit or decrease osteoporosis so that overweight menopausal women have less fragile bones, and are less likely to develop the dowager's hump, than are underweight women.

Exogenous Hormones

There are many circumstances in which people might take or be given exogenous sex hormones. A rise in hormones might feel pleasant, especially a rise of T (de Beun et al., 1989). Pregnant women have been given hormones by their obstetricians (see Chapter 7). Following are descriptions of the effects of the birth control pill and of the anabolic (androgenic) steroids sometimes used by athletes.

The birth control pill: effects and risks. The birth control pill (also called *the pill*) contains an estrogen and usually a progestin (the *combination* pill). In the last decade, its hormone content has been greatly decreased, leading to fewer side effects and health risks. Women on the pill do not experience the hormone changes or the changes in task performances shown by normally cycling women (Becker et al., 1982; Wuttke et al., 1975). Pill users also tend to have lower levels of free T (Bancroft et al., 1991).

Side effects of pill use range from the merely annoying to the serious. These include weight gain, nausea, circulatory disorders such as strokes, headaches, menstrual problems, cancer, breast enlargement, vaginal infections, sterility, and hair growth. Serious physical disorders can also occur. The risk of heart attacks and embolisms (clots in the blood that can plug blood vessels) is increased, particularly in smoking women older than age 37 (Gaspard, 1987; Jick, Dinan, & Rothman, 1978). The lower-dose pills may be associated with a much reduced risk of embolisms than were the older pills. Previous pill users can have a prolonged period of reduced fertility after they stop using the pill (Linn et al., 1982). However, use of the birth control pill may or may not be related to breast cancer (Gaspard, 1987; Harris, Zang, & Wynder, 1990; Schildkraut, Hulka, & Wilkinson, 1990). This conflict in results is similar to the discrepancies found in the literature that explores the relationship between E replacement therapy and breast cancer in menopausal women.

Women using the pill frequently report nausea and weight gain, but mood changes seem to be rare (Glick & Bennett, 1982). The types of mood changes reported may be related to a woman's level of premenstrual tension and to her genes. In a double-blind, placebo study using combination pills with various estrogen and progestin dosages, Cullberg (1972) found that women with premenstrual tension reacted more negatively (with an increase in what he called "irritability") to the estrogen than to progestin. On the other hand, women without premenstrual tension reacted more negatively (often with depression) to the progestin component. Some women may be genetically predisposed to pill-induced depression. However, the genes involved in the side effects of oral contraceptives may be different from the genes associated with the kind of depression that occurs without the pill (Kendler et al., 1988).

Anabolic steroids.   Many athletes of both sexes take anabolic steroids to increase their power, aggression, and speed (Buckley et al., 1988; Taylor & Black, 1987; Windsor & Dumitru, 1989). In one health club, 90 percent of the members reported using these drugs. Even in high school, 5 to 6 percent of the males may use the hormones, as well as 1 to 2 percent of the females. Ben Johnson, a gold medal winner and record breaker at the 1988 Olympics, had his medal taken from him because he tested positive for steroid use. From athletes' subsequent reports, many of the Olympic athletes had used steroids at some point in their training.

These are called **anabolic** steroids because of their tissue-building effects. Most of these steroids also have androgenic effects. Using these drugs does increase lean body mass (muscles) and strength, but much of this may occur because they allow the athlete to overtrain. Overtraining normally leads to increased secretion of catabolic steroids from the adrenal cortex, which breaks muscles down. The anabolic steroids oppose this effect (Danhaive & Rousseau, 1988; Hickson et al., 1990; Mayer & Rosen, 1977). Since anabolic steroids also

reduce body fat levels, they make whatever muscles are present more visible.

The risks associated with steroid abuse are considerable (Alén et al., 1987; Alén, Reinilä, & Vihko, 1985; Tennant, Black, & Voy, 1988; Zuliani et al., 1988). In males, the testes shrink, normal production of T slows and may even stop, breast development may occur, and damage to the kidney, liver, and heart are common. Psychosis and a type of addiction are also likely to occur. Some of these emotional/motivational changes may be very durable and hard to reverse, making steroid abuse very similar to any other drug addiction.

One football player described his experiences in the September 1988 issue of *Sports Illustrated:*

> *Besides the muscle growth, there were other things happening to me. I got real bad acne on my back, my hair started to come out, I was having trouble sleeping, and my testicles began to shrink—all the side effects you hear about. But my mind was set. I didn't care about that other stuff. In fact, my sex drive during the cycles [of steroid use] was phenomenal. . . . In certain ways I was becoming like an animal. . . . And I was developing an aggressiveness that was scary. . . . I really feel that under certain conditions some of the guys who were on steroids would have been perfectly willing to beat someone to death. . . . One night I pulled a loaded shotgun on the boy delivering pizzas. I thought that was funny. (pp. 90, 92, 98)*

SUMMARY

After puberty and before ovarian senescence, the sexes are exposed to systematically different hormone levels. Not only do individuals differ from each other but people also have circadian, weekly, monthly, and yearly cycles in hormone levels, as well as experiencing what the authors called the special periods in life. Some hormone changes may have important implications for the individual, such as the premenstrual, postpartum, and postmenopausal symptoms experienced by some women.

Sex differences in postpubertal hormone levels vary according to age, to stages of the various cycles, and to special conditions such as pregnancy and hormone use. At some times males may have more of the feminine hormones than females do (after menopause), and sometimes females may have as much androgens in their bloodstreams as males do (pregnancy in mice and rats). Nevertheless, the consistent sex differences can affect neural anatomy, neural responses to sensory stimulation, and brain transmitter levels.

Some consistent behavioral covariates of hormone changes have been found. Emotional reactions seem to covary with hormones, at least in some people, as seen in the PMS, postpartum depression, the use of anabolic steroids, and the use of replacement hormones after menopause. Food intake and sexual activity also show some evidence of hormone sensitivity, although cultural factors are of even greater importance. Performances on some cognitive tasks may also be sensitive to hormones, again as seen in the menstrual cycle data and in the data concerning the use of replacement hormones.

ENDNOTES

1. The labeling is done by a type of immune reaction where the immune system's response to foreign proteins is used and the result radioactively labeled: hence, radioimmunoassay.

2. Bonsall, Rees, & Michael, 1985; Handa, Reid, & Resko, 1986; Handa, Roselli, & Resko, 1988; Michael & Rees, 1982; Rees & Michael, 1983; Sheridan, 1983; Sheridan & Weaker, 1982; Stumpf & Sar, 1978.

3. Only five male brains were examined at autopsy, but there was the suggestion that the higher A receptor levels could be found in the adolescent rather than in the older brain.

4. Booth & Dabbs, preprint; Dabbs, 1972; de la Rue, & Williams, 1990; Dabbs et al., 1987; Dabbs, Hopper, & Jurkovic, 1990; Dabbs & Morris, 1990; Dabbs & Ruback, 1988.

5. *Estrous* is the adjective, and *estrus* is the noun form of the word; thus the cycle is an *estrous* cycle but the time of peak sexual receptivity is *estrus*.

6. As a device to control fertility, temperature measurement leaves a lot to be desired. Not only are early morning temperatures highly variable but the replacement of a declining pattern with a sudden (though small) increase from the preceding morning means that one should have had sex — or abstained from sex — 24 hours ago!

7. Dabbs, 1990a; Gordon, Bernstein, & Rose, 1978; Gordon, Rose, & Bernstein, 1976; Ingemann-Hansen & Halkjaer-Kristensen, 1982; Michael & Zumpe, 1981; Mock et al., 1975; Reinberg & Lagoguey, 1978; Reinberg et al., 1978; Smals, Kloppenborg, & Benraad, 1976.

8. Dabbs, 1990a; Gordon, Bernstein, & Rose, 1978; Gordon, Rose, & Bernstein, 1976; Ingemann-Hansen & Halkjaer-Kristensen, 1982; Michael & Zumpe, 1981; Mock et al., 1975; Reinberg & Lagoguey, 1978; Reinberg et al., 1978; Smals, Kloppenborg, & Benraad, 1976.

9. A similar theme will appear again in Chapter 13 when we discuss possible reasons for more women than men being clinically depressed.

10. Chambers, Hess, & Phoenix, 1981; Chambers & Phoenix, 1984; Chambers, Resko, & Phoenix, 1982; Coquelin & Desjardins, 1982; Phoenix et al., 1989; vom Saal & Finch, 1988.

11. Bergkvist et al., 1989; Hunt, Vessey, & McPherson, 1990; Kampert, Whittemore, & Pfaffenbarger, 1988; Lauritzen, 1987; Lufkins et al., 1988; Paganini-Hill, Ross, & Henderson, 1988; Wingo et al., 1987.

12. In surgical menopause, a woman's ovaries have been removed to treat some medical condition such as cysts or some cancers.

UNIT THREE

ENVIRONMENTAL COVARIATES

Most social scientists believe that sex differences are due largely to the processes that will be covered in Unit Three, the sex differences in developmental environments and in the gender-specific expectations a culture has for the behaviors of its children and adults. However, there are two points of view about how the environment affects sex differences. Developmental psychologists tend to view the unfolding of gender-related differences from an epigenetic perspective, in which the developmental environment, both social and nonsocial, facilitates or hinders basic endogenous growth or developmental processes occurring within the individual. Thus, sex differences in the child's environment can produce durable gender-related differences in adult behaviors. On the other hand, socialization theorists tend to deemphasize any possibility of durable effects of children's experiences.

Unit Three covers the environmental differences between the sexes. In what ways, in any given culture, do the worlds in which women live differ from the worlds in which men live? And how can the differences in environments create gender-related differences in behaviors? The first chapter describes the basic mechanisms of environmental influences; this includes the various kinds of learning, and how the developmental environment has been demonstrated to affect brain anatomy and brain function. Two developmental process theorists and a socialization theorist will also be discussed in Chapter 9. Chapter 10 looks at cultural influences by examining sex differences from a cross-cultural perspective. Although sometimes theorists have used the putative cross-cultural universality of some gender-related differences to argue in favor of biological predispositions, in the logic presented in Unit One, conclusions about biological covariates can be made *only* if biological factors are measured or manipulated. Instead, cross-culturally universal sex differences may mean that many cultures use socialization techniques that are similarly differentiated according to gender because only adult females can lactate. Chapter 11 looks at how cultural sexual stereotypes can affect us — affect the ways we treat our children and each other, and affect how we act and react. Chapter 12 introduces the idea of a **gendered environment,** an environment whose elements and components systematically differ according to the gender of the person occupying the environment. Gendered environments start at home, because parents treat girls differently from boys. The school and work environments are also gendered.

Developmental process theorists would emphasize that *when* (during which developmental phase) the sexes systematically experienced different socializing event would be important to the final outcome. In other words, the outcomes would depend on the ages at which various socialization practices begin (Chapter 10), and when various stereotypes are learned (Chapter 11), and when sex differences in developmental environments occur (Chapter 12). Since the age at which (phase during which) an experience occurs is so important to the ultimate outcome of that experience, sex differences, once developed, would be hard to reverse: the person can never return to an earlier developmental phase. Kohlberg and Freud are the developmental process theorists described in Chapter 9.

Other social scientists, particularly social psychologists, sociologists, and some cultural anthropologists, take the **socialization perspective.** Sex differences in cultural/social environments can create sex differences at any age. Of the Chapter 9 theorists, Bandura is the socialization theorist. From this perspective, the sex differences in cultural socialization practices and expectations (Chapter 10), in stereotypically expected traits and characteristics (Chapter 11), and in the ways people are treated by others (Chapter 12) are always important *regardless* of the ages at which they occur. Furthermore, since the age at which an experience occurs is less important, experiences at older ages might be able to reverse any effects of experiences at earlier ages. Socialization theorists tend to believe that any sex difference, regardless of when and how it developed, could be reversed at any age — as long as the person still had the ability to learn. This conclusion about the reversibility of sex differences contrasts with the conclusions of the proponents of the developmental approach. All the chapters in this unit discuss the issue of reversibility.

To the extent that a behavior is sensitive to its environment — which, for humans, would be to a very large extent — then to that extent, Unit Three documents how environments create sex differences.

CHAPTER 9

LEARNING AND DEVELOPMENT: CONCEPTS AND THEORIES

INTRODUCTION
LEARNING PROCESSES
THEORIES OF HOW GENDER-RELATED DIFFERENCES DEVELOPED
BASIC DEVELOPMENTAL PROCESSES
SUMMARY

> Humans have evolved an advanced capacity for observational learning that is better suited for expeditious acquisition of competencies and survival than is learning solely from the consequences of trial and error.
> —Albert Bandura (1986, p. xii)

In one science fiction story, a werewolf bit a dog. The dog describes his resulting transformation: "Right at first I have only dog's memories. Feelings. Impressions. Odors. Anger. Fear. More emotions . . . but something else was happening. Something weird. All of my memories were being sorted out and put into order. Not necessarily proper order, you understand? It was rather an arbitrary order, chosen to make the past more pleasant and meaningful. Some memories were suppressed, others exaggerated, emphasized. It was an attempt to make something more important than it really was. Me. The concept of me—I was what the process was trying to emphasize, what it was making into the center of the universe. And the universe, and the center, the 'I,' were both only part of that process. It was all illusion, but it was inevitable, inexorable illusion that forced you to accept it as the truth. It was later that I realized what it was: I was becoming human." (Ronald Anthony Cross, "Two Bad Dogs," Isaac Asimov's Science Fiction Magazine, September 1990, pp. 91–93)

From the moment of birth, your environment responded to you, at least in part, in ways that were based on your gender. Because the sexes are reared in systematically different environments, they learn somewhat different things, especially through observational learning. As we develop, we devise changing "stories" of ourselves, with the self as the center of the plot and with a past that has been carefully edited to support the current self-description. Part of that story includes the self's gender, along with gender-biased editing and emphasizing processes.

INTRODUCTION

The fact that organisms change as a function of age is undeniable; therefore, the fact that sex differences also change should not be surprising. As described in the introduction to Unit Three, there are two approaches to the development of sex differences: the **developmental perspective** and the **socialization perspective.** Both can explain age-related changes in behavior, including sexually differentiated behaviors. The developmental theorists describe developmental phases; each is characterized by different processes. This means that even similar experiences will create different outcomes as long as those experiences occur during different phases. Socialization theorists point to age-related changes in cultural expectations and socialization practices and to culturally institutionalized timetables (age for school, age for marriage, etc.) as causing age-related changes in sexually dimorphic behaviors.

However, an integrated perspective seems warranted (Levinson, 1986; Snyder & Ickes, 1985). The developing individual is not just acted upon, he also elicits reactions from others, based uniquely on the personal characteristics of the pair of actors involved. Individuals can also select their environments; for example, children can select playmates and playgrounds. The process is always an interaction between individual characteristics and changes, on the one hand, and environmental characteristics and changes on the other.

Unfortunately, since—with important exceptions—most developmental research projects have not used an integrated perspective, it is necessary to examine developmental and socialization ideas separately. This chapter will first review learning processes, which are the mechanisms by which socializing agents affect children as well as adults. The procedures and explanations of learning, which many social scientists of both points of view claim account for most if not all gender-related differences in behaviors among adult humans, will be surveyed. Next, the chapter will discuss some of the most influential theories, some of which take a developmental perspective (e.g., Freud, Kohlberg, evolutionary theorists) and some of which take a socialization perspective (e.g., Bandura). The last section will attempt to integrate some of the age-related changes. It examines how children themselves change, how their situations change, and how children actively respond to, interpret, and change their situations, their self-descriptions, and their memories of past experiences.

LEARNING PROCESSES

First, it is necessary to distinguish among the concepts of learning, memory, and performance. **Learning** refers to the changes in behavior tendencies produced by having certain kinds of past experiences. **Memory** is what enables past experiences to affect current behaviors. Learning is measured by changes in response frequencies, and memory reflects the changes made in the neural circuitry because of past experiences. The change in circuitry *is* the memory (Black et al., 1987; Neve & Bear, 1989; Squire, 1986; Tulving & Schachter, 1990). To change circuitry, experiences may reactivate the neuronal genes that are also active early in fetal development (Dragunow et al., 1989).

We often think of learning as involving changes in the ability to make, or the likelihood of making, some response. Despite this, it is better to think of learning as a change in the *tendency* to make some response. This learned tendency is often linked to a specific **stimulus** or **cue:** some sight, sound, odor, or feeling coming from something happening in our environment or inside our bodies. Learning can have occurred, and past experiences can be remembered, even if the memory is not currently visible in behavior. This contrasts learning with **performance,** which refers to the visible changes in behavior seen in a situation designed to test learning/memory.

Operational Definitions of Three Learning Paradigms

In defining the three types of learning, operational definitions (see Chapter 2) will be used. Later we will look at mechanisms, explanations, and functions of all three types, including how the developmental theories have related them to sex differences. The three types of laboratory procedures used to produce learning are *classical conditioning, operant conditioning,* and *observational learning.* The distinctions among the three are based on the procedures used to establish each of them. The different procedures may or may not involve different cognitive and physiological mechanisms, as will be discussed.

Classical conditioning procedures.   To produce **classical conditioning** in some subject, two stimuli are *paired,* or presented together (in close temporal proximity), on each of several trials. If, every time you talk to a certain person she said something to make you feel bad, you are experiencing classical conditioning: the sight of the person and her saying things to make you feel bad frequently occur together. Pavlov is given the most credit for discovering these procedures. He used dogs as subjects and paired the sound of bells (an auditory stimulus) with meat powder squirted into their mouths. The sound of the bell and the taste of meat were the stimuli, or **stimulus events,** being paired on each of the **conditioning** trials.

The paired stimulus events are the *conditioned stimulus (CS)* and the *unconditioned stimulus (US).* The **conditioned stimulus** is defined as the stimulus, the response to which changes as a function of the pairing. The **unconditioned stimulus** is the stimulus whose response does not change. In the above examples, the sight of that person and the sound of the bell are CSs; the things that person said and the taste of the meat are the USs. In general, for classical conditioning to most effectively take place, the CS must be presented slightly before (often 0.5 second before) the US. Then some changes in the organism's responses to the CS will occur over trials.

There are two kinds of responses involved in classical conditioning: the *conditioned response (CR)* and the *unconditioned response (UR).* The **unconditioned response** does not change and is the one the organism makes to the US. The UR can be an externally visible response, like running, or a change in some internal process. Pavlov's dogs salivated to the meat powder (the US), and so salivation was the UR. In the case of the person who makes you feel bad, feeling bad is the UR and would be visible only through special testing procedures, perhaps simply by asking you to report on how you felt.

The **conditioned response** is a change in the response to the CS as a consequence of its having been *associated with* (paired with) the US. For Pavlov's dogs, the CR was an increased likelihood of salivation to the bell CS. Over successive conditioning trials, the dogs would salivate more and more to the bell, as tested by special trials when the bell was presented alone, without the meat powder US. Usually, within 40 paired CS-US trials, the dogs would salivate rather copiously to the bell by itself. In the case of the person who makes you feel bad, after several pairings of CS and US, the sight of the person—even before she said anything—could make you feel bad. In this case, feeling bad when seeing the person is the CR. There are many different kinds of CRs. Like the UR, the CR can be **overt** (visible from the outside) or **covert** (involving a change in some internal process). The CR can also either be similar or opposite to the UR (Hollis, 1982, 1984; Hollis, Cadieux, & Colbert, 1989; Turkkan, 1989).

A classically conditioned response can be extinguished by using extinction trials. In an **extinction trial,** the CS is presented without the US. The test trials described above are also extinction trials. If many consecutive extinction trials are given to the subject, the CR will eventually **extinguish,** or will stop occurring. The number of trials that the CR will take to extinguish depends on the details of the training procedure. For example, if the CS had frequently been presented without the US, intermixed with CS-US pairing trials **(partial reinforcement),** extinction takes longer to occur. An extinguished CR is not the same as a forgotten CR. An extinguished CR can be rapidly reconditioned by just a few CS-US pairing trials, but a completely forgotten CR would take just as many trials to recondition it as it did to condition it the first time.

An organism can also be taught a classically conditioned **discrimination.** First, the experimenter might pair a light CS with a shock to the foot as a US. In this case, withdrawal of the foot would be both a CR, when it occurs to the light, as well as a UR, when it occurs after the shock. After the CR has been conditioned, then the experimenter could present a slightly brighter light on some trials. At first, the CR would also occur to the brighter light; the organism has **generalized** the CR so that it occurs to stimuli similar to, but not identical to, the original CS. But further suppose that whenever this second light is presented, the shock never follows. The leg withdrawal CR to the brighter light would extinguish, and the animal would have learned to **discriminate** between the two lights of different brightnesses. The CR would occur only to the dimmer, not to the brighter, light.

Operant conditioning procedures.   In **operant conditioning,** the organism first makes some sort of response. An experimental rat may press a lever[1] down with its paw, or a student may study hard for a test. Then the experimenter presents some sort of stimulus event immediately or shortly after the response. Whatever happens to the organism after it makes its response would be a **consequence.** The types of consequences are defined according to the effect that their presentation has on the organism's future tendencies to make that particular response. **Operant conditioning** involves

a change (an increase or decrease) in the future probability of some response because of the consequences that response had in the past.

Some consequences are rewarding stimulus events. Getting a grade of A on a test is a reward for a student, and getting a bit of sugar water to drink is a reward for a hungry rat. If these stimulus events are presented *contingent on* (shortly after the organism has made the) response, the future probability of the response is increased. Presentation of a grade of A increases the probability that the student will study in the future. A **positive reinforcer** is any stimulus event that, when *presented* contingent on a response, *increases* the future probability of that response. The procedure is called **positive reinforcement.** Over many trials, the rat who receives sugar water contingent on its pressing the lever will begin to press the lever at a fairly high rate because of positive reinforcement. The *increase* in lever pressing *rate* is the operantly conditioned response.

Some stimulus events are unpleasant. If an unpleasant stimulus is removed shortly after the organism made some response, the organism is likely to make that same response again the next time it experiences or feels that unpleasant stimulus. Suppose that a rat has cold air blown on it, but shortly after it presses a lever, the experimenter stops the cold air. The next time the rat is cold, it is likely to press the lever again. A **negative reinforcer** is any stimulus event (such as cold) that, when *removed* contingent on a response, *increases* the future probability of that response. The procedure is called **negative reinforcement.**

A special type of negative reinforcement involves avoidance. The type of conditioning described above is called **escape conditioning:** the negative or unpleasant stimulus is already present and the organism must make some sort of response to remove it. In **avoidance conditioning,** the organism can make some response to *prevent* the negative stimulus from occurring. A rat may run from one side of the box to the other side in order to prevent some shock from being turned on. A boy may brush his teeth every day in hopes of preventing cavities and thus the dentist drilling a hole in one of his teeth. All of these are avoidance behaviors and would also be called **active avoidance,** since organisms actively make some response to avoid unpleasant consequences. In rats, females more rapidly learn active avoidance response than males do (Beatty, 1979; Hoyenga & Hoyenga, 1988).

Positive reinforcers can be *removed,* and negative reinforcers can be *presented,* contingent on some response. Both of these events are called **punishment.** Note that reinforcement always means an increase in response rate, by definition, and punishment always decreases response rates. Suppose that some parent takes a toy away from a child to punish her for stealing a cookie from the cookie jar; that would be removal of a positive reinforcer contingent on the response of stealing. The parent is hoping that the child will not steal from the cookie jar again if she gets punished several times for doing so. Alternatively, the parent could spank the child for stealing the cookie; this would be presentation of a negative reinforcer contingent on a response.

If successful, both types of punishment will mean the organism learns not to make a response. The child will learn not to steal. Restraint will have been operantly conditioned. *Withholding* a response, or restraint, can thus be operantly conditioned. This procedure is also referred to as **passive avoidance,** or the avoidance of unpleasant consequences by learning to refrain from making some response (being passive). Male rats learn passive avoidance responses faster than females (Beatty, 1979; Hoyenga & Hoyenga, 1988).

Operantly conditioned responses can also be extinguished. In this case, during an extinction trial, the organism makes the response but is not given the consequence. The rat presses the lever but no longer receives the sugar water. The child takes another cookie but is not punished. In a few trials, the response will be extinguished or will go back to the way it was before the conditioning occurred. The rat will stop pressing the lever, and the child will go back to stealing from the cookie jar at a high rate. Partial reinforcement (e.g., reinforcing only every tenth response) increases the time the organism will take to have its response extinguished. An extinguished response can be reconditioned quickly, whereas a forgotten response will take as many conditioning trials to reacquire as it took to be learned the first time.

An operantly conditioned response can also be placed under stimulus control. When this is done, the animal acquires an **operantly conditioned discrimination.** The experimenter can use some stimulus such as light or sound to signal the animal when bar pressing will be rewarded. In the absence of the cue, bar pressing is not reinforced, but the reinforcement is available when the cue is present. Over time, the animal will come to press the bar almost exclusively when the cue is present, and not when that cue is absent. It has learned the discrimination between cue present versus absent; the cue is a **discriminative stimulus.**

Observational learning. **Observational learning** procedures involve both an observer (the learning organism) and a model. The model performs some response, usually (but not always) receiving some sort of operant consequence, while the observer watches. Later, when given an opportunity, the observer may perform the same or a similar response. A girl will try to hammer a nail just the way she observed her father doing it. A chicken will avoid eating food of a certain color after it has observed another chicken trying that food and violently rejecting it because it tasted awful.

Observational learning can involve the demonstrator modeling either a classically or operantly conditioned response. In the examples above, the procedures used on the model were operant conditioning. Models can also display classically conditioned emotional reactions that an observer can learn. For example, laboratory-reared monkeys do not normally fear snakes. If monkeys grow up in the wild, they do learn to fear snakes, either by watching other adults or by classical conditioning procedures (being bitten). If a laboratory-reared monkey observes a wild monkey exhibiting extreme fear of a snake, that observer will also subsequently fear snakes (Domjan, 1987). Fear of snakes can also be learned if monkeys watch a videotape of model monkeys reacting fearfully to snakes (Cook & Mineka, 1990).

Cognitive Explanations

Most theorists believe that responses are not simply "stamped in" by conditioning procedures. Cognitive processes play a very important role in what gets learned in all three types of paradigms.

Operant conditioning and expectancies. Tolman (1948) was one of the first to claim that human and nonhuman organisms acquire cognitions about the world based on how they interpret their experiences. More recently, Seligman (1975) said that organisms exposed to conditioning procedures acquire expectancies. In operant conditioning, the organism learns to *expect* that, in a certain situation, if it performs a certain response, it will receive a certain consequence. This is a **response-contingent expectancy.**

The rate at which the organism performs any operant response depends on the organism's confidence in its expectancies and how much the organism values (wants) that particular consequence. The more confident the organism is that performing a particular response will produce a desired consequence, the more it will perform that response. The more the consequence is desired — sugar water is a better reward for a hungry rat than for a nonhungry rat — the more the response will be performed. But the expectancy also depends on what the organism has observed, what its biases are, and what it believes about what is going on. What it does depends on what it believes, and what it believes and expects might not correspond to what actually happened.

Bandura (1986) added an idea critical for human expectancies: a person's belief that he is able to perform the required response. Even if a boy is confident that a given response will produce a given very desirable consequence, if he also believes that he is not able to perform the required response, the behavior will not occur. **Efficacy** is the belief that one is competent to carry out the sequence of actions necessary for a given outcome. A boy who very much desires his father's approval for getting a grade of A in mathematics, and who knows that studying is required, may still not study if he believes that he is incapable of learning to do what will be asked of him on the arithmetic test. An efficacy belief translates an expectancy into action.

Punishment and self-control. The cognitive factor is also overwhelmingly important in punishment. Researchers exploring parental use of punishment have almost universally found that adding verbal explanations to the punishment increases the child's future restraint (Harter, 1983; Maccoby & Martin, 1983). Punishment seems to produce restraint only if the child's cognitive processes, or expectancies, are also changed.

Classical conditioning and expectancies. Classical conditioning also entails expectancies, or learning about the relationships between the CS and the US (Rescorla, 1988). It involves an "inductive change in a cognitive system . . . directed toward the development of mental models of the environment that guide inferences [hypotheses, tentative expectancies] in the course of problem solving" (Holyoak, Koh, & Nisbett, 1989). Mere contiguity between CS and US is not enough. For example, if the CS always occurs before the US, but the US also occurs frequently without any CS,[2] conditioning will not occur. Under these conditions, the animal will not see the CS as being related in any way to the US.

According to Seligman (1975), what the organism learns to expect after classical conditioning is that the US will come after the CS, *independent* of any response that the organism might make. Seligman calls these **response-independent expectancies.** Literally, the organism learns to expect that nothing it does will make any difference: the US always occurs after the CS regardless of what it does or does not do. These response-independent expectancies elicit emotions. Organisms first become anxious at experiencing the loss of control over important events (the US). As they become more confident in their response-independent expectancy, they then become depressed. They have acquired a **conditioned helplessness.**

Conditioned helplessness (a confident response-independent expectancy) can lead to depression in humans and a depressivelike state in animals. In humans, the depression is more severe, durable, and extensive if they also believe they will never regain control, that their lack of control is because of lack of ability (e.g., stupidity) and that many very important events are occurring out of control (e.g., failing school). The conditioned helplessness saps motivation and makes thinking and learning very difficult. Some have tried to see if sex differences in conditioned helplessness can explain why women are more often clinically depressed (see Chapter 13).

Classical conditioning is also believed to be an important part of how we humans acquire our attitudes toward ourselves, toward others of our gender, and toward the other gender. **Attitudes** have three components: (1) affective or emotional, (2) cognitive or categorizing, and (3) behavioral tendencies. The behavioral component simply refers to the fact that our attitudes can affect our behaviors. If we classify someone as a member of a given group, and we feel we dislike that kind of person, we are not likely to act friendly toward that person.

Affects, including the emotional components of attitudes, are usually said to be acquired through classical conditioning procedures (Domjan, 1987; Rescorla, 1987; Turkkan, 1989; Maccoby & Martin, 1983). If a dog bites a child, the CS is the sight of that dog (or, because of generalization, any similar dog) and the US is the pain of the bite itself. Through this asociation of dog + pain, fear may come to be elicited by the CS as well as the US, and so become a fear CR. Many phobias, such as dental phobias, are acquired this way: the child learns to expect the feeling of pain (US) when she sees a dog or a dentist (CSs).

Observational learning.   Observational learning is an indirect way to acquire response-contingent and response-independent expectancies and attitudes. Some forms of observational learning may involve learning simple associations among stimuli and responses: if this specific response or stimulus occurs, then that specific stimulus is expected to follow. Other types of observational learning may involve symbolic associations in which antecedent and consequent events are related on logical (symbolic) grounds. For instance, if you observe one man working on a car, you may then assume that all other people whom you label as being male will also work on cars.

Evolution of Learning

Since human sex differences are importantly affected by learning, understanding the evolution of learning is very important in explaining those sex differences. Two basic questions are currently preoccupying learning theorists: (1) Are there many kinds of learning and memory? If there are, do different species show different kinds and do the different kinds involve different evolutionary histories and mechanisms (Beecher, 1988; Sherry & Schachter, 1987)? (2) How did having the ability to learn facilitate the survival and reproduction of past generations?

Different species, different kinds of learning?
Influential theorists are found on both sides of
this issue. Bolles (1988) said, "The structure of
what the animal must learn to survive is determined by where it lives, how it lives, what kind
of animal it is, how its social system works,
what its reproductive strategy is, in short, by
its manner of solving its various biological
problems. That is how it is; it cannot be any
other way" (p. 5). Tooby and Cosmides (1989)
agreed: "The human psyche cannot, even in
principle, be comprised only of a general purpose learning mechanism" (p. 29). On the other
side, Beecher (1988) said, "There seems fair
agreement that the diversity of learning need
not reflect different learning processes" (pp.
246–247).

Developmental and evolutionary theorists
tend to believe that there might be both species-
specific limitations and individual differences,
including sex differences, in learning processes
(see Chapter 14). For example, as previously
described, male and female rats differ in active
and passive avoidance learning, and the differences are sensitive to hormone manipulations
(Beatty, 1979; Hoyenga & Hoyenga, 1988).
Male rodents learn mazes better than female
rodents do, but only in species in which the
males have the larger home ranges (Gaulin &
FitzGerald, 1988; Gaulin & Wartell, 1990, see
Chapter 14). Both species and sex differences
could reflect differences in the various components of learning. These components include:

1. The value of various consequences
2. Differences in the ability to perceive the relevant
   stimuli (e.g., male humans are more often color
   blind: see Chapter 5)
3. Differences in the ability to learn the relevant expectancy (e.g., through observational learning,
   monkeys can learn to fear snakes but they cannot learn to fear flowers: Cook & Mineka, 1990)

Other evidence supports the idea of multiple and often species-specific forms of memory
and learning. Different species may have different memory systems because they had to
solve different kinds of evolutionary problems

(Sherry & Schachter, 1987). Birds seem to use
a different kind of memory for remembering
courtship songs than for remembering the
spatial locations in which they have stored
food. Humans also seem to have several different kinds of memory systems (Black et al.,
1987; Squire, 1986; Tulving & Schachter, 1990).
In these cases, the mechanisms of one memory
system are functionally incompatible with those
of another.[3] Because of this incompatibility,
the systems are distributed among different
parts of the brain (Black et al., 1987; Squire,
1986). Bandura (1986) believes that humans
have evolved the most extensive capability for
observational learning, leading to qualitative
differences between species. He claims that only
humans can observe a model and then, many
hours or even days later, perform a deliberate
sequence of complex movements (Fragaszy &
Visalberghi, 1989; Menzel & Jung, 1982),
perhaps because only humans have advanced
symbolic capacities (language).

However, some primates other than humans
can show relatively extensive learning through
modeling. For example, Fouts (1989) usually
taught his chimpanzees human sign language
by molding the chimps' hands into the proper
positions (shaping), but one chimp learned sign
language solely by watching other chimps
around him use it. The chimpanzees make extensive use of their acquired sign language not
only to communicate with Fouts and other
humans but also to communicate with each
other when no human is around and to themselves when no other chimpanzee is around.

Costs of learning. As was true of the evolution of sex, one of the more interesting ways
to evaluate the evolution of learning is to
discuss its costs (Johnston, 1982). If organisms
have to learn a great deal before they can
become reproductively competent adults, reproduction will have to be delayed until
"enough" is learned. For example, as brain size
increases (relative to body size), so does the
length of the juvenile period, not only among
primates but across species (Bonner, 1980;

Harvey & Clutton-Brock, 1985; Harvey, Martin, & Clutton-Brock, 1987). Also, predatory birds that require learned skills for capturing prey have a delayed maturity relative to other kinds of birds.

Other costs concern the juvenile period in which much of the learning takes place. Because some organisms, especially many primates, have to learn how to survive and reproduce, they are very vulnerable to starvation and predators during this period. Also, since juveniles must learn what to do, that means that they can also learn to do the wrong things. Juveniles are capable of maladaptive as well as adaptive learning; this might lead to antisocial aggression or mental illness, for example. The offspring are dependent on adult provisioning and protection for a longer period of time than are species that have less to learn. This means that what parents do is particularly important for slow-developing species such as humans.

The larger brain required for complex learning has costs. In humans, the brain is 2 percent of adult weight but takes 20 percent of the oxygen. In the first decade of life, the brain may account for 50 percent of the total basal metabolism. The very complexity of such a brain makes it more vulnerable to disruption. Humans are the only primates to experience extensive brain growth both before and after birth (Harvey & Clutton-Brock, 1985).

Possible benefits of learning. The increasing size of the brain during evolution exceeded that which could be specified by the genome. There are too many possible connections among nerve cells in animal brains for each to be specified by a gene — by several orders of magnitude! Because mutations increase when the size and numbers of chromosomes increase, and most mutations are undesirable, having the brain instructed by the environment (learning) may have been a more efficient way to have larger brains than would be having larger genomes.

Learning may also be important because organisms have to learn where to search for food, and predators may also have to learn how

to catch it. **Optimal foraging theory** is an evolutionary idea that describes this kind of learning. Evolutionary pressures work on species so as to maximize their net rates of energy gain while foraging for food (Fantino & Abarca, 1985; Martin, 1983; Smith, 1983). According to optimal foraging theory, the cognitive capacity of the species is, at least in part, an end product of selection pressures creating whatever was needed (brain capacity) to enable the animal to carry out whatever would be an optimal foraging strategy for that particular species (Milton, 1981).

Although the optimum strategy is selected for, the foraging strategies of any given species are expected only to approach the theoretical optimum, for several reasons. One is particularly relevant to sex differences: optimal foraging may potentially conflict with other evolutionary pressures, such as for optimal reproduction. In most mammals, the major evolutionary force working on females is for survival of herself and her offspring, which would emphasize her ability to find and make efficient use of food supplies. The major evolutionary limitation for males is access to females, because of sex differences in parental investments; thus, sometimes males might sacrifice optimal foraging for reproductive opportunities. This could lead to sex differences in various forms of learning.

Another set of learning benefits has to do with the complexities of social living among the primates (Cheney, Seyfarth, & Smuts, 1986). To receive the benefits of social living, primates have to be able to live cooperatively enough with each other so that the costs (aggression, stress) do not outweigh the benefits. To live with others, primates have to be able to interpret a variety of vocal and gestural signals, many or most of them being learned. They have to learn which cries signify snakes and which flying predators. They have to learn to interpret social signals from other primates, such as a willingness to engage in mutual grooming versus a willingness to attack. Sex differences can appear here as well: pigtailed monkey females learn some of these signals better than do the males (Gouzoules & Gouzoules, 1989).

According to Boyd and Richerson (1985), social living allowed complex observational learning to evolve. The simplest form of modeling is where the offspring copies the parent's behaviors and then, through trial and error learning, makes just a few changes in the modeled behavior. More complex modeling rules would be selected for in more variable environments. In an environment that varies extensively, the most effective behavior can be learned just by watching what those who have been there for some time are doing (when in Rome, do as the Romans do). In some breeding systems, females tend to choose the same males as other females do; modeling may be a "short cut to identifying a mate of high quality" (Pomiankowski, 1990, p. 616; Wade & Pruett-Jones, 1990). The same would be true of the tendency to copy the traits and characteristics of the most prestigious models available to you: if it was good enough for that very successful person, it should be good enough for you too. (The Boyd and Richerson theory is covered much more extensively in Chapter 8.)

THEORIES OF HOW GENDER-RELATED DIFFERENCES DEVELOPED

The four types of theories covered here have been tremendously influential, and all have currently active proponents. However, Bandura is the most influential among social and developmental psychologists today. The research associated with evolutionary developmental theories is also increasing.

All Theories Are Now Cognitive

Although the theories were quite different from each other when originally proposed, today their similarities are more striking than their differences, especially in the emphasis on cognitive processes. Although Freud is dead, his followers have changed **psychoanalytic theory.** "It has become clear, for example, that core feminine gender identity develops very early

and that it is mediated in large part by cognitive development and learning" (Silverman, 1981, p. 602). Kohlberg's theory was always cognitive in nature: the **cognitive-developmental theory.** Bandura now describes his theory as a **social-cognitive theory** and gives "a central role to cognitive, vicarious, self-regulatory, and self-reflective processes" (Bandura, 1986, p. xi).

Freud and Psychoanalytic Theory

Freud was a tremendously influential theorist (Bandura, 1986; Miller, 1989). Although he may not have been correct about how gender differences and identity develop, because of his influence, our sex stereotypes are related to psychoanalytic concepts. Described here is Freud's original, influential theory rather than any more recent revision.

Psychosocial stages.   Freud thought that the various experiences a child could have during each **psychosocial** developmental stage had different implications for the adult personality (Freud, 1953, 1961, 1964). If a psychosocial stage was not resolved correctly, the adult personality could be permanently impaired. Although the stages are marked by physiological changes, differences in adult personalities are the outcomes of having had different childhood experiences during one or more of those stages. During the **oral** and **anal stages,** since there are no systematic sex differences in developmental experiences, those experiences could not lead to any sex differences in adult behaviors. Systematic sex differences in developmental experiences begin in the third stage, the **phallic stage,** during which the most pleasurable stimulations come from the boy's penis and the girl's clitoris. During this stage, gender identity is constructed, the core of adult sex differences in personality is created, and the child's conscience (super-ego) is formed.

The Oedipal complex in boys.   At the beginning of the phallic stage, the boy begins masturbating. Because of this, the boy also begins to fantasize about sexually possessing his mother, creating an **Oedipal complex.** Sometime during this stage, the boy would notice that some people did not have penises (e.g., sisters, mother). He would then remember his parents' attempts to limit his masturbation—attempts that may have included threats such as, "If you don't stop doing that, I'll cut it off." The boy would begin to worry that the father, out of jealousy over the son's desire for the mother, might cut off the boy's penis.

The resulting **castration anxiety** brings the Oedipal complex to a close. The boy begins to identify with the father: out of fear, he begins to copy and incorporate the father's characteristics (the Freudian version of observational learning), in hopes that the father would not carry out such a horrible act on a miniature version of himself. Also, by identifying with the father, the boy could, at least vicariously, have sex with his mother. Identification with the father gave the boy his gender identity (male, just like daddy), his characteristically masculine behaviors, and his super-ego. To form the super-ego, the father's values and morals are assimilated by the boy. During the next two and last stages, the **latent stage** and the **genital stage,** the boy further develops and expands on the traits and characteristics he acquired in the first three stages.

The Electra complex in girls.

Freud believed that the girl's progress through the phallic stage was much more difficult. She, too, starts out by masturbation and some sexual thoughts of her father, but in her case, she discovers that it was she who had already been castrated. She finds out that some people have penises, but she does not! Obviously, someone had removed hers. She blames her mother; her mother doesn't have a penis either, so maybe her mother had become jealous not only of her daughter's thoughts of the father but also of the daughter's penis and so cut it off. The daughter angrily turns to the father, hoping that he will give her a penis like his. This wish is later transformed into a desire for the father to give her a male baby, carrying the much desired penis.

As just described, the boy's fear of castration ends his Oedipal complex and so he resolves his phallic stage. In contrast, for the female, the "fact" of her castration starts the Oedipal complex (often called the **Electra complex**). Because of this sex difference, the Electra complex is only slowly resolved during the latent and genital phases for the female. Out of fear, she slowly turns toward identifying with her mother. If she identifies with her mother, she believes that her mother will refrain from further acts of jealousy. Because of this slow, prolonged process of resolution in females, Freud thought that the complex would never would get as completely concluded in the female as in the male, leading inevitably to sex differences in adult personalities.

Sex differences in adults.

Because of the systematic sex differences in phallic phase experiences, Freud thought that male and female adults would have different personalities. Because males' paternal identifications are stronger than females' maternal identifications, he believed that males must be more masculine than females are feminine. Males would therefore have a more secure gender identity. Males would also have a stronger super-ego: "I cannot escape the notion (though I hesitate to give it expression) that for women the level of what is ethically normal is different from what it is in men. Their super-ego is never so inexorable, so impersonal, so independent of its emotional origins as we require it to be in men" (Freud, 1953).

Freud hypothesized that beliefs of female inferiority, both cultural and sexual, and females' jealousy of males, would also be inevitable outcomes of the sex differences in developmental experiences. Females would be more jealous than males are, and both sexes would be convinced of the inferiority of women because, Freud said, women lack a penis. In reaction to their loss of their penises, he said that women become defensively vain. Since the sexuality of females is permanently suppressed by their phallic experiences, and since redirected sexual energy is responsible for the creation of culture, "women have made few contributions to the discoveries and inventions in the history of civilization" (Freud, 1964). Thus, Freud's theory incorporated (thereby apparently "explaining") sex-role stereotypes, giving them an aura of scientific validity, and even more firmly embedding them into our culture.

Despite what Freud claimed, few of his predicted sex differences have been confirmed by research, as indicated here with a few examples. Males (rather than females) have more gender-identity problems (see Chapters 10 and 11). Also, sex differences in moral reasoning are seldom found and may even favor females (Thoma, 1986; Walker, 1984). Even if there are sex differences in styles of moral reasoning as proposed by Gilligan (1982), the highest form of reasoning may involve combining both the masculine and feminine styles (Rogers, 1987, as cited by Cohn, 1991). Sex differences in cultural contributions can be explained by socialization and prejudice (see Chapter 12) rather than by gender differences in sexuality.

Kohlberg and Cognitive-Developmental Theory

Kohlberg modeled his theory on Piaget's description of stagelike developmental changes in children's cognitive capabilities (Miller, 1989). What Kohlberg added were ideas about how children viewed their gender identities, and how children came to believe certain behaviors were appropriate to those identities. Children's gender concepts went through consistent cognitive transformations as they moved from one stage to another.

Kohlberg's five mechanisms of development. Kohlberg (1966, 1969; Kohlberg & Zigler, 1967) saw development as "experience-linked changes in modes of cognition" (1966, p. 83). He, like Freud, thought that childhood experiences were important for the adult personality: "There are important linkages between childhood experiences and adult psychopathology" because "basic cognitive categorizations are irreversible"

(1966, p. 88). He, like Piaget, said that the major motive driving child development was a desire for competence. In fact, Kohlberg saw intelligence as determining how fast cognitive structures could be developed during the child's active interactions with his environments. Kohlberg's research showed that the higher the child's IQ, the sooner he reached each successive developmental stage.

Rather than describe gender development in terms of clearly defined stages, Kohlberg discussed five basic developmental mechanisms. Since he said that (just as Freud claimed) "the interpretation of developmental mechanisms of identifications in girls is much more complex and ambiguous" (1966, p. 124), boys' development is described first, followed by a discussion of sex differences.[4]

The first mechanism describes how the infant schematizes interests so as to respond to new events and stimuli in ways that are consistent with old responses to old stimuli. The child tends to repeat what he did in the past with similar stimuli (people, toys). The **consistency mechanism** occurs in the sensorimotor period and can include sex differences: "By the age of two, there are a number of quite clear sex differences in behavior and interests" (Kohlberg, 1966, p. 112). According to Kohlberg, these sex differences appear because of innate differences between the sexes and because parents treat boys and girls differently (e.g., giving them different toys). Children as young as 18 months show sex-stereotyped toy choices (Caldera, Huston, & O'Brien, 1989), and boys show them even before they have any knowledge of gender stereotypes (Perry, White, & Perry, 1984).

The second mechanism begins to affect behavior when the child values his own gender identity and things associated with that identity. The child should be able to label his own gender by age 3. Because of this mechanism, there is "a clear preference for sex-typed objects and activities by age 3" (Kohlberg, 1969, pp. 457–458). During the ages (3 to 5 years) when this **labeling mechanism** is most strongly operating, the boy indiscriminately imitates adults' behaviors.

As part of the third mechanism, prestige, competence, or goodness get attached to masculine stereotypic characteristics. The little boy perceives that to be masculine is to have prestigious characteristics and to be competent. If you are a boy, it is also good to be masculine, to engage in masculine behaviors, and to have masculine preferences and interests. This **prestige mechanism** seems to most strongly operate from 5 to 8 years of age.

Between 6 to 7, **gender constancy** appears. The child begins to realize that his gender (and, later, the genders of other people) will *not* change with age or behaviors. Once gender constancy develops, the boy realizes that having long hair or wearing skirts will not change him into a girl. Gender constancy develops just after the age at which the child recognizes that mass or volume do not change even when the object's appearance is altered, as when a piece of clay is reshaped.

The fourth mechanism involves the child's belief that conformity to one's own sex role is moral. This **moral mechanism** seems to increase in the years from 5 to 8 (Kohlberg, 1966, p. 123) and then declines. One little boy with whom the authors are acquainted, age 6, found out that the female Hoyenga worked (his own mother was a full-time housewife). He at first angrily denied the possibility of a mother who worked, and then announced, in tones of great disgust, "But mothers are not supposed to work!"

The fifth mechanism involves **modeling** or imitation. The boy tends to imitate the behaviors of certain models he has observed. Boys selectively imitate models they perceive as having prestige and competence and who are perceived as being in some way similar to the self, such as in gender. Boys begin selectively modeling boys more than girls starting by age 5 (Kohlberg, 1969, p. 458). Later, the boy selectively imitates the father more than the mother. Imitation that occurs during the morality period may be especially selective. In fact, because of the immorality of acting out of role and the prestige associated with masculinity, little boys of this age may copy masculine behavior more than feminine, and then only when that behavior is being displayed by a male rather than a female model (Barkley et al., 1977). Kohlberg also describes this modeling as being a kind of identification process, but in this case, not only the like-sexed parent but any prestigious or competent model tends to be imitated.

Sex differences in the third and fifth mechanisms. The developmental process is somewhat different for girls because children associate prestige and competence preferentially with masculine rather than with feminine traits and characteristics. Before age 4, both boys and girls perceive males to be bigger and stronger than females. By age 6 or 7, social power and prestige are perceived to be sex-typed as masculine. Thus, the third and fifth mechanisms will operate quite differently for females than for males. Because of this, girls show no particular age-related sequence in the development of same-sex modeling tendencies: girls should always tend to imitate the masculine more than boys imitate the feminine.[5] Girls will value masculine traits and characteristics more than boys will value feminine characteristics (see Chapters 11 and 12 for documentation of these points).

Bandura's Social-Cognitive Theory

Bandura's 1986 book deviated in some important respects from his former *social learning theory.* In his former theory, the major developmental mechanisms were thought to be conditioning and modeling (Bandura, 1977; Mischel, 1966). Cognitive mechanisms were not only added but given great emphasis in the new theory.

Major developmental mechanisms in social learning theory. Boys become masculine and girls feminine because they are reinforced for acting that way by parents, teachers, and peers. Rewards and punishments are **sex typed** by the environment, meaning that whether any given type of behavior will be rewarded or punished depends on the gender of the child displaying the behavior. Crying is tolerated in girls but punished in boys. Rough and tumble play and aggression is tolerated or even rewarded in boys but punished in girls. What is learned could be generalized to new situations.

Children also model the behaviors of those around them, and most of what they see is males acting masculine and females acting feminine. Children may also learn discriminations by observing such models. They might learn that cooking in the home was inappropriate for males but that being the cook in an expensive restaurant was inappropriate for females. Because boys act masculine and girls feminine, they develop the gender identity to match their behaviors (e.g., "I am acting feminine, therefore I must be a girl.").

Bandura's cognitive learning. In 1986, Bandura made some dramatic changes in the theory, saying that all kinds of conditioning cause changes in responses only to the extent that conscious thoughts are changed. If a child does not notice or think about a CS and a US, she will not acquire a CR. As in Piaget's and Kohlberg's theories, the child actively processes information about her world. She constructs hypotheses about events and tests them. How a child develops, and what develops, is determined by what the child believes about herself and about the nature of her past experiences.

Both forms of Bandura's theory differ in certain critical ways from those of Freud and Kohlberg. Bandura's theory has no stages only the cumulative, incremental effects of experience. Although Bandura does not see knowledge as reversible (we may change our minds but we remember past beliefs), he does not think that childhood experiences have any marked or durable effect on adult personality. Bandura deemphasized any possible biological component to development: experiences and not any endogenous physiological changes are

what drive development. Thus, he also deemphasized biology's role in creating individual differences, or in providing any constraints on what people can learn about (although Bandura does feel that humans have more capacity for symbolic modeling than does any other species). Bandura emphasized the necessity for consciousness, whereas Freud said that unconscious processes are extremely important. Evidence relevant to these points will be presented throughout the rest of this unit.

Evolutionary Concepts of Parental Care

From an evolutionary point of view, age-related changes in sex differences would be expected, for at least two major reasons. First, frequently there is conflict between sexual and natural selection pressures that would limit sex differences to certain phases of life. In other words, if a sexually selected trait impaired survival, natural selection would tend to limit the life periods during which the trait was displayed. Second, since organisms of different ages must solve different developmental tasks, evolutionary pressures acting at different ages can have very different effects on adult phenotypes. These effects are described by theories of **life-history strategies** (Charlesworth, 1980). To the extent that the sexes have different developmental "problems" to solve, they will develop different life-history strategies, different patterns of sex differences as a function of age.

Learned traits can be transmitted from one generation to the next among nonhuman animals, especially among the higher primates (e.g., Cheney, Seyfarth, & Smuts, 1986). However, deliberate instruction of young may be unique to the human primate. As described in Chapter 5, **maternal effects**[6] include parental instruction (Atchley & Newman, 1989; Kirkpatrick & Lande, 1989; Lande & Price, 1989; Stamps, 1991). **Maternal inheritance** includes not only genes but also parental care and cultural socialization. In **maternal selection,** the eventual phenotype of the offspring is an interaction between the maternal phenotype and the offspring's current phenotype. For example, some types of mothers may favor male offspring (invest more in them, instruct them more), whereas other types of mothers may favor females (see Chapter 4). Thus, the eventual phenotypes of males and females would depend on which type of mother each gender had. Maternal effects alter the effects of natural selection pressures in predictable though very complex ways. For example, maternal effects cause phenotypic changes to occur for many generations after natural selection had stopped, and they can also lead to maladaptive outcomes.

Three evolutionary ideas will be discussed here. First, not only should parents invest in their young but there is inherent conflict in the parent-child relationship. Second, attachments between infant and mother may be adaptive, as may variations in those attachments. Third, if development is open to environmental influences, adult mating strategies may depend on the child's developmental environment.

Parent-offspring conflict. Since parents share genes equally with all offspring—past, present, and future—they should not invest so much (risk, effort, resources) in the present offspring that their capacity to invest in future offspring is impaired (Trivers, 1974). As an offspring matures and becomes increasingly more capable of feeding itself, the benefit to it of nursing decreases. At the same time, the costs to its mother increase because she may be losing weight due to the energy drain of lactation. As the offspring grows, its energy requirements also increase. In any childhood period, there should come a point at which the cost/benefit ratio to the mother favors her reducing her parental investment at the same time that the cost/benefit ratio for the offspring favors its demanding still more investment. Hence, there is conflict.

The most likely evolutionarily stable strategy is for a compromise. The nature of the compro-

mise is expected to vary according to the age of the parents and the mating system. Parents will be selected to give offspring more than parents would like but less than what offspring would like. As the mother ages, her cost decreases: she does not expect to have many more offspring. This would decrease conflict. The greatest parent-offspring conflict occurs when both parents are equally affected, as when there is extensive parental investment and monogamy (Parker & MacNair, 1979).

Primate infant-rearing patterns reveal this conflict (Dunbar, 1988; Nicolson, 1987; Whitten, 1987). The mother-offspring conflict becomes most acute at two stages: (1) weaning and (2) when the mother stops carrying the infant everywhere and the youngster now has to walk on its own. At both times, the mother may physically rebuff the infant's attempt to nurse or to be carried, and the infant may respond with temper tantrums.

The interactions of primate males with infants sometimes dramatically reflects the conflict between the adults' and the infant's interests (Dunbar, 1988; Nicolson, 1987; Whitten, 1987). Primate males may sometimes pick up offspring (often their own) when they are in conflict with another male. This puts the infant at risk but also often decreases the level of conflict, perhaps because the other male is afraid the infant's mother would also attack if the fight continued.

Infanticide also occurs among primates (Dunbar, 1988; Nicolson, 1987; Whitten, 1987). Most typically, the offspring are not their own and so any "request" for investment on the part of the youngster is likely to lead to conflict. When a new male takes over a group of females, he may kill their infants. By killing their offspring, he brings the females back into estrous sooner and thus maximizes his reproduction. Female infanticide occurs most often in older females, higher-ranking females, and females not closely related to mother or infant. This action may decrease the competition that the infanticidal female's own offspring will have to face as adults. In general, child abuse and neglect is also more common in humans when the adult is not biologically related to the child (e.g., stepparent) and among the younger and more impoverished mothers (who have more to lose and less to invest) (Daly & Wilson, 1980, 1985; Wilson, Daly, & Weghorst, 1980).

Attachment.   The degree to which a parent and child become attached to each other not only varies from family to family, it has durable developmental implications. **Attachment** refers to bonding relationships and interactions, usually between child and care-giver. The theory came originally from Bowlby, and a recent surge of research occurred when Ainsworth devised an interesting way to test attachment in human infants (Ainsworth, 1973, 1979; Lamb et al., 1984).

Bowlby's theory was evolutionary in nature. He proposed that a system of secure attachments between infant and mother was evolutionarily adaptive. It ensured protection and care from the mother and it ensured that infants would tend to stay close, away from possible predators. Selection pressures favored mothers and infants who became emotionally attached to each other early during infancy. Evolution also selected for behaviors on the part of the infant that would maintain caretaking (e.g., staying close, distress calls when mother is absent) and for appropriate caregiving behaviors on the part of the mother (going to infant after it makes a distress call).

Ainsworth designed the **Strange Situation** to test attachment in 12-month-old human infants. The infant was left in a room (the Strange Situation), and the mother (or father) and experimenter went through a scheduled series of departures and returns. The infant's responses to the returns of her mother were recorded. If the infant made contact with the mother upon her return, either physically or verbally, the infant was classified as securely attached. If the infant either avoided contact or expressed anger while making contact, the infant was classified

as insecurely attached. Secure attachment was regarded as the adaptive behavior.

Recent research has exposed both the power and the limitations of the Strange Situation measure (Hinde, 1981; Lamb et al., 1984). Responsive, sensitive, caring mothers are more likely to have attached infants, and attached infants are more likely to show healthy, intelligent, and adaptive behaviors 3 or more years later. However, it is not clear that attachment is the critical variable. The predictive validity of the Strange Situation depends on the family situation remaining constant between when attachment and when the adaptive behaviors are measured. In view of this, maybe some aspect of the family situation, such as stability versus instability, rather than attachment per se, is the important factor. The large cultural differences seen in the proportion of infants scored as being securely attached suggest that the measure may be valid only for the American culture. Attachment may also reflect infant characteristics as much as parenting styles. Finally, the often large sex differences suggest that whatever attachment is, it has different implications for male and female developments.

As Hinde (1981) suggested, perhaps evolution created not a closed by an **open** parental system. Rather than secure attachment being the most adaptive for all circumstances and so occurring in all healthy relationships (closed system), maybe different types of infant behavior are more adaptive for different cultures. If so, parenting as well as childhood behaviors might be open systems; parents could alter their child-rearing practices and thus their child's behaviors according to their own culture (environment). This could include adjusting child-rearing practices according to the child's gender.

Paternal absence and mating strategies. Draper and her colleagues (Draper & Belsky, 1990; Draper & Harpending, 1982) formulated an epigenetic model: because of genes selected by evolution, early childhood environment affects later adult behaviors, especially reproductive behaviors. The child is sensitive to the family environment because it provides cues as to what types of reproductive strategies might be most effective in his adult environment. Over time, genes sensitive to such aspects of the developmental environment would have been selected for because of cultural variations in conditions across time or across space. In particular, Draper thought that the presence versus the absence of a father during early development provided a cue as to whether monogamous or polygamous mating strategies might be more effective. In the reviews of relevant research, Draper and colleagues concluded that there were supportive findings for both sexes.

The effects of father absence are more dramatic the earlier and the longer the father is absent from the home. This is true whether the absence was due to death, desertion, being in a single-parent family, or role constraints (job, war).[7] Father-absent, compared to father-present, adult males are more aggressive and competitive, less likely to form long-term bonds with a woman or a child, and more often express unfavorable attitudes toward females and femininity. These males also tend to have higher verbal but lower spatial abilities. Father-present males are more occupationally stable. Other reviews and research of father-absent versus father-present children have confirmed that the father-absent children of both sexes are more aggressive (Allison & Furstenberg, 1989; Amato & Keith, 1991; Stevenson & Black, 1988).

Similar effects are found for females (Cherlin et al., 1991; Fleck et al., 1980; McLanahan & Bumpass, 1988). Father-absent females are sexually active earlier, have poorer abilities to establish long-term relationships with just one male, and have more negative attitudes toward men. Father-present females have more interest in marriage. Draper and Harpending (1982) reported that when both father-present and father-absent females were interviewed in research done by Hetherington, the father-absent females were more likely to flirt with the male interviewer. When the effects of divorce and remarriage are studied (Hetherington, 1989), the presence of biological fathers had more effects on the antisocial behaviors of girls, whereas either biological or stepfathers affected boys' behaviors.

The effects of the father's presence can be explained by modeling and attachments (proximal causes) and by paternal investments (ultimate cause). Mothers of the father-absent children more often have negative attitudes towards males, which could be modeled by their daughters. Another mechanism might be the security of the child's attachment to the parents. Parental absence would lead to less trust, which would lead to a more polygamous mating strategy. Furthermore, anything that is associated with insecure attachment relationships is also associated with higher levels of aggression later in childhood (Belsky, 1988). Father-absent families also experience less paternal investment, and the results can be viewed from this perspective as well. The greater the paternal investment (father-present children), the more likely that the offspring of both sexes are to pursue a reproductive strategy of great parental investment (monogamy) themselves. The next chapter will describe how human developmental processes may be sensitive to the paternal investment patterns of a culture as well as to those of a family.

BASIC DEVELOPMENTAL PROCESSES

Development is a complicated network of processes (Hogan, 1988). This section will first discuss processes for which there are obvious changes with age. The brain of a 1-year-old is markedly different from the brain of a 70-year-old. Puberty creates dramatic changes in internal processes and in external appearances. Presented next are the processes that are carried on throughout a lifetime, though the details can change with age. Whether there are qualitative or stagelike changes partially depends on how the researcher/theorist mentally visualizes development. If only a few ages are visualized, steplike changes might seem to occur, but if many, closely spaced ages are visualized, the processes would seem to be continuously changing.

Processes that Change with Development

Several processes change qualitatively as well as quantitatively as the child matures. This includes cognitive strategies, memory capacity, ability to inhibit responses, and increasing differentiation of various emotional reactions to situations. Some changes reflect the changes in brain anatomy occurring during early childhood and some depend on changes in environment.

Genes and environment sometimes act on growth and development in very similar ways. Consequently, any phenotype might come either from a gene or from a given developmental environment (or both) (Cairns, Gariépy, & Hood, 1990; Cheverud, 1988; Gottlieb, 1987; Hogan, 1988; Wake & Larson, 1987; see Chapter 5). One could develop a small body size either because of genes or because of not being fed enough sometime during development. One basic mechanism for evolution is to accelerate or delay developmental processes— something that can be accomplished by genes or the environment (e.g., diet). Life-history strategies can therefore be altered both by genes and the developmental environments. Changes in developmental rate allow new organizations or systems of behavior to appear.

In fact, both genes (evolution) and environment may tend to act on the same developmental processes, with equivalent outcomes (though through different mechanisms). The systems most susceptible to modification by selection pressures (evolution or selective breeding) might also be the ones most sensitive to the environment. Thus, both genes and developmental environments might similarly affect brain bio-

chemistry and thus adult behaviors.

Brain development. Brain organization changes with development. The brain's developing organization may be especially sensitive to the environment during times of rapid developmental changes, which could include some of the sensitive periods for sex hormone effects. Epigenetic development may have been selected for, as already described, because it is more efficient to use learning than to use an enlarged genome to specify some of the connections to be formed in a large brain. Epigenetic development also allows the construction of a brain optimally suited for processing information about the developmental environment, which will probbly be similar to the environment in which the adult will have to compete for survival and reproduction. A brain open to environmental programming would "tailor" the brain for that particular environment. One implication of this is that if the postnatal environments of the sexes are systematically different, because, for example, parents treat boys differently from girls, the sexes would develop some systematic differences in brain organization that did *not* come from genes or hormones. This research is extremely important because it documents the extent to which sex differences in developmental environments could produce sex differences in adult brains and behaviors.

Although postnatal development probably does not involve the creation of new nerve cells for humans and other primates, creation of new cells well after birth has been seen in other species (see Chapter 6). Postnatal brain reorganization involves nerve cells competing with each other to form synapses. Only those synpses that are used (activated by events in the environment) survive, and only those nerves that form synapses survive (Greenough, Black, & Wallace, 1987; Hoyenga & Hoyenga, 1988; Nowakowski, 1987; Rakic & Riley, 1983). The competitive developmental changes depend on neural activity, which depends on the young organism's environment (van Huizen, Romijn,

& Corner, 1987; Nelson et al., 1989). In rhesus monkeys, the time of greatest change in brain structure (2 to 4 months) is also the time at which there are marked changes in sensory-motor coordination and cognitive/memory skills (Rakic et al., 1986).

The developmental environment does affect the adult's brain and behaviors (Bertenthal & Campos, 1987; Cooper & Zubek, 1958; Greenough, Black, & Wallace, 1987; Harwerth et al., 1986; Hirsch & Tieman, 1987; Hoyenga & Hoyenga, 1988). Although most research has focused on the visual system, similar effects of the developmental environment are seen in other sensory systems. To some extent, what the adult organism can see and what kinds of stimuli it is particularly likely to pay attention to depends on what kinds of stimuli were present in its developmental environment. For many species, being raised in a developmentally enriched environment (lots of things to see and do), as opposed to being raised alone in empty metal cages, changes the brain as well as improves some learning performances. In one set of studies, not only did enrichment affect the microanatomy of the hippocampus and the visual cortex but there were sex differences in the degree to which the anatomy was sensitive to experience (Juraska, 1990, 1991; Juraska, Kopcik, Washburne, & Perry, 1988). Some of the sex differences depended on neonatal hormones (Juraska et al., 1988).

Some developmental events modify the duration of the sensitive period. Certain genes in primate visual cortical neurons remain active as long as the newborn animals are deprived of light. This suggests that the light exposure during normal development deactivates some genes in the process of forming specific synaptic interconnections (Neve & Bear, 1989). Exposure to mild stress during the neonatal period may prolong the epigenetic brain development period, allowing even more opportunity for experiences to "instruct" brain connections (Altman, Das, & Anderson, 1968).

Some developmental changes in the human brain are presented in Figures 9.1 and 9.2. The number of neurons, synapses, and receptors for transmitter substances show age-related changes. Human development may also have sensitive periods (Hoyenga & Hoyenga, 1988; Money & Annecillo, 1987). For example, early in development, children learn to perceive the sounds associated with the language of their culture. If, as adults, they attempt to learn a language that has sounds not present in their childhood language, they will be unable to hear the differences among words using those sounds (Snow, 1987).

Sex differences in brain developmental rates are also seen. The ability to inhibit a response seems to depend on the development of the frontal cortex (Diamond & Doar, 1988; Diamond & Goldman-Rakic, 1989; Diamond, Zola-Morgan, & Squire, 1989). Both the frontal cortex and response inhibition develop faster in a male monkey because of his prenatal testosterone (T) (Clark & Goldman-Rakic, 1989; Goldman et al., 1974). On the other hand, not only do human females develop inhibition sooner but boys are relatively more often impulsive and girls more often controlled. Although the frontal cortex develops faster in male monkeys, other parts of the cortex seem to develop faster in both human and nonhuman primate females. The higher the neonatal T level, the slower the development.[8] Perhaps because of this, only in females do some infant traits (hand preferences, vocalizations) predict later traits (intellectual development) (Cameron, Livson, & Bayley, 1967; Gottfried & Bathurst, 1983).

Cognitive and emotional changes. One recent theory (Case et al., 1988) related the cognitive developmental changes, viewed from a Piagetian perspective, to age-related changes in emotional reactions. Since children actively interpret and attempt to control emotion-producing situations, their emotional reactions change as their cognitive complexity increases. Thus, adult sex differences in emotional

FIGURE 9.1   *Lifetime Developmental Changes in the Human Brain*
Part A: Mean number of synapses per neuron in the frontal cortex. Synaptic density increases
during infancy, remains stable through adulthood, and then declines. Part B: The number
of spines (synapses) per neuron in the visual cortex. Part C: Another look at changes in synaptic density as a function of age in the visual cortex. The closed circles are synaptic densities,
and the open circles are the volumes of that part of the brain at those ages, for comparison.
Part D: Changes in the number of dopamine receptors with age in the substantia nigra (a motor
area). NB = not born; 33w and 28w = weeks from conception.

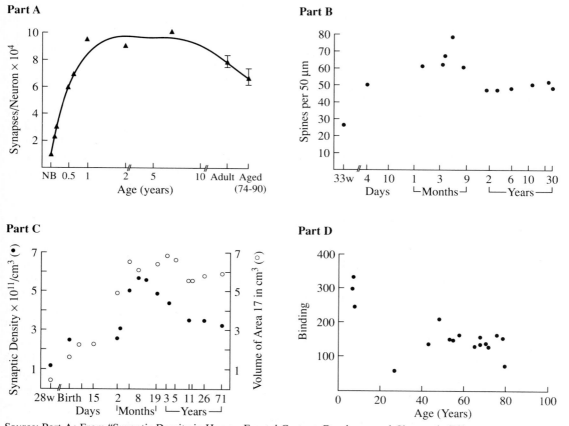

Source: Part A: From "Synaptic Density in Human Frontal Cortex—Developmental Changes in Effects
of Aging" by P. R. Huttenlocher, 1979, *Brain Research, 163,* p. 203. Copyright 1979 by Elsevier Scientific Publishers Ireland Ltd. Reprinted by permission. Part B: From "The Development of Dendritic Spines
in the Human Visual Cortex" by A. E. Michel and L. J. Garey, 1984, *Human Neurobiology, 3,* p. 226.
Copyright 1984 by Springer-Verlag, Neidelberg. Reprinted by permission. Part C: From "Synaptogenesis
in Human Visual Cortex—Evidence for Synapse Elimination during Normal Development" by P. R.
Huttenlocher, C. de Courten, L. J. Garey, and H. van der Loos, 1982, *Neuroscience Letters, 33,* p. 250.
Copyright 1982 by Elsevier Scientific Publishers Ireland Ltd. Reprinted by permission. Part D: Reprinted
with permission from *Neuroscience, 28* (2), 263–273, R. Cortés, B. Gueye, A. Pazos, A. Probst, and
J. M. Palacios, Dopamine receptors in human brains: Autoradiographic distribution of D_1 sites, Copyright
1989, Pergamon Press plc.

Part A

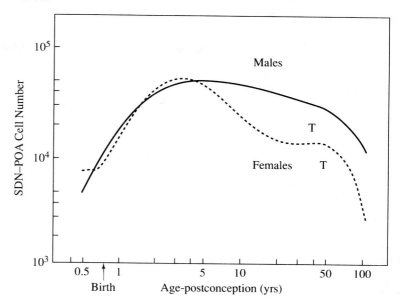

FIGURE 9.2 *Development and Sexual Dimorphism in the Human SDN-POA* This figure shows how the sexually dimorphic nucleus of the preoptic area (SDN-POA) develops in the human brain. Sexual differentiation appears around 2 to 4 years of age, due to a loss of cell numbers in females. Later in life (50 to 80 years of age), the nucleus is also dimorphic, but it is now larger in females because of a loss of cells in aging males. Part A: Cell number, in both sexes, concentrating on early life. The *T*s correspond to the size of the SDN-POA found in two male-to-female transsexuals. Part B: Sex ratio (M/F) of cell number, showing how aging affects the sexual dimorphism of this area.

Source: From "The Sexually Dimorphic Nucleus of the Preoptic Area in the Human Brain: A Comparative Morphometric Study" by M. A. Hofman and D. F. Swaab, 1989, *Journal of Anatomy, 164,* p. 64. Reprinted by permission from Cambridge University Press.

Part B

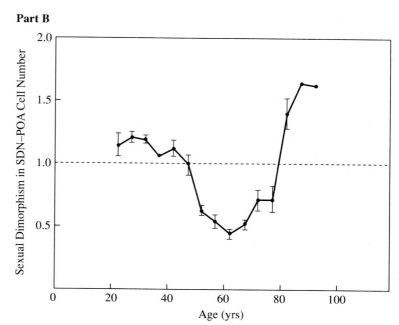

reactions could depend on the age at which the sexes experienced systematically different events or treatments by parents.

Cognitive skills also systematically change during development in both humans and nonhumans (Amsel, 1986; Green & Stanton, 1989; White, 1965). Memory capacity increases (Bandura, 1986; Case et al., 1988; Miller, 1989).

As was just described, the ability to delay a response starts developing during infancy.

Puberty. Puberty is a time of dramatic changes. There is an increased rate of change of bones, height, weight, body fat, size of secondary sex characteristics, and hormone levels (Brooks-Gunn & Warren, 1985b). Puberty may be another sensitive period for the epigenetic control of brain development. Certainly some important neural changes do occur then (see Part C of Figure 9.1; Benes, 1989; Meyer, Ferres-Torres, & Mas, 1978). Compared to other primates, a greater proportion of the human life span occurs before puberty (Savin-Williams & Weisfeld, 1989). Since the timing of puberty is sexually dimorphic (see Chapter 8), so may its effects be. Some cognitive and behavioral traits seem to depend on the timing of puberty, perhaps because puberty timing reflects general developmental rate (see Chapter 14). As such, the timing of puberty may be an important marker or an indication of the effects that changes in developmental rates may have on human traits and characteristics.

Some males and females mature early and some mature late, compared to their age-mates. The effect of this timing depends on one's peers as well as other events in one's life (Brooks-Gunn, Peterson, & Eichorn, 1985; Hill et al., 1985; Peterson, 1988; Simmons et al., 1979). Having puberty around the same time most of one's peers do may be less stressful than having an unusually early or an unusually late — and hence potentially stigmatizing — puberty. If pubertal events occur at the same time in life that other important changes also occur, such as changing schools, the combined effects can be much more extensive than the effects of each by itself.

During puberty, both conflict with and distance from parents increase, especially with regard to mothers (Steinberg, 1989). This may reflect changing patterns of parental investment and the need for offspring to become independent of their parents. For males, conflict with mothers decreases after puberty, largely because mothers begin deferring more often to their sons. In fact, for boys, moderate as opposed to either high or low levels of conflict with parents leads to higher self-reliance, more resistance to peer pressure, and greater psychological health. For girls, closeness to parents seems to delay maturation; girls raised in intact households have a later puberty than do girls raised in nonintact homes (Surbey, as described by Steinberg, 1989).

Puberty has traditionally been seen as a period of marked changes in traits, attitudes, and behaviors (Peterson, 1988). One extensive longitudinal study examined changes in self-concept over three periods in various groups of adolescents ranging from age 11 to 18 and found considerable change as well as significant stability in attitudes toward the self (Dusek & Flaherty, 1981). Rutter and Garmezy (1983) described evidence for rather dramatic changes in emotional disorders. Few childhood emotional disorders persist past puberty into adult life. Depression can occur before adolescence, but its frequency dramatically increases at that time, especially in females. Delinquent activity peaks during adolescence, especially in males, but drops afterwards.

Environmental changes. There are also extremely important and systematic age-related changes in a child's environment. As pointed out, sometimes the effects of puberty's timing depend on the time of other events in the person's life. In our culture, children go to school at around age 6, which is a dramatic change in environment that must affect cognitive, emotional, and social development. For the first time, children are being graded and actively compared to their age-peers. Later, children must shift schools and thus peer groups. According to cultural practices, parents also decide when their children will have to cope with weaning and toilet training and when the children will be given responsibility for various tasks (see Chapter 10).

Many stagelike changes in children could reflect environmental changes rather than any endogenous process. This is important because boys and girls of the same physical age are often at different developmental ages, with females being more advanced (Tanner, 1981). For example, throughout childhood and adolescence, girls are more emotionally, motivationally, and socially mature than boys of the same chronological age (Cohn, 1991). Because of this, the dramatic environmental changes just described could impact girls and boys differentially.

Processes Occurring Throughout Development

Other aspects of the developmental sequence are more continuous in nature. Some processes act throughout development. In other cases, once a process appears, it remains throughout the rest of development, even though its structure can be altered by subsequent experiences. Our ways of describing ourselves as males or females is one example.

Self-concept and gender identity. Harter (1983) described developmental changes in self-concept. The self is both a subject and an object of cognitive processes. The self as a subject is that which does the thinking, behaving, and deciding; it is an active, independent, causal agent. The self as an object is a category of attributes defined as being related in some way to the self. The object self is categorized in the same way as is any external object or person. Just as with other categories, the self category is associated with certain self-relevant attitudes. When we perceive ourselves as thinking about ourselves, we are using both senses of self.

A central part of the concepts of self and others is gender identity and gender-role identity. According to Kohlberg, gender labeling occurs from ages 2 to 3, and gender constancy appears between ages 6 to 7. Young children may also use the words *mommy* and *daddy* to distinguish between any female and male adults

even before they identify themselves as girls or boys (Cahill, 1986). Our gendered self-concepts reflect cultural gender stereotypes and the gender dimorphic environments of our rearing (see Chapters 11 and 12).

Some people, called **transsexuals,** at some point begin to believe that their bodies do not match their gender identities (Abramowitz, 1986; Blanchard, Clemmensen, & Steiner, 1987; Brown, 1990; Bullough, Bullough, & Smith, 1983; Gooren, 1984, 1986a, 1986b; also see references in Hoyenga & Hoyenga, 1993). A genetically, hormonally, and anatomically normal male may decide that she is really a female in a male's body (or vice versa, for a female transsexual). Treatment options include both sex-change surgery and psychotherapy. Currently, both environmental and biological developmental covariates are being explored. When researchers understand how transsexuals developed their transsexual identities, there will be a better understanding of how any gender identity develops.

Language and culture may affect gender-identity development. Some languages distinguish the gender not only of people (e.g., *him* versus *her* in English) but of all objects, and maybe even verbs. Gender identity may undergo somewhat more rapid development when a child grows up learning a very gender-differentiated language (Abelson, 1979; Beit-Hallahmi et al., 1974). Among adolescents, gender forms a more important part of the social identity of some groups, such as Asians and Hispanics, than of other groups, such as American Caucasians (Garza & Herringer, 1988).

Modeling. Modeling starts very early in development and continues throughout life. Paralleling the development of symbolic capacity, the child becomes more selective as to models and actions to be imitated (Maccoby & Martin, 1983). Kohlberg's research described earlier suggested that boy's preferential imitation of male over female models could begin as early as age 5; same-sex modeling is not as strong a mechanism in girls.

Appropriate versus inappropriate models. Perry and Bussey (1979) confirmed that children do not automatically, nonspecifically model any same-sex adult in preference to any opposite-sex adult. They also found important sex differences. In one experiment, 8-year-old children, 42 boys and 42 girls, were assigned to 1 of 6 different kinds of modeling conditions. In *Phase I*, half the children observed 8 adult models, 4 of each gender, making choices among 16 pairs of objects. The children viewed a videotape of 8 adults, 4 of each sex, each one of whom made a series of 16 choices between each of 16 different pairs of objects. For each choice, one of the female models made the same choice that three of the male models did, and one of the male models matched the choices of three of the females. The same man and the same woman played the discrepant role throughout all the object choices, which made each one of them an inappropriate model for a same-sex child.

In *Phase II,* all the children viewed another videotape showing either a same-sex model (for half the children of each sex) or an opposite-sex model making choices among a different 16 pairs of objects. Half the children saw one of the models who had agreed with the choices made by the other people of his or her gender in the Phase I videotape: these children saw an appropriate model. Half the children saw the model who had disagreed with the other people of his or her gender: an inappropriate model. Some control children just saw the Phase II videotape, not the Phase I videotape, and so they had never seen their Phase II model before. Children in the no-model control group did not see any videotape in either Phase I or II.

Each child's score was based on the number of choices she or he made that matched the choices made by the model that child had observed in the Phase II videotape.[9] In Table 9.1, notice that in the appropriate model condition, the boys exposed to a male model matched that model's choices on nearly 15 of the 16 trials, on the average. Likewise, the girls exposed to an appropriate female model

TABLE 9.1 *Imitative Performance Means for Interaction of Sex of Subject, Sex Appropriateness of Model, and Sex of Model (Experiment 2).*
Each mean is based on six subjects' scores; each score is based on the number of choices made that matched those made by that child's model in Phase II. Cells *not* sharing a common subscript differ significantly from each other.

| Subject and Model | Sex Appropriateness of Model | | | No-Model Control (from Experiment 1) |
	Appropriate	*Inappropriate*	*No-Premodeling Control*	
Boys				
Male model	14.7_f	4.3_a	13.2_{def}	8.5
Female model	3.5_a	9.3_{bc}	12.0_{de}	
Girls				
Male model	8.2_b	11.2_{cd}	12.7_{def}	8.2
Female model	14.3_{ef}	8.3_b	12.8_{def}	

Source: From "The Social Learning Theory of Sex Differences: Imitation Is Alive and Well" by D. G. Perry and K. Bussey, 1979, *Journal of Personality and Social Psychology, 37,* p. 1707. Copyright 1979 by the American Psychological Association. Reprinted by permission.

matched that model's choices on just over 14 of the 16 trials. There are three other, even more important, outcomes of this experiment. First, there was no differential same-sex modeling seen in the no-premodeling control group where the children had no prior information about their model. Second, when exposed to an inappropriate model, children tended to avoid that model's choices rather than model them. Third, boys showed significantly more avoidance of an appropriate but opposite-sex model's choices, and significantly more avoidance of an inappropriate same-sex model's choices than girls did.

Just as Kohlberg's and Bandura's theories would predict, children do not uncritically model the behaviors of any model to which they are exposed. They actively process information about the model, and only if they decide that the model can provide "good" information do their choices significantly match those of their models. Even more important, boys are more sensitive to the gender of the models than girls are—or else girls do more opposite-sex modeling because of the greater prestige and competence associated with the male role in our society.

Attributions and goal orientations. As children mature, their explanations for their behavior, or their **attributions,** change. The attributional changes affect how they react to successes and failures, leading to changes in goal orientations (Dweck & Elliot, 1983). After age 7, children begin to explain their own behaviors more in terms of personal traits rather than situations. A 7-year-old girl might explain why she had hit a boy by saying, "I find it hard to control my temper" rather than, "He made me very angry."

Because of this attributional shift, children begin reacting differently to successes and failures. Although kindergarten and first-grade children rank other children's relative academic abilities just as the teacher does, most rank themselves as being at the top of the class. After

this age, children's rankings of themselves come more in line with the teacher's rankings. They start reacting negatively to failure, saying they will never be able to do some task at which they had just failed, probably because they explain the failure as being due to their own lack of ability (an internal or personal attribution). At this point, children become susceptible to learned helplessness. The age-related changes occur earlier in girls than in boys, so girls experience shame in the school environment sooner than boys do.

Theories of self and others. All of these developmental changes affect the child's concept of himself and others. The child begins constructing a theory or story with himself as a central character (Epstein, 1973; Greenwald, 1980; Kihlstrom & Cantor, 1984; McAdams, 1989; Ross, 1989). The story incorporates both self as object and self as subject: the subject of the child's story both acts and is the object of self-descriptions and attitudes. The story has a past, a present, and continuity, the protagonist being viewed as being the same person throughout life.

The developing life story has some fictional elements. To protect self-esteem, judicious editing of present and past always occurs: there is bias in both memories and in current perceptions. Sometimes the past is rewritten to bring it more in line with descriptions of the current self. Recurrent or continuous mood states can affect the story. People who are not depressed exaggerate the degree of control they have had and will have over other people and things. However, depressed people do not do much of this ego-protecting exaggeration, and women are more likely to develop depression than men are (see Chapter 13). A person's gender identity, gender-role identity, and acceptance of cultural sex-role stereotypes will bias the storytelling (see Chapter 11).

Dweck has proposed a very intriguing variant of this idea (Dweck & Elliot, 1983; Dweck & Leggett, 1988). She and her colleagues suggested that children think of intelligence as being either **fixed** or **incremental** in nature. A child with an incremental theory views her intelligence as being increased with effort and learning. On the other hand, if the child views intelligence as being fixed, she believes that intelligence cannot be increased. Her intelligence can be believed to be fixed either high or low, and her ability to perform any task would indicate her fixed intelligence. Having an incremental theory may lead to better study habits and may account for the better academic achievements of Chinese and Chinese-American students compared to white American students (Chen & Uttal, 1988; Nolen, 1988). Although both theories of intelligence appear equally often in both sexes, among the children who are fixed theorists, low task confidence (low efficacy) appears more often in girls than in boys (also see Bandura, 1986). As a consequence, more girls would have low task confidence and would show avoidance of difficult tasks, emotional distress, and helplessness.

Huston's Concepts of Sex Typing

Sex typing is the development of gender-related differences in children (Huston, 1983). Sex typing changes continuously with age. It was viewed as a desirable process until around 1973, but since then, sex typing has been increasingly regarded as putting limitations on children's capabilities. Table 9.2 presents Huston's (1983) theory of the nature and content of sex typing. Children form attitudes toward aspects of their gender as well as toward people of the other gender. Areas about which children form these attitudes are found in the five rows of Table 9.2 (under the column label "Area"). The aspects or contents of each attitude area are indicated in the last four columns of that table, corresponding to each of the five rows or areas. Gender-related differences are found in all areas, and the child's models will express those differences. According to Bandura's and Kohlberg's theories, the gender-dimorphic culture will then be perpetuated from one generation to the next.

In each content area, children acquire beliefs, perceptions of self, affective responses (preferences and values), and behavioral tendencies. These are acquired through conditioning, modeling, and direct instruction, as described by Bandura and Kohlberg. Children are active agents, and what they learn will critically depend on what they believe and perceive during their developmental experiences. Self-perception of interests develops before gender identity, and self-perception of one's own personality traits develops even later.

Predictability and Stability

In **longitudinal research,** a group of people are repeatedly measured at several different ages (Mussen, 1987). Two aspects of longitudinal research are particularly important for sex differences, as will be explained. One concerns the extent to which an adult's traits can be predicted either from the traits he had as a child or from the way he was treated as a child. The second is the extent to which traits remain a stable part of a person from childhood through adulthood. Even if an adult trait is not stable, it may still be predictable: a given childhood trait could reliably develop into a qualitatively different adult trait.

Developmental process theorists would expect both predictability and stability, but socialization theorists would not be surprised at the lack of either. With regard to sex differences, if sex differences found among children are to be relevant to gender-related differences among adults, the adult traits must be either stable or predictable. There is also the possibility that similar childhood traits or parental treatment may develop into distinctly different adult traits, depending on gender.

Parental behaviors. Research has seen few consistencies between child-rearing practices and adult outcomes (Maccoby & Martin, 1983;

TABLE 9.2   *Matrix of Sex-Typing Attitudes: Area in which the Attitude is Expressed, by Aspect of Attitude (e.g., Cognitive, Affective, etc.)*

Area	Cognitive: Beliefs	Cognitive: Self-Perception	Affective: Preferences and Values	Behavior Tendencies
1. Genital gender	Gender constancy	Gender identity; gender-role identity	Wish to be male or female; value attached to each gender	Displaying gender through clothing, body type, hair, etc.
2. Activities and interests: toys, play, occupations, tasks, achievement areas	Beliefs about gender-related differences in abilities and interests; attributions of others	Self-perception of interests and abilities; attributions of self	Preferences for toys, games, activities, achievements	Engaging in games, toy play, activities, toy play, occupations
3. Personal-social attributes, personality, social behavior	Beliefs about gender-related differences in personality and social behaviors	Perception of own personality	Preference for certain traits and characteristics	Displaying sex-typed personal-social behavior
4. Gender-based social relationships; sex of peers, models, etc.	Beliefs about sex-typed norms for gender-related differences in social relationships	Self-perception of own patterns of friendships or sexual orientation	Preference for male or female friends; wish to be feminine or masculine	Engaging in social or sexual activity with others on the basis of their gender
5. Stylistic and symbolic content; nonverbal behavior, speech patterns, styles of play and fantasy, etc.	Beliefs about gender-related differences in nonverbal behaviors and speech patterns	Self-perception of speech and gestures	Preference for certain styles of speech and gestures	Displaying certain styles of speech and gestures, etc., drawing male versus female figures first

Source: From A. C. Huston in P. H. Mussen and E. M. Hetherington (Eds.), *Handbook of Child Psychology,* copyright © 1983, John Wiley & Sons. Adapted by permission of John Wiley & Sons, Inc.

Note: Some entries have been changed to make the terminology more consistent with that used in this book.

McCrae & Costa, 1988a, 1988b; Mussen, 1987). The relationships observed between specific parental behaviors and the child's adult behaviors are never large, and they vary from one study to another. The most consistency comes from the contrast of various kinds of parental styles of discipline and control. The most desirable outcomes seem most often to be associated with parents setting clear limits but allowing flexibility within those limits. Even here, the outcome depends on the child's gender, with clearer effects seen for boys than for girls (see Chapter 12). If parental behaviors are important, they probably have different effects on children according to their age, birth order, genotype, and gender (L. W. Hoffman, 1991). This means that, in humans, most maternal effects take the form of maternal selection.

One productive line of research looks at how both genes and parental behaviors and family environments contribute to developmental processes and adult traits and characteristics (see documentation in Hoyenga & Hoyenga, 1993). The designs employed in these studies are quite powerful; since genetic similarities among family members can be controlled (by being measured), similarities and differences in traits must be due to similarities and differences in environments. This makes genetic research a potentially powerful technique for demonstrating which, and when, sex differences in developmental environments and experiences are important to adult gender-related differences. The interactive effects of parental genes as well as parentally structured environments can be investigated. For example, parents with a high IQ supply not only IQ genes to their offspring but may also provide a rich developmental environment.

Children's genes also affect to which developmental experiences the children will tend to expose themselves. In fact, people's genes can be correlated with their developmental environments (Loehlin & DeFries, 1987). An **active correlation** would occur if a child, because of possessing certain genes, actively selected certain environments in which to develop (friends, toys). A **reactive correlation** could occur if the child, because of having certain genes, tended to provoke certain responses from people in the environment. If the same parents who supplied the child's genes also supplied the environment, there would be a **passive correlation.** This could be true for sex-linked and sex-limited genes as well. Rose (1988) found that the nature of the interaction between genes and environments often depended on gender.

Gene-trait correlations also depend on the child's age (see Hoyenga & Hoyenga, 1993). Adoptive studies have shown that the natural parent-child correlations often increase with the age of the offspring. For example, the similarity of the IQs of natural parents and their children increases with age, whereas the similarity for adoptive parents and their children decreases with age. Similarly, Plomin (1991) found that the correlations between the IQs of adoptive pairs of siblings decreased from .26 when they were about age 8, to .02 when they were about age 18. On the other hand, twin studies have shown that with most trait measures, both personality and cognitive, twins tend to become more *dissimilar* the older they get, suggesting that the aspects of their environments unique to each affect their traits, making them different. Twins do, however, show very similar developmental trends, having growth spurts at the same ages. Overall, traits seem to depend most on genes and unique environments, *not* on who the parents are or their style of parenting. Who parents are is often less important than how one parent treated one specific child differently from all that child's siblings.

Stability over age. Stability of traits, characteristics, and attitudes over age is very moderate (Kagan, 1984; Rutter & Garmezy, 1983). The most stable traits are intelligence and aggression (Parke & Slaby, 1983; see Chapter 13). One review (Kohlberg, Ricks, & Snarey, 1984) concluded that only a few adult traits (e.g., IQ, schizophrenia, and sociopathy) could be predicted from childhood characteristics. Measures of IQ generally are not only stable but are also associated with adult adjustment. Higher IQ children are somewhat more likely than lower IQ children to develop into well-adjusted, productive adults. Adult sociopathy and schizophrenia can be predicted by using information about genes, environments, and childhood behaviors, although the predictability for schizophrenia in males is better than for females.

The ability to delay gratification may also predict adult traits (Funder, Block, & Block, 1983; Mischel, Shoda, & Peake, 1988; Mischell, Shoda, & Rodriguez, 1989). Delay of gratification can be measured in several ways, not all of which may have the same predictive ability. Often the child is given a choice between an immediate, less desirable reward and a delayed but more desirable reward. In other instances, the child is asked not to touch an attractive toy. The ability to delay is greater among girls than among boys, but in both sexes, the ability to delay as a child can predict adolescent characteristics. Children who could delay longer developed into more cognitively and socially competent adolescents, and even got higher scores on the scholastic aptitude test scores, both verbal and quantitative. However, the correlations between delay and the traits measured later tended to be higher for males, and the size of the correlations tended to decrease with age for females but actually to increase with age for males.

Two other characteristics, children's shyness and ill temper, also predict adult characteristics and do so differentially by gender (Caspi, Elder, & Bem, 1987, 1988). Overall, more girls than boys were shy, and more boys than girls were ill-tempered. In a longitudinal study, men with histories of childhood temper tantrums developed into adults in whom job changes and divorce were common. Ill-tempered girls developed into women who married low-status men, frequently got divorced, and were ill-tempered as mothers. Shy boys were developmentally delayed with regard to the major milestones of marriage, parenthood, and stable careers. Shy girls developed into women who married, bore children, and made a stable home, interrupting any job to take on these duties. In fact, their husbands had higher occupational status than the husbands of the comparison women. However, the sex differences in the outcomes probably depend on historical conditions, since young women now are expected to be more occupationally assertive (see Chapter 12). Still, this suggests that similar childhood traits can develop into different kinds of adult life patterns, depending on gender.

Stability, or its lack, does not allow one to conclude anything about the comparative roles of genes versus environments. Stability could reflect one's unchanging genes or could reflect the influence of a stable environment. Lack of stability may reflect environmental change, but it may also have a large genetic component, such as the pubertal appearance of the genetically biased trait of schizophrenia in males.[10] Genetically influenced family traits can change over time: the increasing correlations found among family members as the children mature. Models that incorporate both are the only way to assess how genes and stable environments both contribute to stability, and how genes and environmental changes both contribute to longitudinal discontinuities.

SUMMARY

Development is an epigenetic processes, with continuities and apparent discontinuities and with some stability and predictability despite the discontinuities. The environment affects development and adult behaviors through operant conditioning, classical conditioning, and observational learning. However, since the brain develops epigenetically and seems to be especially open to influence during early childhood and perhaps during puberty (discontinuities), both learning and types of experiences other than learning can affect brain anatomy and adult behaviors and capabilities. Among the theorists covered in this chapter, Freud and Kohlberg emphasized developmental processes and thus continuities. Bandura emphasized the temporary nature of socialization influences and thus discontinuities.

The developmental process at all times reflects the impact of both genes and environmental experiences. Both affect brain anatomy, both affect the child's developing traits and intellectual skills, and both can lead to stability or change. This should be as true of sexually dimorphic developmental processes as it is of development in general, with one added factor: gender may affect the form of the interaction.

The concepts and principles of this chapter are applied in the rest of this unit. Since observational learning evolved, we can acquire culture and so can seek out models and learn rules and proscriptions for sex typing that vary according to our culture. Because modeling is important for sex typing, gender stereotypes will be passed on from parent to child, from one generation to the next, and from one child to the next. Girls are also systematically exposed to fewer same-sex models that have prestige and power than boys are, which must affect their development.

ENDNOTES

1. This is a ledgelike bar that extends out from the side of the experimental apparatus.

2. Note that this is *not* an extinction trial.

3. The physiological and biochemical mechanisms required to form the neural connections of one type of memory system are entirely different from the mechanisms required for another system.

4. Kohlberg died before he had completely developed his theory as it applied to girls. The names given to Kohlberg's stages are those of the authors', not Kohlberg's.

5. Exceptions do occur, but may be related to differences in the attractiveness of the modeled behaviors versus the other behaviors available (e.g., Barkley et al., 1977).

6. Since these effects also can include fathers, the name is somewhat of a misnomer.

7. Except where explicitly cited, see Draper's reviews for the relevant research.

8. Bachevalier et al., 1990; Bachevalier, Hagger, & Bercu, 1989; Bauer et al., 1986; Creighton, 1984; Held, Bauer, & Gwiazda, 1988; Held, Shimojo, & Gwiazda, 1984.

9. For the no-model control group, the score was based on the number of choices that an appropriate same-sex model had made, which, of course, that child had never seen.

10. One of the best documented results of studies of sex differences in schizophrenia is that it appears about five years earlier in males than in females (Angermeyer & Kühn, 1988; Bardenstein & McGlashan, 1990; Haffner et al., 1989).

CHAPTER 10

CULTURAL INFLUENCES ON GENDER-RELATED DIFFERENCES

INTRODUCTION
CONCEPTS AND TENSIONS IN CURRENT ANTHROPOLOGY
EVOLUTION OF SOCIAL BEHAVIOR AND CULTURE
CULTURE AND CHILD SOCIALIZATION
CULTURAL VARIABILITY AMONG ADULTS
SUMMARY

Scientific understanding of human development can only advance when findings reported in one culture are tested cross-culturally.
—B. Whiting and C. P. Edwards (1988, p. ix)

Early twentieth-century theorists claimed that hunting was an exclusively male activity in all primates, including the human. Because of this assumption, most descriptions of human evolution and of the behaviors of primitive peoples included male hunters and female gatherers: the **hunter-gatherer** *theory of human evolution. But primate females do hunt. In one group of olive baboons, hunting of small animals was observed to increase from 1970 to 1974, and females did 14 percent of the killing, particularly of small game such as hares and birds (Strum, 1975). Among the Agta hunter-gatherers of the Philippines, women also hunt; indeed, "women seem to account for not much less than half of the total kill of major prey" (Goodman, Griffin, Estioko-Griffin, & Grove, 1985). So why don't all primate females hunt?*

An evolutionary theory of human psychology, including sex differences in traits and behavioral tendencies, can be tested only in a cross-cultural context (Barkow, 1989). What sorts of environments (social and ecological) lead to what sorts of sex differences? Although past anthropologists have looked at gender-related differences solely from the point of view of a hunter-gatherer evolutionary past, that story has changed and will probably change again. Just how does being male and female vary from culture to culture and from evolutionary past to present? Since "gender is, in its various forms, a fundamental structuring principle" (Wylie, 1991, p. 41), how does culture depend on gender?

INTRODUCTION

This chapter describes how culture may affect gender-related differences in human behaviors. The first section discusses anthropology as a discipline of human knowledge. The next section describes the evolution of social behavior and culture. It includes the possibility that hunting affected the evolution of sex differences and thereby affected the roles assigned to the two genders. These role assignments are similar (but *not* universally the same) in many different cultures. The last section documents the extensive cross-cultural variability in gender differences, as well as the commonalities. It also looks at some possible mechanisms and covariates for the role assignments and the social status of women relative to the status of men.

CONCEPTS AND TENSIONS IN CURRENT ANTHROPOLOGY

Anthropology as a discipline of human knowledge has experienced a philosophical split. Although the roots of the split can be traced to the nineteenth century, the approaches of the two anthropological groups have become even more strongly dichotomized in the last 40 years, and the dichotomies have created tensions. Most likely the tensions have served to advance the field; criticism from one "camp" causes the other "camp" to rethink its positions.

Historical

"From its inception, anthropology has been concerned with the search for general or universalistic laws that 'explain' social and cultural phenomena" (Moles, 1977). Hunter-gatherers having minimal contact with civilization and people with more technological cultures were both studied. The aim was to combine all the data sets and devise a theory that used a limited number of principles to explain any culture.

The techniques and assumptions used by early anthropologists differ from those used today. Early observers of primitive peoples were military men, missionaries, explorers, traders, and colonial administers who recorded their observations. Later, anthropologists were trained largely in universities and felt rushed in their attempts to describe the many rapidly disappearing cultures. All of these data were added to the **ethnographic record** of the customs, beliefs, and behaviors of peoples of various cultures.

Doubts began to creep in. Were the ethnographic records accurate and objective recordings of the people? The rise of the social sciences of psychology and sociology led to the recognition of possible biases. Anthropologists viewed other cultures in terms of their own — they described a culture according to the categories and schema they learned by growing up in their own cultures. However, the categories used by any anthropologist may not be relevant to the way the primitive people view their worlds and lives. For example, cultural biases have been recognized in Margaret Mead's landmark study of cultural variability in sex roles (Gewertz, 1984). How the people of the Tchambuli culture of Papua New Guinea felt about themselves was inadvertently distorted by Mead's attempts to fit them to her Western ideas of masculinity and femininity.

The rise of feminism in anthropology has dramatically accelerated the discovery of bias (Atkinson, 1982). The biased view of women was created by having largely male anthropologists interviewing mostly male native peoples. In fact, the view of native women was sent through two sets of biasing "filters." One was created by the culture of the male anthropologist and one was created by the views that the men of the culture being studied had about the women (as opposed to the views women have about themselves).

The indigenous people also have biases about themselves. People may say they believe something and then act in quite another way. Anthropologists made extensive use of interviews of selected people of a culture, especially the males, to gather their data about customs and beliefs. But are the beliefs as described in the interview the ones that actually affect the peoples' day-to-day behaviors? As Moles (1977) described it, when anthropologists asked informants to explain why certain things were done in certain ways, "perhaps they had never had a reason to explain it verbally or consider the reason for it until the question was raised. In order to please the strange new friends [the anthropologists], informants may make an effort to devise some reasonable explanation for their behavior, and, as a consequence, culture is invented" (p. 255).

Perhaps both behaviors and beliefs should be studied, looking for areas of agreement and discrepancy. For example, the residents of an Israeli kibbutz (a settlement or farm founded on explicitly sex-egalitarian principles) say they believe that roles and traits should not be distinguished on the basis of gender. Despite this, they act as though there were gender-related differences (Rosner, 1967). Chagnon (1988b) described how the Yanomamo people flexibly used their kinship terms. Who was or was not a socially eligible marriage partner for a bachelor depended on the rules of the society, but sometimes the same women were redefined so as to become eligible during periods when marriageable females were in short supply. Cultures differ in the degree to which people's beliefs and behaviors are congruent with each other (Harpending & Pennington, 1991). Cultures may also differ in the extent to which attitudes and behaviors are expected to be congruent. For example, U.S. culture expects far more congruity between individuals' attitudes and their behaviors than does Japanese culture (Triandis, private communication; Markus & Kitayama, 1991).

The anthropological data that were gathered were sometimes used by the administrators of some more powerful culture. These uses were dictated by the biases of the people in the more powerful culture and were often to the detriment of the people in the less powerful culture. The treatment of native Indians by various administrations of elected officials in the United States is an example of how biased assumptions often lead to policies and programs that are not in the best interest of native people (Albert & Romos, 1989; Myers, 1988; Tax, 1988; Wright, 1988).

Current: Humanistic versus Scientific Paradigms

Recognition of the biases and abuses led to several attempted remedies, but the various anthropologists' use of different kinds of remedies led to the tensions that exist today. The remedies attempted can be classified into two different clusters, based on common themes: scientific versus humanistic approaches. This classification is an expository fiction—something that will enable you to understand some of the basic conflicts among anthropologists but that does not accurately describe any one anthropologist.

Some anthropologists thought that biases could be controlled (though never totally eliminated) by using the same techniques of scientific observation and theory building employed by other behavioral scientists. One model that proved useful was based on the techniques of the animal ethologists, who specialized in observing animals in their natural habitats. By using such techniques, the biases contained in the peoples' report of themselves could be detected. Such anthropologists often recommended standardization, because if ethnographers all used similar measurement techniques, the ethnographic reports could be more easily synthesized and integrated into theories (Moles, 1977). From this point of view, observer biases could be best controlled by having ethnographic data replicated by observers with different viewpoints, and so the focus was on the validity and reliability of the data.

On the other hand, humanists were more concerned with examining their own biases to control for their effects on reports and theories. The techniques of humanistic anthropologists are largely those of academic literary critics: analyzing the peoples' culture as though it was a piece of literature to be interpreted (Alexander, 1988; Maynard Smith, 1988). These anthropologists gathered information about a people's beliefs, myths, customs, and social codes, and then attempted to interpret them as an organic whole. Each anthropologist's goal was to write convincingly so that her interpretation would become the generally accepted one. As one such anthropologist wrote, "A characteristic feature of good ethnography is to . . . bring out the uniqueness of each human situation by evoking responses similar to the ones encountered during fieldwork" (Momin, 1977, p. 248). In other words, an ethnographic record is judged according to the criterion of being able to evoke the same responses (emotions, feelings, beliefs) in the reader as the culture itself did in the ethnographer.

The tension between humanists and scientists created conflict. From the scientists' point of view, humanists will never make any progress; there could never be an accumulation of generally acceptable data and theory from such an approach. The humanists accuse the scientists of biases. "The humanistic thrust of the discipline has been lost in the wilderness created by the fetishization of method and measurement" (Momin, 1977, p. 248). "The obnoxious scientism . . . is the unstated premise of all standardizers and metricians" (Ferreira, 1977, p. 245). As Bell (1977) stated, mere data cannot contribute to understanding, and relying on data will "prevent us from appreciating the quality of [any] interaction" (p. 181).

Tensions also appeared as anthropologists wrestled with currently important problems, such as the status of women relative to that of men. Humanistic feminists have frequently been concerned with trying to interpret and explain the cross-culturally common (or even universal) lower status of women. The scientific feminists have been more concerned with careful, accurate data concerning the lives of women in very different cultures, and with making sure that the data and the theories based on the data are not misused against women.

A final tension emerged when anthropologists looked for the explanations of behavior or for the ultimate causes of culture and society among humans. The humanists, particularly the feminists, reacted strongly against the nineteenth-century abuses of evolutionary theory and data. "Many anthropologists find the Darwinian assumptions of evolutionary ecology, when applied to humans, highly implausible" (Blundell, 1983, p. 642). Silverblatt (1988) said "I strongly dispute the implications of inevitability contained in evolutionary 'law'" (p. 455). "Anthropologists . . . have continued to assume . . . that human behavior is infinitely malleable and that sex roles are determined by culture and not by hormones or cognitive processes" (Whiting & Edwards, 1988). Humanists look for socioeconomic factors to explain aspects of culture. Marxism, with its emphasis on politics and economics as explaining aspects of culture, including the status of women, became a dominant force.

Some scientific anthropologists have applied evolutionary theory to human cultures. In the process, they discovered some fascinating facts about being human. Some examples can be found in *Human Reproductive Behaviour: A Darwinian Perspective,* edited by Laura Betzig, Monique Borgerhoff Mulder, and Paul Turke. Humanists have criticized this approach (see Alexander's chapter in that book and Maynard Smith's discussions in *Did Darwin Get It Right?*, 1988).

EVOLUTION OF SOCIAL BEHAVIOR AND CULTURE

Before culture could evolve, group living would have had to evolve. Across species, group living might have evolved for several reasons: defense, foraging, competition, reproduction, parental care, and various combinations. The ancestors of any currently living social group may have been more likely to survive by being in a group, for any of these reasons.

The group could defend individuals from predators or competitors. For some foraging methods (e.g., hunting) being in a group and cooperating might improve food-getting efficiency. Forming a coalition may have increased ccess to potential mating partners; for example, a coalition of males could better defend a harem of females from potential male competitors than could just one male. Group living might increase the degree to which food resources could be defended against possible competitors. Being in a group would offer a ready supply of mates and so could facilitate reproduction. A group could also provide young with alternate care-givers, or **alloparents,** making the rearing of offspring easier.

To illustrate how these selection pressures work, this section describes how forming social groups can affect foraging success and how, eventually, the evolution of social groups might have led to culture. Among mammals, for various reasons, this process is inherently sexually dimorphic. An alternative to the ideas being presented here would emphasize the role that defense against predators played in primate social evolution (Dunbar, 1988). Although the issue is as yet undecided, Wrangham's theory is discussed because it emphasizes sex differences and females' interests as being major evolutionary selection pressures.

Wrangham's Theory of Primate Social Structures

Wrangham (1980, 1987) used optimal foraging theory (see Chapter 9) to explain social structures among various primates. For some species, forming a social group enables its members to use more efficient foraging strategies. According to Wrangham, this has been particularly important to the evolution of social structures in female mammals in general, and primate females in particular.

Theory. The key resource for reproductive success in female mammals is *food,* whereas the key resource for males is *access to females.* Female mammals usually have more parental investment than do males, and thus females are the limiting resource for males and females do the choosing of mates, rather than vice versa

(see Chapter 4). Another way of looking at this is to realize how much energy is required for pregnancy, lactation, and provisioning the helpless young among mammals. For some primates, lactation increases food requirements by as much as 50 percent (Dunbar, 1988). Primate females also carry their young for many months after birth. Although food is obviously important to males too, their reproductive success depends even more on females, since sometimes effort put into mating can yield more babies than effort put into acquiring food or safety.

The evolution of social structures is driven by (dependent on) the optimal foraging strategies for females. In turn, the males distribute themselves among the females so as to maximize their own mating opportunities. If the optimal strategy for females is to form groups, males will distribute themselves within or among those female groups in such a way so as to maximize their own reproductive success. The key for understanding the evolving social structure is the nature of the food patches used by the species. This would be particularly true of the food patches used during times of relative food shortages. At those times, the animals are more likely to starve, which leads to greater selection among the gene patterns affecting social tendencies among the females.

If each patch is relatively large, containing more food than can be eaten by one female, females will tend to form groups that search for and then defend those patches against other groups. One or more males may join each group, or males may just wander between groups; different males, because of variations in health, size, and age, may have different optimal mating strategies. Given that the females cooperate to defend food patches against competitors, inclusive fitness would predict that they should be kin. Cooperation will be most strongly selected for if it benefits those who share genes. Since most social primates live in patchy environments, most socially living (two or more adults) primate groups are **matrilineal,** consisting of sisters, mothers, daughters, and one or more unrelated males (uni-male and multimale groups).

Under other conditions, female social structures would be less likely to develop and male social structure might then evolve. If food is distributed evenly, coalitions of females would not be selected for: the food could not be defended. Social groups may still form for defense but not for foraging. In other cases, the food patches are too small to be exploited by more than one female so that competition among females will inhibit social groupings. If social groups still did form, it might be because of selection pressures working on males or because of a need for predator defense. Male groups might form because of the value of the larger males for increased defense against predators and for the defense of females against other male competitors. Again, if male groups formed, kin groupings would be selected for because cooperation would therefore be able to increase inclusive fitness (see Chapter 4).

Having either female- or male-biased types of social kin groupings leads to sex-biased **dispersal.** To avoid the deleterious effects of inbreeding, either males or females (or both) disperse, leaving their natal group. Otherwise, brother would mate with sister and mother. In birds, it is usually the female that disperses, but among most mammals, it is the young males that leave home upon attaining reproductive maturity (Greenwood, 1980; Holekamp & Sherman, 1989; Pusey & Packer, 1987a, 1987b). If the social groupings are formed on the basis of female kin groups, males should disperse, since staying at home would benefit female more than male reproductive success under these conditions.

Especially in primates, sex-biased dispersal may be incomplete. Some males stay at home and breed with sisters. Here, it is helpful to differentiate between ultimate and proximal causes. Although the evolutionary selection pressure leading to sex-biased dispersal may be inbreeding avoidance, the mechanism is likely to be the attraction of new mates, or the attraction of even more mates being offered by other social groups or other territories. Thus, evolution selected for a mechanism that led to incest avoidance in most conditions—it did *not* select for incest avoidance per se. As long as inbreeding is not consistently practiced, the deleterious effects, especially for offspring mortality, would not be great. Furthermore, some inbreeding would be desirable for many species so that adaptive gene patterns would not be broken up (see Chapter 3).

Evidence consistent with Wrangham's theory from nonprimates. Females' spacing does seem to affect how males space themselves, more than the spacing of males affects that of females (Greenwood, 1980; Ims, 1987, 1988; Ostfeld, 1985, 1986). The distribution of female mammals has been manipulated either by putting out food supplies regularly in various locations or by placing females in cages in various locations. The range and **territoriality**[1] of males depended on how the females were spaced and thus on how a male could best optimize his mating opportunities. Furthermore, if clumping of food resources produced clumping of females, the females were often friendly toward each other, sharing food and even parental chores. The females were hostile towards females of other groups.

Ground squirrels provide an interesting illustration of these ideas (Holekamp & Sherman, 1989). The location of reliable sources of food and good nesting sites is more important to female than to male reproductive success in this species, and so males disperse at maturity (see documentation in Hoyenga & Hoyenga, 1993). Males travel to other female groups and attempt to defend them against other males. Evidently to prevent incest, if a male is successful in his mating attempts with a given female group during one season, he will travel to another group for the next season. An unsuccessful male will remain in the same group for another season. Perinatal hormone levels covary with the sex-biased dispersal. If females were given an injection of testosterone (T) shortly after their birth, they dispersed at a rate typical of males.

Female kin groups among primates. Most socially living primates form groups of related females (Cheney, Seyfarth, & Smuts, 1986; Pusey & Packer, 1987a; Wrangham, 1980, 1987). Females usually stay with the group into which they were born, eventually achieving a dominance rank just below or above their mother's. Groups of related females forage together and defend each food patch they discover against other female groups. Most of the group's social interactions take the form of mutual grooming, usually between related females.

The males emigrate from their birth group. One or more unrelated males will join a group of females, sometimes only temporarily. At times a small group of related males (brothers) may join the same group. These brothers are particularly likely to form coalitions against other males to maintain dominance rankings and access to mating opportunities, just as inclusive fitness would predict. Unrelated males will also sometimes form coalitions for the same reasons, thus showing cooperative behaviors.

Although there are other exceptions to primate matrilineal social groupings, chimpanzees are one of the more important ones. Both our ancestor hominids and the chimpanzee evolved from a common ancestor, and we are more genetically similar to chimpanzees than to any other living species. Wrangham believed that the typical food patch of the chimpanzee is too small to provide food for more than one female, so competition among females prevented the evolution of female-bonded groups. Instead, males stay with the group into which they are born while females leave to join other groups of females and males all unrelated to them. Thus, a very loosely structured group of unrelated females will forage, often

individually or with an offspring, over a home range.

A group of related male chimpanzees will also forage on that home range, defending it against other males (Boesch & Boesch, 1989; Goodall, 1986; Goodall et al., 1979; de Waal, 1982). Males' reproductive success depends on the quality and size of the home range they can successfully defend against other males: larger ranges incorporate several female ranges into the males' mutually defended range. Groups of males will also go on raiding parties to neighboring home ranges, killing any males they find (see Chapter 13).

Hunting and Kin Groups

According to the ethnographic records of all available cultures, human social structures depend on kin groups, and most of them have been patrilineal and patrilocal (D'Andrade, 1966). **Patrilineal** versus **matrilineal** refers to whether property is passed on through the male or the female line (father to son or mother to daughter). **Patrilocal** versus **matrilocal** refers to whether the newly married couple lives with the husband's or the wife's relatives. There are other possibilities, such as **neolocal** (the married couple take up residence in a new area) and **bilineal** (property passed on to both daughters and sons). If primate "residence" and passing on of relative dominance status are viewed as theoretical approximations of the human concepts, the human situation is the reverse of what is the case for most of our primate relatives (except the chimpanzee). The reason sometimes given for this is that hunting increased among human ancestors.[2]

Hill's (1982) review of the history of human evolutionary theories described a recent decrease in the tendency to think of hunting as an important evolutionary factor. Hill said the decrease occurred for two reasons. First, the male bias of anthropology meant that most theories originally described only selection pressures working on males. The emphasis on hunting was later seen as a bias favoring males, ignoring what female ancestors had been doing. Second, evidence pointed out how important the vegetable material gathered by women was to the diet of foraging groups: women gatherers contribute more to the society's daily food intake than do the men hunters.[3]

Despite this, hunting might still have been important (Hill, 1982). In fact, the selection pressures associated with hunting could have led to patrilocal kin groups. To compare hunting by the various primates, hunting in two nonhuman primate groups will be examined, followed by a discussion of hunting in human foraging societies. The next major section focuses on the evolution of culture.

Evolution of human kin grouping: hunting and parental investment.

Meat might have been important to human evolution. When measured by amount of meat gathered per hour of foraging, humans are much more efficient hunters, even when hunting just with bare hands, than are other primates. Also, humans eat more meat than do other primates measured either in terms of kilogram of body weight or percent of total calories (Hill, 1982). During human evolution, this food supply might have become increasingly important to females as the nutritional demands that an infant made on the mother increased (e.g., larger brains, longer dependency periods). Meat provides a richer (more calories per bite) food source than does any vegetable product. If cooperative hunting by males was the optimal foraging strategy for meat, cooperation among males might contribute somewhat more to the reproductive success of females than would various forms of cooperation among females. This would increase the likelihood of male kin groupings. According to these ideas, hunting evolved because of its effect on *female* reproductive success.

Male hunting might explain, at least indirectly, why patrilocal systems are so common. Cooperative hunting among men might have biased human culture toward patrilineal residence, because males could then more easily hunt and gather (D'Andrade, 1966). A husband's reproductive success can be strongly related to how closely he lives to his father (Flinn, 1986). In another patrilocal culture, both husband and wife had greater reproductive success the more of the husband's kin they lived around (Berté, 1988). On the other hand, if women's cooperation in gathering and infant care were more important to their reproductive success than men's cooperation in hunting, that could produce a bias for matrilocal residences. In one culture, having the wife's mother living nearby had more effect on the reproductive success of the couple than did the location of any other maternal or paternal relative. That culture was matrilocal (Turke, 1988).

Comparing infant mortality in various primates can provide further clues as to the evolutionary utility of hunting. Chimpanzees have high levels of infant mortality, caused by their prolongation of infancy and childhood. This might be the reason that monkeys with shorter periods of infancy, such as the macaque, have been evolutionarily more successful than the chimpanzee, despite the chimpanzee's greater cognitive development. Chimpanzee infant mortality is due largely either to inadequate mothering or to injuries caused by the infant falling from the mother.

The evolution of parental strategies could have been important (Lovejoy, 1981), perhaps because it reduced infant mortality in hominids below the levels seen in chimpanzees. Hominids might have been more successful than chimpanzees because they increased parental investments beyond the chimpanzee level and so reduced offspring mortality. Specifically, paternal investment, in the form of providing meat, could decrease the home range size needed by females and thus decrease the risk to their offspring. Direct care by fathers or alloparents would also have decreased offspring mortality during the periods in which the mother carried out her necessary subsistence activities.

Baboon hunting. One troop of baboons learned to hunt (Strum, 1975). From 1970 to 1971, adult males did 94 percent of the killing and 98 percent of the eating. From December 1972 to January 1974, males did 61 percent of the killing, whereas females did 14 percent (the sexes cooperated in the other hunts). Over this same period of time, the amount of hunting increased and the group showed some interesting changes in social structure. Males began to form hunting coalitions that were quite successful in getting larger prey, such as juvenile gazelles and other larger herbivores. Because of these hunting expeditions, males began spending increasing amounts of time away from, and traveling further from, the troop. Only specific individual females were interested in meat, and the ones that did the most killing were not the ones that got the most meat from the animals killed by others. Females sometimes lost their meat to males. Females shared with offspring, and males sometimes shared with females. Some of the females with whom a male shared meat were his consorts (sexual relationships) and some were not. Females killed mostly the smaller animals, such as hares.

Hunting was observed in another troop of baboons as well (Hamilton & Busse, 1982). Hunting was not so extensive in that group, perhaps because they faced considerably more risk of predation by leopards during any hunting forays. Also, cooperative hunting was rarely observed. However, interestingly enough, food sharing (in the sense of more than one baboon eating from a carcass at any given time) was observed only at times when cooperative hunting had occurred.

There are several possible implications of the above observations. The change in the social structure of the first group (food sharing, hunting coalitions) was obviously too rapid for genetic evolution. Different females were showing two different strategies: hunting for their own meat versus sharing the meat caught by a particular male or males. Females did not share

meat with each other despite being related, perhaps because of the small size of their typical prey animals. Females foraged for meat closer to home than males did, maybe because they are smaller and/or because they were caring for their offspring. Given these current evolutionary pressures, baboons could develop a male-bonded, hunting-cooperative social system, as chimpanzees apparently have, which represents another step on the way to human foraging groups.

Chimpanzee hunting. Chimpanzees also hunt, often for smaller primates (Boesch & Boesch, 1989; Cheney et al., 1986; Goodall, 1986; Kaplan & Hill, 1985a, 1985b; Teleki, 1973; McGrew, 1979; Wrangham, 1980). Males do most of the hunting, although the degree to which females also hunt varies from one group to the next. Males also often show some cooperative patterns of hunting. Although foraged vegetable products are shared by the mother with her offspring, the only foods shared among adults are meat and some large, highly favored fruits that occur in small quantities.

The sharing of meat is extensive, and rarely involves overt aggression, as was the case in baboons. A group of chimpanzees that more often cooperatively hunts also does more sharing than do other groups. Males share more often than females do, and they share with other males more than with females. One chimpanzee would request meat, and the possessor of the carcass would sometimes grant the request, especially to older males or to less dominant males. Male chimpanzees are more likely to share with estrous females than with females during any other stage of their menstrual cycle. Males will also share with females with whom they have a friendly (grooming) relationship.

Male hunting in human hunter-gatherer societies. According to Foley and Lee (1989), meat is a high-quality but patchy resource. Thus, an increased reliance on meat would select for different optimal foraging strategies. If they are correct, protohumans may have shifted from a female-bonded kin grouping to a male-bonded kin grouping as male cooperation during hunting became more important to the food supply and thus to females' reproductive success.

Hunting among the Efe pygmy peoples of Zaire somewhat resembles chimpanzee hunting (Bailey & Aunger, 1989). The Efe are predominantly patrilocal and hunt in male kin groups. They are also monogamous. The animals killed on any given hunt are shared equally among all the men on the hunt, and each man then brings home his share to his own family. A group of related males (a **patriclan**) has acknowledged rights to a specific area of the forest for hunting, and some groups have more valuable areas (areas more attractive to females?) than do other groups. Groups of males also defend their females from other groups.

The Ache of eastern Paraguay were full-time hunter-gatherers until they settled at mission-sponsored colonies in the 1980s (Hill & Hurtado, 1989; Hill & Kaplan, 1988a, 1988b; Hurtado et al., 1985; Kaplan & Hill, 1985a, 1985b). They are essentially monogamous, but both marital relationships and group memberships during hunting trips are variable and often very temporary. Although the Ache now combine foraging with some agriculture in their settlements near the missions, the Ache still have hunting-foraging trips into the forest. Extensive data have been collected from several of those trips and have been combined with data from precontact trips obtained by interviewing older adults.

On hunting-foraging trips, a different camp site is established every one to three days. Females forage around and between campsites, whereas males range much more widely in search of food. Males supply 87 percent of the total calories consumed by the group, largely in the form of meat and honey. From 46 percent to 66 percent of their calories come from mammalian meat, and 60 percent of all game

is captured through cooperative male hunting. All food produced by males is shared equally among all members of the group: 90 percent of the meat a hunter acquires is consumed by people not in his immediate family.

Although all male-produced food is shared equally, males who are better at hunting have more reproductive success, as seen in Figure 10.1. More children born to the good hunters survive, perhaps because other members of the group give more consideration to their children than to the children of poor hunters. This may persuade good hunters to stay with that particular group, benefitting everyone. The good hunters also have more extramarital sexual liaisons than do the poor hunters since women favor them as lovers.

Females do very little hunting. In this hostile environment (from 38 to 51 percent of all children die before adulthood, largely from homicide and illness), young children have to

FIGURE 10.1 *Effect of Hunting Prowess on Reproductive Success*
This figure shows the mean number of children surviving to the present time for both poor and good hunters. For children of sure paternity ("Sure" children), $p = 0.15$; for possible children and for all children, $p = 0.05$.

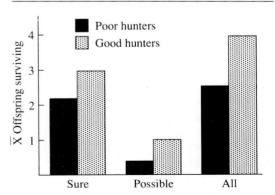

Source: From *Human Reproductive Behaviour* (p. 283) by L. Betzig, M. B. Mulder, and P. Turke, 1988, Cambridge: Cambridge University Press. Reprinted by permission.

be carried everywhere, and females do most of the carrying. The females do little gathering as they carry their children from one camp to the next, and females nursing infants almost never gather. Mothers leave their children with other females, or occasionally with their husbands, to forage away from the camp. The females also share what they gather, but less than do the males. About 30 to 40 percent of good gathered by Ache females is eaten solely by their immediate families. So, males hunt and share, and females gather to feed their families.

The Agta.   Why don't all the females hunt for their own meat, as do many of the female Agta hunter-gatherers of the Philippines? Although more Agta men than women hunt, the women who do hunt contribute about half the meat supplies of the group. Both sexes hunt both alone and in same-sex and mixed-sex groups, but women more often than men hunt in a group "for social reasons and for the sake of increased efficiency" (Goodman et al., 1985, p. 1204). Women also usually hunt with close relatives. Women who hunt have the same reproductive success (e.g., number of surviving children) as do the women who do not hunt, as can be seen in Table 10.1. Hunting women

carry nursing infants with them on the hunt and leave toddlers in the camp under the care of female relatives, often grandmothers or the oldest female sibling.

The researchers suggested that Agta women hunt while Ache women do not because of differential costs of hunting for the two groups. For Agta women, game can be found very close to camp, and so they do not have to carry their infants very far. Also, the Agta women hunt with dogs, which provide further protection and foraging efficiency. The Ache men forage very far from camp, and the campsites are changed every one to three days in order to find game; the Ache women would have to carry their infants considerable distance to find game. So, would women hunt if game were close by and they had dogs to help? And in the absence of dogs and nearby game, did men specialize in hunting?

Evolution of Culture among Humans

Human cultures involve far more than just social groupings and interactions. Observational and symbolic learning abilities are also necessary if culture is to be transmitted from one person to the next (Barkow, 1989; Boyd &

TABLE 10.1   *Comparison of Reproductive Successes and Other Characteristics of Agta Female Hunters and Nonhunters*

	Hunters			**Nonhunters**			
	N	*Mean*	*SD*	*N*	*Mean*	*SD*	*t*
Age	86	30.91	12.95	18	32.61	11.20	−0.52
Age at menarche	78	17.12	0.77	18	17.22	0.73	−0.53
Age at first pregnancy	73	19.58	2.68	16	20.25	3.73	−0.85
Age of youngest child	61	6.30	8.09	16	5.00	5.83	0.60
Total living children	70	2.69	2.23	16	2.75	2.18	−0.10
Height in cm	66	141.50	4.89	14	140.04	5.08	1.01
Weight in kg	66	36.36	5.39	14	38.40	6.20	−1.25
Skinfold triceps	59	9.25	3.35	13	12.62	7.64	−1.56

Source: From "Compatibility of Hunting and Mothering" by M. J. Goodman, P. B. Griffin, A. A. Estioko-Griffin, and J. S. Gove, 1985, *Sex Roles, 12,* p. 1203. Copyright 1985 by Plenum Publishing Corporation. Reprinted by permission.

Richerson, 1985). Language is required for symbolic modeling, a critical part of human socialization. Walking erect, leaving the forest, and changes in diet all occurred before our brains began to enlarge (Corballis, 1989; Lovejoy, 1981). Our ability to completely understand human cultural evolution is going to have to wait for us to understand how both language and complex, symbolically mediated, observational learning skills evolved.

Culture in the higher primates. The essentials for culture are present in the higher primates (Bonner, 1980; Fragaszy & Visalberghi, 1989; Goodall, 1986; Goodall et al., 1979; McGrew, 1979; Nishida, 1987; see Chapter 9). They are capable of symbolic representation of objects and people, they can manufacture and use tools, and they can transmit culture from one member of a group to another. Female chimpanzees extensively use tools that they have somewhat modified from their natural state (e.g., peeled sticks) for gathering ants and termites, and male chimpanzees have been observed throwing rocks at enemy and prey animals. Primates can instruct their young; for example, when one type of fruit was drugged with toxic cynalin, any juvenile baboon attempting to eat that fruit was threatened by the adult male who had already tested and rejected it. Chimpanzees, but perhaps not other primates, are also capable of fairly sophisticated kinds of observational learning, as when a baby chimpanzee learns how to catch and eat termites by watching its mother.

Gene-culture coevolution. Since cultural evolution and the genetic capacities for language, social structure, and the brain have continuously interacted as modern humans evolved, **gene-culture co-evolution** is a good way to describe the process. Durham (1982) provided some models, examples, and a framework. Evolutionary theory talks about changes in gene frequency across generations. Similarly, cultural "units," such as values, ideas, and

beliefs, can either decrease or increase in frequency in future generations. The number of people "carrying" a cultural unit would change, depending on what effect those units had on the ability of a person who possesses those units to adapt to and succeed in a particular natural and social environment. This adaptation and success would include, but not be limited to, successful reproduction.

Whereas genes are transmitted in sexually reproducing species by meiosis and fertilization, cultural units are transmitted by parental treatment, observational learning or imitation, and deliberate instruction or schooling. Although genes are transmitted only from parents to offspring, cultural units can be transmitted to offspring not only by parents but also by other relatives, peers, teachers, and the mass media. Cultural units will increase in frequency only as long as they can be successfully transmitted from one generation to the next. Their transmission will depend on the usefulness of the units to the students, as well as the effectiveness of the instructional methods being employed.

Durham (1982) described how genes and cultural units might be expected to interact. First, culture might influence the effect that genes have on phenotypes. For example, the sickle cell anemia gene may have evolved because it enabled its possessors to resist malaria. If people with the sickle cell anemia gene, either in a homozygous or heterozygous state, eat yams, the sickling of their red blood cells is reduced. The sickling can lead to death from lack of oxygen. In many cultures in which the sickle cell gene is widespread, people commonly eat yams—except during malaria season, where yam eating decreases the heterozygote's resistance to malaria. Culture (yam-eating practices) moderates the effects of the sickle cell gene on phenotypic sickling of red blood cells.

Durham described other types of interactions. Genes may affect the transmissibility of cultural units. We humans find some things easier to learn than others. For example, we find it easy to learn an aversion to a taste but difficult to learn an aversion to food of a given color, such as green (Davis & Dougan, 1988). That bias will affect the degree to which aversion for alcohol versus an aversion for green foods could be transmitted. The degree to which a unit of culture affects the fitness of people in a particular culture will depend on what other features the culture has. What is deemed to be "good" in a culture could be genetically adaptive (in terms of reproductive success), genetically neutral, or genetically maladaptive. The same trait could be all three things, in three different cultures.

The Boyd and Richerson gene-culture co-evolution theory.   Boyd and Richerson (1985) stated that the major mechanism for the cultural transmission of traits is modeling and direct instruction (though the latter is viewed as a special case of the former). Boyd and Richerson carried out the math modeling required to see how culture could evolve.

Although most species are capable of trial-and-error learning (operant conditioning), cultural evolution requires observational learning. If acquisition of traits having survival value were promoted in any socially living species that had a bias for, and the capability of, observational learning, this could lead to culture. It turned out that such evolution would be unlikely overall,[4] but would be most likely under changing environmental conditions, where being able to use information from a variety of models would be advantageous. Observational learning is much faster than trial-and-error learning and can incorporate the experiences of many other organisms. Observational learning would also be able to dilute the effects of poor models, including poor parental models. But observational learning also means that children can acquire prestigious cultural traits that impair survival or reproduction (such as becoming a priest). Thus, culture-producing species should have a mix of both observational and trial-and-error learning to take advantage of the efficiency of observational learning, as well as the lower error rate (acquisition of traits that impair survival or reproduction) of trial-and-error learning.

Children acquire units of culture by observing parents, other adults, and peers. Children actively try out some traits to see if they might be of some benefit to them. In some cases, more common traits may be preferentially modeled — doing what most other people are doing, especially people perceived to have needs similar to oneself, such as same-sex, same-age models. In other cases, the rarer traits may be selected: the child may do what will make him different from most of the rest of the crowd. Finally, particular types of models — those having prestigious roles or those who are wealthy and influential — may be preferentially copied.

Bandura (1986) and Boyd and Richerson provide many intriguing and well-documented examples of research showing how these principles affect the transmission of cultural traits among people of a particular social group. Many sponsors of children's TV programs use these facts to get children to more readily "copy" (buy and use) their products. Government agencies use these techniques to get cooperation from their constituencies, as when farm bureaus try to get the most influential local farmers to be the first to try some new farming technique advocated by the government.

Units of culture "evolve" by increasing in frequency, and individuals are thought to be motivated to be cultural parents as well as parents of children. A teacher would be a cultural parent. An author has been known to treat her book as though it were some kind of offspring. In some cases, genetic evolution and cultural evolution can come into conflict for the individual, as when being a cultural parent would involve curtailing biological reproduction (e.g., writing books takes up too much time for a woman, and so she forgoes having children).

The role of cooperation.   Boyd and Richerson have also argued that cooperation is required for cultural evolution. Cavalli-Sforza and Feldman (1983) added the idea that the evolution of the ability to communicate symbolically may presuppose the ability to cooperate: the evolution of cooperation may have been what allowed language to evolve. Cooperation would also fit into Tooby and Cosmides's (1989) model of cultural evolution as being one of the psychological mechanisms that could "generate and shape culture." Simon (1990) talked about **docility,** by which he means the ability to learn skills and proper behaviors from other people. Docile people will tend to be cooperative as well as altruistic.

Certainly cooperation can increase reproductive success and survival. Among primates, pairs of animals who mutually groom each other will also tend to come to each other's defense when either is attacked by another animal (Walters & Seyfarth, 1987).[5] Another example comes from hunting-gathering groups in New Guinea. Since 1930, the number of male births has steadily surpassed the number of female births until there are now 25 men for every 15 women (*Peoria Journal Star,* 1989). In this monogamous culture, bachelors were traditionally low-status people with little or no chances of reproducing. Since there are now so many of them, they have begun to cooperate with each other. They hunt in groups (married men are required to hunt by themselves), and since group hunting is more efficient, they supply much food to their group. With this kind of leverage, they changed the cultural rules: adultery is now common and more or less acceptable. A bachelor can have sex with any wife and the husband is required to support any resulting offspring!

Lack of reciprocation can bring cooperation to an end. The Australian Aborigines require couples who run out of food and so who cannot contribute to group welfare to break up their marriage (Sansom, 1978). Unless they can find kin to feed them, they are encouraged to leave the group. Running out of food is common, and it is the woman who decides who she

will feed (who will "take tucker" from her kitchen). Since women prefer relatives, current Aborigine groups are often female kin groups.

CULTURE AND CHILD SOCIALIZATION

Although there are cross-cultural commonalities, cultures also differ in how they socialize their children. Child rearing is done almost universally by females. Of the 80 cultures surveyed in one study, in only 10 percent did a father assume major responsibility for child rearing (Katz & Konner, 1981). One of the major works in the field is *Children of Different Words* by Whiting and Edwards (1988). Mothers of different cultures have different theories of children, and these theories affect how their children are socialized and, ultimately, how those children will behave as adults. One parental theory, which is important to gender differences and is endorsed by the people of some cultures, is that males are more important than females.

The data from Whiting and Edwards are used throughout this section. Their book describes the results of extensive behavioral samplings of children in 14 different communities: 6 in Africa (5 in Kenya), 2 in the United States, and 1 each in the Philippines, Okinawa, Mexico, Guatemala, and Peru. Different communities were studied by different observers, but observations could be classified according to the techniques used into three types of communities: New Sample; Six Culture; and Spot Observation. (Some communities were studied by more than one method.) Children were observed, their age and sex noted, and their companions and behaviors recorded. Although statistical tests were rarely carried out, the researchers recorded sex differences in child-rearing practices and children's behaviors.

Types of Parental Care

Although some maternal behaviors seem to vary consistently from one culture to the next, there are more common elements than you might expect. For example, mothers of all cultures frequently carry their infants while engaging in other chores and tasks. In fact, just as among the nonhuman primates, weaning from carrying seems as stressful for children as is weaning from the breast or bottle. As Whiting and Edwards described, mothers everywhere must:

1. Maintain the physical well-being of their children.
2. See to their emotional comfort when they get distressed.
3. Teach them toilet training and hygiene.
4. Teach them etiquette and appropriate social behaviors.
5. Teach them the skills required by like-sexed adults in that culture.

Mothers of various cultures differ only with regard to task emphases or proportions (Arrindell et al., 1986; Whiting & Edwards, 1988).

Three kinds of mothers. Whiting and Edwards described three kinds of mothers, classified according to the components of child rearing the mother emphasized. The **training mother** displayed the least amount of nurturance and the greatest amount of training behaviors (items 3, 4, and 5 from the list above). These included the mothers of Kenya. This type of mother, cross-culturally, is engaged in the most extensive amounts of subsistence activity and so emphasizes responsibility in her children because she needs help with her own extensive workload. They issue more commands to their children than do the other types of mothers, especially **prosocial** commands that enjoin the child to be obedient for the good of others (e.g., "to help other people") or for the good of society.

The other two types of mothers have somewhat lighter workloads. The **controlling mother** also tends to be involved in relatively high levels of subsistence agriculture. Their child-rearing strategies emphasize obedience. These mothers,

such as in the Philippines, do a tremendous amount of work but also get much help both from adult kin and from older children. They often issue more **egoistic** commands, emphasizing the child's obedience to the mother's desires. The **sociable mother,** such as those from the United States, emphasizes control the most. Their next most important child-rearing characteristic is their frequent, positive interactions with their children. Sociable mothers are frequently isolated from all other kin. When women share living space with other women, they seem to interact less with their children.

The mother's environment affects her beliefs about children. Overall, mothers who need more help with their work tend to believe that younger children can be trained to be responsible. For example, among the Ye'kwana villagers, an agricultural community next to the forest in Venezuela, infant care takes more than 90 percent of a mother's total labor time, and her labor is essential to the family. In this culture, female children are socialized early, even by age 4, to care for younger siblings in order to free the mother for her gardening and gathering (Hames, 1988). In societies where mothers have more free time, the mothers tend to believe that children younger than 6 or 7 cannot be trained for useful work.

There are few instances of cross-culturally consistent differences in how mothers treat boys versus girls. But what few there are may be of considerable cultural significance, as will be covered later. The major relevance of these data for gender-related differences is that children everywhere largely see mothers as being responsible for children. Children would be expected to incorporate at a very young age the fact that if they are female, they are going to have to grow up to take care of children, but if they are male, their wives will do it.

Paternal care. Paternal care in humans takes many different forms, just as was the case in the nonhuman primates. Fathers may provide food and direct protection or they may provide resources for one or more wives and their off-spring. Here, the authors concentrate on direct paternal involvement in caregiving, which is relatively rare but is also tremendously variable across cultures (Katz & Konner, 1981; Mackey, 1979; West & Konner, 1976; Whiting & Edwards, 1988; Whitten, 1987). The extent to which fathers are found to be physically close to their children during the periods of experimental observation also varies but is always less than that of women (see documentation in Hoyenga & Hoyenga, 1993).

In a different sample of 80 cultures surveyed by Konner and colleagues, in 20 percent of them fathers were rarely or never found near their infants. In only 4 percent were father-infant relationships close. And even in one of the close societies, such as the hunting gathering !Kung San, fathers spent only 14 percent of their time with their infants, about the same amount of time as did the most active father in industrialized societies. Even among the !Kung, the male did only 6 percent of the actual infant caregiving. In most societies, the major form of paternal interaction is play.

One cultural factor affecting the degree of paternal involvement is the mating system. Although most human societies are monogamous by rule, most human societies are at least mildly polygynous in practice, given the frequency of divorce/remarriage and extramarital affairs in most (but not all) societies (Alexander et al., 1979; Brown & Hotra, 1988). Mating systems affect paternal investment and thus paternal care (see Chapter 4): paternal care is most common in monogamous societies.

Monogamous societies can also be divided into those that are socially imposed versus ecologically imposed. In the latter, the living conditions are such that the attentions of both parents are necessary to rear offspring. In the former, the society's rules prescribe monogamy, just as our own does. Paternal care would be more common in ecologically monogamous societies, such as the !Kung San, just as is the case in the nonhuman primates. Hewlett (1988)

pointed out that not only does monogamy increase paternal investment but so does an increase in the man's certainty of paternity in either monogamous or polygamous societies. Where extramarital affairs are common and paternity is therefore uncertain, paternal care is less likely.

Across cultures, if women contribute substantially to the food supply of the group, polygyny, along with less extensive paternal care, becomes more likely (Berté, 1988; Burton & White, 1984; Ember, 1983; Katz & Konner, 1981; Schlegel & Barry, 1988; Low, 1988). Another way of stating it is that if the woman is unable to provide enough food for her offspring by herself, then monogamy becomes more likely. The rise of intensive agriculture (including the plow) increased monogamy, decreased the amount the woman directly contributed to the food consumed by herself and her offspring, and increased the proportion of childcare provided by the mother. The crops produced by intensive agriculture often require that someone spend much time in the home in food preparations, such as grinding grain. Thus, the woman could do both food preparations and childcare at home. Intensive agriculture also increased the number of calories per person and so increased a woman's fertility. An increase in fertility means that more children are produced and so more time is needed for childcare, as opposed to production of food and resources.

None of these factors can account for the high levels of paternal care that Hewlett found among the Aka net-hunting pygmies of Africa. These people are patrilocal and patrilineal, with some polygynous marriages, and everyone of both sexes participates in the net hunt for game. Hewlett suggested that the unusually high level of paternal care found in this society can be attributed to the females' participation in the net hunt that requires traveling great distances. Given these conditions, having the father help to carry an infant might prove very necessary. But even among the Aka pygmies, some fathers participate a great deal more in childcare than do other fathers (Hoyenga & Hoyenga, 1993).

Fathers also tend to invest differentially in, or pay attention to, boys more than girls. Men are found more often around boys than around girls (Hoyenga & Hoyenga, 1993). For example, Mackey (1979) went to public places in 10 different cultures and counted how frequently adult men and women were found in the company of male and female children. Girls were more often found in groups that had no adult men in them, whereas boys were often found in men-only groups. This sex difference increased with the age of children; the older the boy was, the more likely he was to be in the company of men rather than women.

Another way to look at paternal behaviors is to contrast them with maternal behaviors. As already described, cross-culturally, fathers interact less overall with their children than do mothers (and often female relatives), fathers take less responsibility for actual care, and fathers tend to do more playing. In Whiting and Edwards's cross-cultural study, fathers did less teaching of toddlers, so lessons in how to perform chores and symbolic aspects of culture came from mothers. Fathers mostly did the disciplining. Among the hunting-gathering Aka pygmies of Africa, mothers teach gathering and infant care skills, whereas fathers teach mating skills, ritual knowledge, and dancing/singing traits (Hewlett & Cavalli-Sforza, 1986).

Alloparents.   In most cultures, mothers have help with their childcare chores (Weisner & Gallimore, 1977), especially if paternal involvement is low and maternal work load is high (Katz & Konner, 1981). The helpers are almost female kin: grandmothers are involved more often than grandfathers, and older sisters are involved more often than older brothers. In several national surveys of childcare arrangements in the United States, over half of all children of working women are cared for by family members (Gerson, Alpert, & Richard

son, 1984). Sisters are more often involved in childcare than are brothers (Hoyenga & Hoyenga, 1993). The sex difference is particularly marked for younger children, where girls are twice as likely to be involved. Gender differences in childcare duties are largest in the lower-status families. In the United States, however, older children are seldom put in complete charge of younger children.

Sexually Dimorphic Developmental Environments

Chapter 9 described how childhood environments can affect adult traits and behaviors. Thus, sex differences in developmental environments that are cross-culturally common will produce sex differences among adults that are similar across cultures as well.

Chores.   Girls more often have chores than boys do in most of the Six Culture and Spot Observation data, even when childcare was excluded. In Munrow, Munroe, and Shimmin's (1984) sample of four cultures (Kenya, Belize, Nepal, and Samoa), they found that the mean level of girls' work was higher in all of them. Furthermore, the chores themselves are often gender differentiated. Girls do childcare, household chores, and most economic tasks except those connected to the care of large animals. Even when boys are assigned feminine tasks because of a lack of female children, the boys often perform the tasks in a different manner or style. They carry water in a different way or care for younger siblings with a somewhat different style.

Distance from home.   Another cross-cultural commonality is that boys are found further from home than girls are (Hoyenga & Hoyenga, 1993). The sex difference occurs for both directed (chores) and undirected (play) activities, but is greatest for the latter. The Munroes found similar sex differences in Kenya (Munroe & Munroe, 1971; Nerlove, Munroe & Munroe,

1971). This, combined with the fact that boys are more commonly found without adults being present than girls are, means that environments are sexually differentiated in very important ways.

Cross-cultural commonalities in socialization pressures.

Barry, Bacon, and Child (1957) used published ethnographic reports to gather data on sex differences in child socialization practices across various cultures. (See Hoyenga and Hoyenga, 1993, for a more complete presentation of their results). In 82 percent of the cultures, girls were socialized more than boys were to be nurturant; there were *no* reversals. Girls were socialized to be more obedient than boys in 35 percent of the cultures and to be more responsible than boys in 61 percent of the cultures. In 87 percent of the cultures ($n = 31$, reversals in 3 percent), boys were socialized to strive more for achievement than girls were. And in 85 percent of the cultures ($n = 82$, no reversals), boys were socialized to be more self-reliant than girls were.

Similarly sexually differentiated child socialization practices were later found in many other cultures. Welch and Page (1981) divided 108 societies into five different regions, and the sex differences described above were found in each of those five regions. Furthermore, there is more pressure on boys than on girls to conform to their socialization, and so boys are more anxious over their performances than girls are. Overall, girls tend to vary more from the roles into which they are being socialized than do boys. More deviance is tolerated in girls than in boys and in definitions of *femininity* versus definitions of *masculinity*.

Whiting and Edwards also found sex differences in maternal training, or in the extent to which the mother made task commands and suggestions related to proper social behavior. Girls received more training from their mothers than boys did in 21 of the 28 comparisons that Whiting and Edwards were able to make. Daughters are also trained earlier than sons are,

possibly because of the relatively faster development of females.

Cultural differences in sexually dimorphic socialization pressures.

Schlegel and Barry (1986) and Welch (1978) found that socialization practices differed according to the degree to which women were involved in subsistence labor. If mothers were more heavily involved, girls were more likely to be socialized to be industrious and less likely to be taught sexual restraint. If mothers were more involved in subsistence activities, boys tended to be more anxious than girls about conforming to expected behaviors.

Low (1989) carried out the most extensive analysis on variations in the socializations of boys versus girls, relating them to polygyny and stratification. She measured polygyny by both intensity (maximum harem size) and degree (percentages of men and women married polygynously). **Stratification** refers to fairly rigid social classification or ranking of people by wealth or heredity. Although the effects of polygyny varied according to stratification, the greater the intensity or the degree of polygyny in the culture, the more boys but not girls were taught to show fortitude, to be aggressive (degree of polygyny) or competitive (intensity of polygyny), and to be industrious. In nonstratified societies with intense polygyny, boys but not girls were taught sexual restraint and obedience. Girls but not boys were socialized to be responsible in nonstratified polygynous societies. In stratified societies, older girls but not boys were taught to be sexually restrained, obedient, but not necessarily self-reliant. In such societies, chastity and obedience would increase a girl's chances of **hypergyny** (marrying upwards in status).

Low found that group size and women's power were also important. The more that women controled important resources, the less daughters were taught to be submissive. In fact, the more formal power that women had within kin groups, the more daughters were taught to be aggressive, and the less they were taught to be industrious. As the size of the group increased, socialization of the sexes tended to become more similar, emphasizing obedience, sexual restraint, and submissiveness in both.

Socialization and social behaviors.   Sex differences in childhood environments and chores can also be related to sex differences in the social behaviors of children, and hence, by extension, to the social behaviors of adults (Munroe et al., 1984; Whiting & Edwards, 1973, 1988). Girls were found more often in charge of younger children and in the presence of adults, whereas boys were left more free to interact with same-sex, same-age peers. Across cultures, if children were more involved in childcare, they also engaged in more nurturant behaviors, not only to their charges but also to same-sex, same-age peers.

The more time children spent segregated into age groups, the more they engaged in dominance struggles and competitions. Whiting and Edwards also identified a cross-culturally universal tendency for both boys and girls to prefer to interact with same-sex peers rather than opposite-sex peers. Peer groups are where challenge behavior is likely to be practiced (dominance conflicts). Thus, peer group socialization is likely to have important effects on across all cultures in which extensive peer interaction occurs.

Across cultures, if children are frequently involved in domestic and subsistence activities (most often female), they were also more likely, even when not working, to make responsible suggestions, to reprimand others, and to seek help from others. These children were described as "businesslike, efficient, purposeful" (Munroe et al., 1984). On the other hand, children who did relatively little work (most often male) were more likely to behave in a strictly sociable fashion, to engage in rough-and-tumble play, and to seek attention from others.

Peer group orientation and traveling far from home in the absence of adults encourages independence, competitiveness, and self-reliance. On the other hand, nurturing and helping behaviors directed toward younger children and adults develop social responsibility. As Whiting and Edwards suggested (p. 273), children socialized in the former way may find it difficult to offer help except to people with whom they have no direct contact and may learn to treat their peers largely as competitors.

CULTURAL VARIABILITY AMONG ADULTS

Since Margaret Mead (1939) published her classic work, *Sex and Temperament,* researchers have recognized just how culturally variable definitions of masculinity and femininity are. There are only two possible cultural universals:

1. Every society assigns tasks and traits on the basis of gender to at least some degree.
2. In no society is the overall status of women seen as superior to the status of men, but the reverse is quite common.

Jobs and Tasks

Tables 10.2 and 10.3 present some cross-cultural data based on an analysis of the ethnographic record of 224 different societies (D'Andrade, 1966). For every society in which a given job or task was performed, D'Andrade classified the division of labor into men always, men usually, either sex, women usually, or women always. Men usually go further from home, they are more often involved in gathering meat, and they are more involved in manufacturing objects made of metal and objects for warfare and hunting. Women carry out tasks that can be done closer to the home and manufacture objects used in the home (except the home itself).

Cross-culturally, men are more likely to be involved in political activities than women are (Masters, 1989; Ross, 1986). Warm and affectionate child-rearing practices are associated

TABLE 10.2 *Cross-Cultural Data from 224 Societies on Subsistence Activities and Division of Labor by Sex*

Activity	Number of Societies in Which Activity Is Performed by				
	Men Always	*Men Usually*	*Either Sex*	*Women Usually*	*Women Always*
Pursuit of sea mammals	34	1	0	0	0
Hunting	166	13	0	0	0
Trapping small animals	128	13	4	1	2
Herding	38	8	4	0	5
Fishing	98	34	19	3	4
Clearing land for agriculture	73	22	17	5	13
Dairy operations	17	4	3	1	13
Preparing and planting soil	31	23	33	20	37
Erecting and dismantling shelter	14	2	5	6	22
Tending fowl and small animals	21	4	8	1	39
Gathering shellfish	9	4	8	7	25
Making and tending fires	18	6	25	22	62
Bearing burdens	12	6	35	20	57
Preparing drinks and narcotics	20	1	13	8	57
Gathering fruits, berries, nuts	12	3	15	13	63
Gathering fuel	22	1	10	19	89
Preservation of meat and fish	8	2	10	14	74
Gathering herbs, roots, seeds	8	1	11	7	74
Cooking	5	1	9	28	158
Carrying water	7	0	5	7	119
Grinding grain	2	4	5	13	114

Source: Reprinted from *The Development of Sex Differences,* edited by Eleanor E. Maccoby with the permission of the publishers, Stanford University Press. © 1966 by the Board of Trustees of the Leland Stanford Junior University.

Note: Every job or task was not done in every society, thus the rows do not always add up to 224.

with more political involvement by women. Females are also more politically involved in societies with high levels of internal conflict, as though alliances with women become more important in those circumstances—or women perceive it to be more necessary to get involved to protect their own interests. Conversely, high levels of conflict with other societies reduces the extent of women's political involvement. In some societies, particularly those in which the sexes' socioeconomic roles are very differentiated, the sexes tend to have separate political structures.

Traits

D'Andrade (1966), as well as others, have presented some data on sex differences in

TABLE 10.3   *Cross-Cultural Data on the Manufacture of Objects and Division of Labor by Sex*

Activity	Number of Societies in Which Activity Is Performed by				
	Men Always	*Men Usually*	*Either Sex*	*Women Usually*	*Women Always*
Metalworking	78	0	0	0	0
Weapon making	121	1	0	0	0
Boat building	91	4	4	0	1
Manufacture of musical instruments	45	2	0	0	1
Work in wood and bark	113	9	5	1	1
Work in stone	68	3	2	0	2
Work in bone, horn, shell	67	4	3	0	3
Manufacture of ceremonial objects	37	1	13	0	1
House building	86	32	25	3	14
Net making	44	6	4	2	11
Manufacture of ornaments	24	3	40	6	18
Manufacture of leather products	29	3	9	3	32
Hide preparation	31	2	4	4	49
Manufacture of nontextile fabrics	14	0	9	2	32
Manufacture of thread and cordage	23	2	11	10	73
Basket making	25	3	10	6	82
Mat making	16	2	6	4	61
Weaving	19	2	2	6	67
Pottery making	13	2	6	8	77
Manufacture and repair of clothing	12	3	8	9	95

Source: Reprinted from *The Development of Sex Differences,* edited by Eleanor E. Maccoby with the permission of the publishers, Stanford University Press. © 1966 by the Board of Trustees of the Leland Stanford Junior University.

Note: Every job or task was not done in every society, thus the rows do not always add up to 224.

personality traits. Since only a few cultures were represented in most of the comparisons, making conclusions about general trends would not be warranted. Cross-cultural studies on dominance, sexual behaviors, mate preferences, and aggression are covered in Unit Four. The following section presents data concerning traits whose names appear on typical measures of sex roles (see Chapter 2; e.g., *sensitive to others*), as well as data about sex differences measured with standardized paper-and-pencil personality and sex-role tests.

Variations in sex roles.   Mead's 1939 book, which analyzed the temperaments of both sexes in three cultures of New Guinea, dramatically demonstrated how much masculinity and femininity can vary across cultures. Viewed through the eyes of someone from a Western civilization, the Arapesh males and females were feminine: cooperative, unaggressive, and responsive to the needs and demands of others. The Mundugumor males and females were masculine: ruthless, aggressive, very sexually active, and having little interest in childcare. The Tchambuli were reversed: the women were somewhat masculine whereas the men were somewhat feminine. "The woman [was] the dominant, impersonal, managing partner, the man the less responsible and the emotionally dependent person" (p. 190).

The cultural flexibility of gender roles is not diminished by realizing that the reversal among the Tchambuli reflected somewhat unusual circumstances (Gewertz, 1984). The Tchambuli had been exiled for over 20 years and had been returned to their island by Australian officials just a few years before Mead began to study them. Most of the males were away from the villages, having temporarily migrated to find jobs. With so few men present, women began to dominate the trading relationships that had been carried out by men before the exile. The traits may have shifted as the jobs and tasks shifted—a very important possibility.

Kibbutzim were established before the 1920s in Israel. One of the major tenets of each commune is that women should have equal status, equal responsibility, and perform all jobs as much as men do (Nevo, 1977; Rosner, 1967; Snarey & Son, 1986; Spiro, 1956; Tiger, 1987). Although most kiubbutzniks see few personality differences between the sexes, three traits are still seen by a majority of those tested to be feminine: a tendency to become emotional, a readiness to feel insulted, and shyness. It should also be pointed out that women have taken the lead in making some changes. Women now perceive cosmetics to be desirable, and they are putting pressure on to disband the nurseries and have their children reared at home. Female occupational groups (cooking, nurseries, service activities) have resisted having men join them more than male occupational groups (heavy farming) have resisted female coworkers.

People who prefer to act out certain aspects of the roles and behaviors and traits of the opposite sex have appeared in many cultures, both past and present. They have been most intensively studied in past North American Indian cultures, where such people have been labeled **Berdaches** (Bolin, 1987; Callender & Kochems, 1983; Hultkrantz, 1983; Schlegel, 1983; Whitehead, 1981). Cultures differed in how they viewed such people's gender status and their roles in the culture. In some, male Berdaches who acted out feminine roles were figures of scorn and derision, whereas in others they could achieve high status and were often assigned roles in rituals that could be done only by a Berdache. In some cultures, homosexual activity occurred before the person assumed a Berdache status, but in others it occurred afterwards, if ever. Different cultures believed that a person could become a Berdache as a result of other childhood "inclinations," or an adult decision, or after having received a vision.

Male Berdaches were more common than females. This might be because, paradoxically, males often have higher status than females do, as will be noted in the next section. Because of the higher status of males and of being masculine, perhaps a desire to have the culturally less desirable feminine traits was seen as needing special explanations and labels. Thus, a man wanting to express some feminine traits would be labeled and given a special status in order to "explain" him. A woman desiring to have some masculine traits might have been more comprehensible to these peoples and so these women would not need explaining and special labeling.

Cross-cultural studies of sex differences.   One study gave standardized personality measures to high school and college students of four different cultures: United States, France, Tunisia, and Mexico (Almeida Acosta & Sanchez de

Almeida, 1983). More cultural than gender differences were found. The subjects were also asked about how important they perceived various life goals. Although overall women gave more importance to marriage than men, this was true of only two cultures individually (Tunisia and United States). In the other two cultures, men rated marriage higher than women did. In France and the United States, women desired to have more children than men did, but the reverse was true in the other two countries. In three cultures, men valued competition more than women did; women emphasized personal mastery of skill more than competition. Women valued altruism in occupations and males valued independence, prestige, and salary.

Traits have also been measured with sex-role questionnaires in many studies, two of which will be described by way of example. In the four-culture study just described, men were more instrumental than women were in all four cultures, and women were more expressive than men were (Personal Attributes Questionnaire or PAQ). However, in at least one culture (Tunisia), the women were more instrumental than were the males of another culture (France). Tunisian males were more expressive than were Mexican females.

Williams and Best (1990) asked approximately 100 university students of each sex in each of 14 different cultures to rate themselves and their ideal selves on a standardized list of adjective traits. The masculinity of a trait was defined in terms of which traits were stereotypically associated more often with males than with females in that particular culture (William & Best, 1982). The masculinity of a given subject was assessed by what percent of the stereotypically masculine items for that subject's culture were endorsed by that subject as true of himself or herself. Although which traits were masculine and which feminine varied from one culture to the next, there were some interesting commonalities. Whatever traits were

masculine in a culture, men saw themselves as possessing them to a greater degree than did women. Both sexes in all cultures wanted to be more masculine than they actually saw themselves as being. Overall, men saw themselves more often as dominant and women saw themselves more often as having prosocial traits (see Chapter 13).

Other cross-cultural studies not only confirm that the higher levels of aggression are seen more often in boys than in girls but are also more often seen in adult men than in adult women (see Chapter 13). The United States has the highest rate of homicides among all developed countries. "Cross-cultural research has shown an association between relative father absence and violent or hypermasculine behavior" (Katz & Konner, 1981, p. 173; Whiting, 1965). In cross-cultural research, the father is "absent" because he is uninvolved in childcare, and the children do not often see him interacting with their mothers. Father absence is often associated with polygyny, and both would be expected to increase adult levels of aggression in males (see Chapter 9).

Status of Women

Since the 1970s, the question of the status of women has been a prominent issue in cultural anthropology. Some feminist anthropologists claimed that in every culture, women had a lower status than men did—no matter what men did versus what women did, whatever it was that men did, it was valued by the culture more than whatever it was that women did. Recently, for various reasons, this has been challenged.

Some very influential early work was published in 1974 in the volume entitled *Women, Culture, and Society,* edited by Michelle Zimbalist Rosaldo and Louise Lamphere. Although many chapters were very influential, those written by Rosaldo, Chodorow, and Ortner will be examined here. All three used as the basis for their arguments the fact that women have primary responsibility for child-care in nearly every culture.

Early work. Rosaldo (1974) equated women with domestic life and men with public life. Since women took care of the children, they also took care of other household or domestic functions. Men worked further from the home and so performed more public and there-fore visible tasks and jobs. This meant that men also tended to take charge of the political jobs. Since the public spheres of activity done by men are those that have the most status and prestige, this would explain the lower status of women.

Chodorow (1974, 1978), a psychoanalyst, pointed out that since daughters are raised by a same-sex adult, they develop a primitive attachment to, and sense of continuity with, their mothers. Boys are reared by an opposite-sex adult and must break that initial attachment to form a male identity and gender role. This means masculinity will be more prob-lematic for boys than femininity will be for girls. To become masculine, the boy must deny femininity, which leads to both "the repression and the devaluation of femininity on both psychological and cultural levels" (p. 51). This fact leads to sex differences in both personali-ty traits and in social status. Women have lower status than men do (at least in men's eyes) because to make the difficult transition from femininity and attachments to mother to masculinity, boys must deny the value of femininity and of being female. A girl's sense of continuity with her mother leads her to feel socially connected or related to other people. On the other hand, a boy's developmental ex-periences cause him to perceive himself as an individual, distinct, unique, and separate from everyone else.

Ortner (1974) equated male with culture and female with nature. Females "create" (by giv-ing birth to) imperfect children who develop into imperfect people. Males can create culture,

which involves enduring, perfectible works of art and science. Females lactate and menstru-ate, keeping them symbolically closer to nature, whereas men are responsible for culture, re-moving men from nature. Men transform im-perfect nature into perfectible art. Ortner (Ortner & Whitehead, 1981) later extended this idea, pointing out that women are frequently defined in terms of kinship and men in terms of occupation. Women are mothers and sisters and daughters, whereas men are hunters and bosses and warriors. Again, this makes women seem closer to nature and men closer to culture. Ortner also pointed out that women's prestige relative to men's varies from one culture to the next. In cultures where a man's prestige depends on how much his wife does or how she acts, then women's menstrual blood is more often perceived to be polluting, causing disease and even death to men exposed to it.[6] If a women's products are valued, her natural attributes are culturally exaggerated and made more salient, as if to reaffirm the nature-culture distinction.

Challenges. These early ideas have shifted, sometimes because the theorists changed their minds, sometimes because of challenges from data and other theorists. For example, MacCormack and Strathern (1980) edited a volume of works in which the equation of male with culture and women with nature was ques-tioned. Rosaldo (1980) accordingly altered her theory:

> *My earlier account of sexual asymmetry in terms of the inevitable ranking of opposed domestic and public spheres is not, then, one that I am will-ing to reject for being wrong. Rather, I have sug-gested that the reasons that account made sense are to be found* not in empirical detail, *but in the categories, biases, and limitations of a tradi-tionally individualistic and male-oriented sociology. (p. 415, emphasis added)*

Public versus domestic reflected a search for causes, and the search itself reflected a failure to understand that "the individuals who create social relationships and bonds are themselves social creations" (Rosaldo, 1980, p. 416). According to more recent viewpoints, there is nothing inevitable about childcare being domestic, and domestic being low status. Both are social and hence arbitrary constructions of reality, often by the anthropologist herself. Rosaldo now believes that reproduction itself (and who cares for the children) cannot be used to explain or describe sexual hierarchies in either domestic or public life because asymmetries in status and in public versus domestic life are "as fully social as the hunter's or the capitalist's role." Because of this, "we are challenged to provide new ways of linking the particulars of women's lives, activities, and goals to inequalities wherever they exist" (p. 417).

Even the conclusion that women have lower status than men do in all cultures has been challenged (Mukhopadhyay & Higgins, 1988; Silverblatt, 1988). Both the meaning of status and the creation of any kind of universal dichotomy have been questioned.

First, status does not, in fact, have one simple meaning or referent that transcends cultural specifics. Instead, there are many different kinds of statuses, and so many different ways of defining and measuring it. **Status** can be defined in terms of:

1. Prestige systems of the culture
2. Ownership of or control over material resources
3. Political power
4. Prestige accruing from exercise of personal skill, as in hunting or gathering prowess
5. Number of connections (through kinship or exchange relationships) to the wealthy, mighty, or skilled
6. Prestige of roles played in ritual or myth (e.g., male or female priests or gods)
7. Having personal, physical autonomy or independence of action

Thus, the questions should be: What are women's status*es* relative to those of men? And

how are those different ways of defining status interrelated?

Second, people suggested that claims of *anything* being cross-culturally universal invited "inappropriate biologism" or explanations in terms of the biology of females versus males. Although biological determinism is a myth (see Chapter 1), anything associated with the concept has been distrusted. Since all three explanations of women's status described above involved women's reproductive abilities, they were seen as problematical because they equated *women* with *mother,* as if that were the only social role that women could play.

Current types of research. Mukhopadhyay and Higgins (1988) pointed out that gender must be studied in the context of the history and economics of a society, as well its social systems, myths, beliefs, and rituals. Anthropologists must always keep their own biases and culture in mind. Descriptions of a homogenous "woman" must give way to descriptions of individual and diverse women, recognizing differences within as well as between cultures.

Female contributions to subsistence are related to their status. In current research, cultural correlates of women's subsistence labor are examined in ethnographic records. Schlegel and Barry (1986) compared cultures where women contributed more than 35 percent to the subsistence of a culture to societies where women contributed less. They found that high versus low female contribution societies differed in the following ways, all of which seem to reflect the status of women relative to the status of men:

1. High female contribution societies were more often polygynous.
2. Among matrilineal societies, high female contribution societies more often had bridewealth (payment made by a husband to his wife's relatives).
3. High female contribution societies had shorter periods after birth where sex was culturally prohibited.

4. In high female contribution societies, female children were more likely to be taught industriousness and less likely to be taught sexual restraint.

5. In high female contribution societies, boys were less likely to be valued more than girls were (this was also true of matrilineal versus patrilineal societies).

6. There was a harsher attitude towards premarital sex in low female contribution societies, and rape was more common.

In other investigations, status is given a specific definition such as literacy or social influence. For example, sex differences in illiteracy are found all over the world (Finn, Dulberg, & Reis, 1979). There are more female than male illiterates, ranging from a ratio of 2 to 1 in Europe and Russia to about 1.3 to 1 in Africa. Another study operationalized status as people's answers to the question of which 10 women's advice was followed in doing things (Werner, 1984). When the women of the Mekranoti of central Brazil were asked, women who spent more time in childcare were found to have less influence. Such women are apparently unable to maintain the personal connections and contacts needed to maintain influence. Thus, specific questions can lead to specific answers, which then need to be incorporated into some theory of the cultural constructions of gender and status.

Possible Reasons for Gender-Related Role Assignments and Evaluations

Gender-related differences have been most often explained by using ideas of function, child-rearing duties, and economic organizations. In the following discussion, you should realize that no single-factor theory is being proposed; instead, the authors are suggesting that all these factors, plus others, *combine* and *interact* to determine the roles and relative statuses of the sexes.

Functional analyses.   Functional explanations are based on analyzing the functions served when a society makes various kinds of gender distinctions. A gender distinction might increase the survival and reproduction of individuals or the survival and the smooth operation of the society. If gender distinctions are made in job assignments, boys and girls could be separately socialized so as to develop maximally the traits necessary for the performance of their separate, to-be-assigned jobs. People often relate this type of analysis to evolutionary theory, though there is no logical necessity for it. Given that culture evolves separately from genes, there is no reason why a given cultural trait would necessarily have to have any function for an individual human's survival or reproduction.

D'Andrade (1966) used functional kinds of analyses when looking at why most societies assigned certain jobs and objects of manufacture to people based on their genders, as did Murdock and Provost (1973). In some cases, the assignment of the task is related to a culture's beliefs about the differential skills and abilities of the sexes, such as the assigning of jobs requiring greater strength to males. In other cases, the job assignment is based on its compatibility with childcare: men get the jobs that cannot be done while caring for children, and women get the others. Women's jobs are thus not too dangerous, they do not require much traveling, and they are interruptible (because children frequently interrupt adults, as any parent can tell you). Alternatively, women are assigned the jobs that must be done nearly every day and so cannot be interrupted by battles or hunts. The rise of certain kinds of agriculture, which produced crops requiring extensive preparation for consumption, moved women out of the fields and back into the houses. This also switched the processing of animal products (e.g., preparation of skins, butchering, net making) from a female into a male job.

Other functional reasons for gender differentiation have more to do with the survival society itself. If males and females do different jobs, one of each sex will be required for any household to function. This mutual dependency reinforces marital bonds, perhaps leading to greater social stability. (Having the woman not know how to change the furnace filter and the man not know how to defrost the refrigerator may help keep marriages together!) If, because of gender-specific socialization, you know what traits a person you meet for the first time is likely to possess, just because of that person's gender, this might facilitate social interactions.

Child rearing. Women's roles in pregnancy and lactation have played an important part in many of the explanations given above, both functional and feminist. The fact that only women lactate means that they are associated with domestic tasks, including child rearing. Women are then devalued because they are domestic, or closer to nature, or to make male development easier. In today's technological societies, lactation is seen as problematic because it means that mothers have to stay home to care for their babies. Breast feeding babies has repeatedly gone in and out of favor. Currently, the existence of formula and bottles is seen as potentially liberating for females — someone else, even including dad, can now take care of the baby. Still, infant formula does not have the disease-fighting substances in it that the mother's first milk does (Barkow, 1989, his Chapter 12). It is also interesting to note that the women of the Israeli kibbutzim are now demanding to raise their own children in their own homes.

Social, political, and economic organization. Among the feminist sociologists and anthropologists, the Marxists are particularly likely to relate the sociopolitical features of a culture to who controls the society's means of economic production. The more that women control the means of production, the closer women's status will be to that of men. In prestate societies (no centralized government), women controlled more of the production than was true in state societies, so prestate societies were relatively egalitarian compared to state societies. Women's relative contributions to subsistence are related to many other features of the society as well, including marriage system and child-rearing practices. Furthermore, when intensive agriculture moved women back into the home, their contribution to subsistence declined along with their status relative to men.

Questions of women's statuses. Do the females of a culture share the male status system or do they have one of their own? Do they share the male valuation of them and their system? Or, from their point of view, do males have lower position or importance or influence (or whatever it is that females perceive gives them status)? If there are women's status systems, do most women personally believe in and value them?[7] Any system that does not engender much belief is vulnerable to replacement by some other cultural system. If the sexes have separate status system, why have males' systems so often become the preeminent ones? Have women simply adopted men's systems? If so, why? As yet, we have no answers to these questions, but we will look at some clues in Unit Four.

SUMMARY

Variability is the most important theme of this chapter. There is variability among the anthropologists with regard to how best to approach the understanding of humankind. There is variability in the social systems of primates from one species to the next, and variability in the roles and traits of the sexes from one culture to the next. There is also variability within each species or culture. There are the human Berdaches and the Israeli kibbutzim. The degree of paternal investment varies among primates and among human societies. In some human societies females hunt; in others they do not. Any explanation of the cross-cultural commonalities will also have to be able to explain the great variability.

Hunting, the degree of subsistence activity, and childcare are some of the most cross-culturally consistent gender-related differences. In most societies, men do the hunting and share what they get; women do the gathering and feed mostly their own families. The amount that the average woman contributes to the subsistence activities of her social group affects the rest of the political/social structure of that group. And the amount that the woman can contribute is often constrained by the amount of time she has to devote to childcare. Lactation (at least before bottles) means that some woman (mother or wet nurse) has to stay with the un-weaned infant or carry the infant with her, thus limiting what she can do. Hunting may occur among women only if it involves short trips that could feasibly be made by a lactating woman carrying an infant.

After weaning, the mother can leave the child with alloparents, who are also almost always females (older sisters, grandmothers, mothers with whom she is taking turns with babysitting chores). Particularly in societies in which women play a large role in subsistence activities, older siblings are the most likely alloparents, freeing the mother for her very necessary work. These child-rearing patterns mean that girls are reared by same-sex care-givers, and boys by opposite-sex care-givers.

Despite the large amounts of data gathered there are many questions left. Why are female care-givers preferred? And just how are children affected by different child-rearing styles: Do children reared by other children act differently than children reared by mothers? By fathers? What are the status systems of men and women, and how much overlap is there? How each culture answers these questions varies tremendously according to the myths and symbols used by each to explain itself.

ENDNOTES

1. *Territoriality* is the extent to which the male defends a particular area as his own against other males.

2. Although most (58 percent) foraging societies are patrilocal, many subsistence-level horticultural (farming) societies are matrilocal, and horticultural societies with surplus supplies are again patrilocal (D'Andrade, 1966; Nielsen, 1990).

3. The hunting-foraging Ache are an interesting exception, which will be discussed later.

4. This is a strength of the theory, since only we humans have done it so far.

5. However, the relationship may be that you groom those who have supported you, but those who groom you may not necessarily receive support from you (Hemelrijk & Ek, 1991).

6. One wonders about the functions of menstrual myths. Among the Gimi of New Guinea, menstrual blood — or the touch of a menstruating woman — causes devastation: "Wooden bowls will crack, stone axes will misbehave in the hands of their male owners and inflict upon them otherwise inexplicable wounds, crops will wither and die, even the ground over which the menstruator steps will lose its fertility . . . contact with it [menstrual blood] may cause the . . . male body to die" (Gillison, 1980, pp. 149–150). And yet, the men also find menstruating women to be very erotic and women cannot convince their husbands or lovers to stay away from them when the women are menstruating.

7. Or are they like those males that believe menstrual blood will kill them but still persist in attempting to have sex with menstruating women?

CHAPTER 11

STEREOTYPES AND SEX TYPING

INTRODUCTION
GENDER CATEGORIES
WHEN STEREOTYPES BECOME PREJUDICES
THE DEVELOPMENT OF STEREOTYPES
SUMMARY

> *One fourth-grade male reported that if he saw a boy playing with a doll, "I'd yell at him first, but if he didn't stop, I'd punch him in the nose and call the police."*
> —D. B. Carter and L. A. McCloskey (1983/1984, p. 300)

Ann Beuf (1974) asked 63 children, 3 to 6 years old, what they would do if, when they grew up, they were the other sex. More girls had answers, meaning that they had already thought about the possibility. Boys didn't want to answer the question. "That's a weird question, you know," one replied. When another boy was pressed, he said, "If I were a girl I'd have to grow up to be nothing."

This chapter describes sex or gender stereotypes, including their contexts and how they affect our lives. Because of sex stereotypes, some boys believe that if they were girls, their lives might well be empty. A number of boys also believe that boys playing with dolls should be severely punished.

INTRODUCTION

Gender stereotypes are attitudes with three components: cognitive, affective, and behav-ioral. The first section describes stereotypes as cognitive categories. People inherently categorize things. When we divide up the "nonperson" aspects of our world into different groups, the groups are called **natural language categories.** For example, we make categories of various animals and flowers, furniture and rocks, numbers and colors, and so on. When we divide other people into groups, we are making **social categories.** We have, in addition to gender categories, categories based on race and age. Natural language and social categories show some interesting differences as well as similarities. Sexual prejudice, which is described in the second section, can occur either because of the cognitive component of gender stereotypes or because of the cognitive plus the affective component. Gender stereotypes are acquired by all of us, from our parents and from the mass media. The third section describes the processes by which they are learned.

GENDER CATEGORIES

Our theories of stereotypes have changed during the last 20 years (McCauley, Stitt, & Segal, 1980; Messick & Mackie, 1989). Stereotypes used to be regarded as a form of pathology. Stereotypes now are seen as an inevitable consequence of our inherent tendency to classify or categorize objects, including people, into various concepts or groupings. "What is wrong with stereotyping is no more and no less than what is wrong with human conceptual behavior generally" (McCauley et al., 1980, p. 195).

Categorization Processes

When we encounter an object, whether it is animate, inanimate, or human, we tend to place it into certain categories that we have constructed out of our past experiences. If the object matches some of the defining/distinguishing characteristics of one of our already existing mental categories, we **assimilate** the object into that category. If the object does not fit any of our categories very well, we may **accommodate** by changing one or more categories — or creating a new one — to fit the object.

Categorization is inherent in our brains' processing of information. One way our brains process information is to categorize it and then store it (remember it) based on its category. Even the brains of birds perform some primitive categorizations (Nelson & Marler, 1989). Because an object's category determines where in the brain its memory is stored, if a certain area of the cortex is damaged, the person may be able to remember the names of concrete, inanimate objects such as *bricks* and *toasters,* but be unable to remember the names of animals such as *dogs* or *cats* (McCarthy & Warrington, 1988; Warrington & McCarthy, 1987; Warrington & Shallice, 1984). Another area, when damaged, may produce the reverse set of deficits. Men's and women's names may also be stored in somewhat different areas of the

brain since one brain-damaged patient showed a somewhat better memory for girls' than for boys' names.

Categories and fuzzy sets. Categories have a certain cognitive structure (Armstrong, Gleitman, & Gleitman, 1983; Caramazza, Hersh, & Togerson, 1976; Rips, Shoben, & Smith, 1973; Rosch, 1975a, 1975b; Rosch & Mervis, 1975). To explore the structure, subjects might be given pairs of objects, such as *chair-table, duck-eagle,* and *chair-eagle,* to rate for similarity to each other.[1] The subjects' ratings are combined and transformed mathematically into a picture of what subjects' mental categories of those objects "look like." Part A of Figure 11.1 shows the structure of male categories and Part B shows females' categories. The two dimensions involved for females seem to be (left versus right) progressive versus conservative, and (up versus down) bad (e.g., *tart*) versus good (e.g., *straightforward, ecologist, maternal*). The dimensions for males were not as clearly definable, but the authors thought that one dimension (left versus right) was tough-minded or hard (e.g., *bourgeois*) versus tender-minded or soft (e.g., *softy*), and the other dimension (up versus down) was reliable or predictable types (e.g., *career man*) versus unreliable, unpredictable types (e.g., *gambler*).

Subjects can also be asked to define **prototypical** members of any category. In this case, subjects are asked to rate how typical each object is of the category itself (Armstrong et al., 1983; Caramazza et al., 1976; Osherson & Smith, 1981; Rosch & Mervis, 1975). One group of subjects rated the degree to which a given item represented "their idea or image of the meaning of each category term" on a scale of 1 to 7, with 1 being most representative (Armstrong et al., 1983, p. 275). Those subjects produced the ratings presented in Table 11.1, reflecting the prototypicality of various female subtypes. The most prototypical females were *sister* and *mother.* Even the clearly defined categories of odd and even numbers have been

Part A. Male Subtypes

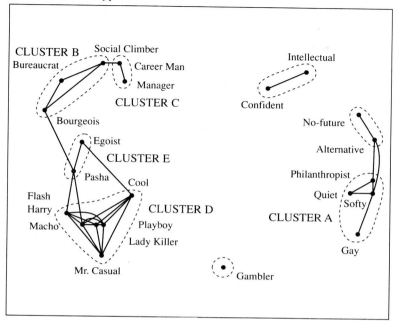

Part B. Female Subtypes

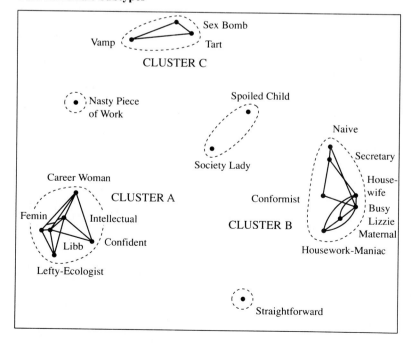

FIGURE 11.1 *The Structure of Cognitive Sexual Categories*
The structure of cognitive categories of various male (Part A) and female (Part B) subtypes, where distance between subtypes on the graphs is assumed to correspond to cognitive "distances" in people's stereotypic concepts. Some subtypes are closely related to each other, as indicated by the dotted lines that surround them to form the various clusters.

Source: From "A Closer Look at the Complex Structure of Gender Stereotypes" by B. Six and T. Eckes, 1991, *Sex Roles, 24,* p. 64. Copyright 1991 by Plenum Publishing Corporation. Reprinted by permission.

TABLE 11.1 *The Prototypicality of Female Subtypes*
This table presents the average "typicality" scores of items according to subjects who were judging the degree to which each item represents, or is typical of, the category *female*. The higher the score, the less typical is that subtype of the category *female*.

Mother	1.7	Sister	1.8
Housewife	2.4	Ballerina	2.0
Princess	3.0	Actress	2.1
Waitress	3.2	Hostess	2.7
Policewoman	3.9	Chairwoman	3.4
Comedienne	4.5	Cowgirl	4.5

Source: From "What Some Concepts Might Not Be" by S. L. Armstrong, L. R. Gleitman, and H. Gleitman, 1983, *Cognition, 13,* p. 276. Copyright 1983 by Elsevier Sequoia. Reprinted by permission.

found to have more prototypical (e.g., *4, 2, 3,* and *7*) and less prototypical (e.g., *106* and *91*) members.

Each member of a category, as well as the category's name, has certain **attributes** (properties) associated with it. In one experiment, subjects were told to list "the characteristics and attributes that people feel are common to and characteristic of different kinds of ordinary everyday objects" (Rosch & Mervis, 1975, p. 578). Prototypical objects of categories shared more attributes in common than did less prototypical objects.[2] Furthermore, the most prototypical members of any two different categories tended to share fewer attributes in common than did less prototypical members. Prototypes are typical and also **differentiating**, maximizing differences and minimizing the overlap of attributes possessed by the members of any two different categories.

Basic categories have some special properties:

The division of the world into categories is not arbitrary. The basic category cuts [divisions] are those which separate the information-rich

bundles of attributes which form natural discontinuities. Basic categories have, in fact, been shown to be the most inclusive categories in which all items in the category possess significant numbers of attributes in common. . . . Basic categories are, thus, the categories which mirror the correlational structure of the environment. (Rosch & Mervis, 1975, p. 602)

The subtypes of men and women rated for the data of Figure 11.1 are examples of **basic-level social gender categories.**

Because of shared attributes, categories become **fuzzy sets** of objects. Fuzzy set do not have clear boundaries or clearly delineated and differentiating properties because objects from one category often share attributes with objects from some other category. People categorize any given object by analyzing the cues shared by the object-to-be identified and a prototype of the fuzzy set category. People are thought to unconsciously compute some kind of cognitive "distance" between that object and various prototypes (Osherson & Smith, 1981; Rosch & Mervis, 1975). If a distance is "small," the object will be mentally placed into the category defined by that particular prototype.

Since categories have subcategories and sub-subcategories, they also have vertical and horizontal associations. Going from a supraordinate category (e.g., *animal*) to a lower level (e.g., *mammal*) to a still lower level (e.g., *homo sapiens*) would define a set of **vertical associations.** Describing different categories of objects that are all at the same level of some category (e.g., both cats and humans are mammals) would be to move horizontally. **Horizontal associations** might be based on the structure of shared versus differentiating attributes. In Figure 11.1, *vamp, sex bomb,* and *tart* might involve one subcategory of females, and *career woman, feminist, intellectual,* and so on, would belong to another subcategory. These two categories would share the attribute "progressive," but would be differentiated by the degree of "good" versus "bad" possessed by their two sets of members.

Differences between natural object and social categories.   Our most common social categories are based on race, age, and sex, categories formed on the basis of shared attributes (Cantor & Mischel, 1979; Messick & Mackie, 1989). However, there are some important differences between social and natural object categories. Social categories not only have prototypes but also memories of specific individuals that can be recalled when asked to make judgments about the group as a whole (Kraft et al., 1991). Therefore, members of subordinate categories (e.g., *businesswoman*) can contain many idiosyncratic associations not shared by the prototype of the category (e.g., *mother* and *sister*). This suggests that vertical and horizontal associations might be less prominent in social categories than in natural object categories.

Furthermore, in the structure of natural object categories, the basic level of objects (e.g., *tables* and *chairs*) has more characteristics associated with it than does the higher-level category that includes several basic-level objects (e.g., *furniture*). This is not true of gender categories. Deaux and her colleagues (Deaux & Kite, 1985; Deaux & Lewis, 1984; Deaux et al., 1985) systematically explored gender subtypes by having subjects "list all the characteristics that they associated with the particular group." For example, although *mother* (basic level) had more attributes associated with it than did *woman* (higher level), *fat woman* had fewer attributes than did *woman,* and no difference was significant. Different attributes were linked to the different gender subcategories, and few were shared with the higher-level category name.

Social categories also contain sets of behavioral traits. Both trait and group stereotypes exist, but the trait stereotypes may be subordinate to the group stereotypes (Anderson & Klatzky, 1987; Fiske, Neuberg, Beattie, & Milberg, 1987). We might have a social stereotype of an *ambitious person* (a trait stereotype), believing that ambitious people share other attributes, such as being determined, resolute, decisive,

stubborn, and so on. However, that stereotype might be subordinate to a group stereotype such as *politician,* since we see politicians as being not only ambitious but also self-assured and diplomatic.

The most important difference between social and nonsocial categories comes from their definitions. When we categorize another person, we must also simultaneously (though not necessarily consciously) categorize ourselves as either being in the same or in some contrasting category (e.g., same versus other sex or race). Our own personal identities are often involved, at least potentially and tangentially, in all of our social categorizations. Probably because of this, people are more likely to remember the subordinate attributes of a member of their own group than those of some other group. When subjects were given stories about various people to remember, two days later, females were more apt to recall the occupations of females than the occupations of males, but males better remembered males' rather than females' occupations (Park & Rothbart, 1982). Children also tend to positively evaluate other children of their own sex and negatively evaluate children of the opposite sex (Martin, 1991).

Content of Gender Categories

Ashmore and Del Boca (1979) define **gender stereotypes** as "the structured sets of beliefs about the personal attributes of women and men" (p. 222). Stereotypes "summarize and organize what the individual has learned about social groups" (Ashmore, Del Boca, & Wohlers, 1986, p. 90) such as men and women. If stereotypes are part of the reason for sex differences, it is important to explore the stereotypes' contents. It is also important to establish how the *content* of the stereotypes depends on the *method* used to measure them.

Methods of studying.   Researchers have explored gender stereotypes with an astonishingly wide variety of inferences and instruments in all combinations of the possibilities described below (Ashmore, 1981; Ashmore & Del Boca, 1979; Ashmore et al., 1986).

1. *Checklists versus rating scales versus open-ended formats.* Some measures use **trait lists** and ask subjects to indicate which are feminine and which are masculine. A feminine stereotypic trait is one that subjects agree (criteria ranging from 40 to 75 percent agreement have been used) is feminine rather than masculine; a masculine trait is defined similarly. In **rating scales,** subjects rate each trait's femininity and masculinity. A masculine stereotypic trait is one on which a majority of subjects agree is more masculine than feminine, and a feminine stereotypic trait is defined similarly. In **open-ended research,** subjects are asked to list several traits and characteristics that are typical of men and/or typical of women. Any trait occurring significantly more often on men's than on women's lists are gender stereotypic. Cowan and Stewart (1977) compared those three techniques and found that they lead to gender stereotypes with different contents.

2. *Type of stimulus figure to be rated.* Sometimes subjects are asked to rate categories (*woman* versus *man*) or various subcategories (*businesswoman* versus *businessman*) (see Figure 11.1). Rating subcategories proves that there are several different gender stereotypes (Ashmore, 1981).

Deaux and her colleagues (Deaux & Kite, 1985; Deaux & Lewis, 1984; Deaux et al., 1985) asked subjects to rate how likely each type of subcategory person would be to have various male and female traits, roles, occupations, and physical characteristics. A *homosexual male* and a *homosexual female* were judged less likely to have sex typical traits, roles, occupations, and physical characteristics than were *heterosexual male* and *heterosexual female* stimulus figures. An *athletic woman* was judged more likely to have male traits, roles, occupations, and physical characteristics than were a *woman,* a *housewife,* or a *sexy woman.* All males were seen as likely to perform male role behaviors, such as being a *financial provider,* and were perceived as unlikely to perform female role behaviors, such as *cooks meals,* or to have female occupations or physical characteristics. "Images of men may be centered around a single concept, one that acknowledges little diversity. . . . Im-

ages of women, in contrast, appear to be segmented more sharply" (Deaux et al., 1985, p. 166).

3. *Types of characteristics to be rated.* Though personality traits are the most frequently researched components of gender stereotypes, other attributes include recreational activities, vocational interests, and types of social interactions and social behaviors (Orlofsky, Cohen, & Ramsden, 1985). As just described, Deaux and colleagues have shown that the structure of gender stereotypes depends on which attributes are used to study them.

4. *Personal versus cultural instructions.* Sometimes subjects are instructed to rate traits according to the subject's own impressions of the beliefs of "society" or of "other people." In other cases, subjects are asked to rate traits according to their "own personal beliefs." A personal stereotype is likely to incorporate several culturally stereotypic items, but is also likely to include some unique items (Eagly & Mladinic, 1989).

5. *Typical versus ideal.* Subjects can be asked to indicate what men and women are "really like" or what men and women "should be like." The **typical** stereotype measures subjects' beliefs as to the attributes most typical of men versus women, and the **ideal** stereotype measures subjects' beliefs as to what attributes women and men ought to ideally possess. There is some but not complete overlap between the traits identified according to each procedure (Archer, 1980, 1984; Stoppard & Kalin, 1978; the Bem Sex Role Inventory [BSRI] versus the Spence Personal Attributes Questionnaire [PAQ], Chapter 2).

6. *Identification versus differentiation.* In all the techniques so far described, **identification** is unavoidably confused with **differentiation.** As described above, items are identified with a particular social group usually because of being possessed by over half of the people in the group. The same item characteristics would also be seen as being possessed by fewer than half of the people in some contrasting social group. For example, a trait that is seen as atypical of women may be perceived as being possessed by anywhere from 0 to 49 percent of all women, but a typical trait could be possessed by 51 to 100 percent of all women. In contrast, a differentiating stereotype identifies those traits on which subjects feel that women and men *most differ* from each other. One trait might be possessed by 51 percent

of all men versus 49 percent of all women, and another might be possessed by 99 percent of all women versus 1 percent of all men. The second trait would be strongly differentiating and the first one would be identifying but not differentiating. A gender-differentiating stereotypic trait might also be identified with both genders: subjects could believe that 99 percent of all women versus 55 percent of all men had the trait.

An **identifying stereotypic trait** is identified with more than half of one group versus less than half of the other. In contrast, a **differentiating stereotypic trait** may be typical of both sexes (or atypical of both) but is also perceived as being more common in one sex than in the other. For example, being a murderer is perceived as atypical of both sexes, but it is also differentiating. Far more men than women are perceived to be murderers.

Research has demonstrated that identifying and differentiating traits are not always the same. In De Lisi and Soundranayagam's (1990) study, only 8 of the 10 identifying (core) are differentiating (when differentiating is defined as an average difference in the subjects' ratings of men versus women of 1 or more). Furthermore, four of the noncore traits *(motherly, soft, softhearted,* and *aggressive)* are differentiating traits. Figure 11.2 depicts a differentiating approach to sex stereotyping. Subjects were asked to rank both *man* and *woman* along a series of rating scales. As you can see, *woman* differs most from *man* on the masculine-feminine rating scale. It is not yet known which type of traits are more important for sex-typing socialization (see Chapter 9).

Contents of selected stereotype lists. Although stereotypic traits contain a number of themes, two of most prevalent are instrumental versus expressive and hard versus soft (Hoyenga & Hoyenga, 1993). In fact, Spence has suggested that the PAQ and the BSRI measure largely instrumental and expressive traits rather than sex roles (see Chapter 2;

Spence, 1991). **Instrumental traits** refer to behaviors useful for accomplishing tasks, and **expressive traits** reflect an ability to express emotions and a sensitivity to the emotions of others. Best, Williams, and Briggs (1980) found that, across cultures, the more masculine a trait was rated, the more potent and strong the trait was also judged to be. When multidimensional scaling techniques were used to place trait adjectives into a cognitive space defined by three dimensions, as shown in Figure 11.3, the male/female dimension almost perfectly corresponded to a hard/soft dimension (Ashmore, 1981). The male end of the dimension was also closer to the *good-intellectual* adjectives than was the female end.

Social desirability of femininity versus masculinity. There has been some controversy over whether masculine stereotypes are more socially desirable than are feminine stereotypes.[3] Since femininity is complex and multidimensional, so is its favorability. For example, Eagly and Mladinic pointed out that status and favorability (evaluation) should be clearly distinguished. Although women have lower social status and power, stereotypes about women may be more favorable than stereotypes about men. Each sex has a somewhat more favorable impression of its own than of the other sex.

Variations in cultural stereotypes. Different social groups often have somewhat different stereotypes. This is true when males' stereotypes are compared to females', and when whites' stereotypes are compared to those of African-Americans (Smith & Midlarsky, 1985; see Hoyenga & Hoyenga, 1993). In Burns's research (1977), females believed that males perceived them to be less dominant than either sex actually perceived females to be. Males thought that females viewed them as being more aggressive than was actually true. Most interesting, neither sex perceived any sex

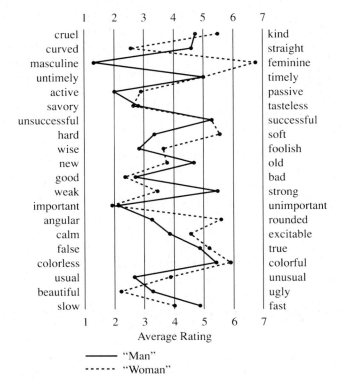

FIGURE 11.2   *The Concepts of Man and Woman*
How subjects rate the concepts of *man* and *woman* along several different dimensions (e.g., the "cruel" to "kind" dimension).

Source: From "An Atlas of Semantic Profiles for 360 Words" by J. J. Jenkins, W. A. Russell, and G. J. Suci, 1958, *American Journal of Psychology, 71,* pp. 688–699. Copyright 1985 by the Board of Trustees of the University of Illinois. Reprinted by permission of the University of Illinois Press.

difference in intelligence when rating themselves or each other. Despite this, males perceived women as thinking of men as being more intelligent, and females saw men as thinking of women as being less intelligent, than was actually true. Overall, females were worse at inferring how males actually view females than males were at inferring how females actually view males.

Cross-cultural research on gender stereotypes has also been carried out. Williams and Best used their checklist technique (Williams & Best, 1982; Williams et al., 1977). Across 30 different countries, men tended to be seen as being more autonomous, more exhibitionistic, more aggressive, more dominant, more achievement-oriented, and as having more endurance. The female stereotype included having greater needs for deference, abasement, succorance, nurturance, affiliation, intraception, and

heterosexuality. There were also cultural differences. For example, Ireland tended to have less differentiating stereotypes than did England or the United States. Eagly and Kite (1987) compared stereotypes of nationalities to sex stereotypes and found that U.S. college students perceived the men of 14 different countries as being higher in agency and women higher in communion.[4] Men were also seen as being more similar to the national stereotype than were women. Accordingly, men of different cultures are perceived quite differently, but women of all cultures are perceived as being high in communion but relatively low in agency (except U.S. women, who are perceived to be the highest in agency of any cultural group).

Change over time.   The degree of change in gender stereotypes seen over time depends on

FIGURE 11.3   *Male and Female Cognitive Categories*
This figure presents another way to look at the cognitive categories of *male* and *female*. To produce this figure, special statistical scaling techniques were used to show how the structure of a gender category compared to the dimensions of *Hard-Soft, Social Desirability* (Good-Social to Bad-Social), and *Intellectual Desirability*. Note that the distinction between Male-Female is closest to that between Hard-Soft.

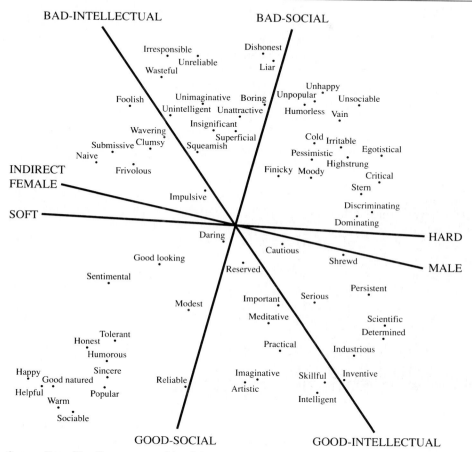

Source: From "Sex Stereotypes and Implicit Personality Theory. I. A Personality Description Approach to the Assessment of Sex Stereotypes" by R. D. Ashmore and M. L. Tumia, 1980, *Sex Roles, 6,* p. 511. Copyright 1980 by Plenum Publishing Corporation. Reprinted by permission.

how the stereotypes are measured. Overall, the favorability of the female stereotype may have increased and egalitarianism may have decreased. However, the stereotypes' contents do not seem to have changed much (Helmreich, Spence, & Gibson, 1982; Lueptow, 1985; Lewin & Tragos, 1987; Slevin & Wingrove, 1983). Another way to look for change is to do a longitudinal study. Etaugh and Spandikow (1981) found that college students' attitudes towards women's roles tended to become more liberal after two years of college. On the other hand, Galambos, Almeida, and Peterson (1990) found that, between the sixth and eighth grades, girls became increasingly more favorable toward the idea of equality between the sexes, but boys became less approving.

Maintenance and Change

Why do stereotypes appear to have "a life of their own"?

Stereotypes modify social behaviors. Stereotypes can create their own reality (Jones, 1986; Jussim, 1986; Snyder, 1984; see Chapter 2). Even when our expectancies might originally have been in error, they can come to be true because those expectancies affect the way we treat each other, which can cause us to come to act in stereotypic ways. Expectancies can even change the self-perceptions of the person exposed to them (Fazio, Effrein, & Falender, 1981; Snyder & Swann, 1978).

In one example of expectancy effects, pairs of subjects decided who would perform various masculine and feminine tasks while having their pictures taken (Skrypnek & Snyder, 1982). Each male subject was led to believe that the person with whom he was working was either a male or a female, although all males were actually working with (unseen) female partners. The subjects, working in separate rooms, used pushbuttons and lights to communicate to each other which task out of each pair each subject preferred. In the first phase, the male subject indicated his choice first, and in the second phase, the female went first. In the first phase, the partners believed to be female chose more feminine tasks than did those labeled as male. This difference persisted into the second phase where the female now indicated her choices first. If she was a "female" rather than a "male," she still indicated a greater preference for feminine tasks. Male subjects induced the "female" female subjects to act more feminine.

Memory processes. Our stereotypes are also durable because they affect how we remember

things. First, merely thinking about a person about whom we have stereotyped perceptions can increase our negative responses to that person (Leone & Ensley, 1985). Second, we simply tend to ignore people (and their characteristics) who are unimportant to us (Rodin, 1987). Younger people tend to ignore older people and so do not even remember what they look like; male (but not female) subjects tend to ignore unattractive females.

A third memory process affecting our stereotypes has to do with whether a person's actions are consistent with, inconsistent with, or irrelevant to our stereotypic expectations, based on the category to which we have assigned that person. Relevant information, either consistent or inconsistent, is remembered better than irrelevant information (Ruble & Stangor, 1986). Consistent information may be remembered better because we have many attributes and traits with which to associate it, and our memory for traits is directly related to the number of associations we can make with some fact we are trying to remember (Higgins, King, & Mavin, 1982). Inconsistent information may elicit more processing and so be remembered better (Branscombe & Smith, 1990). Because it is inconsistent, we may think about it more in an effort to understand why that inconsistent behavior occurred. Inconsistent information may also be salient because it is surprising to us, and salient information elicits more thinking (processing).

Fourth, stereotypes affect memories because of response biases (Ruble & Stangor, 1986). If we are unsure if a given trait was presented in some material that we are supposed to remember, and given that we have to make a choice, we often decide that stereotype-consistent rather than stereotype-inconsistent information had been presented (Furnham & Singh, 1986; Furnham & Duignan, 1989). Snyder and Uranowitz (1978, described in Snyder, 1984) provided a dramatic example of recall bias. They gave college student subjects a description of a woman named Betty K. to remember. One week later, half were told that she was a lesbian, and half were told that she was living with her husband. Then both groups were asked to recall the other information they had been given about her. The subjects reconstructed their memories so as to support their own beliefs and assumptions about lesbians versus heterosexual women. The subjects given the lesbian label remembered that Betty K. had never had a steady boyfriend but did not recall that she had also gone out on many dates in college.

Ego involvement in categorizations. We tend to be egoinvested in our own opinions; we want to believe that we are correct and accurate in our perceptions. At the same time, we might also want to believe that we are not stereotyped (a process that will be discussed later). Power and competition can affect how ego-involved subjects will be (Ashmore et al., 1986; Messick & Mackie, 1989). Members of low-power status groups tend to perceive members of high-power status groups as being more differentiated from each other and more variable, and members of low-power status groups are often perceived as relatively homogeneous by high-status people. When a member of one group thinks that there might be conflict with a member of another group, stereotypic perceptions are likely to be very resistant to change.

Effects of disconfirming examples. How do people cope when stereotyped **targets** (hypothetical or stimulus people used in research) display inconsistent traits? For example, how do people cope with rational, intelligent, agentic, instrumental, nonnurturant women? Locksley and her colleagues (Locksley et al., 1980; Locksley, Hepburn, & Ortiz, 1982) suggested that subjects abandon their stereotypes. When their subjects were faced with disconfirming information (e.g., a female target who was assertive), they did not use gender stereotypes to judge that target. Locksley and colleagues concluded that stereotypes would af-

fect judgments only if gender were the only information provided about people. To reach the conclusion they did, Locksley and associates assumed that an assertive behavioral act was equally **diagnostic** of an assertiveness trait in both sexes, or that being assertive once means that you will be perceived as equally likely to be assertive in the future, regardless of your gender.

Behaviors are not always perceived as having equal diagnostic value for both genders. Sometimes subjects act as if a sex-linked behavior were more predictive, or more indicative of the presence of the corresponding trait, in "appropriate"-sex people—people whose actions match the stereotype (Berndt & Heller, 1986; Kulik, 1983). On other occasions, sex-linked behavior is seen as more indicative of traitedness in "inappropriate"-sex people (Gerber, 1984; Jackson & Cash, 1985; Hansen & O'Leary, 1985; Wallston & O'Leary, 1981). Finally, sometimes behaviors displayed by a woman are more often attributed to personality traits ("That's just the way she is") and the same behaviors displayed by a man are attributed to the situation ("Something made him act that way") (Cowan & Koziej, 1979; Hansen & O'Leary, 1985; Wallston & O'Leary, 1981).

The research that does *not* use the assumption of equal diagnostic value continues to find that gender stereotypes affect people's judgments. For example, Rasinski, Crocker, and Hastie (1985) attempted to replicate the Locksley study except that they replaced the assumption of equal diagnostic value with subjects' actual estimates of the future probability of assertion for male and female targets separately. In this research, stereotypes were demonstrated to affect subjects' ratings. Other research has found similar effects (Futoran & Wyer, 1986). Even when rating the same trait, subjects use different rating scales for male and female stimulus figures (Biernat, Manis, & Nelson, 1991).

Sometimes targets can force a change in the stereotypic perceptions of somebody with whom they interact (Hilton & Darley, 1985). As Rothbart and John (1985) pointed out, if a woman is aware of the stereotype, she can act in such a way so as to force perceivers to change their perceptions—at least of that particular woman. The stereotype itself may be left intact. The atypical woman may simply be placed into a subcategory not directly related to the category woman. They described a colleague who, at a conference, expressed "less than flattering" sentiments about blacks. When one of them asked that colleague about his obviously intelligent and scholarly coauthor and copresenter who was also black, the colleague's response was, "I never think of him as black" (p. 93). No matter how competent a woman is, if she is perceived as an atypical female ("one of the boys"), the gender stereotypes of the people around her will not change.

Rothbart and John (1985) suggested that stereotypes are most likely to change when people are forced to confront targets who are both nonconforming and for whom the original category remains salient, or difficult if not impossible to ignore. For example, an intelligent, competent female computer engineer may change the stereotypes of the people with whom she interacts only if they cannot "forget" she is a female because of her salient femininity. The irony of this is that acting and dressing feminine may cause an otherwise competent female to be perceived as somewhat less competent (Moore, 1984). Still, this may be the only way to get the stereotypes themselves to change.

Individual Differences in Stereotyping

What types of people are particularly likely to use gender stereotypes? If we know something about who they are, how they think, and why they think that way, we will be better able to create any cultural changes deemed desirable.

Types of people by types of stereotypes. Just as there are different types of gender stereotypes, there must also be different kinds of

stereotyping people. A person might deny having any gender stereotypic categories either because his cognitions concerning the genders are not organized that way or because the cognitive categories are organized along gender stereotypic lines but the person is unwilling to admit it. This last idea will be expanded on the discussion of prejudice.

Measuring tendencies and attitudes. Researchers have looked at who tends to sex type other people. The Attitudes towards Women Scale (AWS) (see Hoyenga & Hoyenga, 1993) has often been used to measure individual differences in gender-stereotyping attitudes. It measures the degree to which social prejudice against women is perceived as acceptable (Archer, 1989b; Spence & Helmreich, 1980).

Several characteristics have frequently been found to differentiate between the people who do and the people who do not use the cultural sexual stereotypes (see documentation in Hoyenga & Hoyenga, 1993). For example, sex-typed people do seem to do more stereotyping. In one study, children were asked to rate "what boys are like" and "what girls are like." They were then asked to rate, either "as a boy, I am like" or "as a girl, I am like" (Burke & Tully, 1977). Boys who saw themselves as possessing many girlish traits also saw other boys as being more girlish as well, or as being less different from girls; girls showed a similar pattern. People who get better grades, or who are better educated, or women who have careers (versus homemakers) also all tend to have more liberal attitudes toward women's roles. However, none of these studies indicated the degree to which difference subjects saw men and women as being different from each other. Therefore, none looked for individual differences in the degree to which differentiating stereotypes were being used, or for individual differences in the degree of **stereotypy**.

Characteristics of high-stereotypy people. The authors and Alphons Richert have been looking at the cognitive processes of high- versus low-stereotypy people (Richert & Hoyenga, 1982, 1986; Hoyenga & Richert, 1990). To measure a differentiating stereotype, subjects are asked to make a series of judgments about the proportion of women (or men) who possess a certain BSRI trait, compared to the number of people in the world who possess that trait. Subjects are also asked to judge how many of the people in the world are women. These numbers are then combined into a ratio score (McCauley, Stitt, & Segal, 1980):

$$P \left(\frac{\text{Trait}}{\text{Gender Group}} \right)$$

$$= P \text{ (Trait)} \times \frac{P \left(\dfrac{\text{Gender Group}}{\text{Trait}} \right)}{P \text{ (Group)}}$$

A gender group refers either to men or women. Therefore, this formula says that the probability of women (for example) possessing a given trait (e.g., what proportion of women are assertive?) is equal to the judged probability of the trait existing in anyone (what proportion of people are assertive?), multiplied by the ratio of the last two terms. The last two terms are the probability that a person possessing the trait would be a female (how many assertive people are female?), and the proportion of females in the world.

An individual's degree of **stereotypy** is the rated probability of a women possessing the trait, divided by the rated probability of anyone having the trait. This ratio is calculated for each trait the subject rates women or men on, and the subject's average ratio is then transformed into logarithms.[5] Martin (1987) has used a similar ratio to measure sex stereotyping, showing that individuals do differ in the degree to which they stereotype others. She also found that those who sex stereotype people using the feminine terms on the BSRI and PAQ also stereotype people when using the masculine and the neutral terms. Similarly, Eagly and Mladinic (1989) stated that "subjects'

ratings of a group on *any* list of evaluative traits reveal their attitude toward the group" (p. 548).

Data from the authors' stereotypy research described above revealed that subjects' average stereotypy scores are not related to their scores on the AWS or on the Attitudes Toward Men Scale developed by Iazzo (1983), or to the subjects' own self-ratings of instrumentality and expressiveness. The ratio scores are also moderately stable over time (reliable).

The cognitive space of high-stereotyping people was also found to differ from that of low-stereotyping people. To explore this, the high- and low-stereotypy subjects were asked to rate a variety of gender subtypes on a number of different traits. The traits were then reduced, based on standardized ratings, to the dimensions of potency, activity, and evaluation (good/bad). The various gender subtypes being rated were also classified into male versus female stimulus people (e.g., *male nurse* versus *female doctor*) and into masculine versus feminine occupations (e.g., *doctor* versus *nurse*). The dimension along which subjects most differentiated the genders was the one of potency illustrated in Figure 11.4. High-stereotypy male subjects differentiated male and female stimulus figures more than did any other group, but high-stereotypy females differentiated between masculine and feminine occupations more than they did male and female stimulus figures. With this, we can begin to see how people of different stereotypy levels tend to organize their gender belief systems.

WHEN STEREOTYPES BECOME PREJUDICES

This section discusses some of the processes that affect when and how stereotypes become prejudice. This will include emotional reactions as well as behavioral tendencies. Evidence for change over the years and examples of prejudice are also presented.

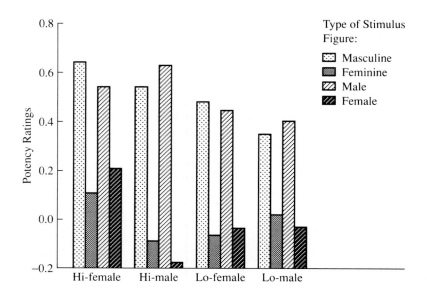

FIGURE 11.4 *Stereotypy Level and Gender of Subject*
This shows the degree to which the various types of subjects differentiate between male and female stimulus figures, compared to their differentiation between masculine and feminine occupations.

Definitions and Processes

Gender differentiation becomes **prejudice** when our reactions to men and women begin to hinder their ability to freely chose their actions. Because of prejudice, people of some groups have different kinds of social, professional, and educational options available to them, compared to people of other groups.

Legal prejudice.   Some of the prejudicial laws in the United States, past and present, were intended to protect certain target groups rather than limit their opportunities (Chamallas, 1984; Powers, 1979). Women in the military have been prohibited from carrying out any combat role, though this seems to be changing. In the past, jobs requiring heavy lifting were restricted to men to supposedly protect the physically weaker woman from damage. Occupations can still be restricted to one gender or another on a certain basis, such as privacy. For example, if strip searching is required, hiring can legally

be limited to same-sex employees. Only male employees may be required to keep their hair short. On the other hand, customer preferences for one sex or the other, such as the airlines' claim that flight passengers preferred female to male flight attendants, would not be a legal basis for gender discrimination.

Cognitive factors in prejudice.   In some cases, prejudicial discrimination can occur even when a person harbors no bad feelings toward the target person's group. Belief can produce prejudice because of discrepancies between what the discriminating person believes about the traits of the target person being judged, compared to the traits believed to be appropriate for a job. A female might be judged less likely to be competent in a given job if the job required some masculine characteristics that females were believed less likely to possess. Both sexes do have stereotypes not only about men and women but also about job requirements (Mellon, Crano, & Schmitt, 1982).

Stereotypes can create prejudice because they affect memory (Deaux & Major, 1987). An interviewer may remember only the stereotypic traits of an applicant, for example, and so reach a prejudicial job decision. Or jurors may have their recall of trial material affected by their gender stereotypes and so come to a prejudicial decision of guilt versus innocence. Potentially disconfirming behaviors of a member of a stereotyped group may be forgotten or "explained away."

Affective component of attitudes and prejudice. The cognitive and affective components of attitudes can operate somewhat independently of each other (Taylor & Falcone, 1982). Frable (1989) found that sex-typed people are more likely to be sexually prejudiced, perhaps because of their affective reactions to nonconforming people. In her first study, subjects were asked to judge the appropriateness of gendered rules for behavior.[6] Sex-typed subjects disliked gender rule violators more. In particular, instrumental men disliked male rule violators. In her second study, subjects evaluated videotaped job interviews of males and females. Sex-typed subjects rated the women applicants lower than they rated the male applicants and were more likely to spontaneously mention gender when they were asked to recall the applicant's characteristics. Despite this, all subjects, including the prejudiced sex-typed subjects, insisted that sex should be irrelevant to employment decisions.

Factors affecting the extent to which subjects will act on their prejudicial tendencies. As Frable (1989) found, whether subjects will display their prejudice often depends on how it is measured. Since sexual prejudice is currently seen as socially undesirable, subjects may claim that prejudice should not occur and might even deliberately favor women (Branscombe & Smith, 1990). Those same subjects may act prejudiced when their behaviors are measured in more subtle ways. Deaux and Major (1987)

presented an extensive model of how stereotypes may be related to behaviors. The degree to which stereotypes are enacted (and so lead to prejudice) depends on several factors, three sets of which are discussed below.

1. *The expectations of the perceiver will affect the way the target acts.* If the perceiver has stereotypic expectations that affect the target's behaviors, the target may enact the expectancy and so lead to prejudice. As an example, if an interviewer expects women to be less competent in a masculine-typed job, and some female applicant acts less competent because of the interviewer's expectancy, the job possibilities of women will be restricted. This process might be intensified if the perceiver has a very differentiated stereotype.

2. *The self-systems of the target will affect how the target reacts to the situation.* Because of the internalized gender stereotypes, women may have more doubts about their abilities in masculine areas, such as those requiring math, strength, or assertiveness. In these areas, women might tend to conform more to interviewers' stereotypes than men would, and they also might interpret ambiguous interviewer behaviors in a more negative fashion then men would because of these self-doubts (Christensen & Rosenthal, 1982). Furthermore, targets who are more concerned with presenting themselves in a favorable light than with verifying their own views of themselves would be more likely to conform to a perceiver's expectations. For example, in situations in which women are more concerned with being liked than with being perceived as competent, women might conform more to the gender stereotypes. In situations where men are more concerned with being liked than with being perceived as being involved with their children, men might conform more to stereotypes.

The target's self-concept might also change as a result of what the target does in the stereotyping situation. For instance, presenting yourself in a negative way can decrease your self-esteem. Subjects who are already mildly depressed are particularly likely to experience a decrease in self-esteem if they present themselves in a negative way in an interview situation (Rhodewalt & Agustsdottir, 1986). Because of this effect of depression, and since women are more likely to be depressed (see Chapter 13), women might be particularly vulnerable to the long-term effects of conforming to negative gender stereotypes.

Hogg and Turner (1987) used an experimental situation in which two males debated with two females on an issue that all subjects were told the sexes had very different opinions. Afterwards, both sexes perceived themselves in more gender-stereotypic ways, but this led to an increase in self-esteem for males and a decrease in self-esteem for females.

3. *Situational cues affect the likelihood of stereotypes being enacted in behavior.* Relevant situational cues include the social desirability of the expected behavior, the degree to which the behavior might be subjected to future public scrutiny, dating versus job situations, and the ratio of women to men in the situation. Applying for a "wrong-gender" job, or a job in which most applicants are of the other sex, would make gender-linked traits more salient to both interviewer and applicant (Heilman, 1980).

Paulhus (1984) described two ways in which people change their initial tendencies toward behaviors that the current situation indicates would be more socially desirable. One was **self-deception,** where the person actually believes her socially desirable responses and thus is lying to herself. The second is **impression management,** where the person consciously dissembles, being aware at the time that she is lying to make a good impression. If people lied to themselves about being prejudiced, they would be careful to act in nonprejudicial ways so as to confirm their own impression of themselves. If people tended to lie to others about being prejudiced so as to appear in a more favorable light, then, at least in public situations, those people would also be careful to act in nonprejudicial ways.

Only methods that can measure prejudice in ways that could not be consciously dissembled might be able to detect its presence, especially in people with strong impression management and self-deception tendencies. For example, Devine (1989) divided his white subjects into high- and low-prejudice groups based on their scores on a racism scale. In a high-awareness condition, low-prejudiced subjects did express less prejudiced thoughts and values. In a low-awareness condition, both high- and low-prejudice subjects showed equal evidence of prejudice. Thus, the affective components of the racial stereotypes were equally present in both high- and low-prejudice groups, and were equally expressed in behaviors in the low-awareness condition, but only low-prejudiced men were shown to be consciously trying to inhibit these tendencies in the high-awareness condition. The same could be true of prejudice against women.

Changes Over Time?

Perhaps not the prejudice itself, but only the ways of expressing it have changed. Since sexual prejudice is now less socially desirable, maybe it is expressed more covertly. Three very influential sets of early studies found evidence of sexual prejudice that later research did not replicate.

Influential early research. Some influential early research was done by Goldberg and his colleagues. First, female subjects rated papers written in either feminine or masculine fields (Goldberg, 1968). Each subject rated six articles, three supposedly written by a man and three by a woman. The total evaluation scores were significantly biased in favor of men only for the three masculine fields. However, Goldberg also compared male versus female authors' ratings for each of the sex articles on each of nine scales. Of the 54 possible comparisons, 7 favored the females and 44 favored the males. Then, Pheterson, Kiesler, and Goldberg (1971) asked college women to rate paintings, supposedly done by either males or females, that were either "prize-winning" or "contest entries." Only the "contest entry" paintings done by women were devalued. Finally, Abramson, Goldberg, Greenberg, and Abramson (1977) had subjects of both sexes rate a male or a female stimulus person who was also either an attorney or a paralegal worker. Female attorneys were rated as more competent than male attorneys, particularly by the male subjects. The authors described their results as the **talking platypus phenomenon:** Unanticipated success (a female attorney) is magnified because "it matters little what the platypus says, the wonder is that it can say anything at all" (p. 114).

In the type of early and second influential study, clinical psychologists, psychiatrists, and social workers were given a list of stereotypic adjectives (Broverman et al., 1970). Separate groups of both sexes were asked which adjectives would characterize: "normal, adult men," "normal, adult women," or "normal adults." The researchers concluded, "Clinicians are significantly less likely to attribute traits which characterize healthy adults to a woman than they are likely to attribute these traits to a healthy man" (p. 5). If females are to be healthy women, they must be unhealthy adults.

Third, Seavey, Katz, and Zalk (1975) showed how a sex label affected the way adults treated an infant. A three-month-old female infant was presented to three different groups as either being a male, a female, or just a baby with no mention of a sex or name. Subjects were observed to see how they reacted to the infant and which (if any) toy they used (a doll, a toy football, or a teething ring). All subjects used the doll most frequently when the infant was labeled as a female, especially the males. The authors concluded that stereotypic expectations may be more important than sex differences in infant behaviors in determining how adults interact with and so socialize infants.

Recent replications and reviews.   A recent meta-analytic review of research done using the Goldberg type of rating paradigm (Swim et al., 1989) found that "the average difference between ratings of men and women is negligible" (p. 409). The prejudice was marginally greater when: (1) performances in masculine jobs were being rated; (2) when sex-neutral (versus masculine or feminine) material was being rated by subjects; (3) when less information was provided to the subjects about the people being rated; and (4) when what was being rated was a job application or a résumé, as opposed to written work, behavior, or a biography.

Widiger and Settle (1987) extended Broverman and colleagues' (1970) research. In the original study, 71 percent of the socially desirable adjectives used in rating the stimulus

people were masculine. The replication systematically varied the adjective sex ratio (number of desirable masculine adjectives divided by the number of desirable feminine adjectives). Each list was presented to three separate groups of introductory psychology undergraduate students, each group being asked to rate a healthy male, a healthy female, or a healthy adult. Subjects exhibited a bias against men, a bias against women, or no bias, depending on how many desirable male and female traits were on the list they were given to use.

Stern and Karraker (1989) reviewed 23 studies of the gender-labeling effect. They concluded that "knowledge of an infant's gender is not a consistent determinant of adults' reactions, but more strongly influences young children's reactions" (p. 501). The effect observed in any one study (such as the greater use of dolls for females described above) was not replicated across studies, and even within a study, not all the predicted effects were seen.

You might conclude from the evidence just described that gender prejudice has faded. Women's works are no longer devalued (or overrated) simply because they are women, people no longer see healthy women as being unhealthy adults, and adults treat babies in an egalitarian fashion. Before you accept that conclusion, consider some methodological factors.

Methodological considerations.   One important factor is whether the research was done in a psychological laboratory simulation or in some real-life situation that would have greater external validity (Top, 1991). For example, in one study, undergraduate students were given descriptions of high- and low-performing male and female college professors to evaluate (Dobbins, Cardy, & Truxillo, 1986). The descriptions came from actual classroom performances of instructors who had been separately rated as being either effective or ineffective teachers. Subjects exhibited no gender bias when they were told that their ratings would simply be used to validate the ratings scale itself. When the subjects were told their ratings would be used in pay and promotion decisions, male professors were rated higher than their actual level of performance would warrant, and female professors were rated lower.

The workplace may be especially prone to gender stereotyping. Even in the meta-analytic review described above, job applications and résumés showed more bias than did other types of ratings. When other reviewers separately analyzed the literature on hiring prejudice (Nieva & Gutek, 1980; Kalin & Hodgins, 1984; Dipboye, 1985; Lott, 1985; Olian, Schwab, & Haberfeld, 1988; Powell, 1987), all concluded that most (but not all) research demonstrated a pro-male bias. All four reviews included proportionately more studies actually carried out in the workplace than did the meta-analytic review described earlier, including some actual ratings of real employees made by real supervisors or subordinates. Perhaps laboratory research is more affected by social desirability biases than is research in the workplace or other real-life settings.

Rating scales may show less bias than do rankings or having to chose just one applicant to hire. For example, if subjects are asked to rate both male and female applicants, little prejudice is displayed, but when only one applicant can be hired, sex is often a major factor (Dipboye, 1985; Pazy, 1986). Similarly, when Katz and Madden (1984) had female subjects rank-order male and female congressional candidates, 37 percent of the raters were found to have prejudicial attitudes toward other females.

Some Examples of the Effects of Prejudice

How might sexual prejudice be affecting us?

Preference for males.   Overall, people prefer to have boys (Norman, 1974; Gray, 1982; Gray, Bortolozzi, & Hurt, 1979; Williamson, 1976). If a family is to have only a single child, most want a boy. Although people prefer sexual balance in their families if they are to have two or four children, if three children are desired, families prefer two boys and one girl.

The desire for maleness also affects females themselves. In one sample of grade-school students, 4 males said that they would rather be a female, but 31 females said that they would rather be a male (Nash, 1975). Among high school students, only females expressed a wish to be reborn as the opposite sex, though this particular tendency may be decreasing over time (Lewin & Tragos, 1987; Solomon et al., 1985). Female college students say they wish to be reborn as a male to have fewer moral restrictions and responsibilities. These women score higher on a neuroticism scale than do the women who wished to remain female. In similar research, more adolescent males say that it is "great" to be a member of their own sex. This particular sex difference increases with age and has been increasing over time as well (Bush et al., 1978; Simmons & Rosenberg, 1975).

Prejudice in operation.   Several other examples of prejudice are presented in Table 11.2. Real-world examples are emphasized, except in the area of person perception where the differential importance of physical appearance to the sexes is described. The woman is not always the victim. When an incompetent male attempts to buy a used car, or when a man acts feminine, a male may suffer more. Females in male-typed occupations may be evaluated as equal to, or even higher than men, but only if they act masculine. In some cases, there is a same-sex bias. Other evidence of prejudice will be reviewed in Chapter 12 and in Unit Four.

Gender as a diffuse status characteristic. Sociologists and some social psychologists point out that because of the sex stereotypes, gender acts like a diffuse status characteristic, with men having higher status than women. An attribute is a **diffuse status characteristic** if it meets all three criteria listed on page 286 (Berger, Rosenholtz, & Zelditch, 1980; Berger, Wagner, & Zelditch, 1985):

TABLE 11.2 *Some Examples of How Gender Stereotypes Can Have Prejudicial Effects on Both Women and Men*

Area of Effect	Description of Effects	References
Legal system	Gender affects: which factors are weighted in probation decisions; placement of juveniles into juvenile justice versus mental-health settings; perception of traits possessed by social, legal, and sexual deviates; and judgments made by juries.	Erez, 1989; King & Clayson, 1988; Westendorp, Brink, Roberson, & Ortiz, 1986
	Family members receive substantially higher monetary damages in wrongful death suits when a male is killed, primarily because the income loss is expected to be greater after the death of a male, compared to after the death of a female.	Goodman et al., 1991
High school athletic coaches	Both male and female basketball players strongly prefer male coaches to female coaches.	Parkhouse & Williams, 1986
Poverty after age 65	More females than males have incomes below the poverty level, partially because of some of the rules of the Social Security system.	Warlick, 1985; Wolff, 1988
Family planning for careers of their adolescents	In a simulation, family decisions favored the career goals of adolescent males over females by 4 to 1.	Peterson et al., 1982
Medical treatments	White males (compared to African-American males and to females) are more likely to receive dialysis and kidney transplants when needed; males are more likely to be considered for cardiac catherization and bypass surgery than females with equivalent heart damage; physician workups are more extensive for their male patients than for their female patients; after heart surgery, men are more likely to get pain medication and women to get sedatives.	Armitage, Schneiderman, & Bass, 1979; Khan et al., 1990; Kjellstrand, 1988; Kjellstrand & Logan, 1987; Steingart et al., 1991; Tobin et al., 1987
Person perception	Females are perceived as crying more frequently and crying is perceived as being culturally less acceptable for males than for females.	Lombardo et al., 1983
	The "success" of a woman affects the perceived masculinity of her "significant other":	Gerber, 1977, 1984

(continued)

TABLE 11.2 *continued*

Area of Effect	Description of Effects	References
Person perception *(continued)*	1. Male raters see husbands and boy-friends of successful women as less masculine than husbands of unsuccessful wives. 2. Female raters see husbands of successful women as more masculine; their ratings of women's boyfriends are not affected by the women's success.	
	Men are more likely to be perceived as competent and are less likely to be perceived as unattractive than are women; physical attractiveness is more important to the perception of women than to men (though attractive women may also be perceived as less competent for masculine jobs than unattractive women); women are more likely to be labeled as unattractive to others, especially by family members, and more likely than men to respond to that label with hurt, embarrassment, anger, resentment, and sadness; a male stimulus person described as a corporate assistant vice president is seen as more competent if he is also attractive, but a female stimulus person is seen as being less competent if she is attractive.	Heilman & Stopeck, 1985; Spreadbury & Reeves, 1983; Wallston & O'Leary, 1981
	Females in a male sex-typed occupation are evaluated more highly than a comparable male *only* if they acted in a masculine manner; highly performing feminine women are evaluated lower than similarly performing masculine men; among low performers, again masculine females are evaluated more highly than masculine men or feminine females; feminine males are always devalued.	Moore, 1984
Used car buying	Male and female callers, simulating competence (knowledgeability about cars) or incompetence, requested prices for a 1974 Monte Carlo or Grand Prix. Average prices quoted were:	Larrance et al., 1979

	Competent	Incompetent
Male	2,509	3.237
Female	2,648	2,702

TABLE 11.2 *continued*

Area of Effect	Description of Effects	References
Check cashing	Amount of time it takes to cash a check as a function of the gender of teller and customer: Teller/Customer Male Female Male 50.0 79.6 Female 27.2 51.4	Larwood, Zalkind, & Legault, 1975
Book reviews	In book reviews published in *Contemporary Psychology* (1974–1977), reviewers said more positive things about same-sex than about opposite-sex authors. Both male and female reviewers made somewhat more negative comments about books written by males compared to those written by females.	Moore, 1978
	In reviews of articles submitted for publication to scholarly journals, male reviewers showed no bias but female reviewers showed a pro-female bias.	Lloyd, 1990
Newspaper photographs	Of 8,960 pictures of men and women in four Connecticut newspapers, photos of men outnumber those of women; men are most often depicted in sports and professional roles and women in the role of spouse.	Luebke, 1989
Department stores	As customers in a department store, women were served first 32% of the time and men 61% of the time. This gender bias occurred whether the clerk was male or female and whether a "male" or "female" department was involved.	Stead & Zinkham, 1986
Evaluations by supervisors	Supervisors with a conservative attitude toward women's roles evaluated their female employees as being less able than the males, and those supervisors were "reluctant to assign technical, vital high profile projects to female subordinates" (p. 15).	Simpson, McCarrey, & Edwards, 1987
Getting a job	People applying for jobs as a social psychologist at a university: letters of recommendation mentioned the marital and parental status of women more often then of men candidates; even when equated for experience, men got jobs at more prestigious universities.	Bronstein et al., 1986
Leadership evaluations	In a meta-analytic review, female leaders were found to be less favorably evaluated than were male leaders, particularly when the behaviors or the jobs were masculine or when the raters were males.	Eagly, Makhijani, & Klonsky, 1992

1. It has two or more states that are differentially valued (e.g., male versus female).
2. A set of specific expectations is associated with each state, such as the ability to perform mathematical or mechanical tasks (males better), and the ability to perform would be valued more than the inability to perform the task.
3. A set of general expectations regarding valued capacities such as intelligence, capacities not limited to specific tasks, is also associated with each state. Men would be assumed to have more "intelligence," and having intelligence would be valued.

Thus, if gender is a diffuse status characteristic in our culture, that would be another way of indicating the status of women relative to that of men, as described in Chapter 10.

Sex does often seem to function as a diffuse status characteristic (Eagly & Wood, 1982; Howard & Leber, 1988; Pugh & Wahrman, 1983, 1985; Wagner, Ford, & Ford, 1986; Wood & Karten, 1986). When people who are strangers to each other are given some task to perform, both sexes assume that men are the more competent, and men more often work directly on the task while women do more socializing. This assumption of male superiority is not changed even when the group is told ahead of time that females' abilities are equal to those of the males. If the group is told that the females have superior ability, the group members no longer assume men to be superior, and women also engage in more task-related behaviors. But even here, despite what the subjects were told, women are still not assumed to be superior. Also, telling a man he is not very capable of performing a task does not make him feel as incompetent as it does a woman. Conversely, telling a woman she is capable tends not to raise her expectations as much it would raise the expectations of a man.

THE DEVELOPMENT OF STEREOTYPES

This last section looks at how stereotypes are acquired and how the nature of the stereotyping processes may change with age.

Processes of Acquisition

Del Boca, Ashmore, and McManus (1986) identified three types of theories of how gender-related attitudes are acquired:

1. In the **intrapersonal** theories, explanations of how stereotypic beliefs are acquired are related to the individual's own personality, cognition, or motivation. People interested in intrapersonal acquisition processes are taking an individual differences approach: What kinds of people are most likely to learn gender stereotypes? Intrapersonal factors in stereotypes were covered in the discussion about the characteristics of gender-differentiating people.

2. **Intergroup** theories describe how beliefs are acquired through culturally-structured interactions among various social groups, as when men come in conflict with women for jobs, or when traditional cultural values affect political systems about what women should and should not do. Some intergroup theories were described in the section on prejudice, where conflict over jobs was seen to increase sexual prejudice. The Chapter 10 theories describing why women have inferior social status are also of this type.

3. In the **interpersonal** theories, individuals acquire stereotypes during interactions with other people, such as parents, and during interactions with cultural institutions, such as schools and mass media. In the rest of this discussion, an interpersonal approach will be used since most of the developmental research focusing on children's acquisition of sex stereotypes uses it.

Interactions with people of the opposite gender. People could acquire gender-stereotypic beliefs by interacting with people of both genders and then forming cognitive categories of sex-related traits based on those personal experiences. Children's development of same-sex preferences seems to be based on each gender's experiences with each other (Maccoby, 1988, 1990), and this could also lead to gender stereotypes. During social interactions as early as 3 years of age, children discover that their interaction styles are less compatible with those of the opposite sex. Boys concentrate on maintaining status in the male hierarchy, and girls concentrate on maintaining social relationships. Girls' stereotypes of boys can become even more negative when forced to interact with boys (Lockheed & Harris, 1984).

If at least some aspects of gender stereotypes are acquired through personal experiences, they should reflect some "real" sex differences: the **kernel of truth** idea of stereotypes. Gender stereotypes should therefore reflect the associative connections that people form between the categories *male* and *female* and various traits, behaviors, occupations, and characteristics, based on the number of women and men they have observed displaying each of those characteristics. Martin (1987) had one group of people estimate the sex ratio of people possessing the BSRI traits, and she also had other subjects drawn from the same population rate themselves on the same BSRI items. The ratio measure of stereotyping exaggerates the sex difference in self-ratings. Overall, the real sex differences in self-endorsement of masculine traits were more accurately reflected in the stereotype than were the sex differences in feminine or neutral traits. As Martin noted, the bias could have come either from the stereotype itself or from biases that affect the degree to which men and women will accurately report which traits they actually have.

For four reasons, associative connections are not expected to be an entirely accurate image of past experiences. First, since the actions of men and women are in reality quite variable and complex, the information about them must be retained in some simplified form. Hoffman and Hurst (1990) have argued that sex differences are too small and variable to be able to be reliably noticed by naive observers or learners. This might be true, but none of us is naive—we've all been exposed to stereotypes that would structure how we gather sex-related information. Second, just categorizing people into two or more groups, even on a minimal basis such as whether they like some work of art, can lead to systematic biases in the perceptions of **ingroup** (members of your own group) versus **outgroup** members (Hamilton, 1979). People often assume that people in the outgroup will have opinions on various issues that are different from those expressed by people in the ingroup.

Third, Hoffman and Hurst (1990) demonstrated that subjects would create a stereotype simply by being exposed to two different groups of "alien beings" who were distributed differently into various occupations. Since the sexes also have different occupations, that fact affects how our stereotypes form. We assume that the people we find in a certain occupation have the traits that would make them good at that occupation.

Fourth, one bias operates at the first stages of stereotype formation: **illusory correlation** or **shared infrequency** (McArthur & Friedman, 1980; Martin, 1990). This bias can affect information gathered either from interactions with other people or from the mass media. Suppose that some one is attempting to form an impression of people in some other group. Further suppose that members of some group are in a minority and that undesirable behaviors are rarely displayed by anyone from any group. People will erroneously conclude that members of the minority groups more frequently displayed the undesirable behaviors than did members of the majority group. Since children frequently play in same-sex groups (see Chapter 10), members of the opposite sex have a minority status and so will be subject to the illusory correlation process.

When trait associations are learned before trait-relevant behaviors are observed. Stereotypes can also be acquired through direct learning of belief systems, or associations of traits with gender groups. Children can learn gender stereotypes by hearing and then modeling the beliefs their parents verbalize about men and women "in general." Children will also read about and see on television other people expressing certain gender beliefs. Stereotypes acquired this way may have properties different from those of the stereotypes acquired through direct experiences with men's and women's behaviors, as will now be described.

People use different strategies when instructed to form an impression of an individual, compared to an impression of a group of individuals. The differences in strategies illustrate the conditions under which trait belief systems rather than specific memories may come to dominate the individual's belief system (Wyer, Bodenhausen, & Srull, 1984; Wyer & Gordon, 1982). For example, when subjects attempted to form an impression of people who all belonged to a given group, the subjects focused on the traits that were presented as being "typical" more than on actual behaviors. The reverse was true when subjects attempted to form an impression of a given individual.

Furthermore, if a person is attempting to form an impression of some group, the resulting stereotypes depend on whether that person learns first about traits or about actual behaviors (Park & Hastie, 1987). College students were told to form an impression of a group based on a list of behaviors, each of which was performed by a different member of the group (e.g., "wrote a difficult computer program" or "volunteered to introduce the new worker to others"). The subjects were also given trait information in the form of a paragraph supposedly written by some knowledgeable person who described members of the group as collectively being, for example, *intelligent* and *sociable.* Half the subjects were given trait information before they saw the list of behaviors, and half after they saw the list. Subjects described the group as being more homogeneous and less variable if they learned about the group's traits before they learned about the members' behaviors.

This has some important implications. If belief systems are acquired largely before actual behaviors are observed, this could lead to more homogeneous impressions of outgroup members. Since children of many cultures often have more same-sex interactions during childhood, even during the play at schools, trait stereotypes could be acquired before those children have extensive experiences with the behaviors of actual cross-sex others. This would lead to relatively homogenous gender-belief systems. Furthermore, if trait associations exist prior to actual cross-sex interactions, the belief systems could bias the social interactions and thus confirm and even exaggerate the beliefs (Lockheed & Harris, 1984).

Stereotypes in Mass Media

If children acquire stereotypes at least partially from mass media, just what is it that they are learning?

Books and magazines. Children have been exposed to gender stereotypes in their school readers (Graebner, 1972; Jacklin & Mischel, 1973).[7] Men and boys dominated both the illustrations and the texts. Boys were shown as active and independent, girls as passive and dependent. Men were shown in over twice as many different occupations as were women. Men were also more often seen outdoors; women were either at home or in school (teaching).

Children's books also present gender stereotypes. One early influential study done by Weitzman, Eifler, Hokada, and Ross (1972) analyzed prize-winning picture books. Women and girls were simply invisible; even most of the animals were males. Boys were leaders who rescued girls, whereas girls served others. Boys and men performed heroic acts and were then rewarded by being given the girl. In one pair of Hallmark books, *What Boys Can Be* and *What Girls Can Be,* boys were told they could be firemen, cowboys, doctors, pilots, astronauts, and even tigers and Presidents of the United States. Girls were told they could be nurses, models, stars, secretaries, singers, brides, housewives, and — ultimately — mothers.

Followup studies have documented changes

but have also pointed out further room for improvements (Collins, Ingoldsby, & Dellman, 1984; Kolbe & LaVoie, 1981; Moore & Mae, 1987; Tetenbaum & Pearson, 1989). In current books explicitly identified by various groups as being nonsexist, the stereotype is sometimes even reversed, with females being more active and independent than males (Davis, 1984). But even in these books, females are still more nurturant, emotional, and less physically active than males, leading to the conclusion that most "studies do not indicate significant declines in sex-role stereotyping in the post-1960 years" (p. 14). When 62 children's readers in use during 1989 were analyzed, stereotyping was found to be less than in 1972, but boys still seldom did anything domestic, and girls were still weak (Purcell & Stewart, 1990):

> *Even though girls are now shown in active roles, they are still shown as needing rescue in many more instances than are boys. Girls are shown as being very brave while waiting for rescue, but they still cannot help themselves out of trouble. (p. 184)*

The boxes that children's toys come in and the pictures in toy catalogues are also stereotyped (Schwartz & Markham, 1985). Boys are pictured using weapon toys (e.g., toy guns), scientific equipment, models, natural science kits and sets, building sets, and workbenches and tools. Feminine toys include housekeeping and cooking toys and toy beauty sets. Action figure dolls (e.g., G.I. Joe) and mechanical or electrical dolls are pictured with boys, whereas fashion dolls, stuffed dolls, and baby dolls are pictured with girls. Feminine costumes include wedding dresses, cheerleader outfits, nurses' uniforms, and ballerina costumes. Boys are pictured wearing uniforms for soldiers, policemen, astronauts, and doctors. Even when girls do appear in "boy" toy pictures, it is often in a feminine role (a girl just watching two boys play with a road racing set, and a boy pictured with a kitchen set but being served by a girl).

Material read by adults demonstrates how pervasively gender stereotypes permeate our culture. Males outnumbered females in college-level textbooks (Bertilson, Fierke, & Springer, 1981). When magazine advertisements used in 1958 were compared to those used 1983, women were more often portrayed as being employed than they used to be, especially in professional, sales, and midlevel business occupations (Sullivan & O'Connor, 1988). But women were also more likely to be portrayed in a "purely decorative role." Advertisements of pharmaceutical drugs were sampled from 1979 and 1989 issues of the same medical journal. All the physicians pictured in both years were male; patients were also most likely to be male (Bailey, Harrell, & Anderson, 1991; Tietze & Smith, 1990). In U.S. periodicals, in publications from 11 cultures, and in works of art spanning six centuries, men's faces are more prominently displayed than are women's faces, and faces displayed more prominently are rated as being more intelligent, ambitious, and attractive (Archer et al., 1983).

Television. Durkin (1985a, 1985b, 1985c) reviewed the literature on television's sex stereotyping, including children's shows. Some studies found that 70 to 85 percent of the characters were male. Males were more often shown as aggressive, constructive, and seeking aid, whereas females were deferent. There has been considerable inconsistency across studies, perhaps because of changes made in response to public pressures. One interesting study looked at two years of televised toy commercials (Feldstein & Feldstein, 1982). More boys than girls were shown, and girls also tended to act more passively in the commercials. Boys most often appeared in commercials for vehicles, male dolls, and manipulative toys, but boys never appeared in commercials for dolls and accessories or household objects (such as toy irons). Therefore, when the number of doll commercials declined from one year to the next, the number of girls pictured also declined.

Durkin (1985a, 1985b, 1985c) also surveyed

adult programming, finding considerable agreement about the gender stereotypes. Males are more often presented as employed and as having higher-status occupations. Women are usually portrayed as mothers, wives, secretaries, and nurses. Female characters who do hold jobs are less likely to be married than male jobholders, and the marriages of female jobholders are more likely to end in divorce or desertion. Males dominate females; females display more emotions. Males perform more violent acts, and females are more often the victims of violence. More recently, Davis (1990) found there were more males than females in prime-time programs, and fewer of the women were over age 35, especially in action-adventure shows.

A couple of studies had a special focus. McLaughlin (1975) analyzed 15 prime-time doctor shows. Patients were more often female than male, reversing the medical journal drug advertising bias, and female patients were twice as likely to be bedridden as were male patients. When treated, 70 percent of the male patients recovered but 77 percent of the female patients died. Mackey and Hess (1982) randomly selected 10-minute intervals of television shows. Not only did males outnumber females and show more instrumental behaviors but men were frequently found in the presence of other men, yet women were rarely found in the company of other women.

An even more stereotypic view of the sexes appears in television commercials (Bretl & Cantor, 1988; Durkin, 1985a, 1985b, 1985c; Hoyenga & Hoyenga, 1979; see Hoyenga & Hoyenga, 1993). Women more often appeared in domestic roles, serving or cleaning up after men. As in the magazine commercials, women in television commercials were often merely decorative. Men were less likely to be shown using a product and were more likely to appear in alcohol, vehicle, and business advertisements, and more likely to be seen outdoors. The most dramatic difference occurred in the voice-overs: between 84 and 94 percent of the "domi-

nant experts" were men. Similar stereotypes appear in radio advertisements (Furnham & Schofield, 1986; Lont, 1990).

Children's Stereotypes

This section documents and describes how children learn stereotypes. A child's knowledge and application of gender stereotypes often reflect that child's own cognitive development (see Chapter 9; also see Hoyenga & Hoyenga, 1993).

Developmental changes. Developmental changes in stereotypes are often assessed by labeling and sorting tasks. In labeling tasks, children are given verbal descriptions, pictures, or drawings and are asked to indicate the gender of each person, trait, activity, or occupation. In sorting tasks, children are asked to sort a set of cards depicting people or objects into two or more categories. Their ability to sort on the basis of some criterion, such as gender or color, is recorded. Children may also be asked to label or sort a picture of themselves as well.

Children have several systems of gender knowledge, many of which are acquired independently of each other. For example, although the children who tend to use gender as a way of categorizing people and objects depicted on cards also tend to display more gender-related knowledge of tasks and occupations, these tendencies were *not* related to sex-typed preferences or sex-biased memories (Hoyt, Leinbach, & Fagot, 1991). Questionnaire measures of sex typing are often poorly correlated with behavioral observation measures (Katz & Walsh, 1991). The speed with which a child indicates his preference for a sex-typed toy over an opposite-sex-typed toy (a measure of gender schema in children) is correlated with his correct attributions of stereotypic traits to male or female stimulus figures, but gender constancy was not related (Levy & Carter, 1989). Similarly, Fagot (1985b, 1985c) found that whether children 20 to 30 months of age acted masculine or feminine was unrelated to their gender constancy.

As suggested by Constantinople (1979), children's knowledge about gender stereotypes might not be immediately applied to their own self-concepts. Perhaps, as Kohlberg suggested (see Chapter 9), only after gender constancy do children attempt to systematically incorporate their knowledge about stereotypes to their beliefs about themselves. This gender constancy may be acquired earlier than we thought. Leonard and Archer (1989) found that children aged 3 to 4 knew that gender remained stable over time. Those children said that wearing "girl's clothing" might make a boy into a girl, but they also said that this change would be "just pretend."

Two types of knowledge—the contents of gender stereotypes and gender flexibility—have different developmental timetables (Leahy & Shirk, 1984; Ruble & Stangor, 1986). As children go from 3 to 7 years of age, gaining increasing knowledge about the sex typing of occupations and activities, they become less likely to spontaneously sort pictures of people into gender categories and more likely to categorize people based on their behaviors. Children's **gender flexibility,** or the ability to be tolerant of role deviations, increases at the same time that their tendency to use gender for categorization decreases. Thus, as gender knowledge increases, the salience of gender decreases, probably because children become more aware of the variability in people's behaviors. In fact, gender flexibility reflects an increasing cognitive sophistication about stereotypes rather a general tendency to ignore or disregard social rules or natural laws such as gravity (Carter & Patterson, 1982).

Paralleling the increase in gender flexibility, the importance of gender to children may reach a peak at age 6 or 7 and then decline, even though children's knowledge of gender stereotypes continues to increase (Ruble & Stangor, 1986). As gender knowledge increases, the

effects of memory biases also increase. On the other hand, children's tendency to distort material they have heard or read should reflect how important gender is to them and should therefore peak at age 6 or 7. For example, when children aged 5 to 6 viewed a film of a male nurse and a female doctor, over 50 percent of the children claimed they had seen a male doctor and a female nurse (Cordua, McGraw, & Drabman, 1979).

Effects of mass media on children's stereotypes.   The contents of children's gender stereotypes appear in Table 11.3. They seem to parallel almost perfectly the stereotypes of the mass media, particularly television. Despite its theoretical importance, very little research has actually documented the degree to which children exposed to mass media incorporate its stereotypes into their own belief systems (Durkin, 1985b). Only very modest associations between amount of television viewed and degree of stereotyping in children have been demonstrated—and even those associations frequently could not be replicated.

Nevertheless, television viewing can affect both behavior and belief (Murray & Kippax, 1979; Rushton, 1979). One of the more convincing examples of television's effects comes from a research project that took 22 years to complete (Eron, 1987):

> *One of the best predictors of how aggressive a young man would be at age 19 was the violence of the television programs he preferred when he was 8 years old. . . . The more frequently youngsters watched TV at age 8, the more serious were the crimes for which they were convicted by age 30. (pp. 438, 440)*

This was true of both males and females, although males engaged in more aggressive crimes than females did. Further analysis showed that the direction of the effects went in both ways: more aggressive children preferred more aggressive TV shows, and watching

TABLE 11.3   *Some Examples of Gender Stereotypes Endorsed by Children*

Female Stereotypes:

2- and 3-year-old children believe that girls (and not boys):
- Like to play with dolls, like to help mother
- Like to cook dinner, like to clean house
- Talk a lot, never hit, and say "I need some help"

Children 5 years and older believe that girls, more than boys, are:
- Weak, emotional, appreciative, excitable, high-strung, gentle, soft-hearted, sentimental, sophisticated, affected, talkative, rattlebrained, fickle, meek, mild, submissive, dependent, whiny, complaining, frivolous, affectionate, fussy, nagging, flirtatious, charming
- More often happy, sad, and frightened than boys

2- and 3-year-old boys (but not girls) believe that girls:
- Cry sometimes, are slow
- Say "You hurt my feelings" and "You're not letting me have a turn"

2- and 3-year-old girls (but not boys) believe that girls:
- Like to sew, like to play inside, look nice
- Give kisses, never fight
- Say "I can do it best"

2- and 3-year-old children believe that when girls grow up they (and not boys) will:
- Clean the house, be a nurse, be a teacher

2- and 3-year-old girls (but not boys) believe that when girls grow up they (and not boys) will:
- Take care of babies

2- and 3-year-old boys (but not girls) believe that when girls grow up they (and not boys) will:
- Cook the dinner

Male Stereotypes:

2- and 3-year-old children believe that boys (and not girls):
- Like to play with cars, like to help father
- Like to build things
- Say "I can hit you"

Children 5 years and older believe that boys, more than girls, are:
- Strong, robust, aggressive, assertive, disorderly, cruel, coarse, adventurous, daring, independent, ambitious, enterprising, loud, dominant, autocratic, confident, self-confident, steady, stable, jolly, boastful, severe, stern, logical, rational
- More often angry than girls

2- and 3-year-old boys (but not girls) believe that boys:
- Like to play with trains, like to work, work hard
- Are loud, are naughty, can make you cry

2- and 3-year-old girls (but not boys) believe that boys:
- Like to climb a tree, like to fight, fight
- Never cry, are mean, are weak, say "I did it wrong"

2- and 3-year-old children believe that when boys grow up they (and not girls) will:
- Be boss, mow the grass

2- and 3-year-old boys (but not girls) believe that when boys grow up they (and not girls) will:
- Be governor, be a doctor, fly an airplane

aggressive TV also increased their aggressive behaviors.

Because television viewing in children can affect their adult behaviors, the relative weakness of the effect on gender stereotypes needs to be examined more closely. Certainly children can readily apply their knowledge of gender stereotypes to what they see on television. Durkin (1984) found out, for example, that children "knew" that Superwoman could never be as strong as Superman and they "knew" that while knights wearing armor went off to war, ladies stayed home and washed things.

One serious problem with research on gender stereotypes is its correlational nature. For example, children's stereotypy covaries not only with their own television viewing but also with their parents' television viewing (Zuckerman, Singer, & Singer, 1980). Maybe children *separately* acquire television viewing habits and gender stereotypes from their parents. The specific programs watched affect the results. Children exposed either to educational programs or to nonstereotypical models (such as female principals and police officers) have less stereotyped judgments and beliefs (Miller & Reeves, 1976; Repetti, 1984).

One important study correlated television viewing with sexism scores measured a year later in sixth- through tenth-grade children (Morgan, 1982). For boys, amount of television viewing was unrelated to sexism measured a year later; instead, boys who were more sexist at first testing increased the amount of television they watched over the year. Among girls, television viewing did predict sexism scores a year later, but this effect was limited to the girls having the highest IQ. Only among the brightest girls, whose sexism scores at first testing were the lowest of all, did heavy television viewing increase sexism.

Another way to investigate the effect of television is to actively manipulate the children's exposure to it. The relevant literature includes much of the modeling literature, since these models are frequently videotaped, simulating a television "exposure" (Durkin, 1985b). Children tend to copy more modeled behaviors when those behaviors are sex neutral rather than sex inappropriate. Thus, one of the few studies to find rather strong modeling effects used gender-neutral toys (Cobb, Stevens-Long, & Goldstein, 1982).

Adults are also affected by what they watch on television. Female college students exposed to nonstereotypical television commercials were subsequently less conforming and more achievement oriented than women exposed to stereotypical (and typical) commercials (Jennings [Walstedt], Geis, & Brown, 1980). Adults who watch a lot of television look at real-life men and women in more stereotypical terms than do those who watch less television (Zemach & Cohen, 1986). In fact, television viewing correlated with stereotypy better than did gender, education, and occupational status. However, it is not known whether stereotypy caused television watching or vice versa.

Attempts to change children's stereotypes. In other research, children are exposed to material that attempts to reverse an already existing belief. When Durkin (1985c) reviewed this literature, he concluded that changes are more likely to occur when the counterstereotypical material "attempts to build upon the diversity of the child's social knowledge rather than directly to contradict or undermine it" (p. 211). A later research project found that the children most resistant to change (adolescent boys and boys aged from 5 to 6) were more receptive to change if the male modeling the gender-inappropriate behaviors (cleaning a house) was also described as having a prestigious and masculine occupation (Jeffery & Durkin, 1989). Similarly, the mere presence of a male during the test may increase children's willingness to model counterstereotypic behaviors (Katz & Walsh, 1991). Interventions that focus on changing cognitive systems rather than behaviors may also be more effective (Bigler & Liben, 1990).

Overall, exposure to same-sex models displaying nonstereotypical attitudes and behaviors may be more likely to change the subject's own behaviors than exposure to opposite-sex models (Matteson, 1991). In fact, sometimes exposure to opposite-sex nonstereotypic models *increases* stereotyping. Same-sex models may lead the subject to copy the model's attitudes. Exposure to opposite-sex models may lead to anxiety and thus to defensive enhancement of the subject's own prior beliefs.

Effects of parents and parental stereotypes. Parental stereotypes and behaviors also affect their children's stereotypes. If mothers are nonstereotypical models, by virtue of being employed outside the home, their children have less stereotypical beliefs (Broverman et al., 1972; Etaugh & Spiller, 1989; Hoffman, 1989; Perloff, 1977; Weinraub et al., 1984; Zuckerman et al., 1980; but also see Albert & Porter, 1986). Children's gender stereotypes also vary according to their culture and their own parents' stereotypes (Albert & Porter, 1986; Perloff, 1977; Weinraub et al., 1984; Zammuner, 1987).

Older siblings may also be models. Although Zuckerman and her colleagues (1980) were unable to demonstrate any effect of birth order and numbers of siblings on children's stereotypes, the effects of siblings may depend not only on their age but also on their gender. Girls with older brothers and boys with older sisters tend to show less gender stereotyping than do other sibling-child pairs (Stoneman, Brody, & MacKinnon, 1986).

Effects on children's behaviors. Children's behaviors can be predicted from their stereotypic beliefs. In one example, children from kindergarten through sixth grade were asked to select toys and occupations under one of the following three conditions: (a) for a girl, (2) for a boy, or (3) choose the best one (Teglasi, 1981). Boys' choices of the "best" matched the choices they made "for a boy." However, girls'

"best" choices did not match the choices they made "for a girl." The girls seemed to have internalized the belief that girls do not get the "best." In another example, children aged 21 months to 40 months were given a test measuring gender constancy (Fagot, Leinbach, & Hagan, 1986). Although aggression in boys was unrelated to their performance on the gender-constancy task, the aggression of girls who passed the test significantly decreased over time. Once girls knew they would always be girls, their tendencies to act aggressively decreased as they matured, as though they now knew that acting aggressively would always be "inappropriate" for them.

Boys will often firmly resist any attempt made to get them to perform a gender-inappropriate behavior. Preschool boys were given a chance to choose which one toy they would like to be given, and they all chose a masculine toy. Then their teacher encouraged them to choose a feminine toy. Only 5 boys did what their teacher had requested; 14 boys refused to change their toy preference (1 boy switched but not to the teacher-recommended toy). The boys subsequently expressed beliefs that, to have made such a suggestion, their teacher must have been "sick" or "overworked" that day or must have suffered from amnesia.

Although children become more gender flexible, their personal reactions to nonconformity may remain extreme even up to the age of college, especially when males are asked about their attitudes toward "sissies" (Martin, 1990). Children from kindergarten through sixth grade were asked how they would respond to someone who acted in a gender-inappropriate manner (e.g., a boy playing with a baby doll) (Carter & McCloskey, 1983/1984). Older children were more negative than were younger children, and children were more negative to cross-gender behavior in males than in females. The reactions varied from avoidance to statements of possible violence: "I would push him and call him a weirdo"; "I'd punch him in the nose and call the police."

Children also enact stereotypes in their fantasy play. Matthews (1981) recorded what same-sex pairs of 4-year-old children said as they played "house." They said that mothers did the ironing and mothers needed to have the fathers plug the iron in for them before they could begin. Mothers cook and fathers work away from home. When a boy played "Mommy," the only thing he did was cook, but girls displayed a much greater variety in "Mommy's" behaviors. Girls were even less likely than boys to enact the role of the opposite-sex parent; if one girl was "Mommy," the other might be a grandmother or a sister.

SUMMARY

The cognitive component of gender stereotypes reflects our universal tendency to construct categories. These cognitive categories have sets of vertical and horizontal associations between traits, characteristics, and various subtypes. Stereotypes are maintained by social pressures, memory biases, and ego involvement. Different people may have different cognitive stereotype structures. Prejudice, or the deleterious effects of stereotypes on the ability of the person being stereotyped to make free choices, can occur either because of the cognitive component alone or because the affective responses to category members biases the behavioral reactions. We may believe that women simply lack the ability to perform a certain kind of task or we may believe that it would be very unpleasant to have to work with women. Demonstrating these forms of sexual prejudice often demands more subtle techniques than those employed in early research.

Children show the three aspects of gender attitudes: cogntive, affective, and behavioral. Their cognitive component undergoes systematic developmental changes representing not only an increase in knowledge but also an increase in cognitive complexity. They acquire the stereotypes from personal experiences with peers, mass media, parents, and other adults.

Children say that they would react negatively to "out-of-role" behavior, just as adults often do (at least when measured with more subtle research techniques). Children then enact the stereotypes in their own behaviors. Once the stereotype is formed, all the biases will come into play, leading to further distortions. People remember more details about members of ingroups than outgroups. They also perceive the members of the outgroup in more stereotypic terms, perceive members of the ingroup to be more variable (differentiated) than outgroup members, and perceive ingroup members more favorably. Because gender is a diffuse status characteristic, men should perceive women as relatively homogeneous, and women should perceive men in a more differentiated fashion, just as Eagly and Kite found with their study of U.S. college students' gender stereotypes of the people of various countries. On the other hand, Deaux found that in the United States, various subtypes of women were more sharply differentiated from each other than were male subtypes.

There are several lessons in this chapter for combating our own sexual stereotypes and those of our children. Learning to make yourself to think of, and to educate children about, the tremendous variability among men and among women will make the stereotypes more flexible. We also need to directly combat the negative reaction to deviations; children need to know that women can be competent in masculine occupations and this does not necessarily reduce their "femaleness."

ENDNOTES

1. For example, subjects are asked how similar a chair is to a table, compared to how similar a duck is to an eagle or a chair is to an eagle.

2. For example, all objects in the category of *vehicles* might share the attributes of wheels and engines.

3. Ashmore, 1981; Ashmore et al., 1986; Belk & Snell, 1986; Broverman, et al., 1970, 1972; Del Boca, Ashmore, & McManus, 1986; Eagly & Mladinic, 1989; Etaugh & Stern, 1984; McGee & Sherriffs, 1957; Sherriffs & McKee, 1957; Widiger & Settle, 1987.

4. **Agentic** describes a constellation of traits that includes self-assertion and concern with mastering the environment. Agency thus extensively overlaps, but is not synonymous with, instrumentality. **Communal** refers to being selfless and concerned with the welfare of other people, and so would include some of the traits previously described as expressive.

5. This equates the size of the ratios for traits typical of a gender group to the ratios for traits atypical for that group.

6. These included, "Ned should not wear nail polish," "William should not cry when he feels sad and a little rejected," "Mary should not take Rick to a restaurant and expect to be the one to order dinner, smell the wine cork, and taste the wine," "Beth should not engage in and enjoy casual sex even though her male friends may."

7. There seems to be no recent research on this subject.

CHAPTER 12

GENDERED ENVIRONMENTS

INTRODUCTION
HOME ENVIRONMENT
SCHOOL ENVIRONMENT
DIMORPHIC EFFECTS
WORK ENVIRONMENT
SUMMARY

If you get left home with the baby you do a lot of things you never knew how to do—or thought you didn't. The only problem is I destroy everything.

—Ahmad Rashad, describing how he cares for his daughter
(*TV Guide,* September 2, 1989, p. 24)

A headline in the Sunday, November 5, 1989, issue of the Macomb Journal *read: "Mother and daughter alike when it comes to shopping." Daughters shop like their mothers do: being first to try a new style, paying attention to coordination of wardrobe, and shopping in several stores to get the best prices. The authors (Sally Francis and Leslie Davis) theorized that the daughters had learned by watching their mothers shop.*

This chapter describes how environments are *gendered,* differing according to our sex. Environments are gendered because our same-sex models act differently: It is most often mothers who take children shopping; females care for children competently, but when males try, they "destroy everything." Environments are also gendered because those around us react to us differently, depending on our sex, even if we act exactly alike (Condry & Ross, 1985).

INTRODUCTION

Gendered environments lead to sex differences in developmental processes (Archer, 1989a; David & Brannon, 1976; Richards & Larson, 1989). The three stages of boys' development all appear in this chapter: avoidance of femininity, the physical role of boyhood, and the achievement roles of adulthood. Female role development is more continuous, at least until puberty. Then concerns with achievement decline, and concerns with social approval and getting married increase at least temporarily. This chapter looks at gendered environments from a life-span developmental point of view, beginning with the home environment. Subsequent sections look at gendered school environments and at environments that create sex differences because boys and girls react differently to them (Rowe, 1982). The last section describes gendered work environments.

HOME ENVIRONMENT

In Chapter 9, it was mentioned that researchers have not been able to demonstrate that parental behaviors dramatically affect their offspring, either as children or as adults. However, environments that are unique to each individual do have large effects on children, and this would include parents treating siblings differentially based on their gender (Hoffman, 1991).

Basic Background Information

Parental child-rearing practices affect children, but children's behaviors also affect what their parents do. Children can directly learn their parents' beliefs and values through modeling, as well as learning them indirectly because children learn that parents' attitudes affect how they treat their children (Antill, 1987). To demonstrate that parents affect sex differences, researchers must have valid measurements of parental behaviors and children's sex typing. According to Huston's model of sex typing (Huston, 1983; see Table 9.2), if researchers measure only one aspect of parental behaviors and only one aspect of children's sex typing, this ignores most of the possible relationships. Various measures of sex typing are not highly interrelated (Hoyt, Leinbach, & Fagot, 1991).

Measurement issues.   Parental attitudes and child-rearing practices are most frequently measured by scales or questionnaires, but there has been little consistency in results across studies (Maccoby & Martin, 1983). One reason is that different studies not only use different questionnaires but the scales themselves have questionable reliability and validity (Holden & Edwards, 1989). In fact, researchers often find very little relationship between what parents *say* they do, and what parents are actually *observed* to do (Fagot, 1974, 1978). In one study, although parents said that the child's gender was not a factor in deciding how to dress that child, 90 percent of the infants were dressed in sex-typed clothes[1] (Shakin, Shakin, & Sternglanz, 1985). Although sex-typed parents said that they wanted their children to be more sex typed than did other parents, these parents' child-rearing practices differed only slightly from those of the other parents[2] (Flake-Hobson, Robinson, & Skeen, 1981). Thus observational rather than questionnaire studies are emphasized here.

Brooks-Gunn (1986) was able to find a relationship between mothers' beliefs about children's sex differences and how those mothers acted. However, a mother's beliefs were related to her behaviors only for daughters. The more stereotypic the mother's beliefs, the less she engaged in active toy play with her daughter and the less often her daughter sought out maternal comfort in a experimental observation situation. The greater the mother's stereotypic beliefs, the lower the daughter's IQ score.

Mechanisms.   Observational   learning, especially symbolic modeling, plays an important role in life-span developmental changes. However, children differ in their tendency to copy the behaviors of a parent. Eron (1987) found that if a boy modeled (closely identified with) his father, the more the boy was punished for aggression at home, the less aggressive he tended to be at either home or school. If a boy was not closely identified with his father, the more often he was punished, the more aggressive he was both in school and at home. The less that children (male or female) had identified with their parents at age 8, the more aggressive they were at age 18. Thus, differences in modeling will affect the relationship between parents' and children's behaviors.

Given Bandura's emphasis on the cognitive aspects of sex typing (see Chapter 9), children will be affected by classical and operant conditioning procedures only if their cognitions are changed. In fact, boys and girls seem well aware that adults have different expectancies for them because of their sex. Muller and Goldberg (1980) asked 3-, 4-, and 5-year-old children what adults (mother, father, and teacher) would do if children engaged in various sex-appropriate and sex-inappropriate activities. The older the children were, the more aware they were that adults would behave differentially toward male and female children doing those activities.

Types of Parenting

The huge parenting literature includes not only observed variations among types of parents but also the effects of parental attitudes and child-rearing practices as measured by questionnaires.

Parental beliefs: content. Parents do not universally believe that the sexes differ, and even the gender differences that parents do believe in do not necessarily match reality (Fagot, 1981b). Sometimes parental beliefs are differentiated not only by the child's gender but also by the parent's gender (Power & Shanks, 1989). For example, British parents of 2-year-old children were asked about gender differences in children's behaviors (McGuire, 1988). Concerns about physical appearance seemed to typify femininity to these parents, particularly the mothers. Fathers saw femininity when children played with dolls in a nurturant way, were gentle, and did housework. Physical ability and athletic skill were viewed as masculine traits, along with enjoying getting dirty, being rough, and being interested in vehicles and tools. Overall, more than half the parents thought there were gender differences in the behaviors of young children, but most (63 percent of the mothers and 72 percent of the fathers) thought that these differences were caused solely by environmental factors. Only a few talked about biological factors.

Although experiments exploring the effects of parental attitudes often have discrepant results, three themes are commonly corroborated (Block, 1973; Lytton & Romney, 1991; Siegal, 1987): (1) Fathers have more gender-differentiated attitudes than mothers (also see Lynn, 1976; Marcus & Corsini, 1978). (2) Mothers and fathers have different attitudes toward their children. (3) Some parental attitudes depend on their child's gender, such as greater encouragement of dependency for daughters.

Father absence. Althogh early research commonly ignored fathers, the possible effects of paternal absence are becoming increasingly important to our society. If "current patterns continue, nearly 60 percent of children born in 1982 will spend at least 1 year living in a single-parent home before they reach 18 years of age and children who spend their entire childhood in two-parent families will be the minority" (Dubowitz et al., 1988, p. 1293). The most rapid increase in mother-headed households has been in the category of "never married."

Recent reviews have revealed some important facts about paternal absence (Amato & Keith, 1991; Cashion, 1982; Cherlin et al., 1991; Dubowitz et al., 1988; Hetherington, 1989; Hetherington, Camara, & Featherman, 1983; Lamb et al., 1983; McLanahan & Bumpass, 1988). The effects depend on the child's age, the reasons for the absence (e.g., death, divorce, desertion), and the financial status of the family left behind. Although the effects are generally more dramatic the younger the child was when the father left, many effects are due to the ensuing poverty rather than paternal absence per se. Still, even when the financial situation is statistically controlled for, "individuals raised in single parent homes are found to have *lower educational, occupational, and economic* attainment when compared to young adults raised in two parent homes" (Dubowitz et al., 1988, p. 1295, italics in original). This is particularly true of males living in single-parent households during their preschool years. Aggression and sexual activities are also often increased (see Chapter 9). Although paternal absence has only small, inconsistent effects on IQ scores, these children are more likely to do poorly in school. Having control and structure in their lives (for boys) and having warm, expressive mothers (for girls) ameliorates these effects (Hetherington et al., 1983). Also, father-absent boys do better academically if they have male relatives who frequently take them on outings (Riley & Chochran, 1987).

Maternal employment.   In families in which only the father is employed outside the home, mothers and fathers present different models for their children. Any possible effects of this should be attenuated if the mother and father are similarly employed outside the home. In fact, an increasing number of mothers work outside the home even when their children are young. Nearly half of women with children under 3 years of age were employed outside the home in 1984, and nearly 60 percent of those with children under age 6 were working (Dubowitz et al., 1988). From 1960 to 1985, the percent of working married women with children under age 6 increased from 19 to 53 percent.

It is difficult to assess the effects of maternal employment on the development of children because the direction of the effects depend on so many other variables (Clarke-Stewart, 1987; Dubowitz et al., 1988; Etaugh, 1984; Gottfried & Gottfried, 1988; Gottfried, Gottfried, & Bathurst, 1988; Hetherington, 1989; Hoffman, 1989; Huston, 1983; Lamb et al., 1983). Relevant moderating variables include the family's economic level; the mother's type of job; the age and gender of her children when she returns (or continues) to work; how the husband views her employment; how much she values her job; the amount of time she spends with her children; the way she interacts with her children; the quality and type of substitute childcare; what the mother herself believes the effects of her working on her children will be; and whether she is single, divorced, or married.

These points can be illustrated by some examples of possible direct and indirect effects of maternal employment. Mothers who do and who do not work outside the home have different personalities (Hock, DeMeis, & McBride, 1988). The degree to which the mother is satisfied with her role, regardless of what it is, is often more important than is her employment status (Lerner & Galambos, 1988). For example, maternal employment was not directly related to the child's development, but being dissatisfied with employment led, several years later, to a tendency to reject the child. The rejection, in turn, was associated with having a child with more problems. Similarly, children's achievements were not directly affected by their mothers' employments. Nevertheless, several years later, employed mothers had higher educational aspirations for their children, and these aspirations had directly affected their children's achievements (Gottfried & Gottfried, 1988; Gottfried et al., 1988). Divorced mothers' employment often seems beneficial for their daughters' development, but is less so for their sons (Hetherington, 1989). Siegal (1987) also found evidence that families with employed mothers gave girls more attention than boys, but the reverse was true for families with nonemployed mothers. (Remember that employed mothers tend to have a more liberal attitude toward the roles of women, as discussed in Chapter 11.)

Employed mothers also often expose their children to environments systematically different from those experienced by the children of mothers not employed outside the home. The socioeconomic status of the family may be higher, and the father will often become more involved in child rearing (Hoffman, 1989; Siegal, 1987). However, this may mean that the husband ends up being less satisfied with his work, his marriage, and his personal life (Stanley, Hunt, & Hunt, 1986). Children of employed mothers who are being cared for outside the home will often have more extensive peer involvement (e.g., in daycare centers) (Clarke-Stewart, 1987; Dubowitz et al., 1988). One example comes from a university daycare setting, where working mothers often have husbands who are completing their educations:

A teacher explained [to the children] that her husband, who had stopped by, could not stay to play with them because he had to go to work. She was immediately corrected by a not-quite-three-year-old boy, who stated emphatically, "No — mommies work, daddies go to school." All the other children present concurred. (Wynn & Fletcher, 1987, pp. 86–87)

Parental Behaviors: Objective Data

To what extent does a child's gender affect how the parents treat that child? The research cited in this section focuses on observational studies or on parental behaviors with documentable outcomes.

Abuse. Child abuse has long-term consequences (Browne & Finkelhor, 1986; Bryer et al., 1987). Furthermore, Wilson and Daly found that parents do discriminate between the sexes in their patterns of abuse (Daly & Wilson, 1980, 1988b; Wilson & Daly, 1985; Wilson, Daly, & Weghorst, 1980, 1981). One explanation may be differential parental investment (see Chapters 4 and 9) as a function of the child's age and gender. Female infanticide may occur more frequently than male infanticide, especially in couples of higher social status in societies that tolerate infanticide.[3] Daughters are more often sexually abused, whether by fathers, stepfathers, or men unrelated to the family. When physical abuse is separated from sexual abuse per se (though there is *much* overlap), mothers do more abusing than fathers do, and fathers abuse sons more often than daughters. Stepparents direct their physical abuse mostly toward same-sex children.

Wilson and Daly also found that the sex ratio of abuse varies with the child's age. Among the youngest U.S. infants, girls may be more frequently abused and neglected, perhaps because of a cutural preference for males. In slightly older children, especially 2-year-olds, males are at greater risk of abuse than females are, perhaps because males are more likely to display physical and behavioral problems that stress their parents. Adolescent girls are more often abused than boys, even when sexual abuse is excluded. Although physical abuse often involves unreported sexual abuse, explaining part of the greater female risk, parents may also be trying to control daughters (and their sexuality) more than sons.

Observational studies. Maccoby and Jacklin's (1974) comprehensive review concluded that few sex-differentiating behaviors of parents had been reliably documented. Exceptions were that parents tended to play more vigorously with sons, and both parents tended to encourage sex typing. Other reviews published afterwards have suggested that there are other differences as well (Block, 1983; Fagot & Leinbach, 1987; Hoyenga & Hoyenga, 1993).

Some generalizations can be made (Block, 1983; Fagot & Leinbach, 1987; Hoffman, 1977; Hoyenga & Hoyenga, 1993). Both parents seem to encourage proximity and dependency behaviors more often in girls. Boys experience more physical types of play, especially by fathers. Aggression is equally likely to be punished in both sexes. Fagot and Leinbach (1987) also concluded that "we were unable to find a single study in which boys were given less opportunity to explore, less encouragement of achievement, or more emotional support than girls" (p. 96). Although sex differences in verbal interactions (stimulations) are not reliable (Lytton & Romney, 1991), boys may receive more of the types of stimulation that best facilitate cognitive development. Weitzman, Birns, and Friend (1985) recorded mothers' communications with their 2½- to 3½-year-old children as the two interacted during various types of tasks. Boys were given significantly more cognitively stimulating kinds of communications, including most kinds of questions, discussions of number, verbal teaching, and the use of action verbs.

Meta-analytic reviews of the developmental literature (Lytton & Romney, 1991; Siegal, 1987) have concluded that both parents tend to reward "appropriate" sex-typed activities and punish "inappropriate" activities. These tendencies tend to be stronger for fathers and for boys. The reviews combined questionnaire and observational studies, but the conclusions held for both types separately.

Fagot and Leinbach research. Fagot and Leinbach (1987, 1989) observed 48 children (22 boys and 26 girls) at 18 months of age at home with their parents. Those same children at 27 to 30 months of age were given various gender-typing tasks and tests. By relating parental behaviors measured at one point to children's behaviors measured at a later time, the researchers could see which parental behaviors were related to the children's gender identity, gender-role identity, and gender constancy.

The more intensely the parents reacted to the child's sex-typed behaviors at 18 months, either positively or negatively, the sooner the child correctly labeled the gender of children's photographs. Early gender-labeling children also had fathers with a traditional attitude toward the roles of women. Weinraub and her coworkers (1984) found similar effects of fathers' beliefs. Interestingly, when the children were 27 months of age, Fagot and Leinbach found that the parents of early versus late gender-labeling children no longer differed even though now their children did. Both parent groups reacted positively to girls engaging in female-typical behaviors and to boys engaging in male-typical behaviors. However, the children who had labeled early had also become more aware of sex-role stereotypes.[4] Early-labeling girls played more with female-typed toys and showed significantly less aggression and more communications with adults.

Not only did parents differentiate between boys and girls but fathers also differed from mothers. When the marriage was not good, children were punished more, especially the boys. Boys were also punished more *by both parents* if the father said he did not enjoy the child. Girls got more instructional types of feedback from their parents than did boys, and mothers gave more instructional types of feedback than did fathers. Fathers, on the other hand, responded more emotionally to their children than did mothers, especially to their sons. Overall, fathers did more sex typing.

The example of play. Parents, especially fathers, are very likely to sex type the play styles and preferences of their children. In fact, in one study, one girl's father refused to use trucks to play with her (Caldera, Huston, & O'Brien, 1989). Sex-consistent play is reinforced and sex-inconsistent play is ignored or even punished. Fathers engage in more physical styles of play, particularly with sons (Lytton & Romney, 1991).

Different styles of play may have more to do with choice of toys than with parental gender (Caldera et al., 1989; Pellegrini & Perlmutter, 1989; Ross & Taylor, 1989). Parents play differently with their children depending on whether masculine or feminine toys are being used. Both parents show a more physical style of play when using masculine toys. When playing with feminine toys, parents had more physical contacts and more verbal interactions with their children. Children of both sexes seemed to prefer the physical play style.

Parents' play may have some long-term effects on the children's behaviors. In the Brooks-Gunn study cited earlier, perhaps the more active play styles of the less sex-typed mothers were at least partially responsible for the higher IQs of their daughters. Physical styles of play may facilitate the development of intellectual competence (particularly in daughters) and social competence (particularly in sons) (MacDonald & Parke, 1984; Tauber, 1979a, 1979b).

Parents of Sex-Atypical Children

Another way to look for parental effects is to contrast the parents of two very different groups of children: masculine versus feminine boys and masculine versus feminine girls.

Masculine versus feminine boys. In longitudinal studies (Green, 1976, 1985, 1987; Green et al., 1987; Green, Williams, & Goodman, 1985), boys who acted in a feminine manner (e.g., dress, toy preference, preference for female versus male playmates) were more likely to become homosexuals[5] and perhaps even male-to-female transsexuals as adults. Parents of feminine boys reported having spent less time with them, compared to the parents of masculine boys. Feminine boys were also hospitalized at an earlier age for illnesses and were separated from their fathers at an earlier age because of divorce. Overall, less father-son shared time and poorer father-son relationships were more common in the families of feminine than masculine boys. Most important, both parents of the feminine boys also tended to report having more accepting attitudes towards cross-gender behaviors.

Fagot has recorded the reactions of parents, teachers, and peers to masculine versus feminine boys (Fagot, 1974, 1977, 1978; Fagot & Patterson, 1969). Parents, especially fathers, are likely to punish boys engaged in feminine activities such as playing with baby dolls or other soft toys. Teachers do not react differentially to these two types of boys, reinforcing feminine activities equally in both groups. Feminine boys do receive more negative and less positive feedback from their male peers. The feminine boys are more often reinforced for feminine behaviors (from teachers and from girls) than for masculine ones, since other boys tend to totally ignore them. Being reinforced more often for acting feminine than for acting masculine may at least partially explain why their feminine behaviors persist.

Masculine versus feminine girls. The environments of masculine and feminine girls have also been contrasted (Fagot, 1974, 1977, 1978; Fagot & Patterson, 1969; Thorne, 1986;

Williams, Goodman, & Green, 1985). Averaging over all sources of reward and punishment (parents, peers, and teachers), although masculine behaviors are not reinforced as often in girls as in boys, the masculine and feminine girls get roughly equal overall amounts of praise and punishment. Furthermore, the masculine girls are not socially isolated. Although it is an insult for a boy to be called a girl by other boys, girls who interact regularly with boys have high status with both sexes, at least prior to puberty.

There are also some differences in their home environments. The masculine girls (tomboys) are more likely to copy their fathers' behaviors, and are less likely to copy their mothers' behaviors. Tomboys' mothers are likely to have been tomboys themselves and are more likely to be the family disciplinarian. The husband is less likely to be the clear boss of the family in the tomboys' homes. Thus, tomboys' environments at least tolerate, if not actively support, their masculine behaviors.

Parents as Models: Sexual Division of Child-Rearing Labors

Parents are also models of household behaviors for their children. Since parents who do different kinds of chores are also likely to differ in other ways as well, it will be difficult to say just what is affecting their child. For example, a father who takes primary responsibility for child rearing will differ from other fathers not only in terms of behaviors that can be modeled but also in his attitudes toward women and toward sex typing in children, and in how he treats his own children (see page 305).

Maternal as opposed to paternal investment: time studies. In some studies, parents simply estimated the number of hours they spent per week on various childcare tasks. In other studies, the parents kept detailed time diaries. Table 12.1 describes some of both kinds of studies. Since time spent in childcare depends on maternal employment level, data for

TABLE 12.1 *Sex-Differentiated Housework*

Housework done by husbands versus wives, in terms of both hours spent and types of tasks performed.

Time Studies

Husbands				Wives				
Children		No Children		Children		No Children		
Wife Working	Wife Not Working	Wife Working	Wife Not Working	Wife Working	Wife Not Working	Wife Working	Wife Not Working	**References**
8.6 h/w		6.3		24.6		18.4		Yogev, 1981
1.38–1.74 h/d	1.34–1.77	1.76	1.64	3.48–3.71	5.25–5.97	3.02	5.62	STU
2.08–2.15 h/d	1.81–1.88	1.82	1.63	4.57–4.79		3.72		QES
5.1 h/w	4.8			6.5	7.0			Levant, Slattery, & Loiselle, 1987
11.6 h/w				26.9				Lawrance et al., 1987

Types of Household Tasks Performed by Husbands versus Wives

Types of Tasks	Husbands	Wives	References
	Household repair; changes lightbulbs; repairs car; prepares tax returns, drives, & pays bills when with wife; mows lawn	Washes dishes; does laundry; cleans house; changes beds; cleans oven; cooks	Yogev, 1981; Krausz, 1986
Average number of tasks done*	16.15	23.46	Gunter & Gunter, 1990
Total domestic labor time including childcare*	25.09 h/w	47.12 h/w	Coverman, 1983
Outdoor tasks	3.3 h/w	2.8 h/w	Levant, Slattery, & Loiselle, 1987
Housework	2.2 h/w	3.2 h/w	Levant, Slattery, & Loiselle, 1987
Meals	2.7 h/w	3.6 h/w	Levant, Slattery, & Loiselle, 1987
Cooking, cleaning up after meals, house-cleaning, laundry, ironing	4.1 h/w	16.1 h/w	Levant, Slattery, & Loiselle, 1987 Robinson, 1988
Outdoor chores, repairs, garden and pet care, bills	5.9 h/w	3.4 h/w	Robinson, 1988

Notes: STU and QES, large questionnaire studies: see documentation in Hoyenga and Hoyenga, 1993.

h/d = hours per day

h/w = hours per week

*All these wives were employed outside the home.

mothers working outside the home are compared to data for stay-at-home mothers.

Maternal employment affects the mother's time more than the father's time (Douthitt, 1989; see other documentation in Hoyenga & Hoyenga, 1993). Fathers do not increase their childcare time much even when their wives become employed outside the home. Paternal involvement in the care of preschool children is determined by the mother's work pattern: the sooner the wife returns to work, the more involved her husband tends to be (Baruch & Barnett, 1981). Neither the husband's or wife's occupational or educational level is strongly related to how much the husband gets involved, suggesting that the variations are directly related to maternal employment per se (Nyquist et al., 1985).

Effects of childcare on various family members. The family is an interacting set of relationships. The way one member acts affects the others, and how they react will affect children's later behaviors. Although the father may do more sex typing, children do have less rigid gender stereotypes if the father is more involved in their care. Infants do form attachments to fathers (Lamb, Pleck, & Levine, 1983), and the greater the degree of paternal involvement, the more achievement oriented and self-controlled his children may be, especially the sons (Hoyenga & Hoyenga, 1993).

When both parents are present, families usually prefer that the major portion of childcare be done by the mother. For example, McGuire (1988) asked the London parents of a child no older than 33 months how they felt about the idea of fathers staying home and taking over the role of principal care-giver. Only one-fourth were positive about the idea. Parents of girls were more likely to be against the idea than were parents of boys.

Three studies (see documentation in Hoyenga & Hoyenga, 1993) described what can happen when a father takes over sole care of

the children and the mother is still present. In some cases, the father took over primary responsibility for childcare because of the mother's career (the United States). In other cases, the decision was entirely the father's idea, childcare being something he really wanted to do (Israel). Few effects on the children were seen, but paternal care children did feel more in charge and in control of their own lives.[6] More involved fathers also spent more time trying to foster their children's cognitive development, especially that of their daughters. In Israel, children of more involved fathers had less stereotyped views of paternal roles, and the daughters were less feminine.[7]

Types of men who parent. Researchers have attempted to find out what kind of man willingly takes on parental responsibilities (Hoyenga & Hoyenga, 1993). Both parents' experiences with their own parents, as well as their attitudes toward the roles of women, differentiate between fathers who do and do not parent. Thus, whether *he* parents at least partially depends on *her.* There may be cultural differences: both Israel and Norway seem to show more intragenerational stability of child-rearing patterns than does the United States (Hoyenga & Hoyenga, 1993; von der Lippe, 1985).

Parents as Models: Sexual Division of Household Labor

Tasks other than childcare are also gendered for adults and children.

Paternal versus maternal household tasks. Table 12.1 and Figure 12.1 present some results of household labor research. In the figure, tasks located higher on the ordinate tend to be done by both parents, and tasks lower on the ordinate are likely to be highly sex differentiated. Tasks low on the ordinate are usually either masculine (to the right) or feminine (to the left). Cooking and cleaning are feminine, but care and house repair are masculine;

FIGURE 12.1   *Proportionate Contribution of Wives and Husbands to Household Tasks*
Participation of husbands and wives in household activities (*n* = 120).

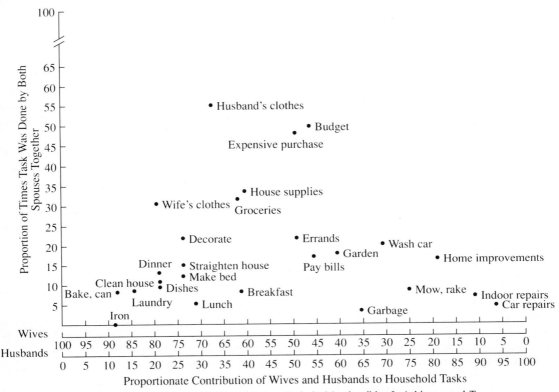

Source: From "Sex Role Orientation and Division of Labor Early in Marriage" by J. Atkinson and T. L. Huston, 1984, *Journal of Personality and Social Psychology, 46,* p. 338. Copyright 1984 by the American Psychological Association. Reprinted by permission.

shopping is unisex. Some errands and bill paying are done by husbands, others by wives.

The characteristics of both the husband and the wife affect his housework. If the wife is employed outside the home, the husband may not necessarily do more housework (Table 12.1; Levant et al., 1987; Hartman, 1981). One longitudinal study found that when wives became employed, 44 percent of their husbands increased the number of household tasks they did, 45 percent performed the same number of

tasks, and 11 percent actually did fewer tasks than before (Presser, 1977, as cited by Pleck, 1985). On the other hand, the presence of children tends to increase the amount of housework done by husbands. Husbands who have nontraditional attitudes toward women do more housework and do more of the feminine types of household tasks[8] (Antill & Cotton, 1988; Atkinson & Huston, 1984; Gunter & Gunter, 1990; Nyquist et al., 1985; Seccombe, 1986). Also, if the man is married to a woman that is either highly expressive or instrumental, or if he himself is expressive (BSRI & PAQ), he tends to do more housework.

The household time studies are nearly unanimous in finding that wives want husbands to do more housework than they actually do. In fact, the more housework is done by the husband, the happier the wife is with her role. This is true even of the wives who did *not* want their husbands to be more involved in childcare. Moreover, in recent years the housework done by men has tended to increase (Robinson, 1988).

Wives' housework is decreased by their employment but increased by children. Mothers with paid employment outside the home and mothers who do less housework also have more influence over family decisions than do non-working wives and mothers (Krausz, 1986; Nyquist et al., 1985). When hours of paid work are added to housework time plus childcare time, employed mothers work more hours per week than do unemployed mothers or their own husbands (Table 12.1). Thus, the mother employed outside the home has less free time than any of the other mothers, which could affect her child-rearing styles as well as her behaviors as a model.

Effects. Weinraub and her coworkers (Weinraub et al., 1984) found that fathers who did more feminine types of housework had less stereotyped children. The children of these fathers were less likely to correctly label other people's genders, and they had lower scores on a gender-identity task. They also had lower scores on a test measuring gender stereotyping of adults' possessions (e.g., clothing and makeup). This work suggests that a gender-dimorphic home-labor environment does affect children. On the other hand, Serbin and her colleagues (Serbin et al., 1990) did not find parental division of home labor to have any effect on the academic performances of their children. Obviously, more research needs to be done.

Children's chores. Overall, girls do more housework than boys do, replicating the cross-cultural research (Bloch, 1987; Goodnow, 1988; Goodnow & Delaney, 1989; Mauldin & Meeks, 1990; White & Brinkerhoff, 1981; Chapter 10). Girls' tasks include working in the kitchen and general household cleaning. Boys' tasks include farmwork, taking out the garbage, and outdoor work. Even paid employment is differentiated: girls babysit and boys mow lawns and shovel sidewalks. In a few families, self-care is sex typed; girls but not boys are asked to make siblings' beds and pick up others' toys. In general, males, older people, and lower SES people are more in favor of gender stereotyping children's tasks than are females, younger people, and higher SES people (Lackey, 1989).

Gendered Toys

"The evidence is overwhelmingly in support of children exhibiting sex-typed toy preference and playing behavior" (Tracy, 1987, p. 124). Children begin reacting to toys' genders starting as early as 14 to 18 months of age (Caldera et al., 1989; O'Brien & Huston, 1985). Even though 2-year-old boys cannot successfully label the sex typing of a toy, those boys still prefer the boys' toys (Blakemore, LaRue, & Olejnik, 1979; Perry, White, & Perry, 1984).[9] Although the correlations were not significant, the types of toys parents purchased were more consistently related to their son's toys preferences in a play situation ($r = .35$) than to their daughters' preferences ($r = .08$) (O'Brien & Huston, 1985).

Gendered toy environments of children. There are two methods by which the gendered toy environments have been documented. The first type of study analyzed the toys requested by children compared to those actually purchased by their parents. Robinson and Morris (1986) found that boys got more toys and a greater variety of toys. Among the toys picked out by the parents, no boy received a cross-sexed toy, although 8 percent of the toys that parents picked out for girls were cross sexed. Boys received more musical/camera and more arts/crafts sex-neutral toys that had not been requested. From 72 to 77 percent of the toys requested by boys were masculine sex typed, and the percentage did not vary by age. Only one boy requested (and received) a cross-sex toy, whereas 5 percent of the toys requested by girls were cross sexed. Older girls requested more sex-typed toys than did younger girls, varying from 29 percent at age 3 to 73 percent at age 5.

In the other type of study, the researchers went into children's homes and counted the types of toys found (Bybee, Glick, & Zigler, 1990; Cole, Zucker, & Bradley, 1982; O'Brien & Huston, 1985; Rheingold & Cook, 1975). Boys had a greater variety of toys as well as more vehicles. Boys' rooms also had more animal furnishings; more educational and art materials; more toys that emphasized the properties of space, matter, energy, and time (e.g., outer-space toys, magnets, clocks); more sports equipment; more tools; and more toy animals. Other toys in boys' rooms reflected outdoor and farm chores and the military. Boys had more blue, red, and white clothes, and more blue was used to furnish their rooms.

Girls' rooms reflected childcare and household chores, and were more often decorated in yellow, with more floral and ruffled furnishings. Girls were also more likely to have pink and multicolored clothes and doll toys. Only a few boys' rooms had even one female doll, and even fewer had a baby doll; only a few girls' rooms had male dolls. Girls' rooms were much more likely to have doll carriages, strollers, swings, and toy household appliances.

Some developmental implications of gendered toy environments. Although both sexes react in the same way to similar toys (Karpoe & Olney, 1983; Liss, 1981; Pellegrini & Perlmutter, 1989), since the sexes are exposed to different toys, their developments could be differentially affected. Boys' toys have more inventive possibilities (Block, 1983; Tracy, 1987). Girls' toys also encourage more imitation and keep them closer to their care-givers. Play with boys' toys might promote the development of spatial ability and science and mathematics achievements (Fagot & Littman, 1976; Serbin et al., 1990; Chapter 14).[10] Toy preferences and styles of play are also embedded in a sex-typing context and so are related to other characteristics such as gender of playmate preferred and maternal employment (Eisenberg-Berg, Boothby, & Matson, 1979; Tauber, 1979b). Serbin and her colleagues found that the higher the status of the mother's occupation, the more likely that children of both sexes had masculine toys in their rooms.

Table 12.2 presents Miller's (1987) description of the dimensions on which boys' and girls' toys differ. She had undergraduate psychology students rate 25 toys on each of 12 dimensions and also had them rate each toy's appropriateness for boys or girls. Boys' and girls' toys have several important differentiating characteristics. Girls seem to be encouraged to be nurturant by their toys, and boys are encouraged to compete.

SCHOOL ENVIRONMENT

Unless they have been in some type of daycare center, school is the first time U.S. children have extensive contact with nonparental adults—their teachers. They also for the first time interact with large numbers of children of their own age.

Observational Studies of Teachers' Behaviors

Table 12.3 presents some observational studies of teachers' behaviors. The lack of consistency should not be a surprise. As almost all the researchers clearly recognize, external validity is limited since only a few teachers are studied in any one study and they are neither a random nor a representative sample. Teachers are as

TABLE 12.2 *Characteristics of Masculine versus Feminine Toys*
This table presents descriptions of categories used in the toy rating study, along with sample ratings for each category.

Sex Rating of Toy	Category and Description	Sample Ratings
♀	Manipulability ("How easy or difficult is it for a child to manipulate parts of this toy, e.g., to remove and replace parts?")	1. Is generally a stationary, self-contained toy; there are no movable or removable parts. 5. Has movable/removable parts, but such manipulation is not necessary for proper functioning of this toy. 9. Has movable/removable parts that *require* manipulation for proper functioning of this toy.
♂	Symbolic play ("Is this toy very realistic or can it be used by the child for fantasy play?")	1. Toy is used primarily for fantasy play. 5. Toy can be used equally for either fantasy or reality play. 9. Toy is entirely reality based; cannot be used for fantasy play.
♀	Creativity ("How much does this toy exploit the child's imagination, i.e., can it be used in more than one way, does it encourage imaginative uses, etc.?")	1. There is only one way that this toy can be used for play; there is no room for imagination. 5. There is generally only one use of this toy, but a very imaginative child could easily make up others. 9. The toy is intended to exploit the child's imagination; it can be used in many different and creative ways.
♂	Sociability ("To what extent does this toy encourage sociability, i.e., using the toy to play with another child?")	1. The toy can be played with only by one child at a time. 5. The toy can be played either alone or with one or more other children. 9. The toy requires at least two children to play; cannot be played with by only one child at a time.
♂	Competition ("To what extent does this toy encourage cooperation vs competition among two or more children?")	1. Play with this toy encourages cooperation among two or more children. 5. This toy can be used either cooperatively or competitively by two or more children. 9. This toy encourages competition among children.
♂	Handling ("How easy or difficult is it for a child to manipulate this toy, i.e., pick up, turn around, move about, etc.?")	1. Cannot be handled; too large and/or cumbersome to pick up, turn around, move about, etc. 5. Can be handled, but handling is not necessary when playing with this toy. 9. Is easily handled; functions best as a toy when handled.

(continued)

TABLE 12.2 *(continued)*

Sex Rating of Toy	Category and Description	Sample Ratings
♀	Nurturance ("To what extent can the child cuddle and/or nurture this toy?")	1. This toy cannot be cuddled and/or nurtured. 5. This toy can be cuddled, but this is not generally how the toy is used for play. 9. The primary function of this toy is for the child to cuddle.
♂	Constructiveness ("To what extent can this toy be used for constructive purposes, i.e., by adding pieces together or combining with another toy to create something new?")	1. Toy is self-contained; must be used "as is." 5. Toy can either be used "as is" or can be combined with another toy to construct something new. 9. The primary function of the toy is for constructive purposes (by adding parts together, taking pieces apart, or combining with another toy to create something new); the toy is useless by itself.
♂	Aggressiveness ("To what extent can this toy be used for aggressive purposes, i.e., in aggressive actions against an object or against another child?")	1. This toy cannot be used aggressively against an object or another child. 5. This toy can be used for aggressive purposes, but this is not generally how the toy is used for play. 9. The primary functions of this toy is for aggressive purposes.
♀	Attractiveness ("Based on whatever features you think are relevant, e.g., color, texture, complexity, etc., how physically attractive would this toy to be a child who had never seen it before?")	1. Not at all attractive. 5. Moderately attractive. 9. Extremely attractive.

Source: From "Qualitative Differences among Gender-Stereotyped Toys: Implications for Cognitive and Social Development in Girls and Boys" by C. L. Miller, 1987, *Sex Roles, 16,* p. 479. Copyright 1987 by Plenum Publishing Corporation. Reprinted by permission.

likely to differ from one another as are their students.

Preschool studies. Preschool children of both sexes are most frequently rewarded for feminine behaviors. Since feminine activities are also the ones most likely to facilitate classroom instruction, the preschool teachers may be trying to encourage their children to behave in ways more appropriate to the classroom as opposed to trying to sex type them. It is the experienced teacher who is most likely to reinforce these girl-preferred behaviors. At least one boy-preferred activity, block play, is also relevant to the classroom and is also reinforced by teachers. Preschool teachers also treat the sexes similarly, except that block play may be reinforced more often in boys. More importantly, girls may be given more direction, especially when they are very close to the teacher. The implications of this will be discussed later.

Primary grades. By the primary grades, many of the gender-differentiated teacher behaviors

TABLE 12.3 *Sex-Differentiated Teacher Behaviors*
The following are observational studies of teachers' behaviors toward male and female children, organized by age of child.

Age of Child	References
Preschool	
Feminine behaviors (e.g., painting and artwork) were reinforced for both sexes, but boys more often than girls were reinforced for masculine activities (e.g., play with blocks and transportation toys, rough-and-tumble play, carpentry play).	Etaugh, Collins, & Gerson, 1975; Fagot, 1985b; Fagot & Patterson, 1969; McCandless, Bush, & Carden, 1976
Boys were given more criticism for dress-up behaviors and more reinforcement for block play (masculine) and art play (feminine) than were girls; girls were given more criticism for sandbox play (masculine) than boys.	Fagot, 1977a
Compared to other girls, girls who were low in both task and overall activity levels got more positive reactions, whereas high-activity girls got more negative reactions; boys who were low in task involvement but high in overall activity got less positive feedback and more negative feedback, compared to other boys.	Fagot, 1984a
Both boys and girls who were low in masculine but high in feminine behaviors got more positive reactions than did other boys and girls, respectively; girls who were high in masculine but low in feminine activities got more negative feedback compared to other girls.	Fagot, 1984a
Teachers initiated more activity and behaviors for girls and responded more to girls' questions, and gave girls more favorable comments and more direction.	Fagot, 1973
Teachers were more likely to respond to male than to female aggression (with punishment or distraction) and attended more to girls when they were close as opposed to far away from the teachers (effect of proximity was not seen with boys); more directions and instructions were given to boys.	Serbin et al., 1973
Male teachers were likely to reinforce masculine behaviors in boys than in girls, and more likely to reinforce masculine than feminine behaviors in boys (maybe because of having less experience than the average female teacher, since this is also the pattern of reinforcements given by less experienced female teachers as well; this pattern was also seen in Dutch preschool teachers).	Fagot, 1977b, 1981a; McCandless et al., 1976
Primary Grades (1–6)	
Boys were scolded by both sexes of teachers and praised more than girls by female teachers (no sex differences existed in students' behaviors).	Etaugh & Harlow, 1975; Katz & Stake, 1980

(continued)

TABLE 12.3   *(continued)*

Age of Child	References
Teachers made more academic contacts and spent more instructional time with girls in reading classes; they spent more time with boys in math classes; by the end of the year, girls were better than boys in reading.	Leinhardt, Seewald, & Engel, 1979
Dweck and colleagues found that teachers responded differentially to different aspects of task performances; not replicated by the other studies.	Dweck et al., 1978; Heller & Parsons, 1981; Parsons, Kaczala & Meece, 1982
Teachers reprimanded girls but not boys for calling out questions in class without being called on; boys' answers were responded to more specifically and at length, whereas more bland and diffuse reactions were given to girls.	Sadker & Sadker, 1985
Boys got more talk directed at them, especially informative types of talk; communications directed toward girls focused on academic performances and those directed toward boys focused on procedural issues (i.e., misbehavior).	Eccles & Blumenfeld, 1985
High-achieving boys received the most praise of all student groups; low achieving, misbehaving boys received the most criticism.	Brophy, 1985; Brophy & Good, 1974 (reviews)
Secondary Grades Girls got more approval than boys from female teachers, especially highly expressive but low instrumental teachers.	Bledsoe, 1983
Math Classrooms in Secondary Grades Girls received less criticism; low-achieving boys received the most criticism; high-achieving girls received the least praise of all achievement/sex groups.	Eccles & Blumenfeld, 1985; Frey, 1979 (as cited by Block, 1983); Parsons, Kaczala, & Meece, 1982
The sex-differentiated pattern of teacher feedback observed by Dweck and colleagues in primary grades was not observed here in a study devoted only to mathematics classrooms.	Heller & Parsons, 1981
Boys received more teacher contacts in math classes.	Brophy, 1985; Brophy & Good, 1974 (reviews)
In high school geometry classes, teachers more often called on boys, more often allowed boys to call out answers without being called on, gave more feedback to boys than to girls following incorrect answers, and more often encouraged and praised the boys.	Becker, 1981

are elicited by the students and so do not reflect sexism on the teachers' part (Brophy, 1985; Brophy & Good, 1974; Block, 1983; Table 12.3). Boys are more active and more often disrupt the classroom, whereas girls are more teacher oriented. Overall, boys seem to receive more criticism and, in some studies, more praise. The criticism is usually directed toward a small group of misbehaving boys, and the praise is directed toward a small group of highly achieving boys who are well adjusted to the student role. Sex-differentiated teacher behaviors are more likely to be seen when specific types of classes are compared, such as math and science versus reading.

Secondary grades.   Much of the research has concentrated on mathematics classrooms because, although girls continue to get higher grades in math, girls' scores on math achievement tests start to lag behind those of boys. Starting at the fourth grade, girls' self-confidence in math is lower than that of boys (Fennema & Peterson, 1985), and both children and their mothers believe that boys are better at math and girls are better at reading. These beliefs appear as early as the first grade in Taiwan, Japan, and the United States (Lummis & Stevenson, 1990).[11] Although there is considerable variability, boys often seem to have an advantage over girls in secondary mathematics classrooms. Sometimes the differences are striking, as in the Becker study. Other differences are far more subtle — bright girls receive the least praise, and it is the brighter girls and the less able boys who receive the most criticism. Because of the feedback they get from teachers, girls could be less likely to develop **autonomous learning behaviors** in mathematics. Those behaviors "include working independently on high-level tasks, persisting at such tasks, choosing to do and achieving success in such tasks" (Fennema & Peterson, 1985, p. 20).

Peer Interactions

There is a children's subculture. It is passed on from one generation to the next, and deviations from one's appropriate role can be severely punished. To the extent that male and female peer or subculture groups have different kinds of social interactions, the sexes will also get differential practice in various social behaviors.

Same-sex groupings.   During all the years between preschool and puberty, the free play of children occurs largely in gender-segregated groups (Carter, 1987; Feiring & Lewis, 1987; Jacklin, 1989; La Freniere, Strayer, & Gauthier, 1984; Maccoby, 1987, 1988, 1990; Maccoby & Jacklin, 1987; Thorne, 1986). Children will preferentially asociate with same-sex peers before the age at which they can even reliably label the sex of the children with whom they are associating: by 27 months of age, girls show a preference for same-sex play partners. By age 6½, children are spending 11 times as much time with same-sex as with opposite-sex partners (Maccoby, 1990). Even when cross-sex interactions are encouraged in a classroom, children still prefer same-sex children as friends (Lockheed, 1985b).

Why do these same-sex preferences appear (Maccoby, 1988, 1990; Maccoby & Jacklin, 1987)? According to the cognitive hypothesis (e.g., Kohlberg), once children label their own and others' gender, the value of things "like the self" leads them to prefer their own gender in play partners. Children could also be differentially reinforced by peers and/or adults for same-sex as opposed to cross-sex peer play. Or children may be attracted to same-sex others because of sex differences in preferred styles of play. These ideas are now described.

Cognitive factors.   Gendered cognitions develop in parallel with same-sex preferences. Even children as young as 6 months of age react differently to male and female faces (Fagan &

Shepherd, 1981; Fagan & Singer, 1979), providing a cognitive basis for the same-sex preferences that occur before the age of labeling. When children from 21 to 40 months of age were tested, children who could correctly categorize people by gender had a greater same-sex peer preference (Fagot et al., 1986). Some children identified gender reliably at 24 months.

According to another version of the cognitive theory, people who share interests might be more enjoyable companions. The sexes could develop differing interests because of parental treatment, including toy purchases. Similar to Kohlberg's reasoning, children might prefer to play with people who play with similar toys. In support of this, children with stronger same-sex playmate preferences also tend to have stronger same-sex toy preferences (Eisenberg-Berg, Boothby, & Matson, 1979; Fagot et al., 1986). If a child prefers to play with same-sex peers, that child also prefers same-sex adults and same-sex toys and occupations (Serbin & Sprafkin, 1986). However, other research has not been able to confirm these associations. "Frequency of play with sex-stereotypical toys was not related to a child's preference for same-sex playmates" (Maccoby & Jacklin, 1987, p. 257). Only playmate preferences and not toy preferences could be related to the child's ability to categorize others on the basis of their gender (Fagot et al., 1986).

Given these data, same-sex playmate preferences and toy preferences may be independently acquired through different processes, but same-sex playmate preferences might be able to strengthen preferences for sex-specific toys (or vice versa). For example, the presence of boys inhibits girls from playing with masculine toys. Boys are inhibited from playing with feminine toys by the presence of any peer, but particularly by girls (Serbin et al., 1979). The kind of toy that a child is playing with affects whether boys or girls will join the child's play (Eisenberg, Tryon, & Cameron, 1984; Wynn & Fletcher, 1987). This is especially true for boys. If being joined by same-sex others is more reinforcing than being joined by opposite-sex others, for reasons to be described now, same-sex playmate preferences could lead to increased sex-typical toy preferences.

Differential reinforcement and different play styles. Cognitive process alone cannot account for gender segregation (Carter, 1987; Maccoby & Jacklin, 1987; Serbin & Sprafkin, 1986; Thompson, 1975). Maybe girls simply find the company of other girls to be more enjoyable (Maccoby, 1988, 1990). When boys are in the group, they dominate the girls. In a small group learning situation, when a girl and boy disagree as to the correct answer, the boy's answer more commonly prevails (Wilkinson, Lindow, & Chiang, 1985). Preschool boys also tend to dominate girls (Pellegrini & Perlmutter, 1989). Girls might prefer not to be dominated and so seek the company of other girls.

These differential play and dominance styles begin as early as 13 months of age (Goldberg & Lewis, 1969). Jacklin and Maccoby (1978) observed 33-month-old children interacting in pairs. They found that there was more social activity among same-sex than among opposite-sex pairs. Girls paired with boys tended to stand by, just passively watching their partner. Among most kinds of playmate pairs, when one said "No!", the other responded by stopping whatever he or she was doing. But boys ignored the prohibitions of girls, which apparently made the girls withdraw from the play. Also, boys tend to play in larger groups, but girls prefer to play in groups of just two (Waldrop & Halverson, 1975). Girls may learn to avoid playing with boys because the consequences of doing so are often unpleasant for them, and boys may learn to avoid playing with girls because girls do not often play in the way that boys prefer (Maccoby & Jacklin, 1987). "The rough-and-tumble play style characteristic of boys and their orientation towards issues of competition and dominance appear to be somewhat aversive to most girls" (Maccoby, 1990, p. 515).

Some of the segregation may occur because peers often react negatively to the possible sexual connotations of opposite-sex relationships (Thorne, 1986). If cross-sex friendships do form, the children get together only at home, where the other children will not see them playing together. One female child of age 11 described what her peers would do if she were friends with a boy: "Tease me. People would not be my friends. They would scorn me" (Maccoby & Jacklin, 1987, p. 245). When the authors asked one preadolescent boy if he ever thought he'd have a girlfriend, he paused and then responded, "No. My friends would kill me."

Parents and peer relationships.   Parents affect their children not only directly but also indirectly, by means of their influence on peer interaction patterns. For example, when parents' tendencies to direct their children were assessed in a play session, more directive fathers had less popular sons and daughters. On the other hand, directive mothers had popular daughters, but maternal directiveness did not seem to affect their son's popularity (MacDonald & Parke, 1984). If fathers had played physically with their daughters, these daughters became popular and had stronger same-sex play preferences in nursery school (Maccoby & Jacklin, 1987; MacDonald & Parke, 1984).

There are at least a couple of reasons why these relationships may develop. Children may learn certain patterns of social interactions with their parents that affect later peer interactions. More social children could also elicit different parental behaviors and at the same time they responded differently to peers.

Peer reinforcement patterns.   Knowledge of an infant's gender consistently influences how children react to that infant (Stern & Karraker, 1989). Overall, peers tend to reinforce sex-typical behavior and punish sex-atypical behavior in each other (Fagot, 1977a, 1984a; Langlois & Downs, 1980; McCandless, Bush, & Carden, 1976; Lamb & Roopnarine, 1979).

Table 12.4 presents some representative data. Both sexes get more rewards for engaging in sex-typical than for sex-atypical activity. Boys acting in male-typical ways are more likely to be rewarded by both sexes. The converse was true for females.

Both imitation and punishment may be masculine patterns of peer feedback. Being imitated often acts like a positive reinforcer for children, but boys do more imitating and are imitated

TABLE 12.4   *Sex-Typed Rewards*
Sources of rewards for male and female children displaying male-typical or female-typical behaviors from either male or female peers.

Source of rewards	Males	Males	Females	Females	Total	Total
Target of rewards	Males	Females	Males	Females	Males	Females
Male-typical behavior	2.75	1.58	1.47	1.13	4.26	2.68
Female-typical behavior	1.63	2.71	0.93	1.69	2.58	1.42

Source: From "Peer Influences on Sex-Role Development in Preschoolers" by M. E. Lamb and J. L. Roopnarine, 1979, *Child Development, 50,* p. 1219. Copyright 1979 by The Society for Research in Child Development. Reprinted by permission.

more often than girls (Abramovitch & Grusec, 1978). Also, at least among preschoolers, boys may administer more negative feedback to their peers than girls do (Roopnarine, 1984).

Effectiveness of feedback from girls versus boys. Children are more sensitive to some than to other types of feedback. For example, being reinforced for acting feminine affects girls more than boys, whereas being reinforced for acting masculine affects boys more (Lamb & Roopnarine, 1979). Fagot has explored the differential sensitivity of children to same-sex versus opposite-sex peer feedback by looking at how the feedback affects the behavior (Fagot, 1985b, 1985c; Fagot & Hagen, 1985; Fagot et al., 1985). Once the feedback occurs, does the behavior continue or does the child quit doing whatever it is? Girls' feedback influences the behaviors of other girls but not those of boys, and boys' feedback influences the behaviors of other boys but not those of girls. In other words, girls ignore what boys say about them, and vice versa.

More specifically, Fagot has found that boys tend to ignore girls' aggressive/assertive acts. Being ignored also seems to be the feedback that most promptly makes any child stop acting aggressive. Both boys and girls respond to the aggressive/assertive acts of boys, often negatively. Seemingly perversely, this kind of feedback makes boys continue rather than cease their aggression, even those as young as 25 months of age. Thus, boys receive the message that their behaviors have an impact on others. Girls, performing apparently the same kinds of activities, are ignored.

The peer culture. Once in peer groups, boys and girls tend to engage in different kinds of games and interactions (Maccoby, 1988, 1990). One difference is that boys have extensive peer systems and girls have intensive peer systems. For example, if boys were friendly at age 2½, at age 7½ those same boys tended to play with large groups of other boys (Waldrop & Halver-

son, 1975). On the other hand, girls who were friendly at age 2½ tended at age 7½ to play intensively with only one other girl at a time.

Observational studies have found other gender differences in peer interactions (Sanders & Harper, 1976; Stoneman, Brody, & MacKinnon, 1984; Tauber, 1979b; Tizard, Philps, & Lewis, 1976; also see reviews in Maccoby & Jacklin, 1987; Maccoby, 1988, 1990). Girls are more likely to accept suggestions or respond to requests, and they are also more sedentary and nurturant. Boys are more likely to play outside and in more public places, in larger groups, and further away from adults. Girls are more likely to choose a domestic theme for play, whereas boys more often pretend to be driving vehicles, fighting, and killing. In play groups, girls' verbal communications involve maintaining relationships, whereas boys' involve dominance attempts or attempts to attract attention. Boys' groups also more readily form dominance, toughness, or status hierarchies (Maccoby, 1988, 1990; Savin-Williams, 1977, 1979; Omark & Edelman, 1975; Chapter 13). Thus, status differentials are an early characteristic of boys' play groups.

Several reviews of children's play have focused on the types of games played (Freedman & DeBoer, 1979; Hughes, 1988; Lever, 1976; Parker, 1984). Girls more often join boys' games than boys join girls' games. When boys do join girls' games, it is usually to disrupt them. The games of boys last longer than those of girls, perhaps because conflict often breaks up girls' games but boys do not terminate a game because of a quarrel. Boys' games more often involve throwing (e.g., baseballs and footballs).

Rough-and-tumble play is a particularly masculine form of play (Freedman & DeBoer, 1979; Humphreys & Smith, 1984; DiPietro, 1981; Maccoby & Jacklin, 1987; Pelligrini, 1988). **Rough-and-tumble** play refers to active, physical forms of play that have the appearance of aggression but that the participants view as play. In play wrestling, the participants will take turns as winner and loser, whereas in aggressive wrestling, there is no turn taking. Rough-and-tumble pay is seen more often in boys in most, if not all, cultures, and may also more often be seen among the male juveniles in many other species (Hoyenga & Hoyenga, 1984). The presence of male playmates stimulates rough-and-tumble play, particularly among other males. However, the magnitude of the sex difference does vary across cultures and across settings, being less in more structured settings, for example.

Peers versus Teachers

Overall, peers do more sex typing than teachers do.

Which behaviors are differentially reinforced?

Several studies have compared the sex typing of peers and teachers (Fagot, 1977a, 1984a, 1985b; Fagot et al., 1985; Fagot & Patterson, 1969). Preschool teachers tend to reinforce feminine behaviors in both sexes, whereas peers reinforce mostly same-sex others. Boys criticize other boys for engaging in feminine activities, something that teachers do not tend to do.

In most studies, peers discriminate more among sex-typed peer behaviors than do teachers. Only peers criticize boys for doll play. Only peers are less likely to reinforce boys than girls for kitchen play, and they are less likely to reinforce girls than boys for hammering (Fagot, 1977b). Although high-activity levels in girls are not rewarded by either teachers or peers, high-activity boys receive more positive peer feedback and more negative teacher feedback than do low-activity boys (Fagot, 1984a).

One study contrasted the sex typing of peers versus adults by observing the same children, first at 13 to 14 months of age and then again at 24 to 25 months of age (Fagot et al., 1985b, 1985c). There were no sex differences in children's communications (verbal) or assertiveness behaviors or in peer feedback at the

earlier ages. However, girls' assertiveness attempts were far more often ignored by the adults, and boys had to be more vigorous in their attempts to communicate to get the same attention that girls got with much less vigorous (less shouting) attempts. Eleven months later, the boys were more assertive and the girls talked to the teachers more. Now the adults no longer differentiated between sexes, but peers did, reacting negatively to boys' assertion attempts and ignoring those of girls. Perhaps the adults helped create the sex differences that peer feedback then served to maintain. Or maybe adults, because of their own past experiences, were just anticipating the sex differences that would eventually appear.

Effectiveness of teacher versus peer feedback.

Girls' behaviors are affected by both teachers' and peers' reactioons, but boys respond mostly to feedback from other boys (Fagot, 1985b, 1985c). If a girl is reinforced (as by a peer coming to play with her or by a teacher's praise) for *any* activity (male-typical, female-typical, or gender-neutral), she is more likely to continue that activity than if she were punished. If boys engage in female-typical activities, they are less likely to continue these activities if punished by their male peers than if they had been reinforced, and male peers are very unlikely to reinforce such behaviors. Boys are particularly likely to get negative sex-typed reaction from other boys when playing with girls' toys: "That's dumb, boys don't play with dolls" and "You're silly, that's for girls." On the other hand, as described before, the negative peer response to aggression in a boy is more likely to make the boy continue doing it than to make him quit!

DIMORPHIC EFFECTS

The same environment can have different impacts on the sexes. Both Block's and Baumrind's research has shown how apparently similar styles of parenting can have differential effects on how the sexes develop (Baumrind,

1968, 1971a, 1982, 1991; Block, von der Lippe, & Block, 1973; Costos, 1986). Sex-typing socialization seems to expand men's adult options but seems to restrict the options for women (Block et al., 1973).

This section examines the dimorphic effects of three types of school environments. First, females and males may react differentially to competition among peers. Second, girls and boys have different task preferences. Third, the effects of social comparison processes may depend on gender. For example, one study compared three different ways to improve student performances in sixth-grade social studies classes (Ward & Jungbluth, 1980). Females improved more in the situation in which adults delivered reinforcements for correct performances, whereas males improved more in the situation in which students rewarded themselves.

Competition

Females can compete as vigorously as males do and be as likely to succeed; many may also enjoy it. However, exposure to competitive environments may more often have detrimental long-term effects on a girl's than on a boy's development and self-concept.

Preferences for competitive versus cooperative environments. In this section, **cooperation** refers to the tendency to work for and value the rewards given to other people. It also refers to the tendency to value rewards achieved while working jointly with certain others at least as much as, if not more than, rewards achieved while working alone or in competition with others. **Competition** refers to the tendency to value rewards for the self much more than rewards for others. Competition also refers to situations in which one can get more rewards than anyone else, compared to situations in which rewards are equally shared among group members. Although there are exceptions, when given a choice, more boys than girls prefer com-

petition, and more girls than boys prefer cooperation (Ahlgren, 1983; Ahlgren & Johnson, 1979; Boehnke et al., 1989; Charlesworth & Dzur, 1987; Charlesworth & La Freniere, 1983; Knight & Kagan, 1977; Moely, Skarin, & Weil, 1979).

Algren's research found that females have more positive attitudes toward cooperation than do males, and males have more positive attitudes toward competition than do females. The differences are largest at grades 8 through 10. With age, males lose most of their negative attitudes toward competition, but females do not. Although males who like competing also tend to like themselves, liking cooperation is associated with favorable self-concepts only in older female children.

Boys more often play competitive types of games (Freedman & DeBoer, 1979; Hughes, 1988; Lever, 1976; Parker, 1984). Even when boys and girls play the same game, boys compete with everyone, but girls form cooperative friendship groups. Girls' games more often involve strict turn taking, as in jump rope and hopscotch, again making them more cooperative than competitive.

Hughes (1988) described some sex differences in how fourth- and fifth-grade boys and girls reacted to the same competitive game. According to the rules, every player should compete with every other player. This was how males played it. Girls turned it into a team sport, cooperating with their close friends and competing with other friendship groups. In this context, competing was not being "mean," because one had to compete to help one's friends win. But if girls competed too vigorously against their friends, they risked that friendship.

Spence and Helmreich (1983) have done extensive work with achievement values. They measured **work values** (value of working hard, importance of doing well), **mastery values** (importance of challenge) and **competitiveness** (valuing and enjoying competition). Across very different samples, from college students to business people, males valued competitiveness more than females did.

Sex differences in behaviors in competitive situations. The sexes often have different reactions to competition. In Charlesworth's experiments involving same-sex and cross-sex competition among children (Charlesworth & Dzur, 1987; Charlesworth & La Freniere, 1983), boys displayed more physical behaviors and girls were more verbal. When dominance was measured by who won the competition, only the dominant girls, not the dominant boys, acted cooperatively. However, sometimes women describe themselves as acting cooperatively even when they are acting nearly as competitively as men are (Stockard, Van de Kragt, & Dodge, 1988). Especially after adolescence, females may dislike competition more often than males do because winning means that someone else will have to lose, which is inconsistent with the stereotype of the ideal female held by their male peers (Curry & Hock, 1981).

Adolescent females will sometimes deliberately become less competitive when playing with male opponents who are less skilled than they are at some game (Cronin, 1980; Weisfeld, Weisfeld, & Callaghan, 1982). Often the females may be unaware of what they are doing. Even among adults, although males report that they may frequently "play dumb" in front of bosses and coworkers, females are more likely to say they "play dumb" in front of husbands and boyfriends (Gove, Hughes, & Geerken, 1980). Only women, not men, who compete successfully against the opposite sex seem to get tense and nervous (Morgan & Mausner, 1973).

Effects of competition. Competition can have different effects on task motivation in the two sexes. Boys may be more motivated by competition per se, especially competition at which they have been successful (Weinberg & Jackson, 1979; Weinberg & Ragan, 1979). Using Spence's measure of mastery motivation, only in boys was mastery directly related to enjoyment of competition; in girls, mastery was related to math ability, teachers' support for them, and the girls' degree of support for women working (Farmer, 1985).

Frankenhaeuser and her colleagues have demonstrated that the sexes have different physiological responses to competitive situations.[12] Men show higher levels of adrenaline, suggesting greater arousal levels.[13] The more men's adrenaline increases during competitive stress, such as taking an important examination, the better they tend to do. Women's changes in adrenaline are unrelated or negatively related to their performances. One group of women who got high scores on an important examination had their adrenaline levels increase just as did males—but these females, unlike the high-scoring males, had low levels of self-esteem.

Despite getting higher grades, women are more likely to drop out at all stages of higher education (Berg & Ferber, 1983; Widnall, 1988). Reactions to competition are part of the cause. Widnall (1988) pointed out:

> *Men often feel comfortable with a communication style that seeks to reduce one of the protagonists to rubble in the course of a scientific discussion. After the storm is over, they quickly forget about the incident. For many women this style of interaction is unacceptable, either as giver or receiver. A women student may take weeks or months to recover from such an interchange, and it may contribute to a permanent loss of self-esteem. Women report that a process in which points are won at the expense of putting someone else down is to them an unacceptable mode of scientific debate. (pp. 1744–1745)*

Women are more likely than men to suffer when exposed to a competitive school or work environment. In a medical school program, the more competitive the atmosphere was perceived to be by a female student, the lower were her grade point average and her score on the medical boards tests. The relationships were in the opposite direction for males (Inglehart & Brown, 1988; Inglehart, Nyquist, Brown, &

Moore, 1987). Fewer female than male psychology professors reported that they were able to ignore a rude editorial rejection of a research paper that had been submitted for possible publication (Boice, Shaughnessy, & Pecker, 1985). If having males around creates a competitive environment, and that environment has more detrimental effects on females, this could explain why single-sex schooling improves the achievements of female students relative to coeducational schooling (Lee & Bryk, 1986).

Competitiveness may more often benefit males. Spence and her colleagues found that although scores on their scale of competitiveness are only weakly associated with college grade point average, the association is significant and positive only for males (Spence, Helmreich, & Pred, 1987). Small but facilitating effects of competitiveness for males also showed up in business persons' salaries and in the number of publications that professional psychologists had (Spence & Helmreich, 1983).

Task Preferences and Peer versus Adult Orientation

Sex differences in task preferences can create differences in environments with potentially large developmental implications. Some researchers looked at what activities children chose during their free-play periods at school and found that females liked structured activities more than males did (Carpenter & Huston-Stein, 1980; Huston & Carpenter, 1985; Huston et al., 1986). **Structured activities** are those in which there are adult-provided rules, guidelines, or suggestions about what should be done. Adults can provide structure by verbal feedback or by modeling ways of performing an activity. A given activity may be either low or high in structure, depending on whether an adult is interacting with the children who are engaging in the activity.

The greater female preference for structure is visible from age 2½ to at least age 7 and does not depend on the nature of the task per se. The

researchers found that an activity such as art might be a high structure activity in one classroom yet a low-structure activity in another classroom. Regardless of what the activity was, there were always more girls than boys in high-structure activities, and more boys than girls in low-structure activities. Females also displayed a greater preference for structure in a daycare camp setting.

The reason for the sex difference may be boys' competitiveness. According to Maccoby's review (1990) of research done by Greeno and by Powlishta in Maccoby's laboratory, the reason for the female preference for structure is related to boys' competitiveness and dominance attempts. In the presence of an adult, boys are less like to dominate girls. Therefore, girls stay close to the teacher for "protection." By doing so, girls therefore engage in more highly structured activities.

Once engaged in the activities, by preference or by experimental assignment, the sexes react the same way to the structure level. In high-structure activities, both sexes are oriented toward adults — making bids for adult recognition, seeking adult help, and complying with the adult's requests — and show only low rates of peer interactions. Children engaged in low-structure acctivities are peer oriented — directing high rates of leadership and other social behaviors to peers rather than to adults. Novel (creative?) forms of play also occurred more often in low-structure activities. Since girls engage more often in high-structured activities and boys in low-structured activities, girls will have more practice in fitting into adults' structures, whereas boys will have more practice in creating their own structures. Boys practice taking the initiative, planning and creating structures, whereas girls practice conforming and fitting into the structures provided by others.

Social Comparison Processes

One part of academic life is being compared with the performances of peers. Estimates of one's own ability depend on the outcome of that comparison. Although both sexes engage in social comparisons, the outcome tends to have dimorphic effects perhaps because comparisons of grades in school versus performances on standardized academic achievement tests produce the opposite sex differences. Females of all ages and in all kinds of classes tend to get higher grades than males do (e.g., Burke, 1989), but males tend to get higher scores on standardized tests of mathematics and science (see Chapter 14). The types of motivation involved with getting high grades in a college classroom are not the same as those associated with a high SAT score (Wentzel, 1989). For example, concerns with social responsibility (feminine) predicted grade point average but not SAT scores, whereas SAT scores were better predicted by reported attempts to try to be better than others (competition: masculine).

Sex differences.   In one study, children from ages 5½ to 10 were watched while spontaneously making social comparisons in a classroom (Frey & Ruble, 1985, 1987). Girls were more likely to make self-critical comments and to praise peers' efforts and achievements than were boys. Girls sometimes attributed their poor performances on school tasks to lack of ability, but boys never did.[14] More specifically, girls are more likely than boys to attribute failures in math and science to lack of ability, whereas boys are more likely than girls to attribute successes in those areas to having ability (Ryckman & Peckham, 1987).

Veroff (1969) described sex differences in the development of achievement motives that depended on the outcome of the social comparison processes. He claimed that males are more often able to successfully master social comparisons, thus developing a more independent achievement motivation. The male's advantage may be due to greater socialization for independence prior to entering school. Girls' socialization for conformity to adults and so to social cues provided by those adults could

also be a factor, with boys reacting more negatively to conformity pressures, especially when applied by an adult. It is interesting how many of Veroff's hypotheses have been confirmed by the recent data cited above.

On certain tasks, males have a higher expectancy for future success than do females, and when given a choice, males also are more likely to select the more difficult task to perform.[15] Females are more likely to underrate their ability levels when "real" ability ratings are derived from teachers' ratings of competence than when the ability ratings come from scores on standardized tests. After having experienced both successes and failures, females' estimates of future successes are more adversely affected by the failures than are those of males. Since life is always a mixture of successes and failures, this sex difference has extensive implications.

Sex differences are more common in tasks for which children have no past experiences on which to base estimates of their own abilities. For kindergarten children, school is novel, and males have higher expectancies than do females. Math may continually change—division is different from addition, and both differ from calculus and algebra. Math may therefore present repeated novelties to students. Females tend to have lower expectancies in this area. People who have low expectancies for their performances tend to attribute task failures to lack of ability, which leads to a downward spiral.

Women in management or in graduate schools also have lower levels of self-confidence (Berg & Ferber, 1983; Fiorentine, 1987, 1988a; White, De Sanctis, & Crino, 1981; Widnall, 1988). This probably accounts for another part of females' lower persistence rates. Among undergraduate college students interested in science and engineering careers, the more ability the students perceived themselves to have with regard to the required coursework, the higher the students' grades and the more likely the students were to continue with those career plans in later years (Lent, Brown, & Larkin, 1984).

Bright, high-achieving females. The brightest girls may be the most likely to have low aspirations and low estimates of their own ability levels (Dweck, 1986; Peterson, 1987; Rauste-von Wright et al., 1981; Tapasak, 1990). High-achieving girls may have lower expectancies for future successes than do low- or average-achievement girls (Crandall, Katovsky & Preston, 1962; Stipek & Hoffman, 1980). In fact, girls' expectations of task successes may actually be negatively related to their actual intelligence scores. Among boys, the less able children are most likely to have their performances adversely affected by having material irrelevant to solving a problem also presented. But among girls, it was the intellectually most able ones who were disrupted (Licht & Dweck, 1984).

Peterson (1987) found that girls in the seventh grade who were the most academically successful were also the ones most likely to report a poor self-image or to be depressed. If the girls decreased their academic achievements, particularly in the areas of math and science, their depression and self-image tended to improve. Probably because of all this, the more intelligent men were as children, the more their IQ scores increased in later years. For women, the more intelligent they had been, the less they gained in later years (Kangas & Bradway, 1971).

WORK ENVIRONMENT

Since women and men have systematically different kinds of jobs, they experience different kinds of job environments.

Income Differentials

A major part of the sex difference in work environments is the pay differential. Almost 50 percent of children living in single-parent homes with their mothers live in poverty (Bane & Ellwood, 1989).

Some data showing sex differences in pay are presented in Table 12.5. When job categories are taken into account, women earn from 51.2 to 73.4 percent of what men do, except for laborers and service workers, with the pay differential decreasing from 1981 to 1990. On study looked at the pay of male versus female administrators in a university that practiced affirmative action policies (Sigelman, Milward, & Shepard, 1982). Even when controlling for job level, experience, and the amount of responsibility required by the job, men still earned $2,000 more per year than did women. Most recently, *Science* (1991) published data on the median annual salaries of employed Ph.D. scientists and engineers. The gap between males' and females' salaries varied from $15,800 per year (medical scientists) to $7,000 per year (psychologists). When males and females were equated for years of professional experience, the wage gap was present at all levels, and even tended to increase with greater numbers of years of experience.

The wage gap in the United States has several components (U.S. Bureau of the Census, 1991; U.S. Department of Labor, 1983). Education level and measures of attachment to the labor force (e.g., absenteeism, plans to quit a job) account for only a very small part of it. In a nine-nation study on sex and earnings (Treiman & Roos, 1983), the wage gap was found in all countries and was not due to sex differences in job prestige or education. Instead, a person's education and occupational prestige contributed more to men's than to women's income, just as they do in the United States. Furthermore, according to government statistics, 54.6 percent of white men versus 35.6 percent of white women have the uninterrupted, continuous pattern of employment that is associated with higher wages (the sex ratio is the same among African Americans) (U.S. Department of Labor, 1983). Only 2.8 percent of white men versus 11.8 percent of white women had at least five distinct working/nonworking periods in their lives.

Job segregation is also a very important part

TABLE 12.5 *Median Earnings of Year-Round Full-Time Civilian Workers, by Occupation Group and Sex (Persons 15 Years of Age and Over)*

Occupation Group	Women	Men	Dollar Gap	Women's Earnings as a Percent of Men's	Percent Men's Earnings Exceeded Women's
1981*					
Total	$12,001	$20,260	$ 8,259	59.2	68.8
Professional and technical workers	16,523	26,544	10,021	62.2	60.6
Managers and administrators	14,979	26,856	11,877	55.8	79.3
Sales workers	11,353	22,169	10,816	51.2	95.3
Clerical workers	11,703	17,310	5,607	67.6	47.9
Craft and kindred workers	13,212	20,659	7,447	64.0	56.4
Operatives, including transport	10,316	17,159	6,843	60.1	66.3
Laborers (except farm)	10,414	15,098	4,684	69.0	45.0
Service workers (except private household	8,162	11,472	3,310	71.1	40.6
1990**					
Total	$19,816	$27,866	$ 8,050	71.1	40.6
Managers and administrators	25,861	40,573	14,712	63.7	56.9
Sales workers	16,986	29,652	12,666	57.3	74.6
Clerical workers	18,477	26,186	7,709	70.6	41.7
Craft and kindred workers	18,739	26,510	7,771	70.7	41.5
Transportation	16,003	24,550	8,547	55.6	53.4
Laborers (not including farming, forestry, and fishing	13,650	18,378	4,728	74.3	34.6
Service workers (except private household)	12,285	18,566	6,281	66.2	51.1

Source: From Women's Bureau, U.S. Department of Labor. Reprinted by permission.

*Current Population Reports, P-60, No. 134, U.S. Department of Commerce, Bureau of the Census.

**U.S. Bureau of the Census (1991). *Money, income of households, families, and persons in the United States: 1990.* Washington, DC: U.S. Government Printing Office (pp. 106 & 107).

of the gender gap. Women are disproportionately confined to the lower-paying jobs both at the level of professional subspecialties and at the level of job titles across employers. Feminine jobs, regardless of title, pay less (Blau, 1982; Borker, 1987; England, 1979; Gutek, 1988). The fewer females there are in a given level of the occupation, the lower the salary of females compared to males at that level. As Smith (1984) has pointed out, most of the new jobs available to the recent flood of women into the marketplace were in the services sector, such as fast-food restaurants, that have very low wages.

Job Segregation

Women's roles in the marketplace have undergone dramatic changes during the last couple of decades (Briggs, 1987). The percent of women working has increased from 33.9 percent in 1950 to 54.4 percent in 1986. Women constituted about 45 percent of the civilian labor force in 1986, and this percentage should increase to 47 percent in 1995. The rise in women's participation in the labor force is particularly marked for mothers (Hayghe, 1986). In polls of women, 52 percent in 1974, versus 63 percent in 1985, say that combining marriage, career, and children is the best alternative for a satisfying and interesting life (Wilkins & Miller, cited by Borker, 1987).

Women have also made impressive gains in jobs traditionally designated as masculine (Beller, 1985). For example, the proportion of doctorates in science and engineering given to women increased from 7 percent in 1965 to 23 percent in 1980 (Vetter, 1981). However, fewer students got science and engineering degrees in 1987 than in 1985, and this included fewer women (Vetter, 1989). The percent of medical school applicants who are women increased from 9 percent in 1965/1966 to 35.1 percent in 1985/1986 (Wilson, 1987). In 1991, 29.1 percent of the medical scientists were female (Holden, 1991).

Despite all this, jobs still remain segregated. Although government statistics indicate declining job segregation (see Beller, 1985), the actual job segregation is hidden in the kind of statistics used and published by the government in two ways (Baron, Davis-Blake, & Bielby, 1986; Bielby & Baron, 1986; Gutek, 1988; Presser, 1987):

1. Some jobs that are entirely male in one corporation are entirely female in another; these differences are averaged out in the aggregate statistics.
2. Even within a given corporation, careers that are considered the same by the government are divided into sections by the corporation, with each section within the company getting a different job title, and all being gender segregated.

In fact, jobs are often highly segregated. In one study, researchers randomly dialed and interviewed working men and women; 72 percent of men and 60 percent of women worked in jobs surrounded mostly by members of their own sex (Gutek, 1988). At the level of job titles, only 8 percent of workers in one sample of 290 businesses in California (the study was done between 1964 and 1979) shared titles with members of the opposite sex. In another sample of civil service personnel in California (done at the end of 1984), 66 percent of the state jobs were perfectly segregated (Bielby & Baron, 1986). In still another sample of 100 establishments (with the data gathered between 1965 and 1979), of the 1,071 jobs with two or more workers in them, only 73 had both males and females (Baron et al., 1986).

The sexes often have different types of jobs or careers within the same professions (Gutek, 1988). Male and female physicians have different specialty choices and have different kinds of practices (Maheaux et al., 1988; Weisman et al., 1986; Wilson, 1987). Among people with a Ph.D. in psychology, less than 15 percent of cognitive, comparative, engineering, industrial/organizational, and psychopharmacology degree holders are females, whereas 30 percent or more of developmental, general, and school psychology degree holders are females. Male psychologists are more likely to work in business and governments (15.1 percent female) and females are more commonly seen in school settings (Russo et al., 1981). Salaries are lower in school settings: $63,100 versus $53,100 (Holden, 1991). This can explain at least part of the income gap.

Why Are Jobs Segregated?

There are several possible answers to the question of why jobs are segregated.

Socialization.   Socialization factors are of major importance. One excellent review can be found in Marini and Brinton (1982). The most important factors mentioned by that review, and some of their implications, are given here.

Many jobs are perceived as being either masculine or feminine. Table 12.6 compares the results of a 1975 and a 1990 study concerning the sex typing and status rankings of various occupations (Evans-Rhodes, Murrell, & Dietz, 1990). Occupational stereotypes have changed little over the years, although the job of teacher did become gender neutral. Female subjects also saw masculine occupations to be more gender neutral than males did. Both masculine and neutral occupations are rated as having higher status than feminine occupations; both the former types of jobs also tend to command higher salaries.[16] In other research, occupations rated low in prestige and power were also feminine (cheerleader, housecleaner, secretary, etc.) (O'Connor, 1982).

These stereotypes do affect children. Girls who perceive that many occupations are limited to one sex have stronger preferences for feminine careers (Lavine, 1982). Even though boys' estimates about which occupations were "best" corresponded to the occupations they had chosen for a male stimulus figure, the same was not true of girls (Teglasi, 1981). Explicitly

teaching children about how both sexes can perform sex-typed jobs decreased the degree to which they stereotyped occupations, but did not affect their own, highly sex-typed occupational preferences (Bigler & Liben, 1990).

The sexes also differ in job values (Bridges, 1989; Betz & O'Connell, 1987; Fiorentine, 1988b). From 1969 to 1984, women have put increasing emphasis on status-achievement goals (e.g., being financially well-off), equalling the emphasis of men (Fiorentine, 1988b). However, in making their occupational choices, women continue to place more emphasis than men do on jobs that will allow them to help others (Bailyn, 1987; Betz & O'Connell, 1987; Bridges, 1989; Inglehart et al., 1987). Only women believe that sex discrimination and the opportunities a job offers for pursuing an interrupted career pattern, as described above, would be important to their decisions (Bridges, 1989). More males than females rank job prestige as being a very important, and more females than males rank job prestige as being one of the least important factors.

Table 12.7 summarizes some of the other developmental and sex-typing factors most consistently related to career socialization and choices. For example, women in masculine occupations are less likely to be married, rate being married and having children as being less important, and, if they do marry and have children, they do so later in life than do women in feminine occupations. Women who aspire to masculine jobs also tend to be more instrumental, have more educated parents, receive more encouragement from their fathers, and have fewer brothers. Marini and Brinton (1982) also pointed out that girls more often aspire to jobs that have lower status. They also pointed to the influence of parental expectations, parents as role models, the effects of teachers' and counselors' expectations, and the effects of stereotyping in the textbooks and on television, as well as the sex typing of toys. Also, parents may support the career goals of males more than those of females (Peterson et al., 1982).

TABLE 12.6   *Gender and Status Ratings of Occupations*

Job	1991 Ratings	Census Data*	Previous Ratings (Shinar '75)**	Perceived Status
Accountant	1.6	45.7	nr	3.3
Artist	2.1***	45.9	nr	2.9
Computers	1.7	36.6	3.4	3.2
Dentist	1.2	8.9	2.1	3.6
Engineer	1.4	6.9	1.9	3.6
Housewife	2.9	nr	nr	2.7
Insurance Sales	1.5	27.4	2.8	2.8
Lawyer	1.5	19.7	nr	3.8
Librarian	2.8	85.6	nr	2.5
Military	1.2	nr	nr	3.1
Minister	1.2****	46.6	nr	3.2
Nurse	2.9	95.1	6.6	3.2
Pharmacist	1.7	nr	3.0	3.5
Photographer	1.8	nr	nr	2.8
Physician	1.5	19.5	2.7	3.8
Psychologist	2.0	54.6	nr	3.4
Receptionist	2.8	97.5	nr	2.5
Social Worker	2.6	65.6	4.7	2.8
Teacher	2.3	73.6	5.6	3.1
Typist	2.8	94.6	nr	2.4
Veterinarian	1.7	nr	2.7	3.4
Writer	1.9	45.9	3.8	3.1

Source: From "Gender Stereotyping of Occupations: Is Women's Work Still Women's Work?" by D. Evans-Rhodes, A. Murrell, and B. Dietz. Poster presented at the Eastern Psychological Association at the 61st Annual Conference, April 1990. Adapted by permission.

   Prior occupational gender ratings taken from Shinar (1975).

   Gender ratings from Shinar are 1 = masculine, 4 = neutral, 7 = feminine.

   Current gender ratings are 1 = masculine, 2 = neutral, 3 = feminine.

   *Occupations not listed in current U.S. Census data are represented by "nr." 1987 Census Data reflects the percentage of *females* in each occupation.

   **Occupations not rated in the Shinar (1975) study are represented by "nr."

   ***Percentages reflect global category: Writers, Artists, Entertainers, & Athletes.

   ****Percentages reflect global category: Social, Recreation, & Religious Workers.

Prejudice/discrimination. Economics and competition are major factors. By identifying jobs as feminine and hiring only women, employers can often pay lower salaries and still get workers, as there are more workers than jobs. As Taylor and Lobel (1989) pointed out, negative reactions to outgroups (e.g., negative reactions of men to women) are particularly likely under conditions of threat, or when the person's self-esteem or social status is low. Men have a vested interest in restricting the access of women to the men's types of jobs (Miller & Labovitz, 1975). There are also fewer promotion opportunities in feminine than in masculine

TABLE 12.7 *Occupational Socialization*
Socialization of occupational preferences and choices: A description of some of the major factors involved.

Socialization Factors	References
Instrumentality and Expressiveness	
Adolescent females who were high in I (PAQ) had higher educational and occupational aspirations	Holmes & Esses, 1988
College women in engineering and management were higher in I and lower in E (PAQ & BSRI) than women in home economics or secretarial training.	Jones & Lamke, 1985; Strange & Rea, 1983; Sztaba & Colwill, 1988
Vocational Identity (having "a clear and stable picture of one's goals, interests and talents") was positively associated with I (PAQ) in both sexes; competitiveness was negatively related to vocational interest in females.	Grotevant & Thorbecke, 1982
In college males, E (BSRI) was positively related to the amount of household work done by father; in females, E was negatively related to the household work of father and positively related to maternal employment.	De Fronzo & Boudreau, 1979
Math efficacy scores positively related to I (BSRI).	Betz & Hackett, 1983
Family versus Career Values	
Adolescent females with high commitment to marriage and family had lower educational and occupational aspirations.	Holmes & Esses, 1988
Women's attitudes toward the ability to combine careers with childrearing predicted their own career aspirations and expectations.	Lyson & Brown, 1982
High school females were more likely to anticipate conflict between children and career (83%) than were males (58%); when asked how concerned they were over the conflict, 75% of the males said they were not concerned at all, but 42% of the females expressed great concern; a majority of the females planned to withdraw from the labor force when their children were young.	Archer, 1985
Plans to combine family with career affected career planning of females but not males; conflict was greater in women who perceived that others had traditional (stereotypic) expectations of them.	Tipping & Farmer, 1991
College females with high educational aspirations planned to defer marriage and children.	Zuckerman, 1980
When asked why they might in later life have to change a chosen career, males more often mentioned starting their own business and changing jobs; females more often mentioned getting married and having children— and these responses in females were *not* related to the prestige ratings of their chosen career.	Feather & Said, 1983

(continued)

TABLE 12.7 *(continued)*

Socialization Factors	References
Family/career conflicts were common in dual-employed couples and negatively affected the education and career of the wife more often than of the husband; however, these conflicts may *not* account for the lower research productively of female compared to male scientists; conflicts and depression for wife can be eased if husband helps with childcare and if stable childcare arrangements are available.	Bailyn, 1987; Cole & Zuckerman, 1987; Etzion, 1988; Goldscheider & Waite, 1981; Heckman, Bryson, & Bryson, 1977; Ross & Mirowsky, 1988
Among female scientists, both being childless and having children under 10 years of age decreased productivity; the same two variables had little effect on males productivity; women with children more than 10 years of age were as productive in publication frequency as were married men with children.	Kyvik, 1990
Questionnaire items related to the perceived value of parenting were the ones most strongly related to career choices in young women.	Jensen, Christensen, & Wilson, 1985
Males were positive than females toward the idea of wives not working and toward the idea of wives taking full responsibility for childcare; high E females (BSRI) were less positive than high I females toward having full responsibility for child rearing.	Allgeier, 1981

People in Sex-Atypical Occupations or Majors

College women majoring in engineering had lower self-esteem than women in home economics, especially if those women were high in I (PAQ).	Jones & Lamke, 1985
Nontraditional females were higher in I, parental education, foreign ancestry, family stability, being first-born, maternal employment, and paternal encouragement, and had fewer brothers, compared to females in traditionally feminine occupations or majors.	Lemkau, 1979 (review)
Females were higher in I (PAQ & BSRI) if they preferred or were interested in male-dominated occupations.	Feather & Said, 1983; Jones & Lamke, 1985; Strange & Rea, 1983; Sztaba & Colwell, 1988
Nontraditional males had lower I (BSRI), did more household tasks, had more distant fathers and more employed mothers, had more often experienced parental death or divorce, were members of racial minorities and/or lower SES, were less satisfied with jobs, and were less likely to be or to have been married, compared to males in male-dominated occupations.	Lemkau, 1984

TABLE 12.7   *(continued)*

Socialization Factors	References
Atypical female job applicants considered being married and having children as less important, perceived families as being more compatible with careers, planned on getting married and having children later in life, and more often had supportive boyfriends, compared to female applicants for female-typical jobs.	Baber & Monaghan, 1988; Betz & O'Connell, 1987; Bruns-Hillman, 1980; Fuchs, 1986; Gutek, 1988 (review); Ruggiero & Weston, 1988; Trigg & Perlman, 1976
Nontraditional females got higher scores on competitiveness scales.	Bruns-Hillman, 1980; Sztaba & Colwill, 1988
In male-dominated occupations, females had lower self-confidence than males did; more in females than in males: self-confidence positively related to success in lives outside of work and negatively related to perceived opportunities to gain technical job expertise.	Bailyn, 1987
Sex-atypical females perceived their mothers to have had more power in decision making in their families.	Lavine, 1982

Models

Females were less likely to have atypical occupational aspirations or be in male-dominated careers if they had more brothers.	Abrams, Sparkes, & Hogg, 1985; Grotevant, 1978; Lemkau, 1979 (review)
Having had a same-sex high school science teacher increased commitment to science career.	Stake & Granger, 1978
The fewer female models they had seen in male-dominated occupations, the less ability that females thought they would have in those occupations.	Matsui, Ikeda, & Ohnishi, 1989
When using slides of people performing various types of jobs to assess occupational interests in students from grades 5–11, gender of model used affected stated preferences.	Tétreau & Traham, 1988

Self-Efficacy
(Task Confidence or Ability Self-Estimates)

Males in 8th and 9th grades and college males, in both the U.S. and Japan, had equal self-efficacy for 10 female and 10 male occupations; females had higher self-efficacy for traditional female than for traditional male occupations; ACT scores did not predict number of occupations that college females had considered, but math ACT scores did predict the number of male-dominated occupations that had been considered by males.	Betz & Hackett, 1981; Matsui et al., 1989; Post-Kammer & Smith, 1985
Self-confidence in math tasks (problems, courses) was higher for college males than for college females.	Betz & Hackett, 1983

(continued)

TABLE 12.7   *(continued)*

Socialization Factors	References
Self-efficacy ratings in various sex-typed occupations were strongly related to occupational preferences among both young men and young women.	Janman, 1987
Self-estimates of general ability were positively related to self-estimates of math ability only among male—not female—college students; male and female students had equal self-assessment of math ability, but scholastic ability scores predicted math-related career aspirations only in females; math confidence predicted self-efficacy ratings for male-dominated occupations only in females.	Matsui et al., 1989; Singer & Stake, 1986

Notes: BSRI = Bem Sex Role Inventory; PAQ = Personal Attributes Questionnaire (Spence); I = instrumentality; E = expressiveness; SES = socioeconomic status

jobs (Baron et al., 1986). In one study, in 73.3 percent of the women's jobs that had promotion opportunities, the superordinate jobs included only men. In another 10 percent of those jobs, the superordinate jobs included only women. This minimizes competition with and for men.

Sometimes as the number of women in a masculine job increases, the men's hostility toward them also increases, as though the men were reacting negatively to the increased competition (Zimmer, 1988). Among university faculty women in Israel, the lower the proportion of women in a given scientific field, the more likely that the academic ranks of the sexes would be equivalent (Toren & Kraus, 1987). In a large federal bureaucracy, the higher the rank of the male, the more support he reports receiving from other men; the higher the rank of the women, the less support she receives from men (South et al., 1987). Among steel workers threatened by layoffs, only men whose wives were employed supported the hiring of women (Livingstone & Luxton, 1989).

Women are more often subjected to and negatively affected by sexual harassment on the job (Gutek & Cohen, 1987; Gutek &

Dunwoody, 1987). Women feel uncomfortable and have to quit the job to get away from the harassment, or they pay the price in terms of stress-induced decreases in productivity. Men's responses to the rare harassment they receive are often humorous ("There was this little blond who had the hots for me").

Discrimination also occurs at the time of hiring. Several studies have shown how women can be discriminated against, particularly when applying for masculine jobs (Fidell, 1970; Firth, 1982; Levinson, 1976; Nieva & Gutek, 1980; Chapter 11). Laboratory studies of sexual discrimination have emphasized that males are most likely to display discrimination if they expect to have to work with the person they pick (Hagen & Kahn, 1975; Nieva & Gutek, 1980). This is, of course, the case in the real world.

Affirmative action policies can also have negative effects. Some subjects (college students) were told that they had been selected to be the leader of a certain group because they had high levels of skill on some task. Others were told that because "too few" women or men had been tested, they were "picked" to be leaders to "balance" the study (Heilman, Simon, & Repper, 1987). Men were not affected by the manipulation. But "affirmative action" women, compared to other women, had lower perceptions of their leadership abilities, took less credit for successful outcomes, and were less interested in being leaders at another time.

Ability/trait congruence. Employers may believe that some jobs require certain sex-limited abilities or traits (Mellon, Crano, & Schmitt, 1982; O'Connor, 1982; Chapter 11). Table 12.7 also presents data showing that students' self-efficacies in sex-typed areas affect their job aspirations. When Bielby and Baron (1986) evaluated ability and trait job requirements as possible reasons for job segregation, they found that women were most likely to be excluded from certain jobs. Characteristics of those jobs included: (1) required heavy lifting; (2) did not require finger dexterity, verbal aptitude, or clerical skills; (3) had long training requirements; (4) required spatial skills or eye/hand/foot coordination; and (5) were in companies with unions. Actual sex differences in these areas are much too small to support the observed levels of sex segregation, so factors such as socialization or discrimination must be more important.

Integration of career and family. Women believe that they should have (should want to have?) major responsibilities for child-rearing chores and so plan for careers that minimize job-family conflicts (Baber & Monaghan, 1988). Men are not as concerned with these conflicts in their career planning.

As pointed out in Table 12.7, job-family conflicts affect women's careers more often than those of men. Employers prefer men for jobs requiring extensive training (Bielby & Baron, 1986) because they are aware that females more often have interrupted job patterns. Females in male-dominated careers are less likely to have children and have fewer children. Although both sexes in demanding careers are equally heavily invested and involved in their work, women in those same

careers also invest heavily in their families (Spence & Helmreich, 1983). Success in work and in family are compatible for male engineers, but there is a conflict for female engineers (Etzion, 1988).

Females may pick sex-typed occupations, at least in part, because they perceive those kinds of careers to be more compatible with interruptions for child rearing. Stewart (1980) did a longitudinal study of young women who graduated from a prestigious New England women's college. Of the women who had careers (114), 55 percent had interrupted careers. The best predictor of interrupted versus continuous careers, and of masculine versus feminine careers, was the presence of children. Polacheck (1976, 1978, 1979, 1981) suggested that feminine jobs suffer less loss of pay from interruptions than do masculine jobs. Although England (1984) could find no evidence for this, the job categories she used combined masculine and feminine subspecialties. When two specific jobs were compared (librarian and MBA), job interruptions did have a more negative effect on the salaries of women in business than on the salaries of librarians (Olson, Frieze, & Detlefsen, 1990). Furthermore, a recent study by Jacobson and Levine (1992) found that women who interrupted their careers for child rearing had lower salaries than those of their women peers who had never left their jobs, even 20 years after the interruption.

Moreover, some effect of interruption could be at the level of expectancies. As long as women perceive that their status would suffer less from interruptions in feminine than in masculine jobs, compared to other people in the same jobs with continuous careers, they might chose feminine jobs out of a desire to avoid being "second-class citizens" among their coworkers. As Table 12.7 documents, combining children with a career is a prominent focus in most females' career planning. Farmer has developed a way to measure home-career conflict and its effects in women (Tipping & Farmer, 1991), which should be of use in further explorations of the effects of child-rearing expectations.

SUMMARY

Males and females are exposed to gendered environments from birth to death. Whether a child's behavior — such as assertion/aggression, for example — is reinforced, punished, or ignored by peers, parents, and teachers depends on the child's gender. Adults also supply different toys for boys and girls, and peers react differentially to toy play based on the child's gender. The behaviors of same-sex models are also gendered. Relevant data come from the effects of father absence, maternal employment, paternal versus maternal child care, and the division of household chores between the parents. Women who had employed mothers are more likely to have sex-atypical career aspirations, and the women who had many brothers are more likely to have sex-typical aspirations.

If the environment is gendered, the sexes will be getting systematically different practice on various skills. This would include intimate social interactions for females, versus the egoistic dominance and competitive interactions for males. The sex differences in toy play and peer interactions may predict sex differences in social and task skill acquisition. The differences in job environments — lower pay and fewer promotion opportunities for women's than for men's jobs — elicit different work behaviors.

Even if the environment is not gendered per se, it may still elicit gender-differentiated responses. Males and females may respond in systematically different fashions to competition and to social comparison, and may have different preferences for structured versus unstructured tasks. Because most women still believe that they will have the major responsibility for any children they have, women's and men's careers will remain different. In these last examples, only a change of the environment will change the outcome. Perhaps it is the case that

men spend too much time on their jobs (and not enough time with their families) rather than women spending too little time. Maybe instead of female scientists not publishing often enough, male scientists publish too much, with detrimental consequences for both the quality of research and the quality of family lives.

ENDNOTES

1. Girls were labeled by having clothes that were pink, yellow, ruffled, and puffy-sleeved. Boys wore blue and/or red.

2. Non-sex-typed fathers emphasized achievement more than sex-typed fathers did.

3. In many societies, parental inheritance goes preferentially to sons.

4. In a later study, some other effects of early versus late gender labeling were not replicated, except for a trend for early labelers to have more gender-related knowledge (Hoyt, Leinbach, & Fagot, 1991).

5. Two-thirds of the feminine boys were reinterviewed as adults, and 75 percent were homosexual or bisexual; treatment of the feminine behavior in childhood had no effect on the adult sexual outcome, but treated boys had higher self-concepts (Green, 1987).

6. This attitude reflects an internal **locus of control;** people who have an external locus of control tend to feel that other people are in control of their lives instead of they themselves being in control.

7. As measured by the It scale for children.

8. On the other hand, the wife's outside employment had little effect on her becoming involved in the masculine household tasks — they remained his.

9. In Blakemore's research, 3-year-old girls significantly prefer girls' toys only when they are first asked to label the same toys.

10. However, the linkage may not be direct: when girls who had been exposed to different levels of prenatal hormones were tested later in life, they not only got higher spatial scores but they also preferred more masculine types of toys as children. However, toy preferences were *not* directly related to spatial scores: both were independently associated with prenatal hormonal levels (see Chapter 14).

11. However, in the United States, parental expectations depend on socioeconomic status (SES): middle-class mothers actually had higher math expectations of their daughters than of their sons. Also, regardless of SES, high maternal expectations led to higher mathematics performances only in sons, not in daughters (Baker & Entwisle, 1987: see their Table 1, pp. 684–685).

12. Bergman & Magnusson, 1979; Collins, 1985; Collins & Frankenhaeuser, 1978; Frankenhaeuser, 1982; Lundberg, de Château, Winberg, & Frankenhaeuser, 1981; Rauste-von Wright, von Wright, & Frankenhaeuser, 1981.

13. On the other hand, men and women are equally as physiologically aroused by having to take a 3-year-old child to the hospital for a checkup.

14. There is a possibility that girls were simply *saying* that they lacked ability and what they said did not correspond to their beliefs; they may only have been displaying public modesty rather than indicating a true lack of self-confidence.

15. Crandall, 1975; Frey & Ruble, 1985; Parsons et al., 1982; Hughes, Sullivan, & Beaird, 1986; Lippa & Beauvais, 1983; Lee, Hall, & Carter, 1983; Lenny, 1977; Parsons & Ruble, 1977; Stake, 1979; Veroff, 1969.

16. Using another measuring instrument, England (1979) found no difference in the prestige of sex-typed jobs; however, her calculations did not take into account the fact that several masculine and feminine subspecialities were combined into a given job category.

UNIT FOUR

SEX AND STATUS

The obsession of our species with sex and status will never be successfully explained in other than Darwinian terms, and this preoccupation will be found to underlie most (but not all) social phenomena.
—J. H. Barkow (1991, p. 301)

The two chapters of this last unit cover only a few of the many ways our species' preoccupation with sex and status may reveal itself, some of which are sexually dimorphic. Chapter 13 argues that the sexes sometimes seek different kinds of status. Males are more often concerned with **egoistic dominance,** which serves to maintain or increase one's own social status in some group. Women are more often concerned with **prosocial dominance,** which serves the purpose of influencing other people in a group while maintaining the social relationships within that group. Egoistic dominance has long been stereotypically associated with males. Between 1956 and 1982, little change had occurred in the degree to which adolescent males emphasized male dominance and female subordination in their sexual stereotypes (Lewin & Tragos, 1987).

The contrast between acts of egoistic versus prosocial dominance encompasses the difference between hierarchical status versus mutual influence. Concerns with egoistic dominance are concerns over one's relative social status within one's group, when status can be classified along a hierarchy from superior to subordinate. Orders, commands, and influence go predominately in one way: down the hierarchy. On the other hand, prosocial dominance involves having an impact on other people in one's groups. In this case, not only can one person affect another but the second person can, in turn, affect the first person's behaviors and beliefs. The influence exerted by prosocial dominance acts can be mutual as well as consistent with relatively egalitarian friendship bonds.

Chapter 13 describes the sex differences in dominance, and then goes on to describe what can happen to individuals who carry out these concerns to a maladaptively (for both the individual and the group) exaggerated degree. Acts of egoistic dominance, unleavened by a concern for the feeling of others, can lead to homicide.

Attempting to maintain social relationships without thought for one's own ego can lead to an affective disorder, such as clinical depression. As will be described, low-status males are more likely to commit murders, but, if anything, high-status women are more likely to develop affective disorders. Thus, much of Chapter 13 deals with sex differences in homicides and in the incidence of clinical depression, two of the largest and best documented gender-related differences in the human species.

Chapter 14 discusses two other possible manifestations of our obsession with sex and status. According to evolutionary theory, men seek high social status because, in the past, high status gave men increased access to females. Is there any evidence of this in the criteria we humans, male and female, use for selecting our mates? Gaining social status demands not only opportunities but also the relevant motives and skills. For example, becoming a dominant male is only one of several reproductive strategies open to male savanna baboons (Noë & Sluijter, 1990). Similarly, there are several strategies available to human males and females, depending on their motives, skills, and physical attributes. Among humans, having high levels of certain kinds of skills can lead to high-status jobs; this is true with regard to mathematical skills, which may be related to spatial skills. In fact, two of the best predictors of professional career development in young women are marriage and early motherhood (negative) and high levels of mathematical interests and abilities (positive) (Astin & Myint, 1971). Furthermore, spatial scores are highly correlated with school achievements (assessed with standardized test scores) in reading, math, and language, in both sexes (Thompson, Detterman, & Plomin, 1991).

Thus, Chapter 14 discusses gender-related differences in attitudes toward sexual behaviors, mate selection criteria, and performances on various kinds of spatial tasks. Interestingly, both sexual behaviors and spatial skills may covary with developmental rate in females, as measured by timing of puberty. Early maturing girls are more sexually active, more aggressive, and may have higher IQs, but the later maturing girls may tend to do better on at least some kinds of spatial tasks.

CHAPTER 13

PROSOCIAL VERSUS EGOISTIC DOMINANCE: MURDER VERSUS DEPRESSION?

INTRODUCTION
THE CONCEPT OF PERSONALITY
HOMICIDES
DEPRESSION
SUMMARY

> *For our present purposes, the most interesting thing about all-boy and all-girl groups [among children] is the divergence in the interactive styles that develop in them. In male groups, there is more concern with issues of dominance . . . [and] among boys, speech serves largely egoistic functions and is used to establish and protect an individual's turf. Among girls, conversation is a more socially binding process.*
> —E. E. Maccoby (1990, p. 516)

> *There is no doubt that, across cultures, girls get more practice in nurturance and prosocial dominance, boys in egoistic dominance and challenge.*
> —B. Whiting and C. P. Edwards (1988, p. 278)

Depression: Nancy Andreasen (1987) found that of 30 writers attending a prestigious workshop, 80 percent had some history of depressive disorder, compared to 30 percent of a comparison group. The most common disorder was manic-depressive illness. Even the relatives of the writers more often had disorders.

Aggression: While writing this chapter, the authors were struck by two small articles appearing in the Saturday, March 3, 1990, Peoria Journal Star, *both taken from the AP wire service. One article was concerned with an incident from Grand Rapids, Michigan: "A man angry that his Social Security check was late wounded a postman and three passers-by in a 25-round barrage of shotgun fire, authorities said Friday." The article from Bartow, Florida, said: "The mother of a toddler who died after repeatedly being dunked head first into a toilet struck a deal with prosecutors Friday, pleading*

337

no contest to a second-degree murder charge. . . . [Two-year-old] Bradley died July 28 after he was dunked head first into a toilet for soiling his pants, authorities charge."

Depression and aggression are the major themes of this chapter. Women are more likely to become clinically depressed, but men are more likely to commit homicide. And when women do commit homicide, they are more likely than men to kill members of their personal families, such as their own children. Are these two gender-related differences in any way related to the sex differences in egoistic versus prosocial dominance?

INTRODUCTION

This chapter discusses gender-related differences in some personality characteristics. Gender differences per se are not emphasized; instead, the material presented in the earlier units is applied to demonstrations of how we can understand, explain, and change any gender-related difference. The first section looks at the concept of personality, including meta-analytic reviews of some sex differences. A common theme is sex differences in prosocial versus egoistic dominance.

Egoistic dominance and prosocial concerns, when exaggerated, can become pathological, turning into homicide and clinical depression, respectively (Buss, 1990; Lewis, 1985). The last two sections look at gender-related differences in homicide and in depression. However, nothing stated here should lead you to conclude that depression is in any sense a consequence of refraining from homicide; although the sexes differ in opposite ways on these two traits, the presence of one is never a necessary consequence of the absence of the other. Most people of both genders avoid both pathological consequences.

THE CONCEPT OF PERSONALITY

Before describing sex differences in personality, the concept of personality must be dis-

cussed. Following Spence's idea (Chapters 2 and 11) about what her Personal Attributes Questionnaire (PAQ) and Bem's Sex Role Inventory (BSRI) actually measure, this section will focus on the traits of instrumentality and expressiveness. Descriptions of prosocial and egoistic dominance are also presented.

Measuring Personality Traits

The **concept of personality** means being able to predict someone's future behaviors by knowing something about that person's traits and characteristics, especially interpersonal ones. If peoples' personalities are consistent across time, their future behaviors in specific situations can be predicted, based on their past behaviors in those situations. The concept of personality would be meaningful if we could use it to predict behaviors across different situations, including predicting "real-life" behaviors from test-taking behaviors (personality test scores). Any scale is an adequate measure of some personality trait to the extent that its scores can provide socially and interpersonally useful predictions of future behaviors.

Before continuing, three important concepts must be emphasized. First, by the very nature of science, one can probably never adequately predict the behaviors of an individual. Nevertheless, a scale would be valid if groups of people who differed in average trait-level scores also had different probabilities of engaging in certain behaviors. Second, the authors emulate Buss (Buss & Craik, 1983) in viewing personality as serving "descriptive and forecasting functions" (p. 106), but not as providing causal explanations. If scores on an aggressiveness scale predicted future aggressive acts, one could *not* explain the acts by saying the person was aggressive. One would have to search for an explanation elsewhere, by looking at the biological, developmental, and motivational covariates of both the behavioral acts and the personality test scores.

Third, people with certain personality characteristics and the situations in which they find themselves are not just passively or accidentally linked. This will affect how one looks at prediction. Buss (1987) described the active links that selection, evocation, and manipulation create between people and situations. **Selection** deals with people's choices of which situations to enter or leave. Individuals unintentionally elicit or **evoke** reactions from others. **Manipulation** refers to how people intentionally change their social environments by altering or exploiting the people in that environment. Thus, some environmental covariates of traits can occur because the individual creates that environment for himself.

Conceptualizing a personality trait. The cognitive revolution that occurred in psychology has changed how prediction from a personality trait is conceptualized (Carson, 1989; Pervin, 1985). David Buss used cognitive prototype theory (see Chapter 11) to define behavioral acts and traits (Buss, 1984a, 1984b, 1987b; Buss & Craik, 1983, 1985). Buss asked undergraduates to think of acts that would be more or less prototypical of the personality traits of agreeable, aloof, dominant, gregarious, quarrelsome, and submissive.[1] Each subject was asked to think of three same-sex people who were very high in one particular trait and then to write down the "five acts or behaviors they have performed that reflect or exemplify" that trait (Buss & Craik, 1983, p. 109).

After a list of 100 acts for each trait were generated, a second group of judges rated how good an example each one was. For example, "I picked a fight with the stranger at the party" was judged to be very prototypical of quarrelsomeness, but "I insisted upon doing the driving on the trip" was seen as much less prototypical. Then married people were asked to indicate, on two different occasions, how frequently each act had been performed both by themselves and by their spouses. When the acts within each disposition were aggregated, the stability across time (which is a type of predic-

tability) was .68 for self-ratings and .65 for ratings of spouses.

Relationships among traits. The organization among traits can be studied in several ways. Factor analyses can be performed on people's scale scores, after each person had taken many different personality trait tests (e.g., see Zuckerman, Kuhlman, & Camac, 1988). Category structure analysis can also be done. To do this, subjects could be given all possible pairs from a list of traits and asked to rate how similar to each other each possible pair is (e.g., White, 1980).

Wiggins' **circumplex model of personality traits** combined both techniques (Wiggins, 1979; Wiggins & Broughton, 1985; Wiggins & Holzmuller, 1978, 1981; Wiggins, Phillips, & Trapnell, 1989). The Figure 13.1 model is somewhat revised to make its relevance to instrumentality and expressiveness clearer. Wiggins selected and then factor analyzed traits to place them into a space defined by two independent trait dimensions: dominance versus submission; and nurturance/warmth versus hostile/cold. Each trait at each end of a dimension is measured by self-ratings on the associated adjectives. Traits at opposite ends of any line drawn through the center should be negatively correlated. For example, the more frequently someone displays dominant behavioral acts, the less frequently that person should display submissive acts. Traits close to each other on the circumference should be positively correlated — a warm person would also be gregarious and ingenuous. Traits at right angles to each other, such as dominance and warmth/nurturance, should be unrelated (independent).

In tests of this model, its ability to actually predict people's behaviors were confirmed (Buss & Craik, 1983; Gifford & O'Connor, 1987). Wiggins's model can also be related to other personality research (Trapnel & Wiggins, 1990). The five basic factors of personality found in other research (extroversion, agreeableness, conscientiousness, neuroticism, and openness

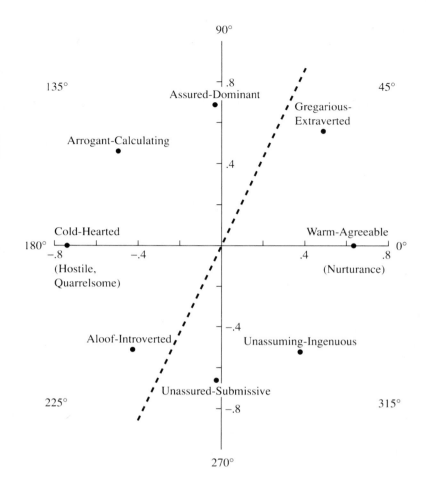

FIGURE 13.1 *The Circumplex Model of Personality*
In most studies, men score higher on the traits located above and to the left of the dotted diagonal line. Women score higher, on the average, on trait dimensions located below and to the right of that dotted diagonal. For example, women more often rate themselves as *warm* (feminine), and men more often rate themselves as *cold* (masculine).

Source: From "Circular Reasoning about Interpersonal Behavior" by J. S. Wiggins, 1989, *Journal of Personality & Social Psychology, 56,* p. 297. Copyright 1989 by the American Psychological Association. Reprinted by permission.

to experiences) can be viewed as related to, and an extension of, the two basic dimensions of the circumplex (dominance and nurturance).

In unselected samples of college students who rated themselves on the appropriate adjectives, sex differences were found for all traits (Paulhus, 1987; Wiggins & Holzmuller, 1978, 1981). Males got higher scores on all traits located above and to the left of the diagonal line. Females got higher scores on the other traits. The sex difference was largest for arrogant/calculating (in favor of males) and for ingenuous/assuming (in favor of females). Sex differences in extraversion and introversion are small.

Because of the reliable sex differences, Wiggins's model is a useful way to conceptualize gender-related differences in personality traits. The dominance and warmth/nurturance trait dimensions (instrumental and expressive) are the ones emphasized by the masculine (M) and feminine (F) scales found on the PAQ and on the BSRI. The overlap with the BSRI would be even greater if that scale measured just an M and an F factor. When Wiggins and Holzmuller eliminated three items from the M scale (athletic, individualistic, and masculine) and four items from the F scale (childlike, shy, flatterable, gullible), the correlation between dominant and M was .826 and the correlation between warmth and F was .892. According to Wiggins's model, Bern and Spence found M and F to be independent traits because the scale developers focused on dominance and warmth (see Chapter 2). Had they chosen dominance and submission, or warmth and quarrelsomeness, M and F would have been found to be bipolar opposites.

Cross-cultural research. The instrumentality/expressiveness circumplex also appears in other cultures. White (1980) found it when he analyzed personality trait names in three languages. Perhaps personality traits reflect basic interpersonal behaviors such as cooperation/conflict and dominance/submission. Williams and Best (1990) had people in 14 different countries rate themselves on over 200 different trait adjectives. The masculinity-femininity of a trait was measured by what proportion of males endorsed it: a score of 93 meant that 93 percent of the people who endorsed that trait as being characteristic of themselves were male. Traits with scores below 50 are therefore feminine. The authors compared the circumplex model to Williams and Best's results (Hoyenga & Hoyenga, 1993). Self-ratings on the traits found on the circumplex (or any trait that seemed to be a close synonym to a circumplex trait) were examined and the average masculinity score of that trait across the 14 different cultures was computed. Traits on the introversion-extroversion diagonal showed little sex differentiation, as predicted. For the other dimensions, as one moves from the lower right to the upper left, more males endorsed the trait, as predicted.

Meta-Analytic Studies

Eagly (1987; Eagly & Wood, 1991) suggested that the typical division of labor in most societies, women being assigned to child rearing, has shaped gender roles. Because of this, instrumentality and expressiveness traits appear not only in our gender stereotypes but also in our behaviors. Even when two fictitious groups of aliens were described to college students as "child raisers" versus "city workers," subjects allocated instrumental and expressive traits differentially to the two groups (Hoffman & Hurst, 1990).

Table 13.1 summarizes some meta-analytic studies of instrumental and expressive traits. Table 13.2 presents Hall's (1984) analysis of the relative sizes of sex differences, including some expressive and instrumental traits, for comparison. The first part of Table 13.2 describes traits that might be called instrumental; certainly they seem to reflect traits found above and to the left of the diagonal line of Figure 13.1.

Some instrumental and expressive behaviors. Males show more of all kinds of aggression (or else in the group of very aggressive people, there are more males than females). The effect sizes tend to be larger for children than for adults. Most of the adults were college students, and a college group might include relatively fewer of the very aggressive individuals than would a group of children. The effect sizes are largest in those situations in which fear of consequences or empathy for the victim's suffering would be expected; these characteristics inhibit aggression in females more than in males (Eagly & Steffen, 1986). The data also reflect, at least in part, a bias on the part of observers to rate males as more aggressive even when both sexes act the same way (Lyons & Serbin, 1986). Although males are also more active than females, Maccoby and Jacklin (1980) concluded that sex differences in aggression were not just an artifact of activity levels.

The sex differences in leadership described in Table 13.1 can be changed. For example, in one study, subjects watched one of two sets of TV commercials, depicting either competent or incompetent women (Geis, Boston, & Hoffman, 1985). Then the subjects interacted in mixed-sex groups to recommend solutions to a problem.[2] In the competent condition, male

TABLE 13.1 *Meta-Analytic Studies of Instrumental and Expressive Traits*

Area	Effect Sizes/Description	References
Aggression in children	$z = 5.776$ for physical aggression; $z = 5.342$ for verbal aggression	Maccoby & Jacklin, 1980
Aggression in adults	1. Effect size larger for laboratory than for field study (.35 vs. .21). 2. Effect size larger for physical than for psychological aggression (.40 vs. .18). 3. Effect size largest when only the experimenter or target was present, compared to being totally alone or being observed by several others (.38 vs. .17 & .21). 4. Effect size larger when aggression was the only response, compared to when choice among responses was allowed (.37 vs. .24). 5. More aggression directed toward men than toward women (sex of target effect size = .13). 6. No sex of author effect.	Eagly & Staffen, 1986
Aggression in both children adults	1. Effect size larger for subjects under age 6 than than for college students (.58 vs. .27). 2. Effects size larger for naturalistic than for laboratory studies (.56 vs. .29). 3. Effect size largest for projective tests, next largest for projective tests, next largest for peer reports, and smallest for self-reports of aggression (.86, .63, & .40). 4. More recent studies tend to have smaller effect sizes. 5. Effect sizes for types of aggression: physical + verbal .43 physical .60 verbal .43 fantasy .84 willingness to shock .39 imitative .49 hostility scale .02 other .43	Hyde, 1986
Activity level	1. Effect size for age of subject: prenatal .33 infant .29 preschool .44 older .64 2. Effect size also larger under low stress conditions, low restrictions, and presence of peers. 3. No effect of year of publication or sex of author.	Eaton & Enns, 1986
Social influence	1. In studies in which the male subjects are given the advantage ($n = 8$): 100% report males higher in power & prestige.	Lockheed, 1985a

TABLE 13.1   *(continued)*

Area	Effect Sizes/Description	References
	2. Studies in which sexes have equal skills ($n = 32$): 62% report males higher and 3.1% report females higher in power & prestige. 3. Female advantage studies ($n = 6$): 17.5% report males higher and 33.3% report females higher in power.	

Behavior in groups	1. Initiating structure (instrumental) $-.03$
	2. Consideration (expressive) $-.047$
	3. Subordinate satisfaction $-.079$
	4. Leadership effectiveness:
	  Laboratory setting $.246$
	  Field setting $.040$
		Dobbins & Platz, 1986

Group performance	1. Active task behavior $.58$ 2. Positive social behavior $-.58$ 3. Equality in division $-.10$ 4. Equity of rewards $.20$ 5. Smaller rewards for self $-.28$	Carli, 1982 (as cited by Hall, 1984)
	1. Overall, all male groups performed better than all female groups either as individuals within groups ($.38$) or collectively, comparing male to female groups ($.39$). 2. The presence of females facilitated performance of tasks requiring positive social activities (group performance, $-.58$). 3. Men's task orientation style slightly facilitated performance on tasks requiring that behavior (group performance, $.34$).	Wood, 1987
Leadership	1. Women adopt a more democratic leadership style, compared to men's more autocratic or directive style ($d = .20-.29$). 2. Authors tend to portray their own sex more favorably (sex of author effects). 3. Sex differences larger in more recent studies. 4. Sex differences tend to be larger in studies that used more reliable measures.	Eagly & Johnson (1990)
	1. Men tended to emerge as task leaders, especially in short-term groups, in groups carrying out tasks that did not require complex social interactions, and in groups with an equal number of men and women ($d = .41$, and 79% of the results were in this direction). 2. Women tended to emerge as social leaders ($d = .18$, and 87% of the results were in this direction). 3. Year of publication had no significant effect.	Eagly & Karau, 1991

(continued)

TABLE 13.1 *(continued)*

Area	Effect Sizes/Description			References
Conformity/ influence-ability	1. Overall:	$z =$	3.04	Cooper, 1979
	2. Group pressure	$z =$	4.03	
	3. Fictitious group norm:	$z =$	$-.91$	
	4. Persuasive communication	$z =$	1.10	
	1. Overall:	.26		Eagly & Carli, 1981
	2. Group pressure	.32		
	3. Persuasion	.16		
	4. Other	.28		
	5. Effect size larger for male authors but no effect of publication date.			
	1. Persuasion studies	.11		Becker, 1988
	[American subjects	.13		
	Foreign subjects	$-.04$]		
	2. Group pressure	.28		
	[American subjects	.29		
	Foreign subjects	.19]		
	3. Other	.13		
	4. Effect size larger for male authors, but this is confounded with large norm groups, longer tests, and stronger pressure.			
Decoding nonverbal cues	1. Visual	$-.32$		Hall, 1978
	2. Auditory	$-.18$		
	3. Both	-1.02		
	4. Total	$-.40$		
	5. Larger effect sizes seen in more recent studies.			
	1. PONS test		$-.41$	Hall, 1984, 1987
	2. All tests		$-.43$	
	3. Face recognition		$-.32$	
	4. Accuracy of facial expressions		$-.52$	
	5. No sex of author effects.			
Nonverbal communica-tion	1. Social smiling			Hall, 1984, 1987; Hall & Halberstadt, 1986
	Children		.04	
	Adults		$-.63$	
	2. Gazing			
	Children		$-.39$	
	Adults		$-.68$	
	3. Body expressiveness		$-.58$	
	4. Speech error		.68	
	5. Filled pauses ("um")		1.18	
	6. No sex of author effect.			
Changes in effect sizes over the years	No consistent effect or trend.			Eagly, 1987

Note: All effect sizes are in terms of d, unless otherwise noted; z is another measure of effect size; positive effect sizes mean larger in males; negative effect sizes mean larger in females; PONS = a standardized test of sensitivity to moods and facial expressions.

TABLE 13.2 *Average Size of Sex Differences from 1975 to 1984**

Grade Point Average	Effect Size	Number of Studies
Grade point average	− .04	5
Self-esteem	+ .12	10
Masculine (instrumentality)	+ .52	12
Feminine (expressiveness)	− .80	12
Liberality of sex role attitude	− .52	6
Fear of Success	− .06	11
Achievement motivation	+ .10	13
Dominance/assertiveness	+ .12	14
Anxiety	− .32	14
Loneliness	+ .16	6
Depression	− .16	5
Neuroticism	− .32	14
Psychoticism	+ .28	8
Having an external locus of control (feeling that others control your life)	− .24	16
Extroversion	− .04	17
Liking and closeness to others	− .45	10
Self-disclosure (tendency to reveal oneself to others)	− .36	10

Source: Hall, Judith A. *Nonverbal Sex Differences.* The Johns Hopkins University Press, Baltimore/London, 1985. Reprinted by permission.

*Taken from Hall, 1984, based on research published in four journals between those two dates; r transformed into d scores by $d = 2r/(1 - r^2)^{1/2}$. Positive d scores indicate that males' average scores were higher than females'; negative d scores indicate that females have the higher average scores.

and female subjects displayed equal numbers of dominance behaviors, and their leadership was equally recognized by their peers. In the incompetent condition, although men and women performed equally, only men were recognized as having been leaders.

Women show higher average levels of most other expressive traits. As shown in Table 13.1, this includes the ability to decode nonverbal cues as to people's feeling and motives. Women are also more willing to adjust their opinions according to the opinions of others around them, especially friends. Although this behavior is usually called **conformity,** it could also be seen as an attempt to preserve group harmony (Hyde, 1990). When female scientists study primates, they are significantly more likely to focus on cooperative behaviors than are male primatologists (Adams & Burnett, 1991). Empathy may be required for optimal parenting (Dix, 1991), a cultural task that females are more likely to perform than are males (see Chapters 10 and 12).

There is a reversal of the expected sex difference in helping behaviors. Women may perceive more danger to themselves than men do in the situations experimenters typically use to measure helping (e.g., helping a person being assaulted or raped, offering to fix a flat tire on an empty road at night) (Eagly & Crowley, 1986). The situations in which help is requested also often involve tasks on which men have had more practice (e.g., changing a tire). It is also interesting that the effect size increases when other people are observing the subjects' behaviors. Private, confidential helping actually shows women being more likely to help. Also, women may be more likely to help friends and family members, which was not tested in the typical research.

Relevant ideas from past chapters. Some of the gender-related differences documented in past chapters provide an important context for this chapter. For example, women seem to suffer more debilitating long-term consequences from competitive situations (see Chapter 12). The sexes also tend to segregate themselves according to gender (see Chapters 10 and 12). To the extent that boys and girls are involved in different games, play patterns, and work patterns, the sexes will practice and acquire different skills. The tasks of any society are also differentially allocated according to gender (see Chapters 10 and 12). If Eagly is right, consistent sex differences in instrumental and expressive traits would then appear in every society with similar labor divisions. Because of this, gender may function as a diffuse status characteristic (see Chapter 11). If so, one would predict that men would dominate women and would display more task-related behaviors. Women would display social, friendly, and cooperative behaviors to make up for their "inferior" status and thereby gain a right to contribute to the group.

Prosocial versus Egoistic Dominance

Acts of prosocial versus egoistic dominance can be located along the circumplex of Figure 13.1. Acts of egoistic dominance would appear in the upper left quadrant, whereas acts of prosocial dominance would appear in the upper right quadrant. Egoistic dominance attempts would be more likely to include overt aggression as well as direct competition. Prosocial attempts would more often include persuasion and nurturance.

Several lines of evidence can be used to support this point of view. For example, although what men tend to do in groups is usually called *leadership,* it could also be called *egoistic dominance.* In fact, Eagly and Karau (1991) concluded from their meta-analytic review that although men were more often **task leaders,** women were more often **social leaders,** as measured by social contributions, positive social behaviors, and ratings of likableness. Carli (1989), in studying sex differences in influence, found that feminine interaction styles (agreeing with partner) were more influential in changing a partner's opinion than were masculine interaction styles (disagreeing with or interrupting partner). Also, in terms of effectiveness, what men do in groups will generate more solutions to specific, concrete problems. On the other hand, what women do in groups will gen-

erate higher-quality solutions to discussion problems, such as deciding on the one best solution (Wood, Polek, & Aiken, 1985).

Social interrelatedness among women. Women's prosocial dominance means that their concepts of self are centered more around relationships with others, whereas men's egoistic dominance means that their self-concepts are centered more around task performances and skills. "Women, in particular, tend to measure their well-being in life in terms of the strength and quality of their close relationships, whether these be with kin, spouse, lover, or friends" (Worell, 1988, p. 478). When men and women view two conflicting stimuli in a stereoscope, males more often see the object than the person stimulus, but females more often see the person (McGuinness & Symonds, 1977).

Triandis (1989) found that one dimension that differentiates both the sexes as well as cultures is that of **individualism** versus **collectivism.**[3] In individualistic cultures, such as the United States, people tend to develop an image of themselves as private and autonomous. In collectivist cultures, such as Japan and China, people view themselves as being more related to others. Competition tends to be interpersonal in individualistic and to be between groups in collectivist cultures. People in individualistic cultures value autonomy, independence, and self-reliance, whereas conformity is more valued in collectivist cultures.

The corresponding terms for individuals are **idiocentric** and **allocentric.** Idiocentrics report themselves to be concerned with achievement, whereas allocentrics report receiving more social support and say they feel more connected to other people. Across cultures, women are more allocentric than men, being more concerned with maintaining social and family relationships and more often caring for family members, including elderly parents (Bybee, Glick, & Zigler, 1990; Dittmar, 1989; House, Umberson, & Landis, 1988; Houser, Berkman, & Bardsley, 1985; Triandis, 1989). Dittmar

(1989) found that women value possessions that were gifts from someone close to them, and men value possessions in terms of status and prestige. Lykes (1985) also said that men emphasize autonomous individualism and women emphasize social individuality in their self-images.

Developmental research.   The cross-cultural research project on children's behaviors published by Whiting and Edwards (1988) led to one of the quotes presented at the beginning of this chapter. In the Six Culture study, boys more often than girls engaged in rough-and-tumble play, assaults, and miscellaneous aggressive acts in most cultures. Boys were also more likely to seek attention and engage in acts of egoistic dominance. This included issuing challenges (dominance conflicts) to same-age peers. Girls were more likely to exhibit nurturance and general sociability.

Maccoby also reviewed the evidence concerning sex differences in children's social behaviors and came to similar conclusions, as indicated in the other quote presented at the beginning of this chapter (Maccoby, 1988, 1990). She cited sex differences in the behaviors of both children and adults, in situations ranging from playgrounds to social conversations to parenting. Males were described as being more dominance or "turf oriented," and females as being more oriented toward the maintenance of group relationships. These sex differences begin to appear by 3 years of age.

One large-scale recent study used a representative population sample of 2- and 4-year-old Dutch children (Koot & Verhulst, 1991). In that study, boys were more aggressive, as measured by the following behaviors: destroys things, hits, fights, and attacks people. On the other hand, girls showed more inhibited behaviors: more guilt, more sensitivity to punishment, more fear, and more shyness. Similarly, in describing his research on childhood shyness, Kagan, Reznick, and Snidman (1988) said that "during the initial selection at 21 or 31 months,

it was most difficult to find extremely inhibited boys" (p. 171).

Act frequency research.   Buss (1981) used his act frequency approach to personality to see how women and men expressed a dominance trait. Male raters judged self-enhancing acts as being more socially desirable than did females, and females judged group-oriented dominance acts (e.g., introducing a speaker at a meeting) as being more socially desirable than men did. Of the 100 dominant acts studied, men performed 22 of them more often than women did, and women performed only 2 more often than men did. People of both sexes who scored high on some measure of a dominance trait performed prosocial dominance acts frequently, but dominant men performed many more egoistic acts than did women.

The Megargee paradigm.   Research done with the Megargee paradigm also shows that women and men express dominance in different ways (Carbonell, 1984; Davis & Gilbert, 1989; Fleischer & Chertkoff, 1986; Megargee, 1969; Nyquist & Spence, 1986). In this type of research, dyads (pairs of subjects) are asked to decide which of them is to act as the leader during the performance of some task. In addition, both members of the dyad were previously given a dominance scale and had scored either low or high. Of most interest are the dyads containing one man and one women who differed in dominance levels. Looking across these studies, the more dominant member of the dyad generally decides who will be the leader. A dominant male decides he will be the leader, and the dominant female decides that the male will be the leader. However, if the dominant female interacts with her male partner before having to decide, she then bases her decision on his desires. She assumes leadership herself if he is low in dominance and so probably does not desire leadership. Thus, his dominance acts elevate his status and her dominance acts maintain interpersonal relationships.

Situations that increase aggression.   Duncan and Hobson (1977) had college students "state the situations in which they were most likely to be aggressive." Personal threats and problems at work were likely to produce aggressive responses in both sexes. Males listed sporting events as making them aggressive more often than females did, but females more often said "to help others." Also, only males listed drinking, sex, being with the opposite sex, money matters, and fighting. Conversely, only women listed unfairness, it being a matter of principles, being in groups, being frustrated, being in authority, being under pressure, and when family welfare was being threatened. Thus, males described sexual conflicts and females described defense of others and family. Many of these differences correspond to the distinction between prosocial dominance and egoistic dominance or aggression.

Comparisons of human and chimpanzee dominance relationships.   Humans are not the only primates in which struggles for status have been observed. For example, two types of chimpanzee groups have been extensively studied, one living in a semi-natural environment in the Arnheim Zoo (de Waal, 1982, 1984, 1986) and the other living in the Gombe preserve in Africa (Goodall, 1986). Both the Arnheim and the Gombe chimpanzee males seem preoccupied with attaining — or regaining — status. "The 'desire' to dominate is, in fact, one of the most common causes of aggression among adult males at Gombe" (Goodall, 1988, p. 325). "At Gombe some males strive with much energy to better their social status over a period of years; others work hard for a short while, but give up if they encounter a serious setback; a few seem remarkably unconcerned about their social rank" (p. 415). de Waal spoke of a *dominance drive* and said that male coalitions "seem to serve status competition" and entitled his book *Chimpanzee Politics.*

There are several routes to high status for male chimpanzees. It does not hurt to be large

and aggressive. However, a male can also acquire high status by being intelligent and creative. One Gombe male became dominant by creatively using oil drums in his dominance displays to intimidate his opponents. Other males achieved status by forming coalitions, often with other males but sometimes with females. Particularly in the Arnheim chimps, the females sometimes played a critical role in determining which male became alpha, which sounds similar to the outcome of research with the Megargee paradigm in humans. Sapolsky similarly found that adult male baboons could be dominant either because of social skills or because of aggressiveness (Sapolsky, 1987, 1989; Sapolsky & Mott, 1987; Sapolsky & Ray, 1989).

Human males also tend to arrange themselves into dominance hierarchies. Males' hierarchies tend to be more stable and reliable than are the ones formed by females, and males' hierarchies also involve more aggression (Freedman, 1980a, 1980b; Mazur, 1985; Omark, 1980; Omark & Edelman, 1975; Savin-Williams, 1976, 1979, 1980a, 1980b; Weisfeld, 1980; Weisfeld & Weisfeld, 1984). Across cultural groups, males seem more concerned with maintaining and acquiring personal status than females are. Males also tend to overestimate their own status, relative to that of other males. The *lack* of overestimation in a male may be a sign he has some problems.[4] As males age, the basis for dominance and status shifts from "toughness" to athletic ability and then to whatever the male's culture uses as a measure of status. However, Crosbie (1979) demonstrated that, even among college students, one male's ability to dominate another, as well as his ability to dominate females, was related to his physical size.

Other similarities between human and chimpanzee dominance acts have also been noted. For example, researchers have found that nonverbal behaviors, such as posture, eye contact, and speech style, are reliable indicators of a human male's dominance status (Mazur,

1985; Weisfeld, Omark, & Cronin, 1980). Similarly, the most reliable way of measuring dominance in chimps is by greeting behaviors. The submissive chimpanzee makes a specific gesture and sound when greeting a more dominant chimp (de Waal, 1982). When dominance is measured this way, the male determined to be dominant sometimes loses competitive contests. He shares food with, and is displaced from favorite sleeping places by, less dominant animals, including females.

The last similarity is that, just as with humans, chimpanzee males' actions are more egoistic and females' more prosocial (see references cited above; also see Hemelrijk & Ek, 1991; Strayer & Noel, 1986). If the male chimp becomes dominant, he intervenes preferentially on the behalf of anyone being attacked, even when the attacker is related to the dominant male or is a grooming partner. Thus, dominant males defend victims. Males form shifting coalitions of defense and alliance, coalitions that seem to have little to do with the friendship patterns measured by mutual grooming. Females form more stable coalitions that strongly overlap with social (grooming and kin) bonds. As de Waal (1982) said, "Male coalitions seem to serve status competition. Males may form flexible coalitions in order to rise in rank, and may adopt the role of group protector in order to maintain a high rank. Female coalitions seem to serve the protection of particular individuals, namely friends and kin" (p. 239).

The tendency to seek either egocentric or prosocial status may have evolved in primates because it could at times have increased reproductive success. Some earlier work did find that dominance increased reproductive success among female primates (Abbott & Hearn, 1978; Dunbar & Dunbar, 1977; Estep et al., 1988; Meikle, Tilford, & Vessey et al., 1984; Silk, 1983; Wasser & Barash, 1983; Zumpe & Michael, 1987). For example, the correlation between mean offspring per female and the female's rank in free-living baboons was .667.

Dominant females will often harrass subordinates, inhibiting their sexual activity or causing them to abort their babies. However, dominance may strongly affect reproductive success only when food supplies are scarce and dominant animals would have preferential access to what food there is (Boccia, Laudenslager, & Reite, 1988; Whitten, 1983). Among groups given food supplements, dominant females do not consistently have greater reproductive success than do subdominants (Fedigan et al., 1986; Gouzoules, Gouzoules, & Fedigan, 1982; Meikle et al., 1984; Nieuwenhuijsen et al., 1985).

Until very recently, measures of how dominance was related to reproductive success in male primates involved their sexual behaviors rather than paternity. However, the two are not highly correlated (Curie-Cohen et al., 1983). When more adequate measures of paternity are used (blood tests), dominant males do tend to have more reproductive success than do subdominant males, although the most prolific breeder may not necessarily be the currently most dominant male (Cowlishaw & Dunbar, 1991; Curie-Cohen et al., 1983; Smith & Smith, 1988; Vessey & Meikle, 1987). Among the Arnheim male chimps, dominance is closely relted to the ability to reproductively monopolize the females. Since males often become dominant just by long-term residency in a group, perhaps dominance seeking could also represent parental investment or inclusive fitness. Dominance would be selected for because the survival and reproduction of the offspring they sired before becoming dominant would be increased by their subsequent ability to defend those offspring.

Furthermore, different male chimps have different reproductive strategies, and becoming the dominant male is only one of them. Another strategy is to persuade (sometimes with force) a female to go off with him on a *consortship*, where the two forage for food by themselves for several days, hopefully (for the male) including the female's fertile period.

Different baboon males also use different reproductive strategies (Noë & Sluijter, 1990). Thus, any correlation between dominance and reproductive success would be expected to be weak, since dominance is only one possible reproductive strategy out of several from which a male can choose.

Does dominance lead to reproductive success in male humans? *Dominance* has been variously defined as being rich, being intelligent, being the group leader, owning more land or other valued possessions, or having successfully killed the enemy. In various cultures, all of these have been shown to at least sometimes lead to greater reproductive success in human males, usually because "successful" males had more wives than other males did (polygyny) (Betzig, 1982; Chagnon, 1988a; Essock-Vitale, 1984; Flinn, 1986; Hill, 1984; Mulder, 1987).

However, as Chapter 9 noted, although there is tremendous cultural variability, cultures also tend to socialize their male children to strive for status more than they do their female children. As an end result of evolutionary (sex limitation) as well as socialization pressures, the sexes may have come to differ in the frequency with which they express traits on the circumplex. One possible outcome is sex differences in homicides and depressive disorders.

Homicide versus depression: Exaggerated effects of egoistic versus prosocial tendencies?
Both homicide and depression can be related to the circumplex of Figure 13.1. Depression can be viewed as reflecting traits in the lower right quadrant (Wiggins, 1982). Depression can involve a heightened sensitivity to the opinions of others, as well as a lack of dominance feelings. For example, Schwartz (1991) has suggested that women living in the kinds of social groups that emphasize altruism over egoism are more vulnerable to depression but are less vulnerable to antisocial personality disorders. Similarly, high levels of interpersonal sensitivity, including sensitivity to others' opinions, can

predict a depressive episode following a stressing condition such as childbirth (Boyce & Parker, 1989; Boyce et al., 1990; Hirschfeld et al., 1989). Homicide would most often reflect aggression, or egoistic dominance unleavened by concerns for the feeling of others. This would appear in the upper left quadrant. In fact, incarcerated male criminals show personality profiles matching the upper left quadrant (Wiggins, Phillips, & Trapnell, 1989).

Because the dimension running from the upper left to the lower right quadrants is sexually dimorphic, sex differences in the antecedents of depression would not be surprising. For example, physically abused children most often grow up to be perfectly normal adults. But if problems do develop, abused boys are at a greater risk of developing excessive aggression as adults than are abused girls. On the other hand, girls are at a greater risk for developing depression (Dodge, Bates, & Pettit, 1990; Widom, 1989a, 1989b).

What is surprising is that, for boys, aggression can actually turn into depression. Block and his colleagues did a longitudinal study to look at the developmental predictors of depressive symptoms at age 18. They found that boys who became depressed at age 18 were, at age 14, power oriented, hostile, physically attractive, and interested in the opposite sex; they were not liked or warm, and did not have close relationships with others (Block, Gjerde, & Block, 1991). In contrast, from ages 3 through 7, girls who later became depressed were admired and sought out by other children, got along well with other children, and recognized the feelings of others. They were not dominating. By age 14, these to-be-depressed girls began feeling inadequate and lost their social poise and presence. Furthermore, in girls, IQ at ages 3–4 was positively related to depression, but for boys, the relationship was negative.

Brain biochemistry.
Depression and aggression may covary with brain levels of the transmitter substance serotonin. Serotonin has

mixed effects on the activities of neurons, but often seems to inhibit high levels of neural activity (Hoyenga & Hoyenga, 1988). Brain serotonin levels are increased in times of stress or high arousal. This increase may act as a homeostatic mechanism, controlling activity and preventing long periods of hyperactivity in limbic system neurons.

Serotonin levels are related to gender, depression, aggression, and dominance. Serotonin levels are low in the brains of impulsively aggressive people (Linnoila et al., 1983; Virkkunen et al., 1989; Virkkunen & Linnoila, 1990). Drugs that increase brain levels of serotonin tend to inhibit aggression (Eichelman, 1987; Miczek & Donat, 1989; Mos, Olivier, & van Oorschot, 1990; Olivier & Mos, 1988) and decrease depression (see Table 13.6, later in this chapter). Levels of serotonin rise in the brains of male nonhuman primates when they assume a dominant social position within their group (Raleigh et al., 1984). Females, both primates and rats, may have higher serotonin levels (Higley, Suomi, & Linnoila, 1991; Carlsson et al., 1985; Kennett et al., 1986; Seegal, 1985; Young & Ervin, 1984). While the sex difference in serotonin seems consistent with the sex difference in aggression, it is inconsistent with the sex differences in depression and dominance. One possible explanation for the depression effects will be provided later in this chapter.

HOMICIDES

Most definitions of **aggression** claim that the individual's motives are critically important (Hoyenga & Hoyenga, 1984). If you harm someone by accident, with no specific intent to create harm, your act would usually not be defined as aggressive. In our legal system, a verdict of first-degree murder demands that the prosecution prove that a guilty intent was present. Despite this, it is difficult to include intent as part of the definition of aggression. In nonhuman animals, we cannot determine in-

tent, and humans can also lie about what their true intentions were. Although the intent is crucial to the concept both theoretically and socially, this section concentrates on homicidal acts that usually would be seen as aggressive, regardless of motive. This approach is not uncommon among researchers studying cultural patterns of homicide.

To understand sex differences in aggression as something other than an aberration that males have more often than females do, homicide is presented in an evolutionary context and aggressiveness in a developmental context. Both are necessary to explain why there are more aggressive men than women.

Gender-Related Differences in Homicides

Martin Daly and Margo Wilson (Daly & Wilson, 1982, 1988a, 1988b; Daly, Wilson, & Wegnorst, 1982; Wilson & Daly, 1985) described how sex differences in reproductive roles and inclusive fitness could predict who was likely to kill whom.[5] Sex differences in reproductive roles produce sex differences in the content of aggression. In most mammals, especially those with polygynous mating systems, females invest more in offspring and so females should be more aggressive around children. Whether the aggression would be directed at the children or at some threat to their welfare would depend on relative costs and benefits. The costs would be measured in the loss of future reproductive opportunities. Benefits would be measured by changes in the likelihood of the child surviving and reproducing. Because of the sex difference in parental investment (reproductive roles), males are more subjected to sexual selection pressures. If males' reproductive roles involved conflict with each other to gain access to females, males would become aggressive in conflicts over status and females. Females may be less concerned with conflicts over certain kinds of status, if that kind of status affects their reproduction less than it affects the reproduction of males.

Homicide rates.   Across cultures and time, crimes against persons (including homicide) and crimes against properties (e.g., theft) are more likely to be committed by men than by women (see documentation in Hoyenga & Hoyenga, 1993). Cultures tend to be high or low in both types of crimes simultaneously. Men are more likely to kill than women are; and when they kill, men are more likely to kill other men than to kill women. The more developed the country, the more likely females are to be killed, relative to males. When women kill, they are more likely to kill family members than men are. In the United States in 1984, women committed 38 percent of all the murders of spouses, compared to only 14 percent of the homicides not involving family members (Straus, 1986).

The sex difference in assaults and homicides starts at puberty (Weisheit, 1984). In a national probability sample of 1,626 adolescents who were privately interviewed, males admitted to more assaults than did females. Many homicides and serious assaults among juveniles are part of gang wars. Females are associated with male gangs but they seldom form gangs of their own. The effect of age and gender on the rate of committing violent crimes in the United States is depicted in Figure 13.2—this is the largest sex difference to be found in this book.

Homicide and kinship.   Wilson and Daly pointed out that both sexes are more likely to kill unrelated individuals than blood relatives. Blood relatives are more likely to be partners in crimes, including homicide. Since relatives share genes, not only should people be more likely to aid relatives than nonrelatives but people should be less likely to kill relatives. Killing of spouses is a widespread form of homicide; although it involves family, it does not involve blood relatives.

The sex differences are much smaller in the assault or killing of spouses, compared to the assault and killing of friends and strangers. In two large national probability samples of violence in the home, one carried out in 1975 and

the other in 1985, few sex differences in the use of violence were noted (Straus, 1980, 1986; Straus & Gelles, 1986). When calculated as rate per 1,000 couples, husband-to-wife violence occurred at the rate of 121 in 1975; the rate of wife-to-husband violence was 116. In 1985, the figures were 113 and 121. Similarly, in data cited by Wilson and Daly, there are some cultures and time periods in which husbands greatly outnumber wives in spousal homicides, but in other areas at other times, wives commit more.

The violent acts and homicides committed by wives were more likely to be in self-defense. Sometimes the husband only laughs at his wife's blows, knowing they cannot do him any damage. The more violence used by a wife against her husband, the more violence he uses in return. A wife tends to avoid the use of severely violent measures (knives and guns) at all levels of marital conflict, up to the point where her husband had committed 20 or more separate assaults on her during the preceding year. Then she becomes quite violent herself. Wives most often kill husbands when the husbands had been regularly beating them; wives often perceive that their only safe way out is to kill their tormenter (Andrews & Brown, 1988; Saunders, 1988; Steinmetz, 1980; Walker, 1989; Browne & Williams, 1989). Many of the homicidal women hd attempted to leave their spouses, but the men had tracked them down and assaulted them again. Women may also be trapped by economic circumstances. If the family is poor and she has no job, she would have no way to feed herself and her children. On the other hand, in high-status families, women seem reluctant to give up that status by leaving their husbands.

For several reasons, providing women with options may decrease the frequency with which wives kill husbands (Andrews & Brown, 1988; Saunders, 1988; Steinmetz, 1980; Walker, 1989; Browne & Williams, 1989). If wives have no friends or family members to provide support, they may be more likely to be battered and also

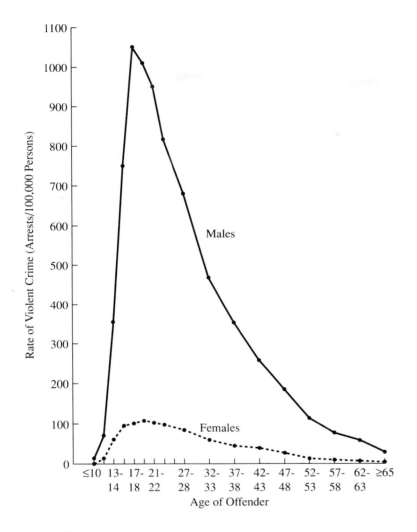

FIGURE 13.2 *Arrest Rates for Violent Crime in the United States as a Function of Age and Gender*

Source: From "An Evolutionary and Developmental Perspective on Aggressive Patterns" by R. B. Cairns in M. C. Zahn-Waxler, E. M. Cummings, and R. Tonnotti (Eds.), *Altruism and Aggression,* 1986, Cambridge: Cambridge University Press. Reprinted by permission.

more likely to kill in return. Threatening divorce may at least temporarily stop a husband's attacks, but the initiation of divorce proceedings often leads the husband to escalate his violence. Passing laws for the punishment of spouse abusers and providing safe houses as refuges for abused wives significantly decreases the rate at which wives kill husbands. Ironically, the laws and safe houses do not affect the rate at which husbands kill wives.

Sexual jealousy often seems to precipitate a husband's assaults on his wife. Marriages in which the male was clearly the dominant partner tended to be the most violent (Straus, 1980, 1986; Straus & Gelles, 1986). Premarital pregnancy is a risk factor in wife abuse (Andrews & Brown, 1988). Some abusive husbands are generally violent; others are violent only in the home (Saunders, 1987). High levels of conflict in the marriage and low socioeconomic status (SES) are also important risk factors (Sugarman & Hotaling, 1989). The techniques used by abusive husbands even have characteristics in common with the techniques used by captors to control prisoners of war (Romero, 1985).

Many of the references cited in the paragraphs above point out that societies grant the husband a "right" to assault his wife. In fact, marital rape and severe assault were not legally prosecutable crimes in our culture until recently. When bystanders see a man assaulting a women, they often assume that the two are related (lovers, married) and are not likely to intervene to protect the woman. If bystanders believe that the two are strangers, then at least males are more likely to intervene (Borofsky, Stollak, & Messé, 1971.

Buss (1988, 1989a) examined reproductive conflicts in couples, using his act frequency approach described earlier. He asked couples to describe what acts they had performed "in the context of their relationship with their romantic partner" (p. 300, 1988) to see how humans attempt to retain a mate or "prevent their partner from getting involved with someone else" (p. 296). Although acts of violence among members of dating or married couples were rare, males more often than females reported using threats and violence. The longer the couple had been together, the more likely the man was to use punishment and violence. Violence (abuse), along with being unfaithful, were judged to be the most upsetting acts that a mate could perform.

This fits Wilson and Daly's model of the abusive, potentially homicidal husband trying to control his wife's behavior and sexuality with violence. His violence makes his wife afraid to leave him. If he is certain she is going to leave — or has already left him — then he may kill her. From an evolutionary point of view, by killing his wife, he may ruin his reproductive success but at least his rivals will not succeed with "his" wife.

Infanticide is not uncommon among hunter-gatherers; thus, infanticide is not just a disease of the modern world (see Chapter 10). Wilson and Daly's data show that, overall, mothers are somewhat more likely than fathers to kill their children, reversing the typical sex difference in homicide. The sex difference in infanticide is largest for the youngest children (less than 1 year old). Younger mothers are also more likely to kill their offspring than are older mothers. The older the child is, the more his or her parents have invested in him or her, so the less likely they are to kill the child. Younger mothers have more reproductive potential than older mothers, so older mothers, having less to lose, might be more willing to invest in a risky child and less likely to kill that child.

Several risk factors for child abuse and potential infanticide have been identified (Gelles & Straus, 1979; Winpisinger et al., 1991; Wolfe, 1985). During one year alone, Gelles and Staus suggested that between 1.4 and 1.9 million children in the United States are injured by their parents. Mothers were more often responsible than fathers. Children of younger, or unmarried, mothers are at much greater risk. Child abusers were likely to have been abused themselves as children and tend to have low SES and low occupational status. They are also likely to have recently moved to a new area and so have no friends or relatives living nearby. High levels of marital conflict are common.

Children are also killed by nonrelatives. Children are more likely to be killed if there is a stepparent (not a blood relative) in the home. In this case, there would be more conflict about how much to invest. Because of inclusive fitness, the blood relative parent would want to invest more than would the stepparent. In Cook County, Illinois, from 1977 through 1982, mothers' boyfriends were not infrequently responsible for the children's deaths (Christoffel, Anzinger, & Merrill, 1989). Although younger chldren are more at risk from their parents, Wilson and Daly pointed out that older children are more likely to die at the hands of nonrelatives.

Since mammalian females invest more in children, mothers might be more reluctant to risk further investment in any one child than would fathers. Wilson and Daly suggested that this is one reason for the sex differences in infanticide and abuse. Furthermore, since child rearing is cross-culturally assigned to females, mothers are left alone with the children far more than are fathers. Proximity could be an important factor, especially when this is combined with isolation from friends and relatives.

Intermale conflicts and homicides. Wilson and Daly said that males often kill each other as part of a generalized conflict over status and females. The most prevalent type of urban homicide in the United States involves an "altercation of relatively trivial origin; insult, curse, jostling, etc." (Wolfgang, as cited by Daly & Wilson, 1988b, p. 125). If a man allowed another man to get away with insulting him, the first man would lose status in the eyes of his peer group. Sometimes men engage in showing-off disputes, where one tries to best the other in front of witnesses. In Detroit in 1972, 26 male homicides occurred as a result of this. In another three cases, a woman did the killing. In two of those cases, the woman was intervening in a showing-off dispute between males, killing one male to protect the other. Only one homicide involved a showing-off dispute between females.

In one incident described by Daly and Wilson, both the killer and his eventual victim had been drinking together. The future killer placed his night stick between the victim's legs, lifting him in the air and thereby embarrassing him. People laughed at the victim, who then hit the offender. Both men were asked to leave the bar, but the killer said that the victim hit him again as the killer left the bar—so he shot him.

Katz (1988) also described how concerns over status lead males to violence. He quoted one criminal who described himself and other criminals as, "We the show people. The glamour people. Come on the set with the finest car, the finest woman. . . . Hear people talking about you. Hear the bar get quiet when you walk in the door" (p. 315). In their own words, for the career or "heavy" stickup man, peremptory and excessive violence may be the way he

markets his reputation as a "badass." In effect, robbers can use irrational violence against victims as a way of building their "careers as immoral entrepreneurs" (p. 184). "The construction of a career as a heavy in stickups requires living as a hardman—a person who anticipates mobilizing violence at any moment" (p. 219). In an interview, Katz said the males he studied killed in "order to appear to be killers, to sustain that kind of general appearance among the people they are familiar with" (quote taken from the *Peoria Journal Star,* January 1, 1989). These killers almost take pleasure at becoming outraged by insult, and they become shamed at being humiliated, feeling that they *must* defend themselves.

The male status offenders are disproportionately young, unemployed, and single. From an evolutionary point of view, they have few prospects for status or reproductive success and have little to lose. Risk taking might have been selected for under those conditions. Cross-cultural studies have also shown that crimes against people are more prevalent in polygynous than in monogamous cultures (Bacon, Child, & Barry, 1963). Polygyny would be predicted to increase male conflicts for status, especially among young males with few prospects.

Men also fight over goods and over women. Robberies and drug crimes provide the wherewithal to improve status. Crime-specific homicides—deaths occurring during crimes—are also preponderantly committed by males. Wilson and Daly said that in Detroit in 1972, 95 percent of these offenders were male. Of the burglaries committed during 1980 in the United States, 94 percent were committed by males, even though far more females than males live in poverty. Men sometimes fight over women because they are attempting to control women's sexuality. Evolutionary theory points out that males must "guard" the females from other males if they are to be certain of their paternity. Sometimes this takes the form of beating or killing the girlfriend or wife, and other times the rival is killed. Of the 47 homicides involving jealous males that occurred in Detroit during 1972, 16 of the jealous men killed the female and 17 killed the rival male. Of the 11 homicides involving jealous females, 6 killed the offending male and 3 killed the rival female.

These crimes are also uniquely common in the United States, compared to all other developed countries (Fingerhut & Kleinman, 1990; Rockett & Smith, 1989). In most countries, the rate of male deaths from homicide (largely because of other males) during the ages of 25 to 34 is almost twice what it is during the ages of 55 to 64, and both are under 5/100,000 population. The 21-country average for homicide deaths of males aged 15 to 24 per 100,000 population was 1.9. In the United States, the rate of deaths by homicide for males aged 55 to 64 is just above 10/100,000, and the rate for men aged 25 to 34 is somewhere between 21.9 to 33/100,000, which is four to six times the average. The more individualistic orientation of the U.S. culture may increase intermale conflicts over status.

Developmental Covariates

The relationship between evolutionary pressures and aggression is probably not direct. Evolution would have created the ability to learn aggression in certain developmental environments and to learn that aggressive acts are one way to satisfy certain motives and emotions, such as jealousy. The developmental mechanisms described in Unit Three of this book affect aggression (Eron, 1987; Loeber & Dishion, 1983; Loeber & Schmaling, 1985; Parke & Slaby, 1983). What parents do, such as tolerating rather than punishing aggressive acts, affects what the child learns. Children model both parental behaviors and the behaviors of aggressive TV models.

Gendered-developmental environments. Several sex differences in developmental environments could lead to sex differences in

adult aggression (Chapter 12). Boys' toys more often involve aggressive themes and concepts than do girls' toys (Miller, 1987). As soon as little girls learn to reliably label their own gender (around age 27 months), their level of aggression drops; this does not happen in boys (Fagot & Leinbach, 1989; Fagot, Leinbach, & Hagan, 1986). There are more male than female aggressive models on TV, and the amount of exposure to aggressive TV predicts adult aggression (Eron, 1987). Thus, children are taught that aggression is masculine, and girls seem to incorporate that lesson into their self-concepts, using it to guide future behaviors.

People in the environment of children also respond differentially to aggression in boys and girls (Fagot, 1985b; Fagot & Hagan, 1985; Fagot et al., 1985). Both peers and teachers are more likely to ignore aggression in girls than in boys. Furthermore, although teachers and peers often respond negatively to aggression in boys, this is a positive reinforcer for boys, so parents and teachers may be inadvertently reinforcing aggression in boys and extinguishing it in girls.

Fathers seem to be important to aggression in boys. Boys from single-parent families are more aggressive in peer interactions (Romney, 1965; Weigel, 1985; Chapter 12). From an evolutionary point of view, father absence leads to a more competitive mating strategy (see Chapter 10). Boys also end up being more aggressive if their mothers were negative toward them during the first years of their lives, and if the father had abused the mother (Hoffman, 1960; Olweus, 1980a). In fact, abused mothers often feel more negative about their sons. Divorce and maternal custody is more likely to lead to aggression and insecurity in boys (Hetherington, 1989).

Frequent parental use (abuse?) of power also tends to increase aggression in children, especially in sons (Eron, 1980, 1987; Hoffman, 1960; Huesmann et al., 1984; Lefkowitz, Huesmann, & Eron, 1978; Olweus, 1980a, 1980b; Widom, 1989a, 1989b). Although most abused and neglected children do not become delinquent, criminal, or violent, they are at an increased risk. Widom (1989a, 1989b) compared the adult records of abused and neglected children (*n* = 908) to those of controls (*n* = 667). The abused males were more likely to have committed violent crimes.[6] Eron and his colleagues provided one of the most detailed descriptions of how punishment by parents can affect the child's aggression. If a child is punished for aggression and also identifies with his parents (sees himself similar to them), the punishment will suppress aggression. If, however, the child does not identify with his parents, the punishment increases aggressiveness. The researchers also discovered that although parental punishment is not strongly (not significantly) related to adult aggression, the punishment you received as a child predicts how much you will punish your own children.

Other studies have identified additional developmental covariates of male aggression. Hyperactivity is more common in males, and a hyperactive boy may develop an antisocial disorder and then be more likely to become a criminal (Mannuzza et al., 1989). Boys born to older mothers also tend to become more aggressive adults, as well as being more likely to later kill their own mothers (Daly & Wilson, 1988a; Huesmann et al., 1984).

Longitudinal changes in aggression. Aggressiveness changes with age. Physical aggression increases between 2 and 4 years of age, and then tends to decrease in most children. For example, physical aggression among siblings decreases from a level of 90 percent of siblings at ages 3 and 4, to 64 percent at ages 15 and 17 (Straus, Gelles, & Steinmetz, 1980; Hetherington, 1989). Females are somewhat less aggressive toward their siblings than males are. By 10 years of age, males' rate of sibling aggression in all-boy families is more than twice the level found in families with only one boy. *Hostile* physical aggression (aggression out of anger, directed at harming the other person) in-

creases after age 4. Self-reports of aggressive acts increase as boys enter puberty, as does their likelihood of committing a violent crime (Cairns, 1986; Figure 13.2).

Despite the changes with age, aggressiveness is nearly as developmentally stable a characteristic as is IQ (Botha & Mels, 1990; Eron, 1980, 1987; Huesmann et al., 1984; Lefkowitz et al., 1978; Moss & Susman, 1980; Olweus, 1980a, 1980b). Aggression in males at age 8 predicts, 22 years later, spouse abuse, punishment of his own children, criminal justice convictions, commission of serious criminal acts, moving traffic violations, and driving while intoxicated. IQ also interacts with aggression, in that more intelligent males tend to be less aggressive. In Eron's work, aggression in a female at age 8 predicts only how she will punish their own children and the seriousness of her criminal acts at age 30. Nevertheless, very aggressive females tend to be as stable in their aggressiveness across time as males are (Botha & Mels, 1990; Cairns & Cairns, 1984; Huesmann et al., 1984).

Eron and his colleagues found that prosocial behaviors can inhibit the development of aggression in both sexes. The greater the popularity with peers and the greater the avoidance of aggression at age 8, the less aggressive the person was as an adult. For any given level of aggression at age 8, the greater the prosocial behaviors at the same age, the less was the adult aggression. Girls' more prosocial orientation could thus explain why hostile, physical aggression is more common in males. Also, since the social structure of friendship groups is tighter among girls, girls can more effectively use indirect types of aggression such as social ostracism (Cairns, 1986; Lagerspetz, Björkqvist, & Peltonen, 1988).

Biological Covariates

To create sex differences, evolution would select for sex limitation or sex linkage of aggression- or egoistic dominance-promoting genes.

Genetic basis. Research on the genetic control of aggression in rodents leads to two important conclusions (Hoyenga & Hoyenga, 1993): (1) Males and females may have somewhat separate genetic controls (e.g., sex linkage)[7] and (2) Some of these breeding programs have changed developmental timing. If animals are bred according to their aggression levels at 60 days of age, the aggressive strain may simply become aggressive sooner in life than the nonaggressive strain. One or two months later, animals from the two strains may show more nearly equivalent levels of aggression, particularly if the low aggression strain was given some aggressive experiences.

Both twin studies and adoption studies have revealed a genetic basis for personality traits in humans (see documentation in Hoyenga & Hoyenga, 1993). More specifically, genes have some impact on instrumentality, expressiveness, aggressiveness, sociability, criminality, and altruism. Twin studies have shown that scores on sex-role scales (instrumentality and expressiveness) are heritable, though according to research done by Rowe (1982) and by Mitchell, Baker, and Jacklin (1989), instrumentality may have a larger genetic component for adults than does expressiveness. Adoption studies have shown that the traits that increase petty criminality have a hereditary component (Mednick, Gabrielli, & Hutchings, 1984; Baker et al., 1989). Violent criminality may not be inherited, however. Twin studies that used mother's ratings and well as observational data find high levels of heritability for aggression (Ghodsian-Carpey & Baker, 1987; Sines, private communication, 1992).

Rushton and his colleagues (Rushton et al., 1986) gave five questionnaires measuring altruistic and aggressive tendencies to 573 adult twin pairs. They estimated heritability to be from 56 to 72 percent. Not only did they find men to get higher scores on the aggression scales and women higher scores on the altruism scales but aggression scores decreased and altruism scores increased with subjects' ages.

Hormonal covariates in nonhumans. Sex hormone levels covary with adult aggressiveness in most animals (Beatty, 1979; Hoyenga & Hoyenga, 1993). Prenatal androgen treatment increases the adult aggressiveness of nonhuman primate females (Goy & McEwen, 1980; Phoenix, 1974). In adult rodents, different kinds of aggression are controlled by different kinds of postpubertal sex hormones. Neonatal estrogen (E) exposure makes the animals more aggressive in response to adult E injections, and neonatal androgen exposure increases adult aggressive responses to adult androgen injections (Simon & Whalen, 1987). Postpartum aggression can be increased by exposure to prenatal progesterone (P) treatments (Wagner, Kinsley, & Svare, 1986).

The major effect of perinatal androgen is to increase adult sensitivity to testosterone (T) injections (Gandelman, 1980; Gandelman, Rosenthal, & Howard, 1980; Simon, Gandelman, & Gray, 1984; Simon & Whalen, 1987). Exposing a rat or mouse female to repeated T injections as an adult can increase her aggression, even without perinatal androgen treatments. Neonatal exposure to T only makes her aggression appear sooner in response to adult T treatments. However, putting the female in social isolation for eight weeks prior to the T treatment has the same effect on her aggressive response to adult T as does neonatal T. Furthermore, in some strains of rats, both sexes are equally sensitive to the aggression-promoting effects of postpubertal T injections (van de Poll et al., 1982). However, only in adult male rats and primates will the presence of T cause them to durably suppress their aggression after being defeated (Keverne, Eberhart, Yodyingyuad, & Abbott, 1984; Swanson, 1990; van de Poll et al., 1982).

Increases in androgens may increase an adult female's dominance and aggression, and aggressiveness in primate females also varies as a function of both the attacker's and the target's hormone levels (Hoyenga & Hoyenga, 1993). Presumably these attacks are part of the female's reproductive strategy. Carefully timed attacks can suppress a rival's ovulation or can lead her to abort. Females that are close to fertility themselves, or close to giving birth, may be more concerned about competition.

Hormones and dominance in humans. Only a few studies of perinatal hormones found any evidence that exposure to higher than normal levels of androgens or masculinizing progestins could increase adult aggressiveness or assertiveness in humans.[8] Nonetheless, if one was to conceptualize dominance more broadly, viewing a career orientation as a relatively more egoistic type, compared to an orientation toward marriage and motherhood, one would see more evidence that prenatal hormones can covary with egoistic dominance. For example, the most recently published study on adrenogenital females has found them to have less desire "to have their own children" and more desire for "having a career versus staying at home" (Dittmann et al., 1990a, 1990b). Prenatal hormones may affect the size of the bed nucleus of the stria terminalis in the brain, which is related to aggressive behavior and which is also larger in male than in female humans (Allen & Gorski, 1990). Perinatal hormones also change the brain's serotonin metabolism (Hoyenga & Hoyenga, 1988).

Maccoby, Jacklin, and colleagues (Jacklin, Maccoby, & Doering, 1983; Maccoby et al., 1979; Marcus et al., 1985) found that neonatal steroid levels were related to later interpersonal behaviors, but not in expected ways. Neonatal P (negative), T (negative), and E (positive) predicted later timidity in boys. However, even though 6- to 18-month-old girls were more timid than were the same age boys, no neonatal hormone level was related to girls' timidity. Thus, although more girls than boys are shy and timid, replicating the research described earlier, the basis for the sex differences at such an early age does not seem to be related to sex differences in neonatal hormone levels.

Postpubertal hormone levels also covary

with dominance and aggression in humans (see reviews in: Buchanan, Eccles, & Becker, 1992; Hoyenga & Hoyenga, 1993). Exposure to very high levels of androgens — much higher than males typically have — can markedly increase aggression. Another consistent finding is that, for a few women at least, hostility tends to increase during the premenstrual period. Dominance, whether assessed behaviorally or by a paper-and-pencil test, often directly (though weakly) covaries with T levels in both sexes.

Hormone-occupational covariates are also relevant. The greater the income of employed men and women, and the greater the prestige of the job they hold, the more dominant they are, as measured by a personality test (Steil & Weltman, 1991). However, the relationships among T and occupational choices and statuses (prestige) are different for the sexes (Hoyenga & Hoyenga, 1993). High androgen levels in females are associated with a greater preference for having a career and for having a higher status, more masculine career. The relationships are not as consistent in males.

Dabbs (personal communication, 1991) had a model that explained the variability in males. If a male has high T levels, this both directly and indirectly decreases his occupational status. The indirect effect would be mediated by a decrease in IQ and by an increase in antisocial behaviors. Both of these effects of high T would decrease education and so decrease career status. Thus, although T may tend to increase desires for dominance in males, males who are already of lower SES and who have lower IQs will receive less education. The outcome of high T for them might be aggression rather than high social status. Still, high T level men *are* found among entertainers and in skilled manufacturing jobs. Also, the career criminals described earlier can have very high status within their own social groups and could also have high T levels.

All these hormone-behavior relationships could be indirect. For example, both current T levels and career choices might reflect prenatal

T levels. Or high T females may be less interested in motherhood and so are freer to pursue a high-status, time-demanding career. Furthermore, having a high-status career, or behaving in a dominant fashion, may increase T levels.

DEPRESSION

If exaggerated egoistic dominance attempts become warped into acts of homicide in some men, perhaps exaggerated prosocial concerns in women might sometimes turn into clinical depression. Table 13.3 presents some basic facts about depression that will be needed to understand the sex differences.

Sex Differences

This section concentrates on diagnoses of depression rather than on depressive symptoms as measured by scales or questionnaires. If exceeding a given score on some scale is used as a criterion, "depression" identified that way does not extensively overlap with the depression measured by diagnostic interviews (Myers & Weissman, 1980; Oliver & Simmons, 1985). People of lower SES score higher on scales of depression but they do not more often receive diagnoses of depression, even in community survey studies (Crandell & Dohrenwend, 1967; Klerman & Weissman, 1988; Oliver & Simmons, 1985; Seiler, 1973). Questionnaire measures seem to measure general stress and distress, and lower SES people may be more likely to express stress in the form of depressive symptoms.

Even more importantly, the variables that correlate with scale scores often do not correlate with diagnoses (Lewinsohn, Hoberman, & Rosenbaum, 1988; Rohde et al., 1990; Oliver & Simmons, 1985). In the Lewinsohn longitudinal study, cognitive characteristics, such as having low self-esteem, consistently expecting the worse to happen, and perceiving oneself to have little control over events in one's life,

TABLE 13.3 *Facts About Depression*
The table presents some facts about depression that have to be explained by any theory of depression and of sex differences in depression.

1. The symptoms of depression vary from person to person.
2. Dysphoria (painfully depressed mood) is central to depression.
3. There are multiple behavioral and cognitive changes associated with depression.
4. There is a high prevalence (at any given point in time and for a lifetime) of depression in the general population.
5. Age is related to the prevalence of depression.
6. There is a greater prevalence of depression in females (2–3 times higher) and in persons who have had previous depressive episodes.
7. People with a previous history of depression do not differ from controls on most cognitive and affective and behavioral measures.
8. Depression spontaneously disappears with time in most people.
9. Depression can be effectively treated with both drugs and with psychotherapy.
10. Stress and low social support can lead to the onset of depressive episodes.
11. There are genetic risk factors.
12. There has been an increase after World War II, along with a decrease in age of onset.

Source: From "An Integrative Theory of Depression" by P. M. Lewinsohn, H. Hoberman, L. Teri, and M. Hautzinger, 1985, *Theoretical Issues in Behavior Therapy*. Reprinted by permission from Academic Press.

were correlated with future scale scores but not with future depressive episodes. Although women tend to get higher depression scale scores than men do, the gender difference in scores can often be attributed to gender differences in employment, job status, and income (Golding, 1988). As will be seen, the same is not true of gender differences in diagnosed depression.

Sex ratios of depressive disorders. In any 6-month period, 6 percent of the population can be expected to experience a depressive episode as defined by the Diagnostic and Statistical Manual III-R. About 85 percent of the patients have recurrent episodes. Of these, 20 percent may be chronically disabled by their symptoms. Close to 80 percent of depressed people never get any treatment, or only inadequate treatment. Women are from two to three times more likely than men to experience depressive episodes in their lifetimes than are men (Hoyenga & Hoyenga, 1993). The likelihood of having at least one depressive episode is one in four for women, versus one in ten for men. This sex difference has been documented by both literary and quantitative reviews of the literature and appears in many different cultures. It can be seen in community surveys involving semi-random samples of people diagnosed by trained interviewers. The higher the criterion set for a diagnosis to be made, the more likely it is that the person will be a female.

Lewinsohn and his colleagues carried out one of the more impressive, longitudinal studies of depression (Amenson & Lewinsohn, 1981; Lewinsohn, Hoberman, & Rosenbaum, 1988; Lewinsohn et al., 1981; Rohde et al., 1990). Announcements of the research were sent to a random sample of 20,000 residents in two cities in Oregon. Some 2,000 people expressed an interest in participating, and a 938-item questionnaire was later returned by 1,213 of them. Some refused to participate further, and some were excluded for a priori reasons (e.g., high scores on a Lie scale), but 998 people were interviewed and then reinterviewed about 15 months later. There was no sex difference in the number of new cases of depression that developed during that period, but women with a prior history of depression were much more likely to become depressed again than men with the same history.

The major potentially confounding variables are stereotypes and alcoholism. Because of stereotypes, depressed women might be more likely to seek help than would depressed men and so would be more likely to be diagnosed as depressed. However, the Lewinsohn studies found no evidence that depressed women more often sought treatment. Alternatively, since depression and alcoholism both tend to occur in the same families, alcoholism could be the way that men express their depression. If so, just comparing the sexes on depression would overestimate the sex difference in disorder. However, there is evidence that alcoholism and depression are separate diseases, with somewhat different kinds of environmental and genetic backgrounds (Bohman et al., 1987; Schuckit, 1986). Despite this, both questions should still be regarded as open.

Seasonal affective disorders. **Seasonal affective disorder** or **SAD** is a condition in which depressive episodes tend to occur only in a given season (Kasper et al., 1989; Rosenthal et al., 1987; Rosenthal et al., 1984). Although at first only winter depressions **(winter SAD)** were described, recurrent summer depressions **(summer SAD)** were later identified. Even people whose moods never meet the criteria for a major affective disorder frequently show seasonal mood shifts (92 percent). More men than women feel worse in the winter than in the summer, but since the magnitude of the mood swings is much larger in the women, more of them meet the diagnosis of winter SAD (71 percent female). Women are more likely to feel worse in the summer and so more often experience summer SAD (66 percent female).

SAD patients show some interesting contrasts with nonseasonal patients (Eastwood & Peter, 1988; Garvey, Wesher, & Godes, 1988). Episodes for nonseasonal depression are more likely to occur in the spring. SAD patients are more likely to be depressed by cloudy days, to have carbohydrate cravings, and to have premenstrual depressions even between episodes.

Sex differences in depressive symptom patterns. The nature and size of the sex difference does vary. Women from ages 18 to 44 are at greatest risk, relative to men. Married people have lower rates than do single, divorced, or widowed people in both sexes, although unhappily married women have the highest rates of all. The sex difference also takes some interesting forms (Cassano et al., 1988; Roy-Byrne et al., 1985; Spalt, 1980; Sytema, 1991; Taylor & Abrams, 1981). Some people have recurring episodes of depression—these people are even more likely to be females. Female sociopaths are more often depressed than are male sociopaths. Although there is no sex difference in the frequency of manic-depressive disorder per se, women tend to have more depressive episodes and symptoms, and men more manic episodes.

Table 13.4 describes other surprising facts. Even though women are more likely to have depressive episodes than men are, the age of onset is the same. The difference in appetite is particularly interesting, since SAD sufferers also show strong changes in appetite. However, there is a possibility that women more often have increases in appetite with depression because they are more likely to be on a diet. Dieting people are particularly likely to gain weight when depressed (Polivy & Herman, 1976). Long-distance female runners who have stopped menstruating have more affective disorders in themselves and in their relatives than is true of female runners who are still menstruating. These runners are also likely to say that they run to control their depression (Gadpaille, Sanborn, & Wagner, 1987).

Sex Differences in Stress

According to many environmental theories, women are more often depressed than men because women more often experience various kinds of stress, including the stress of having lower social status (see Chapters 10 and 12). To evaluate this idea, the following will examine some ways in which women may be more severely stressed, leading to sex differences in depression.

Stress responses. If normal stress responses are abnormally exaggerated, by a combination of genetic liability and environmental stress, depression may occur. Stress responses and depressive syndrome symptoms do show some impressive overlaps (Gold, Goodwin, & Chrousos, 1988). Both stressed and depressed people often show high levels of **cortisol,** a stress hormone secreted by the adrenal cortex. (However, the cortisol changes may be more closely related to the anxiety than to the depressive symptoms: Meador-Woodruff et al., 1990.) Depression has been described as "a chronic 'flu-like' malaise with poor concentration, tension, and psychomotor retardation" (DePaulo et al., 1989, p. 828). Furthermore, just being under stress, such as facing a surgery, can lead to physiological changes similar to those seen in depression (Ceulemans, Westenberg, & van Praag, 1985).

Animal models of stress-induced depression typically do not show greater effects in females. In the one model that does, female rats may be less affected by the stressful event (being prevented from moving for a brief time) the first time it occurs. However, only male rats are able to **adapt** to the stress (Beatty & Hoyenga, 1992; Heinsbroek et al., 1990; Kennett et al., 1986). That is to say, only in males does the behavioral aftermath of the stress (a model for depression) decreases with or adapt to the repetition of the stress. So, after repeated stresses, the females act more "depressed" than do the males. Since the largest sex difference in human depression is that repetition of episodes is more likely in females, this model presents some intriguing analogues to human depression.

One reason for the sex difference in adaptation may be the greater serotonin level found in female brains (see references in Table 13.6). Perhaps the higher level means that females will not show the effects of the first stressor as strongly as males do (Stone, 1983). But the females' higher levels of serotonin may also limit the brain's ability to adapt. Putting this all together, perhaps the sex difference in

TABLE 13.4 *Sex Differences in the Structure of Depressive Syndrome*
The sexes differ not only in overall frequency but also in symptom patterns displayed within the various depressive syndromes.

Symptoms and Sex Differences	References
1. Clinically depressed females more often report excessive eating and weight gain as one of the symptoms (loss of appetite and weight loss is the most common eating symptom in both sexes).	1, 16 (but also see 6)
2. In nonselected populations, females are more likely than males to report that they eat when they become depressed; women also are more likely to report crying, becoming irritable, and confronting their feelings; males are more likely to report becoming aggressive and engaging in sexual activity.	2
3. Factor structure of depression scales is different for males and females: in nonselected populations. among depressed subjects.	3 4
4. Working females are more likely to go to health services and males to simply miss work when depressed.	5
5. The personality factors that differentiate depressed males from depressed females are the same same factors as those that differentiate nondepressed males from nondepressed females.	7
6. Psychomotor agitation (nervous activity) seems to be more common in female than in male depressives; retardation (inactivity) may be relatively more common in males.	8
7. Among depressed college students (rating scale measure), males are more socially withdrawn, express more motivational and cognitive problems, use drugs, and have somatic symptoms (e.g., aches and pains); women have greater lack of confidence, lack of concern over what happens to them, more self-blame, more crying spells and irritability, and are more hurt by criticism.	2, 9
8. Depression is associated with decreased instrumentality (as measured by sex role scales), but this may be an effect rather than a precursor of depression.	10
9. When under stress, college student females report feeling more depressed and anxious than males do, and females say they are more likely to express their feelings; males become more active in response to stress; stress from school or from intimate relationships depressed personal self-esteem only in females.	11
10. Age of onset of bipolar and unipolar syndromes is the same for both sexes, although female/male ratio for bipolar onset may be greatest from ages 30 to 75.	12, 13, 15
11. Incidence of depression before puberty is the same in both sexes; female incidence of depressive episodes increases at puberty.	12, 14
12. Males more likely to commit suicide; females are more likely to make nonfatal suicide attempts.	17

References:
 1. Casper et al., 1985; Frank, Carpenter, & Kupfer, 1988; Young et al., 1990; Zielinski, 1978
 2. Chino & Funabiki, 1984; Kleinke, Staneski, & Mason, 1982
 3. Clark et al., 1981; Hammen & Padesky, 1977; Kivelä & Pahkala, 1986; Ross & Mirowsky, 1984
 4. Kivelä & Pahkala, 1987
 5. Selzer, Paluszny, & Carroll, 1978
 6. Baron & Joly, 1988; Weissenburger et al., 1986
 7. Hirschfeld et al., 1984
 8. Avery & Silverman, 1984; Kivelä & Pahkala, 1988
 9. Vredenburg, Krames, & Flett, 1986
10. Feather, 1985; Flett, Vredenburg, & Pliner, 1985; Krames, England, & Flett, 1988
11. Zuckerman, 1989
12. Weissman et al., 1987
13. Amenson & Lewinsohn, 1981; Rice et al., 1984; Weissman et al., 1987
14. Angold, 1988; Carlson & Kashani, 1988; Jorm, 1987
15. Sibisi, 1990
16. Stunkard et al., 1990
17. Stillion & McDowell, 1991

depression reflects stress adaptation mechanisms rather than initial responses to stress. The initial response to stress in females may be more adaptive than that of males. On the other hand, the more extreme male response might lead to more adaptation, leaving females more susceptible to a depressionlike syndrome. If so, this would make females more vulnerable to repeated stress, including the stress produced by being depressed. In fact, repeated episodes of depression may heighten sensitivity to future stress. All of this might be particularly true for the stress of affiliative loss, as will now be described.

Life stress and social support.   The fact that life stress is related to depression seems to be clearly established (Brown & Harris, 1986). The occurrence of stress can be used to predict future episodes of depression in both sexes (Coyne & Downey, 1991; Rohde et al., 1990). Table 13.5 presents some of the relevant stressors and references. Furthermore, the death or loss (as through divorce) of a parent in childhood has been found to be a risk factor for adult depression. One study examined adopted children (Cadoret et al., 1985): the parent who died was genetically unrelated to the child who later developed depression as an

TABLE 13.5   *Major Life Event Risk Factors for an Episode of Depressive Disorder*

Type of Risk Factor	References
1. Death or loss of parent (e.g., divorce) in childhood, especially for females.	1
2. Traumatic childhood (e.g., abuse; distant, unaffectionate parents; overprotective parents; or—for males—an adoptive home with alcohol problems).	1, 2
3. Death of family member in adulthood.	3
4. Lack of social support (impairs recovery from episode equally for both sexes).	4
5. Other life event stress (few sex differences), though effects are weak and are less important for later than for first episodes.	6
6. Genes and life event stress interact (e.g., stress may cause episode only in genetically vulnerable people).	1, 6
7. High levels of interpersonal dependency or sensitivity may increase risk.	7

References:
1. Alnaes & Torgersen, 1988, 1989; Cadoret, O'Gorman, Heywood & Troughton, 1985; Kuyler et al., 1980; Lloyd, 1980a; Roy, 1981; for evidence to the contrary, see Ragan & McGlashan, 1986; Zahner & Murphy, 1989
2. Alnaes & Torgersen, 1990; Faravelli et al., 1986; Hällström, 1987; Holmes & Robins, 1988; Parker, 1979
3. Akiskal, 1982; Bruce, Kim, Leaf, & Jacobs, 1990; Lloyd, 1980b
4. Brugha et al., 1990
5. Ezquiaga, Gutierrez, & López, 1987; Perris, 1984a, 1984b, 1984c, 1984d; Surtees et al., 1986
6. Cadoret et al., 1985; Lloyd, 1980b; McGuffin, Katz & Bebbington, 1987; McGuffin et al., 1988; Post, 1992; Swann et al., 1990
7. Birtchnell, Deahl, & Falkowski, 1991; Boyce & Parker, 1989; Mongrain & Zuroff, 1989; Segal, Shaw, & Vella, 1989

adult. In fact, some researchers have claimed that the biochemical and behavioral effects of social losses in nonhuman primates are similar to those of depression in humans (Coe, Rosenberg, & Levine, 1988; Laudenslager, 1988; McKinney, 1985; Petrovich & Gewirtz, 1985).

Having the support of other people **(social support)** can alleviate the effects of stress, and lacking social support can be a stressor in and of itself, as documented in Table 13.5. Gender differences are sometimes found in social support. Wives provide more social support for husbands than husbands do for wives (Vanfossen, 1981). Women also say they are more affected (stressed) by the misfortunes of friends and relatives (other than first-degree relatives) than men do (Kessler & McLeod, 1984; Turner & Avison, 1989). Females also have more social support from friends. Women's more "interconnected" definitions of themselves might explain why they are more likely to be affected by loss of friends and relatives.

Differing levels of stress may not account for all the sex differences in clinical depression. Women are not necessarily more likely than men to have more stressors in their lives (Bebbington, Tennant, & Hurry, 1991). Also, stressful events predict a first episode better than they do recurrences, and, as pointed out, women more often have the repeated episodes.

Emotional reactivity.   The sexes also differ in reactivity to events. Females experience both more joy in response to pleasant events and more negative affect (anxiety and depression) in response to unpleasant events (Wood, Rhodes, & Whelan, 1989). Negative affect is correlated with symptoms of both depression and anxiety, and the *lack* of positive affect is associated specifically with depression (Watson, Clark, & Carey, 1988). Women's opinions of themselves are more affected by both positive and negative evaluations made concerning them than are men's opinions (Roberts & Nolen-Hoeksema, 1989).

Since women have more pleasant as well as unpleasant moods, how this reactivity might be related to sex differences in depressive episodes is unclear. Nonetheless, greater reactivity could mean that women might less often adapt to recurrent stressors, which could lead to depression. Thus, even in research that shows that women do not more often experience adversity than men do, women could react more than men do to the same events, especially negative events befalling friends, as described above.

Passive versus active coping strategies. Thierry, Steru, Chermat, and Simon (1984) have an evolutionary model of stress-related depressions. Organisms facing a problem of survival without any immediately obvious solution face a choice: continued struggle and search or simply wait for some environmental change that might offer a solution. Depression may reflect the waiting strategy. There could be sex differences in the cost/benefit ratios of each strategy, resulting in selection pressures for sex limitation. For example, castrating male mice increases the likelihood of a depressive or waiting response to survival problems (Bernardi et al., 1989). More aggressive male mice are more likely to use active coping strategies, and the less aggressive males the more passive strategies (Benus et al., 1990).

Are there sex differences? In a longitudinal study, human subjects who reported using more passive coping strategies (keeping away from people, waiting for someone to help, staying in bed) were most likely to develop clinical depression at a later time, especially after enduring some stressful events (Rohde et al., 1990). However, *men* rather than women more often said they used these passive strategies.

However, sex differences in passive versus active response styles might account for males' greater propensity for suicide. Across cultures, men are more likely to commit suicide, but women have been more likely to make nonfatal attempts (Åsgård, Nordström, & Råbäck,

1987; Huchcroft & Tanney, 1988; Kessler & McRae, 1983; Monk, 1987; Weissman, 1974). Many suicides occur because of depression, so looking at suicides also provides information about depression. One reason for the sex differences is that men use more lethal means, such as firearms, and so are less likely to be saved by medical attention. The difference between a completed suicide and an nonfatal suicide attempt is often determined by how quickly medical attention can be sought, so at least part of the difference is not related to gender per se. In fact, the incidence of attempted suicide seems to be increasing among males and may even be higher than that in females (Davis & Kosky, 1991).

Differences between male and female suicides have been assessed by interviewing family and friends after the event (Kotila & Lönnqvist, 1988; Monk, 1987; Rich et al., 1988). Both male attempters and male suicide victims tend to use more lethal methods, are more likely to be substance abusers, and are more likely to have economic problems leading to the act. Female suicides are more likely than males to have affective disorders and to commit suicide because of the pain of depressive episodes.

Cultural roles.   Is depression culturally defined as feminine? Children do associate anger with "maleness," and happiness, sadness, and fear with "femaleness" (Birnbaum, Nosanchuk, & Croll, 1980). Furthermore, the increase in individualism (as opposed to collectivism) in our culture may be related to the increase in depression (Glenn, 1987; Seligman, 1988; Weissman, 1987). Given the tendency for women to be more socially interrelated, the increased individualism may have affected their risk of depression even more than that of men because society has moved still further from women's preferences.

Depressogenic cognitions.   According to cognitive theories, people vulnerable to depression have certain thought patterns that lead them to overreact to stress and so become depressed. Depressed people do tend to view themselves more accurately than nondepressed people do (Taylor & Brown, 1988). Healthy people view themselves through rose-colored glasses, exaggerating skills and accomplishments and minimizing deficits. Healthy people also view themselves as having more control over the world than depressed people do. Depressed people have more accurate views concerning their own impact on the events of the world around them. Alloy and Clements (1990) found that this **depressive realism** was not only a consequence of being depressed but it also predicted future increases in depression scale scores after negative life events.

However, Tennen and Herzberger (1987) found depressive realism to be more closely related to lowered self-esteem than to depression per se. Stake (1990) went further and found that only in women did low levels of self-esteem lead to "realism." High self-esteem women and all men showed evidence of ego-enhancing (and distorting) explanations of events. Thus, "realism," low self-esteem, and depression may all go together in some way, but only for certain women.

Nolen-Hoeksema (1987) has suggested that females are more vulnerable to depression because they are more likely to focus on themselves and their pain. Males are more likely to try to block out their feelings by engaging in active, distracting behaviors, such as exercising. She suggested that women's rumination exaggerates a depressed mood, more often turning it into a clinical depression. For example, not only are college females more likely to focus on themselves than on the environment around them but such a self-focus increases depressive moods in response to some negative event (Ingram et al., 1988).

Despite this, such rumination might be adaptive in the long run. Newmann (1987) has suggested that women may be better able to cope with sadness because they are more willing to express it. Wegner (1990) found that *not* thinking about something when one is in a bad mood actually served to classically condition the thought to the bad mood. Every time the thought comes back, do does the bad mood and vice versa. The only way to extinguish the conditioning is to think freely about it — which is what women do.

Brewin's (1985) review of the cognitive theories concluded that the evidence did not suggest that cognitions led directly to depression. Instead, being depressed seems to cause these cognitions. Nevertheless, having the types of cognitions decribed above slows recovery, prolonging the depressive episode. The longitudinal research of Lewinsohn and colleagues described earlier supports this conclusion. Not only did cognitions *not* predict future episodes (though they did predict changes in scale scores) but women — even those who were to become depressed — had more healthy cognitions than men did. Thus, cognitions cannot be used to explain the sex difference.

Biological Covariates

The data just described concerning stress and depression, and sex differences in stress, might seem very convincing. In fact, it does seem as though there is little left for biology to explain. But as pointed out in Chapter 2, establishing environmental covariates does not rule out biological covariates.

Genetics and family history. The depressive syndromes have some genetic basis, as verified by twin, family history, and adoption studies (Hoyenga & Hoyenga, 1993). For example, 13 percent of the male and 30 percent of the female relatives of a person with depressive disorder also suffer from depression. The risks to females who have depressed relatives may have recently increased to 60 percent (Seligman, 1988).

The environmental factors associated with adult depression have been explored in research asking depressed people to describe their child-hoods (Gotlib et al., 1988; Parker, 1981; Perris et al., 1985). Either parental overprotection or lack of parental affection have most often been reported. Overprotection may prevent the person from learning appropriate coping strategies, and lack of affection could lead to a poor self-image. However, it is difficult to disentangle the effect of parental behaviors on their children from the effects that shared genes have on both the parents and the children.

Adoption studies allow one to see how environmental factors affect the likelihood of illness separate from the effects of shared genes. Depression studies have found that biological relatives of adoptees who developed affective disorders were three to eight times more likely to have an affective disorder themselves than are relatives of nondepressed adoptees (Hoyenga & Hoyenga, 1993). Although one study (Wender et al., 1986) found that the adoptive parents of affectively disturbed adoptees had no increase in risk compared to those of healthy adoptees, another study (Von Knorring et al., 1983) did find an increased risk. However, the fathers often became ill after their children had. This suggests that having a depressed child stresses parents, rather than depression in the parent causing depression in the child.

Do mental disorder genes confer any advantages? If depression is promoted by the presence of certain specific genes, why haven't evolutionary selection pressure eliminated those genes? Although depressed people have few children, the biological relatives of those people, particularly their fathers, might have unusually high reproductive success (Wender et al., 1986).

The "depression-promoting" genes may, in some cases, enhance cultural status and so the reproductive success of some family members. People with depressive disorders are often highly creative and achieve high social status (Andreasen, 1987; Coryell et al., 1989; Holden, 1986; Woodruff et al., 1971). The high achievement and creativity is characteristic not only of the sufferers themselves but also of their relatives. This may be somewhat more true of **bipolar** (alternating period of mania and depression) than of **unipolar** disorders (only episode of depression). However, although symptom scales of depression find higher scores in the lower SES, lifetime risks of major (unipolar) depression may be higher in the upper SES (Weissman & Myers, 1978).

More specifically, mood disorders, including depression, are frequently seen in highly achieving women. Of female Ph.D.s and doctors, 30 to 50 percent have depressive disorders (Clayton et al., 1980; Welner et al., 1979). Since in many cases the disorder appeared before the woman's career was started, this cannot be solely due to the stress of a demanding career. Among young women who attempted suicide, the most lethal attempts were made by those of the highest SES (Goldney, 1981). In fact, one review claimed that the sex difference in depression appears only during the periods of history in which there had been increasing opportunities for women (Silverstein & Perlick, 1991). Are these the times when women are most negatively affected by their relatively lower social statuses?

Evidence for sex limitation. Perinatal sex hormone levels may covary with risk. Humans exposed prenatally to DES have an increased risk of major depression (Meyer-Bahlburg et al., 1985; Vessey et al., 1983). The Vessey study involved subjects who had been randomly assigned to DES versus placebo groups. Furthermore, moods in young children covary with their neonatal hormonal levels (Jacklin, Maccoby, & Doering, 1983; Maccoby et al., 1979; Marcus et al., 1985). However, boys and girls did not differ in the frequencies of good and bad moods in the first two years of life, and only in boys were neonatal androgens positively correlated with happy/excited moods.

Table 13.6 presents some indirect evidence of hormone covariance. At one time or another, nearly every major transmitter has been linked to depressive disorders, and sex hormone levels covary with all of them. Only the serotonin data are presented because of the growing focus on serotonin dysfunction in depression. Diseases and hormones can have parallel effects on biochemistry and anatomy, but causation cannot be inferred from these parallels.

Postpubertal hormone levels have sometimes been found to covary with depression (Hoyenga & Hoyenga, 1993). Some women with a family history of depression seem to be at an increased risk for becoming depressed after having giving birth. In fact, Gater, Dean, and Morris (1989) have claimed that females' increased risk for depressive episodes is entirely due to child bearing—females who have never had children have risks equal to those of males.[9] Having been pregnant also causes long-lasting changes in hormone levels (Bernstein et al., 1985). Although menopause does not increase most women's chances for becoming depressed, some women who had depressive episodes before menopause may begin to have more frequent episodes afterwards (Bungay, Vessey, & McPherson, 1980; Hällström & Samuelsson, 1985; Hammar et al., 1984; Winokur, 1973). Furthermore, in double-blind research, menopausal women given either E or E + T scored significantly lower on a depression scale than did women given a placebo (Montgomery et al., 1987).

SUMMARY

The concept of personality implies prediction—the ability to predict differences in behaviors from differences in scores on personality tests. Wiggins's circumplex (Figure 13.1) is one way to visualize sex differences not only in personality traits but also in egoistic dominance (top), prosocial dominance (more to the right), hostile physical aggression (top left), and depression (bottom right). Egoistic versus prosocial dominance seems to be masculine and feminine, respectively, in children

TABLE 13.6 *Hormone-Depression Parallels*

The anatomical and biochemical variables associated with depression also tend to covary with sex hormone levels, which is especially true for 5-HT or serotonin biochemistry. However, covariation does not mean causation.

Disease Association	References	Hormone Covariation	References
Depressive moods more often occur after left- than right-side brain lesions; thus, right hemisphere is more active in depression.	1	Perinatal sex hormones may affect brain organization.	3
5-HT dysfunction important in depression: 5-HT specific drugs are therapeutic; other antidepressant drugs require an intact 5-HT system to work; depletion of blood tryptophan (and hence brain 5-HT) induces depression.	2	Sex hormones affect 5-HT activity (e.g., T suppresses levels); females have greater levels (greater rates of synthesis) and/or their brain is more sensitive to 5-HT.	4
		One 5-HT receptor is coded for by an X-linked gene.	5

References:
1. Altshuler et al., 1990; Otto, Yeo, & Dougher, 1987; Robinson et al., 1985.
2. Byerley et al., 1987; Charney et al., 1990; Curzon, 1988; Delgado et al., 1990; Faustman et al., 1990; Plaznik, Kostowski, & Archer, 1989; Swann et al., 1990; Van de Kar, 1989; Young et al., 1985
3. See Chapter 7
4. Carlsson et al., 1985; Glaser et al., 1990; Goudsmit, Feenstra, & Swaab, 1990; Heinsbroek et al., 1990; Higley et al., 1991; Kendall, Stancel, & Enna, 1981; Kennett et al., 1986; Meyer, Ferres-Torres, & Mas, 1978; Peters, Gray, & Joseph, 1991; Seegal, 1985; Young & Ervin, 1984; Chapter 6
5. Yu et al., 1991

of most cultures, in adults, and even in chimpanzees.

Egoistic dominance gone awry may lead to homicide in males. Paradoxically, aggressive boys may also become depressed as teens as well as being more likely to be aggressive adults. Males more often than females kill for status. Females more often kill their children or kill in self-defense. Although evolution may have selected for a mechanism that increased egoistic dominance and aggression in males, since development is epigenetic, socialization practices are the proximal cause of male aggressiveness.

Neglecting the ego for the sake of prosocial concerns may lead to depression. Women are more likely to become clinically depressed. After a first episode, women are also more likely to have reccurrences. The reasons for the sex difference might include evolutionary selection pressures, hormones, and socialization. Women may be more affected by stressors, particularly the stressors of affiliative losses (death of friends and more distant relatives). Females' brain biochemistry may not adapt in the same way to repeated stressors, making repeated episodes of depression more likely. Women also have lower social status than men do, and the higher-status women—who are presumably most highly motivated for egoistic status—seem to be the most likely to have affective disorders.

ENDNOTES

1. As will be seen later, all of these traits can be related to the concepts of instrumentality and expressiveness, and all show consistent sex differences in self-endorsement frequencies.

2. Rank-order the equipment a space crew would need to survive after a crash landing on the moon.

3. This seems to correspond most closely to the upper left versus the lower right quadrant of the circumplex of Figure 13.1.

4. For example, depressed people are less likely to exaggerate their own status; this has been called **depressive realism** (Alloy & Clements, 1990; Taylor & Brown, 1988).

5. When Daly and Wilson are mentioned, the references just cited are being used.

6. Abused versus control males: 19.4 percent versus 13.5 percent, $p < .05$; females: 3.,4 percent versus 2.4 percent, $p > .05$.

7. The sexes can be subjected to separate breeding programs. Suppose that aggression in females is being selected for and against. In each generation, the most aggressive and the least aggressive females are bred to produce the offspring of the next generation. The males to whom they are bred are the brothers of the other females also selected for breeding in the same line (high or low aggression).

8. Jaffe et al., 1989: only a very weak effect; Meyer-Bahlburg & Ehrhardt, 1982; Reinisch, 1981; Reinisch & Karow, 1977; Reinisch & Sanders, 1984; Reinisch, Ziemba-Davis, & Sanders, 1991; for the negative studies, see Hoyenga & Hoyenga, 1993.

9. Subsequent research confirmed this effect, but a more sophisticated statistical analysis suggested that the most important factor was marriage rather than child bearing, though parity may also have an effect (Bebbington, Dean et al., 1991).

CHAPTER 14

DEVELOPMENTAL RATE: SEXUAL MOTIVES AND SPATIAL VISUALIZATION

INTRODUCTION
BACKGROUND
SEX AND MATING
SPATIAL TASKS
SUMMARY

> *The man's desire is for the woman; but the woman's desire is rarely other than for the desire of the man.*
> —S. T. Coleridge (1827, from Cohen & Cohen, 1960, p. 117)

> *The natural man has only two primal passions—to get and beget.*
> —William Osler (from Fitzhenry, 1987, p. 172)

> *Men and women differ far less in their potential physiological and psychological responses during sexual activities per se than they do in how they negotiate sexual activities and in the kinds of sexual relationships and interactions they are motivated to seek. This may explain the anomaly (from the male point of view) that although women can be strongly aroused by pornography they are unlikely to seek it out.*
> —D. Symons (1979, p. 179)

The three quotations above illustrate the interlocking themes of this chapter. Men focus on desire for women (desire for sex), and women focus on having men desire them. Men and women may have different kinds of sexual and mating preferences, but since successful reproduction must involve one of each sex both conflict and compromise would be unsurprising.

INTRODUCTION

This chapter covers two apparently unrelated kinds of behaviors: sexual behaviors and performances on spatial tasks. Males tend to be more intensely interested in sex, particularly casual sex, whereas females tend to be more selective about their sexual partners. Males also tend to have higher average performances on several different measures of **spatial ability,** or the ability to visualize objects' rotations or to see relationships in three-dimensional space. (More precise definitions will be given later.) As pointed out in the introduction to this last unit, both behaviors may be seen as facets of the human preoccupation with sex and status. Furthermore, both covary (though weakly) with timing of puberty, which suggests some interesting ideas about mechanisms and evolutionary selection pressures.

The first section of the chapter presents the context for pubertal timing and sex differences in spatial tasks. The next section looks at gender-related differences in criteria for mate selection and in attitudes toward sexual activity. The final section covers spatial tasks.

BACKGROUND

The context for spatial performances includes sex differences in the performances on other tasks. This section also presents data on timing of puberty and evolutionary theories of sexual choices and spatial skills. Why have the sexes come to differ from each other?

Sex Differences in Task Performances

McGuinness (1985) reached the following conclusion about sex differences, which applies to a wide variety of cognitive tasks.[1] Some differences depend on whether the task emphasizes interest in people versus objects and things. Females, compared to males, seem more people oriented and often do better on "people" tasks, such as discriminating among the faces of people.

McGuinness's descriptions of differences. The sexes differ in sensitivities to sights and sounds (McGuinness, 1985). Females are more sensitive to sounds, especially to the high-frequency sounds that allow us to tell the difference between consonants and between different peoples' voices. Females are also less comfortable with loud sounds. Females have greater

sensitivity to light under dim viewing conditions, but males are more sensitive under brighter viewing conditions. Males are better at seeing the fine details in either stationary or moving images. Females are better at detecting wide stripes (when the brightness of the stripe differs only slightly from its background), but males are better at detecting very narrow stripes. Males have greater age-related declines in hearing, but age has more severe effects on vision in females.

The sexes also show consistent differences on motor tasks. Boys run faster and are stronger at almost all ages. Females tend to do better on tests of fine-motor skills and in clerical tasks, such as scanning text for the occurrence of certain letters or symbols. On the other hand, males are not only faster but more accurate at tasks that require subjects to self-correct their own movements in responses to shifts in the position of objects in a visual display (such as the typical video-arcade games).

McGuinness found one surprisingly large sex difference. She asked college students to search for target letters (*A* or *I*) in five-letter words. The words were presented either visually or were spoken, and in both cases the subjects were told to search for either a given sound (the sound of *A* or *I*) or a given shape (the appearance of a capital letter *A* or *I*). There were no sex differences during visual presentations. However, during auditory presentations, males were much poorer at detecting a sound and were even worse at detecting whether a given shape was present or not in some word. In fact, in the latter task, males performed at chance levels.

Meta-analytic reviews. According to meta-analytic reviews and studies involving large, representative samples of students, females get higher scores on some kinds of verbal tests (Hyde, 1981; Hyde & Linn, 1988; Rosenthal & Rubin, 1982; Wilder & Powell, 1989). Most research shows that the size of the sex difference has been decreasing in recent years. However, on the verbal portion of the Scholastic Aptitude Test (SAT), scores have favored males since around 1972 when the test was changed (Burton, Lewis, & Robertson, 1988). Boys also lag behind girls in learning to read and are more likely to suffer from **dyslexia** (a reading disorder) (Finucci & Childs, 1981; McGuinness, 1981).

Sex differences in performances on certain types of mathematical performances have also been repeatedly found. Hyde's (1981) early review of studies on sex differences in mathematical performances found an average effect size of .43, just slightly smaller than the one she found for spatial studies. Subsequent re-analyses of her data found that the effect size has been decreasing over time (Becker & Hedges, 1984; Rosenthal & Rubin, 1982). Friedman (1989) published a meta-analytic review of studies done between 1974 and the middle of 1987, coming to similar conclusions and finding an average effect size of only .024.[2]

Hyde and her colleagues later published a much more extensive meta-analytic review (Hyde, Fennema, & Lamon, 1990). They analyzed 100 studies, which produced 254 independent effect sizes and involved 3,175,188 subjects. The overall $d = -.05$. Females had the advantage for computational problems and for understanding mathematical concepts. Only for complex problem solving did the difference reverse: $d = .08$. Even in this area, differences only emerged in high school ($d = .29$) and college ($d = .32$) samples.

Overall, the more selected the sample (e.g., college students as opposed to high school students, or higher- versus lower-ability students), the larger the sex difference in math scores (Hyde et al., 1990; Ramist & Arbeiter, 1986; Rosenthal & Rubin, 1982). The sex differences in the most select samples may be the most important for mathematical genius or the highest levels of mathematical creativity (Lubinski & Humphreys, 1990).

Relationships among tasks. In order to understand spatial tasks, we have to see how performances on them are related to perfor-

mances on other tasks. Math and spatial tasks are frequently found to be interrelated, for example. The kinds of math items on which males do better than females often have a spatial component (Englehard, 1990; Marshall & Smith, 1987; Sabers, Cushing, & Sabers, 1987; Wood, 1976).

Scores on many spatial tests are highly correlated with scores on a variety of mathematical tests, including the Scholastic Aptitude Test, Mathematics Section (SAT-M) (Bieri, Bradburn, & Galinsky, 1958; Benbow et al., 1983; Burnett, Lane, & Dratt, 1979; Fennema & Sherman, 1977; Hyde, Geiringer, & Yen, 1975; Sherman, 1980). Some researchers have shown that if sex differences in scores on spatial tests are statistically controlled, the sex difference on mathematics scores decreases, often to the point of nonsignificance (Burnett, Lane, & Dratt, 1979; Fennema & Sherman, 1977; Johnson, 1984). Other researchers have not found this to be true (Benbow, 1988; Ethington & Wolfle, 1984). Probably the specific nature of the relationship depends on ability level and handedness as well as on gender (Ethington & Wolfle, 1984; Fennema & Tartre, 1985; Pattison & Grieve, 1984). For example, spatial ability may predict mathematics scores better in males and in females with anomalous dominance[3] than in right-handed females (Casey, Pezaris, & Nuttall, 1992).

Math and spatial scores could be related to each other because both are related to other abilities or to the same background developmental variables. One study found that sex differences in math scores disappeared not only when spatial scores were controlled but also when parental behaviors and attitudes were controlled (Fennema & Sherman, 1977). Furthermore, both math and spatial scores are related to language skills in unique ways for females. A female's skill in verbal tasks is associated with a greater dislike of mathematics (Ethington & Wolfle, 1984, 1986; Marsh, 1989). Although both math and English test scores are positively correlated with spatial scores in women, in men, only math scores predict spatial scores (Kyllonen, Lohman, & Snow, 1984; Ozer, 1987; Pearson & Ferguson, 1989).[4] Thus, it seems safe to assume that sex differences in spatial performances affect sex differences in scores on standardized mathematics tests and thus affect the ability of women to choose mathematical type of occupations.

Developmental Rate Covariates

The timing of puberty importantly affects several characteristics, including brain organization. One set of factors controls which side of the brain is responsible for some function *(direction of lateralization)*. Another, separate set of factors controls the degree of difference between the right and left sides *(degree of lateralization)*. Both sets of factors seem to covary with developmental rate and are jointly controlled by genes and by the environment (see documentation in Hoyenga & Hoyenga, 1993). The presence of testosterone (T) during perinatal development may   crease the rate of growth of the smaller side of the brain, whichever one that is (see Chapters 6, 7, and 9; Galaburda et al., 1987; Rosen et al., 1989). Differences in growth rate during specific perinatal periods may translate into differences in adult abilities, including **dyscalculia** (disorder of math performances) and dyslexia (Hynd & Semrud-Clikeman, 1989a, 1989b; Semrud-Clikeman & Hynd, 1990).

Covariates of the timing of puberty. Late maturers of both sexes tend to have higher scores on spatial tests than do earlier maturers, especially if extremely early-maturing are compared to extremely late-maturing females (Hoyenga & Hoyenga, 1993). However, any effect of puberty on spatial task performances has to be interpreted in the context of the developmentally stable scores and stable sex differences. The size of the sex difference varies little with age, appearing at the second grade and lasting well into old age (Czarnota, 1989; Huss & Kayson, 1985; Kerns & Berenbaum,

1991; Robert & Tanguay, 1990; Willis & Schaie, 1988). Spatial scores are also stable across age in longitudinal studies (Goldberg & Meredith, 1975; Ozer, 1987; Witkin, Goodenough, & Karp, 1967).

Other consistent covariates of pubertal timing include hormone levels and sexual behaviors (see documentation in Hoyenga & Hoyenga, 1993). Females with an early puberty have higher levels of at least some hormones, and the higher levels of the estrogens persist throughout their lives. Females with an early puberty also tend to become sexually active earlier, are more likely to commit crimes, have children at a younger age, and have more children. In fact, in both sexes, an early onset of sexual activity is genetically linked to aggressive behaviors (Rowe et al., 1989). However, a *very* early puberty may be associated with reproductive problems and even infertility. Despite having higher IQ scores, early-maturing women get less education.

In industrialized societies, the female's age at puberty affects her changes for **hypergamy** (marrying a man with higher status than her parents) (Elder, 1969; Gibbs, 1986; Hoyenga & Hoyenga, 1993; Jessor et al., 1983; Simmons, Blyth, & McKinney, 1983). Women can increase their chances of hypergamy either by increasing their own status through education or by being attractive to a man of high status. However, becoming sexually active early is associated with lower grades, and women who will eventually marry up in status are less sexually active as adolescents. Thus, females with a later puberty tend to get more education and eventually either a higher status job or a higher status marriage (or both).

In summary, both sexual activities and performances on spatial tasks are related to women's pubertal timing. An early puberty— but not abnormally early—is linked to higher scores on some spatial tasks. It also leads to greater reproductive success and thus to greater value to men in less industrialized countries. On the other hand, in more industrialized countries, a delay of puberty can increase a woman's chances of hypergamy.

Mechanisms. According to the most typical interpretation of the timing covariates, the pubertal hormonal surge affects some developing brain processes. Since the surge occurs at different ages for the sexes, their developmental processes are affected in somewhat different ways. Some of the covariation between post-pubertal hormones and test scores in humans could be used to support this idea. Also, maze-learning scores in female rats decline at puberty (Hoyenga & Hoyenga, 1993).

Alternatively, pubertal timing could be a marker for a developmental timetable. If so, the most critical factor would not be the time of puberty (and the surge of sex hormones) per se. Instead, age at puberty would simply reflect the timing of some other, more directly relevant process, perhaps some process that started prenatally. Perinatal hormones do affect puberty: perinatal T delays it in primates. XXY males also have slowed development, are less likely to be right-handed, and often have developmental learning disorders and atypical lateralization. People with delayed puberties are more likely to be left-handed (Hoyenga & Hoyenga, 1993). The consistency of spatial scores across age would also imply that the group of early maturers is not systematically changing relative to late maturers.

The postnatal developmental environment clearly also affects pubertal timing (Hoyenga & Hoyenga, 1993). Father absence accelerates puberty in females, as does having frequent fights with parents. Eating meat (in females) and overeating (in both sexes) can lead to an earlier puberty.

Evolutionary Theories

This section discusses evolutionary theories of sex differences in mating preferences and spatial performances. The fact that both father absence and pubertal timing affect reproductive behavior supports Draper's ideas about how the developmental environment is related to the selection of polygamous versus monogamous mating strategies in humans (see Chapter 9).

Sexual selection and mate choice. Sexual selection is related to mate choices (see Chapter 4). Female mammals tend to be more selective and they commonly choose males that have gathered resources or that have desirable characteristics such as dominance or "good genes." If males bearing desirable characteristics are preferentially selected by the kinds of females that successfully rear more offspring, sexual selection will affect genetic inheritance patterns even in a monogamous mating system (Andersson, 1986; Fairbairn, 1988).

The more that males invest in offspring (as they tend to do in monogamous system when they are relatively certain of paternity: Chapter 4), the more sexually selective they will be. Under these monogamous conditions, **positive assortive mating** occurs—mating pairs tend to resemble each other on one or more characteristics. For example, females may prefer large males, and vice versa, so that only the largest of each gender gets its preferred partner. Smaller males and females will have to settle for "second best."

In part, the necessity of male parental investment depends on how much resources the female has and on the nature of the competition. The acquisition of resources by the male could signal the genetic quality of the male to the female (female choice, sexual selection) or it could indicate that he has resources that can be invested in their joint offspring. In other words, a rich man may be attractive to females because he possess the traits that lead to accumulation of wealth—traits that can be passed on to his offspring (sexual selection for "good genes"). Or the rich man may be attractive because his wealth means that their offspring can be well fed, given the latest medical care, and be well educated, which would be particularly important if the female herself lacked sufficient resources for successful reproduction.

Types of reproductive strategies.   Although as a species humans are K-selected strategists, sex differences in human reproductive strategies can be described as males being relatively more r- and females more K-selected strategists (see Chapter 4). Furthermore, males would focus more on mate quality (genes) and females on paternal investment (his social status and commitment to her and her offspring).

Individuals within each sex can also be relatively more r- or K-strategists, compared to others of their same sex. Early- versus late-maturing animals, at least in nonhumans, can be viewed as relatively more r-selected strategists. Among gerbils, early-maturing females have greater lifetime reproductive success (under laboratory conditions), have relatively more female offspring, and show reduced maternal behaviors (Clark, Spencer, & Galef, 1986). Choice of strategy might be partially under some genetic control as reflected, for example, in individual differences in developmental rate and timing of puberty (Hoyenga & Hoyenga, 1993). Strategy choice could also be epigenetically selected (Barkow, 1989; Draper & Harpending, 1982; Ellis, 1987; Rushton, 1985; Thornhill & Thornhill, 1983). Critical cues leading to a shift toward a relatively more r-strategy would probably include lack of paternal investment (father absence) and a lower socioeconomic status.

For both sexes, an r-strategy would imply less parental investment, a greater number of sexual (mating) partners, and more offspring. Characteristics of an r-strategy for females would also include selection of a mate based on his qualities (status) rather than on his willingness to make a large paternal investment. A female K-strategist would focus on a male's commitment to her and her offspring. Both sexes would shift to relatively more K-type strategies as they age, and both would be ex-pected to use relatively more r-type strategies in picking partners for shorter-term sexual relationships.

The amount of competition will also affect mating strategies. One way to measure the amount of competition in humans is to look at the sex ratio among mating adults (Secord, 1983; Veevers, 1988). The lower the sex ratio, the more females there are relative to males and the more competition there is among women for males. Low sex ratios may be associated with more illegitimate births, more divorce, more extramarital affairs, and less hypergamy. Women may marry later in life and be more politically active. In the United States, the sex ratio is currently low. According to Secord and Veevers, the effects a high sex ratio has on competition among males does not parallel the effects of a low sex ratio on female competition, because of the greater status and power of men in most societies.

Evolution of sex differences in spatial performances.   The model presented in this section has been derived from the work of the researchers and theorists cited here. In this model, rodents' ability to learn mazes is used as a possible analogue for some human spatial skills (e.g., Gray & Buffery, 1971). Sex differences, favoring males, have also been reported in human maze-learning performances (Halpern, 1986).

Gaulin, FitzGerald, and Wartell (Gaulin & FitzGerald, 1986, 1988, 1989; Gaulin, FitGerald, & Wartell, 1990; Gaulin & Wartell, 1990) related sex differences in maze learning to rodents' reproductive roles. These researchers found that males are better at maze learning only in polygynous and not in monogamous strains of rodents. Also, only in the polygynous strains do males range more widely than females (and then only in breeding season). Given their more extensive home ranges, spatial skills would be more relevant to male than to female reproductive roles but only in polygynous strains.

As will be described in the spatial section of this chapter, rodent sex differences depend on sex differences in strategies. Male rats tend to learn about geometry, whereas female rats attend to a greater variety of location cues. Perhaps learning about the overall geometry of his range enables a polygynous male to more quickly learn about his larger range. The females' focus on all cues allows her to learn more completely about her smaller home range. The differences in reproductive roles may cause the genes associated with each strategy to become sex limited.

Spatial skills are related to some behaviors that are important in human evolutionary history. Spatial skills are related both to throwing skills (Jardine & Martin, 1983) and to people's ability to find their way around their environments (Pearson & Ialongo, 1986). Two studies have explicitly related spatial[5] performances to male and female adults' abilities to locate themselves in a familiar area such as their college campus (Bryant, 1982) or their hometown (Pearson & Ferguson, 1989). The correlations between spatial scores and locational accuracy were not always significantly different from zero, but they were always positive. Across cultures, male children go further from home, and children that go further from home have higher levels of spatial ability (see Chapter 10; also see Hoyenga & Hoyenga, 1993). Male children also make more use of extra visual cues to aid them in performing a spatial task than do female children (Kearins, 1981; Keogh, 1971).

If the genes creating tendencies to use a certain type of spatial strategy (e.g., *visual* versus *geometry* versus *all cues*) provided only benefits and no costs to either gender, there would be no reason to have the genes' activities limited to just one gender. One possibility is that because of brain constraints on the processing of stimulus information, the organism can maximally benefit from only one type of strategy. Which strategy would be of most benefit would depend on home range size.

There would be costs as well as benefits of possessing either strategy, and the cost/benefit ratio could depend on gender. One way this could happen would be if the cost was a by-product of the developmental mechanisms required for the maturation of higher levels of spatial skills. Specifically, a slowed rate of biological maturation might be required. Whatever mechanisms act to affect general developmental rate (e.g., genes, prenatal T), brain developmental rate might also inevitably be affected. Because the brain's developmental rate affects its organization, as just described, a change in rate might indirectly affect spatial skills and strategies. Thus, sex differences in the cost/benefit ratio of early puberty versus high-spatial skills (or differing uses of various kinds of spatial cues) would be measured by how each affected the lifetime reproductive success of each sex.

A developmental timetable that maximizes spatial skills may be more detrimental to a female's ability to reproduce than to a male's ability, especially in polygynous species. In fact, polygynous species are likely to have a delayed reproductive maturity, compared to similar monogamous species. Polygynous species are also more likely to have sex differences in the timing of puberty, the female being earlier (Dewsbury, 1981a; Weisfeld & Berger, 1983). The human species has most frequently been described as mildly polygynous in its evolutionary history (see Chapter 4).

In polygynous species, where there is extensive intermale conflict for mates, a slowed rate of maturation would not affect the reproductive success of males. Younger males that have not yet been able to achieve high social status are unlikely to mate. On the other hand, a delay in sexual maturity would decrease lifetime reproductive success in females. Delaying maturity by a year could cost her one offspring, or one litter, and, in turn, all the offspring of those offspring. This could have been true of humans throughout much of our preindustrialized evolutionary history, although, as just described, industrialization has changed the factors associated with hypergamy in females.

Therefore, early puberty might have provided a relatively more favorable cost/benefit ratio for human females than for males, and delay of puberty a more favorable ratio for males, leading to sex limitation. Sex differences in both sexual activities and in spatial performances might have been the result. The research that documents and describes those sex differences will now be presented.

SEX AND MATING

This section discusses gender-related differences in mating preferences and in attitudes toward sexual activity. Although the material is consistent with the evolutionary models just presented, the models also point out that culture and therefore developmental experiences are expected to have a tremendous impact on both sexes.

Human Mating Preferences

Not all of us want the same things in a mate: beauty may be in the eye of the beholder.

Love and mate selection.   Evolution gave us the propensity to love certain kinds of people, depending in part on who we are. Evolutionary selection pressures are the ultimate cause, but love is the proximal cause, at least in societies in which the people themselves rather than their parents choose their mates.

Sternberg (1986) proposed a triangular theory of love with three components. The first is **intimacy,** or the feelings of closeness, connectedness, and bondedness that occur not only in opposite-sex but also in same-sex and kin relationships. **Passion** involves the drives leading to romance, physical attraction, and sexual activity. The last component, **decision/commitment,** is cognitive and includes both a short-term and a long-term component. The short-term component is the cognitive decision that love is present; the long-term component is the cognitive decision to be committed to maintaining that love. Decision/commitment might reflect long-term or K-type mate selection strategies.

People's mate preferences.   There are more similarities than differences between the sexes when people are asked to rate what qualities they desire in a mate. Nevertheless, the sex differences that do occur, as presented in Table 14.1, are shared by a number of different cultures.

Another way to look at human mate preferences is to examine newspaper advertisements in the classifieds section. As Table 14.1 shows, attractiveness of the potential partner is more important to men, but status is more important to women. The older the man is, the younger he wants his partner to be, relative to his own age. Good-looking women also seek well-to-do men, suggesting that women sometimes exchange attractiveness for status. One study that examined the number of responses a given advertiser received found that thin women and tall men got more responses than did fat women and short men (Lynn & Shurgot, 1984).

Other research has also demonstrated how important attractiveness is for a female (Berscheid & Walster, 1974). If a male dates or marries an attractive female, he is perceived as having higher status. The more self-confident a man feels, the more attracted he is to a physically attractive female confederate (Pellegrini, Hicks, & Meyers-Winton, 1979). Romantic partners also tend to be matched for physical attractiveness, which increases the likelihood that the relationship will continue (Feingold, 1988b). If a female college student is physically attractive, she is also more sexually active (Kaats & Davis, 1970). Table 14.1 presents some data on same-sex versus opposite-sex sexual preferences (homosexual versus heterosexual), showing that men desire attractiveness whether their sexual partners are male or female.

TABLE 14.1 *Mating Preferences in Humans*

Preferred Mate Characteristics	References
Ratings of Desirable Mate Characteristics Both sexes want kindness, understanding, intelligence, physical attractiveness, exciting personality, good health, adaptability, and creativity.	Buss, 1985; Buss & Angleitner, 1989; Buss & Barnes, 1986; Symons,, 1979, 1987

Traits that females rate higher than males do:
   mates taller than they are
   mates older than they are
   good earning capacity
   similarity in educational background
   desire for home & children
   favorable social status
   industriousness
   education
   intelligence
   achievement strivings
 Traits that males rate higher than females do:
   physical attractiveness
   frugality
   mates younger than they are
   chastity
   someone who makes a good impression on friends
	Buss, 1989b; Buss & Angleitner, 1989; Buss & Barnes, 1986; Buss et al., 1990; Howard, Blumstein, & Schwartz, 1987; Langhorne & Secord, 1955; Morse, Gruzen, & Reis, 1976; Thiessen & Ross, 1990

Dominance increases heterosexual attractiveness ratings of males but not of females (dominance does not increase males' desirability as mates).	Sadalla, Kenrick, & Vershure, 1987
Men found high earning potential in women to be attractive only if women were physically attractive; the earning potential of male stimulus figures had more effect on women if males were physically unattractive.	Sprecher, 1989
Sex Differences in the Contents of Newspaper Advertisements Requesting a Heterosexual Partner • Women request* status and offer** appearances, especially thinness; men request appearance and offer status. • Women want taller, older (+ 3 years) men, and men want younger, slender women; the older the man, the younger (relative to his age) he wants the woman to be. • Men more often requested intelligence. • Good-looking advertisers seek good-looking partners, but good-looking women also seek well-to-do men (especially women over 40). • Women more often seek sincerity (commitment?) and offer instrumental traits; men more often offer expressive traits.	Cameron, Oskamp, & Sparks, 1977; Deaux & Hanna, 1984; Harrison & Saied, 1977; Kenrick & Keefe, 1989; Koestner & Wheeler, 1988; Smith, Waldorf, & Trembath, 1990

(continued)

TABLE 14.1 *(continued)*

Preferred Mate Characteristics	References
Sex Differences in Attraction and Retention among Dating (or Potentially Dating) Couples	
Males are evaluated more favorably when wife or dating partner is attractive or intelligent; wife is not rated more favorably for having an attractive husband.	Bar-Tal & Saxe, 1976; Meiners & Sheposh, 1977; Sigall & Landy, 1973
Men more interested than women are in returning a flirtation or in meeting someone in a bar.	Cunningham, 1989; Downey & Vitulli, 1987
Males' interest in a female is directly related to the female's perceived sexiness, but females were more influenced by a male's perceived intelligence.	Cunningham, 1989
Affairs most likely to break up if couples are discrepant in age, educational aspirations, intelligence, and physical attractiveness; matching on attractiveness may be most important at the beginning stages of a relationship; females somewhat more likely to initiate the breakup.	Hill, Rubin, & Peplau, 1976; Feingold, 1988b
Sex of Partner versus Sex of Subject Effects	
In advertisements, female heterosexuals most likely to offer attractiveness and female homosexuals least likely to do so; heterosexuals seek a broader range of characteristics; males, regardless of sexuality, are most concerned about a prospective partner's attractiveness, and female homosexuals are least concerned.	Deaux & Hanna, 1984
Women have stronger preferences for expressive and males for attractive partners; aggressiveness is preferred in a male partner by both heterosexual females and homosexual males, especially the latter; women have stronger preferences for ambitiousness, and ambition is preferred more in men than in women.	Howard, Blumstein, & Schwartz, 1987 (4,314 heterosexual married couples & cohabitors, 969 male homosexual couples, & 788 lesbian couples)
Mating Patterns in Humans	
A person's income negatively affects chances of remarriage after divorce for women and positively affects men; the more children the woman has, or the older she is, the less likely she is to remarry.	Blumstein & Schwartz, 1983; Oh, 1987
Women are more likely to improve social status through marriage if they are thin (in westernized cultures) and attractive; trends for men are in the same direction but much smaller.	Elder, 1969; Goldblatt, Moore, & Stunkard, 1965; Power & Moynihan, 1988; Sobal, 1984
There is assortative mating for psychological variables such as extroversion, dominance, quarrelsomeness, being religious, liking children, & ingenuousness; similarity of pairs decreases as length of marriage increased.	Buss, 1984a, b; Buss & Barnes, 1986; Epstein & Guttman, 1984; Thiessen & Gregg, 1980
There is assortative mating for physical and cognitive variables such as height, degree of overweight, earlobe length, IQ, verbal skills, and neuroticism.	Buss, 1984c, 1985; Epstein & Guttman, 1984; Sobal, 1984; Thiessen & Gregg, 1980; Vandenberg, 1972

TABLE 14.1 *(continued)*

Preferred Mate Characteristics	References
Attraction versus Durability of the Bond (Commitment)	
For females, the importance of the male's intelligence increases as he goes from a potential date to sexual partner to steady date to marriage partner; the ntelligence of a sexual partner is less important to males than to females; for most characteristics *except* attractiveness, men were less selective about sexual partners than about dates; sex differences are usually smallest with regard to preferences for a marriage partner.	Kenrick & Keefe, 1989; Kenrick et al., 1990
There are more sex differences in partner preferences for short-term "sexual" relationships than in long-term "meaningful" relationships; for short-term relationships, males focus only on appearance, but females rank personal qualities, achievement strivings, and money higher than males do.	Nevid, 1984
Preferences for attractive and athletic partners are negatively correlated with satisfaction with relationship and likelihood that relationship will continue.	Howard et al., 1987
Relationship is more likely to continue if couple is more similar to each other in abilities, attractiveness, personalities and values.	Blumstein & Schwartz, 1983; Epstein & Guttman, 1984; Thiessen & Gregg, 1980
• Possessiveness is related to commitment, but only for wives. • In outside sex, men look for variety, whereas women look for some special relationship. • Heterosexuals who are not monogamous are less committed to marriage. • Ambition in wives—and its lack in husbands—leads to breakup.	Blumstein & Schwartz, 1983
Nonmonogamous marriages are more likely to break up.	Blumstein & Schwartz, 1983; Essock-Vitale & McGuire, 1988; Glass & Wright, 1977; Kitson, Babri, & Roach, 1985
Divorce is more likely to be thought of by the female, but in states with no-fault divorce laws, filing by males has greatly increased.	Fletcher, 1983; Kitson et al., 1985
People prefer to match on Type-A/Type-B characteristics,*** but couples with Type-A female partners are more likely to break up.	Morell, Twillman, & Sullaway, 1989; Rosenberger & Strube, 1986

Notes: * = Request means the characteristics desired in a potential partner, as stated by the person advertising in a personals column; ** = Offer means the characteristics that the person writing the advertisement claims to possess; *** = Type A refers to the personality characteristics associated with high risk for heart attacks, and Type B is a heart-attack "resistant" personality.

In one study of a dating service, physical attractiveness was important to the popularity of both men and women (Green, Buchanan, & Heuer, 1984). Women also picked older men and men picked younger women. The only factor that affected the likelihood of a woman being chosen by a man was her physical attractiveness (which is reflected in her age), whereas both having higher status and being attractive affected the likelihood of a man being chosen by a women. A friend of the authors who manages a dating service said that men are adamant about wanting thin women, regardless of their own weight. The weight of men is less important to women.

Researchers have also looked at who marries whom, as well as how long the marriages last, with what reproductive consequences. First, the satisfaction with a relationship may depend more on how the partner is perceived rather than on the partner's actual characteristics (Sternberg & Barnes, 1985). Second, marriages represent assortative mating, with partners being similar to each other on a number of different psychological and physical characteristics. The better matched the pair, the more durable the marital bond tends to be and the more children they tend to have (Epstein & Guttman, 1984; Thiessen & Gregg, 1980). Third, the factors that contribute to original attraction are not always the same that contribute to greater durability of the bond or commitment. A man may prefer to have a very attractive wife, but if she is much more attractive than he is, she is likely to leave him.[6]

Nonmonogamous relationships are more likely to break up (except for homosexual male pairs, where a lack of monogamy is the rule rather than an exception). In fact, people often give infidelity as a reason for divorce (Kitson, Babri, & Roach, 1985). Fisher's (1987) cross-cultural review concluded that divorce most commonly occurs after four years of marriage. She pointed out that the optimal interbirth internal for !Kung is about four years (see Jones, 1986). Thus, male-female bonds often last just

long enough to see the offspring weaned and the woman able to return to her more extensive prechildbirth work patterns. Obviously, many marriages last longer, reflecting greater commitment.

Sex Differences in Sexual Motives

In the past, it was assumed that women had a weaker drive, that women were more difficult to sexually arouse, and that they became aroused far more infrequently than men do. Therefore, scientists exposed male and female subjects to various kinds of erotic material and measured arousal both physiologically (penile erection and vaginal contractions) and through self-reports. The quote from Symons presented at the beginning of this chapter indicates how wrong these ideas proved to be when actually tested this way.

Sex differences in response to erotic stimuli.
Some research finds women to be less sexually arousable than men, but only because of cultural expectancies and because women have had fewer sexual experiences (Griffitt, 1987). Women are culturally *expected* to be less arousable. Sexual arousal can also be conditioned in both nonhumans and humans (Bartos & Trojan, 1985; Rachman & Hodgson, 1968; Zamble, Hadad, Mitchell, & Cutmore, 1985), and males, because of our culture, have had more conditioning opportunities. Of 249 college students who filled out a sexual experiences questionnaire, only 6 percent of males versus 20 percent of females said that they had never had sexual intercourse (Carroll, Volk, & Hyde, 1985). Griffitt (1975) found that amount of past sexual activity strongly affected sexual arousability, as measured in a laboratory, in both sexes.

Although the sexes also tend to be sexually aroused by the same kinds of stimuli, there are some differences. Physiological measures are more strongly related to verbal reports of arousal in males than in females (Heilman,

1980; Steinman et al., 1981, Singer, 1984). Scientists exposed male and female subjects to erotic videotapes and to tapes of crying babies (Furedy et al., 1989). As measured by small magnitude changes in heart rate, men reacted more than women did to the erotic scenes, and women reacted more than men did to the babies. Women also tend to be less sexually aroused by unusual sexual stimuli. Fetishism, where "a person is reiteratively responsive to and dependent on atypical or forbidden stimulus imagery, in fantasy or in practice" (Money, 1981, p. 75), is much more common in males than in females. In one study of the 48 cases of sexual fetishism seen in one London hospital over 20 years, there was only one female, a lesbian with a breast fetish (Chalkley & Powell, 1983). The males had fetishes for underwear, stockings, raincoats, shoes, boots, leather jackets, and rubber items, among others.

Another frequently asked question about human female sexual arousability concerns orgasms (Hrdy, 1979; Jayne, 1981; Symons, 1979). From somewhere between 5 to 25 percent of women never experience orgasm during sexual intercourse, suggesting that the capacity for orgasm in women did not evolve in order to increase the pair bond (her male partner's commitment to her). Hrdy has suggested that sexual activity in females, with or without orgasms, may act to increase paternal investment in her offspring. This may be related to the fact that in nonhuman animals, having sex with a male can decrease the chances that the male will attack any offspring that are born later. Also, Jayne pointed out that many women who get orgasms from masturbation but not from intercourse still prefer intercourse. In fact, many women report that intercourse, even without orgasms, can be very satisfying — though perhaps not for the same reasons as for the male.

Another frequently discussed phenomenon is the **Collidge Effect** (Dewsbury, 1981b; Hoyenga & Hoyenga, 1984), named after an apocryphal incident in which President and Mrs. Coolidge were touring a farm. Mrs. Coolidge noted the vigorous sexual activity of one rooster and asked the aides to tell the president about it. When told, the president reportedly responded, "Was it always the same hen?" The Coolidge Effect refers to the renewal of sexual interest and activity that occurs when the males of some species are presented with a novel sexual partner. In one study, male and female monkeys were caged in pairs for a period of 3.5 years (Michael & Zumpe, 1978). Despite the fact that their female partners were made continuous sexually receptive by the use of hormones, the sexual activity of their male partners steadily declined. If the males were given new females, their sexual activity abruptly increased to the former levels.

Two questions about this phenomenon are important. Does it exist in humans? If it does, do both sexes experience the stimulating effects of a partner change? One relevant source of evidence would be the changes in sexual activity occurring over time in married couples. Early research suggested that their sexual activity declined (Udry & Morris, 1978). However, later research found that, at least after the intense sexual activity of the first months of marriage, levels of sexual activity tend to remain quite stable (Blumstein & Schwartz, 1983; George & Weiler, 1981). Another source of evidence, the number of sexual partners, will be discussed in the next section.

Sex differences in patterns of and motives for sexual activity. Until the last three decades, before marriage, men were more likely to be sexually experienced than were women. This has changed (Biggar, Brinton, & Rosenthal, 1989; Kaats & Davis, 1970). The number of different sexual partners that women have has also been increasing, something that is of concern, given the possibility of acquired immune deficiency syndrome (AIDS).[7]

Some sex differences may remain. Out of 249 college students, 23 percent of the males said that they had had from 6 to 10 different partners, and 13 percent said that they had had over 25 different partners. The comparable percentages of women were 12 percent and 0 percent (Carroll et al., 1985). Also, 23 percent of the women versus only 6 percent of the men had had only one sexual partner. In two different groups of men and women (differentiated by a personality measure), men had had a greater number of sexual partners in the past year than women had (2.18 and 1.12, versus 1.17 and .54) (Snyder, Simpson, & Gangestad, 1986). Similarly, Symons (1979, 1980) reported that, in one study of homosexuals in the San Francisco area, 28 percent of the men but no women had had more than 1,000 partners.[8]

The Blumstein and Schwartz (1983) study of thousands of American couples, married and cohabiting, heterosexual and homosexual, also showed some sex differences in sexual activity. Although there were only minor sex differences in the frequency of having any instance of nonmonogamy (sex with someone other than the partner to whom one commits oneself), males were likely to do so in all types of couples. Among married couples, of the nonmonogamous women, 43 percent had had only one other partner and only 3 percent had had more than 20 other partners. Among the married men, 29 percent had had only one other partner and 7 percent had had more than 20. Among the homosexual couples, 1 percent of the women versus 43 percent of the men had had more than 20 partners.

Men and women often have different attitudes toward sexual activities. Table 14.2 presents some of the items from a sexual questionnaire (Hendrick et al., 1985). Women still feel that it is more important for them than for their mates to be virgins at the time of their marriage, whereas men feel that the reverse is true for them (Kaats & Davis, 1970). The sexes also differ in the reasons they give for having, or for not having, sexual intercourse (Carroll et al., 1985; Leigh, 1989). Some 85 percent of women say that emotional involvement is a prerequisite either always or most of the time,

whereas 60 percent of the men say that it is only sometimes or never important. In response to the question, "What would be your primary reason for refusing to have sexual intercourse with someone?", 56 percent of women mentioned lack of commitment to the potential partner, whereas 46 percent of men said that they'd "never neglect an opportunity." Generally, men attach more importance to sexual pleasure, conquest, and relief of tension, whereas women value emotional closeness.

Unwanted sex. Almost all reported rapes are perpetrated by men, with women as victims. Nevertheless, sometimes men are raped (Moore, Nord, & Peterson, 1989; Muehlenhard & Cook, 1988; Sarrel & Masters, 1982; Siegel et al., 1989). Sometimes men's attackers are women who do not physically overwhelm their victims but rather dominate, intimidate, and seduce them. An adult woman may dominate and seduce a preadolescent boy. Men also say they have been forced into sex by peer pressure and desires for popularity.

The problem of men raping women seems to be increasing in the United States. One research focus is on whether the motive for rape involves sex or violence. However, phrasing the question this way neglects the possibility that some men experience sexual arousal when thinking about, or engaging in, violence against women. Rape could also be a reproductive strategy for low-status men (social "losers") (Thornhill & Thornhill, 1983).

College student males were asked if they would commit a rape if they were sure they would not be caught. About 35 percent indicated some possibility that they would (Malamuth, 1981a, 1981b). Both convicted rapists and those particular college students tend to believe in the rape myths, such that women enjoy being raped. They also tend to become sexually aroused by erotic scenes of violent sex. Either short- or long-term exposure to sexually violent material in the media

TABLE 14.2 *Sex Differences in Sexual Attitudes*
These are selected questionnaire items on which there are significant differences between the sexes in the extent to which subjects indicated disapproval of each of the following sexual attitudes.

Sexual Attitudes	Which Gender Disapproved the Most
I do not need to be committed to a person to have sex with him/her.	Females
I would like to have sex with many partners.	Females
It is okay to have ongoing sexual relationships with more than one person at a time.	Females
It is okay to manipulate someone into having sex as long as no future promises are made.	Females
The best sex is with no strings attached.	Females
It is possible to enjoy sex with a person and not like that person very much.	Females
Unlimited premarital sexual experience is fine.	Females
Extramarital affairs are all right as long as one's partner doesn't know about them.	Females
Extramarital affairs are unacceptable.	Males
To have good sex, two people have to know each other pretty well.	Males
Sex without love is meaningless.	Males
In order for sex to be good, it must also be meaningful.	Males
Sex is a sacred act.	Males
At its best, sex seems to be the merging of two souls.	Males
Sex is primarily emotional.	Males
I could live quite well without sex.	Males
Sex is best when one keeps the emotions under cool control.	Females
Sex and power are highly related.	Females
Good sex gives one a feeling of power.	Females

Source: From "Gender Differences in Sexual Attitudes" by S. Hendrick, C. Hendrick, M. J. Slapion-Foote, and F. H. Foote, 1985, *Journal of Personality and Social Psychology, 48,* pp. 1634 and 1635. Copyright 1985 by the American Psychological Association. Adapted by permission.

(magazines, films) may well make these men more likely to commit rape (Linz, 1989).

One frequent type of rape, which frequently goes unreported, is date or acquaintance rape (Moore, Nord, & Peterson, 1989; Muehlenhard & Cook, 1988; Sarrel & Masters, 1982; Siegel et al., 1989). In one sample of 3,132 Los Angeles residents, 26.3 percent of the white women reported some sexual assault; 47.6 percent of those involved an acquaintance or friend, 13.5 percent involved a lover, and 13.5 percent involved a husband. Men who admit to a history of date rape also tend to score high on a Macho personality scale, which measures enjoyment of violence and danger and having a calloused attitude towards sex (all is fair in love and war) (Mosher & Anderson, 1986; Mosher & Sirkin, 1984; Smeaton & Byrne, 1987). Men generally do not consider date rape to be as serious as stranger rape (Quackenbush, 1989).

Hormones and Sexual Activity

In analyzing the covariation of sexual activity with hormone levels, at least three different aspects of sex must be separately considered. One is the amount of sexual activity, regardless of its type, assuming suitable partners are present. The second question is concerned with the type of sexual activity being displayed: masculine versus feminine. In nonprimates, it is mounting versus lordosis; in primates, it is mounting versus the sexual presentation posture. Although this is the area where researchers have the most data in nonhumans, there is no comparable distinction in humans. Males may be somewhat more likely to take the initiative and be more likely to assume the partner-on-top position, but how these activities may (or may not) covary with hormones is unknown.

The third question concerns partner preferences. In much of this research, after varying hormone treatments, subjects are given a choice between partners, such as a sexually receptive male versus a sexually receptive female. It is difficult to distinguish between purely social and sexual motives. For example, does a prenatally androgenized female rat prefer female to male sexual partners because of the sexual activity or because of the intersocial activities? In humans, the question takes the form of the hormonal covariates of homosexuality, which is discussed later in this chapter.

Lordosis and mounting in rats. Feminine and masculine forms of sexual behavior in rats, as well as in many other nonprimate species, are sensitive to both perinatal and postpubertal levels of sex hormones (Baum, 1979; Feder, 1984; Moore, 1985; Schumacher, Legros, & Balthazart, 1987; Yahr, 1988). Perinatal hormones both masculinize and defeminize adult sexual behavior in rats and other nonprimates. The masculinization occurs largely because the hormones affect the preoptic area (POA), and the defeminization occurs because of hormonally induced changes in the ventromedial hypothalamus (VMH). Both androgens such as dihydrotestosterone (DHT), which cannot be aromatized to estrogens, and estradiol (E) itself contribute to these effects. The magnitude and details of the effects depend on species, strain, prenatal stress, uterine position, and postpubertal experiences (see Chapters 6 and 7).

The sexual activity of adult rats also covaries with their hormone levels as well as with their environments. After castration, sexual activity declines in both sexes, but the decline in females is more rapid and far more complete. However, the effect of castration on males' masculine sexual activity depends on prior sexual experience and genotype (Clemens et al., 1988; Manning & Thompson, 1976; Chapter 6). Forced exercise can increase sexual activity in female rats, and housing a male with other males can decrease sexual activity in mice, independent of changes in hormones (Axelson & Sawin, 1987; de Catanzaro, 1987).

Both masculine and feminine hormones can increase all sexual behaviors in adult rats of both sexes. However, females are more sensitive to the lordosis-stimulating effects of E, and males are more sensitive to the mounting-stimulating effects of T. Perinatal treatment of females with T or E makes them react more like males do to adult hormonal treatments. Consistent with the aromatization hypothesis (see Chapters 6 and 7), both T and E can activate mounting in males. Nevertheless, both androgens and E may be required for complete activation of all aspects of masculine sexual activity in males. T can also facilitate females' sexual activity.

Primates.   Adult, intact male primates are more likely to assume the feminine sexual presentation posture than adult, intact male rats are to display lordosis. The feminine sexual posture in primates is a submissive display, so it has dominance as well as sexual implications. Thus, the effects of perinatal hormones on feminine behaviors are more subtle in the primate than in the rat. Still, prenatal treatments with both aromatizable and nonaromatizable androgens defeminize and masculinize the sexual activities of the adult female (see documentation in Hoyenga & Hoyenga, 1993). Although the effects of the prenatal androgens occur even in females whose external genitals have not been modified, the effects do depend on the details of the testing situation.

Adult hormones also covary with sexual behaviors. Castration decreases the sexual activities of both sexes. Although males' sexual activity declines with age, T injections cannot restore their youthful levels of sexual activity (Phoenix & Chambers, 1986). The effects of menstrual cycle hormone changes depend on the female's environment. If the female is housed with groups of other monkeys of both sexes, she engages in sexual activity most frequently around the time of her ovulation, and the dominant male is most likely to monopolize her sexually at that time (Hoyenga & Hoyenga, 1993). On the other hand, a female housed with just one other animal, a male, engages in sexual activity throughout the menstrual cycle, with just slight evidence of cyclical changes.

Cyclical and noncyclical changes in androgens can sometimes affect sexual activity in female primates. Zumpe and Michael (1985) have said that T increases the sexual motivations (invitations to males) only in one and not in another type of macaque female. Also, a stimulating effect of androgens has only been demonstrated in tests that use just a male-female pair of monkeys, the same conditions that reduce the impact of E and P on sexual behaviors (Lovejoy & Wallen, 1990).

Humans.   Humans' sexual behaviors have sometimes been found to covary with their postpubertal hormone levels. Although a woman's menstrual cycle has only minor effects, postpubertal and pubertal androgens may affect her sexual motivation. A woman's peak T level (late follicular phase) is directly related to her sexual motivation, as measured by masturbation episodes, self-ratings, or female-initiated sexual intercourse. Thus, women with higher T levels also have higher sexual motivation. Much of this research is summarized by Sherwin (1988a). Androgen treatments do not help sexually unresponsive women.

Earlier research that found males' sexual motivation to be unrelated to their androgen levels has been superseded by research employing newer technology (Hoyenga & Hoyenga, 1993; Sherwin, 1988a). Not only do men with higher T have higher levels of sexual motivation but an individual male's changes in T (weekly, seasonally) parallel changes in sexual motivation. Sexual arousal can also increase T levels, so there is a two-way effect. Although XXY men tend to have low levels of T and low levels of sexual motivation, within that group, there is no relationship between hormone level and motivation level. Still, T treatments can increase XXY males' sexual activities. Treatment with drugs that block androgen's effects reduces sexual motivation and has been used to treat sexually aggressive men.

Sexual Preferences in Humans

Researchers have only recently demonstrated how both experiences and hormone levels interact to affect partner preferences in rats, hamsters, ferrets, dogs, pigs, and perhaps primates (Hoyenga & Hoyenga, 1993). If animal research were to be used as a model for homosexuality in humans, the determinants would have to be as complex as those demonstrated in nonhumans.

Until very recently, most researchers, including the authors, have concluded that sexual preferences in humans do not covary with hormone levels at any time of life (e.g., Hoyenga & Hoyenga, 1984, 1988). In fact, homosexuals do not differ from heterosexuals in the postpubertal level of any sex hormone, at least when the effects of contaminating factors such as stress, diet, and activity levels are controlled (Meyer-Bahlburg, 1984; Downey et al., 1987).

Perinatal hormones. Some evidence that prenatal hormone levels may covary with sexual preferences has recently appeared, however (e.g., Ellis & Ames, 1987). Perinatal sex hormone abnormalities sometimes affect level of motivation and partner preferences (see reviews in Hoyenga & Hoyenga, 1993, and Reinisch et al., 1991). Although most women exposed prenatally to DES (diethylstilbestrol) are heterosexual, more were bisexual or homosexual than was true of a matched control group, and the DES women also had lower levels of sexual enjoyment and excitability (Ehrhardt et al., 1985; Meyer-Bahlburg et al., 1985). In Money's (1987) experiences with patients who had some gender/hormone abnormality, prenatal exposure to an androgenic progestin did not affect the sexuality of his female patients, in contrast to the effect of DES. However, he found that adrenogenital females more often grow up to be bisexual or homosexual.

Some XY individuals with varying degrees of androgen insensitivity are reared as females and some as males. There is a smaller likelihood of gender transposition (transsexuality or homosexuality, defined according to the gender of rearing) in those reared as males (Money, 1987; Money, Devors, & Norman, 1986; Money & Norman, 1987). Being stigmatized in childhood was associated with gender transposition in both sexes. The stigmatized children were teased by other children because of the way their genitals looked and were treated with shame by their parents.

The above data might mean that apparently hormonally normal homosexuals did, in fact, have some abnormality prenatally. This might occur because of the way prenatal stress affects hormones and brain development, and might be detected in the way that adult hormone levels are regulated by the hypothalamus and pituitary. Although Dörner (1988) found a change in such regulation,[9] other researchers were unable to replicate his findings (Gooren, 1986a, 1986b; Hendricks, Graber, & Rodriguez-Sierra, 1989). The possibility that the anatomy of the hypothalamus may differ between homosexual and heterosexual men is also being explored (LeVay, 1991).

Genes and family environments. Male homosexuality has some genetic covariates (Bailey & Pillard, 1991; Buhrich, Bailey, & Martin, 1991; Pillard, Poumadere, & Caretta, 1981, 1982; Pillard & Weinreich, 1986). Monozygotic twins are more likely to share sexual preferences than are dizygotic twins; in fact, around 50 percent of monozygotic twins are probably concordant for sexual orientation. Many homosexual males also have families containing several other homosexual males. If prenatal hormone levels are involved, the relevant genes may determine the fetus's sensitivity to the effects of the mother being stressed.

According to Storms's (1981) theory of sexual orientation, male homosexuals have an earlier puberty than do heterosexuals. The earlier puberty could be due either to genes and/or neonatal hormone levels. Thus, the male homosexual becomes sexually arousable at a time when boys are still playing in all-boy groups. His sexual arousal becomes classically conditioned to other boys and he develops a same-sex partner preference.

Cross-culturally, homosexual males are more likely to act feminine, both in their childhoods and their adult lives (Freund & Blanchard, 1983; Green, 1979, 1985, 1987;

McConaghy, 1987; Whitam, 1983; Whitam & Zent, 1984). In a longitudinal study (Green, 1987), feminine boys were more likely to grow up to be bisexual or homosexual than were a matched group of masculine boys, regardless of professional treatment during their childhoods. The typical interpretation is that these boys had a distant, hostile father and so became both feminine and gender transposed. On the other hand, perhaps having a feminine boy makes some fathers feel very uncomfortable or even hostile.

Homosexuality in females may follow a different course. The families of homosexual males show an increased frequency of homosexual males but no increased frequency of homosexual females (Pillard, Poumadere, & Carretta, 1981, 1982; Pillard & Weinrich, 1986). One study of six pairs of monozygotic female twins, all reared apart, found that all were discordant for sexual preference (Eckert et al., 1986). This would be highly unlikely in six male pairs. Since the homosexual member of each pair was, without exception, the one who was taller and had the later puberty, this suggests that the developmental processes leading to homosexuality may be sexually dimorphic.

SPATIAL TASKS

If there is any sex difference in any kind of spatial task, males usually get the higher average scores. Similar sex differences show up in a variety of different tasks involving spatial ability, including — as pointed out previously — throwing accuracy and the ability to find one's way around town using spatial cues.

Sex Differences

This section documents the sex difference by describing the conclusions of meta-analytic studies. Data from representative samples of subjects are also included because these type of data have greater external validity (see Chapter 2).

Meta-analyses and types of spatial tasks. Not only do different spatial tasks measure different skills but sex differences also vary. Examples of various spatial tasks are given in Figure 14.1. There are several types of **Embedded Figures Tests (EFT),** only one of which is shown. The most common rotation task is the **Shepherd-Meltzer Mental Rotations Test (S-M).** The **Block Design Test** requires subjects to mentally rotate a stack of blocks and match it to one of the test figures. Types of tests not illustrated include the **Flags** and **Cards** tests from the French kit, which have subjects mentally rotate a stimulus flag or card to match it with some samples; this is similar to the mental rotation task pictured. In the **Rod and Frame Test (RFT),** the subject is seated in a darkened room looking at a glowing frame (rectangle) that has neither true vertical nor horizontal lines. A glowing rod in the center of the frame can be rotated. The subject's task is to say when the rod is either truly vertical or horizontal. Since the room is darkened and the frame distorted, subjects' only cues are their own bodies.

Hyde (1981) did the first meta-analytic study of spatial tasks. Some reanalyses of her data were later done by Becker and Hedges (1984) and by Rosenthal and Rubin (1982). Hyde's study found a weighted effect size of .43. Effect sizes tended to be even larger for more selected samples: the higher the average ability of the group, the larger the effect size. The effect size has decreased across time (the effect size for date of study = .43).

A subsequent meta-analysis divided spatial tasks into three subtypes (Linn & Peterson, 1985, 1986). The **spatial perception** factor includes the RFT and the water level task and has an average effect size of .64. The **mental rotation** factor is broken down into two groups. One is a S-M type of mental rotation tasks, with an average effect size of .94. The second group includes other rotation tasks, with an average effect size of .26. The third factor is **spatial visualization** and includes EFT, **paper folding** (see Figure 14.1), blocks, and DAT space,

FIGURE 14.1 *Some Spatial Tasks*

Of these spatial tasks, Parts A and C involve some three-dimensional rotations to solve (Answers: [A] = 1 and 3; [B] = each simple figure is present in the complete figure below it; [C] = each test does match its sample; [D] = choice A.) EFT = Embedded Figures Test.

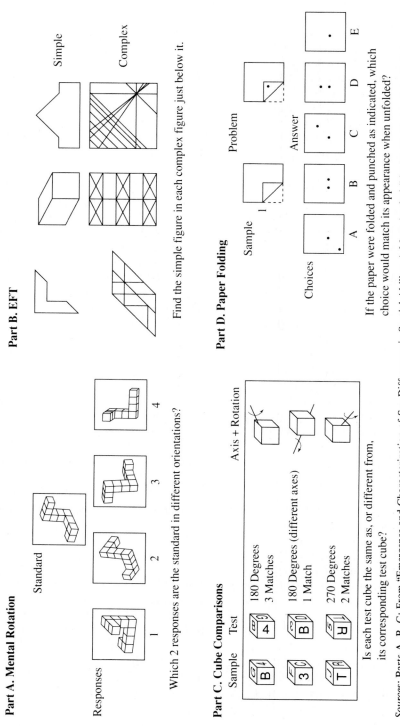

Part A. Mental Rotation

Standard

Responses

1   2   3   4

Which 2 responses are the standard in different orientations?

Part B. EFT

Simple

Complex

Find the simple figure in each complex figure just below it.

Part C. Cube Comparisons

Sample   Test

Axis + Rotation

180 Degrees
3 Matches

180 Degrees (different axes)
1 Match

270 Degrees
2 Matches

Is each test cube the same as, or different from, its corresponding test cube?

Part D. Paper Folding

Sample   Problem

1

Answer

A   B   C   D   E

Choices

A   B   C

If the paper were folded and punched as indicated, which choice would match its appearance when unfolded?

Sources: Parts A, B, C: From "Emergence and Characterization of Sex Differences in Spatial Ability: A Meta-Analysis" by M. C. Linn and A. C. Petersen, 1985, *Child Development, 56*, pp. 1483, 1485. © The Society for Research in Child Development, Inc. Reprinted by permission. Part D: From "Cognitive Coordinate Systems: Accounts of Mental Rotation and Individual Differences in Spatial Ability" by M. A. Just and P. A. Carpenter, 1985, *Psychologial Review, 92*, p. 141. Copyright 1985 by the American Psychological Association. Reprinted by permission.

among others. In the **DAT space** task, a subject is presented with a drawing of a three-dimensional object that had been disassembled and flattened out. The subject's task is to indicate which, among three choices, would best represent the object if it were reassembled by folding it along the lines indicated. The average effect size across studies for visualization was .13, which was not significantly different from zero. The reviewers did not see any effects of subjects' ages.

Data not included in the Linn and Peterson review confirm most of their conclusions.[10] The contrast between the gender effect sizes on the S-M versus the other rotation tasks was confirmed by one study that used the same subjects for both tasks (Sanders, Soares, & D'Aquila, 1982). A later study done by the same researchers found an effect size of .82 for the S-M (Sanders & Soares, 1986). Popiel and De Lisi (1984) found an effect size of .51 for the paper-folding test and one of .50 for the water level task.

However, the effect size for the EFT may actually be greater than zero. A review done earlier included 10 RFT studies and 15 EFT studies (Allen & Cholet, 1978). The authors computed effect sizes and found a weighted effect size of .32 for the RFT, in agreement with Linn and Peterson. However, a similar effect size, .37, was found for the EFT. The authors also examined DAT and EFT effect sizes (weighted by sample size) for studies not included in either review. Effect sizes ranged from .54 to .96 for the EFT, and from .19 to .54 for the DAT, with no consistent trend seen for date of study (Bieri, Bradburn, & Galinsky, 1958; Dorval & Pepin, 1986; Newcombe, Bandura, & Taylor, 1983; Stericker & LeVesconte, 1982; Tapley & Bryden, 1977). Furthermore, according to a correlational study with a large sample, the EFT seems to differ not only from the mental rotation tasks but also from the paper-folding task that Linn and Peterson included in the same category (Loehlin, Sharan, &

Jacoby, 1978). Small but reliable sex differences may exist on both tasks.

Representative samples. Research on the DAT space test finds small effect sizes in favor of males. The effect size found when the DAT was normed by giving it to large, representative samples of twelfth-grade students, as reported in the 1974 manual, was .28 (Burnett, 1986). According to Wilder and Powell's review (1989) of sex differences found in the large, representative samples of the 1980 DAT space data, the effect size was .22. The ratio of males to females scoring above the 90th percentile was almost 2 to 1. Feingold (1988a) also found evidence of a declining sex difference.

Just what are all these tests measuring? The sexes differ in more than just average scores (Tambs, 1989).

The Structure of Spatial Performances

Different spatial tests measure somewhat different abilities in the sexes. One way to look at this is to examine the correlations among the various spatial tests with each other and with other cognitive tests. Another way is to look for sex differences in strategy use.

Correlational studies. The authors looked at the correlations among various tests in a set of 14 studies (Hoyenga & Hoyenga, 1993). Of the 30 possible correlations, 22 were higher for males versus 8 for females, suggesting a gender-differentiated organization of spatial skills. On the other hand, Pearson and Fergusen (1989) examined the correlations of three spatial tasks to each other and to the American College Testing math and English scores. They found females to have higher correlations in all 15 cases, significantly so in 3 cases. Thus, sex differences in structure are commonly found but the direction is not consistent and so is currently uninterpretable.

Strategies.   The tasks on which the largest sex differences are found, the mental rotation tasks, can be approached with one of two different strategies. Subjects can use either a visualization (global, spatial) strategy or an analytic strategy (breaking down figures into component parts to analyze relationships) (Kyllonen, Lohman, & Snow, 1984). The most effective performers on the Cubes task (see Figure 14.1) perform a single mental rotation on the object (Cooper & Shepard, 1984; Corballis, 1986; Just & Carpenter, 1985). Analyses of response latencies show that the more the sample cube must be rotated to potentially match each test cube, the longer the subject takes to respond, as though the subject were mentally rotating the cube through three-dimensional (but imaginary) space. Effective performers can rotate a cube not only horizontally and vertically but also through various oblique angles when necessary, and they often carry out the rotations in one continuous movement. This rotation can apparently still take place in the subject's mind even when the subject temporarily shifts attention to another task.[11]

Nevertheless, some subjects with high spatial scores do not use rotation. Instead, they attempt to verbally encode the spatial relationships among parts of the pattern and then match that code to the test figures. For example, the mental rotation test sample in Figure 14.1 could be encoded as a walk in a building—turn left, walk down a corridor, go up some stairs, and turn right. This strategy requires considerable practice; with practice, this strategy can become quite accurate but remains slow.

Like some of the high-scoring subjects, low-scoring subjects use rotational strategies but do so less effectively. Subjects scoring low on the Cubes problem do not use oblique angles for rotation. They also attempt to first mentally align each cube to an external upright. They carry out rotations in two or more distinct movements instead of just one smooth rotation.

Males and females tend to use different strategies. In one study, the one group of females who outperformed the males on a mental rotation task apparently used a visual, rotational strategy, just as the high-scoring males did. The other groups of females were using verbal encoding strategies (Pezaris & Casey, 1991). In fact, when older female subjects were encouraged to use verbal strategies on the S-M task, their errors decreased (Clarkson-Smith & Halpern, 1983, as cited by Halpern, 1986). In other experiments, the different kinds of rotational strategies just described were not measured (Allen, 1974; Allen & Hogeland, 1978). However, women, more often than men, resorted to using concrete aids ("I used my finger or a pencil") or simply gave up. Based simply on the use of the various strategies, 90 percent of the subjects could be classified correctly according to sex.

Other data also suggest that the sexes differ in strategy use. How fast men can rotate an object in their minds is directly related to how detailed a mental image they can form of an object, but there is no relationship between rotation rate and imagery in women (Tapley & Bryden, 1977). Accuracy of identification also depends on how much the sample must be rotated. Slow reaction times are associated with low accuracy, particularly for the items requiring more rotation (Voyer & Bryden, 1990). When the genders' spatial scores are equated, however, the accuracy of low-ability males are more affected by the amount of rotation required than is the accuracy of low-ability females.

Men carry out mental rotations faster than women do (Kail, Carter, & Pellegrino, 1979; McGlone, 1981; Tapley & Bryden, 1977). Still, the overlap between the sexes is more impressive than the difference. "About 70 percent of the women mentally rotated stimuli at rates comparable to men, while 30 percent of the women did so at a slower rate" (Kail et al., 1979, p. 185). Another study found a sex difference of a similar size, but in this case, the sample size was too small and so the difference was not statistically significant (Van Strien & Bouma, 1990). The slow-rotating women seemed to rotate the objects in parts, which is the strategy used by the poor-performing males described above.

In summary, using a flexible, accurate, single-direction rotation is most characteristic of high-scoring men and a few high-scoring women. Most high-scoring women use verbal encoding strategies. Low-scoring people of both sexes use rotation strategies ineffectively, and there are more women than men in this group. Rotation seems to be the factor that best differentiates between the sexes' performances, leading to the large difference. The question is why?

Developmental and Situational Covariates

Concurrent covariates are variables associated with task performances whose order is uncertain.[12] Conversely, **ordered covariates** are those variables that are known (or commonly assumed) to have occurred before the cognitive ability either developed or else was changed in some way. Practice is an obvious ordered covariate since the practice precedes the observed increase in performances. Parental attitudes and behaviors are usually assumed to be ordered, but in some studies it is entirely possible that the child's skill levels could have affected the parents' attitudes and behaviors (as well as, or instead of, vice versa) (Loehlin & DeFries, 1987).

Cultural variables are usually seen as ordered. However, the way that people in that culture respond to the child may well depend on that child's skills, as well as affecting how those skills develop. Since various cultural activities, including children's play, are sexually stereotyped, the sexes may get different amounts of practice for various cognitive skills. Alterntively, more masculine children could prefer masculine activities and also do better on spatial tasks, but the activities and the task performances might not be directly related to each other.

Play preferences and personality: masculine versus feminine. Children who prefer masculine play activities clearly have higher scores on mathematics, spatial, and science tests, when all are measured at the same time (Tracy, 1987). For example, EFT performances in young boys were correlated with the masculinity of their play patterns ($r = .803$ for boys; $r = .124$ for girls; not significant) (Connor & Serbin, 1977).

In a meta-analysis (Baenninger & Newcombe, 1989), although the effect sizes were small, remembering having participated in spatial activities as a child (e.g., playing with Lincoln logs) was specifically associated with higher spatial scores for adults of both sexes. For males, the association was limited to those activities that were not only spatial but also masculine. Females that participated in either spatial or masculine activities had higher spatial scores. Spatial visualization scores were more strongly related to participation in spatial activities than were performances on mental rotation or spatial perception types of tasks.

Other research looked at stereotyped play preferences as an ordered covariate of cognitive skills. Masculine and feminine play patterns measured in preschool predicted school performances measured several years later (Fagot & Littman, 1976). The degree to which boys helped adults (a feminine activity) as preschoolers was negatively correlated with their later performances in science, math, and art, and with their EFT scores. Degree of masculinity in play preferences was positively correlated with EFT scores three to six years later in both sexes (just failed to reach significance with girls). Also, the greater the masculine play preferences during preschool, the better girls did in science, math, and the language arts. Even here, however, being "masculine" for whatever reason could have preceded both the play preferences as well as the better spatial and math performances.

The sex of the examiner and the sex label attached to the task can affect performances. For example, Berch and Wright (1990) found that both sexes tended to get higher mental rotation scores with opposite-sex than with same-sex examiners. Thus, the sex difference was largest with female examiners and smallest (nonsignificant) with male examiners. Davies (1989/1990) gave the same spatial task to various groups of adolescents, each group being told either that the task was one on which males tend to do better or one on which females tend to do better. Both sexes did better on so-called gender-appropriate tasks, with the gender labeling affecting males' performances more than females'. On the other hand, even though Canadian college students perceived a spatial water level task to be neither feminine nor masculine, male subjects still outperformed females (Robert, 1990). Thus, sex typing of tasks may sometimes follow (rather than causally precede) sex differences in performances.

Spatial tasks also have personality covariates. This research often asks whether gender stereotypic self-descriptions on one of the sex-role scales (the PAQ or BSRI) are related to cognitive performances. On the basis of a meta-analytic review, Signorella and Jamison (1986) concluded that "higher masculine and lower feminine self-concept scores were associated with better performance" (p. 207) on verbal, spatial, and mathematical tasks. The association with sex-role scale scores is often stronger for female adolescents than for older females. Among male adolescents, the more feminine they tended to describe themselves as being, the higher were their scale scores, which reversed the effects found for older males.

Bryant (1982) examined the personality covariates (California Personality Inventory) of mental rotations and environmental localization accuracy. There were no significant covariates of rotation, but those people who more accurately located themselves in their environ-ments were socially outgoing, ambitious, self-assured, and dominant.

Ozer (1987) found that the personality ratings made of his subjects at ages 3 to 14 predicted their rotation scores at age 18. Similar to what Crandall and Sinkeldam (1964) found with children, childhood dependency behaviors were negatively correlated, and childhood achievement behaviors positively correlated with spatial scores. This was especially true for females. As Ozer said, "The intellectual gifts of females who score high on the Mental Rotations Test are apparent to observers as early as 15 years before . . . , whereas those very same intellectual advantages that accrue in males are virtually invisible to observers" (p. 133). Ozer also found that more personality traits measured at age 18 were related to spatial rotation scores in female than in male subjects. High-spatial males were simply not socially repellant, but high-spatial females had a sense of humor and were socially perceptive, warm, empathetic, generous, bright, and not self-defeating or self-defensive.

Some of Ozer's dimensions seem similar to those found in earlier research (Witkin & Goodenough, 1977). Field-independent people, defined as those who got high scores on the RFT or EFT, were found to be more socially perceptive and sensitive to others' feelings (and faces), more open, and liked being closer to people. Puzzlingly, Ozer's high-spatial females sound most like the field-dependent people (low spatial) described earlier, even though the EFT and RFT scores measured earlier in Ozer's subjects' lives were positively correlated with their age 18 rotation scores. Ozer also found that his high-scoring females were relatively insensitive to criticism and to demands made by others, two traits that earlier research suggested were more typical of low- than of high-spatial people. Thus, despite the correlation between EFT and rotation scores, high-spatial EFT people may be quite different from high-spatial rotation people.

The meaning of the personality covariates is obscure, and their interpretation is not aided by the inconsistency. Some variable, such as perinatal hormone level or very early childhood experiences, could separately affect both personality and spatial performances. Nevertheless, cognitive abilities are imbedded in intact people, and task performances are only one way high versus low people differ. In general, high-spatial rotation people tend to be high in instrumentality and social dominance.

Family environment.   Father absence seems to be an important covariate of the spatial skills of both sexes. Whether the father is absent because of divorce, death, or night-shift work, father-absent adolescents and adults score lower on math and spatial tests compared to father-present subjects (Barclay & Cusumano, 1967; Carlsmith, 1964; Landy, Rosenberg, & Sutton-Smith, 1969). The mechanism for this effect remains obscure, but paternal encouragement could be particularly important for a child's cognitive development in these "masculine" areas.

Serbin and her coworkers (Serbin et al., 1990) looked at some home environmental covariates of Block Design performances in elementary school children. The more masculine toys there were in the child's room, the higher was the child's score. In fact, 37 percent of the sex differences in Block Design scores could be accounted for by the difference in the availability of masculine toys. Also, the higher the occupational status of the mother, and the greater the father's educational level, the higher were the child's scores. The mother's occupational status both directly and indirectly affected her child's scores, since the children of high-status mothers also had more masculine toys. The sexual division of labor in the home was not related to the child's score.

Ordered covariates.   College-level coursework increases spatial and math scores. Two years of college study leads to more of an improvement in spatial scores in math and science majors than in humanities majors (Burnett & Lane, 1980). The more math courses taken, the greater the improvement. People's EFT scores also improve when they take a math or drafting course (Johnson, Flinn, & Tyler, 1979).

Practice can improve spatial scores in both sexes. Baenninger and Newcombe's (1989) meta-analytic study of practice effects found that training and/or practice improved spatial test scores equally for both sexes. The longer and the more specific the training, the greater the improvement was. Short training periods did not provide more benefits than did practice on the task itself. Even playing a video game can increase college students' scores on the DAT space test (Dorval & Pépin, 1986).

Sometimes the effects of training depend on both gender and skill patterns (Kyllonen et al., 1984; Willis & Schaie, 1988). For example, Willis and Schaie found that men did worse on spatial tasks as they aged largely because they had slowed down with age. Women showed more of a decline in accuracy. Training improved both the speed and accuracy scores of older women, regardless of whether their scores had declined much with age. Spatial training improved mostly accuracy in the men whose scores had declined with age, and improved mostly speed in the men with stable spatial scores.

Sex differences in various cultural and ethnic groups.   Sex differences vary in size across various cultural and ethnic groups (Hoyenga & Hoyenga, 1993). Thus, although the U.S. pattern of abilities is common, it is by no means universal. One exception might be three-dimensional rotation on which males have a more consistent advantage. Also, cultural variables are covariates not only of spatial scores in both sexes combined but also of the size of the sex difference. Overall, the kinds of cultures that produce people with lower spatial scores, compared to people of other cultures, also tend to have a larger sex difference in spatial scores. Thus, it would seem that cultural factors are more important to women's than to men's scores.

Possible mechanisms for cultural effects include practice opportunities and strategy choices. Pontius (1989) found evidence that sex differences depend on which cultural tasks and roles are carried out by which sex. If a certain task provides extensive practice in a certain kind of skill, and if women more often than men perform that task, then women will get higher test scores. The more a culture distinguishes between men's and women's roles, the lower the average spatial scores of people in that culture (Hoyenga & Hoyenga, 1993).

Biological Covariates

The evolutionary theory presented earlier used rodent sex differences in maze learning as a model for sex differences in spatial tasks. Thus, the sex differences in rodents, along with the biological covariates in both rodents and humans, will be documented and described here. Spatial task performances in humans have one of the highest estimates of heritability of any of the cognitive tasks (Bouchard, Segal & Lykken, 1990; McGue & Bouchard, 1989). Since the gene is not sex linked, it may be sex limited.

Sex differences in maze learning in rodents. The model suggests that sex differences in maze learning in rodents will be commonly but *not* universally seen (Hoyenga & Hoyenga, 1993). The male superiority in rodents' maze-learning performances depends on the task and the developmental environment. Sex differences are most commonly seen in closed mazes and in the more complex open mazes. In an **open maze,** the whole structure is elevated off the floor, and there are no walls, as there are in **closed mazes.** In open mazes, the rodents can see all arms at once as well as all the room stimuli. However, the authors have

seen significant sex differences in their laboratory on both closed and open mazes under normal laboratory rearing conditions.

Just as male and female humans do, male and female rodents differ in maze-learning strategies. In a closed maze, males may be more likely to systematically visit each part in sequence, whereas females skip around. As described previously, in open mazes, males more than females attend to the spatial geometry of the room (where the corners were). Females use both the geometry of the room and specific landmarks (the locations of windows) to learn their way through the mazes. These results suggest that when the maze is closed, depriving females of all their preferred cues, the males' systematic arm-visiting pattern may be the best maze-learning strategy. In complex open mazes, females may sometimes learn the mazes more slowly because they are learning about more cues.

Although perinatal hormone manipulations affect adult maze learning scores in rodents, postpubertal manipulations seldom do so (Hoyenga & Hoyenga, 1993). However, puberty may increase error scores in females. Furthermore, Williams and colleagues (1990) found that castrating males during the neonatal period led them to adopt "female" maze-learning strategies as adults. Treating neonatal females with E caused them to adopt masculine strategies.

Lateralization. If developmental rate is related to brain organization and hence to spatial ability, since the sexes have different developmental rates, the sexes would also differ in brain organization. In support of this model, moderately lateralized[13] (as opposed to either weakly or strongly lateralized) rodents do learn mazes faster (Ettlinger, 1988; Glick, 1985; LeMay, 1985; Noonan & Axelrod, 1989a, 1989b).

Two parts of the brain important to the model are sensitive to both hormones and the developmental environment (Diamond, 1985; Chapter 7). The **corpus callosum** connects the right and left hemispheres, and the **hippo-campus** is important to spatial learning in rodents (Crusio & Schwegler, 1991; Hoyenga & Hoyenga, 1988; Schwegler, Crusio, & Brust, 1990). The anatomy of the corpus callosum, and right-left differences in hippocampal anatomy, covary with sex hormones and with developmental environments. The hippo-campus is sensitive to both perinatal and postpubertal sex hormones (Denenberg & Yutzey, 1985; Diamond, 1985; Denenberg, Berrebi, & Fitch, 1989; Juraska, 1990; Juraska & Kopcik, 1988; Maggi et al., 1989); Meyer, Ferres-Torres, & Mas, 1978). Lateralization of hippocampal anatomy in mice is at least par-tially controlled by a Y-linked gene and covaries with maze performances (van Abeelen et al., 1989). The microanatomy of the hippocampus changes at puberty in male mice, and this change is prevented by prepubertal castration (Meyer, Ferres-Torres, & Mas, 1978).

Human lateralization can be detected dur-ing infancy (Hahn, 1987). The electrical brain wave response to stimulation (**evoked ac-tivity**) has been measured in newborn infants through electroencephalogram (EEG) elec-trodes (Molfese & Molfese, 1985). Some children's left hemispheres responded differen-tially to various speech sounds, and their right hemisphere responses distinguished between speech and nonspeech sounds. Three years later, these particular children scored the highest on the verbal subscale of a children's ability test. The sexes also showed different right versus left patterns of brain activity evoked by speech and nonspeech sounds (Burger-Judisch, Camperlengo, & Molfese, 1989; Burger-Judisch & Molfese, 1991; Molfese & Radtke, 1982; Shucard, Shucard, Campos, & Salamy, 1982; Shucard, Shucard, Cummins, & Campos, 1981), probably because of sex dif-ferences in developmental rates.

Gender, lateralization, handedness, and per-formances on various spatial tasks are all inter-related, but in very complex ways (see documentation in Hoyenga & Hoyenga, 1993). For example, cerebral lateralization may be at least weakly related to cognitive ability patterns (Lewis & Harris, 1988). Left handedness is more likely in both learning-disordered people as well as in people with very high levels of ability. Some professional people of very high ability had learning disorders when younger. The relationships between handedness and ability patterns may vary among racial/ethnic groups. Most important, the sexes very often show different relationships among the various factors.

Handedness in humans shows both gender differences and some genetic basis. Females are more strongly right handed, and there are more left and mixed-handed males (Lansky, Fein-stein, & Peterson, 1988). Despite this, females report greater success in being able to shift handedness in response to pressure from parents or teachers (Porac, Coren, & Searle-man, 1986). More left-handed children are born to parents who are left handed, but the handed-ness of an adoptive parent is not related to the handedness of their adopted children. Mater-nal left handedness is more strongly related to children's handedness than is the father's handedness (Annett, 1985). Twins not only develop more slowly than do singletons, they are also more likely to be left handed (Annett, 1985).

Verbal, spatial, and mathematical tasks are controlled by somewhat different areas of the brain (Annett, 1985; Corbett, McCusker, & Davidson, 1986; Geschwind, 1985; Lewis & Kamptner, 1987; Troup, Bradshaw, & Nettle-ton, 1983). More complex tasks are done better using both hemispheres (Banich & Beler, 1990). Because the corpus callosum is the major struc-ture connecting the left to the right cortex, peo-ple who have had that structure surgically removed to control their epilepsy have *separate* right and left areas. With appropriate use of stimuli (right- versus left-side presentations), spatial tasks can be presented separately to their left and right brains. This research confirms that spatial rotation tasks are carried out in the right hemisphere (Corballis & Sergent, 1988, 1989; Loring, Meador, & Lee, 1989). Lesion research strongly confirms this observation (Ditunno & Mann, 1990). However, in a most dramatic demonstration of practice effects, the left hemisphere *can* learn to carry out rotation tasks.

The sexes show different patterns of losses after damage to various parts of the brain, including left versus right side.[14] Sex-differentiated patterns of deficits appear for both verbal (**aphasia**, or loss of speech) and spatial tasks. Women may also show more recovery after aphasia-producing lesions. Studies of people done shortly after the damage occurred will show smaller sex differences than those done on the people one or more years afterwards. These studies also make it clear that sex differences cannot be described just in terms of lateralization. The lesion's location within a hemisphere makes a difference, and the effects are not the same for the sexes.

Several studies recorded the electrical activity of left and right brains of both sexes, both at rest and during task performances. These studies attempted to relate patterns of electrical activity to the quality of the performances (see documentation in Hoyenga & Hoyenga, 1993). Left versus right side differences in activity may have sexually dimorphic patterns of relationships to spatial performances. In fact, for males, the greater the left-right differences in electrical activity, the higher their spatial scores. The *opposite* relationship was found for females: the higher scoring females showed the *smallest* right-left difference. Bowers and LaBarba (1988) suggested that high-ability (spatial visualization) males may use their right hemispheres and low-ability males their right hemispheres. If so, the same may *not* be true of women. High- versus low-scoring women may use different strategies, but neither strategy is quite the same as what either high- or low-ability men are doing.

Hormonal covariates in humans. As pointed out before, postpubertal hormone manipulations do not affect maze-learning performances

in rodents, so one might not expect to find any postpubertal correlates in humans either. On the other hand, considerable research demonstrates that women's auditory, visual, olfactory, taste, and memory processes covary with the cyclical hormonal changes (Altemus, Wexler, & Boulix, 1989; Creutzfeldt et al., 1976; Dunn & Ross, 1985; Gandelman, 1983; Hapidou & De Catanzaro, 1988; Parlee, 1983). There is also some consistency across studies showing systematic variations in spatial task performances with menstrual cycle phases (Hoyenga & Hoyenga, 1993). Spatial performances tend to be better in the low- (menstrual) than in the high-hormone (follicular and luteal) parts of the cycle. However in two studies, gonadotropic hormone levels seemed to be more strongly related to cognitive task performances than were the sex hormone levels in either gender (Gordon, Corbin, & Lee, 1986; Gordon & Lee, 1986).

The effects of both T and E may be curvilinear. For example, Nyborg (1983) found that he could improve the spatial skills of Turner's syndrome females (XO females) if he gave them some injections of E around puberty. However, a more prolonged exposure to E suppressed spatial scores. Similarly, women with high T levels get higher spatial scores, but men with high T levels get lower spatial scores (Broverman, 1964; Broverman et al., 1964; Broverman, Klaiber, & Vogel, 1980; Gouchie & Kimura, 1991; Peterson, 1976; Shute et al., 1983). Men with high T would have more than optimal levels, according to this model, but women with low T would have lower than optimal levels. On the other hand, Rich and McKeever (1990) interpreted their data according to a reversed optimal hormone level hypothesis: moderate T levels in males would be associated with *lower* spatial scores.

Putting all the research together, the relationship between hormones and spatial scores is clearly not linear. It may even have several optimal points. Given this, it is obviously foolish to conclude that sex differences in hormones explain sex differences in spatial performances. Much more needs to be known before sex differences or the implications of the postpubertal hormonal covariates can be understood.

Postpubertal hormones may also be more closely related to strategy choices than they are to actual skill levels (Chiarello, McMahon, & Shaefer, 1989; Ho, Gilber, & Brink, 1986). Women have a different response criterion for guessing than men do (women are less likely to guess). Whatever determines the criterion (mood? self-confidence?) may vary with hormones in both men and women—and maybe even in rodents. Despite the attractiveness of this possibility, Hampson's data (1990b) showing menstrual cycle changes in performances cannot be easily attributed to changes in her subjects' moods or emotions.

Spatial performances may also covary with prenatal hormone levels in humans (see reviews in Hoyenga & Hoyenga, 1993, and in Reinisch et al., 1991). For example, one study found a large difference in spatial performances, including on the S-M task, between adrenogenital females and their unaffected female relatives (Resnick et al., 1986). Adrenogenital females got the higher scores. They had also more often participated in spatial tasks early in life, including playing with spatial types of toys. Nevertheless, childhood spatial task scores were *not* related to adult spatial performances. The adrenogenital syndrome had no effect on the cognitive task scores of males in this study. On the other hand, Jacklin and her colleagues (Jacklin et al., 1988) found that females' spatial performances, measured at school age, were negatively related to the females' neonatal androgen levels.

The difference between the outcomes of the Resnik study (and earlier research: Hoyenga & Hoyenga, 1993) and the Jacklin study could have at least two explanations. First, the hormone levels of the subjects in the Resnik and earlier studies were all abnormal, maternal hormone intake or abnormal fetal adrenal secretion being superimposed on top of the hormone

levels normally present in fetuses. Abnormal hormone levels could change endogenous processes in unexpected ways. In the Jacklin study, the hormone levels were normal, reflecting normal processes, including the children's developmental rates. Second, the spatial scores of the high hormone group in the Jacklin study might not remain depressed. It is not known what their developmental timetable will be. The effect of perinatal hormones probably depends on the timing of the hormone level increase, relative to which endogenous developmental processes are occurring at that same time. Until more is known about these processes, nothing more can be said about perinatal hormones except that they are likely to be significant covariates of cognitive task performances.

SUMMARY

In mate preferences, women prefer men who have status and resources, and men prefer younger, attractive women. Men are more interested in casual sex; women are more interested in commitment. The more resources a woman accumulates, the more she can invest in her offspring, and she may also be able to attract a higher-status man (though she will also be narrowing her options in current industrialized societies: highly achieving women are less likely to marry, to stay married, and to have several children). Despite all this, the sexes are much more similar than different. Both sexes prefer a kind, considerate, and attractive partner, and both sexes frequently desire status. The greater the potential commitment to each other, the more similar the sexes' mating preferences are.

Whenever there are any sex differences, men tend to get the higher average scores on spatial tests; most of the very high-scoring people, particularly on rotation tasks, are male. The sex difference in spatial performances may affect sex differences in choices of occupations that require these abilities, such as engineering, some types of computer skills, and some types of mathematics. Both biological and environmental covariates have been convincingly demonstrated, but the mechanisms through which each type of influence operate remain obscure. Most important, training and practice can improve the scores of both sexes, suggesting that sex differences in this area are never inevitable.

Developmental rate has been the underlying theme of this chapter. Not only do very late-maturing females score higher on spatial tasks, the magnitude of the sex difference in spatial scores matches the sex difference in the age at which hormone levels begin increasing. However, developmental rate itself is complexly determined by genes, prenatal hormones, and the postnatal environment. No sex difference is purely environmental or purely biological. Sex differences, like developmental rates, are epigenetic phenomena. The major importance of this fact is that sex differences can be manipulated — magnified, minimized, or even reversed — by appropriate manipulations of the relevant environmental factors and developmental experiences.

Given the knowledge you have gained about sex differences from this text, the authors leave you with a problem. From the authors' point of view as feminists, the differential valuation of masculine and feminine is pernicious and should be eliminated even if sex differences are not. If, in addition, you feel that sex differences are undesirable, just what would you change in our society so as to eliminate them? What are some of the other implications of those changes? Would we have to eliminate sexual intercourse (reproduction would have to take place in test tubes, where ova and sperm from completely anonymous and sexually neutral-looking people are mixed)? Why couldn't we eliminate sexual reproduction and just clone ourselves?

ENDNOTES

1. You should always remember that, whatever the direction of the difference, the amount of variability is such that knowledge of gender alone can never be used to adequately predict someone's performance.

2. Although, as Friedman noted, the effect size for sex differences on the mathematics section of the SAT has been steadily decreasing from 1975 to 1986, this reflects changes in variability rather than in the size of the average sex difference: an average difference of 50 was associated with an effect size of .448 in 1978, .414 in 1982, and .395 in 1986.

3. Females who do not strongly prefer the right hand, or females who have nonright-handed relatives.

4. These effects may only occur for spatial visualization/rotation types of tasks (e.g., see Burnett, Lane, & Dratt, 1979).

5. They used the Shepard and Meltzer mental rotation test: see later discussion and Figure 14.1.

6. In one study, men rated the attractiveness of various female faces. The faces that were seen as being most attractive were also seen as belonging to more healthy and fertile women but also to women who were more likely to have extramarital affairs (Cunningham, 1986).

7. This disease is caused by the human immunodeficiency virus (HIV), which can be transmitted sexually or by any exchange of bodily fluids (sharing needles, etc.).

8. This number of partners has decreased since the AIDS epidemic among homosexual partners became better publicized (Blumstein & Schwartz, 1983).

9. An abnormality in the positive feedback regulation of gonadotropic hormone levels (see Chapters 6–8). However, in primates, positive feedback is not sexually dimorphic and so the presence of positive feedback in male homosexuals and its absence in heterosexuals, as found by Dörner, is difficult to interpret.

10. They limited their analysis to studies published between 1974 and 1982 and did not include data from large, representative sampling types of studies.

11. According to the terminology used by cognitive researchers and theorists, this makes rotation an **automatic** rather than a **controlled** process. The most typical example of an automatic process is driving your car to work along the same route you've driven hundreds of times before. On some days you get to work without remembering anything you've seen along the way.

12. That is, whether the covariate or the task performance appeared first during the person's development is unknown.

13. As measured by strength of paw preferences.

14. Annett, 1985; Inglis & Lawson, 1981; Kimura, 1983, 1987; Lewis & Kamptner, 1987; McGlone, 1980; Sundet, 1988. One recent lesion study (Kertesz & Benke, 1989) said that there were no sex differences in brain organization but that study averaged over types of aphasia and over cortical and subcortical damage. Furthermore, that study did find that 61.3 percent of males versus 41.4 percent of females with left brain damage had aphasia. Furthermore, central damage was specifically much more likely to lead to aphasia in males than in females, similar to what Kimura has found (see references above).

REFERENCES

The pages on which each source is cited are indicated in boldface type at the end of the entry.

Abbott, D. H., & Hearn, J. P. (1978). Physical, hormonal and behavioural aspects of sexual development in the marmoset monkey, Callithrix jacchus. *Journal of Reproductive Fertility*, *53*, 155–166. **349**

Abelson, A. G. (1979). Development of psychosexual concepts in relation to expressive language performance. *Psychiatry*, *42*, 274–279. **229**

Abraham, G. E. (1974). Ovarian and adrenal contribution to peripheral androgens during the menstrual cycle. *Journal of Clinical Endocrinology and Metabolism, 39*, 340–346. **178**

Abramovitch, R., & Grusec, J. E. (1978). Peer imitation in a natural setting. *Child Development, 49*, 60–65. **316**

Abramowitz, S. I. (1986). Psychosocial outcomes of sex reassignment surgery. *Journal of Consulting and Clinical Psychology, 54*, 183–189. **229**

Abrams, D., Sparkes, K., & Hogg, M. A. (1985). Gender salience and social identity: The impact of sex of siblings on educational and occupational aspirations. *British Journal of Educational Psychology, 55*, 224–232. **329**

Abramson, P. R., Goldberg, P. A., Greenberg, J. J., & Abramson, L. M. (1977). The talking platypus phenomenon: Competency ratings as a function of sex and professional status. *Psychology of Women Quarterly, 2*, 114–124. **280**

Adams, E. R., & Burnett, G. W. (1991). Scientific vocabulary divergence among female primatologist s working in East Africa. *Social Studies of Science, 21*, 547–560. **345**

Adams, L. A., Vician, L., Clifton, D. K., & Steiner, R. A. (1991). Testosterone regulates pro-opiomelanocortin gene expression in the primate brain. *Edocrinology, 128*, 1881–1886. **136**

Adcock, I. M., & Greenstein, B. D. (1986). Sexual dimorphism of messenger RNA isolated from neonatal rat brain. *Journal of Endocrinology, 109*, 23–28. **138**

Adkins-Regan, E. (1981). Hormone specificity, androgen metabolism, and sexual behavior. *American Zoologist, 21*, 257–271. **141, 142**

Adler, T. (1990). Treatments for PMS are promising, but untested. *American Psychological Association Monitor, 21*, 11–12. **195**

Aguilar, R., Bellido, C., & Aguilar, E. (1987). Differences in prepuberal neonatally estrogenized or androgenized male rats. *Andrologia, 19*, 183–187. **128, 187**

Ahlgren, A. (1983). Sex differences in the correlates of cooperative and competitive school attitudes. *Developmental Psychology, 19*, 881–888. **318**

Ahlgren, A., & Johnson, D. W. (1979). Sex differences in cooperative and competitive attitudes from the 2nd through the 12th grades. *Developmental Psychology, 15*, 45–49. **318**

Ainsworth, M. D. S. (1973). The development of infant-mother attachement. In B. M. Caldwell & H. N. Ricciuti (Eds.), *Review of child development research* (Vol. 3). Chicago: University of Chicago Press. **222**

_____ . (1979). Infant-mother attachment. *American Psychologist, 34*, 932–937. **222** Akiskal, H. S. (1982). Factors associated with incomplete recovery in primary depressive illness. *Journal of Clinical Psychiatry, 43*, 266–271. **364**

Akker, O. van den, & Steptoe, A. (1985). The pattern of prevalence of symptoms during the menstrual cycle. *British Journal of Psychiatry, 147*, 164–169. **192**

Alatalo, R. V., Lundberg, A., & Glynn, C. (1986). Female pied flycatchers choose territory quality and not male characteristics. *Nature, 323*, 152–153. **84**

Albert, A. A., & Porter, J. R. (1986). Children's gender-role stereotypes: A comparison of the United States and South Africa. *Journal of Cross-Cultural Psychology, 17*, 45–65. **294**

Albert, B., & Romos, A. R. (1989). Yanomami Indians and anthropological ethics. *Science, 244*, 632. **239**

Albert, D. J., Jonik R. H., Watson, N. V., Gorzalka, B. B., & Walsh, M. L. (1990). Hormone-dependent aggression in male rats is proportional to serum testosterone concentration but sexual behavior is not. *Physiology & Behavior, 48*, 409–416. **151**

Alén, M., Rahkila, P., Reinilä, M., & Vihko, R. (1987). Androgenic-anabolic steroid effects on serum thyroid, pituitary and steroid hormones in athletes. *American Journal of Sports Medicine, 15*, 357–361. **202**

Alén, M., Reinilä, M., & Vihko, R. (1985). Response of serum hormones to androgen administration in power athletes. *Medicine and Science in Sports and Exercise, 17*, 354–359. **202**

Alexander, R. D. (1988). Evolutionary approaches to human behavior: What does the future hold? In L. Betzig, M. B. Mulder, & P. Turke (Eds.), *Human reproductive behaviour*. Cambridge: Cambridge University Press. **239**

Alexander, R. D., Hoogland, J. L., Howard, R. D., Noonan, K. M., & Sherman, P. W. (1979). Sexual dimorphisms and breeding systems in pinnipeds, ungulates, primates, and humans. In N. Chagnon & W. Irons (Eds.), *Evolutionary biology and human social behavior*. North Scituate, MA:Duxbury Press. **252**

Allen, L. S., & Gorski, R. A. (1990). Sex difference in the bed nucleus of the stria terminalis of the human brain. *Journal of Comparative Neurology, 302*, 697–706. **165, 359**

_____ . (1991). Sexual dimorphism of the anterior commissure and massa intermedia of the human brain. *Journal of Comparative Neurology, 31*, 97–104. **165**

Allen, L. S., Richey, M. F., Chai, Y. M., & Gorski, R. A. (1991). Sex differences in the corpus callosum of the living human being. *Journal of Neuroscience, 11*, 933–942. **164**

Allen, L. S., Hines, M., Shryne, J. E., & Gorski, R. A. (1989). Two sexually dimorphic cell groups in the human brain. *Journal of Neuroscience, 9*, 497–506. **162, 165**

Allen, M. J. (1974). Sex differences in spatial problem-solving styles. *Perceptual and Motor Skills, 39,* 843–846. **392**

Allen, M. J., & Cholet, M. E. (1978). Strength of association between sex and field dependence. *Perceptual and Motor Skills, 47,* 419–421. **391**

Allen, M. J., & Hogeland, R. (1978). Spatial problem-solving strategies as functions of sex. *Perceptual and Motor Skills, 47,* 348–350. **392**

Allgeier, E. R. (1981). The influence of androgynous identification on heterosexual relations. *Sex Roles, 7,* 321–330. **328**

Allison, P. D., & Furstenberg, F. F., Jr. (1989). How marital dissolution affects children: Variations by age and sex. *Developmental Psychology, 25,* 540–549. **223**

Alloy, L. B., & Clements, C. M. (1990, May). *Realism in judging personal control: Antecedent or consequence of depression.* Paper presented at Midwestern Psychological Association Convention, Chicago. **366, 369**

Almeida Acosta, E., & Sanchez de Almeida, M. E. (1983). Psychological factors affecting change in women's roles and status: A cross-cultural study. *International Journal of Psychology, 18,* 3–35. **259**

Alnaes, R., & Torgersen, S. (1988). Major depression, anxiety disorders and mixed conditions: Childhood and precipitating events. *Acta Psychiatrica Scandinavica, 78,* 632–638. **364**

————. (1989). Characteristics of patients with major depression in combination with dysthymic or cyclothymic disorders: Childhood and precipitating events. *Acta Psychiatrica Scandinavica, 79,* 11–18. **364**

————. (1990). Parental representation in patients with major depression, anxiety disorder and mixed conditions. *Acta Psychiatrica Scandinavica, 81,* 518–522. **364**

Altemus, M., Wexler, B. E., & Boulix, N. (1989). Changes in perceptual asymmetry with the menstrual cycle. *Neuropsychologia, 27,* 233–240. **398**

Altman, J., Das, G. D., & Anderson, W. J. (1968). Effects of infantile handling on morphological development of the rat brain: An exploratory study. *Developmental Psychobiology, 1,* 10–20. **225**

Altshuler, L. L., Devinsky, O., Post, R. M., & Theodore, W. (1990). Depression, anxiety, and temporal lobe epilepsy: Laterality of focus and symptoms. *Archives of Neurology, 47,* 284–288. **369**

Alvarez-Buylla, A., Kirn, J. R., & Nottebohm, F. (1990). Birth of projection neurons in adult avian brain may be related to perceptual or motor learning. *Science, 249,* 1444–1446. **142**

Alvarez-Buylla, A., Theelen, M., & Nottebohm, F. (1988). Birth of projection neurons in the higher vocal center of the canary forebrain before, during, and after song learning. *Proceedings of the National Academy of Sciences, USA, 85,* 8722–8726. **142**

Alvir, J., & Thys-Jacobs, S. (1991). Premenstrual and menstrual symptom clusters and response to calcium treatment. *Psychopharmacology Bulletin, 27,* 145–148. **195**

Amatayakul, K., Silvasomboon, B., & Thanangkul, O. (1980). A study of the mechanism of weight gain in medroxyprogesterone users. *Contraception, 22,* 605–622. **189**

Amato, P. R., & Keith, B. (1991). Parental divorce and the well-being of children: A meta-analysis. *Psychological Bulletin, 110,* 26–46. **223, 299**

Amenson, C. S., & Lewinsohn, P. M. (1981). An investigation into the observed sex difference in prevalence of unipolar depression. *Journal of Abnormal Psychology, 90,* 1–13. **361, 364**

American Psychiatric Association. (1987). *Diagnostic and statistical manual of mental disorders* (3rd ed., Rev.). Washington, DC: Author. **361**

Amsel, A. (1986). Developmental psychobiology and behaviour theory: Reciprocating influences. *Canadian Journal of Psychology, 40,* 311–342. **227**

Andersen, S. M., & Klatzky, R. L. (1987). Traits and social stereotypes: Levels of categorization in person perception. *Journal of Personality and Social Psychology, 53,* 235–246. **269**

Anderson, C. M. (1986). Female age: Male preference and reproductive success in primates. *International Journal of Primatology, 7,* 305–326. **19, 375**

Anderson, R. H., Fleming, D. E., Rhees, R. W., & Kinghorn, E. (1986). Relationships between sexual activity, plasma testosterone, and the volume of the sexually dimorphic nucleus of the preoptic area in prenatally stressed and nonstressed rats. *Brain Research, 370,* 1–10. **148**

Andersson, M. (1982). Female choice selects for extreme tail length in a widowbird. *Nature, 299,* 818–820. **85**

————. (1986). Evolution of condition-dependent sex ornaments and mating preferences: Sexual selection based on viability differences. *Evolution, 40,* 804–816. **87**

Andersson, M., Page, D. C., & de la Chapelle, A. (1986). Chromosome Y-specific DNA is transferred to the short arm of X chromosome in human XX males. *Science, 233,* 786–788. **106**

Andreasen, N. C. (1987). Creativity and mental illness: Prevalence rates in writers and their first-degree relatives. *American Journal of Psychiatry, 144,* 1288–1292. **337, 367**

Andrews, B., & Brown, G. W. (1988). Marital violence in the community: A biographical approach. *British Journal of Psychiatry, 153,* 305–312. **352, 353**

Angelbeck, J. H., & DuBrul, E. F. (1983). The effect of neonatal testosterone on specific male and female patterns of phosphorylated cytosolic proteins in the rat preoptic-hypothalamus, cortex and amygdala. *Brain Research, 264,* 277–283. **138**

Angermeyer, M. C., & Kühn, L. (1988). Gender differences in age at onset of schizophrenia: An overview. *European Archives of Psychiatry and Neurological Sciences, 237,* 351–364. **236**

Angold, A. (1988). Childhood and adolescent depression: I. Epidemiological and aetiological aspects. *British Journal of Psychiatry, 152,* 601–617. **363**

Annett, M. (1985). *Left, right, hand and brain: the right shift theory.* London: Lawrence Erlbaum. **397, 400**

Antill, J. K. (1987). Parents' beliefs and values about sex roles, sex differences, and sexuality: Their sources and implications. In P. Shaver & C. Hendrick (Eds.), *Sex and gender.* Beverly Hills: Sage. **298**

Antill, J. K., & Cotton, S. (1988). Factors affecting the division of labor in households. *Sex Roles, 18,* 531–554. **306**

Apter, D., Reinilä, M., & Vihko, R. (1989). Some endocrine characteristics of early menarche, a risk factor for breast cancer, are preserved into adulthood. *International Journal of Cancer, 44,* 783–878. **130**

Apter, D., & Vihko, R. (1990). Endocrine determinants of fertility: Serum androgen concentrations during follow-up of adolescents into the third decade of life. *Journal of Clinical Endocrinology and Metabolism, 71,* 970–974. **130**

Archer, D., Iritani, B., Kimes, D. D., & Barrios, M. (1983). Face-ism: Five studies of sex differences in facial prominence. *Journal of*

Personality and Social Psychology, 45, 725–735. **289**

Archer, J. (1980). The distinction between gender stereotypes and sex-role concepts. *British Journal of Social and Clinical Psychology, 19,* 51. **270**

_____. (1984). Gender stereotype and sex-role concepts: A reply to Stoppard & Kalin. *British Journal of Social Psychology, 23,* 89–91. **270**

_____. (1989a). Childhood gender roles: Structure and development. *The Psychologist: Bulletin of the British Psychological Society, 9,* 367–370. **49, 297**

_____. (1989b). The relationship between gender-role measures: A review. *British Journal of Social Psychology, 28,* 173–184. **49, 276**

_____. (1990). Gender-stereotypic traits are derived from gender roles: A reply to McCreary. *British Journal of Social Psychology, 29,* 273–277. **49**

Archer, J., & Rhodes, C. (1989). The relationship between gender-related traits and attitudes. *British Journal of Social Psychology, 28,* 149–157. **49**

Archer, S. L. (1985). Career and/or family: The identity process for adolescent girls. *Youth & Society, 16,* 289–314. **327**

Archidiacono, N., Rocchi, M., Valente, M., & Filippi, G. (1979). X pentasomy: A case and review. *Human Genetics, 52,* 69–77. **123**

Arendash, G. W., & Gorski, R. A. (1982). Enhancement of sexual behavior in female rats by neonatal transplantation of brain tissue from males. *Science, 217,* 1276–1278. **159**

_____. (1983). Effects of discrete lesions of the sexually dimorphic nucleus of the preoptic area or other medial preoptic regions on the sexual behavior of male rats. *Brain Research Bulletin, 10,* 147–154. **162**

Arimatsu, Y., & Hatanaka, H. (1986). Estrogen treatment enhances survival of cultured fetal rat amygdala neurons in a defined medium. *Developmental Brain Research, 26,* 151–159. **137**

Armitage, K. J., Schneiderman, L. J., & Bass, R. A. (1979). Response of physicians to medical complaints in men and women. *Journal of the American Medical Association, 241,* 2186–2187. **283**

Armstrong, S. L., Gleitman, L. R., & Gleitman, H. (1983). What some concepts might not be. *Cognition, 13,* 263–308. **266, 268**

Arnold, A. P., & Breedlove, S. M. (1985). Organizational and activational effects of sex steroids on brain and behavior: A reanalysis. *Hormones and Behavior, 19,* 469–498. **125**

Arnold, S. J. (1983). Sexual selection: The interface of theory and empiricism. In P. P. G. Bateson (Ed.), *Mate Choice.* Cambridge: Cambridge University Press. **61, 62, 84**

Arnold, S. J., & Wade, M. J. (1984a). On the measurement of natural and sexual selection: Theory. *Evolution, 38,* 709–719. **62, 84**

_____. (1984b). On the measurement of natural and sexual selection: Applications. *Evolution, 38,* 720–734. **62, 84**

Arrindell, W. A., Perris, C., Perris, J., Eisemann, M., van der Ende, J., & von Knorring, L. (1986). Cross-national invariance of dimensions of parental rearing behaviour: Comparison of psychometric data of Swedish depressives and healthy subjects with Dutch target ratings on the EMBU. *British Journal of Psychiatry, 148,* 305–309. **251**

Åsgård, U., Nordström, P., & Rabäck, G. (1987). Birth cohort analysis of changing suicide risk by sex and age in Sweden 1952 to 1981. *Acta Psychiatrica Scandinavica, 76,* 456–463. **366**

Ashmore, R. D. (1981). Sex stereotypes and implicit personality theory. In D. L. Hamilton (Ed.), *Cognitive processes in stereotyping and intergroup behavior.* Hillsdale, NJ: Erlbaum. **270, 271, 295**

Ashmore, R. D., & Del Boca, F. K. (1979). Sex stereotypes and implicit personality theory: Toward a cognitive-social psychological conceptualization. *Sex Roles, 5,* 219–248. **269, 270**

Ashmore, R. D., Del Boca, F. K., & Wohlers, A. J. (1986). Gender stereotypes. In R. D. Ashmore & F. K. Del Boca (Eds.), *The social psychology of female-male relations.* New York: Academic Press. **269, 270, 272, 295**

Astin, H. S., & Myint, T. (1971). Career development of young women during the post-high school years. *Journal of Counseling Psychology, 18,* 369–394. **336**

Atchley, W. R., & Newman, S. (1989). A quantitative-genetics perspective on mammalian development. *American Naturalist, 134,* 486–512. **220**

Atkinson, J. (1987). Gender roles in marriage and the family: A critique and some proposals. *Journal of Family Issues, 8,* 5–41. **6, 40**

Atkinson, J., & Huston, T. L. (1984). Sex role orientation and division of labor early in marriage. *Journal of Personality and Social Psychology, 46,* 330–345. **306**

Atkinson, J. M. (1982). Anthropology.

Signs: *Journal of Women in Culture and Society, 8,* 236–258. **238**

Aureli, F., Schino, G., Cordischi, C., Cozzolino, R., Succhi, S., & van Schaik, C. P. (1990). Social factors affect secondary sex ratio in captive Japanese macaques. *Folia Primatologica, 55,* 176–180. **80**

Avery, D., & Silverman, J. (1984). Psychomotor retardation and agitation in depression: Relationship to age, sex, and response to treatment. *Journal of Affective Disorders, 7,* 67–76. **263**

Axelson, J. F., & Sawin, C. (1987). Effects of voluntary and forced exercise on lordosis behavior in female rats. *Hormones and Behavior, 21,* 384–401. **386**

Ayoub, D. M., Greenough, W. T., & Juraska, J. M. (1983). Sex differences in dendritic structure in the preoptic area of juvenile Macaque monkey brain. *Science, 219,* 197–198. **163**

Baber, K. M., & Monaghan, P. (1988). College women's career and motherhood expectations: New options, old dilemmas. *Sex Roles, 19,* 189–204. **329, 331**

Bachevalier, J., Brickson, M., Hagger, C., & Mishkin, M. (1990). Age and sex differences in the effects of selective temporal lobe lesion on the formation of visual discrimination habits in rhesus monkeys *(Macaca mulatta).* *Behavioral Neuroscience, 104,* 885–899. **236**

Bachevalier, J., Hagger, C., & Bercu, B. B. (1989). Gender differences in visual habit formation in 3-month-old rhesus monkeys. *Developmental Psychobiology, 22,* 585–599. **236**

Bachmann, G. A., Leiblum, S. R., Sandler, B., Ainsley, W., Narcessian, R., Shelden, R., & Hymans, H. N. (1985). Correlates of sexual desire in post-menopausal women. *Maturitas, 7,* 211–216. **199**

Bacon, M. K., Child, I. L., & Barry, H., III. (1963). A cross-cultural study of correlates of crime. *Journal of Abnormal and Social Psychology, 66,* 291–300. **355**

Baenninger, M., & Newcombe, N. (1989). The role of experience in spatial test performance: A meta-analysis. *Sex Roles, 20,* 327–344. **393, 395**

Bailey, J. M., & Pillard, R. C. (1991). A genetic study of male sexual orientation. *Archives of General Psychiatry, 48,* 1089–1096. **388**

Bailey, R. C., & Aunger, R., Jr. (1989). Significance of the social relationships of Efe pygmy men in the Ituri forest, Zaire. *American Journal of Physical Anthropology, 78,* 495–507. **246**

Bailey, W. T., Harrell, D. R., &

Anderson, L. E. (1991, May). *You've come a long way baby; or have you? The image of middle-aged and older women in magazine advertisement*. Paper presented at the annual meeting of the Midwestern Psychological Association, Chicago. **289**

Bailyn, L. (1987). Experiencing technical work: A comparison of male and female engineers. *Human Relations, 40*, 299–312. **325, 328, 329**

Baker, D. P., & Entwisle, D. R. (1987). The influence of mothers on the academic expectations of young children: A longitudinal study of how gender differences arise. *Social Forces, 63*, 670–694. **332**

Baker, L. A., Mack, W., Moffitt, T. E., & Mednick, S. (1989). Sex differences in property crime in a Danish adoption cohort. *Behavior Genetics, 19*, 355–370. **359**

Balazs, R., Gallo, V., Kingsbury, A., Thangnipon, W., Smith, R., Atterwill, C., & Woodhams, P. (1987). Factors affecting the survival and maturation of nerve cells in culture. In H. H. Althaus & W. Seifert (Eds.), *Glial-neuronal communication in development and regeneration*. New York: Springer-Verlag. **139**

Baldwin, A. C., Critelli, J. W., Stevens, L. C., & Russell, S. (1986). Androgyny and sex role measurement: A personal construct approach. *Journal of Personality and Social Psychology, 51*, 1081–1088. **45**

Bancroft, J., Axworthy, D., & Ratcliffe, S. (1982). The personality and psycho-sexual development of boys with 47 XXY chromosome constitution. *Journal of Child Psychology and Psychiatry, 23*, 169–180. **115**

Bancroft, J., Cook, A., & Williamson, L. (1988). Food craving, mood and the menstrual cycle. *Psychological Medicine, 18*, 855–860. **189**

Bancroft, J., Sherwin, B. B., Alexander, G. M., Davidson, D. W., & Walker, A. (1991). Oral contraceptives, androgens, and the sexuality of young women: II. The role of androgens. *Archives of Sexual Behavior, 20*, 121–135. **201**

Bandura, A. (1977). *Social learning theory*. Englewood Cliffs, NJ: Prentice Hall. **219**

_____. (1986). *Social foundations of thought and action*. Englewood Cliffs, NJ: Prentice Hall. **207, 212, 214, 219, 227, 232, 249**

Bane, M. J., & Ellwood, D. T. (1989). One fifth of the nation's children: Why are they poor? *Science, 245*, 1047–1053. **322**

Banich, M. T., & Belger, A. (1990). Interhemispheric interaction: How do the hemispheres divide and conquer a task? *Cortex, 26*, 77–94. **397**

Bar-Tal, D., & Saxe, L. (1976). Physical attractiveness and its relationship to sex-role stereotyping. *Sex Roles, 2*, 123–134. **380**

Barbarino, A., De Marinis, L., & Mancini, A. (1983). Estradiol modulation of basal and gonadotropin-releasing hormone-induced gonadotropin release in intact and castrated men. *Neuroendocrinology, 36*, 105–111. **145**

Barclay, A., & Cusumano, D. R. (1967). Father absence, cross-sex identity, and field-dependent behavior in male adolescents. *Child Development, 38*, 243–250. **395**

Bardenstein, K. K., & McGlashan, T. H. (1990). Gender differences in affective, schizoaffective, and schizophrenic disorders: A review. *Schizophrenia Research, 3*, 159–172. **236**

Bardin, C. W., & Catterall, J. F. (1981). Testosterone: A major determinant of extragenital sexual dimorphism. *Science, 211*, 1285–1294. **152**

Barkley, R. A., Ullman, D. G., Otto, L., & Brecht, J. M. (1977). The effects of sex typing and sex appropriateness of modeled behavior on children's imitation. *Child Development, 48*, 721–725. **219, 236**

Barkow, J. H. (1989). *Darwin, sex, and status: Biological approaches to mind and culture*. Toronto: University of Toronto Press. **237, 247, 263, 376**

_____. (1991). Précis of *Darwin, sex and status: Biological approaches to mind and culture*. *Behavioral and Brain Sciences, 14*, 295–334. **1, 2, 335**

Barlow, G. W. (1991). Nature-nurture and the debates surrounding ethology and sociobiology. *American Zoologist, 31*, 286–296. **13, 15**

Barlow, P. (1973). The influence of inactive chromosomes on human development: Anomalous sex chromosome complements and the phenotype. *Humangenetik, 17*, 105–136. **112**

Barnes, A. B., Colton, T., Gundersen, J., Noller, K. L., Tilley, B. C. Strama, T., Townsend, D. E., Hatab, P., & O'Brien, P. C. (1980). Fertility and outcome of pregnancy in women exposed in utero to diethylstilbestrol. *New England Journal of Medicine, 302*, 609–613. **170**

Barnes, D. M. (1988). Sex hormones linked to task performance. *Science, 242*, 1509–1510. **190, 201**

_____. (1989). "Fragile X" syndrome and its puzzling genetics. *Science, 243*, 171–172. **121**

Baron, J. N., Davis-Blake, A., & Bielby, W. T. (1986). The structure of opportunity: How promotion ladders vary within and among organizations. *Administrative Science Quarterly, 31*, 248–273. **324, 330**

Baron, P., & Joly, E. (1988). Sex differences in the expression of depression in adolescents. *Sex Roles, 18*, 1–8. **363**

Barry, H., III, Bacon, M. K., & Child, I. L. (1957). A cross-cultural survey of some sex differences in socialization. *Journal of Abnormal and Social Psychology, 55*, 327–332. **254**

Bartos, L., & Trojan, S. (1985). Experimentally induced conditioned sexual preference in the laboratory rat. *Physiologia Bohemoslovaca, 34*, 7–8. **382**

Bartsch, W., & Voigt, K. D. (1984). Endocrine aspects of aging in the male. *Maturitas, 6*, 243–251. **199**

Baruch, G. K., & Barnett, R. C. (1981). Fathers' participation in the care of their preschool children. *Sex Roles, 7*, 1043–1056. **305**

Bateson, P. (1982). Preferences for cousins in Japanese quail. *Nature, 295*, 236–237. **87**

Baucom, D. H. (1976). Independent masculinity and femininity scales on the California Personality Inventory. *Journal of Consulting and Clinical Psychology, 44*, 876. **44**

_____. (1980). Independent CPI masculinity and femininity scales: Psychological correlates and a sex-role typology. *Journal of Personality Assessment, 44*, 262–271. **44**

Baucom, D. H., Besch, P. K., & Callahan, S. (1985). Relation between testosterone concentration, sex role identity, and personality among females. *Journal of Personality and Social Psychology, 48*, 1218–1226. **16, 44**

Bauer, H. C., & Bauer, H. (1990). Effects of progesterone, epipregnanolone and RU 38486 on potassium uptake in cultured cortical neurons. *Journal of Steroid Biochemistry, 36*, 269–272. **137**

Bauer, J. A., Shimojo, S., Gwiazda, J., & Held, R. (1986). Sex differences in the development of binocularity in human infants. *Investigative Ophthalmology & Visual Sciences, 27*, 265. **236**

Baulieu, E.-E. (1978). Cell membrane, a target for steroid hormones. *Molecular and Cellular Endocrinology, 12*, 247–254. **136**

Baum, M. J. (1979). Differentiation of coital behavior in mammals: A comparative analysis. *Neuroscience and Biobehavioral Reviews, 3*, 265–284. **141, 386**

_____. (1990). Frank Beach's research on the sexual differentiation of behavior and his struggle with the "organizational" hypothesis. *Neuroscience & Biobehavioral Reviews, 14*, 201–206. **125, 154**

Baum, M. J., Stockman, E. R., & Lundell, L. A. (1985). Evidence of proceptive without increased defeminization in male ferrets. *Behavioral Neuroscience, 99*, 742–750. **141**

Baumann, S. B., Rogers, R. L., Guinto, F. C., Saydjari, C. L., Papanicolaou, A. C., & Eisenberg, H. M. (1991). Gender differences in source location for the N100 auditory evoked magnetic field. *Electroencephalography and Clinical Neurophysiology, 80*, 53–59. **165**

Baumrind, D. (1968). Authoritarian vs. authoritative parental control. *Adolescence, 3*, 255–272. **318**

_____. (1971a). Current patterns of parental authority. *Developmental Psychology, 4*, 1–103. **318**

_____. (1971b). From each according to her ability. *School Review, 80*, 161–197.

_____. (1982). Are androgynous individuals more effective persons and parents? *Child Development, 53*, 44–75. **318**

_____. (1991). To nurture nature. *Behavioral and Brain Sciences, 14*, 386–387. **18, 318**

Bayer, S. A. (1985). Neuron production in the hippocampus and olfactory bulb of the adult rat brain: Addition or replacement? *Annals of the New York Academy of Sciences, 457*, 163–172. **152**

Bayer, S. A., Yackel, J. W., & Puri, P. S. (1982). Neurons in the rat dentate gyrus granular layer substantially increase during juvenile and adult life. *Science, 216*, 890–892. **152**

Beatty, L. A., Hoyenga, K. B. & Hoyenga, K. T. (1992). A sex difference in adaptation to stress: Utility and validity issues in the development of an animal model of depression. Unpublished master's thesis, Western Illinois University. **362**

Beatty, W. E. (1979). Gonadal hormones and sex differences in nonreproductive behaviors in rodents: Organizational and activational influences. *Hormones and Behavior, 12*, 112–163. **211, 214, 358**

Beauchamp, G. K., Yamazaki, K., Bard, J., & Boyse, E. A. (1988). Preweaning experience in the control of mating preferences by genes in the major histocompatibility complex of the mouse. *Behavior Genetics, 18*, 537–547. **74, 87**

Bebbington, P. E., Dean, C., Der, G., Hurry, J., & Tennant, C. (1991). Gender, parity and the prevalence of minor affective disorder. *British Journal of Psychiatry, 158*, 40–45. **370**

Bebbington, P. E., Tennant, C., & Hurry, J. (1991). Adversity in groups with an increased risk of minor affective disorder. *British Journal of Psychiatry, 158*, 33–40. **365**

Beck, L. E., Gevirtz, R., & Mortola, J. F. (1990). The predictive role of psychosocial stress on symptom severity in premenstrual syndrome. *Psychosomatic Medicine, 52*, 536–543. **192**

Becker, B. J. (1988). Influence again: An examination of reviews and studies of gender differences in social influence. In J. S. Hyde & M. C. Linn (Eds.), *The psychology of gender: Advances through meta-analysis*. New York: Academic Press. **82, 344**

Becker, B. J., & Hedges, L. V. (1984). Meta-analysis of cognitive gender differences: A comment on an analysis by Rosenthal and Rubin. *Journal of Educational Psychology, 76*, 583–587. **373, 389**

Becker, D., Creutzfeldt, O. D., Schwibbe, M., & Wuttke, W. (1982). Changes in physiological, EEG and psychological parameters in women during the spontaneous menstrual cycle and following oral contraceptives. *Psychoneuroendocrinology, 7*, 75–90. **190, 201**

Becker, J. (1981). Differential teacher treatment of males and females in mathematics classes. *Journal of Research in Mathematics Education, 12*, 40–53. **312**

Beecher, M. D. (1988). Some comments on the adaptationist approach to learning. In R. C. Bolles & M. D. Beecher (Eds.), *Evolution and learning*. Hillsdale, NJ: Erlbaum. **213, 214**

Beecher, M. D., & Beecher, I. M. (1979). Sociobiology of bank swallows: Reproductive strategy of the male. *Science, 205*, 1282–1285. **78**

Beit-Hallahmi, B., Catford, J. C., Cooley, R. E., Dull, C. Y., Guiora, A. Z., & Paluszny, M. (1974). Grammatical gender and gender identity development: Cross cultural and cross lingual implications. *American Journal of Orthopsychiatry, 44*, 424–431. **229**

Bekoff, M. (1988). Motor training and physical fitness: Possible short-and long-term influences on the development of individual differences in behavior. *Developmental Psychobiology, 21*, 601–612. **75**

Belk, S. S., & Snell, W. E., Jr. (1986).

Beliefs about women: Components and correlates. *Personality and Social Psychology Bulletin, 12*, 403–413. **295**

Bell, C. (1977). Commentary on "My brother's keeper: Child and sibling caretaking." *Current Anthropology, 18*, 181. **240**

Bell, G. (1987). Two theories of sex and variation. In S. C. Stearns (Ed.), *The evolution of sex and its consequences*. Boston: Birkhauser. **68, 71, 72**

Belle, D. (1985). Ironies in the contemporary study of gender. *Journal of Personality, 53*, 400–405. **10, 12, 25**

Beller, A. H. (1985). Changes in the sex composition of U.S. occupations, 1960–1981. *Journal of Human Resources, 20*, 235–250. **324**

Belsky, J. (1988). The "effects" of infant day care reconsidered. *Early Childhood Research Quarterly, 3*, 235–272. **223**

Bem, S. L. (1974). The measurement of psychological androgyny. *Journal of Consulting and Clinical Psychology, 42*, 153–162. **42, 45**

_____. (1975). Sex-role adaptability: One consequence of psychological androgyny. *Journal of Personality and Social Psychology, 31*, 634–643. **45, 48**

_____. (1978). Beyond androgyny: Some presumptuous prescriptions for a liberated sexual identity. In J. Sherman & F. Denmark (Eds.), *Psychology of women: Future directions of research*. New York: Psychological Dimensions. **44, 45**

_____. (1979). Theory and measurement of androgyny: A reply to the Pedhazur-Tetenbaum and Locksley-Colten critiques. *Journal of Personality and Social Psychology, 37*, 1047–1054. **45**

_____. (1981a). Gender schema theory: A cognitive account of sex typing. *Psychological Review, 88*, 354–364. **45, 48**

_____. (1981b). The BSRI and gender schema theory: A reply to Spence and Helmreich. *Psychological Review, 88*, 369–371. **48**

_____. (1982). Gender schema theory and self-schema theory compared: A comment on Markus, Crane, Bernstein, and Siladi's "Self-Schemas and Gender." *Journal of Personality and Social Psychology, 43*, 1192–1194. **45, 48**

_____. (1985). Androgyny and gender schema theory: A conceptual and empirical integration. In T. B. Sonderegger (Ed.), *Nebraska symposium on motivation, 1984: Psychology and gender* (Vol 32). Lincoln: University of Nebraska Press. **30, 45, 49**

Benbow, C. P. (1988). Sex differences in mathematical reasoning ability in intellectually talented preadolescents: Their nature, effects, and possible causes. *Behavioral and Brain Sciences, 11*, 169–232. **373**

Benbow, C. P., Stanley, J. C., Kirk, M. K., & Zonderman, A. B. (1983). Structure of intelligence in intellectually precocious children and in their parents. *Intelligence, 7*, 129–152. **373**

Bender, H. S., King, C. S., & Lin, Y. C. (1988). Decreased serum testosterone response to gonadotropin-releasing hormone in male offspring of diabetic female rats. *Archives of Andrology, 21*, 11–16. **170**

Benes, F. M. (1989). Myelination of cortical-hippocampal relays during late adolescence. *Schizophrenia Bulletin, 15*, 585–593. **228**

Bennett, J. H., Hayman, D. L., & Hope, R. M. (1986). Novel sex differences in linkage values and meiotic chromosome behavior in a marsupial. *Nature, 323*, 59–60. **101**

Benus, R. F., Bohus, B., Koolhaas, J. M., & van Oortmerssen, G. A. (1990). Behavioural strategies of aggressive and non-aggressive male mice in response to inescapable shock. *Behavioural Processes, 21*, 127–141. **365**

Berch, D. B., & Wright, K. P. (1990, May). *Sex-of-examiner effects in assessing spatial ability.* Paper presented at Midwestern Psychological Association, Chicago. **394**

Bercu, B. B., Lee, B. C., Pineda, J. L., Spiliotix, B. E., Denman, D. W., III, Hoffman, H. J., Brown, T. J., & Sachs, H. C. (1983). Male sexual development in the monkey. I. Cross–sectional analysis of pulsatile hypothalamic-pituitary-testicular function. *Journal of Clinical Endocrinology and Metabolism, 56*, 1214–1226. **150**

Bereiter, D. A., & Barker, D. J. (1980). Hormone-induc ed enlargement of receptive fields in trigeminal mechnanorecep tive neurons. I. Time course, hormone, sex, and modality specificity. *Brain Research, 184*, 395–410. **181**

Bereiter, D. A., Standford, L. R., & Barker, D. J. (1980). Hormone-induced enlargement of receptive fields in trigeminal mechnano-receptive neurons. II. Possible mechanisms. *Brain Research, 184*, 411–423. **181**

Berg, H. M., & Ferber, M. A. (1983). Men and women graduate students: Who succeeds and why? *Journal of Higher Education, 54*, 629–648. **319, 321**

Berg, J. M., Karlinsky, H., Korossy, M., & Pakula, Z. (1988). Twenty-six years later: A woman with tetra-X chromosomes. *Journal of Mental Deficiency Research, 32*, 67–74. **123**

Berg, K. (1979). Inactivation of one of the X chromosomes in females is a biological phenomenon of clinical importance. *Acta Medica Scandinavica, 206*, 1–3. **104**

Berger, G. S., & Talwar, P. P. (1978). Oral contraceptive potencies and side effects. *Obstetrics and Gynecology, 51*, 545–547. **189**

Berrger, J., Rosenholtz, S. J., & Zelditch, M., Jr. (1980). Status organizing processes. *Annual Review of Sociology, 6*, 479–508. **285**

Berger, J., Wagner, D. G., & Zelditch, M., Jr. (1985). Introduction: Expectation states theory: Review and assessment. In J. Berger & M. Zelditch, Jr. (Eds.), *Status, rewards, and influence.* San Francisco: Jossey-Bass. **285**

Berger, J. O., & Berry, D. A. (1988). Statistical analysis and the illusion of objectivity. *American Scientist*, March–April, 159–165. **40**

Bergkvist, L., Adami, H.-O., Persson, I., Hoover, R., & Schairer, C. (1989). The risk of breast cancer after estrogen and estrogen-progestin replacement. *New England Journal of Medicine, 321*, 293–297. **203**

Bergman, L. R., & Magnusson, D. (1979). Overachievement and catecholamine excretion in an achievement-demanding situation. *Psychosomatic Medicine, 41*, 181–188. **332**

Berkley, K. J. (1992). Vive la diffrence! *Trends in Neurosciences, 15*, 331–332. **39**

Bermond, B. (1982). Effects of medial preoptic hypothalamus anterior lesions on three kinds of behavior in the rat: Intermale aggressive, male-sexual, and mouse-killing behavior. *Aggressive Behavior, 8*, 335–354. **162**

Bernard, L. C. (1981). The multidimensional aspects of masculinity-femininity. *Journal of Personality and Social Psychology, 41*, 797–802. **48**

_____. (1984). The multiple factors of sex role identification: Rapprochement of unidimensional and bidimensional assessment. *Journal of Clinical Psychology, 40*, 986–991. **48**

Bernardi, M., Genedani, S., Tagliavini, S., & Bertolini, A. (1989). Effect of castration and testosterone in experimental models of depression in mice. *Behavioral Neuroscience, 103*, 1148–1150. **365**

Berndt, T. J., & Heller, K. A. (1986).

Gender stereotypes and social inferences: A developmental study. *Journal of Personality and Social Psychology, 50*, 889–898. **275**

Bernstein, H., Byerly, H. C., Hopf, F. A., & Michod, R. E. (1984). Origin of sex. *Journal of Theoretical Biology, 110*, 323–351. **70**

_____. (1985). Genetic damage, mutation, and the evolution of sex. *Science, 229*, 1277–1281. **70, 368**

Bernstein, H., Hopf, F. A., & Michod, R. E. (1988). Is meiotic recombination an adaptation for repairing DNA, producing genetic variation, or both. In R. E. Michod & B. R. Levin (Eds.), *The evolution of sex: an examination of current ideas.* Sunderland, MA: Sinauer. **64**

Bernstein, I. S., & Ehardt, C. L. (1985). Agonistic aiding: Kinship, rank, age, and sex influences. *American Journal of Primatology, 8*, 37–52. **83**

_____. (1986a). Selective interference in Rhesus monkey *(Macaca mulatta)* intragroup agonistic episodes by age-sex class. *Journal of Comparative Psychology, 100*, 380–384. **79, 83**

_____. (1986b). The influence of kinship and socialization on aggressive behaviour in rhesus monkeys *(Macaca mulatta). Animal Behaviour, 34*, 739–747. **83**

Berscheid, E., & Walster, E. (1974). Physical attractiveness. In L. Berkowitz (Ed.), *Advances in experimental social psychology.* New York: Academic Press. **378**

Berta, P., Hawkins, J. R., Sinclair, A. H., Taylor, A., Griffiths, B. L., Goodfellow, P. N., & Fellous, M. (1990). Genetic evidence equating SRY and the testis-determining factor. *Nature, 348*, 448–450. **123**

Berté, N. A. (1988). K'ekchci' horticultural labor exchange: Productive and reproductive implications. In L. Bertzig, M. B. Mulder, & P. Burke (Eds.), *Human reproductive behaviour.* Cambridge: Cambridge University Press. **244, 252**

Bertenthal, B. I., & Campos, J. J. (1987). New directions in the study of early experience. *Child Development, 58*, 560–567. **225**

Bertilson, H. S., Fierke, K. M., & Springer, D. K. (1981, May). *Distribution of gender referents in introductory college textbooks.* Paper presented at Midwestern Psychological Association, Detroit. **289**

Berzins, J. I., Welling, M. A., & Wetter, R. E. (1978). A new measure of psychological androgyny based on the Personality Research Form. *Journal of Consulting and Clinical Psychology, 46*, 126–138. **45**

Best, D. L., Williams, J. E., & Briggs,

S. R. (1980). A further analysis of the affective meanings associated with male and female sex-trait stereotypes. *Sex Roles, 6*, 735–747. **271**

Betz, M., & O'Connell, L. (1987). Gender and work: A look at sex differences among pharmacy students. *American Journal of Pharmaceutical Education, 51*, 39–42. **325, 329**

Betz, N. E., & Hackett, G. (1981). The relationship of career-related self-efficacy expectations to perceived career options in college women and men. *Journal of Counseling Psychology, 28*, 399–410. **329**

_____. (1983). The relationship of mathematics self-efficacy expectations to the selection of science-based college majors. *Journal of Vocational Behavior, 23*, 329–345. **327, 329**

Betzig, L. L. (1982). Despotism and differential reproduction: A cross-cultural correlation of conflict asymmetry, hierarchy, and degree of polygyny. *Ethology and Sociobiology, 3*, 209–221. **350**

Betzig, L., Mulder, M. B., & Turke, P. (Eds.). (1988). *Human reproductive behavior: A Darwinian perspective.* Cambridge: Cambridge University Press. **246**

Beuf, A. (1974). Doctor, lawyer, household drudge. *Journal of Communication, 24*, 142–145. **265**

Beyer, C., & Feder, H. H. (1987). Sex steroids and afferent input: Their roles in brain sexual differentiation. *Annual Review of Physiology, 49*, 349–364. **157**

Bibbo, M., Haenszel, W. M., Wied, G. L., Hubby, M., & Herbst, A. L. (1978). A twenty-five-year follow-up study of women exposed to diethylstilbestrol during pregnancy. *New England Journal of Medicine, 298*, 763–767. **170**

Bielby, W. T., & Baron, J. N. (1986). Men and women at work: Sex segregation and statistical discrimination. *American Journal of Sociology, 91*, 759–799. **324, 321**

Bielert, C., & Busse, C. (1983). Influences of ovarian hormones on the food intake and feeding of captive and wild female chacma baboons (Papio ursinus). *Physiology & Behavior, 30*, 103–111. **189**

Bieri, J., Bradburn, W. M., & Galinsky, M. D. (1958). Sex differences in perceptual behavior. *Journal of Personality, 26*, 1–12. **373, 391**

Biernat, M., Manis, M., & Nelson, T. E. (1991). Stereotypes and standards of judgment. *Journal of Personality and Social Psychology, 60*, 485–499. **275**

Bierzychudek, P. (1987). Resolving the paradox of sexual reproduction: A review of experimental tests. In S. C. Stearns (Ed.), *The evolution of sex and its consequences.* Boston: Birkhauser. **71, 72**

Biggar, R. J., Brinton, L. A., & Rosenthal, M. D. (1989). Trends in the number of sexual partners among American women. *Journal of Acquired Immune Deficiency Syndrome, 2*, 497–502. **383**

Bigler, R. S., & Liben, L. S. (1990). The role of attitudes and interventions in gender-schematic processing. *Child Development, 61*, 1440–1452. **293, 325**

Birnbaum, D. W., Nosanchuk, T. A., & Croll, W. L. (1980). Children's stereotypes about sex differences in emotionality. *Sex Roles, 6*, 435–443. **364**

Birtchnell, J., Deahl, M., & Falkowski, J. (1991). Further exploration of the relationship between depression and dependence. *Journal of Affective Disorders, 22*, 221–233. **364**

Bittles, A. H., Mason, W. M., Greene, J., & Rao, N. A. (1991). Reproductive behavior and health in consanguineous marriage. *Science, 252*, 789–794. **73**

Black, I. B., Adler, J. E., Dreyfus, C. F., Friedman, W. F., LaGamma, E. F., & Roach, A. H. (1987). Biochemistry of information storage in the nervous system. *Science, 236*, 1263–1268. **208, 214**

Blakemore, J. E. O., LaRue, A. A., & Olejnik, A. B. (1979). Sex-appropriate toy preference and the ability to conceptualize toys as sex-role related. *Developmental Psychology, 15*, 339–340. **307**

Blanchard, R., Clemmensen, L. H., & Steiner, B. W. (1987). Heterosexual and homosexual gender dysphoria. *Archives of Sexual Behavior, 16*, 139–152. **229**

Blau, F. C. (1982). Occupational segregation and labor market discrimination. In B. F. Reskin (Ed.), *Sex segregation in the workplace: Trends, explanations, remedies.* Washington, DC: National Academy Press. **324**

Bledsoe, J. C. (1983). Sex differences in female teachers' approval and disapproval behaviors as related to their self-definition of sex-role type. *Psychological Reports, 53*, 711–714. **312**

Bloch, M. N. (1987). The development of sex differences in young children's activities at home: The effect of the social context. *Sex Roles, 16*, 279–302. **307**

Block, J., Gjerde, P. F., & Block, J. H. (1991). Personality antecedents of depressive tendencies in 18-year-olds: A prospective study. *Journal of Personality and Social Psychology, 60*, 726–738. **350**

Block, J., von der Lippe, A., & Block, J. H. (1973). Sex-role and socialization patterns: some personality concomitants and environmental antecedents. *Journal of Consulting and Clinical Psychology, 41*, 321–341. **299**

Block, J. H. (1973). Conceptions of sex role: some cross-cultural and longitudinal perspectives. *American Psychologist, 28*, 512–526. **318**

_____. (1983). Differential premises arising from differential socialization of the sexes: Some conjectures. *Child Development, 54*, 1335–1354. **301, 308, 312, 313**

Blumstein, P., & Schwartz, P. (1983). *American couples.* New York: William Morrow. **380, 381, 383, 384, 400**

Blundell, V. (1983). Commentary on "Anthropological applications of optimal foraging theory: A critical review." *Current Anthropology, 24*, 641–642. **240**

Boccia, M. S., Laudenslager, M., & Reite, M. (1988). Food distribution, dominance, and aggressive behaviors in bonnet macaques. *American Journal of Primatology, 16*, 123–130. **349**

Boehnke, K., Silbereisen, R. K., Eisenberg, N., Reykowski, J., & Palmonari, A. (1989). Developmental pattern of prosocial motivation: A cross-national study. *Journal of Cross-Cultural Psychology, 20*, 219–243. **318**

Boesch, C., & Boesch, H. (1989). Hunting behavior of wild chimpanzees in the Ta National Park. *American Journal of Physical Anthropology, 78*, 547–573. **243, 245**

Bogren, L. Y. (1983). Couvade. *Acta Psychiatrica Scandinavica, 68*, 55–65. **198**

_____. (1984). The couvade syndrome: Background variables. *Acta Psychiatrica Scandinavica, 70*, 316–320. **198**

Bohman, M., Cloninger, R., Sigvardsson, S., & von Knorring, A.-L. (1987). The genetics of alcoholism and related disorders. *Journal of Psychiatric Research, 21*, 447–452. **361**

Boice, R., Shaughnessy, P., & Pecker, G. (1985). Women and publishing in psychology. *American Psychologist, 40*, 577–578. **320**

Bolin, A. (1987). Transsexualism and the limits of traditional analysis. *American Behavioral Scientist, 31*, 41–65. **258**

Bolles, R. C. (1988). Nativism, naturalism, and niches. In R. C. Bolles & M. D. Beecher (Eds.), *Evolution and learning.* Hillsdale, N. J.: Lawrence Erlbaum. **214**

Bonner, J. T. (1980). *The evolution of culture in animals.* Princeton, NJ:

Princeton University Press. **215, 248**

Bonsall, R. W., Rees, H. D., & Michael, R. P. (1985). The distribution, nuclear uptake and metabolism of [3H]dihydrotestosterone in the brain, pituitary gland and genital tract of the male rhesus monkey. *Journal of Steroid Biochemistry, 23*, 389–398. **203**

Booth, A., & Dabbs, J. M. (under review, 1991). Hormones and marriage: The case for testosterone poisoning. **203**

Booth, W. (1988). The social lives of dolphins. *Science, 240*, 1273–1274. **80**

_____. (1989). "Oh, I thought you were a man." *Science, 243*, 475. **105**

Borghgraef, M., Fryns, J. P., Dielkens, A., Pyck, K., & van den Berghe, H. (1987). Fragile (X) syndrome: A study of the psychological profile in 23 prepubertal patients. *Clinical Genetics, 32*, 179–186. **121**

Borker, S. R. (1987). Sex roles and labor force participation. In D. B. Carter (Ed.), *Current conceptions of sex roles and sex typing*. New York: Praeger. **324**

Born, G., Grutzner, P., & Hemminger, H. (1976). Evidenz fur eine mosaikstruktur der netzhaut bei konduktorinnen fur dichromasie. [Evidence for reduced color vision in carriers of congenital color vision deficiencies.] *Human Genetics, 32*, 189–196. **105**

Borofsky, G. L., Stollak, G. E., & Mess, L. A. (1971). Sex differences in bystander reactions to physical assault. *Journal of Experimental Social Psychology, 7*, 313–318. **354**

Borrill, J., & Reed, B. (1986). Are British psychologists interested in sex differences? *Bulletin of the British Psychological Society, 39*, 286–288. **39**

Botha, M. P., & Mels, G. (1990). Stability of aggression among adolescents over time: A South African study. *Aggressive Behavior, 16*, 361–380. **357**

Bottjer, S. W., & Dignan, T. P. (1988). Joint hormonal and sensory stimulation modulate neuronal number in adult canary brains. *Journal of Neurobiology, 19*, 624–635. **142**

Bouchard, T. J., Jr. (1984). Twins reared together and apart: What they tell us about human diversity. In S. W. Fox (Ed.), *Individuality and determinism*. New York: Plenum. **108**

Bouchard, T. J., Jr., Lykken, D. T., McGue, M., Segal, N. L., & Tellegen, A. (1990). Sources of human psychological differences: The Minnesota study of twins

reared apart. *Science, 250*, 223–228. **14**

Bouchard, T. J., Segal, N. L., & Lykken, D. T. (1990). Genetic and environmental influences on special mental abilities in a sample of twins reared apart. *Acta Genetica Medical Gemellology, 39*, 193–206. **396**

Boué, J., Bou, A., & Lazar, P. (1975). Retrospective and prospective epidemiological studies of 1500 karyotyped spontaneous human abortions. *Teratology, 12*, 11–26. **111**

Bowen, D. J., & Grunberg, N. E. (1990). Variations in food preference and consumption across the menstrual cycle. *Physiology & Behavior, 47*, 287–291. **189**

Bowers, C. A., & LaBarba, R. C. (1988). Sex differences in the lateralization of spatial abilities: A spatial component analysis of extreme group scores. *Brain and Cognition, 8*, 165–177. **398**

Boyar, R. M., Rosenfeld, R. S., Finkelstein, J. W., Kapen, S., Roffwarg, H. P., Weitzman, E. D., & Hellman, L. (1975). Ontogeny of luteinizing hormone and testosterone secretion. *Journal of Steroid Biochemistry, 6*, 803–808. **181**

Boyce, P., Hickie, I., & Parker, G. (1991). Parents, partners or personality? Risk factors for postnatal depression. *Journal of Affective Disorders, 21*, 245–255. **197**

Boyce, P., & Parker, G. (1989). Development of a scale to measure interpersonal sensitivity. *Australian and New Zealand Journal of Psychiatry, 23*, 341–351. **350, 364**

Boyce, P., Parker, G., Hickie, I., Wilhelm, K., Brodaty, H., & Mitchell, P. (1990). Personality differences between patients with remitted melancholic and nonmelancholic depression. *American Journal of Psychiatry, 147*, 1476–1483. **350**

Boyd, R., & Richerson, P. J. (1985). *Culture and the evolutionary process*. Chicago: University of Chicago Press. **216, 248, 249**

Brand, T., & Slob, A. K. (1988). Peripubertal castration of male rats, adult open field ambulation and partner preference behavior. *Behavioural Brain Research, 30*, 111–117. **150**

Branscombe, N. R., & Smith, E. R. (1990). Gender and racial stereotypes in impression formation and social decision-making processes. *Sex Roles, 22*, 627–648. **274, 279**

Breden, F., & Stoner, G. (1987). Male predation risk determines female preference in the Trinidad guppy. *Nature, 329*, 831–833. **85**

Breedlove, S. M. (1984). Steroid influences on the development and

function of a neuromuscular system. *Progress in Brain Research, 61*, 147–170. **163**

Bremermann, H. J. (1987). The adaptive significance of sexuality. In S. C. Stearns (Ed.), *The evolution of sex and its consequences*. Boston: Birkhauser. **70, 71, 72**

Brennan, J. R. (1986). *Patterns of human heredity: An introduction to human genetics*. Englewood Cliffs, NJ: Prentice-Hall. **56, 64**

Brenowitz, E. A., & Arnold, A. P. (1990). The effects of systemic androgen treatment on adrogen accumulation in song control regions of the adult female canary brain. *Journal of neurobiology, 21*, 837–843. **142**

Bretl, D. J., & Cantor, J. (1988). The portrayal of men and women in U.S. television commercials: A recent content analysis and trends over 15 years. *Sex Roles, 18*, 595–610. **290**

Brewin, C. R. (1985). Depression and causal attributions: What is their relation? *Psychological Bulletin, 98*, 297–309. **367**

Bridges, J. S. (1989). Sex differences in occupational values. *Sex Roles, 20*, 205–212. **325**

Briggs, V. M., Jr. (1987). The growth and composition of the U.S. labor force. *Science, 238*, 176–180. **324**

Bronstein, P., Black, L., Pfenning, J., & White, A. (1986). Getting academic jobs: Are women equally qualified and equally successful? *American Psychologist, 41*, 318–322. **285**

Brooks, L. D. (1988). The evolution of recombination rates. In R. E. Michod & B. R. Levin (Eds.), *The evolution of sex: an examination of current ideas*. Sunderland, MA: Sinauer. **66, 100**

Brooks-Gunn, J. (1986). The relationship of maternal beliefs about sex typing to maternal and young children's behavior. *Sex Roles, 14*, 21–35. **298**

Brooks-Gunn, J., Peterson, A. C., & Eichorn, D. (1985). The study of maturational timing effects in adolescence. *Journal of Youth and Adolescence, 14*, 149–161. **228**

Brooks-Gunn, J., & Warren, M. P. (1985a). The effects of delayed menarche in different contexts: Dance and nondance students. *Journal of Youth and Adolescence, 14*, 285–300. **228**

_____. (1985b). Measuring physical status and timing in early adolescence: A developmental perspective. *Journal of Youth and Adolescence, 14*, 163–189. **228**

Brophy, J. (1985). Interactions of male and female students with male and female teachers. In L. C.

Wilkinson & C. B. Marrett (Eds.), *Gender-related differences in the classroom*. New York: Academic Press. **312, 313**

Brophy, J., & Good, T. (1974). *Teacher*–student relationships: Causes and consequences. New York: Holt, Rinehart & Winston. **312, 313**

Broverman, D. M. (1964). Generality and behavioral correlates of cognitive styles. *Journal of Consulting Psychology, 28*, 487–500. **398**

Broverman, D. M., Broverman, I. K., Vogel, W., Palmer, R. D., & Klaiber, E. L. (1964). The automatization cognitive style and physical development. *Child Development, 35*, 1343–1359. **398**

Broverman, D. M., Klaiber, E. L., & Vogel, W. (1980). Gonadal hormones and cognitive functioning. In J. E. Parsons (Ed.), *The psychobiology of sex differences and sex roles*. New York: McGraw-Hill. **398**

Broverman, I. K., Broverman, D. M., Clarkson, F. E., Rosenkrantz, P. S., & Vogel, S. R. (1970). Sex-role stereotypes and clinical judgments of mental health. *Journal of Consulting and Clinical Psychology, 34*, 1–7. **281, 295**

Broverman, I. K., Vogel, S. R., Broverman, D. M., Clarkson, F. E., & Rosenkrantz, P. S. (1972). Sex-role stereotypes: A current appraisal. *Journal of Social Issues, 28*, 59–78. **44, 47, 294, 295**

Brown, D. E., & Hotra, D. (1988). Are prescriptively monogamous societies effectively monogamous? In L. Betzig, M. B. Mulder, & P. Burke (Eds.), *Human reproductive behaviour*. Cambridge: Cambridge University Press. **252**

Brown, G. R. (1990). A review of clinical approaches to gender dysphoria. *Journal of Clinical Psychiatry, 51*, 57–64. **229**

Brown, G. W., & Harris, T. (1986). Stressor, vulnerability and depression: A question of replication. *Psychological Medicine, 16*, 739–744. **364**

Brown, R. E. (1985). Hormones and paternal behavior in vertebrates. *American Zoologist, 25*, 895–910. **141**

Brown, S., & Rastan, S. (1988). Age-related reactivation of an X-linked gene close to the inactivation centre in the mouse. *Genetical Research, 52*, 151–154. **105**

Brown, T. J., Hochberg, R. B., Zielinski, J. E., & MacLusky, N. J. (1988). Regional sex differences in cell nuclear estrogen-binding capacity in the rat hypothalamus and preoptic area. *Endocrinology, 123*, 1761–1770. **138**

Browne, A., & Finkelhor, D. (1986). Impact of child sexual abuse: A review of the research. *Psychological Bulletin, 99*, 66–77. **301**

Browne, A., & Williams, K. R. (1989). Exploring the effect of resource availability and the likelihood of female-perpetrated homicides. *Law & Society Review, 23*, 75–94. **352**

Bruce, M. L., Kim, K., Leaf, P. J., & Jacobs, S. (1990). Depressive episodes and dysphoria resulting from conjugal bereavement in a prospective community sample. *American Journal of Psychiatry, 147*, 608–611. **364**

Brugha, T. S., Bebbington, P. E., MacCarthy, B., Sturt, E., Wykes, T., & Potter, J. (1990). Gender, social support and recovery from depressive disorders: A prospective clinical study. *Psychological Medicine, 20*, 147–156. **364**

Bruns-Hillman, M. (1980, May). *Traditional and nontraditional female achievers: Factors which may account for divergent modes of expression of achievement motivation.* Paper presented at Midwestern Psychological Association, St. Louis. **329**

Bryant, K. J. (1982). Personality correlates of sense of direction and geographical orientation. *Journal of Personality and Social Psychology, 43*, 1318–1324. **377, 394**

Bryer, J. B., Nelson, B. A., Miller, J. B., & Krol, P. A. (1987). Childhood sexual and physical abuse as factors in adult psychiatric illness. *American Journal of Psychiatry, 144*, 1426–1430. **301**

Buchanan, C. M., Eccles, J. S., & Becker, J. B. (1992). Are adolescents the victims of raging hormones: Evidence for activational effects of hormones on moods and behavior at adolescence. *Psychological Bulletin, 111*, 62–107. **359**

Buchsbaum, M. S., & Henkin, R. I. (1980). Perceptual abnormalities in patients with chromatin negative gonadal dysgenesis and hypogonadotropic hypogonadism. *International Journal of Neuroscience, 11*, 201–209. **114**

Buckle, V., Mondello, C., Darling, S., Craig, I. W., & Goodfellow, P. N. (1985). Homologous expressed genes in the human sex chromosome pairing region. *Nature, 317*, 739–741. **104**

Buckley, W. E., Yesalis, C. E., III, Friedl, K. E., Anderson, W. A., Streit, A. L., & Wright, J. E. (1988). Estimated prevalence of anabolic steroid use among male high school seniors. *Journal of the American Medical Association, 260*, 3441–3445. **202**

Buhrich, N., Bailey, J. M., & Martin, N. G. (1991). Sexual orientation, sexual identity, and sex-dimorphic behaviors in male twins. *Behavior Genetics, 21*, 75–96. **388**

Bullough, V., Bullough, B., & Smith, R. (1983). A comparative study of male transvestites, male to female transsexuals, and male homosexuals. *Journal of Sex Research, 19*, 238–257. **229**

Bungay, G. T., Vessey, M. P., & McPherson, C. K. (1980). Study of symptoms in middle life with special reference to the menopause. *British Medical Journal, 281*, 181–183. **368**

Burd, G. D., & Nottebohm, F. (1985). Ultrastructural characterization of synaptic terminals formed on newly generated neurons in a song control nucleus of the adult canary forebrain. *Journal of Comparative Neurology, 240*, 143–152. **142**

Burger-Judisch, L. M., Camperlengo, L. L., & Molfese, D. L. (1989, May). *Electrophysiological correlates of speech and nonspeech perception in human newborn infants.* Paper presented at Midwestern Psychological Association Convention, Chicago. **397**

Burger-Judisch, L. M., & Molfese, D. L. (1991, May). *Maturational sex differences in the auditory evoked respnse to speech and nonspeech stimuli.* Paper presented at Midwestern Psychological Association, Chicago. **397**

Burgoyne, P. S., Levy, E. R., & McLaren, A. (1986). Spermatogenic failure in male mice lacking H-Y antigen. *Nature, 320*, 170–172. **106**

Burke, P. J., & Tully, J. C. (1977). The measurement of role identity. *Social Forces, 55*, 881–896. **276**

Burke, R. J. (1989). Gender identity, sex, and school performance. *Social Psychology Quarterly, 52*, 159–169. **321**

Burley, N. (1981). Sex ratio manipulation and selection for attractiveness. *Science, 211*, 721–722. **85**

————. (1986). Sex-ratio manipulation in color-banded populations of zebra finches. *Evolution, 40*, 1191–1206. **85**

————. (1988). Wild zebra finches have band-colour preferences. *Animal Behaviour, 36*, 1235–1237. **85**

Burnett, S. A. (1986). Sex-related differences in spatial ability: Are they trivial? *American Psychologist, 41*, 1012–1014. **391**

Burnett, S. A., & Lane, D. M. (1980). Effects of academic instruction on spatial visualization. *Intelligence, 4*, 233–242. **395**

Burnett, S. A., Lane, D. M., & Dratt, L. M. (1979). Spatial visualization and sex differences in quantitative ability. *Intelligence, 3*, 345–354. **373, 400**

Burns, R. B. (1977). Male and female perceptions of their own and the other sex. *British Journal of Social and Clinical Psychology, 16*, 213–220. **271**

Burt, A., & Bell, G. (1987). Mammalian chiasma frequencies as a test of two theories of recombination. *Nature, 326*, 803–805. **66, 73, 102**

Burton, M. L., & White, D. R. (1984). Sexual division of labor in agriculture. *American Anthropologist, 86*, 568–583. **252**

Burton, N. W., Lewis, C., & Robertson, N. (1988). Sex differences in SAT scores. *College Board Report*, No. 88–9. **372**

Bush, D. E., Simmons, R. G., Hutchinson, B., & Blyth, D. A. (1978). Adolescent perception of sex-roles in 1968 and 1975. *Public Opinion Quarterly, 41*, 459–474. **282**

Bush, T. L., Cowan, L. D., Barrett-Connor, E., Criqui, M. H., Karon, J. M., Wallace, R. B., Tyroler, H. A., & Rifkind, B. M. (1983). Estrogen use and all-cause mortality: Preliminary results from the Lipid Research Clinics Program Follow-up Study. *Journal of the American Medical Association, 249*, 903–906. **201**

Buss, D. M. (1981). Sex differences in the evaluation and performance of dominant acts. *Journal of Personality and Social Psychology, 40*, 147–154. **347**

_____. (1984a). Evolutionary biology and personality psychology: Toward a conception of human nature and individual differences. *American Psychologist, 39*, 1135–1147. **2, 339, 380**

_____. (1984b). Toward a psychology of person-environment (PE) correlation: The role of spouse selection. *Journal of Personality and Social Psychology, 47*, 361–377. **339, 380**

_____. (1984c). Marital assortment for personality dispositions: Assessment with three different data sources. *Behavior Genetics, 14*, 111–123. **380**

_____. (1985). Human mate selection. *American Scientist, 73*, 47–51. **2, 379, 380**

_____. (1986). Can social science be anchored in evolutionary biology? Four problems and a strategic solution. *Revue Europenne des Sciences Sociales, 24*, 41–50. **2**

_____. (1987a). Sex differences in human mate selection criteria: An evolutionary perspective. In C. Crawford, M. Smith, & D. Krebs (Eds.), *Sociobiology and psychology: Ideas, issues, and applications.* Hillsdale, NJ: Erlbaum. **2**

_____. (1987b). Selection, evocation, and manipulation. *Journal of Personality and Social Psychology, 53*, 1214–1221. **339**

_____. (1988). From vigilance to violence: Tactics of mate retention in American undergraduates. *Ethology and Sociobiology, 9*, 291–317. **2, 354**

_____. (1989a). Confict between the sexes: Strategic interference and the evocation of anger and upset. *Journal of Personality and Social Psychology, 56*, 735–747. **354**

_____. (1989b). Sex differences in human mate preferences: Evolutionary hypotheses tested in 37 cultures. *Behavioral and Brain Sciences, 12*, 1–49. **2, 379**

_____. (1990). Unmitigated agency and communion: An analysis of the negative components of masculinity and femininity. *Sex Roles, 22*, 555–568. **338**

Buss, D. M. (plus 49 others). (1990). International preferences in selecting mates: A study of 37 cultures. *Journal of Cross-Cultural Psychology, 21*, 5–47. **379**

Buss, D. M., & Angleitner, A. (1989). Mate selection preferences in Germany and the United States. *Personality and Individual Differences, 10*, 1269–1280. **379**

Buss, D. M., & Barnes, M. (1986). Preferences in human mate selection. *Journal of Personality and Social Psychology, 50*, 559–570. **379, 380**

Buss, D. M., & Craik, K. H. (1983). The act frequency approach to personality. *Psychological Review, 90*, 105–126. **338, 339**

_____. (1985). Why not measure that trait? Alternative criteria for identifying important dispositions. *Journal of Personality and Social Psychology, 48*, 934–946. **339**

Butera, P. C., & Czaja, J. A. (1984, May). *Species differences and similarities in the physiological and behavioral responsivity of castrated males to dihydrotestosterone.* Paper presented and Midwestern Psychological Association, Chicago. **142**

_____. (1985). Maintenance of target tissue and sexual behavior with dihydrotestosterone and male rats and guinea pigs. *Physiology & Behavior, 34*, 319–321. **142**

Bybee, J., Glick, M., & Zigler, E. (1990). Differences across gender, grade level, and academic track in the content of the idal self-image. *Sex Roles, 22*, 349–358. **308, 346**

Byerley, W. F., Judd, L. L., Reimherr, F. W., & Grosser, B. I. (1987). 5-hydroxytryptophan: A review of its antidepressant efficacy and adverse effects. *Journal of Clinical Psychopharmacology, 7*, 127–137. **369**

Byne, W., & Bleier, R. (1987). Medial preoptic sexual dimorphisms in the guinea pig. I. An investigation of their hormonal dependence. *Journal of Neuroscience, 7*, 2688–2696. **163**

Cadoret, R., O'Gorman, T. W., Heywood, E., & Troughton, E. (1985). Genetic and environmental factors in major depression. *Journal of Affective Disorders, 9*, 155–164. **364**

Cahill, S. E. (1986). Language practices and self definition: The case of gender identity acquisition. *Sociological Quarterly, 27*, 295–311. **229**

Cairns, R. B. (1986). An evolutionary and developmental perspective on aggressive patterns. In C. Zahn-Waxler, E. M. Cummings & R. Ionnotti (Eds.), *Altruism and aggression.* New York: Cambridge University Press. **357**

Cairns, R. B., & Cairns, B. (1984). Predicting aggressive patterns in girls and boys: A developmental study. *Aggressive Behavior, 10*, 227–242. **357**

Cairns, R. B., Garipy, J.-L., & Hood, K. E. (1990). Development, microevolution, and social behavior. *Psychological Review, 97*, 49–65. **224**

Caldera, Y. M., Huston, A. C., & O'Brien, M. (1989). Social interaction and play patterns of parents and toddlers with feminine, masculine, and neutral toys. *Child Development, 60*, 70–76. **218, 302, 307**

Callan, H. G., & Perry, P. E. (1977). Recombination in male and female meiocytes contrasted. *Philosophical Transactions of the Royal Society of London, Series B, 277*, 227–233. **101**

Callard, G. V. (1983). Androgen and estrogen actions in the vertebrate brain. *American Zoologist, 23*, 607–620. **157**

Callender, C., & Kochems, L. M. (1983). The North American berdache. *Current Anthropology, 24*, 443–470. **258**

Cameron, C., Oskamp, S., & Sparks, W. (1977). Courtship American style: Newspaper ads. *The Family Coordinator, 26*, 27–30. **379**

Cameron, J., Livson, N., & Bayley, N. (1967). Infant vocalizations and their relationship to mature intelligence. *Science, 157*, 331–333. **225**

Canonaco, M., O'Connor, L. H., Pfaff, D. W., & McEwen, B. S. (1989). Longer term progesterone treatment induces changes of

GABAA receptor levels in forebrain sites in the female hamster: Quantitative autoradiography study. *Experimental Brain Research, 77,* 407–411. **139**

Cantor, N., & Mischel, W. (1979). Prototypes in person perception. In L. Berkowitz (Ed.), *Advances in experimental social psychology* (Vol. 12). NY: Academic Press. **269**

Caramazza, A., Hersh, A., & Torgerson, W. S. (1976). Subjective structures and operations in semantic memory. *Journal of Verbal Learning and Verbal Behavior, 15,* 103–117. **266**

Carbonell, J. L. (1984). Sex roles and leadership revisited. *Journal of Applied Psychology, 69,* 44–49. **347**

Carli, L. L. (1989). Gender differences in interaction style and influence. *Journal of Personality and Social Psychology, 56,* 565–576. **346**

Carlier, M., Roubertoux, P. L., Kottler, M. L., & Degrelle, H. (1990). Y chromosome and aggression in strains of laboratory mice. *Behavior Genetics, 20,* 137–156. **117**

Carlsmith, L. (1964). Effect of early father absence on scholastic aptitude. *Harvard Educational Review, 34,* 3–21. **395**

Carlson, E. R., & Carlson, R. (1960). Male and female subjects in personality research. *Journal of Abnormal and Social Psychology, 61,* 482–483. **39**

Carlson, G. A., & Kashani, J. H. (1988). Phenomenology of major depression from childhood through adulthood: Analysis of three studies. *American Journal of Psychiatry, 145,* 1222–1225. **363**

Carlson, J. C., Gruber, M. Y., & Thompson, J. E. (1983). A study of the interaction between progesterone and membrane lipids. *Endocrinology, 113,* 190–194. **133, 137**

Carlson, R. (1985). Masculine/feminine: A personological perspective. *Journal of Personality, 53,* 384–399. **46**

Carlsson, M., Svensson, K., Eriksson, E., & Carlsson, A. (1985). Rat brain serotonin: Biochemical and functional evidence for a sex difference. *Journal of Neural Transmission, 63,* 297–313. **351, 369**

Carothers, A. D., Collyer, S., De Mey, R., & Frackiewicz, A. (1978). Parental age and birth order in the aetiology of some sex chromosome aneuploidies. *Annals of Human Genetics, London, 41,* 277–287. **111, 112**

Carpenter, C. J., & Huston-Stein, A. (1980). Activity structure and sex-typed behavior in preschool children. *Child Development, 51,* 862–872. **320**

Carrigan, T., Connell, B., & Lee, J. (1985). Toward a new sociology of masculinity. *Theory and Society, 14,* 551–604. **41, 49**

Carroll, J. L., Volk, K. D., & Hyde, J. S. (1985). Differences between males and females in motives for engaging in sexual intercourse. *Archives of Sexual Behavior, 14,* 131–139. **382, 384**

Carson, R. C. (1989). Personality. *Annual Review of Psychology, 40,* 227–248. **339**

Carter, D. B. (1987). The roles of peers in sex role socialization. In D. B. Carter (Ed.), *Current conceptions of sex roles and sex typing.* New York: Praeger. **313, 314**

Carter, D. B., & McCloskey, L. A. (1983/1984). Peers and the maintenance of sex-typed behavior: The development of children's conceptions of cross-gender behavior in their peers. *Social Cognition, 2,* 294–314. **265, 294**

Carter, D. B., & Patterson, C. J. (1982). Sex roles as social conventions: The development of children's conceptions of sex-role stereotypes. *Developmental Psychology, 18,* 812–824. **291**

Case, R., Hayward, S., Lewis, M., & Hurst, P. (1988). Toward a neo-Piagetian theory of cognitive and emotional development. *Developmental Review, 8,* 1–51. **225, 227**

Casey, M. B., Pezaris, E., & Nuttall, R. L. (1992). Spatial ability as a predictor of math achievement: The importance of sex and handedness patterns. *Neuropsychologia, 30,* 35–45. **373**

Cashion, B. G. (1982). Female-headed families: Effects on children and clinical implications. *Journal of Marital and Family Therapy,* April, 77–85. **299**

Casper, R. C. Redmond, D. E., Jr., Katz, M. M., Schaffer, C. B., Davis, J. M., & Koslow, S. H. (1985). Somatic symptoms in primary affective disorder: Presence and relationship to the classification of depression. *Archives of General Psychiatry, 42,* 1098–1104. **363**

Casper, R. F., Yen, S. S. C., & Wilkes, M. M. (1979). Menopausal flushes: A neuroendocrine link with pulsatile luteinizing hormone secretion. *Science, 205,* 823–825. **200**

Caspi, A., Elder, G. H., Jr., & Bem, D. J. (1987). Moving against the world: Life-course patterns of explosive children. *Developmental Psychology, 23,* 308–313. **235**

_____. (1988). Moving away from the world: Life-course patterns of shy children. *Developmental Psychology, 24,* 824–831. **235**

Cassano, G. B., Musetti, L., Perugi, G., Soriani, A., Mignani, V., McNair, D. M., & Akiskal, H. S. (1988). A proposed new approach to the clinical subclassification of depressive illness. *Pharmacopsychiatrica, 21,* 19–23. **362**

Caton, H. (1984). Margaret Mead and Samoa: In support of the Freeman critique. *Quadrant,* March, 28–32. **10**

Cauley, J. A., Cummings, S. R., Black, D. M., Mascioli, S. R., & Seeley, D. G. (1990). Prevalence and determinants of estrogen replacement therapy in elderly women. *American Journal of Obstetrics and Gynecology, 163,* 1438–1444. **200**

Cavalli-Sforza, L. L., & Feldman, M. W. (1983). Paradox of the evolution of communication and of social interactivity. *Proceedings of the National Academy of Sciences, USA, 80,* 2017–2021. **250**

Ceulemans, D. L. S., Westenberg, H. G. M., & van Praag, H. M. (1985). Effect of stress on the dexamethasone suppression test. *Psychiatry Research, 14,* 189–195. **362**

Chagnon, N. A. (1988a). Life histories, blood revenge, and warfare in a tribal population. *Science, 239,* 985–992. **91, 350**

_____. (1988b). Male Yanomam manipulations of kinship classification of female kin for reproductive advantage. In L. Betzig, M. B. Mulder, & P. Burke (Eds.), *Human reproductive behaviour.* Cambridge: Cambridge University Press. **239**

Chakraborty, R. (1989). Can molecular imprinting explain heterozygote deficiency and hybrid vigor? *Genetics, 122,* 713–717. **102, 103**

Chalkley, A. J., & Powell, G. E. (1983). The clinical description of forty-eight cases of sexual fetishism. *British Journal of Psychiatry, 142,* 292–295. **383**

Chamallas, M. (1984). Exploring the "entire spectrum" of disparate treatment under Title VII: Rules governing predominatly female jobs. *University of Illinois Law Review, 1984,* 1–51. **278**

Chambers, K. C., Hess, R. L., & Phoenix, C. H. (1981). Relationship of free and bound testosterone to sexual behavior in old rhesus males. *Physiology & Behavior, 27,* 615–620. **203**

Chambers, K. C., & Phoenix, C. H. (1984). Testosterone and the decline of sexual behavior in aging male rats. *Behavioral and Neural Biology, 40,* 87–97. **203**

Chambers, K. C., Resko, J. A., & Phoenix, C. H. (1982). Correlation of diurnal changes in hormones with sexual behavior and age in male rhesus macaques. *Neurobiology of Aging, 3*, 37–42. **182, 183, 203**

Chapais, B. (1988a). Rank maintenance in female Japanese macaques: Experimental evidence for social dependency. *Behaviour, 104*, 41–59. **79**

———. (1988b). Experimental matrilineal inheritance of rank in female Japanese macaques. *Animal Behaviour, 36*, 1025–1037. **79**

Chapais, B., & Larose, F. (1988). Experimental rank reversals among peers in *Macaca fuscata:* Rank is maintained after the removal of kin support. *American Journal of Primatology, 16*, 31–42. **79**

Chappel, S. C. (1985). Neuroendocrine regulation of luteinizing hormone and follicle stimulating hormone: A review. *Life Sciences, 36*, 97–103. **145**

Charlesworth, B. (1978). Model for evolution of Y chromosomes and dosage compensation. *Proceedings of the National Academy of Sciences, USA, 75*, 5618–5622. **117**

———. (1980). *Evolution in age-structured populations.* Bristol, Great Britain: J. W. Arrowsmith. **220**

———. (1991). The evolution of sex chromosomes. *Science, 251*, 1030–1033. **104**

Charlesworth, W. R. (1986a). *Darwin* and developmental psychology: 100 years later. *Human Development, 29*, 1–35 (see pages 1–4). **2**

———. (1986b). *Darwin* and developmental psychology: From the proximate to the ultimate. *Developmental Psychology, 29*, 22–35. **2**

Charlesworth, W. R., & Dzur, C. (1987). Gender comparisons of preschoolers' behavior and resource utilization in group problem solving. *Child Development, 58*, 191–200. **319**

Charlesworth, W. R., & La Freniere, P. (1983). Dominance, friendship, and resource utilization in preschool children's groups. *Ethology and Sociobiology, 4*, 175–186. **318, 319**

Charney, D. S., Krystal, J. H., Delgado, P.L., & Heninger, G. R. (1990). Serotonin-specific drugs for anxiety and depressive disorder. *Annual Review of Medicine, 41*, 437–446. **369**

Charnov, E. L., Los-den Hartogh, R. L. Jones, W. T., & van den Assem, J. (1981). Sex ratio evolution in a variable environment. *Nature, 289*, 27–33. **62**

Chen, C., & Uttal, D. H. (1988). Cultural values, parents' beliefs, and children's achievement in the United States and China. *Human Development, 31*, 351–358. **232**

Chen, H., Faigenbaum, D., & Weiss, H. (1981). Psychosocial aspects of patients with the Ullrich-Turner syndrome. *American Journal of Medical Genetics, 8*, 191–203. **114**

Cheney, D., Seyfarth, R., & Smuts, B. (1986). Social relationships and social cognition in nonhuman primates. *Science, 234*, 1361–1366. **80, 83, 215, 220, 243, 245**

Cherfas, J. (1991). Sex and the single gene. *Science, 252*, 782. **106**

Cherlin, A. J., Furstenberg, F. F., Jr., Chase-Lansdale, P. L., Kiernan, K. E., Robins, P. K., Morrison, D. R., & Teitler, J. O. (1991). Longitudinal studies of divorce on children in Great Britain and the United States. *Science, 252*, 1386–1389. **223, 299**

Cheverud, J. M. (1988). A comparison of genetic and phenotypic correlations. *Evolution, 42*, 958–968. **224**

Chiarello, C., McMahon, M. A., & Schaefer, K. (1989). Visual cerebral lateralization over phases of the menstrual cycle: A preliminary investigation. *Brain and Cognition, 11*, 18–36. **399**

Chino, A. F., & Funabiki, D. (1984). A cross-validation of sex differences in the expression of depression. *Sex Roles, 11*, 175–188. **363**

Chodorow, N. (1974). Family structure and feminine personality. In M. Z. Rosaldo & L. Lamphere (Eds.), *Woman, culture, and society.* Stanford: Stanford University Press. **260**

———. (1978). *The reproduction of mothering: Psychoanalysis and the sociology of gender.* Berkeley: University of California Press. **260**

Christensen, D., & Rosenthal, R. (1982). Gender and nonverbal decoding skill as determinants of interpersonal expectancy effects. *Journal of Personality and Social Psychology, 42*, 75–87. **279**

Christensen, L. W., & Gorski, R. A. (1978). Independent masculinization of neuroendocrine systems by intracerebral implants of testosterone or estradiol in the neonatal female rat. *Brain Research, 146*, 325–340. **159**

Christiansen, K., & Knussman, R. (1987). Sex hormones and cognitive functioning in men. *Neuropsychobiology, 18*, 27–36.

Christoffel, K. K., Anzinger, N. K., & Merrill, D. A. (1989). Age-related patterns of violent death, Cook County, Illinois, 1977 through 1982. *American Journal of Diseases of Children, 143*, 1403–1409. **354**

Chudley, A. E., & Hagerman, R. J. (1987). Fragile X syndrome. *Journal of Pediatrics, 110*, 821–831. **121**

Chumlea, W. C., Siervogel, R. M., Roche, A. F., Mukherjee, D., & Webb, P. (1982). Changes in adipocyte cellularity in children ten to 18 years of age. *International Journal of Obesity, 6*, 383–389.

Clark, A. S., & Goldman-Rakic, P. S. (1989). Gonadal hormones influence the emergence of cortical function in nonhuman primates. *Behavioral Neuroscience, 103*, 1287–1295. **225**

Clark, M. M., & Galef, B. G., Jr. (1989). Male pups are more hesitant to urinate in response to anogenital stimulation than are their female sibs. *Developmental Psychobiology, 22*, 81–85. **17**

———. (1990). Sexual segregation in the left and right horns of the gerbil uterus: "The male embryo is usually on the right, the female on the left" (Hippocrates). *Developmental Psychobiology, 23*, 29–37. **107**

Clark, M. M., Spencer, C. A., & Galef, B. G., Jr. (1986). Reproductive life history correlates of early and late sexual maturation in female Mongolian gerbils *(Meriones unguiculatus). Animal Behaviour, 34*, 551–560. **376**

Clark, V. A., Aneshensel, C. S., Frerichs, R. R., & Morgan, T. M. (1981). Analysis of effects of sex and age in response to items on the CES-D scale. *Psychiatry Research, 5*, 171–181. **363**

Clarke, B. C. (1979). The evolution of genetic diversity. *Proceedings of the Royal Society of London, Series B, 205*, 453–474. **72**

Clarke-Stewart, A. (1987). The social ecology of early childhood. In N. Eisenberg (Ed.), *Contemporary topics in developmental psychology.* New York: Wiley. **300**

Clayton, P. J., Marten, S., Davis, M. A., & Wochnik, E. (1980). Mood disorder in women professionals. *Journal of Affective Disorders, 2*, 37–46. **368**

Clemens, L. G., Wee, B. E. F., Weaver, D. R., Roy, E. J., Goldman, B. D., & Rakerd, B. (1988). Retention of masculine sexual behavior following castration in male B6D2F1 mice. *Physiology & Behavior, 42*, 69–76. **147, 386**

Clements, C. D. (1985). "Therefore choose life": Reconciling medical and environmental bioethics. *Perspectives in Biology and Medicine, 28*, 407–425. **21**

———. (1989). Biology, man, and culture: A unified science based on hierarchy levels. *Perspectives in Biology and Medicine, 33*, 70–85. **10, 13, 21**

Clutton-Brock, T. H. (1985). Reproductive success in red deer. *Scientific American, 252,* 86–92. **62**

_____. (1989). Female transfer and inbreeding avoidance in social mammals. *Nature, 337,* 70–71. **93**

Clutton-Brock, T. H., Albon, S. D., & Guinness, F. E. (1986). Great expectations: Dominance, breeding success and offspring sex ratios in red deer. *Animal Behaviour, 34,* 460–471. **62**

Clutton-Brock, T. H., & Iason, G. R. (1986). Sex ratio variation in mammals. *Quarterly Review of Biology, 61,* 339–374. **80**

Cobb, N. J., Stevens-Long, J., & Goldstein, S. (1982). The influence of televised models on toy preferences in children. *Sex Roles, 8,* 1075–1080. **293**

Coe, C. L., Rosenberg, L. T., & Levine, S. (1988). Immunological consequences of psychological disturbance and maternal loss in infancy. In C. Rovee-Collier & L. P. Lipsitt (Eds.), *Advances in infant research.* Norwood, NJ: Ablex. **365**

Coe, C. L., Wiener, S. G., Rosenberg, L. T., & Levine, S. (1985). Endocrine and immune responses to separation and maternal loss in nonhuman primates. In M. Reite & T. Field (Eds.), *The psychobiology of attachment and separation.* New York: Academic Press. **365**

Cohen, I. L., Brown, W. T., Jenkins, E. C., Krawczun, M. S., French, J. H., Raguthu, S., Wolf-Schein, E. G., Sudhalter, V., Fisch, G., & Wisniewski, K. (1989). Fragile X syndrome in females with autism. *American Journal of Medical Genetics, 34,* 302–303. **121**

Cohen, I. T., Sherwin, B. B., & Fleming, A. S. (1987). Food cravings, mood, and the menstrual cycle. *Hormones and Behavior, 21,* 457–470. **189**Cohen, J. (1977). *Statistical power analysis for the behavioral sciences* (2nd ed.) New York: Academic Press. **37**

Cohen, J. M., & Cohen, M. F. (1960). *Penguin dictionary of quotations.* New York: Viking Penguin. **371**

Cohn, L. D. (1991). Sex differences in the course of personality development: A meta-analysis. *Psychological Bulletin, 109,* 252–266. **218, 229**

Cole, H. J., Zucker, K. J., & Bradley, S. J. (1982). Patterns of gender role behavior in children attending traditional and non-traditional daycare centers. *Canadian Journal of Psychiatry, 27,* 410–414. **308**

Cole, J. R., & Zuckerman, H. (1987). Marriage, motherhood and research performance in science. *Scientific American, 256 (2),* 119–125. **328**

Collins, A. (1985). Interaction of sex-related psychological characteristics and psychoneuroendocrine stress responses. *Sex Roles, 12,* 1219–1230. **332**

Collins, A., & Frankenhaeuser, M. (1978). Stress responses in male and female engineering students. *Journal of Human Stress, 4,* 43–48. **332**

Collins, L. J., Ingoldsby, B. B., & Dellmann, M. M. (1984). Sex role stereotyping in children's literature: A change from the past. *Childhood Education,* March/April, 278–285. **289**

Commins, D., & Yahr, P. (1984a). Adult testosterone levels influence the morphology of a sexually dimorphic area in the Mongolian gerbil brain. *Journal of Comparative Neurology, 224,* 132–140. **163**

_____. (1984b). Lesions of the sexually dimorphic area disrupt mating and marking in male gerbils. *Brain Research Bulletin, 13,* 185–193. **163**

Condon, J. T., & Watson, T. L. (1987). The maternity blues: Exploration of a psychological hypotheses. *Acta Psychiatrica Scandinavica, 76,* 164–171. **197**

Condry, J. C., & Ross, D. F. (1985). Sex and aggression: The influence of gender label on the perception of aggression in children. *Child Development, 56,* 225–233. **297**

Connell, R. W., & Radican. N. (1987). The evolving man. *New Internationalist,* September, 18–20. **50**

Connor, J. M., & Serbin, L. A. (1977). Behaviorally based masculine- and feminine-activity-preference scales for preschoolers: Correlates with other classroom behaviors and cognitive tests. *Child Development, 48,* 1411–1416. **393**

Constantinople, A. (1973). Masculinity-femininity: An exception to a famous dictum? *Psychological Bulletin, 80,* 389–407. **42**

_____. (1979). Sex-role acquisition: In search of the elephant. *Sex Roles, 5,* 121–134. **291**

Cook, M., & Mineka, S. (1990). Selective associations in the observational conditioning of fear in rhesus monkeys. *Journal of Experimental Psychology: Animal Behavior Processes, 16,* 372–389. **212, 214**

Cooke, H. J., Brown, W. A. R., & Rappold, G. A. (1984). Closely related sequences on human X and Y chromosomes outside the pairing region. *Nature, 311,* 259–261. **101**

Cooper, H. M. (1979). Statistically combining independent studies: A meta-analysis of sex differences in conformity research. *Journal of Personality and Social Psychology, 37,* 131–146. **82, 343**

Cooper, L. A., & Shepard, R. N. (1984). Turning something over in the mind. *Scientific American,* December, 102–107. **392**

Cooper, R. M., & Zubek, J. P. (1958). Effects of enriched and restricted early environments on the learning ability of bright and dull rats. *Canadian Journal of Psychology, 12,* 159–164. **225**

Coquelin, A., & Desjardins, C. (1982). Luteinizing hormone and testosterone secretion in young and old male mice. *American Journal of Physiology, 243,* E257–E263. **203**

Corballis, M. C. (1986). Is mental rotation controlled or automatic? *Memory & Cognition, 14,* 124–128. **392**

_____. (1989). Laterality and human evolution. *Psychological Review, 96,* 492–505. **248**

Corballis, M. C., & Sergent, J. (1988). Imagery in a commissurotomized patient. *Neuropsychologia, 26,* 13–26. **397**

_____. (1989). Mental rotation in a commissurotomized subject. *Neuropsychologia, 27,* 585–597. **397**

Corbett, A. J., McCusker, E. A., & Davidson, O. R. (1986). Acalculia following a dominant-hemisphere subcortical infarct. *Archives of Neurology, 43,* 964–966. **397**

Corbier, P. (1985). Sexual differentiation of positive feedback: Effect of hour of castration at birth on estradiol-induced luteinizing hormone secretion in immature male rats. *Endocrinology, 116,* 142–147. **145, 150**

Corbier, P., Roffi, J., & Rhoda, J. (1983). Female sexual behavior in male rats: Effect of hour of castration at birth. *Physiology & Behavior, 30,* 613–616. **150, 160**

Cordua, G. D., McGraw, K. O., & Drabman, R. S. (1979). Doctor or nurse: Children's perception of sex typed occupations. *Child Development, 50,* 590–593. **291**

Coren, S., & Halpern, D. F. (1991). Left-handedness: A marker for decreased survival fitness. *Psychological Bulletin, 109,* 90–106.

Coryell, W., Endicott, J., Keller, M., Andreasen, N., Grove, W., Hirschfeld, R. M. A., & Scheftner, W. (1989). Bipolar affective disorder and high achievement: A familial association. *American Journal of Psychiatry, 146,* 983–988. **367**

Costa, P. T., & McCrae, R. R. (1987). On the need for longitudinal evidence and multiple measures in behavioral-genetic studies of adult personality. *Behavioral and Brain Sciences, 10,* 22–23. **43**

Costos, D. (1986). Sex role identity in young adults: Its parental antecedents and relation to ego development. *Journal of Personality and*

Social Psychology, 50, 602–611. **318**

Cousins, L., Karp, W., Lacey, C., & Lucas, W. E. (1980). Reproductive outcome of women exposed to diethylstilbestrol in utero. *Obstetrics & Gynecology, 56,* 70–76. **170**

Couwenbergs, C., Knussmann, R., & Christiansen, K. (1986). Comparisons of the intra- and inter-individual variability in sex hormone levels of men. *Annals of Human Biology, 13,* 63–72. **130, 147**

Coverman, S. (1983). Gender, domestic labor time, and wage inequality. *American Sociological Review, 48,* 623–637. **304**

Cowan, G., & Koziej, J. (1979). The perception of sex-inconsistent behavior. *Sex Roles, 5,* 1-14. **275**

Cowan, M. L., & Stewart, B. J. (1977). A methodological study of sex stereotypes. *Sex Roles, 3,* 205–216. **270**

Cowan, W. M., Fawcett, J. W., O'Leary, D. D. M., & Stanfield, B. B. (1984). Regressive events in neurogenesis. *Science, 225,* 1258–1265. **152**

Cowlishaw, G., & Dunbar, R. I. M. (1991). Dominance rank and mating success in male primates. *Animal Behaviour, 41,* 1045–1056. **349**

Coyne, J. C., & Downey, G. (1991). Social factors and psychopathology: Stress, social support, and coping processes. *Annual Review of Psychology, 42,* 401–425. **364**

Craig, I., Levy, E., & Fraser, M. (1987). The mammalian Y chromosome: Molecular search for the sex-determining gene summary and perspectives. *Development, 101* (Supplement), 185–190. **104**

Crandall, V. C. (1975). Sex differences in expectancy of intellectual and academic reinforcement. In R. K. Unger & F. L. Denmark (Eds.), *Woman: Dependent or independent variable?* New York: Psychological Dimensions. **333**

Crandall, V. C., Katkovsky, W., & Preston, A. (1962). Motivational and ability determinants of young children's intellectual achievement behaviors. *Child Development, 33,* 643–661. **322**

Crandall, V. J., & Sinkeldam, C. (1964). Children's dependent and achievement behaviors in social situations and their perceptual field dependence. *Journal of Personality, 32,* 1–22. **394**

Crandell, D. L., & Dohrenwend, B. P. (1967). Some relations among psychiatric symptoms, organic illness, and social class. *American Journal of Psychiatry, 123,* 1527 –1538. **394**

Crane, M., & Markus, H. (1982).

Gender identity: The benefits of a self-schema approach. *Journal of Personality and Social Psychology, 6,* 1195–1197. **45**

Crawford, C. B. (1989). The theory of evolution: Of what value to psychology? *Journal of Comparative Psychology, 103,* 4–22. **60**

Creighton, D. E. (1984). Sex differences in the visual habituation of 4-, 6- and 8-month-old infants. *Infant Behavior and Development, 7,* 237–249. **236**

Creutzfeldt, O. D., Arnold, P.-M., Becker, D., Langenstein, S., Tirsch, W., Wilhelm, H., & Wuttke, W. (1976). EEG changes during spontaneous and controlled menstrual cycles and their correlation with psychological performance. *Electroencephalography and Clinical Neurophysiology, 40,* 113–131. **398**

Crews, D. (1984). Gamete production, sex hormone secretion, and mating behavior uncoupled. *Hormones and Behavior, 18,* 22–28. **141**

Cronin, C. L. (1980). Dominance relations and females. In D. R. Omark, F. F. Strayer, & D. G. Freedman (Eds.), *An ethological view of human conflict and social interaction.* New York: Garland. **319**

Crosbie, P. V. (1979). The effects of sex and size on status ranking. *Social Psychology Quarterly, 42,* 340–354. **348**

Crow, J. F. (1958). Some possibilities for measuring selection intensities in man. *Human Biology, 30,* 1-13 [reprinted in *Human Biology, 61* (1989), 763–775]. **59**

_____. (1987). Muller, Dobzhansky, and overdominance. *Journal of the History of Biology, 20,* 351–380. **58**

_____. (1989). Update to "some possibilities for measuring selection intensities in man." *Human Biology, 61,* 776–780. **59, 103**

Crow, T. J. (1987). Integrated viral genes as potential pathogens in the functional psychoses. *Journal of Psychiatric Research, 21,* 479–485. **75**

_____. (1988). Sex chromosomes and psychosis: The case for a pseudoautosomal locus. *British Journal of Psychiatry, 153,* 675–683. **67, 103**

Crusio, W. E., & Schwegler, H. (1991). Early postnatal hyperthyroidism improves both working and reference memory in a spatial radial-maze task in adult mice. *Physiology & Behvior, 50,* 259–261. **397**

Cullberg, J. (1972). Mood changes and menstrual symptoms with different gestagen/estrogen combinations: A

double blind comparison with a placebo. *Acta Psychiatrica Scandinavica, Supplement 236,* 1–86. **202**

Culliton, B. J. (1987). Osteoporosis reexamined: Complexity of bone biology is a challenge. *Science, 235,* 833–834. **200**

Cunningham, J. D., & Antill, J. K. (1980). A comparison among five masculinity-femininity-androgyny instruments and two methods of scoring androgyny. *Australian Psychologist, 15*(3), 437–448. **46**

Cunningham, M. R. (1986). Measuring the physical in physical attractiveness: Quasi-experiments on the sociobiology of female facial beauty. *Journal of Personality and Social Psychology, 50,* 925–935. **400**

_____. (1989). Reactions to heterosexual opening gambits: Female selectivity and male responsiveness. *Personality and Social Psychology Bulletin, 15,* 27–41. **380**

Curfs, L. M. G., Borghgraef, M., Wiegers, A., Schreppers-Tijdink, G. A. J., & Fryns, J. P. (1989). Strengths and weakness in the cognitive profile of fra(X) patients. *Clinical Genetics, 36,* 405–410. **121**

Curie-Cohen, M., Yoshihara, D., Luttrell, L., Benforado, K., MacCluer, J. W., & Stone, W. H. (1983). The effects of dominance on mating behavior and paternity in a captive troop of rhesus monkeys (Macaca mulatta). *American Journal of Primatology, 5,* 127–138. **349**

Currey, J. F., & Hock, R. A. (1981). Sex differences in sex role ideals in early adolescence. *Adolescence, 16,* 779–789. **319**

Curry, J. J., III, & Heim, L. M. (1966). Brain myelination after neonatal administration of oestradiol. *Nature, 209,* 915–916. **157**

Curzon, G. (1988). Serotonergic mechanisms of depression. *Clinical Neuropharmacology, 11* (Suppl. 2), S11–S20. **369**

Curzon, G., & Green, A. R. (1968). Effect of hydrocortisone on rat brain 5-hydroxytryptamine. *Life Sciences, 7,* 657–663. **369**

Cutler, W. B., Garcia, C. R., & Krieger, A. M. (1979). Sexual behavior frequency and menstrual cycle length in mature premenopausal women. *Psychoneuroendocrinology, 4,* 297–309. **190**

Cutler, W. B., Preti, G., Huggins, G. R., Erickson, B., & Garcia, C. R. (1985). Sexual behavior frequency and biphasic ovulatory type menstrual cycles. *Physiology & Behavior, 34,* 805–810. **190**

Cutler, W. B., Schleidt, W. M., Friedmann, E., Preti, G., & Stine, R. (1987). Lunar influences on the reproductive cycle in women.

Human Biology, 59, 959–972. **191**

Cutolo, M., Balleari, E., Giusti, M., Intra, E., & Accardo, S. (1991). Androgen replacement therapy in male patients with rheumatoid arthritis. *Arthritis and Rheumatism, 34*, 1–5. **173**

Cutolo, M., Balleari, E., Giusti, M., Monachesi, M., & Accardo, S. (1988). Sex hormone status of male patients with rheumatoid arthritis: Evidence of low serum concentrations of testosterone at baseline and after human chorionic gonadotropin stimulation. *Arthritis and Rheumatism, 31*, 1314–1317. **173**

Czarnota, M. (1989, May). *Gender differences in the spatial abilities of grade school children.* Paper presented at Midwestern Psychological Association Convention, Chicago. **374**

Dabbs, J. M., Jr. (1990a). Age and seasonal variation in serum testosterone concentration among men. *Chronobiology International, 7*, 245–249. **182, 199, 203**

————. (1990b). Salivary testosterone measurements: Reliability across hours, days, and weeks. *Physiology & Behavior, 48*, 83–86. **130, 182**

————. (1992). Testosterone and occupational achievement. *Social Forces, 70*, 813–824.

Dabbs, J. M., Jr., & de La Rue, D. (1991). Salivary testosterone measurements among women: Relative magnitude of circadian and menstrual cycles. *Hormone Research, 35*, 182–184. **182**

Dabbs, J. M., Frady, R. L., Carr, T. S., & Besch, N. F. (1987). Saliva testosterone and criminal violence in young adult prison inmates. *Psychosomatic Medicine, 49*, 174–182. **176, 203**

Dabbs, J. M., Hopper, C. H., & Jurkovic, G. J. (1990). Testosterone and personality among college students and military veterans. *Personality and Individual Differences, 11*, 1263–1269. **176, 203**

Dabbs, J. M., & Ruback, R. B. (1988). Saliva testosterone and personality of male college students. *Bulletin of the Psychonomic Society, 26*, 244–247. **16, 203**

Dahlgren, J. (1990). Females choose vigilant males: An experiment with the monogamous grey partridge, Perdix perdix. *Animal Behaviour, 39*, 646–651. **86**

Dai, W., Kuller, L., LaPorte, R., Gutai, J., Falvo-Gerard, L., & Caggiula, A. (1981). The epidemiology of plasma testosterone levels in middle-aged men. *American Journal of Epidemiology, 114*, 804–816. **130**

Daitzman, R., & Zuckerman, M.

(1980). Disinhibitory sensation seeking, personality and gonadal hormones. *Personality and Individual Differences, 1*, 103–110. **16**

Daly, M., & Wilson, M. (1980). Discriminative parental solicitude: A biological perspective. *Journal of Marriage and the Family, 42*, 277–288. **222, 301**

————. (1982). Homicide and kinship. *American Anthropologist, 84*, 372–378. **351**

————. (1983). *Sex, evolution, and behavior* (2nd ed.). Boston: Willard Grant Press. **2, 15, 70, 76, 78, 79, 81, 84, 90, 91**

————. (1985). Child abuse and other risks of not living with both parents. *Ethology and Sociobiology, 6*, 197–210. **222**

————. (1988a). *Homicide.* Hawthorne, NY: Aldine De Gruyter. **351, 357**

————. (1988b). Evolutionary social psychology and family homicide. *Science, 242*, 519–524. **86, 301, 351, 355**

Daly, M., Wilson, M., & Weghorst, S. J. (1982). Male sexual jealousy. *Ethology and Sociobiology, 3*, 11–27. **351**

D'Andrade, R. G. (1966). Sex differences and cultural institutions. In E. E. Maccoby (Ed.), *The development of sex differences.* Stanford: Stanford University Press. **243, 244, 255, 256, 262, 264**

Danhaive, P. A., & Rousseau, G. G. (1988). Evidence for sex-dependent anabolic response to androgen steroids mediated by muscle glucocorticoid receptors in the rat. *Journal of Steroid Biochemistry, 29*, 575–581. **202**

Darras, B. T., & Francke, U. (1987). A partial deletion of the muscular dystrophy gene transmitted twice by an unaffected male. *Nature, 329*, 556–558. **119**

Darwin, C. (1871). *The descent of man, and selection in relation to sex.* London: John Murray. **76, 83, 84, 90**

Davenport, Y. B., & Adland, M. L. (1982). Postpartum psychoses in female and male bipolar manic-depressive patients. *American Journal of Orthopsychiatry, 52*, 288–297. **198**

David, D. S., & Brannon, R. (1976). The male sex role: Our culture's blueprint of manhood, and what it's done for us lately. In D. S. David & R. Brannon (Eds.), *The forty-nine percent majority: The male sex role.* Reading, MA: Addison-Wesley. **297**

Davidson, J., & Robertson, E. (1985). A follow-up study of postpartum illness, 1946–1978. *Acta Psychiatrica Scandinavica, 71*, 451–457. **197, 198**

Davidson, J. M. (1985). Sexual behavior and its relationship to ovarian hormones in the menopause. *Maturitas, 7*, 193–201. **200**

Davies, D. R. (1989/1990). The effects of gender-typed labels on children's performance. *Current Psychology: Research & Reviews, 8*, 267–272. **394**

Davis, A. J. (1984). Sex-differentiated behaviors in nonsexist picture books. *Sex Roles, 11*, 1–16. **289**

Davis, A. T., & Kosky, R. J. (1991). Atempted suicide in Adelaide and Perth: Changing rates for males and females, 1971–1987. *Medical Journal of Australia, 154*, 666–670. **366**

Davis, B. M., & Gilbert, L. A. (1989). Effect of dispositional and situational influences on women's dominance expression in mixed-sex dyads. *Journal of Personality and Social Psychology, 57*, 294–300. **347**

Davis, D. M. (1990). Portrayals of women in prime-time television: Some demographic characteristics. *Sex Roles, 23*, 325–332. **290**

Davis, R. T., & Dougan, J. D. (1988). The phylogeny of information processing. In R. C. Bolles & M. D. Beecher (Eds.), *Evolution and learning.* Hillsdale, NJ: Erlbaum. **249**

Dawood, M. Y., & Saxena, B. B. (1977). Testosterone and dihydrotestosterone in maternal and cord blood and in amniotic fluid. *American Journal of Obstetrics and Gynecology, 129*, 37–42. **197**

Deaux, K. (1984). From individual differences to social categories: Analysis of a decade's research on gender. *American Psychologist, 39*, 105–116. **33, 35, 41**

————. (1985). Sex and gender. *Annual Review of Psychology, 36*, 49–81. **6**

Deaux, K., & Hanna, R. (1984). Courtship in the personals column: The influence of gender and sexual orientation. *Sex Roles, 11*, 363–375. **379, 380**

Deaux, K., & Kite, M. E. (1985). Gender stereotypes: Some thoughts on the cognitive organization of gender-related information. *Academic Psychology Bulletin, 7*, 123–144. **269**

Deaux, K., & Lewis, L. L. (1984). Structure of gender stereotypes: Interrelationships among components and gender label. *Journal of Personality and Social Psychology, 46*, 991–1004. **48, 269**

Deaux, K., & Major, B. (1987). Putting gender into context: An interactive model of gender-related behavior. *Psychological Review, 94*, 369–389. **279**

Deaux, K., Winton, W., Crowley, M., & Lewis, L. L. (1985). Level of categorization and content of gender stereotypes. *Social Cognition, 3,* 145–167. **269, 270**

De Beer, E. L., & Keizer, H. A. (1982). Direct action of estradiol-17 on the atrial action potential. *Steroids, 40,* 223–231. **152**

de Beun, R., Geerts, N. E., Vreeburg, J. T. M., Slangen, J. L., & van de Poll, N. E. (1989). Sex differences in luteinizing hormone releasing hormone-induced conditioned place preference in the rat. *Drug Development Research, 16,* 375–383. **201**

de Catanzaro, D. (1987). Differential sexual activity of isolated and grouped male mice despite testosterone administration. *Behavioral and Neural Biology, 48,* 213–221. **386**

Deckard, B. S., Wilson, J. R., & Schlesinger, K. (1989). Behavioral and reproductive differences in mice as a function of inbreeding. *Behavior Genetics, 19,* 433–445. **75**

Decker, S. N., & Bender, B. G. (1988). Converging evidence for multiple genetic forms of reading disability. *Brain and Language, 33,* 197–215. **113**

De Fronzo, J., & Boudreau, F. (1979). Further research into antecedents and correlates of androgyny. *Psychological Reports, 44,* 23–29. **327**

DeJong, R., Rubinow, D. R., Roy-Byrne, P., Hoban, M. C., Grover, G. N., & Post, R. M. (1985). Premenstrual mood disorder and psychiatric illness. *American Journal of Psychiatry, 142,* 1359–1361. **193**

De Jonge, F. H., Muntjewerff, M.-W., Louwerse, A. L., & van de Poll, N. E. (1988). Sexual behavior and sexual orientation of the female rat after hormonal treatment during various stages of development. *Hormones and Behavior, 22,* 100–115. **150**

De Kloet, E. R., Voorhuis, Th. A. M., & Elands, J. (1985). Estradiol induces oxytocin binding sites in rat hypothalamic ventromedial nucleus. *European Journal of Pharmacology, 118,* 185–186. **136**

de la Chapelle, A. (1981). The etiology of maleness in XX men. *Human Genetics, 58,* 105–116. **106, 113**

_____. (1986). Genetic and molecular studies on 46,XX and 45,X males. *Cold Spring Harbor Symposia on Quantitative Biology, 51,* 249–255. **106**

_____. (1987). The Y-chromosomal and autosomal testis-determining genes. *Development, 101* (Suppl.), 33–38. **106**

Del Boca, F. K., Ashmore, R. D., & McManus, M. A. (1986). Gender-related attitudes. In R. D. Ashmore & F. K. Del Boca (Eds.), *The social psychology of female-male rela-*

tions. New York: Academic Press. **286, 295**

Delgado, P. L., Charney, D. S., Price, L. H., Aghajanian, G. K., Landis, H., & Heninger, G. R. (1990). Serotonin function and the mechanism of antidepressant action: Reveral of antidepressant-induced remission by rapid depletion of plasma tryptophan. *Archives of General Psychiatry, 47,* 411–418. **369**

De Lisi, R., & Soundranayagam, L. (1990). The conceptual structure of sex role stereotypes in college students. *Sex Roles, 23,* 593–612. **271**

Demotes-Mainard, J., Arnauld, E., & Vincent, J. D. (1990). Estrogen modulate the responsiveness of in vivo recorded striatal neurons to iontophoretic application of dopamine in rats: Role of D1 and D2 receptor activation. *Journal of Neuroendocrinology, 2,* 825–832. **139**

Denenberg, V. H., Berrebi, A. S., & Fitch, R. H. (1989). A factor analysis of the rat's corpus callosum. *Brain Research, 497,* 271–279. **397**

Denenberg, V. H., & Yutzey, D. A. (1985). Hemispheric laterality, behavioral asymmetry, and the effects of early experience in rats. In S. D. Glick (Ed.), *Cerebral lateralization in nonhuman species.* New York: Academic Press. **397**

Dennerstein, L., Spencer-Gardner, C., Gotts, G., Brown, J. B., Smith, M. A., & Burrows, G. D. (1985). Progesterone and the premenstrual syndrome: A double blind crossover trial. *British Medical Journal, 290,* 1617–1621. **195**

DePaulo, J. R., Simpson, S. G., Folstein, S., & Folstein, M. F. (1989). The new genetics of bipolar affective disorder: Clinical implications. *Clinical Chemistry, 35,* B28–B32. **362**

Devine, P. G. (1989). Stereotypes and prejudice: Their automatic and controlled components. *Journal of Personality and Social Psychology, 56,* 5–18. **280**

DeVoogd, T. (1984). The avian song system: Relating sex differences in behavior to dimorphism in the central nervous system. *Progress in Brain Research, 61,* 171–183. **123, 142**

DeVoogd, T. J., Brenowitz, E. A., & Arnold, A. P. (1988). Small sex differences in song control dendrites are associated with minimal differences in song capacity. *Journal of Neurobiology, 19,* 199–209. **142**

DeVoogd, T., & Nottebohm, F. (1981). Gonadal hormones induce dendritic growth in the adult avian brain. *Science, 214,* 202–204. **142**

de Waal, F. (1982). *Chimpanzee politics.* New York: Harper & Row. **243, 348, 349**

_____. (1984). Sex differences in

the formation of coalitions among chimpanzees. *Ethology and Sociobiology, 5,* 239–255. **348**

_____. (1986). The integration of dominance and social bonding in primates. *Quarterly Review of Biology, 61,* 459–479. **348**

Dewsbury, D. A. (1981a). An exercise in the prediction of monogamy in the field from laboratory data on 42 species of muroid rodents. *The Biologist, 63,* 138–162. **377**

_____. (1981b). Effects of novelty on copulatory behavior: The Coolidge effect and related phenomena. *Psychological Bulletin, 89,* 464–482. **383**

Diamond, A., & Doar, B. (1988). The performance of human infants on a measure of frontal cortex function, the delayed response task. *Developmental Psychobiology, 22,* 271–294. **225**

Diamond, A., & Goldman-Rakic, P. S. (1989). Comparison of human infants and rhesus monkeys on Piaget's AĀ task: Evidence for dependence on dorsolateral prefrontal cortex. *Experimental Brain Research, 74,* 24–40. **225**

Diamond, A., Zola-Morgan, S., & Squire, L. R. (1989). Successful performance by monkeys with lesions of the hippocampal formation on AĀ and object retrieval, two tasks that mark developmental changes in human infants. *Behavioral Neuroscience, 103,* 526–537. **225**

Diamond, J. M. (1986). Variation in human testis size. *Nature, 320,* 488–489. **88**

Diamond, M. C. (1985). Rat forebrain morphology: Right-left; male-female; young-old; enriched-impoverished. In S. D. Glick (Ed.), *Cerebral lateralization in nonhuman species.* New York: Academic Press. **396, 397**

Diczfalusy, E. (1977). Interrelations between plasma levels of biologically active LH and ovarian and adrenal steroids in the normal menstrual cycle. *Journal of Reproductive Fertility, 51,* 193–201. **197**

Dieringer, C. S., Lamartiniere, C. A., & Lucifer, G. W. (1980). Neonatal treatment with testosterone propionate or diethylstilbestrol alters sex differentiation of 5-reductase and 16-hydroxylase. *Journal of Steroid Biochemistry, 13,* 1449–1453. **152**

Dipboye, R. L. (1985). Some neglected variables in research on discrimination in appraisals. *Academy of Management Review, 10,* 116–127. **282**

DiPietro, J. A. (1981). Rough and tumble play: A function of gender. *Developmental Psychology, 17,*

50–58. **316**

Dittman, R. W., Kappes, M. H., Kappes, M. E., Börger, D., Meyer-Bahlburg, H. F. L., Stegner, H., Willig, R. H., & Wallis, H. (1990). Congenital adrenal hyperplasia II: Gender-related behavior and attitudes in female salt-wasting and simple-virilizing patients. *Psychoneuroendocrinology, 15,* 421–434. **169, 359**

Dittman, R. W., Kappes, M. H., Kappes, M. E., Börger, D., Stegner, H., Willig, R. H., & Wallis, H. (1990). Congenital adrenal hyperplasia I: Gender-related behavior and attitudes in female patients and sisters. *Psychoneuroendocrinology, 15,* 401–420. **169, 349**

Dittmar, H. (1989). Gender identity-related meanings of personal possessions. *British Journal of Social Psychology, 28,* 159–171. **346, 347**

Ditunno, P. L., & Mann, V. A. (1990). Right hemisphere specialization for mental rotation in normals and brain damaged subjects. *Cortex, 26,* 177–188. **398**

Dix, T. (1991). The affective organization of parenting: Adaptive and maladaptive processes. *Psychological Bulletin, 110,* 3–25. **345**

Dobbins, G. H., Cardy, R. L., & Truxillo, D. M. (1986). Effects of ratee sex and purpose of appraisal on the accuracy of performance evaluations. *Basic and Applied Social Psychology, 7,* 225–241. **281**

Dobbins, G. H., & Platz, S. J. (1986). Sex differences in leadership: How real are they? *Academy of Management Review, 11,* 118–127. **348**

Dodge, K. A., Bates, J. E., & Pettit, G. S. (1990). Mechanisms in the cycle of violence. *Science, 250,* 1678–1683. **350**

Doering, C. H., Kraemer, H. C., Brodie, H. K. H., & Hamburg, D. A. (1975). A cycle of plasma testosterone in the human male. *Journal of Clinical Endocrinology and Metabolism, 40,* 492–500. **195**

Döhler, K. D. (1986). The special case of hormonal imprinting, the neonatal influence of sex. *Experientia, 42,* 759–769. **157, 158, 174**

Döhler, K. D., Coquelin, A., Davis, F., Hines, M., Shryne, J. E., & Gorski, R. A. (1984). Pre- and postnatal influence of testosterone propionate and diethylstilbestrol on differentiation of the sexually dimorphic nucleus of the preoptic area in male and female rats. *Brain Research, 302,* 291–295. **157, 158, 163, 176**

Döhler, K. D., Coquelin, A., Davis, F., Hines, M., Shryne, J. E., Sickmller, P. M., Jarzab, B., & Gorski, R. A. (1986). Pre- and postnatal influence of an estrogen antagonist and an androgen antagonist on differentiation of the sexually dimorphic nucleus of the preoptic area in male and female rats. *Neuroendocrinology, 42,* 443–448. **163**

Döhler, K. D., Hancke, J. L., Srivastava, S. S. Hofmann, C., Shryne, J. E., & Gorski, R. A. (1984). Participation of estrogens in female sexual differentiation of the brain; neuroanatomical, neuroendocrine and behavioral evidence. *Progress in Brain Research, 61,* 99–117. **163**

Döhler, K. D., Srivastava, S. S., Shryne, J. E., Jarzab, B., Sipos, A., & Gorski, R. A. (1984). Differentiation of the sexually dimorphic nucleus in the preoptic area of the rat brain is inhibited by postnatal treatment with an estrogen antagonist. *Neuroendocrinology, 38,* 297–301. **158**

Dominey, W. J. (1980). Female mimicry in male bluegill sunfisha genetic polymorphism? *Nature, 284,* 546–548. **61**

Domjan, M. (1987). Animal learning comes of age. *American Psychologist, 42,* 556–564. **212, 213**

Dörner, G. (1988). Neuroendocrine response to estrogen and brain differentiation in heterosexuals, homosexuals, and transsexuals. *Archives of Sexual Behavior, 17,* 57–75. **388**

Dorval, M., & Ppin, M. (1986). Effect of playing a video game on a measure of spatial visualization. *Perceptual Motor Skills, 62,* 159–162. **391, 395**

Douthitt, R. A. (1989). The division of labor within the home: Have gender roles changed? *Sex Roles, 20,* 693–704. **305**

Downey, J., Ehrhardt, A. A., Gruen, R., Bell, J. J., & Morishima, A. (1989). Psychopathology and social functioning in women with Turner syndrome. *Journal of Nervous and Mental Disease, 177,* 191–201. **114**

Downey, J., Ehrhardt, A. A., Shiffman, M., Dyrenfurth, I., & Becker, J. (1987). Sex hormones in lesbian and heterosexual women. *Hormones and Behavior, 21,* 347–357. **388**

Downey, J. L., & Vitulli, W. F. (1987). Self-report measures of behavioral attributions related to interpersonal flirtation situations. *Psychological Reports, 61,* 899–904. **380**

Dragunow, M., Currie, R. W., Faull, R. L. M., Robertson, H. A., & Jansen, K. (1989). Immediate-early genes, kindling and long-term potentiation. *Neuroscience & Biobehavioral Reviews, 13,* 301–313. **208**

Draper, P. (1987). Testing sociobiological hypotheses ethnographically. *Behavioral and Brain Sciences, 10,* 74-75. **41**

Draper, P., & Belsky, J. (1990). Personality development in an evolutionary perspective. *Journal of Personality, 58,* 141–161. **222**

Draper, P., & Harpending, H. (1982). Father absence, and reproductive strategy: An evolutionary perspective. *Journal of Anthropological Research, 38,* 255–273. **222, 223, 376**

Dubey, A. K., Zeleznik, A. J., & Plant, T. M. (1987). In the rhesus monkey (Macaca mulatta), the negative feedback regulation of follicle-stimulating hormone secretion by an action of testicular hormone directly at the level of the anterior pituitary gland cannot be accounted for by either testosterone or estradiol. *Endocrinology, 121,* 2229–2237. **145**

Dubowitz, H., Newberger, C. M., Melnicoe, L. H., & Newberger, E. H. (1988). The changing American family. *Pediatric Clinics of North America, 35,* 1291–1311. **299, 300**

Dufy, B., Vincent, J.-D., Fleury, H., Du Pasquier, P., Gourdji, D., & Tixier-Vidal, A. (1979). Membrane effects of thyrotropin-releasing hormone and estrogen shown by intracellular recording from pituitary cells. *Science, 204,* 509–511. **139, 152**

Dunbar, R. I. M. (1988). *Primate social systems.* New York: Cornell University Press. **221, 241**

Dunbar, R. I. M., & Dunbar, E. P. (1977). Dominance and reproductive success among female gelada baboons. *Nature, 266,* 351–352. **349**

Duncan, P., & Hobson, G. N. (1977). Toward a definition of aggression. *Psychological Record, 3,* 545–555. **348**

Dunlap, K. D., & Sridaran, R. (1988). Plasma levels of dihydrotestosterone in the cycling rat: Implications for the regulation of lordosis behavior. *Physiology & Behavior, 42,* 199–202. **146**

Dunn, C., & Ross, H. E. (1985). Gender, the menstrual cycle and visual contrast sensitivity. *Journal of Physiology, 367,* 19P. **398**

Dupon, C., & Kim, M. H. (1973). Peripheral plasma levels of testosterone, androstenedione, and oestradiol during the rat oestrous cycle. *Journal of Endocrinology, 59,* 653–654. **183**

Durham, W. H. (1982). Interactions of genetic and cultural evolution: Models and examples. *Human Ecology, 10,* 289–323. **248**

Durkin, K. (1984). Children's accounts of sex-role stereotypes in television. *Communication Research, 11,*

341–362. **293**

_____. (1985a). Television and sex-role acquisition 1: Content. *British Journal of Social Psychology, 24*, 101–113. **289, 290**

_____. (1985b). Television and sex-role acquisition 2: Effects. *British Journal of Social Psychology, 24*, 191–210. **289, 290, 291, 293**

_____. (1985c). Television and sex-role acquisition 3: Counterstereotyping. *British Journal of Social Psychology, 24*, 211–222. **289, 290**

Dusek, J. B., & Flaherty, J. F. (1981). The development of the self-concept during the adolescent years. *Monographs of the Society for Research in Child Development, 46*(191), 1–60. **228**

Dweck, C. S. (1986). Motivational processes affecting learning. *American Psychologist, 41*, 1040–1048. **322**

Dweck, C. S., Davidson, W., Nelson, S., & Enna, B. (1978). Sex differences in learned helplessness: II. The contingencies of evaluative feedback in the classroom, and III. An experimental analysis. *Developmental Psychology, 14*, 268–276. **312**

Dweck, C. S., & Elliot, E. S. (1983). Achievement motivation. In E. M. Hetherington (Ed.), *Socialization, personality, and social development. Handbook of child psychology* (4th ed.), P. H. Mussen (Series Ed.). New York: Wiley. **231**

Dweck, C. S., & Leggett, E. L. (1988). A social-cognitive approach to motivation and personality. *Psychological Review, 95*, 256–273. **20, 231**

Eagly, A. H. (1978). Sex differences in influenceability. *Psychological Bulletin, 85*, 86-116. **35**

_____. (1983). Gender and social influences: A social psychological analysis. *American Psychologist, 36*, 971–981. **9, 13, 33, 39**

_____. (1987). *Sex differences in social behavior: A social-role interpretation.* Hillsdale, NJ: Erlbaum. **35, 341, 344**

Eagly, A. H., & Carli, L. L. (1981). Sex of researchers and sex-typed communications as determinants of sex differences in influenceability: A meta-analysis of social influence studies. *Psychological Bulletin, 90*, 1–20. **35, 39, 82, 344**

Eagly, A. H., & Crowley, M. (1986). Gender and helping behavior: A meta-analytic review of the social psychological literature. *Psychological Bulletin, 100*, 283–308. **345**

Eagly, A. H., & Johnson, B. T. (1990). Gender and leadership style: A meta-analysis. *Psychological Bulletin, 108*, 233-256. **343**

Eagly, A. H., & Karau, S. J. (1991). Gender and the emergence of leaders: A meta-analysis. *Journal of Personality and Social Psychology, 60*, 685–710. **343, 346**

Eagly, A. H., & Kite, M. E. (1987). Are stereotypes of nationalities applied to both women and men? *Journal of Personality and Social Psychology, 53*, 451–462. **272**

Eagly, A. H., Makhijani, M. G., & Klonsky, B. G. (1992). Gender and the evaluation of leaders: A meta-analysis. *Psychological Bulletin, 111*, 3–22. **285**

Eagly, A. H., & Mladinic, A. (1989). Gender stereotypes and attitudes towards women and men. *Personality and Social Psychology Bulletin, 15*, 543-558. **270, 277, 295**

Eagly, A. H., & Steffen, V. J. (1984). Gender stereotypes stem from the distribution of women and men into social roles. *Journal of Personality and Social Psychology, 46*, 735–754. **47**

Eagly, A. H., & Steffen, V. J. (1986). Gender and aggressive behavior: A meta-analytic review of the social psychological literature. *Psychological Bulletin, 100*, 309–330. **341, 342**

Eagly, A. H., & Wood, W. (1982). Inferred sex differences in status as a determinant of gender stereotypes about social influence. *Journal of Personality and Social Psychology, 43*, 915–928. **286**

_____. (1985). Gender and influenceability: Stereotype versus behavior. In V. E. O'Leary, R. K. Unger, & G. S. Wallston (Eds.), *Women, gender, and social psychology.* Hillsdale, NJ: Erlbaum. **47**

_____. (1991). Explaining sex differences in social behavior: A meta-analytic perspective. *Personality and Social Psychology Bulletin, 17*, 306–315. **341**

Eastwood, M. R., & Peter, A. M. (1988). Epidemiology and seasonal affective disorder. *Psychological Medicine, 18*, 799-806. **361**

Eaton, W. O., & Enns, L. R. (1986). Sex differences in human motor activity level. *Psychological Bulletin, 100*, 19–28. **342**

Ebbin, A. J., Howell, V. V., & Wilson, M. G. (1980). Deficits in space-form perception in patients with sex chromosome mosaicism (45,X/46,XY). *Developmental and Medical Child Neurology, 22*, 352–361. **114**

Eccles, J. S., & Blumenfeld, P. (1985). Classroom experiences and student gender: Are there differences and do they matter? In L. C. Wilkinson & C. B. Marrett (Eds.), *Gender influences in classroom interaction.*

New York: Academic Press. **312**

Eckert, E. D., Bouchard, T. J., Bohlen, J., & Heston, L. L. (1986). Homosexuality in monozygotic twins reared apart. *British Journal of Psychiatry, 148*, 421–425. **389**

Edwards, D. A., & Einhorn, L. C. (1986). Preoptic and midbrain control of sexual motivation. *Physiology & Behavior, 37*, 329–335. **162**

Edwards, D. P., DeMarzo, A. M., Oate, S. A., Beck, C. A., Estes, P. A., & Nordeen, S. K. (1991). Mechanisms controlling steroid receptor binding to specific DNA sequences. *Steroids, 56*, 271–278. **136**

Egid, K., & Brown, J. L. (1989). The major histocompatibility complex and female mating preferences in mice. *Animal Behaviour, 38*, 548–550. **74**

Egid, K., & Lenington, S. (1985). Responses of male mice to odors of females: Effects of T- and H-2-locus genotype. *Behavior Genetics, 15*, 287–295. **74**

Eguchi, Y., Arishima, K., Morikawa, Y., & Hashimoto, Y. (1976). Changes in the weight of the adrenal glands and in the concentration of plasma corticosterone in perinatal rats after prenatal treatment with oestradiol benzoate. *Journal of Endocrinology, 69*, 427–431. **128**

Ehardt, C. L., & Bernstein, I. W. (1986). Matrilineal overthrows in rhesus monkey groups. *International Journal of Primatology, 7*, 157–181. **83**

Ehrhardt, A. A., Meyer-Bahlburg, H. F. L., Rosen, L. R., Feldman, J. F., Veridiano, M. P., Zimmerman, I., & McEwen, B. S. (1985). Sexual orientation after prenatal exposure to exogenous estrogen. *Archives of Sexual Behavior, 14*, 57–77. **388**

Eichelman, B. (1987). Neurochemical and psychopharmacologic aspects of aggressive behavior. In H. Y. Meltzer (Ed.), *Psychopharmacology: The third generation of progress*, pp. 697–704. New York: Raven Press. **351**

Eicher, E. M., & Washburn, L. L. (1986). Genetic control of primary sex determination in mice. *Annual Review of Genetics, 20*, 327–360. **106, 118**

Eisenberg, N., Tryon, K., & Cameron, E. (1984). The relation of preschoolers' peer interaction to their sex-typed toy choices. *Child Development, 55*, 1044–1050. **314**

Eisenberg-Berg, N., Boothby, R., & Matson, T. (1979). Correlates of preschool girls' feminine and masculine toy preferences. *Devel-*

opmental Psychology, 15, 354–355. **308, 314**

Elder, G. H., Jr. (1969). Appearance and education in marriage mobility. *American Sociological Review, 34*, 519–533. **374, 380**

Ellis, L. (1987). Criminal behaviaor and r/K selection: An extension of gene-based evolutionary theory. *Deviant Behavior, 8*, 149–176. **376**

Ellis, L., & Ames, M. A. (1987). Neurohormonal functioning and sexual orientation: A theory of homosexuality-heterosexuality. *Psychological Bulletin, 101*, 233–258. **388**

Ember, C. R. (1983). The relative decline in women's contribution to agriculture with intensification. *American Anthropologist, 85*, 285–304. **252**

Ember, M. (1985). Evidence and science in ethnography: Reflections on the Freeman-Mead controversy. *American Anthropologist, 87*, 906–910. **10**

Emlen, S. T., & Oring, L. W. (1977). Ecology, sexual selection, and the evolution of mating systems. *Science, 197*, 215–223. **87, 88**

Endicott, J., & Halbreich, U. (1982). Psychobiology of premenstrual change. *Psychopharmacology Bulletin, 18*, 109–112. **192**

————. (1988). Practical problems in evaluation. In L. H. Gise (Ed.), *The premenstrual syndromes.* New York: Churchhill Livingstone. **192**

Engele, J., Pilgrim, C., & Reisert, I. (1989). Sexual differentiation of mesencephalic neurons in vitro: Effects of sex and gonadal hormones. *International Journal of Developmental Neuroscience, 7*, 603–611. **137**

England, P. (1979). Women and occupational prestige: A case of vacuous sex equality. *Signs: Journal of Women in Culture and Society, 5*, 252–265. **324, 333**

————. (1984). Wage appreciation and depreciation: A test of neoclassical economic explanations of occupational sex segregation. *Social Forces, 62*, 726–749. **331**

Englander-Golden, P., Whitmore, M. R., & Dienstbier, R. A. (1978). Menstrual cycle as focus of study and self-reports of moods and behaviors. *Motivation and Emotion, 2*, 75–86. **192**

Englehard, G., Jr. (1990). Gender differences in performances on mathematics items: Evidence from the United States and Thailand. *Contemporary Educational Psychology, 15*, 13–26. **373**

Epple, G., Alveario, M. C., & St. Andre, E. (1987). Sexual and social behavior of adult saddle-back Tamarins (Saguinus fascicollis), castrated as neonates. *American Journal of Primatology, 13*, 37–49. **150**

Epstein, E., & Guttman, R. (1984). Mate selection in man: Evidence, theory, and outcome. *Social Biology, 31*, 143–277. **380, 381, 382**

Epstein, S. (1973). The self-concept revisited: Or a theory of a theory. *American Psychologist* (May), 404–416. **231**

Erez, E. (1989). Gender, rehabilitation, and probation decisions. *Criminology, 27*, 307–327. **283**

Eron, L. D. (1980). Prescription for reduction of aggression. *American Psychologist, 35*, 244–252. **356, 357**

————. (1987). The development of aggressive behavior from the perspective of a developing behaviorism. *American Psychologist, 42*, 435–442. **291, 298, 356, 357**

Erulkar, S. D., & Wetzel, D. M. (1989). 5-dihydrotestosterone has nonspecific effects on membrane channels and possible genomic effects on ACh-activated channels. *Journal of Neurophysiology, 61*, 1036–1052. **137**

Essock-Vitale, S. M. (1984). The reproductive success of wealthy Americans. *Ethology and Sociobiology, 5*, 45–49. **350**

Essock-Vitale, S. M., & McGuire, M. T. (1988). What 70 million years hath wrought: Sexual histories and reproductive success of a random sample of American women. In L. L. Betzig, M. G. Mulder, & P. Turke (Eds.), *Human reproductive behaviour: A Darwinian perspective.* Cambridge: Cambridge University Press. **381**

Estep, D. Q., Nieuwenhuijsen, K., Bruce, K. E. M., De Neef, K. J., Walters, P. A., Baker, S. C., & Slob, A. K. (1988). Inhibition of sexual behaviour among subordinate stumptail macaques, Macaca arctoides. *Animal Behaviour, 36*, 854–864. **349**

Etaugh, C. (1984, May). *Effects of maternal employment on children: an updated review.* Paper presented at Midwestern Psychological Association, Chicago. **300**

Etaugh, C., Collins, G., & Gerson, A. (1975). Reinforcement of sex-typed behaviors of two-year-old children in a nursery school setting. *Developmental Psychology, 11*, 255. **311**

Etaugh, C., & Harlow, H. (1975). Behaviors of male and female teachers as related to behaviors and attitudes of elementary school children. *Journal of Genetic Psychology, 127*, 163–170. **311**

Etaugh, C., & Spandikow, D. B. (1981). Changing attitudes toward women: A longitudinal study of college students. *Psychology of* Women Quarterly, 5, 591–594. **273**

Etaugh, C., & Spiller, B. (1989). Attitudes toward women: Comparison of traditional-aged and older college students. *Journal of College Student Development, 30*, 41–46. **294**

Etaugh, C., & Stern, J. (1984). Person perception: Effects of sex, marital status, and sex-typed occupation. *Sex Roles, 11*, 413–424. **296, 300**

Etgen, A. M. (1987). Inhibition of estrous behavior in rats by intrahypothalamic application of agents that disrupt nuclear binding of estrogen-receptor complexes. *Hormones and Behavior, 21*, 528–535. **136**

Ethington, C. A., & Wolfle, L. M. (1984). Sex differences in a causal model of mathematics achievement. *Journal for Research in Mathematics Education, 15*, 361–377. **373**

————. (1986). A structural model of mathematics achievement for men and women. *American Educational Research Journal, 23*, 65–75. **373**

Ettlinger, G. (1988). Hand preference, ability, and hemispheric specialization: In how far are these factors related in the monkey? *Cortex, 24*, 389–398. **396**

Etzion, D. (1988). The experience of burnout and work/non-work success in male and female engineers: A matched-pairs comparison. *Human Resource Management, 27*, 163–179. **328, 331**

Evans-Rhodes, D., Murrell, A., & Dietz, B. (1990, April). *Gender stereotyping of occupations: Is women's work still women's work?* Paper presented to the Eastern Psychological Association, Philadelphia. **325**

Ezquiaga, E., Gutierrez, J. L. A., & Lpez, A. G. (1987). Psychosocial factors and episode number in depression. *Journal of Affective Disorders, 12*, 135–138. **364**

Facchinetti, F., Martignoni, E., Petraglia, F., Sances, M. G., Nappi, G., & Genazzani, A. R. (1987). Premenstrual fall of plasma -endorphin in patients with premenstrual syndrome. *Fertility and Sterility, 47*, 570–573. **193**

Fagan, J. F., III, & Shepherd, P. A. (1981). Theoretical issues in the early development of visual perception. In M. Lewis & L. T. Taft (Eds.), *Developmental disabilities: Theory, assessment, and intervention.* New York: Spectrum. **314**

Fagan, J. F., III, & Singer, L. T. (1979). The role of simple feature differences in infants' recognition of faces. *Infant Behavior and Development, 2*, 39–45. **314**

Fagot, B. I. (1973). Influence of teacher behavior in the preschool. *Developmental Psychology, 9,* 198–206. **311**

_____. (1974). Sex differences in toddlers' behavior and parental reaction. *Developmental Psychology, 10,* 554–558. **298, 303**

_____. (1977a). Consequences of moderate cross gender behavior in preschool children. *Child Development, 48,* 902–907. **44, 303, 313, 315, 317**

_____. (1977b). Teachers' reinforcement of sex-preferred behaviors in Dutch preschools. *Psychological Reports, 41,* 1249–1250. **303, 311, 317**

_____. (1978). The influence of sex of child on parental reactions to toddler children. *Child Development, 49,* 459–465. **298, 303**

_____. (1981a). Male and female teachers: Do they treat boys and girls differently? *Sex Roles, 7,* 263–271. **311**

_____. (1981b). Stereotypes versus behavioral judgments of sex differences in young children. *Sex Roles, 7,* 1093–1096. **299**

_____. (1984a). Teacher and peer reactions to boys' and girls' play styles. *Sex Roles, 11,* 691–702. **311, 315, 317**

_____. (1985a). A cautionary note: Parents' socialization of boys and girls. *Sex Roles, 12,* 471–476. **290, 298**

_____. (1985b). Beyond the reinforcement principle: Another step toward understanding sex role development. *Developmental Psychology, 21,* 1097–1104. **290, 311, 316, 317, 356**

_____. (1985c). Changes in thinking about early sex role development. *Developmental Review, 5,* 83–98. **290, 316, 317**

Fagot, B. I., & Hagan, R. (1985). Aggression in toddlers: Responses to the assertive acts of boys and girls. *Sex Roles, 12,* 341–352. **316, 356**

Fagot, B. I., Hagan, R., Leinbach, M. D., & Kronsberg, S. (1985). Differential reactions to assertive and communicative acts of toddler boys and girls. *Child Development, 56,* 1499–1505. **316, 317, 356**

Fagot, B. I., & Leinbach, M. D. (1987). Socialization of sex roles within the family. In D. B. Carter (Ed.), *Current conceptions of sex roles and sex typing.* New York: Praeger. **301**

_____. (1989). The young child's gender schema: Environmental input, internal organization. *Child Development, 60,* 663–672. **301, 356**

Fagot, B. I., Leinbach, M. D., & Hagan, R. (1986). Gender labeling and the adoption of sex-typed behaviors. *Developmental Psychology, 22,* 440–443. **294, 314, 356**

Fagot, B. I., & Littman, I. (1976). Relation of preschool sex-typing to intellectual performance in elementary school. *Psychological Reports, 39,* 699–704. **44, 308, 393**

Fagot, B. I., & Patterson, G. R. (1969). An in vivo analysis of reinforcing contingencies for sex-role behaviors in the preschool child. *Developmental Psychology, 1,* 563–568. **303, 311, 317**

Fairbairn, D. J. (1988). Sexual selection for homogamy in the Gerridae: An extension of Ridley's comparative approach. *Evolution, 42,* 1212–1222. **375**

Fantino, E., & Abarca, N. (1985). Choice, optimal foraging, and the delay-reduction hypothesis. *Behavioral and Brain Sciences, 8,* 315–362. **215**

Faravelli, C., Sacchette, E., Ambonetti, A., Conte, G., Pallanti, S., & Vita, A. (1986). Early life events and affective disorder revisited. *British Journal of Psychiatry, 148,* 288–295. **364**

Farmer, H. S. (1985). Model of career and achievement motivation for women and men. *Journal of Counseling Psychology, 32,* 363–390. **319**

Farrer, L. A., & Conneally, P. M. (1985). A genetic model for age at onset in Huntington Disease. *American Journal of Human Genetics, 37,* 350–357. **103**

Faulk, W. P., McIntyre, J. A., & Coulam, C. B. (1988). Immunology of recurrent spontaneous abortions. *ISI Atlas of Science: Immunology,* 31–34. **74**

Faustman, W. O., Faull, K. F., Whiteford, H. A., Borchert, C., & Csernansky, J. G. (1990). CSF 5-HIAA, serum cortisol, and age differentially predict vegetative and cognitive symptoms in depression. *Biological Psychiatry, 27,* 311–318. **369**

Fazio, R. H., Effrein, E. A., & Falender, V. J. (1981). Self-perceptions following social interaction. *Journal of Personality and Social Psychology, 41,* 232–242. **274**

Feather, N. T. (1985). Masculinity, femininity, self-esteem, and subclinical depression. *Sex Roles, 12,* 491–500. **363**

Feather, N. T., & Said, J. A. (1983). Preference for occupations in relation to masculinity, femininity, and gender. *British Journal of Social Psychology, 22,* 113–127. **327, 328**

Feder, H. H. (1984). Hormones and sexual behavior. *Annual Review of Psychology, 35,* 165–200. **151, 153,** **156, 386**

Fedigan, L. M., Fedigan, L., Gouzoules, S., Gouzoules, H., & Koyama, N. (1986). Lifetime reproductive success in female Japanese macaques. *Folia Primatologica, 47,* 143–157. **349**

Fedor-Freybergh, P. (1977). The influence of oestrogens on the well-being and mental performance in climacteric and postmenopausal women. *Acta Obstetricia et Gynecologica Scandinavica, Supplement 64,* 3–91. **201**

Feek, C. M., Tuzi, N. L., & Edwards, C. R. W. (1989). The adrenal gland and progesterone stimulates testicular steroidogenesis in the rat *in vivo. Journal of Steroid Biochemistry, 32,* 573–579. **178**

Feingold, A. (1988a). Cognitive gender differences are disappearing. *American Psychologist, 43,* 95–103. **391**

_____. (1988b). Matching for attractiveness in romantic partners and same-sex friends: A meta-analysis and theoretical critique. *Psychological Bulletin, 104,* 226–235. **378, 380**

Feiring, C., & Lewis, M. (1987). The child's social network: Sex differences from three to six years. *Sex Roles, 17,* 621–636. **313**

Feldstein, J. H., & Feldstein, S. (1982). Sex differences on televised toy commercials. *Sex Roles, 8,* 581–588. **289**

Fennema, E., & Peterson, P. (1985). Autonomous learning behavior: A possible explanation of gender-related differences in mathematics. In L. C. Wilkinson & C. B. Marrett (Eds.), *Gender-related differences in the classroom.* New York: Academic Press. **313**

Fennema, E., & Sherman, J. (1977). Sex-related differences in mathematics achievement, spatial visualization and affective factors. *American Educational Research Journal, 14,* 51–71. **373**

Fennema, E., & Tartre, L. A. (1985). The use of spatial visualization in mathematics by girls and boys. *Journal for Research in Mathematics Education, 16,* 184-206. **373**

Ferin, M. (1980). The neuroendocrinologic control of the menstrual cycle. In D. T. Krieger & J. C. Hughes (Eds.), *Neuroendocrinology,* New York: Sinauer Associates. **187**

Ferreira, J. V. (1977). Commentary on "Standardization and measurement in cultural anthropology: a neglected area." *Current Anthropology, 18,* 245. **240**

Fetherstone, M., & Hepworth, M. (1985). The male menopause: Lifestyle and sexuality. *Maturitas, 7,*

235–246. **199**

Fidell, L. S. (1970). Empirical verification of sex discrimination in hiring practices in psychology. *American Psychologist, 25*, 1094–1098. **330**

Filicori, M., Flamigni, C., Campaniello, E., Ferrari, P., Meriggiola, M. C., Michelacci, L., Parechi, A., & Valiserri, A. (1989). Evidence for a specific role of GnRH pulse frequency in the control of the human menstrual cycle. *American Journal of Physiology, 257*, E930–E936. **150**

Fillit, H., Weinreb, H., Cholst, I., Luine, V., Amador, R., Zabriskie, J. B., & McEwen, B. S. (1986). Hormonal therapy for Alzheimer's disease. In T. Crook, R. Bartus, S. Ferris, & S. Gershon (Eds.), *Treatment development strategies for Alzeimer's disease.* Madison, WI: Mark Powley. **181**

Fine, M. (1985). Reflections on a feminist psychology of women: Paradoxes and prospects. *Psychology of Women Quarterly, 9*, 167–183. **39**

Fingerhut, L. A., & Kleinman, J. C. (1990). International and interstate comparisons of homicides among young males. *Journal of the American Medical Association, 263*, 3292–3295. **356**

Finlay, B. L. , & Slattery, M. (1983). Local differences in the amount of early cell death in neocortex predict adult local specializations. *Science, 219*, 1349–1351. **152**

Finn, C. A. (1986). Implantation, menstruation and inflammation. *Biological Reviews, 61*, 313–328. **184, 186**

_____. (1987). Why do women and some other primates menstruate? *Perspectives in Biology and Medicine, 30*, 566–574. **184, 186**

Finn, J. D., Dulberg, L., & Reis, J. (1979). Sex differences in educational attainment: a cross-national perspective. *Harvard Educational Review, 49*, 477–503. **262**

Finnell, R. B. (1988). Daughters or sons. *Natural History, 4*, 63–83. **62**

Finucci, J. M., & Childs, B. (1981). Are there really more dyslexic boys than girls? In A. Ansara, N. Geschwind, A. Galaburda, M. Albert, & N. Gartrell (Eds.), *Sex differences in dyslexia.* Towson, Md: Orton Dyslexia Society. **373**

Fiorentine, R. (1987). Men, women, and the premed persistence gap: A normative alternatives approach. *American Journal of Sociology, 92*, 1118–1139. **321**

_____. (1988a). Sex differences in success expectancies and causal attributions: Is this why fewer women become physicians? *Social Psychology Quarterly, 51*, 236–249.

321

_____. (1988b). Increasing similarity in the values and life plans of male and female college students? Evidence and implications. *Sex Roles, 18*, 143–158. **325**

Firth, M. (1982). Sex discrimination in job opportunities for women. *Sex Roles, 8*, 891–902. **330**

Fisher, H. E. (1987). The four-year itch. *Natural History, 96*, 22–29. **382**

Fisk, D. W. (1971). *Measuring the concepts of personality.* Chicago: Aldine. **48**

Fiske, S. T., Neuberg, S. L., Beattie, A. E., & Milberg, S. J. (1987). Category-based and attribute-based reactions to others: Some informational conditions of stereotyping andindividuating processes. *Journal of Experimental Social Psychology, 23*, 399–427. **269**

Fitzhenry, R. I. (Ed.). (1987). *Barnes & Noble revised and enlarged book of quotations.* New York: Harper & Row. **371**

Flake-Hobson, C., Robinson, R. E., & Skeen, P. (1981). Relationship between parental androgyny and early child-rearing ideals and practices. *Psychological Reports, 49*, 667–675. **298**

Fleck, J. R., Fuller, C. C., Malin, S. Z., Miller, D. H., & Acheson, K. R. (1980). Father psychological absence and heterosexual behavior, personal adjustment and sex-typing in adolescent girls. *Adolescence, 15*, 847–860. **223**

Fleischer, R. A., & Chertkoff, J. M. (1986). Effects of dominance and sex on leader selection in dyadic work groups. *Journal of Personality and Social Psychology, 50*, 94–99. **347**

Fletcher, G. J. O. (1983). Sex differences in causal attributions for marital separation. *New Zealand Journal of Psychology, 12,* 82–89. **381**

Flett, G. L., Vredenburg, K., & Pliner, P. (1985). Sex roles and depression: A preliminary investigation of the direction of causality. *Journal of Research in Personality, 19*, 429–435. **363**

Flinn, M. V. (1986). Correlates of reproductive success in a Caribbean village. *Human Ecology, 14*, 225–243. **244, 350**

Flint, M. (1982). Anthropological perspectives of the menopause and middle age. *Maturitas, 4*, 173–180. **200**

Foley, R. A., & Lee, P. C. (1989). Finite social space, evolutionary pathways, and reconstructing hominid behavior. *Science, 243*, 901–906. **245**

Forger, N. G., & Breedlove, S. M.

(1986). Sexual dimorphism in human and canine spinal cord: Role of early androgen. *Proceedings of the National Academy of Sciences, USA, 83*, 7527–7531. **163, 165**

Fouts, R. (1989, June 16). *Chimpanzees in sign.* Talk given at the ECNS summer lecture series. **214**

Frable, D. E. S. (1989). Sex typing and gender ideology: two facets of the individual's gender psychology that go together. *Journal of Personality and Social Psychology, 56*, 1–14. **49, 279**

Fragaszy, D. M., & Visalberghi, E. (1989). Social influences on the acquisition of tool-using behaviors in tufted capuchin monkeys (Cebus apella). *Journal of Comparative Psychology, 103*, 159–170. **214, 248**

Francke, U., Felsenstein, J., Gartler, S. M., Migeon, B. R., Dancis, J., Seegmiller, J. E., Bakay, B., & Nyhan, W. L. (1976). The occurrence of new mutants in the X-linked recessive Lesch-Nyhan disease. *American Journal of Human Genetics, 28*, 123–137. **119**

Frank, E., Carpenter, L. L., & Kupfer, D. J. (1988). Sex differences in recurrent depression: Are there any that are significant? *American Journal of Psychiatry, 145*, 41–45. **363**

Frankenhaeuser, M. (1982). Challenge-control interaction as reflected in sympathetic-adrenal and pituitary-adrenal activity: Comparison between the sexes. *Scandinavian Journal of Psychology, Suppl. 1*, 158–164. **332**

Fredrickson, W. T., & Sackett, G. P. (1984). Kin preferences in primates (Macaca nemestrina): Relatedness or familiarity. *Journal of Comparative Psychology, 98*, 29–34. **93**

Freedman, D. G. (1980a). Cross-cultural notes on status hierarchies. In D. R. Omark, F. F. Strayer, & D. G. Freedman (Eds.), *An ethological view of human conflict and social interaction.* New York: Garland STPM Press. **348**

_____. (1980b). Sexual dimorphism and the status hierarchy. In D. R. Omark, F. F. Strayer, & D. G. Freedman (Eds.), *An ethological view of human conflict and social interaction.* New York: Garland STPM Press. **348**

Freedman, D. G., & DeBoer, M. M. (1979). Biological and cultural differences in early child development. *Annual Review of Anthropology, 8*, 579–600. **316, 318**

Freeman, D. (1983). *Margaret Mead and Samoa: The making and unmaking of an anthropological myth.* Cambridge, MA: Harvard University Press. **10**

_____. (1985a). A reply to Ember's reflections on the Freeman-Mead controversy. *American Anthropologist, 87,* 910–917. **10**

_____. (1985b). Open letter to the president and board of the American Anthropological Association. *Anthropology Newsletter, 26,* 1–2. **10**

Freud, S. (1953). Some psychological consequences of the anatomical distinctions between the sexes. In J. Strachey (Ed. and Trans.), *Collected papers.* London: Hogarth Press. **216, 217**

_____. (1961). Female sexuality. In J. Strachey (Ed. and Trans.), *Complete edition of the psychological works of Sigmund Freud, vol. 21, The future of an illusion, civilization and its discontents and other works.* London: Hogarth Press. **216**

_____. (1964). Lecture 33: Femininity. In J. Strachey (Ed. and Trans.), *Complete edition of the psychological works of Sigmund Freud, Vol. 22, New introductory lectures on psycho-analysis and other works.* London: Hogarth Press. **216, 218**

Freund, K., & Blanchard, R. (1983). Is the distant relationship of fathers and homosexual sons related to the sons' erotic preference for male partners, or to the sons' atypical gender identity, or to both? *Journal of Homosexuality, 9,* 7–25. **388**

Frey, K. S., & Ruble, D. N. (1985). What children say when the teacher is not around: Conflicting goals in social comparison and performance assessment in the classroom. *Journal of Personality and Social Psychology, 48,* 550–562. **321, 333**

Frey, K. S., & Ruble, D. N. (1987). What children say about classroom performance: Sex and grade differences in perceived competence. *Child Development, 58,* 1066–1078. **321**

Fride, E., Dan, Y., Feldon, J., Halevy, G., & Weinstock, M. (1986). Effects of prenatal stress on vulnerability to stress in prepubertal and adult rats. *Physiology & Behavior, 37,* 681–687. **148**

Friedman, L. (1989). Mathematics and the gender gap: A meta-analysis of recent studies on sex differences in mathematical tasks. *Review of Educational Research, 59,* 185–213. **373**

Frodi, A., Macaulay, J., & Thome, P. R. (1977). Are women always less aggressive than men? A review of the experimental literature. *Psychological Bulletin, 84,* 634–660. **35**

Frohman, L. A. (1980). Neurotransmitters as regulators of endocrine function. In D. T. Krieger & J. C.

Hughes (Eds.), *Neuroendocrinology.* Sunderland, MA: Sinauer Associates. **150**

Fryns, J. P. (1984). The fragile X syndrome. *Clinical Genetics, 26,* 497–528. **121**

Fryns, J. P., Kleczkowska, A., Petit, P., & van den Berghe, H. (1983). X-chromosome polysomy in the female: Personal experience and a review of the literature. *Clinical Genetics, 23,* 341–349. **123**

Fuchs, V. R. (1986). Sex differences in economic well-being. *Science, 232,* 459–464. **329**

Funder, D. C., Block, J. H., & Block, J. (1983). Delay of gratification: Some longitudinal personality correlates. *Journal of Personality and Social Psychology, 44,* 1198–1213. **234**

Funderburk, S. J., Valente, M., & Klisak, I. (1981). Pentasomy X: Report of patient and studies of X-inactivation. *American Journal of Medical Genetics, 8,* 27–33. **123**

Furedy, J. J., Fleming, A. S., Ruble, D., Scher, H., Daly, J., Day, D., & Loewen, R. (1989). Sex differences in small-magnitude heart-rate responses to sexual and infant-related stimuli: A psychophysiological approach. *Physiology & Behavior, 46,* 903–905. **383**

Furnham, A., & Duignan, S. (1989). The selective recall of attitude consistent information: A study concerning sex differences. *Psychologia, 32,* 112–119. **274**

Furnham, A., & Schofield, S. (1986). Sex-role stereotyping in British radio advertisements. *British Journal of Social Psychology, 25,* 165-171. **290**

Furnham, A., & Singh, A. (1986). Memory for information about sex differences. *Sex Roles, 15,* 479–486. **274**

Futoran, G. C., & Wyer, R. S., Jr. (1986). The effects of traits and gender stereotypes on occupational suitability judgments and the recall of judgment-relevant information. *Journal of Experimental Social Psychology, 22,* 475–503. **275**

Gadpaille, W. J., Sanborn, C. F., & Wagner, W. W., Jr. (1987). Athletic amenorrhea, major affective disorders, and eating disorders. *American Journal of Psychiatry, 144,* 939–942. **362**

Galaburda, A. M., Corsiglia, J., Rosen, G. C., & Sherman, G. F. (1987). Planum temporale asymmetry, reappraisal since Geschwind and Levitsky. *Neuropsychologia, 25,* 853–868. **172, 374**

Galambos, N. L., Almeida, D. M., & Peterson, A. C. (1990). Masculinity, femininity, and sex role attitudes in early adolescence: Ex-

ploring gender intensification. *Child Development, 61,* 1905-1914. **274**

Galli, L., & Maffei, L. (1988). Spontaneous impulse activity of rat retinal ganglion cells in prenatal life. *Science, 242,* 90–91. **139**

Gandelman, R. (1980). Gonadal hormones and the induction of intraspecific fighting in mice. *Neuroscience & Biobehavioral Reviews, 4,* 133–140. **398**

_____. (1983). Gonadal hormones and sensory function. *Neuroscience & Biobehavioral Reviews, 7,* 1–17. **358**

Gandelman, R., Rosenthal, C., & Howard, S. M. (1980). Expsosure of female mouse fetuses of various ages to testosterone and the later activation in intraspecific fighting. *Physiology & Behavior, 25,* 333–335. **137**

Garcia-Segura, L. M., Baetens, D., & Naftolin, F. (1985). Sex differences and maturational changes in arcuate nucleus neuronal plasma membrane organization. *Developmental Brain Research, 19,* 146–149. **137**

Garcia-Segura, L. M., Olmos, G., Tranque, P., & Naftolin, F. (1987). Rapid effects of gonadal steroids upon hypothalamic neuronal membrane ultrastructure. *Journal of Steroid Biochemistry, 27,* 1–3. **137**

Gardner, L. I. (1979). Polysomy X masquerading as Down's syndrome: The necessity of being earnest about karyotype analysis in the diagnosis of mongolism. *American Journal of the Diseases of the Child, 133,* 254–255. **123**

Garris, D. R., Billiar, R. B., Takaoka, Y., White, R., & Little, B. (1983). Autoradiographic localization of estradiol- and progesterone-concentrating neurons in the isolated rhesus monkey hypothalamus. *Neuroscience Letters, 37,* 149–154. **180**

Gartler, S. M., & Riggs, A. D. (1983). Mammalian X-chromosome inactivation. *Annual Review of Genetics, 17,* 155–190. **104**

Garvey, M. J., Wesner, R., & Godes, M. (1988). Comparison of seasonal and nonseasonal affective disorders. *American Journal of Psychiatry, 145,* 100–102. **361**

Garza, R. T., & Herringer, L. G. (1988). Social identity: A multidimensional approach. *Journal of Social Psychology, 127,* 299–308. **229**

Gaspard, U. J. (1987). Metabolic effects of oral contraceptives. *American Journal of Obstetrics and Gynecology, 157,* 1029–1041. **201**

Gater, R. A., Dean, C., & Morris, J. (1989). The contribution of childbearing to the sex difference in first admission rates for affective psychosis. *Psychological Medicine, 19*, 719–724. **368**

Gaulin, S. J. C., & FitzGerald, R. W. (1986). Sex differences in spatial ability: An evolutionary hypothesis and test. *American Naturalist, 127*, 74–88. **376**

———. (1988). Home-range size as a predictor of mating systems in Microtus. *Journal of Mammology, 69*, 311–319. **214, 376**

———. (1989). Sexual selection for spatial-learning ability. *Animal Behaviour, 37*, 322–331. **376**

Gaulin, S. J. C., FitzGerald, R. W., & Wartell, M. S. (1990). Sex differences in spatial ability and activity in two vole species (Microtus ochrogaster and M. pennsylvanicus). *Journal of Comparative Psychology, 104*, 88–93. **376**

Gaulin, S. J. C., & Wartell, M. S. (1990). Effects of experience and motivation on symmetrical-maze performance in the prairie vole (Microtus ochrogaster). *Journal of Comparative Psychology, 104*, 183–189. **214, 376**

Gayton, W. G., Havu, G. F., Ozmon, K. L., & Tavormina, J. (1977). A comparison of the Bem Sex Role Inventory and the PRF ANDRO scale. *Journal of Personality Assessment, 41*, 619–621. **46**

Geis, F. L., Boston, M. B., & Hoffman, N. (1985). Sex of authority role models and achievement by men and women: Leadership performance and recognition. *Journal of Personality and Social Psychology, 49*, 636–653. **341**

Geis, F. L., Brown, V., Jennings (Walstedt), J., & Porter, N. (1984). TV commercials as achievement scripts for women. *Sex Roles, 10*, 513–525. **293**

Gelles, R. J., & Straus, M. A. (1979). Violence in the American family. *Journal of Social Issues, 35*, 15–39. **354**

George, L. K., & Weiler, S. J. (1981). Sexuality in middle and late life: The effects of age, cohort, and gender. *Archives of General Psychiatry, 38*, 919–923. **383**

Gerall, A. A., Dunlap, J. L., & Hendricks, S. E. (1973). Effect of ovarian secretions on female behavioral potentiality in the rat. *Journal of Comparative and Physiological Psychology, 82*, 449–465.

Gerber, G. L. (1977). The effect of competition on stereotypes about sex-role and marital satisfaction. *Journal of Psychology, 97*, 297–308. **283**

———. (1984). Attribution of feminine and masculine traits to opposite-sex dyads. *Psychological Reports, 55*, 907–918. **275, 283**

Gerdes, L. C., Sonnendecker, E. W. W., & Polakow, E. S. (1982). Psychological changes effected by estrogen-progestogen and clonidine treatment in climacteric women. *American Journal of Obstetrics and Gynecology, 142*, 98–104. **201**

Gerson, M. J., Alpert, J. L., & Richardson, M. S. (1984). Mothering: The view from psychological research. *Signs: Journal of Women in Culture and Society, 9*, 434–453. **253**

Geschwind, N. (1985). Implications for evolution, genetics, and clinical syndromes. In S. D. Glick (Ed.), *Cerebral lateralization in nonhuman species*. New York: Academic Press. **397**

Geschwind, N., & Galaburda, A. M. (1985a). Cerebral lateralization: Biological mechanisms, associations, and pathology: I. A hypothesis and a program for research. *Archives of Neurology, 42*, 428–459. **172**

Geschwind, N., & Galaburda, A. M. (1985b). Cerebral lateralization: Biological mechanisms, associations, and pathology: II. A hypothesis and a program for research. *Archives of Neurology, 42*, 521–552. **172**

Geschwind, N., & Galaburda, A. M. (1985c). Cerebral lateralization: Biological mechanisms, associations, and pathology: III. A hypothesis and a program for research. *Archives of Neurology, 42*, 634–654. **172**

Gewertz, D. (1984). The Tchambuli view of persons: A critique of individualism in the works of Mead and Chodorow. *American Anthropologist, 86*, 615–629. **238, 258**

Ghiselin, M. T. (1986). The assimilation of Darwinism in developmental psychology. *Human Development, 29*, 12–21. **2**

Ghodsian-Carpey, J., & Baker, L. A. (1987). Genetic and environmental influences on aggression in 4- to 7-year-old twins. *Aggressive Beahvior, 13*, 173–186. **358**

Gibber, J. R., & Goy, R. W. (1985). Infant-directed behavior in young rhesus monkeys: Sex differences and effects of prenatal androgens. *American Journal of Primatology, 8*, 225–227. **150**

Gibbs, H. L., Weatherhead, P. J., Boag, P. T., White, B. N., Tabak, L. M., & Hoysak, D. J. (1990). Realized reproductive success of polygyous red-winged blackbirds revealed by DNA markers. *Science, 250*, 1394–1397. **78**

Gibbs, J. T. (1986). Psychosocial correlates of sexual attitudes and behaviors in urban early adolescent

females: Implications for intervention. *Journal of Social Work and Human Sexuality, 5*, 81–97. **374**

Gifford, R., & O'Connor, B. (1987). The interpersonal circumplex as a behavior map. *Journal of Personality and Social Psychology, 52*, 1019–1026. **339**

Gilbert, L. A. (1985). Measures of psychological masculinity and femininity: A comment on Gaddy, Glass, and Arnkoff. *Journal of Counseling Psychology, 32*, 163–166. **49**

Gilligan, C. (1982). *In a different voice: Psychological theory and women's development*. Cambrige, MA: Harvard University Press. **218**

Gillison, G. (1980). Images of nature in Gimi thought. In C. P. MacCormack & M. Strathern (Eds.), *Nature, culture and gender*. Cambridge: Cambridge University Press. **264**

Gise, L. H., Lebovits, A. H., Paddison, P. L., & Strain, J. J. (1990). Issues in the identification of premenstrual syndrome. *Journal of Nervous and Mental Disease, 178*, 228–234. **192**

Gittelman, J. L., & Thompson, S. D. (1988). Energy allocation in mammalian reproduction. *American Zoologist, 28*, 863–875. **78**

Gladue, B. A. (1984). Dihydrotestosterone stimulates mounting behavior but not lordosis in female rats. *Physiology & Behavior, 33*, 49–53. **146**

Glaser, J., Russell, V. A., de Villiers, A. S., Searson, J. A., & Taljaard, J. F. (1990). Rat brain monoamine and serotonin S2 receptor changes during pregnancy. *Neurochemical Research, 15*, 949–956. **369**

Glass, S. P., & Wright, T. L. (1977). The relationship of extramarital sex, length of marriage, and sex differences on marital satisfaction and romanticisms: Athanasiou's data reanalyzed. *Journal of Marriage and the Family, 39*, 691–703. **381**

Glenn, N. D. (1987). Social trends in the United States: Evidence from sample surveys. *Public Opinion Quarterly, 51*, S109–S126. **366**

Glick, I. D., & Bennet, S. E. (1982). Oral contraceptives and the menstrual cycle. In R. C. Friedman (Ed.), *Behavior and the menstrual cycle*. New York: Marcel Dekker. **201**

Glick, S. D. (1985). Heritable differences in turning behavior of rats. *Life Sciences, 37*, 499–503. **396**

Gold, P. W., Goodwin, F. K., & Chrousos, G. P. (1988). Clinical and biochemical manifestation of depression: Relation to the neurobioogy of stress (in two parts). *New*

England Journal of Medicine, 319, 348–353, 413–420. **362**

Goldberg, J., & Meredith, W. (1975). A longitudinal study of spatial ability. *Behavior Genetics, 5*, 127–135. **374**

Goldberg, P. (1968). Are women prejudiced against women? *Transaction*, April, 28–30. **280**

Goldberg, S., & Lewis, M. (1969). Play behavior in the year-old infant: Early sex differences. *Child Development, 40*, 21–31. **314**

Goldblatt, P. B., Moore, M. E., & Stunkard, A. J. (1965). Social factors in obesity. *Journal of the American Medical Association, 192*, 1039–1044. **380**

Golding, J. M. (1988). Gender differences in depressive symptoms: Statistical considerations. *Psychology of Women Quarterly, 12*, 61–74. **360**

Goldman, P. S., Crawford, H. T., Stokes, L. P., Galkin, T. W., & Rosvold, H. E. (1974). Sex-dependent behavioral effects of cerebral cortical lesions in the developing rhesus monkey. *Science, 186*, 540–542. **225**

Goldman, S. A., & Nottebohm, F. (1983). Neuronal production, migration, and differentiation in a vocal control nucleus of the adult female canary brain. *Proceedings of the National Academy of Sciences, 80*, 239–2394. **142**

Goldney, R. D. (1981). Attempted suicide in young women: Correlates of lethality. *British Journal of Psychiatry, 139*, 382–390. **368**

Goldscheider, F. K., & Waite, L. J. (1981). Sex differences in the entry into marriage. *American Journal of Sociology, 92*, 91–109. **328**

Gomendio, M., Clutton-Brock, T. H., Albon, S. D., Guinness, F. E., & Simpson, M. J. (1990). Mammalian sex ratios and variation in costs of rearing sons and daughters. *Nature, 343*, 261–263. **80**

Gomez, M. R., Engel, A. G., Dewald, G., & Peterson, H. A. (1977). Failure of inactivation of Duchenne dystrophy X-chromosome in one of female identical twins. *Neurology, 27*, 537–541. **105**

Gong, E. J., Garrell, D., & Calloway, D. H. (1989). Menstrual cycle and voluntary food intake. *American Journal of Clinical Nutrition, 49*, 252–258. **189**

Goodall, J. (1986). *The chimpanzees of Gombe: Patterns of behavior*. Cambridge, MA:Belknap Press of Harvard University. **243, 245, 248, 348**

Goodall, J., Bandora, A., Bergmann, E., Busse, C., Matama, H., Mpongo, E., Pierce, A., & Riss, D. (1979). Intercommunity interactions in the chimpanzee population

of the Gombe national park. In D. A. Hamburg & E. R. McCown (Eds.), *The great apes*. Menlo Park, CA: Benjamin/Cummings. **243, 248**

Goodfellow, P. J., Darling, S., & Wolfe, J. (1985). The human Y chromosome. *Journal of Medical Genetics, 22*, 329–344. **117**

Goodfellow, P. J., Pritchard, C., Tippett, P., & Goodfellow, P. N. (1987). Recombination between the X and Y chromosomes: Implications for the relationship between *MIC2*, *XG*, and *YG*. *Annals of Human Genetics, 51*, 161–167. **104**

Goodfellow, P. N., Davies, K. E., & Ropers, H. H. (1985). Human gene mapping. 8. Report of the committee on the genetic condition of the X and Y chromosomes. *Cytogenetics and Cellular Genetics, 40*, 295–352. **117, 119**

Goodman, A. (1991). Organic unity theory: The mind-body problem revisited. *American Journal of Psychiatry, 148*, 553–563. **21**

Goodman, J., Loftus, E. F., Miller, M., & Greene, E. (1991). Money, sex, and death: Gender bias in wrongful death damage awards. *Law & Society Review, 25*, 263–285. **283**

Goodman, M. J., Griffin, P. B., Estioko-Griffin, A. A., & Grove, J. S. (1985). The compatibility of hunting and mothering among the Agta hunter-gatherers of the Philippines. *Sex Roles, 12*, 1199–1209. **237, 247**

Goodnow, J. J. (1988). Children's household work: Its nature and functions. *Psychological Bulletin, 103*, 5–26. **307**

Goodnow, J. J., & Delaney, S. (1989). Children's household work: Task differences, styles of assignment, and links to family relationships. *Journal of Applied Developmental Psychology, 10*, 209–226. **307**

Gooren, L. (1984). Androgens and sexual functions in the human male. A study with cyproterone acetate. *Neuroendocrinology Letters, 6*, 183–186. **229**

_____. (1986a). The neuroendocrine response of luteinizing hormone to estrogen administration in heterosexual, homosxual, and transsexual subjects. *Journal of Clinical Endocrinology and Metabolism, 63*, 583–588. **229, 388**

_____. (1986b). The neuroendocrine response of luteinizing hormone to estrogen administration in the human is not sex specific but dependent on the hormonal environment. *Journal of Clinical Endocrinology and Metabolism, 63*, 589–593. **229, 388**

Gordon, H. W., Corbin, E. D., & Lee,

P. A. (1986). Changes in specialized cognitive function following changes in hormone levels. *Cortex, 22*, 399–415. **398**

Gordon, H. W., & Lee, P. A. (1986). A relationship between gonadotropins and visuospatial function. *Neuropsychologia, 24*, 563–576. **398**

Gordon, T. P., Bernstein, I. W., & Rose, R. M. (1978). Social and seasonal influences on testosterone secretion in the male rhesus monkey. *Physiology & Behavior, 21*, 623–627. **203**

Gordon, T. P., Rose, R. M., & Bernstein, I. S. (1976). Seasonal rhythm in plasma testosterone levels in the rhesus monkey (Macaca mulatta): A three year study. *Hormones and Behavior, 7*, 229–243. **203**

Gorski, R. A. (1984). Critical role for the medial preoptic area in the sexual differentiation of the brain. *Progress in Brain Research, 61*, 129–146. **162, 163**

_____. (1985). The 13th J. A. F. Stevenson Memorial Lecture: Sexual differentiation of the brain: Possible mechanisms and implications. *Canadian Journal of Physiology and Pharmacology, 63*, 577–594. **151**

Gotlib, I. H., Mount, J. H., Cordy, N. I., & Whiffen, V. E. (1988). Depression and perceptions of early parenting: A longitudinal investigation. *British Journal of Psychiatry, 152*, 24–27. **367**

Gottfried, A. E., & Gottfried, A. W. (1988). Maternal employment and children's development: An integration of longitudinal findings with implications for social policy. In A. E. Gottfried & A. W. Gottfried (Eds.), *Maternal employment and children's development*. New York: Plenum Press. **300**

Gottfried, A. E., Gottfried, A. W., & Bathurst, K. (1988). Maternal employment, family environment, and children's development: infancy through the school years. In A. E. Gottfried & A. W. Gottfried (Eds.), *Maternal employment and children's development*. New York: Plenum Press. **300**

Gottfried, A. W., & Bathurst, K. (1983). Hand preference across time is related to intelligence in young girls, not boys. *Science, 221*, 1074–1076. **225**

Gottlieb, G. (1987). The developmental basis of evolutionary change. *Journal of Comparative Psychology, 101*, 262–271. **224**

Gouchie, C., & Kimura, D. (1991). The relationship between testosterone levels and cognitive ability patterns. *Psychoneuroendocrinology, 16*, 323–334. **398**

Goudsmit, E., Feenstra, M. G. P.,

& Swaab, D. F. (1990). Central monoamine metabolism in the male brown-Norway rat in relation to aging and testosterone. *Brain Research Bulletin, 25*, 755–763. **369**

Goudsmit, E., Fliers, E., & Swaab, D. F. (1988). Testosterone supplementation restores vasopressin innervation in the senescent rat brain. *Brain Research, 473*, 306–313. **199**

Gouzoules, H., & Gouzoules, S. (1989). Sex differences in the acquisition of communicative competence by pigtail macaques (Macaca nemestrina). *American Journal of Primatology, 19*, 163–174. **216**

Gouzoules, H., Gouzoules, S., & Fedigan, L. (1982). Behavioural dominance and reproductive success in female Japanese monkeys (Macaca fuscata). *Animal Behaviour, 30*, 1138–1150. **349**

Gove, W. R., Hughes, M., & Geerken, M. R. (1980). Playing dumb: A form of impression management with undesirable side effects. *Social Psychology Quarterly, 43*, 89–102. **319**

Goy, R. W., Bercovitch, F. B., & McBrair, M. C. (1988). Behavioral masculinization is independent of genital masculinization in prenatally androgenized rhesus macaques. *Hormones and Behavior, 22*, 552–571. **150**

Goy, R. W., & Jakway, J. S. (1959). The inheritance of patterns of sexual behaviour in female guinea pigs. *Animal Behaviour, 7*, 142–149. **147**

Goy, R. W., & McEwen, B. S. (1980). *Sexual differentiation of the brain.* Cambridge, MA: MIT Press. **358**

Graebner, D. B. (1972). A decade of sexism in readers. *The Reading Teacher, 26*, 1–7. **288**

Grant, S. G., & Chapman, V. M. (1988). Mechanisms of X-chromosome regulation. *Annual Review of Genetics, 22*, 199–233. **104**

Gray, E. (1982). Transgeneration analyses of the human sex ratio. *Journal of Heredity, 73*, 123–127. **282**

Gray, E., Bortolozzi, J., & Hurt, V. K. (1979). Desired family size and sex of children in Botucatu, Brazil. *Journal of Heredity, 70*, 67–69. **282**

Gray, J. A., & Buffery, A. W. H. (1971). Sex differences in emotional and cognitive behaviour in mammals including man: Adaptive and neural bases. *Acta Psychologica, 35*, 89–111. **376**

Green, R. (1976). One-hundred ten feminine and masculine boys: Behavioral contrasts and demographic similarities. *Archives of Sexual Behavior, 5*, 425–446. **303**

——— . (1979). Childhood cross-gender behavior and subsequent sexual preference. *American Journal of Psychiatry, 136*, 106–108. **388**

——— . (1985). Gender identity in childhood and later sexual orientation: Follow-up of 78 males. *American Journal of Psychology, 142*, 339–341. **303, 388**

——— . (1987). *The "sissy boy syndrome."* New Haven, CT: Yale University Press. **303, 332, 389**

Green, R., Roberts, C. W., Williams, K., Goodman, M., & Mixon, A. (1987). Specific cross-gender behvior in boyhood and later sexual orientation. *British Journal of Psychiatry, 151*, 84–88. **303**

Green, R., Williams, K., & Goodman, M. (1985). Masculine or feminine gender identity in boys: Developmental differences between two diverse family groups. *Sex Roles, 12*, 1155–1162. **303**

Green, R. J., & Stanton, M. E. (1989). Differential ontogeny of working memory and reference memory in the rat. *Behavioral Neuroscience, 103*, 98–105. **227**

Green, S. K., Buchanan, D. R., & Heuer, S. (1984). Winners, losers, and choosers: A field investigation of dating initiation. *Personality and Social Psychology Bulletin, 10*, 502–511. **382**

Greene, J. G., & Cooke, D. J. (1980). Life stress and symptoms at the climacterium. *British Journal of Psychiatry, 136*, 486–491. **200**

Greenough, W. T., Black, J. E., & Wallace, C. S. (1987). Experience and brain development. *Child Development, 58*, 539–559. **224, 225**

Greenwald, A. G. (1980). The totalitarian ego: Fabrication and revision of person history. *American Psychologist, 35*, 603–618. **231**

Greenwood, P. J. (1980). Mating systems, philopatry and dispersal in birds and mammals. *Animal Behaviour, 28*, 1140–1162. **242**

Griffitt, W. (1975). Sexual experience and sexual responsiveness: Sex differences. *Archives of Sexual Behavior, 4*, 529–540. **382**

——— . (1987). Females, males, and sexual responses. In K. Kelley (Ed.), *Females, males, and sexuality.* Albany: State University of New York Press. **382**

Grigsby, J. P., Kemper, M. B., Hagerman, R. J., & Myers, C. S. (1990). Neuropsychological dysfunction among affected heterozygous fragile X females. *American Journal of Medical Genetics, 35* 28–35. **121**

Grotevant, H. D. (1978). Sibling constellations and sex typing of interests in adolescence. *Child Development, 49*, 540–542. **329**

Grotevant, H. D., & Thorbecke, W. L. (1982). Sex differences in styles of occupational identity formation in late adolescence. *Developmental Psychology, 18*, 396–405. **327**

Grumbach, M. M. (1980). The neuroendocrinology of puberty. In D. T. Krieger & J. C. Hughes (Eds.), *Neuroendocrinology.* New York: Sinauer Associates. **178**

Gubbay, J., Collignon, J., Koopman, P., Capel, B., Economous, A., Mnsterberg, A., Vivian, N., Goodfellow, P., & Lovell-Badge, R. (1990). A gene mapping to the sex-determining region of the mouse Y chromosome is a member of a novel family of embryonically expressed genes. *Nature, 346*, 245–250. **123**

Guignard, M. M., Pesquies, P. C., Serrurier, B. D., Merino, D. B., & Reinberg, A. E. (1980). Circadian rhythms in plasma levels of cortisol, dehydroepiandrosterone, 4-androstenedione, testosterone and dihydrotestosterone of healthy young men. *Acta Endocrinologica, 94*, 536–545. **182**

Gunter, N. C., & Gunter, B. G. (1990). Domestic division of labor among working couples: Does androgyny make a difference? *Psychology of Women Quarterly, 14*, 355–370. **304, 306**

Gupta, D., Rager, K., Attianasia, A., Klemm, W., & Eichner, M. (1975). Sex steroid hormones during multiphase pubertal developments. *Journal of Steroid Biochemistry, 6*, 859–868. **177**

Gur, R. C., Mozley, P. D., Resnick, S. M., Gottleib, G. L., Kohn, M., Zimmereman, R., Herman, G., Atlas, S., Grossman, R., Berretta, D., Erwin, R., & Gur, R. E. (1991). Gender differences in age effect on brain atrophy measured by magnetic resonance imaging. *Proceedings of the National Academy of Sciences, USA, 88*, 2845–2849. **166**

Gutek, B. A. (1988). Sex segregation and women at work: a selective review. *Applied Psychology: An International Review, 37*, 103–120. **324, 329**

Gutek, B. A., & Cohen, A. G. (1987). Sex ratios, sex role spillover, and sex at work: A comparison of men's and women's experiences. *Human Relations, 40*, 97–115. **330**

Gutek, B. A., & Dunwoody, V. (1987). Understanding sex in the workplace. In A. H. Stromberg, L. Larwood, & B. A. Gutek (Eds.), *Women and work, an annual review, volume 2.* Beverly Hills: Sage. **330**

Gwynne, D. T. (1981). Sexual difference theory: Mormon crickets show role reversal in mate choice. *Science, 213*, 779–780. **84**

Gwynne, D. T., & Simmons, L. W. (1990). Experimental reversal of courship roles in an insect. *Nature, 346*, 172–174. **84**

Haffner, S. M., Katz, M. S., Stern, M. P., & Dunn, J. F. (1989). Relationship of sex hormone binding globulin to overall adiposity and body fat distribtion in a biethnic population. *International Journal of Obesity, 13*, 1–9. **236**

Hagen, C., Christiansen, C., Christensen, M. S., & Transbl, I. (1982). Climacteric symptoms, fat mass, and plasma concentrations of LH, FSH, Prl, oestradiol-17 and androstenedione in the early postmenopausal period. *Acta Endocrinologica, 101*, 87–92. **200**

Hagen, R. L., & Kahn, A. (1975). Discrimination against competent women. *Journal of Applied Social Psychology, 5*, 362–376. **330**

Hahn, W. K. (1987). Cerebral lateralization of function: From infancy through childhood. *Psychological Bulletin, 101*, 376–392. **397**

Halbreich, U., Alt, I. H., & Paul, L. (1988). Premenstrual changes: Impaired hormonal homeostasis. *Endocrinology of neuropsychiatric Disorders, 6*, 173–194. **191, 193**

Halbreich, U., & Endicott, J. (1985). Relationship of dysphoric premenstrual changes to depressive disorders. *Acta Psychiatrica Scandinavica, 71*, 331–338. **193**

Halbreich, U., Endicott, J., Goldstein, S., & Nee, J. (1986). Premenstrual changes and changes in gonadal hormones. *Acta Psychiatrica Scandinavica, 74*, 576–586. **193, 195**

Halbreich, U., Endicott, J., & Nee, J. (1983). Premenstrual depressive changes: Value of differentiation. *Archives of General Psychiatry, 40*, 535–542. **193**

Hall, J. A. (1978). Gender effects in decoding nonverbal cues. *Psychological Bulletin, 85*, 845–857. **35, 344**

——. (1984). *Nonverbal sex differences*. Baltimore, MD: Johns Hopkins University Press. **341, 343, 344, 345**

——. (1987). On explaining gender differences: the case of nonverbal communication. In P. Shaver & C. Hendrick (Eds.), *Sex and gender*. Beverly Hills, CA: Sage. **344**

Hall, J. A., & Halberstadt, A. G. (1986). Smiling and gazing. In J. S. Hyde & M. C. Linn (Eds.), *The psychology of gender: Advances through meta-analysis*. Baltimore, MD: Johns Hopkins University Press. **344**

Hall, J. G. (1990). Genomic imprinting: Review and relevance to human diseases. *American Journal of Human Genetics, 46*, 857–873. **102, 103**

Hall, W. D., Douglas, M. B., Blumenstein, B. A., & Hatcher, R. A. (1980). Blood pressure and oral progestational agents. *American Journal of Obstetrics and Gynecology, 136*, 344–348. **189**

Hällström, T. (1987). Major depression, parental mental disorder and early family relationships. *Acta Psychiatrica Scandinavica, 75*, 259–263. **364**

Hällström, T., & Samuelsson, S. (1985). Mental health in the climacteric: The longitudinal study of women in Gothenburg. *Acta Obstetrica Gynecologica Scandinavica, Suppl. 130*, 13–18. **200, 368**

Halpern, D. F. (1986). *Sex differences in cognitive abilities*. Hillsdale, NJ: Erlbaum. **376, 392**

Hames, R. B. (1988). The allocation of parental care among the Ye'kwana. In L. Betzig, M. B. Mulder, & P. Turke (Eds.), *Human reproductive behaviour*. Cambridge: Cambridge University Press. **251**

Hamilton, D. L. (1979). A cognitive-attributional analysis of stereotyping. In J. Berkowitz (Ed.), *Advances in experimental social psychology* (Vol 12). New York: Academic Press. **287**

Hamilton, J. A., & Alagna, S. W. (1988). Toward a clinical perspective. In L. H. Gise (Ed.), *The premenstrual syndromes*. New York: Churchill Livingstone. **192, 193**

Hamilton, W. D. (1963). The evolution of altruistic behavior. *The American Naturalist, 97*, 354–356. **81**

——. (1964). The genetical evolution of social behaviour. I. *Journal of Theoretical Biology, 7*, 1–16. **81, 82**

——. (1990). Memes of Haldane and Jayakar in a theory of sex. *Journal of Genetics, 69*, 17–32. **72**

Hamilton, W. D., Axelrod, R., & Tanese, R. (1990). Sexual reproduction as adaptation to resist parasites (a review). *Proceedings of the National Academy of Sciences, USA, 87*, 3566–3573. **71, 72**

Hamilton, W. D., & Zuk, M. (1982). Heritable true fitness and bright birds: A role for parasites? *Science, 218*, 384–387. **87**

Hamilton, W. J., III, & Busse, C. (1982). Social dominance and predatory behavior of chacma baboons. *Journal of Human Evolution, 11*, 567–573. **245**

Hammar, M., Berg, G., Fåhraeus, L., & Larsson-Cohn, U. (1984). Climacteric symptoms in an unselected sample of Swedish women. *Maturitas, 6*, 345–350. **368**

Hammen, C. L., & Padesky, C. A. (1977). Sex differences in the expression of depressive responses on the Beck Depression Inventory. *Journal of Abnormal Psychology, 86*, 609–614. **363**

Hammer, R. P., Jr. (1985). The sex hormone-dependent development of opiate receptors in the rat medial preoptic area. *Brain Research, 360*, 65–74. **162**

——. (1988). Opiate receptor ontogeny in the rat medial preoptic area is androgen-dependent. *Neuroendocrinology, 48*, 336–341. **162**

Hammer, R. P., Jr., & Jacobson, C. D. (1984). Sex difference in dendritic development of the sexually dimorphic nucleus of the preoptic area in the rat. *International Journal of Developmental Neuroscience, 2*, 77–85. **163, 200**

Hampson, E. (1990a). Estrogen-related variations in human spatial and articulatory-motor skills. *Psychoneuroendocrinology, 15*, 97–111. **190**

——. (1990b). Variations in sex-related cognitive abilities across the menstrual cycle. *Brain and Cognitions, 14*, 26–43. **190, 399**

Hancke, J. L., & Dhler, K. D. (1984). Sexual differentiation of female brain function is prevented by postnatal treatment of rats with the estrogen antagonist tamoxifen. *Neuroendocrinology Letters, 6*, 201–206. **158**

Handa, R. J., Reid, D. L., & Resko, J. A. (1986). Androgen receptors in brain and pituitary of female rats: Cyclic changes and comparisons with the male. *Biology of Reproduction, 34*, 293–303. **180, 203**

Handa, R. J., Roselli, C. E., & Resko, J. A. (1988). Distribution of androgen receptor in microdissected brain areas of the female baboon (Papio cynocephalus). *Brain Research, 445*, 111–116. **180, 203**

Hansen, J. W., Hoffman, H. J., & Ross, G. T. (1975). Monthly gonadotropin cycles in premenarcheal girls. *Science, 190*, 161–163. **177**

Hansen, R. D., & O'Leary, V. E. (1985). Sex-determined attributions. In V. E. O'Leary, R. K. Unger, & B. S. Wallstron (Eds.), *Women, gender, and social psychology*. Hillsdale, NJ: Erlbaum. **275**

Hapidou, E. G., & De Catanzaro, D. (1988). Sensitivity to cold pressor pain in dysmenorrheic and non-dysmenorrheic women as a function of menstrual cycle phase. *Pain, 34*, 277–283. **398**

Harcourt, A. H., Harvey, P. H., Larson, S. G., & Short, R. V. (1981). Testis weight, body weight and breeding system in primates. *Nature, 293,* 55–60. **88**

Harding, S. (1987). The instability of the analytical categories of feminist theory. In S. Harding & J. F. O'Barr (Eds.), *Sex and scientific inquiry.* Chicago: University of Chicago Press. (Original work published 1986) **15**

Hare-Mustin, R. T., & Maracek, J. (1988). The meaning of difference: Gender theory, postmodernism, and psychology. *American Psychologist, 43,* 455–464. **25, 26**

Harlan, R. E. (1988). Regulation of neuropeptide gene expression by steroid hormones. *Molecular Neurobiology, 2,* 183–200. **139**

Harpending, H. C., & Pennington, R. (1991). Age structure and sex-biased mortality among hetero pastoralists. *Human Biology, 63,* 329–353. **239**

Harpending, H., Rogers, A., & Draper, P. (1987). Human sociobiology. *Yearbook of Physical Anthropology, 30,* 127–150. **82, 91**

Harris, R. E., Zang, E. A., & Wynder, E. L. (1990). Oral contraceptives and breast cancer risk: A case-control study. *International Journal of Epidemiology, 19,* 240–246. **201**

Harrison, A. A., & Saied, L. (1977). Let's make a deal: An analysis of revelations and stipulations in lonely hearts advertisements. *Journal of Personality and Social Psychology, 35,* 257–264. **379**

Harrison, W. M., Sandberg, D., Gorman, J. M., Fyer, M., Nee, J., Uy, J., & Endicott, J. (1989). Provocation of panic with carbon dioxide inhalation in patients with premenstrual dysphoria. *Psychiatry Research, 27,* 183–192. **192**

Hart, B. L. (1974). Gonadal androgen and sociosexual behavior of male mammals: A comparative analysis. *Psychological Bulletin, 81,* 383–400. **141**

——————. (1979). Activation of sexual reflexes of male rats by dihydrotestosterone but not estrogen. *Physiology & Behavior, 23,* 107–109. **146**

——————. (1983). Role of testosterone secretion and penile reflexes in sexual behavior and sperm competition in male rats: A theoretical contribution. *Physiology & Behavior, 31,* 823–827. **151**

Harter, S. (1983). Developmental perspectives on the self-system. In E. M. Hetherington (Ed.), *Socialization, personality, and social development. Handbook of child psychology* (4th ed.), P. H. Mussen, (Series Ed.) New York:

Wiley. **212, 229**

Hartmann, H. I. (1981). The family as the locus of gender, class, and political struggle: The example of housework. *Signs: Journal of Women in Culture and Society, 6,* 366–394. **306**

Hartung, J. (1985). Matrilineal inheritance: New theory and analysis. *Behavioral and Brain Sciences, 8,* 661–688. **62**

Harvey, P. H. (1986). Birds, bands and better broods? *Trends in Ecology and Evolution, 1,* 8–9. **85**

Harvey, P. H., & Clutton-Brock, T. H. (1985). Life history variation in primates. *Evolution, 39,* 559–581. **215**

Harvey, P. H., Martin, R. D., & Clutton-Brock, T. H. (1987). Life histories in comparative perspective. In B. Smuts, D. L. Cheney, R. M. Seyfarth, R. W. Wrangham, & T. T. Struhsaker (Eds.), *Primate societies.* Chicago: University of Chicago Press. **215**

Harvey, P. H., & May, R. M. (1989). Out for the sperm count. *Nature, 337,* 508–509. **151, 186**

Harvey, P. H., & Read, A. F. (1988). When incest is not best. *Nature, 336,* 514–515. **75**

Harwerth, R. S., Smith, E. L., III, Duncan, G. C., Crawford, M. L. J., & von Noorden, G. K. (1986). Multiple sensitive periods in the development of the primate visual system. *Science, 232,* 235–238. **225**

Haskett, R. F., Steiner, M., Osmun, J. N., & Carroll, B. J. (1980). Severe premenstrual tension: Delineation of the syndrome. *Biological Psychiatry, 15,* 121–139. **193**

Haskins, J. T., & Moss, R. L. (1983). Action of estrogen and mechanical vaginocervical stimulation on the membrane excitability of hypothalamic and midbrain neurons. *Brain Research Bulletin, 10,* 489–496. **181**

Hassold, T., Benham, F., & Leppert, M. (1988). Cytogenetic and molecular analysis of sex-chromosome monosomy. *American Journal of Human Genetics, 42,* 534–541. **112**

Hassold, T. J., Sherman, S. L., Pettay, D., Page, D. C., & Jacobs, P. A. (1991). XY chromosome nondisjunction in man is associated with diminished recombination in the pseudoautosomal region. *American Journal of Human Genetics, 49,* 253–260. **112**

Hatton, J. D., & Ellisman, M. H. (1982). A restructuring of hypothalamic synapses is associated with motherhood. *Journal of Neuroscience, 2,* 704–707. **127, 138**

Hauck, W. W., & Ober, C. (1991). Statistical analysis of outcomes from repeated pregnanacies: Effects of HLA sharing on fetal loss

rates. *Genetic Epidemiology, 8,* 187–197. **74**

Haug, H., Khl, S., Mecke, E., Sass, N.-L., & Wasner, K. (1984). The significance of morphometric procedures in the investigation of age changes in cytoarchitectonic structures of human brain. *International Journal of Brain Research and Neurobiology, 25,* 353–374. **165**

Haus, E., Lakatua, D. J., Halberg, F., Halberg, E., Cornelissen, G., Sachett, L. L., Berg, H. G., Kawasaki, T., Ueno, M., Uezono, K., Matsuoka, M., & Omae, T. (1980). Chronobiological studies of plasma prolactin in women in Kyushu, Japan, and Minnesota, USA. *Journal of Clinical Endocrinology and Metabolism, 51,* 632–640. **196**

Hausfater, G., & Skoblick, B. (1985). Perimenstrual behavior changes among female yellow baboons: Some similarities to premenstrual syndrome (PMS) in women. *American Journal of Primatology, 9,* 165–172. **192**

Hayghe, H. (1986). Rise in mothers' labor force activity includes those with infants. *Monthly Labor Review, 109,* 43–45. **324**

Hayman, D. L., Moore, H. D. M., & Evans, E. P. (1988). Further evidence of novel sex differences in chiasma distribution in marsupials. *Heredity, 61,* 455–458. **100, 101**

Heckman, N. A., Bryson, R., & Bryson, J. B. (1977). Problems of professional couples: A content analysis. *Journal of Marriage and the Family, 39,* 323–330. **328**

Hedges, L. V., & Becker, B. J. (1986). Statistical methods in the meta-analysis of research on gender differences. In J. S. Hyde and M. C. Linn (Eds.), *The psychology of gender: Advances through meta-analyses.* Baltimore, MD: Johns Hopkins University Press. **37**

Heerboth, J. R., & Ramanaiah, N. V. (1985). Evaluation of the BSRI masculine and feminine items using desirability and stereotype ratings. *Journal of Personality Assessment, 49,* 264–270. **44**

Heilbrun, A. B., Jr. (1976). Measurement of masculine and feminine sex role identities as independent dimensions. *Journal of Consulting and Clinical Psychology, 44,* 183–190. **44**

Heilman, M. E. (1980). The impact of situational factors on personnel decisions concerning women: Varying the sex composition of the applicant pool. *Organizational Behavior and Human Performance, 26,* 386–395. **280**

Heilman, M. E., Simon, M. C., & Repper, D. P. (1987). Intentionally favored, unintentionally harmed? Impact of sex-based preferential selection of self-perceptions and self-evaluations. *Journal of Applied Psychology, 72,* 62–68. **330**

Heilman, M. E., & Stopeck, M. H. (1985). Attractiveness and corporate success: Different causal attributions for males and females. *Journal of Applied Psychology, 70,* 379–388. **284**

Heim, L. M., & Timiras, P. S. (1963). Gonad-brain relationship: Precocious brain maturation after estradiol in rats. *Journal of Physiology, 72,* 598–606. **157**

Heiman, J. R. (1980). Female sexual response patterns: interactions of physiological, affective, and contextual cues. *Archives of General Psychiatry, 37,* 1311–1316. **382–383**

Heinsbroek, R. P. W., van Haaren, F., Feenstra, M. G. P., van Galen, H., Boer, G., & van de Poll, N. E. (1990). Sex differences in the effects of inescapable footshock on central catecholaminergic and serotonergic activity. *Pharmacology, Biochemistry & Behavior, 37,* 539–550. **362, 369**

Held, R., Bauer, J., & Gwiazda, J. (1988). Age of onset of binocularity correlates with level of plasma testosterone in male infants. *Investigative Opthamology & Visual Science, 29,* 60. **236**

Held, R., Shimojo, S., & Gwiazda, J. (1984). Gender differences in the early development of human visual resolution. *Investigative Opthalmology & Visual Science, 25,* 220. **236**

Heller, K. A., & Parsons, J. E. (1981). Sex differences in teachers' evaluative feedback and students' expectancies for success in mathematics. *Child Development, 52,* 1015–1019. **312**

Helmreich, R. L., Spence, J. T., & Gibson, R. H. (1982). Sex-role attitudes: 1972-1980. *Personality and Social Psychology Bulletin, 8,* 656–663. **273**

Helmreich, R. L., Spence, J. T., & Holahan, C. K. (1979). Psychological androgyny and sex role flexibility: A test of two hypotheses. *Journal of Personality and Social Psychology, 37,* 1631–1644. **45**

Helmreich, R. L., Spence, J. T., & Wilhelm, J. A. (1981). A psychometric analysis of the Personal Attributes Questionnaire. *Sex Roles, 7,* 1097–1108. **48**

Hemelrijk, C. K., & Ek, A. (1991). Reciprocity and interchange of grooming and "support" in captive chimpanzees. *Animal Behaviour, 41,* 923–936. **264, 369**

Henderson, B. E., Paganini-Hill, A., & Ross, R. K. (1991). Decreased

mortality in users of estrogen replacement therapy. *Archives of Internal Medicine, 151,* 75–78. **201**

Hendrick, S., Hendrick, C., Slapion-Foote, M. J., & Foote, F. H. (1985). Gender differences in sexual attitudes. *Journal of Personality and Social Psychology, 48,* 1630–1642. **384**

Hendricks, S. E., Graber, B., & Rodriguez-Sierra, J. F. (1989). Neuroendocrine responses to exogenous estrogen: No differences between heterosexual and homosexual men. *Psychoneuroendocrinology, 14,* 177–185. **388**

Hendricks, S. E., Lehman, J. R., & Oswalt, G. (1982). Responses to copulatory stimulation in neonatally androgenized female rats. *Journal of Comparative and Physiological Psychology, 96,* 834–845. **125**

Hennessey, A. C., Wallen, K., & Edwards, D. A. (1986). Preoptic lesions increase the display of lordosis by male rats. *Brain Research, 370,* 21–28. **162**

Hepper, P. G. (1986). Kin recognition: Functions and mechanisms, a review. *Biological Reviews, 61,* 65–93. **83**

Hepper, P. G., Shahdullah, S., & White, R. (1990). Origins of fetal handedness. *Nature, 347,* 431. **173**

Herdt, G. H., & Davidson, J. (1988). The Sambia "Turnim-man": Sociocultural and clinical aspects of gender formation in male pseudohermaphrodites with 5-alpha-reductase deficiency in Papua New Guinea. *Archives of Sexual Behavior, 17,* 33–56. **169**

Heritage, A. S., Stumpf, W. E., Sar, M., & Grant, L. D. (1980). Brainstem catecholamine neurons are target sites for sex steroid hormones. *Science, 207,* 1377–1379. **139**

Herre, E. A., Leigh, E. G., Jr., & Fischer, E. A. (1987). Sex allocation in animals. In S. C. Stearns (Ed.), *The evolution of sex and its consequences.* Boston: Birkhauser. **69**

Herron, W. G., Goodman, C. K., & Herron, M. J. (1983). Comparability of sex-role measures. *Psychological Reports, 53,* 1087–1094. **46**

Hetherington, E. M. (1989). Coping with family transitions: Winners, losers, and survivors. *Child Development, 60,* 1–14. **223, 299, 300, 356, 357**

Hetherington, E. M., Camara, K. A., & Featherman, D. L. (1983). Achievement and intellectual functioning of children in one-parent households. In J. T. Spence (Ed.), *Achievement and achievement motives.* San Francisco: W. H. Freeman. **299, 300**

Hewlett, B. S. (1988). Sexual selection

and paternal investment among Aka pygmies. In L. Betzig, M. B. Mulder, & P. Turke (Eds.), *Human reproductive behaviour.* Cambridge: Cambridge University Press. **252**

Hewlett, B. S., & Cavalli-Sforza, L. L. (1986). Cultural transmission among Aka pygmies. *American Anthropologist, 88,* 922–934. **253**

Heywood, J. S. (1989). Sexual selection by the handicap mechanism. *Evolution, 43,* 1387–1397. **87**

Hickson, R. C., Czerwinski, S. M., Falduto, M. T., & Young, A. P. (1990). Glucocorticoid antagonism by exercise and androgen-anabolic steroids. *Medicine and Science in Sports and Exercise, 22,* 331–340. **202**

Hier, D. B., Atkins, L., & Perlo, V. P. (1980). Learning disorders and sex chromosome aberrations. *Journal of Mental Deficiency Research, 24,* 17–26. **113**

Higgins, E. T., King, G. A., & Mavin, G. H. (1982). Individual construct accessibility and subjective impressions and recall. *Journal of Personality and Social Psychology, 43,* 35–47. **274**

Higley, J. D., Suomi, S. J., & Linnoila, M. (1991). CSF monoamine metabolite concentrations vary according to age, rearing, and sex, and are influenced by the stressor of social separation in rhesus monkeys. *Psychopharmacology, 103,* 551–556. **351, 369**

Hill, C. T., Rubin, Z., & Peplau, L. A. (1976). Breakups before marriage: The end of 103 affairs. *Journal of Social Issues, 32,* 147–168. **380**

Hill, G. E. (1990). Female house finches prefer colourful males: Sexual selection for a condition-dependent trait. *Animal Behaviour, 40,* 563–572. **87**

————. (1991). Plumage coloration is a sexually selected indicator of male quality. *Nature, 350,* 337–339. **86**

Hill, J. (1984). Prestige and reproductive success in man. *Ethology and Sociobiology, 5,* 77–95. **350**

Hill, J. P., Holmbeck, G. N., Marlow, L., Green, T. M., & Lynch, M. E. (1985). Menarcheal status and parent-child relations in families of seventh-grade girls. *Journal of Youth and Adolescence, 14,* 301–316. **228**

Hill, K. (1982). Hunting and human evolution. *Journal of Human Evolution, 11,* 521–544. **243, 244**

Hill, K., & Hurtado, A. M. (1989). Hunter-gatherers of the New World. *American Scientist, 77,* 437–443. **245**

Hill, K., & Kaplan, H. (1988a). Tradeoffs in male and female reproductive strategies among the Ache: Part 1. In L. Betzig, M. B. Mulder, & P. Turke (Eds.), *Human reproductive behaviour.* Cambridge: Cambridge University Press. **245**

_____. (1988b). Tradeoffs in male and female reproductive strategies among the Ache: Part 2. In L. Betzig, M. B. Mulder, & P. Turke (Eds.), *Human reproductive behaviour.* Cambridge: Cambridge University Press. **245**

Hilton, J. L., & Darley, J. M. (1985). Constructing other persons: A limit on the effect. *Journal of Experimental Social Psychology, 21,* 1–18. **276**

Hinde, R. A. (1981). Attachment: Some conceptual and biological issues. In J. Stevenson-Hinde & C. Murray Park (Eds.), *The place of attachment in human behavior.* New York: Basic Books. **222**

_____. (1989). Relations between levels of complexity in the behavioral sciences. *Journal of Nervous and Mental Disease, 177,* 655–667. **21**

Hines, M., Alsum, P., Roy, M., Gorski, R. A., & Goy, R. W. (1987). Estrogenic contributions to sexual differentiation in the female guinea pig: Influences of diethylstilbestrol and tamoxifen on neural, behavior, and ovarian development. *Hormones and Behavior, 21,* 402–417. **158**

Hirsch, J. V. B., & Tieman, S. B. (1987). Perceptual development and experience-dependent changes in cat visual cortex. In M. H. Bornstein (Ed.), *Sensitive periods in development.* Hillsdale, NJ: Ehrlbaum. **225**

Hirschfeld, R. M. A., Klerman, G. L., Clayton, P. J., Keller, M. B., & Andreasen, N. C. (1984). Personality and gender-related differences in depression. *Journal of Affective Disorders, 7,* 211–221. **363**

Hirschfeld, R. M. A., Klerman, G. L., Lavorit, P., et al. (1989). Premorbid personality assessments of first onset of major depression. *Archives of General Psychiatry, 46,* 345–350. **350**

Ho, H.-Z., Gilger, J. W., & Brink, T. M. (1986). Effects of menstrual cycle on spatial information-processes. *Perceptual and Motor Skills, 63,* 743–751. **399**

Hobson, W., Coulston, F., Faiman, C., Winter, J. S. D., & Reyes, F. (1976). Reproductive endocrinology of female chimpanzees: A suitable model of humans. *Journal of Toxicology and Environmental Health, 1,* 657–668. **197**

Hock, E., DeMeis, D., & McBride, S. (1988). Maternal separation anxiety: Its role in the balance of employment and motherhood in mothers of infants. In A. E. Gottfried & A. W. Gottfried (Eds.), *Maternal employment and children's development.* New York: Plenum. **300**

Hodgen, C. D., Goodman, A. L., O'Connor, A., & Johnson, D. K. (1977). Menopause in rhesus monkeys: Model for study of disorders in the human climacteric. *American Journal of Obstetrics and Gynecology, 127,* 581–584. **189**

Hoelzer, G. A. (1989). The good parent process of sexual selection. *Animal Behaviour, 38,* 1067–1078. **86**

Hoepfner, B. A., & Ward, I. L. (1988). Prenatal and neonatal androgen exposure interact to affect sexual differentiation in female rats. *Behavioral Neuroscience, 102,* 61–65. **150**

Hoffman, C., & Hurst, N. (1990). Gender stereotypes: Perception or rationalization? *Journal of Personality and Social Psychology, 58,* 197–208. **287, 341**

Hoffman, L. W. (1977). Changes in family roles, socialization, and sex differences. *American Psychologist, 32,* 644–657. **301**

_____. (1989). Effects of maternal employment in the two-parent family. *American Psychologist, 44,* 283–292. **294, 300**

_____. (1991). The influence of family environment on personality: Accounting for sibling differences. *Psychological Bulletin, 110,* 187–203. **233, 298**

Hoffman, M. (1991a). How parents make their mark on genes. *Science, 252,* 1250–1251. **103**

_____. (1991b). Unraveling the genetics of fragile X syndrome. *Science, 252,* 1070. **121**

Hoffman, M. L. (1960). Power assertion by the parent and its impact on the child. *Child Development, 31,* 129–143. **356**

Hofman, M. A., & Swaab, D. F. (1991). Sexual dimorphism of the human brain: Myth and reality. *Experimental and Clinical Endocrinology, 98,* 161–170. **165**

Hogan, J. A. (1988). Cause and function in the development of behavior systems. In E. M. Blass (Ed.), *Handbook of behavioral neurobiology, Vol. 9, Developmental psychobiology and behavioral ecology.* New York: Plenum. **223, 224**

Hogg, M. A., & Turner, J. C. (1987). Intergroup behaviour, self-stereotyping and the salience of social categories. *British Journal of Social Psychology, 26,* 325–340. **280**

Holden, C. (1986). Manic depression and creativity. *Science, 233,* 725. **367**

_____. (1991). Career trends for the '90s. *Science, 252,* 1–24 (special insert). **324, 325**

Holden, G. W., & Edwards, L. A. (1989). Parental attitudes toward child rearing: Instruments, issues, and implications. *Psychological Bulletin, 106,* 29–58. **298**

Holekamp, K. E., & Sherman, P. W. (1989). Why male ground squirrels disperse. *American Scientist, 77,* 232–239. **242**

Hollis, K. L. (1982). Pavlovian conditioning of signal-centered action patterns and autonomic behavior: a biological analysis of function. *Advances in the study of behavior, 12,* 1–64. **209**

_____. (1984). The biological function of Pavlovian conditioning: the best defense is a good offense. *Journal of Experimental Psychology: Animal Behavior Processes, 10,* 413–425. **209**

Hollis, K. L., Cadieux, E. L., & Colbert, M. M. (1989). The biological function of Pavlovian conditioning: A mechanism for mating success in the blue gourami (Trichogaster trichopterus). *Journal of Comparative Psychology, 103,* 115–121. **209**

Holmes, S. J., & Robins, L. N. (1988). The role of parental disciplinary practices in the development of depression and alcoholism. *Psychiatry, 51,* 24–35. **364**

Holmes, V. L., & Esses, L. M. (1988). Factors influencing Canadian high school girls' career motivation. *Psychology of Women Quarterly, 12,* 313–328. **327**

Holmes, W. G. (1988). Kinship and the development of social preferences. In E. M. Blass (Ed.), *Handbook of behavioral neurobiology, Vol. 9, Developmental psychobiology and behavior ecology.* Ann Arbor: University of Michigan. **93**

Holyoak, K. J., Koh, K., & Nisbett, R. E. (1989). A theory of conditioning: Inductive learning within rule-based default hierarchies. *Psychological Review, 96,* 315–340. **212**

Hook, E. B. (1979). Extra sex chromosomes and human behavior: The nature of the evidence regarding XYY, XXY, XXYY, and XXX genotypes. In H. L. Vallet & I. H. Porter (Eds.), *Genetic mechanisms of sexual development,* pp. 437–464. New York: Academic Press. **114, 115**

Hook, E. B., Schreinemachers, D. M., Willey, A. M., & Cross, P. K. (1983). Rates of mutant structural chromosome rearrangements in human fetuses: Data from prenatal cytogenetic studies and associations with maternal age and parental mutagen exposure. *American Journal of Human Genetics, 35,* 96–109. **111**

_____. (1984). Inherited structural cytogenetic abnormalities detected incidentally in fetuses diagnosed prenatally: Frequency, parental-age associations, sex-ratio trends, and comparisons with rates of mutants. *American Journal of Human Genetics, 36,* 422–443. **111**

House, J. S., Umberson, D., & Landis, K. R. (1988). Structures and processes of social support. *Annual Review of Sociology, 14,* 293-318. **346**

Houser, B. B., Berkman, S. L., & Bardsley, P. (1985). Sex and birth order differences in filial behavior. *Sex Roles, 13,* 641–652. **346**

Howard, J. A., Blumstein, P., & Schwartz, P. (1987). Social or evolutionary theories? Some observations on preferences in human mate selection. *Journal of Personality and Social Psychology, 53,* 194–200. **379, 380, 381**

Howard, J. A., & Leber, B. D. (1988). Social-izing attribution: Generalization to "real" social environments. *Journal of Applied Social Psychology, 18,* 664–687. **286**

Hoyenga, K. B., & Hoyenga, K. T. (1979). *The question of sex differences: Psychological, cultural, and biological issues.* Boston: Little, Brown. **15, 17, 137, 197, 290**

_____. (1984). *Motivational explanations of behavior: Evolutionary, physiological, and cognitive ideas.* Monterey, CA: Brooks/Cole. **11, 12, 14, 15, 17, 36, 40, 91, 317, 351, 383, 388**

_____. (1988). *Psychobiology: The neuron and behavior.* Monterey, CA: Brooks/Cole. **2, 14, 17, 21, 134, 137, 138, 152, 168, 179, 180, 195, 211, 214, 224, 225, 351, 359, 388, 397**

_____. (1993). *A manual to accompany Gender-Related Differences: Origins and Outcomes.* Allyn & Bacon. **30, 45, 46, 79, 105, 112, 113, 133, 148, 149, 160, 161, 166, 168, 170, 173, 174, 183, 190, 191, 199, 229, 234, 242, 252, 253, 254, 271, 276, 290, 301, 304, 305, 341, 351, 358, 359, 361, 367, 368, 370, 374, 375, 376, 377, 387, 388, 391, 395, 396, 397, 398, 399**

Hoyenga, K. I., & Richert, A. J. (1990, May). *Differences in cognitive structure as a function of level of stereotyping of women.* Paper presented at Midwestern Psychological Convention, Chicago. **277**

Hoyt, B., Leinbach, M. D., & Fagot, B. I. (1991). Is there coherence among the cognitive components of gender acquisition? *Sex Roles, 24,* 195–209. **290, 298, 332**

Hrdy, S. B. (1979). The evolution of human sexuality: The latest word and the last. *Quarterly Review of Biology, 54,* 309–314. **383**

Hu, D.-N., Qiu, W.-Q., Wu, B.-T., Fang, L.-Z., Zhou, F., Gu, Y.-P., Zhang, Q.-H., Yan, J.-H., Ding, Y.-Q, & Wong, H. (1991). Genetic aspects of antibiotic induced deafness: Mitochondrial inheritance. *Journal of Medical Genetics, 28,* 79–83. **98**

Huang, H. H., Steger, R. W., Bruni, J. F., & Meites, J. (1978). Patterns of sex steroid and gonadotropin secretion in aging female rats. *Endocrinology, 103,* 1855–1859. **198**

Huchcroft, S. A., & Tanney, B. L. (1988). Sex-specific suicide trends in Canada, 1971-1985. *International Journal of Epidemiology, 17,* 839–843. **366**

Huesmann, L. R., Eron, L. D., Lefkowitz, M. M., & Walder, L. O. (1984). Stability of aggression over time and generations. *Developmental Psychology, 20,* 1120–1134. **356, 357**

Hughes, B. J., Sullivan, H. J., & Beaird, J. (1986). Continuing motivation of boys and girls under differing evaluation conditions and achievement levels. *American Educational Research Journal, 23,* 660–667. **333**

Hughes, L. A. (1988). "But that's not really mean": Competing in a cooperative mode. *Sex Roles, 19,* 669–687. **316, 318**

Hultkrantz, A. (1983). Commentary on "The North American berdache." *Current Anthropology, 24,* 459. **258**

Humphreys, A. P., & Smith, P. K. (1984). Rough-and-tumble in preschool and playground. In P. K. Smith (Ed.), *Play in animals and humans.* New York: Basil Blackwell. **316**

Hunt, K., Vessey, M., & McPherson, K. (1990). Mortality in a cohort of long-term users of hormone replacement therapy: An updated analysis. *Journal of Obstetrics and Gynaecology, 97,* 1080–1086. **203**

Hunter, M. S. (1990). Psychological and somatic experience of the menopause: A prospective study. *Psychosomatic Medicine, 52,* 357–367. **200**

Hurtado, A. M., Hawkes, K., Hill, K., & Kaplan, H. (1985). Female subsistence strategies among Ache hunter-gatherers of eastern Paraguay. *Human Ecology, 13,* 1–28. **246**

Huss, E. T., & Kayson, W. A. (1985). Effects of age and sex on speed of finding embedded figures. *Perceptual and Motor Skills, 61,* 591–594. **374**

Huston, A. C. (1983). Sex-typing. In P. H. Mussen & E. M. Hetherington (Eds.), *Handbook of child psychology, Vol. 4, Socializations, personality, and social behavior,* (4th ed.). New York: Wiley. **9, 12, 232, 298, 300**

Huston, A. C., & Carpenter, C. J. (1985). Gender differences in preschool classrooms: The effects of sex-typed activity choices. In L. C. Wilkinson & C. B. Marrett (Eds.), *Gender-related differences in the classroom.* New York: Academic Press. **320**

Huston, A. C., Carpenter, C. J., Atwater, J. B., & Johnson, L. M. (1986). Gender, adult structuring of activities, and social behavior in middle childhood. *Child Development, 57,* 1200–1209. **320**

Hutchison, J. B., & Steimer, Th. (1984). Androgen metabolism in the brain: Behavioural correlates. *Progress in Brain Research, 61,* 23-51. **156**

Hutter, H. S., & Gibson, M. J. (1988). Effect of neonatal androgenization on positive feedback in female mice. *Biology of Reproduction, 38,* 636–638. **145**

Hyde, J. S. (1981). How large are cognitive gender differences? A meta-analysis using 2 and d. *American Psychologist, 36,* 892–901. **372, 373, 389**

_____. (1986). Gender differences in aggression. In J. S. Hyde & M. C. Linn (Eds.), *The psychology of gender: advances through meta-analysis.* Baltimore, MD: Johns Hopkins University Press. **341**

_____. (1990). Meta-analysis and the psychology of gender differences. *Signs: Journal of Women in Culture and Society, 16,* 55–73. **345**

Hyde, J. S., Geiringer, E. R., & Yen, W. M. (1975). On the empirical relation between spatial ability and sex differences in other aspects of cognitive performance. *Multivariate Behavioral Research* (July), 289–309. **373**

Hyde, J. S., Fennema, E., & Lamon, S. J. (1990). Gender differences in mathematics performance: A meta-analysis. *Psychological Bulletin, 107,* 139–155. **373**

Hyde, J. S., & Linn, M. C. (1988). Gender differences in verbal ability: A meta-analysis. *Psychological Bulletin, 104,* 53–69. **372**

Hynd, G. W., & Semrud-Clikeman, M. (1989a). Dyslexia and neurodevelopmental pathology: Relationships to cognition, intelligence, and reading skill acquisition. *Journal of Learning Disabilities, 22,* 204–220. **374**

Hynd, G. W., & Semrud-Clikeman, M. (1989b). Dyslexia and brain morphology. *Psychological Bulletin, 106*, 447–482. **374**

Iazzo, A. N. (1983). The construction and validation of attitudes toward men scale. *Psychological Record, 33*, 371–378. **277**

Imperato-McGinley, J., & Gautier, T. (1986). Inherited 5-reductase deficiency in man. *Trends in Genetics* (May), 130–133. **168**

Imperato-McGinley, J., Peterson, R. E., & Gautier, T. (1976). Gender identity and hermaphroditism. *Science, 191*, 872. **169**

Imperato-McGinley, J., Peterson, R. E., Leshin, M., Griffin, J. E., Cooper, G., Draghi, S., Berenyi, M., & Wilson, J. D. (1980). Steroid 5-reductase deficiency in a 65-year-old male pseudohermaphrodite: The natural history, ultrastructure of the testes, and evidence for inherited enzyme heterogeneity. *Journal of Clinical Endocrinology and Metabolism, 50*, 15–22. **168, 169**

Imperato-McGinley, J., Pichardo, M., Gautier, T., Voyer, D., & Bryden, M. P. (1991). Cognitive abilities in androgen-insensitive subjects: Comparison with control males and females from the same kindred. *Clinical Endocrinology, 34*, 341–347. **168**

Ims, R. A. (1987). Responses in the spatial organization and behaviour to manipulations of the food resource in the vole Clethrionomys rufocanus. *Journal of Animal Ecology, 56*, 585–596. **242**

——————. (1988). Spatial clumping of sexually receptive females induces space sharing among male voles. *Nature, 335*, 541–543. **242**

Ingemann-Hansen, T., & Halkjr-Kristensen, J. (1982). Seasonal variation of maximal oxygen consumption rate in humans. *European Journal of Applied Physiology, 49*, 151–157. **203**

Ingemar, P., Hans-Olov, A., Reinhold, B., Brith, K. U., & robert, H. (1990). Survival in women receiving hormone replacement therapy. A record-linkage study of a large population-based cohort. *Journal of Clinical Epidemiology, 43*, 677–685. **201**

Inglehart, M., & Brown, D. R. (1988, April). *Competition and gender differences in academic achievementa longitudinal analysis.* Paper presented at Midwestern Psychological Association, Chicago. **319**

Inglehart, M. R., Nyquist, L., Brown, D. R., & Moore, W. (1987, May). *Gender differences in academic achievement--the result of cognitive or affective factors?* Paper presented at Midwestern Psychological Association, Chicago. **320, 325**

Inglis, J., & Lawson, J. S. (1981). Sex differences in the effects of unilateral brain damage on intelligence. *Science, 212*, 693–695. **400**

Ingram, R. E., Cruet, D., Johnson, B. R., & Wisnicki, K. S. (1988). Self-focused attention, gender, gender role, and vulnerability to negative affect. *Journal of Personality and Social Psychology, 55*, 967–978. **366**

Jablonka, E., & Lamb, M. J. (1988). Meiotic pairing constraints and the activity of sex chromosomes. *Journal of Theoretical Biology, 133*, 23–36. **104**

Jacklin, C. N. (1989). Female and male: Issues of gender. *American Psychologist, 44*, 127-133. **313**

Jacklin, C. N., & Maccoby, E. E. (1978). Social behavior at thirty-three months in same-sex and mixed-sex dyads. *Child Development, 49*, 557–569. **314**

Jacklin, C. N., Maccoby, E. E., & Doering, C. H. (1983). Neonatal sex-steroid hormones and timidity in 6-18-month-old boys and girls. *Developmental Psychobiology, 16*, 163–168. **171, 359, 368**

Jacklin, C. N., Maccoby, E. E., Doering, C. H., & King, D. R. (1984). Neonatal sex-steroid hormones and muscular strength of boys and girls in the first three years. *Developmental Psychobiology, 17*, 301–310. **171**

Jacklin, C. N., & Mischel, H. N. (1973). As the twig is bentsex role stereotyping in the early readers. *School Psychology Digest,* (Summer), 30–38. **288**

Jacklin, C. N., Wilcox, K. T., & Maccoby, E. E. (1988). Neonatal sex-steroid hormones and cognitive abilities at six years. *Developmental Psychobiology, 21*, 567–574. **171, 399**

Jackson, L. A., & Cash, T. F. (1985). Components of gender stereotypes: Their implications for inferences on stereotypic and nonstereotypic dimensions. *Personality and Social Psychology Bulletin, 11*, 326–344. **275**

Jacobs, G. H., & Neitz, J. (1985). Color vision in squirrel monkeys: Sex-related differences suggest the mode of inheritance. *Vision Research, 25*, 141–143. **105**

Jacobsen, J., & Levin, L. (1992). Research reported in, "Lower pay persists for women 'gappers.'" Peopria Journal Star, January 11. **331**

Jacobson, C. D., Arnold, A. P., & Gorski, R. A. (1987). Steroid autoradiography of the sexually dimorphic nucleus of the preoptic area. *Brain Research, 414*, 349–356. **162**

Jacobson, C. D., Davis, F. C., & Gorski, R. A. (1985). Formation of the sexually dimorphic nucleus of the preoptic area: Neuronal growth, migration and changes in cell number. *Developmental Brain Research, 21*, 7–18. **163**

Jaffe, B., Shye, D., Harlap, S., Baras, M., & Lieblich, A. (1989). Aggression, physical activity levels and sex role identity in teenagers exposed in utero to MPA. *Contraception, 40*, 351–364. **370**

Jáger, R. J., Anvret, M., Hall, K., & Scherer, G. (1990). A human XY female with a frame shift mutation in the candidate testis-determining gene SRY. *Nature, 348*, 452–455. **123**

James, W. (1890). *The principles of psychology.* New York: Holt. **5**

James, W. H. (1987a). The human sex ratio. Part 1: A review of the literature. *Human Biology, 59*, 721–752. **80**

James, W. H. (1987b). The human sex ratio. Part 2: A hypothesis and a program of research. *Human Biology, 59*, 873–900. **80**

Janman, K. (1987). Achievement motivation theory and occupational choice. *European Journal of Social Psychology, 17*, 327–346. **329**

Jardine, R., & Martin, N. G. (1983). Spatial ability and throwing accuracy. *Behavior Genetics, 13*, 331–340. **377**

Jarett, L. R. (1984). Psychosocial and biological influences on menstruation: Synchrony, cycle length, and regularity. *Psychoneuroendocrinology, 9*, 21–28. **191**

Jarman, P. (1983). Mating system and sexual dimorphism in large, terrestrial, mammalian herbivores. *Biological Review, 58*, 485–520. **88**

Jayne, C. (1981). A two-dimensional model of female sexual response. *Journal of Sex & Marital Therapy, 7*, 3-30. **383**

Jean-Faucher, Ch., Berger, M., Gallon, Ch., de Turckheim, M., Veyssiere, G., & Jean, Cl. (1987). Sex-related differences in renal size in mice: Ontogeny and influence of neonatal androgens. *Journal of Endocrinology, 115*, 241–246. **152**

Jeffery, L., & Durkin, K. (1989). Children's reactions to televised counter-stereotyped male sex role behaviour as a function of age, sex and perceived power. *Social*

Behaviour, 4, 285–310. **293**

Jenkins, J. S., & Hall, C. J. (1977). Metabolism of [^{14}C]testosterone by human foetal and adult brain tissue. *Journal of Endocrinology, 74*, 415–429. **180**

Jennings (Walstedt), J., Geis, F. L., & Brown, V. (1980). Influence of television commercials on women's self-confidence and independent judgment. *Journal of Personality and Social Psychology, 38*, 203–210. **293**

Jensen, A. R. (1983). Effects of inbreeding on mental-ability factors. *Personality and Individual Differences, 4*, 71–87. **75**

Jensen, D. D. (1989). Pathologies of science, precognition, and modern psychophysics. *The Skeptical Inquirer, 13*, 147-160. **10, 18**

Jensen, L. C., Christensen, R., & Wilson, D. J. (1985). Predicting young women's role preference for parenting and work. *Sex Roles, 13*, 507–514. **328**

Jessor, R., Costa, F., Jessor, L., & Donovan, J. E. (1983). Time of first intercourse: A prospective study. *Journal of Personality and Social Psychology, 44*, 608–626. **374**

Jick, H., Dinan, B., & Rothman, K. J. (1978). Oral contraceptives and nonfatal myocardial infarction. *Journal of the American Medical Association, 239*, 1403–1406. **201**

Joffe, L. S., Vaughn, B. E., Barglow, P., & Benveniste, R. (1985). Biobehavioral antecedents in the development of infant-mother attachment. In M. Reite & T. Field (Eds.), *The psychobiology of attachment and separation*. New York: Academic Press. **148**

Johnson, E. S. (1984). Sex differences in problem solving. *Journal of Educational Psychology, 76*, 1359–1371. **373**

Johnson, J. A. (1987). Dominance rank in juvenile olive baboons, Papio anubis: The influence of gender, size, maternal rank and orphaning. *Animal Behaviour, 35*, 1694–1708. **79**

Johnson, S., Flinn, J. M., & Tyler, Z. E. (1979). Effect of practice and training in spatial skills on embedded figures scores of males and females. *Perceptual and Motor Skills, 48*, 975–984. **395**

Johnston, T. D. (1982). Selective costs and benefits in the evolution of learning. *Advances in the Study of Behavior, 12*, 65–106. **214**

Jolly, A. (1985). The evolution of primate behavior. *American Scientist, 73*, 230–239. **80**

Jones, E. E. (1986). Interpreting interpersonal behavior: The effects of expectancies. *Science, 234*, 41–46. **41, 274, 382**

Jones, J. S., & Harvey, P. H. (1987). It pays to be different. *Nature, 328*, 575–576. **68**

Jones, K. J., McEwen, B. S., & Pfaff, D. W. (1988). Quantitative assessment of early and discontinuous estradiol-induced effects on ventromedial hypothalamic and preoptic area proteins in female rat brain. *Neuroendocrinology 48*, 561–568. **150**

Jones, R. A., Sensenig, J., & Haley, J. V. (1974). Self-descriptions: Configurations of content and order effects. *Journal of Personality and Social Psychology, 30*, 36–45. **47, 50**

Jones, S. L., & Lamke, L. K. (1985). The relationship between sex role orientation, self esteem, and sextyped occupational choice of college women. *Psychology of Women Quarterly, 9*, 145–152. **327, 328**

Jorm, A. F. (1987). Sex and age differences in depression: A quantitative synthesis of published research. *Australian and New Zealand Journal of Psychiatry, 21.* 46–53. **363**

Jost, A. (1983). Genetic and hormonal factors in sex differentiation of the brain. *Psychoneuroendocrinology, 8*, 183–193. **156**

Juraska, J. M. (1990). Gender differences in the dendritic tree of granule neurons in the hippocampal dentate gyrus of weaning age rats. *Developmental Brain Research, 53*, 291–294. **225, 397**
————. (1991). Sex differences in cognitive regions of the rat brain. *Psychoneuroendocrinology, 16*, 105–109. **137, 222**

Juraska, J. M., Fitch, J. M., & Washburne, D. L. (1989). The dendritic morphology of pyramidal neurons in the rat hippocampal CA3 area. II. Effects of gender and the environment. *Brain Research, 479*, 115–119. **137**

Juraska, J. M., & Kopcik, J. R. (1988). Sex and environmental influences on the size and ultrastructure of the rat corpus callosum. *Brain Research, 450*, 1–8. **397**

Juraska, J. M., Kopcik, J. R., Washburne, D. O., & Perry, D. L. (1988). Neonatal castration of male rats affects the dendritic response to differential environments in granule neurons of the hippocampal dentate gyrus. *Psychobiology, 16*, 406–410. **225**

Jusssim, L. (1986). Self-fulfilling prophecies: A theoretical and integrative review. *Psychological Review, 93*, 429–445. **274**

Just, M. A., & Carpenter, P. A. (1985). Cognitive coordinate systems: Accounts of mental rotation and individual differences in

spatial ability. *Psychological Review, 92*, 137–172. **392**

Kaats, G. R., & Davis, K. E. (1970). The dynamics of sexual behavior of college students. *Journal of Marriage and the Family, 32*, 390–399. **378, 383, 384**

Kacser, H., & Burns, J. A. (1981). The molecular basis of dominance. *Genetics, 97*, 639–666. **58**

Kadowaki, T., Bevins, C. L., Cama, A., Ojamaa, K., Marcus-Samuels, B., Kadowaki, H., Beitz, L., McKeon, C., & Taylor, S. I. (1988). Two mutant alleles of the insulin receptor gene in a patient with extreme insulin resistance. *Science, 240*, 787–790. **58**

Kagan, J. (1984). *The nature of the child*. New York: Basic Books. **234**

Kagan, J., Reznick, J. S., & Snidman, N. (1988). Biological bases of childhood shyness. *Science, 240*, 167–171. **374**

Kahn, A. S., & Jean, P. J. (1983). Integration and elimination or separation and redefinition: The future of the psychology of women. *Journal of Women in Culture and Society, 8*, 659–671. **12, 25, 26**

Kail, R., Carter, P., & Pellegrino, J. (1979). The locus of sex differences in spatial ability. *Perception & Psychophysics, 26*, 182–186. **392**

Kaiser, E., Kies, M., Maass, G., Schmidt, H., Beach, R. C., Bormacher, K., Herrmann, W. M., & Richter, E. (1978). The measurement of the psychotropic effects of an androgen in aging males with psychovegetative symptomatology: A controlled double blind study of mesterolone versus placebo. *Progress in Neuro-Psychopharmacology, 2*, 505–515. **199**

Kalin, M. G., & Zumoff, B. (1990). Sex hormones and coronary disease: A review of the clinical studies. *Steroids, 55*, 330–352. **201**

Kalison, B., Warshaw, M. L., & Gibori, G. (1985). Contrasting effects of prolactin on luteal and follicular steroidogenesis. *Journal of Endocrinology, 104*, 241–250. **177, 282**

Kallman, K. D., & Borkoski, V. (1978). A sex-linked gene controlling the onset of sexual maturity in female and male platyfish (*Xiphophorus maculatus*), fecundity in females and adult size in males. *Genetics, 89*, 79–119. **98**

Kampert, J. B., Whittemore, A. S., & Pfaffenbarger, R. S. Jr. (1988). Combined effect of childbearing menstrual events, and body size on age-specific breast cancer risk. *American Journal of Epidemiology, 128*, 962–979. **203**

Kangas, J., & Bradway, K. (1971).

Intelligence at middle age: A thirty-eight-year follow-up. *Developmental Psychology, 5,* 333–337. **322**

Kaplan, H., & Hill, K. (1985a). Hunting ability and reproductive success among male Ache foragers: Preliminary results. *Current Anthropology, 26,* 131–133. **245, 246**

——. (1985b). Food sharing among Ache foragers: Tests of explanatory hypotheses. *Current Anthropology, 26,* 223–246. **245, 246**

Kaplan, J. R., Adams, M. R., Koritnik, D. R., Rose, J. C., & Manuck, S. B. (1986). Adrenal responsiveness and social status in intact and ovariectomized Macaca fascicularis. *American Journal of Primatology, 11,* 181–193. **128**

Kaplan, M. S. (1985). Formation and turnover of neuron in young and senescent animals: An electron-microscopic and morphometric analysis. *Annals of the New York Academy of Sciences, 457,* 173–192. **152**

Karpoe, K. P., & Olney, R. L. (1983). The effect of boys' or girls' toys on sex-typed play in preadolescents. *Sex Roles, 9,* 507–518. **308**

Karsch, F. J. (1987). Central actions of ovarian steroids in the feedback regulation of pulsatile secretion of luteinizing hormone. *Annual Review of Physiology, 49,* 365–382. **145**

Karsch, F. J., Dierschke, D. J., & Knobil, E. (1973). Sexual differentiation of pituitary function: apparent difference between primates and rodents. *Science, 179,* 484–486. **145**

Kasper, S., Wehr, T. A., Bartko, J. J., Gaist, P. A., & Rosenthal, N. E. (1989). Epidemiological findings of seasonal changes in mood and behavior: A telephone survey of Montgomery County, Maryland. *Archives of General Psychiatry, 46,* 823–833. **361**

Katz, D. L., Frankenburg, F. R., Benowitz, L. I., & Gilbert, J. M. (1987). Psychosis and prenatal exposure to diethylstilbestrol. *Journal of Nervous and Mental Disease, 175,* 306–308. **170**

Katz, E. J., & Madden, J. M. (1984). Using policy capturing to measure prejudicial attitudes of women toward women. *Bulletin of the Psychonomic Society, 22,* 90–91. **282**

Katz, J. (1988). *Seductions of crime: Moral and sensual attractions in doing evil.* New York: Basic Books. **355**

Katz, J. F., & Stake, J. E. (1980, May). *Responses of men and women teachers to boys and girls in the elementary school classroom.* Paper presented at Midwestern

Psychological Association, St. Louis. **311**

Katz, M., & Konner, M. (1981). The role of the father: An anthropological perspective. In M. Lamb (Ed.), *The role of the father in child development.* New York: Wiley. **250, 252, 253, 259**

Katz, P. A., & Walsh, P. V. (1991). Modification of children's gender-stereotyped behavior. *Child Development, 62,* 338–351. **290, 293**

Kaufert, P. A. (1982). Anthropology and the menopause: The development of a theoretical framework. *Maturitas, 4,* 181–193. **200**

Kauppila, A., Kivel, A., Pakarinen, A., & Vakkuri, O. (1987). Inverse seasonal relationship between melatonin and ovarian activity in humans in a region with a strong seasonal contrast in luminosity. *Journal of Clinical Endocrinology and Metabolism, 65,* 823–828. **196**

Kaye, A. M. (1983). Enzyme induction by estrogen. *Journal of Steroid Biochemistry, 19,* 33–40. **136**

Ke, F.-C., & Ramirez, V. D. (1990). Binding of progesterone to nerve cell membranes of rat brain using progesterone conjugated to 125I-bovine serum albumin as a ligand. *Journal of Neurochemistry, 54,* 467–472. **136**

Kearins, J. M. (1981). Visual spatial memory in Australian aboriginal children of desert regions. *Cognitive Psychology, 13,* 434–460. **377**

Keddy, A. C. (1986). Female mate choice in vervet monkeys (Cercopithecus aethiops sabaeus). *American Journal of Primatology, 10,* 125–134. **83**

Kelly, J. A., Caudill, M. S., Hathorn, S., & O'Brien, C. G. (1977). Socially undesirable sex-correlated characteristics: Implications for androgyny and adjustment. *Journal of Consulting and Clinical Psychology, 41,* 1185–1186. **48**

Kelly, J. A., Furman, W., & Young, V. (1978). Problems associated with the typological measurement of sex roles and androgyny. *Journal of Consulting and Clinical Psychogy, 46,* 1574–1576. **46**

Kemnitz, J. W. (1981). Ovarian hormones and eating behavior in rhesus monkeys. *Neuroscience Abstracts, 7,* 615. **189**

Kemnitz, J. W., Gibber, J. R., Lindsay, K. A., & Eisele, S. G. (1989). Effects of ovarian hormones on eating behaviors, body weight, and glucoregulation in rhesus monkeys. *Hormones and Behavior, 23,* 235–250. **189**

Kendall, D. A., Stancel, G. M., & Enna, S. J. (1981). Imipramine:

Effects of ovarian steroids on modifications in serotonin receptor binding. *Science, 211,* 1183–1185. **369**

Kendler, K. S. (1988). Indirect vertical cultural transmission: A model for nongenetic parental influences on the liability to psychiatric illness. *American Journal of Psychiatry, 145,* 657–665. **202**

Kennett, G. A., Chaoloff, F., Marcou, M., & Curzon, G. (1986). Female rats are more vulnerable than males in an animal model of depression: The possible role of serotonin. *Brain Research, 382,* 416–421. **351, 362, 369**

Kenrick, D. T., & Keefe, R. C. (1989). Time to integrate sociobiology and social psychology. *Behavioral and Brain Sciences, 12,* 24–26. **379, 381**

Kenrick, D. T., Sadalla, E. K., Groth, G., & Trost, M. R. (1990). Evolution, traits, and the stages of human courtship: Qualifying the parental investment model. *Journal of Personality, 58,* 97–116. **381**

Keogh, B. K. (1971). Pattern copying under three conditions of an expanded spatial field. *Developmental Psychology, 4,* 25–31. **377**

Kerlinger, F. N. (1986). *Foundations of behavioral research* (3rd ed.). New York: Holt, Rinehart & Winston. **27, 28**

Kerns, K. A., & Berenbaum, S. A. (1991). Sex differences in spatial ability in children. *Behavior Genetics, 21,* 383–396. **374**

Kertesz, A., & Benke, T. (1989). Sex equality in intrahemispheric language organization. *Brain and Language, 37,* 401–408. **400**

Kessler, R. C., & McLeod, J. D. (1984). Sex differences in vulnerability to undesirable life events. *American Sociological Review, 49,* 620–631. **365**

Kessler, R. C., & McRae, J. A., Jr. (1983). Trends in the relationship between sex and attempted suicide. *Journal of Health and Social Behavior, 24,* 98–110. **366**

Keverne, E. B., Eberhart, J. A., Yodyingyuad, U., & Abbott, D. H. (1984). Social influences on sex differences in the behaviour and endocrine state of talapoin monkeys. *Progress in Brain Research, 61,* 331–347. **358**

Khan, S. S., Nessim, S., Gray, R., Czer, L. S., Chaux, A., & Matloff, J. (1990). Increased mortality of women in coronary artery bypass surgery: Evidence for referral bias. *Annals of Internal Medicine, 112,* 561–567. **283**

Kihlstrom, J. F., & Cantor, N. (1984). Mental representations of the self. *Advances in Experimental Social Psychology, 17,* 1–47. **46, 47,**

50, 231

Kilbourne, E. D., Easterday, B. C., & McGregor, S. (1988). Evolution to predominance of swine influenza virus hemagglutinin mutants of predictable phenotype during single infections of the natural host. *Proceedings of the National Academy of Sciences, USA, 85,* 8098–8101. **72**

Kimball, M. M. (1986). Developing a feminist psychology of women: Past and future accomplishments. *Canadian Psychology, 27,* 248–259. **25**

Kimlicka, T. M., Wakefield, J. A., Jr., & Friedman, A. F. (1980). Comparison of factors from the Bem Sex-Role Inventory for male and female college students. *Psychological Reports, 46,* 1011–1017. **47**

Kimura, D. (1983). Sex differences in cerebral organization for speech and praxic functions. *Canadian Journal of Psychology, 37,* 19–35. **400**

_____. (1987). Are men's and women's brains really different? *Canadian Psychology, 28,* 133–147. **400**

King, K. P., & Clayson, D. E. (1988). The differential perceptions of male and female deviants. *Sociological Focus, 21,* 153–164. **283**

Kirkpatrick, M. (1982). Sexual selection and the evolution of female choice. *Evolution, 36,* 1–12. **84**

_____. (1985). Evolution of female choice and male parental investment in polygynous species: The demise of the "sexy son." *American Naturalist, 125,* 788–810. **61, 84, 86, 87**

Kirkpatrick, M., & Lande, R. (1989). The evolution of maternal characters. *Evolution, 43,* 485–503. **61, 98, 220**

Kirkpatrick, M., & Ryan, M. J. (1991). The evolution of mating preferences and the paradox of the lek. *Nature, 350,* 33–38. **84, 86**

Kitcher, P. (1982). *Vaulting ambition: sociobiology and the quest for human nature.* Boston: MIT Press. **62**

_____. (1985). Confessions of a curmudgeon. *Behavioral and Brain Sciences, 10,* 89–99. **62**

Kitson, G. C., Babri, K. B., & Roach, M. J. (1985). Who divorces and why: A review. *Journal of Family Issues, 6,* 255–293. **381, 382**

Kivelä, S.-L., & Pahkala, K. (1986). Sex and age differences of factor pattern and reliability of the Zung Self-rating Depression Scale in a Finnish elderly population. *Psychological Reports, 59,* 587–597. **363**

_____. (1987). Factor structure of the Zung Self-rating Depression Scale among a depressed elderly population. *International Journal of Psychology, 22,* 289–300. **363**

_____. (1988). Symptoms of depression in old people in Finland. *Zeitschrift fr Gerontologie, 21,* 257–263. **363**

Kjellstrand, C. M. (1988). Age, sex, and race inequality in renal transplantation. *Archives of Internal Medicine, 148,* 1305–1309. **283**

Kjellstrand, C. M., & Logan, G. M. (1987). Racial, sexual and age inequalities in chronic dialysis. *Nephron, 45,* 257–263. **283**

Klaiber, E. L., Broverman, D. M., Vogel, W., Kennedy, J. A., & Nadeau, C. J. L. (1982). Estrogens and central nervous system function: Electroencephalography, cognition, and depression. In R. C. Friedman (Ed.), *Behavior and the menstrual cycle.* New York: Marcel Dekker. **183, 190**

Kleinke, C. L., Staneski, R. A., & Mason, J. K. (1982). Sex differences in coping with depression. *Sex Roles, 8,* 877–890. **363**

Klerman, G. L., & Weissman, M. M. (1988). The changing epidemiology of depression. *Clinical Chemistry, 34,* 807–812. **360**

Knight, G. P., & Kagan, S. (1977). Development of prosocial and competitive behaviors in Anglo-American and Mexican-American children. *Child Development, 48,* 1385–1394. **318**

Knoppien, P. (1985). Rare male mating advantage: A review. *Biological Reviews, 60,* 81–117. **68**

Koch, S. (1981). The nature and limits of psychological knowledge: Lessons of a century qua Science. *American Psychologist, 36,* 257–269. **11**

Kochersperger, L. M., Parker, E. L., Siciliano, M., Darlington, G. J., & Denney, R. M. (1986). Assignment of genes for human monoamine oxidases A and B to the X chromosome. *Journal of Neuroscience Research, 16,* 601–616. **119**

Koenig, M., Moisan, J. P., Heilig, R., & Mandel, J. L. (1985). Homologies between X and Y chromosomes detected by DNA probes: Localization and evolution. *Nucleic Acids Research, 13,* 5485–5501. **118**

Koestner, R., & Wheeler, L. (1988). Self-presentation in personal advertisements: The influence of implicit notions of attraction and role expectations. *Journal of Social and Personal Relationships, 5,* 149–160. **379**

Kohlberg, L. (1966). A cognitive-developmental analysis of children's sex-role concepts and attitudes. In E. E. Maccoby (Ed.), *The development of sex differences.* Stanford: Stanford University Press. **218, 219**

_____. (1969). Stage and sequence: The cognitive-developmental approach to socialization. In D. A. Goslin (Ed.), *Handbook of socialization theory and research.* Chicago: Rand McNally. **218, 219**

Kohlberg, L., Ricks, D., & Snarey, J. (1984). Childhood development as a predictor of adaptation in adulthood. *Genetic Psychology Monographs, 110,* 91–172. **234**

Kohlberg, L., & Zigler, E. (1967). The impact of cognitive maturity on the development of sex-role attitudes in the years 4 to 8. *Genetic Psychology Monographs, 75,* 89–165. **218**

Kolata, G. (1986). Maleness pinpointed on Y chromosome. *Science, 234,* 1076–1077. **97, 106**

Kolbe, R., & LaVoie, J. C. (1981). Sex-role stereotyping in preschool children's picture books. *Social Psychology Quarterly, 44,* 369–374. **289**

Kolbinger, W., Trepel, M., Beyer, C., Pilgrim, C., & Reisert, I. (1991). The influence of genetic sex on sexual differentiation of diencephalic dopaminergic neurons in vitro and in vivo. *Brain Research, 544,* 349–352. **140**

Kondrashov, A. S. (1988). Deleterious mutations and the evolution of sexual reproduction. *Nature, 336,* 435–440. **64**

Konishi, M., & Akutagawa, E. (1988). A critical period for estrogen action on neurons of the song control system in the zebra finch. *Proceedings of the National Academy of Sciences, 85,* 7006–7007. **142**

Konner, M., & Worthman, C. (1980). Nursing frequency, gonadal functions, and birth spacing among !Kung hunter-gatherers. *Science, 207,* 788–791. **197**

Koopman, P., Gubbay, J., Vivian, N., Goodfellow, P., & Lovell-Badge, R. (1991). Male development of chromosomally female mice transgenic for Sry. *Nature, 351,* 117–121. **123**

Koopman, P., Múnsterberg, A., Capel, B., Vivian, N., & Lovell-Badge, R. (1990). Expression of a candidate sex-determining gene during mouse testis differentiation. *Nature, 348,* 450-452. **123**

Koot, H. M., & Verhulst, F. C. (1991). Prevalence of problem behavior in Dutch children aged 2-3. *Acta Psychiatrica Scandinavica, Supplementum, 83,* 1-37 (No. 367). **347**

Kotila, L., & Lönnqvist, J. (1988). Adolescent suicide attempts: Sex differences predicting suicide. *Acta Psychiatrica Scandinavica, 77,* 264–270. **366**

Kow, L.-M., & Pfaff, D. W. (1973/74). Effects of estrogen

treatment on the size of the receptive field and response threshold of pudendal nerve in the female rat. *Neuroendocrinology, 13,* 299–313. **181**

———. (1982). Responses of medullary reticulospinal and other reticular neurons to somatosensory and brainstem stimulation in anesthetized or freely-moving ovariectomized rats with or without estrogen treatment. *Experimental Brain Research, 47,* 191–202. **181**

———. (1985). Estrogen effects on neuronal responsiveness to electrical and neurotransmitter stimulation: An in vitro study on the ventromedial nucleus of the hypothalamus. *Brain Research, 347,* 1–10. **181**

Kraft, R. N., Smith, S., Dick, K., Francis, A., & Bower, S. (1991, May). *Attitudes about minorities and women: The influence of autobiographical memories.* Paper presented at the annual meeting of the Midwestern Psychological Association, Chicago. **269**

Krames, L., England, R., & Flett, G. L. (1988). The role of masculinity and femininity in depression and social satisfaction in elderly females. *Sex Roles, 19,* 713–722. **363**

Krausz, S. L. (1986). Sex roles within marriage. *Social Work, 31,* 457–464. **304, 307**

Kruijt, J. P., Bossema, I., & Lammers, G. J. (1982). Effects of early experience and male activity on mate choice in mallard females (Anas platyrhynchos). *Behaviour, 80,* 32–43. **87**

Kulik, J. A. (1983). Confirmatory attribution and the perpetuation of social beliefs. *Journal of Personality and Social Psychology, 44,* 1171–1181. **275**

Kupfer, D. J., Carpenter, L. L., & Frank, E. (1988). Is bipolar II a unique disorder? *Comprehensive Psychiatry, 29,* 228–236. **103**

Kuyler, P. L., Rosenthal, L., Igel, G., Dunner, D. L., & Fieve, R. R. (1980). Psychopathology among children of manic-depressive patients. *Biological Psychiatry, 15,* 589–597. **364**

Kyllonen, P. C., Lohman, D. F., & Snow, R. E. (1984). Effects of aptitudes, strategy training, and task facets on spatial task performance. *Journal of Educational Psychology, 76,* 130–145. **374, 392, 395**

Kyvik, S. (1990). Motherhood and scientific productivity. *Social Studies of Science, 20,* 149–160. **328**

Lackey, P. N. (1989). Adults' attitudes about assignments of household chores to male and female children. *Sex Roles, 20,* 271–282. **307**

La Freniere, P., Strayer, F. F., & Gauthier, R. (1984). The emergence of same-sex affiliative preferences among preschool peers: A developmental/ethological perspective. *Child Development, 55,* 1958–1965. **313**

Lagerspetz, K. M. J., Bjrkqvist, K., & Peltonen, T. (1988). Is indirect aggression typical of females? Gender differences in aggressiveness in 11- to 12-year-old children. *Aggressive Behavior, 14,* 403–414. **357**

Laird, C. D. (1988). Fragile-X mutation proposed to block complete reactivation of an inactive X chromosome. *American Journal of Medical Genetics, 30,* 693–696. **122**

———. (1991). Possible erasure of the imprint on a fragile X chromosome when transmitted by a male. *American Journal of Medical Genetics, 38,* 391–395. **122**

Laird, C. D., Lamb, M. M., & Thorne, J. L. (1990). Two progenitor cells for human oogonia inferred from pedigree data and the X-inactivation imprinting model of the fragile-X syndrome. *American Journal of Human Genetics, 46,* 696–719. **122**

Lamb, M. E., Pleck, J. H., & Levine, J. A. (1983). The role of the father in child development: The effects of increased paternal involvement. In B. B. Lahey & A. E. Kazdin (Eds.), *Advances in clinical child psychology,* (vol. 8). New York: Plenum . **299, 300, 305**

Lamb, M. E., & Roopnarine, J. L. (1979). Peer influences on sex-role development in preschoolers. *Child Development, 50,* 1219–1222. **315, 316**

Lamb, M. E., Thompson, R. A., Gardner, W. P., Charnov, E. L., & Estes, D. (1984). Security of infantile attachment as assessed in the "strange situation." *The Behavioral and Brain Sciences, 7,* 127–171. **222**

Lande, R. (1980). Sexual dimorphism, sexual selection, and adaptation in polygenic characters. *Evolution, 34,* 292–305. **84, 99**

Lande, R., & Arnold, S. J. (1985). Evolution of mating preference and sexual dimorphism. *Journal of Theoretical Biology, 117,* 651–664. **61, 84**

Lande, R., & Price, T., (1989). Genetic correlations and maternal effect coefficients obtained from offspring-parent regression. *Genetics, 122,* 915–933. **220**

Landy, F., Rosenberg, B. G., & Sutton-Smith, B. (1969). The effect of limited father absence on cognitive development. *Child Development, 40,* 941–944. **395**

Langhorne, M. C., & Secord, P. F. (1955). Variations in marital needs

with age, sex, marital status, and regional location. *Journal of Social Psychology, 41,* 19–37. **379**

Langlois, J. H., & Downs, A. C. (1980). Mothers, fathers, and peers as socialization agents of sex-typed play behaviors in young children. *Child Development, 51,* 1217–1247. **315**

Lansky, L. M., Feinstein, H., & Peterson, J. M. (1988). Demography of handedness in two samples of randomly selected adults (N = 2083). *Neuropsychologia, 26,* 465–477. **397**

Larrance, D., Pavelich, S., Storer, P., Polizzi, M., Baron, B., Sloan, S., Jordan, R., & Reis, H. T. (1979). Competence and incompetence: Asymmetric [sic] responses to women and men on a sex-linked task. *Personality and Social Psychology Bulletin, 5,* 363–366. **284**

Larwood, L., Zalkind, D., & Legault, J. (1975). The bank job: A field study of sexually discriminatory performance on a neutral-role task. *Journal of Applied Social Psychology, 5,* 68–74. **285**

Laudenslager, M. L. (1988). The psychobiology of loss: Lessons from humans and nonhuman primates. *Journal of Social Issues, 44,* 19–36. **365**

Lauritzen, C. (1987). Results of a 5 years' prospective study of estriol succinate treatment in patients with climacteric complaints. *Hormones and Metabolic Research, 19,* 579–584. **203**

Lavine, L. O. (1982). Parental power as a potential influence on girls' career choice. *Child Development, 53,* 658–663. **325, 329**

Lawrence, F. C., Draughn, P. S., Tasker, G. E., & Wozniak, P. H. (1987). Sex differences in household labor time: A comparison of rural and urban couples. *Sex Roles, 17,* 489–502. **304**

Leahy, R. L., & Shirk, S. R. (1984). The development of classificatory skills and sex-trait stereotypes in children. *Sex Roles, 10,* 281–292. **291**

Lee, A. M., Hall, E. G., & Carter, J. A. (1983). Age and sex differences in expectancy for success among American children. *Journal of Psychology, 113,* 35–39. **333**

Lee, J. R. (1991). Is natural progesterone the missing link in osteoporosis prevention and treatment? *Medical Hypotheses, 35,* 316–318. **200**

Lee, V. E., & Bryk, A. S. (1986). Effects of single-sex secondary schools on student achievement and attitudes. *Journal of Educational Psychology, 78,* 381–395. **320**

Lee, W., Mason, A. J., Schwall, R.,

Szonyi, E., & Mather, J. P. (1989). Secretion of activin by interstitial cells in the testis. *Science, 243,* 396–398. **178**

LeFevre, J., & McClintock, M. K. (1991). Isolation accelerates reproductive senescence and alters its predictors in female rats. *Hormones and Behavior, 25,* 258–272. **198**

Lefkowitz, M. M., Huesmann, L. R., & Eron, L. D. (1978). Parental punishment: A longitudinal analysis of effects. *Archives of General Psychiatry, 35,* 186–191. **356, 357**

Leigh, B. C. (1989). Reasons for having and avoiding sex: Gender, sexual orientation, and relationship to sexual behavior. *Journal of Sex Research, 26,* 199–209. **384**

Leinhardt, G., Seewald, A. M., & Engel, M. (1979). Learning what's taught: Sex differences in instruction. *Journal of Educational Psychology, 71,* 432–439. **312**

LeMay, M. (1985). Asymmetries of the brains and skulls of nonhuman primates. In S. D. Glick (Ed.), *Cerebral lateralization in nonhuman species.* New York: Academic Press. **396**

Lemkau, J. P. (1979). Personality and background characteristics of women in male-dominated occupations: A review. *Psychology of Women Quarterly, 4,* 221–240. **328, 329**

_____. (1984). Men in female-dominated professions: Distinguishing personality and background features. *Journal of Vocational Behavior, 24,* 110–122. **328**

Lenington, S., Egid, K., & Williams, J. (1988). Analysis of a genetic recognition system in wild house mice. *Behavior Genetics, 18,* 549–564. **87**

Lenny, E. (1977). Women's self-confidence in achievement settings. *Psychological Bulletin, 84,* 1–13. **333**

Lent, R. W., Brown, S. D., & Larkin, K. C. (1984). Relation of self-efficacy expectations to academic achievement and persistence. *Journal of Counseling Psychology, 31,* 356–362. **321**

Leonard, J. M., Paulsen, C. A., Ospina, L. F., & Burgess, E. C. (1979). The classification of Klinefelter's syndrome. In H. L. Vallet & I. H. Porter (Eds.), *Genetic mechanisms of sexual development.* New York: Academic Press. **112**

Leonard, S. P., & Archer, J. (1989). A naturalistic investigation of gender constancy in three- to four-year-old children. *British Journal of Developmental Psychology, 7,* 341–346. **291**

Leone, C., & Ensley, E. (1985). Self-generated attitude change: Another look at the effects of thought and cognitive schemata. *Representative Research in Social Psychology, 15,* 2–9. **274**

Lerner, J. V., & Galambos, N. L. (1988). The influences of maternal employment across life: The New York longitudinal study. In A. E. Gottfried & A. W. Gottfried (Eds.), *Maternal employment and children's development.* New York: Plenum. **300**

Leutenegger, W. (1978). Scaling of sexual dimorphism in body size and breeding system in primates. *Nature, 272,* 610–611. **88**

_____. (1982). Scaling of sexual dimorphism in body weight and canine size in primates. *Folia Primatology, 37,* 163–176. **88**

Leutenegger, W., & Kelly, J. T. (1977). Relationship of sexual dimorphism in canine size and body size to social, behavioral, and ecological correlates in anthropoid primates. *Primates, 18,* 117–136. **88**

Levant, R. F., Slattery, S. C., & Loiselle, J. E. (1987). Fathers' involvement in housework and child care with school-aged daughters. *Family Relations, 36,* 152–157. **304, 306**

LeVay, S. (1991). A difference in hypothalamic structure between heterosexual and homosexual men. *Science, 253,* 1034–1037. **165, 388**

Lever, J. (1976). Sex differences in the games children play. *Social Problems, 23,* 478–487. **316, 318**

Levinson, D. J. (1986). A conception of adult development. *American Psychologist, 41,* 3–13. **208**

Levinson, R. M. (1976). Sex discrimination and employment practices: An experiment with unconventional job inquiries. *Social Problems, 23,* 533–543. **330**

Levy, G. D., & Carter, D. B. (1989). Gender schema, gender constancy, and gender-role knowledge: The roles of cognitive factors in preschoolers' gender-role stereotype attributions. *Developmental Psychology, 25,* 444–449. **290**

Lewin, M., & Tragos, L. M. (1987). Has the feminist movement influenced adolescent sex role attitudes? A reassessment after a quarter century. *Sex Roles, 16,* 125–135. **273, 282, 335**

Lewin, R. (1987). The origin of the modern human mind. *Science, 236,* 668–670. **80**

_____. (1988). New views emerge on hunters and gatherers. *Science, 240,* 1146–1148. **91**

Lewinsohn, P. M., Hoberman, H. M., & Rosenbaum, M. (1988). A prospective study of risk factors for unipolar depression. *Journal of Abnormal Psychology, 97,* 251–264. **360, 361**

Lewinsohn, P. M., Hoberman, H., Teri, L., & Hautzinger, M. (1985). An integrative theory of depression. In S. Reiss & R. R. Bootzin (Eds.), *Theoretical issues in behavior therapy.* New York: Academic Press. **360**

Lewinsohn, P. M., Steinmetz, J. L., Larson, D. W., & Franklin, J. (1981). Depression-related cognitions: Antecedent or consequence? *Journal of Abnormal Psychology, 90,* 213–219. **361**

Lewis, H. B. (1985). Depression vs. paranois: Why are there sex differences in mental illness? *Journal of Personality, 53,* 150–178. **338**

Lewis, R. S., & Harris, L. J. (1988). The relationship between cerebral lateralization and cognitive ability: Suggested criteria for empirical tests. *Brain and Cognition, 8,* 275–290. **397**

Lewis, R. S., & Kamptner, N. L. (1987). Sex differences in spatial task performance of patients with and without unilateral cerebral lesions. *Brain and Cognition, 6,* 142–152. **397, 400**

Lewis, W. M., Jr. (1987). The cost of sex. In S. C. Stearns (Ed.), *The evolution of sex and its consequences.* Boston: Birkhauser. **69**

Licht, b. G., & Dweck, C. S. (1984). Determinants of academic achievement: the interaction of children's achievement orientations with skill area. *Developmental Psychology, 20,* 628–636. **322**

Lifschytz, E., & Lindsley, D. L. (1972). The role of X-chromosome inactivation during spermatogenesis. *Proceedings of the National Academy of Sciences, USA, 69,* 182–186. **104**

Linn, M. C., & Peterson, A. C. (1985). Emergence and characterization of sex differences in spatial ability: A meta-analysis. *Child Development, 56,* 1479–1498. **389, 390**

_____. (1986). A meta-analysis of gender differences in spatial ability: Implications for mathematics and science achievement. In J. S. Hyde & M. C. Linn (Eds.), *The psychology of gender: Advances through meta-analysis.* Baltimore: John Hopkins. **389**

Linn, S., Schoenbaum, S. C., Monson, R. R., Rosner, B., & Ryan, K. J. (1982). Delay in conception for former 'pill' users. *Journal of the American Medical Association, 247,* 629–632. **201**

Linnoila, M., Virkkunen, M., Scheinin, M., Nuutila, A., Rimon, R., & Goodwin, F. (1983). Low cerebrospinal fluid 5-hydroxyindoleacetic acid concentration differentiates impulsive from nonimpulsive violent behavior. *Life Sciences, 33*, 2609–2614. **351**

Linz, D. (1989). Exposure to sexually explicit materials and attitudes toward rape: A comparison of study results. *Journal of Sex Research, 26*, 50–84. **385**

Lippa, R., & Beauvais, C. (1983). Gender jeopardy: The effects of gender, assessed femininity and masculinity, and false success/failure feedback on performance in an experimental quiz game. *Journal of Personality and Social Psychology, 44*, 344–353. **333**

Lippe, A. L. von der (1985). Agency and communion in three generations of women and their relation to socialization. *Scandinavian Journal of Psychology, 26*, 289–304. **305**

Lipton, S. A. (1986). Blockade of electrical activity promotes the death of mammalian retinal ganglion cells in culture. *Proceedings of the National Academy of Sciences, USA, U*, 9774–9778. **139**

Liss, M. B. (1981). Patterns of toy play: An analysis of sex differences. *Sex Roles, 7*, 1143–1150. **308**

Lissner, L., Stevens, J., Levitsky, D. A., Rasmussen, K. M., & Strupp, B. J. (1988). Variation in energy intake during the menstrual cycle: implications for food-intake research. *American Journal of Clinical Nutrition, 48*, 56–62. **189**

Litteria, M. (1977a). Effects of neonatal estrogen on *in vivo* transport of -aminoisobutyric acid into rat brain. *Experimental Neurology, 57*, 817–827. **138**

————. (1977b). The effects of neonatal androgenization on the in vivo transport of alpha-amonoisobutyric acid into specific regions of rat brain. *Brain Research, 132*, 287–299. **138**

————. (1980a). Effects of neonatal estrogenization on thymidine kinase activity and DNA content in the cerebellum of the rat. *Developmental Neuroscience, 3*, 209–216. **138**

————. (1980b). The effects of sex and neonatal androgenization on thymidine kinase activity and DNA content in the cerebellum of the rat. *Brain Research, 181*, 401–412. **138**

Litteria, M., & Popoff, C. G. (1984). Ontogeny of thymidine kinase and DNA in the hypothalamus and cerebral cortex of the rat: effects of neonatal estrogen. *Experimental Neurology, 83*, 634–639. **138**

Litteria, M., & Thorner, M. W. (1974). Inhibition in the incorporation of [^{3}H]lysine in the Purkinje cells of the adult female rat after neonatal androgenization. *Brain Research,*

69, 170–173. **138**

————. (1975). Inhibition in the incorporation of [^{3}H]lysine in the proteins of specific hypothalamic nuclei of the adult female rat after neonatal estrogenization. *Experimental Neurology, 49*, 592–595. **138**

————. (1976). Inhibitory action of neonatal estrogenization on the incorporation of [^{3}H]lysine into cortical nucleoproteins. *Brain Research, 103*, 584–587. **138**

Lively, C. M. (1987). Evidence from a New Zealand snail for the maintenance of sex by parasitism. *Nature, 328*, 519–521. **51, 72**

Livingstone, D. W., & Luxton, M. (1989). Gender consciousness at work: Modification of the male breadwinner norm among steelworkers and their spouses. *Canadian Review of Sociology and Anthropology, 26*, 240–275. **330**

Lloyd, C. (1980a). Life events and depressive disorder reviewed. I. Events as predisposing factors. *Archives of General Psychiatry, 37*, 529–535. **364**

————. (1980b). Life events and depressive disorder reviewed. II. Events as precipitating factors. *Archives of General Psychiatry, 37*, 541–548. **364**

Lloyd, M. E. (1990). Gender factors in reviewer recommendations for manuscript publication. *Journal of Applied Behavior Analysis, 23*, 539–543. **285**

Lockheed, M. E. (1985a). Sex and social influence: A meta-analysis guided by theory. In J. Berger & M. Zelditch (Eds.), *Status, rewrds, and influence*. San Franciso: Jossey-Bass. **342**

————. (1985b). Some determinants and consequences of sex segregation in the classroom. In L. C. Wilkinson & C. B. Marrett (Eds.), *Gender-related differences in the classroom*. New York: Academic Press. **313**

Lockheed, M. E., & Harris, A. M. (1984). Cross-sex collaborative learning in elementary classrooms. *American Educational Research Journal, 21*, 275–294. **287, 288**

Locksley, A., Borgida, E., Brekke, N., & Hepburn, C. (1980). Sex stereotypes and social judgment. *Journal of Personality and Social Psychology, 39*, 821–831. **275**

Locksley, A., & Colten, M. E. (1979). Psychological androgyny: A case of mistaken identity? *Journal of Personality and Social Psychology, 37*, 1017–1031. **35, 47, 49**

Locksley, A., Hepburn, C., & Ortiz, V. (1982). Social stereotypes and judgments of individuals: An instance of the base-rate fallacy.

Journal of Experimental Social Psychology, 18, 23–42. **275**

Loeber, R., & Dishion, T. (1983). Early predictors of male delinquency: A review. *Psychological Bulletin, 94*, 68–99. **356**

Loeber, R., & Schmaling, K. B. (1985). The utility of differentiating between mixed and pure forms of antisocial child behavior. *Journal of Abnormal Child Psychology, 13*, 315–336. **356**

Loehlin, J. C., & DeFries, J. C. (1987). Genotype-environment correlation and IQ. *Behavior Genetics, 17*, 263–277. **234, 393**

Loehlin, J. C., Sharan, S., & Jacoby, R. (1978). In pursuit of the "spatial gene": A family study. *Behavior Genetics, 8*, 27–41. **391**

Logue, C. M., & Moos, R. H. (1986). Perimenstrual symptoms: prevalence and risk factors. *Psychosomatic Medicine, 48*, 388–414. **191**

Loh, D. Y., & Baltimore, D. (1984). Sexual preference of apparent gene conversion events in MHC genes of mice. *Nature, 309*, 639–640. **101**

Lombardo, W. K., Cretser, G. A., Lombardo, B., & Mathis, S. L. (1983). Fer cryin' out loud—there is a sex difference. *Sex Roles, 9*, 987–995. **283**

Longcope, C. (1986). Adrenal and gonadal androgen secretion in normal females. *Clinics in Endocrinology and Metabolism, 15*, 213–228. **177, 178, 199**

Longcope, C., Hunter, R., & Franz, C. (1980). Steroid secretion by the postmenopausal ovary. *American Journal of Obstetrics and Gynecology, 138*, 564–568. **199**

Longino, H., & Doell, R. (1987). Body, bias, and behavior: A comparative analysis of reasoning in two areas of biological science. *Journal of Women in Culture and Society, 9*, 206–227. (original work published 1983) **12, 13**

Lont, C. M. (1990). The roles assigned to females and males in non-music radio programming. *Sex Roles, 22*, 661–668. **290**

Loosfelt, H., Fridlansky, F., Atger, M., & Milgrom, E. (1981). A possible nontranscriptional effect of progesterone. *Journal of Steroid Biochemistry, 15*, 107–110. **137**

Lopata, H. Z., & Thorne, B. (1978). On the term "sex roles." *Signs, 3*, 718–721. **9**

Lord, C. G., Ross, L., & Lepper, M. R. (1979). Biased assimilation and attitude polarization: The effects of prior theories on subsequently considered evidence. *Journal of Personality and Social Psychology, 37*, 2098–2109. **9**

Loring, D. W., Meador, K. J., & Lee, G. P. (1989). Differential-handed response to verbal and visual spatial stimuli: Evidence of specialized hemispheric processing following callosotomy. *Neuropsychologia, 27,* 811–827. **398**

Lott, B. (1985). The devaluation of women's competence. *Journal of Social Issues, 41,* 43-60. **282**

Lovejoy, C. O. (1981). The origin of man. *Science, 211,* 341–350. **80, 244, 248**

Lovejoy, J., & Wallen, K. (1990). Adrenal suppression and sexual initiation in group-living female rhesus monkeys. *Hormones and Behavior, 24,* 256–269. **387**

Low, B. S. (1988). Pathogen stress and polygyny in humans. In L. Betzig, M. B. Mulder, & P. Turke (Eds.), *Human reproductive behaviour.* Cambridge: Cambridge University Press. **252**

_____. (1989). Cross-cultural patterns in the training of children: An evolutionary perspective. *Journal of Comparative Psychology, 103,* 311-319. **254**

Loy, R., & Milner, T. A. (1980). Sexual dimorphism in extent of axonal sprouting in rat hippocampus. *Science, 208,* 1282–1284. **138**

Lubahn, D. B., Joseph, D. R., Sullivan, P. M., Willard, H. F., French, F. S., & Wilson, E. M. (1988). Cloning of human androgen receptor complementary DNA and localization to the X chromosome. *Science, 240,* 327–330. **107**

Lubinski, D., & Humphreys, L. G. (1990). Assessing spurious "moderator effects": Illustrated substantively with the hypothesized ("synergistic") relation between spatial and mathematical ability. *Psychological Bulletin, 107,* 385–393. **373**

Luebke, B. F. (1989). Out of focus: Images of women and men in newspaper photographs. *Sex Roles, 20,* 121-133. **285**

Lueptow, L. B. (1985). Concepts of femininity and masculinity: 1974–1983. *Psychological Reports, 57,* 859–862. **273**

Lufkins, E. G., Carpenter, P. C. Ory, S. J., Malkasian, G. D., & Edmonson, J. H. (1988). Estrogen replacement therapy: Current recommendations. *Mayo Clinic Proceedings, 63,* 453–460. **203**

Lui, E. M. K., & Lucier, G. W. (1980). Neonatal feminization of hepatic mono-oxygenase in adult male rats: Altered sexual dimorphic response to cadmium. *Journal of Pharmacology and Experimental Therapeutics, 212,* 211–216. **152**

Lummis, M., & Stevenson, H. W. (1990). Gender differences in beliefs and achievement: A cross-cultural study. *Developmental Psychology, 26,* 254–263. **313**

Luna, F., & Moral, P. (1990). Mechanisms of natural selection in human rural populations, survey of a Mediterranean region (La Alpujarra, SE Spain). *Annals of Human Biology, 17,* 153–158. **59**

Lundberg, U., de Câhteau, P., Winberg, J., & Frankenhaeuser, M. (1981). Catecholamine and cortisol excretion patterns in three-year-old children and their parents. *Journal of Human Stress, 7,* 3–11. **332**

Lykes, M. B. (1985). Gender and individualistic vs. collectivist bases for notions about the self. *Journal of Personality, 53,* 356–383. **347**

Lykes, M. B., & Stewart, A. J. (1986). Evaluating the feminist challenge to research in personality and social psychology: 1963–1983. *Psychology of Women Quarterly, 10,* 393–412. **39**

Lynn, D. B. (1976). Fathers and sex-role development. *The Family Coordinator* (October), 403–409. **299**

Lynn, M., & Shurgot, B. A. (1984). Responses to lonely hearts advertisements: Effects of reported physical attractiveness, physique, and coloration. *Personality and Social Psychology Bulletin, 10,* 349–357. **378**

Lyon, M. F. (1972). X-chromosome inactivation and developmental patterns in mammals. *Biological Review, 47,* 1–35. **104**

Lyon, M. F., & Glenister, P. H. (1980). Reduced reproductive performance in androgen-resistant Tfm/Tfm female mice. *Proceedings of the Royal Society of London, Series B, 208,* 1–12. **127**

Lyons, J. A., & Serbin, L. A. (1986). Observer bias in scoring boys' and girls' aggression. *Sex Roles, 14,* 301–314. **341**

Lyons, P. M., Truswell, A. S., Mira, M., Vizzard, J., & Abraham, S. F. (1989). Reduction of food intake in the ovulatory phase of the menstrual cycle. *American Journal of Clinical Nutrition, 49,* 1164–1168. **189**

Lyson, T. A., & Brown, S. S. (1982). Sex-role attitudes, curriculum choice, and career ambition: A comparison between women in typical and atypical college majors. *Journal of Vocational Behavior, 20,* 366–375. **327**

Lytton, H., & Romney, D. M. (1991). Parents' differential socialization of boys and girls: A meta-analysis. *Psychological Bulletin, 109,* 267–296. **170, 299, 301, 302**

Macaulay, J. (1985). Adding gender to aggression research: Incremental or revolutionary change? In V. E.

O'Leary, R. K. Unger, & B. Wallston (Eds), *Women, gender, and social psychology.* Hillsdale, NJ: Erlbaum. **16**

Maccoby, E. E. (1966). Sex differences in intellectual functioning. In E. E. Maccoby (Ed.), *The development of sex differences.* Stanford: Stanford University Press. **42, 256, 259**

_____. (1987). The varied meanings of "masculine" and "feminine." In J. M. Reinisch, L. A. Rosenblum, & S. A. Sanders (Eds.), *Masculinity/femininity: Basic perspectives.* New York: Oxford University Press. **313**

_____. (1988). Gender as a social category. *Developmental Psychology, 24,* 755–765. **286, 313, 316, 347**

_____. (1990). Gender and relationships: A developmental account. *American Psychologist, 45,* 513–520. **286, 313, 314, 316, 320, 337, 347**

Maccoby, E. E., Doering, C. H., Jacklin, C. N., & Kraemer, H. (1979). Concentrations of sex hormones in umbilical-cord blood: Their relation to sex and birth order of infants. *Child Development, 50,* 632–642. **171, 359, 368**

Maccoby, E. E., & Jacklin, C. N. (1974). *The psychology of sex differences.* Stanford: Stanford University Press. **42, 301**

_____. (1980). Sex differences in aggression: A rejoinder and reprise. *Child Development, 51,* 964–980. **341, 342**

_____. (1987). Gender segregation in childhood. In H. W. Reese (Ed.), *Advances in child development and behavior* (vol. 20). New York: Academic Press. **313, 314, 315, 316**

Maccoby, E. E., & Martin, J. A. (1983). Socialization in the context of the family: Parent-child interaction. In E. M. Hetherington (Ed.), *Socialization, personality, and social development. Handbook of child psychology* (vol. 4), Series ed. P. H. Mussen. **212, 213, 229, 232, 298**

MacCormack, C. P., & Strathern, M. (Eds.). (1980). *Nature, culture and gender.* Cambridge: Cambridge University Press. **260**

MacDonald, K., & Parke, R. D. (1984). Bridging the gap: parent-child play interaction and peer interactive competence. *Child Development, 55,* 1265–1277. **302, 315**

Mackey, W. C. (1979). Parameters of the adult-male-child bond. *Ethology and Sociobiology, 1,* 59–76. **252, 253**

Mackey, W. C., & Hess, D. J. (1982). Attention structure and stereotypy of gender on television: An empirical analysis. *Genetic Psychology*

Monographs, 106, 199–215. **290**

MacLusky, N. J., Chaptal, C., Lieberburg, I., & McEwen, B. S. (1976). Properties and subcellular interrelationships of presumptive estrogen receptor macromolecules in the brains of neonatal and prepubertal female rats. *Brain Research, 114*, 158–165. **157**

MacLusky, N. J., Lieberburg, I., Krey, L. C., & McEwen, B. S. (1980). Progestin receptors in the brain and pituitary of the bonnet monkey (Macaca radiata): Differences between the monkey and the rat in the distribution of progestin receptors. *Endocrinology, 106*, 185–191. **180**

MacLusky, N. J., Luine, V. N., Gerlach, J. L., Fischette, C., Noftolin, F., & McEwen, B. S. (1988). The role of androgen receptors in sexual differentiation of the brain: Effects of the testicular feminization (Tfm) gene on androgen metabolism, binding, and action in the mouse. *Psychobiology, 16*, 381–397. **146**

MacMahon, B., Trichopoulos, D., Brown, J., Andersen, A. P., Cole, P., DeWaard, F., Kauraniemi, T., Polychronopoulou, A., Ravnihar, B., Stormby, N., & Westlund, K. (1982). Age at menarche, urine estrogens and breast cancer risk. *International Journal of Cancer, 30*, 427–431. **127, 130**

Mager, D. L., & Henthorn, P. S. (1984). Identification of a retrovirus-like repetitive element in human DNA. *Proceedings of the National Academy of Sciences, USA, 81*, 7510–7514. **66**

Maggi, A., Susanna, L., Bettini, E., Mantero, G., & Zucchi, I. (1989). Hippocampus: A target for estrogen action in mammalian brain. *Molecular Endocrinology, 3*, 1165–1170. **397**

Magnus, E. M. (1980). Sources of maternal stress in the postpartum period: A review of the literature and an alternative view. In J. E. Parsons (Ed.), *The psychobiology of sex differences and sex roles.* New York: McGraw-Hill. **197**

Magos, A. L., Brincat, M., & Studd, J. W. W. (1986). Treatment of the premenstrual syndrome by subcutaneous oestradiol implants and cyclical oral norethisterone: Placebo controlled study. *British Medical Journal, 292*, 1629–1633. **195**

Maheaux, B., Dufort, F., Lambert, J., & Berthiaume, M. (1988). Do female general practitioners have a distinctive type of medical practice. *Canadian Medical Association Journal, 139*, 737–740. **324**

Maiter, D., Koenig, J. I., & Kaplan,

L. M. (1991). Sexually dimorphic expression of the growth hormone-releasing hormone gene is not mediated by circulating gonadal hormones in the adult rat. *Endocrinology, 128*, 1709–1716. **136**

Majerus, M. E. N., O'Donald, P., Kearns, P. W. E., & Ireland, H. (1986). Genetics and evolution of female choice. *Nature, 321*, 164–167. **87, 88**

Majewska, M. D., Harrison, N. L., Schwartz, R. D., Barker, J. L., & Paul S. M. (1986). Steroid hormone metabolites are barbiturate-like modulators of the GABA receptor. *Science, 232*, 1004–1007. **139**

Major, B., Carnevale, P. J. D., & Deaux, K. (1981). A different perspective on androgyny: Evaluations of masculine and feminine personality characteristics. *Journal of Personality and Social Psychology, 41*, 988–1001. **48**

Malamuth, N. M. (1981a). Rape proclivity among males. *Journal of Social Issues, 37*, 138–157. **384**

_____. (1981b). Rape fantasies as a function of exposure to violent sexual stimuli. *Archives of Sexual Behavior, 10*, 33–47. **384**

Malaspina, P., Persicheti, F., Novelletto, A., Iodice, C., Terrenato, L., Wolfe, J., Ferraro, M., & Prantera, G. (1990). The human Y chromosome shows a low level of DNA polymorphism. *Annals of Human Genetics, 54*, 207–305. **119**

Malmnäs, C. O. (1977). Short-latency effect of testosterone on copulatory behaviour and ejaculation in sexually experienced intact male rats. *Journal of Reproductive Fertility, 51*, 351–354. **151**

Mann, V. A., Sasanuma, S., Sakuma, N., & Masaki, S. (1990). Sex differences in cognitive abilities: A cross-cultural perspective. *Neuropsychologia, 28*, 1063–1077. **36**

Manning, A., & Thompson, M. L. (1976). Postcastration retention of sexual behaviour in the male BDF1 mouse: The role of experience. *Animal Behaviour, 24*, 523–533. **386**

Mannuzza, S., Klein, R. G., Konig, P. H., & Giampino, T. L. (1989). Hyperactive boys almost grown up. IV. Criminality and its relationship to psychiatric status. *Archives of General Psychiatry, 46*, 1073–1079. **357**

Mansfield, P. K., Hood, K. E., & Henderson, J. (1989). Women and their husbands: Mood and arousal fluctuations across the menstrual cycle and days of the week. *Psychosomatic Medicine, 51*, 66–80. **190**

Marcus, J., Maccoby, E. E., Jacklin,

C. N., & Doering, C. H. (1985). Individual differences in mood in early childhood: their relation to gender and neonatal sex steroids. *Developmental Psychobiology, 18*, 327–340. **171, 359, 368**

Marcus, T. L., & Corsini, D. A. (1978). Parental expectations of preschool children as related to child gender and socioeconomic status. *Child Development, 49*, 243–246. **299**

Marini, M. M., & Brinton, M. C. (1982). Sex typing in occupational socialization. In B. F. Reskin (Ed.), *Sex segregation in the workplace: Trends, explanations, remedies.* Washington, DC: National Academy Press. **325**

Markus, H. (1977). Self-schemata and processing information about the self. *Journal of Personality and Social Psychology, 35*, 63–78. **30, 45, 46**

_____. (1983). Self-knowledge: An expanded view. *Journal of Personality, 51*, 543–565. **46, 47, 48**

Markus, H., Crane, M., Bernstein, S., & Siladi, M. (1982). Self-schemas and gender. *Journal of Personality and Social Psychology, 42*, 38–50. **45**

Markus, H. R., & Kitayama, S. (1991). Culture and the self: Implications for cognition, emotions, and motivation. *Psychological Review, 98*, 224–253. **239**

Marsh, H. W. (1989). Sex differences in the development of verbal and mathematics constructs: The High School and Beyond Study. *American Educational Reseach Journal, 26*, 191–225. **373**

Marsh, H. W., Antill, J. K., & Cunningham, J. D. (1987). Masculinity, femininity, and androgyny: Relations to self-esteem and social desirability. *Journal of Personality, 55*, 661–685. **46**

Marshall, S. P., & Smith, J. D. (1987). Sex differences in learning mathematics: A longitudinal study with item and error analysis. *Journal of Educational Psychology, 79*, 372–383. **373**

Martin, C. J., Brown, G. W., Goldberg, D. P., & Brockington, I. F. (1989). Psycho-social stress and puerperal depression. *Journal of Affective Disorders, 16*, 283–293. **197, 198**

Martin, C. L. (1987). A ratio measure of sex stereotyping. *Journal of Personality and Social Psychology, 52*, 489–499. **277, 287**

_____. (1990). Attitudes and expectations about children with nontraditional and traditional gender roles. *Sex Roles, 22*, 151–166. **287, 294**

_____. (1991, May). *Age changes*

in gender stereotypes. Invited address presented at the meetings of the Midwestern Psychological Association, Chicago. **269**

Martin, J. F. (1983). Optimal foraging theory: A review of some models and their applications. *American Anthropologist, 85,* 612–629. **215**

Marx, J. L. (1988a). A parent's sex may affect gene expression. *Science, 239,* 352–353. **102**

_____. (1988b). Sexual responses are—almost—all in the brain. *Science, 241,* 903–904. **177, 198**

Masters, R. D. (1989). Gender and political cognition: Integrating evolutionary biology and political science. *Political and Life Sciences, 8,* 3–39. **255**

Matsui, T., Ikeda, H., & Ohnishi, R. (1989). Relations of sex-typed socializations to career self-efficacy expectations of college students. *Journal of Vocational Behavior, 35,* 1–16. **329, 330**

Matsumoto, A., Kobayashi, S., Murakami, S., & Arai, Y. (1984). Recovery of declined ovarian function in aged female rats by transplantation of newborn hypothalamic tissue. *Proceedings of the Japan Academy, 60,* 73–76. **198**

Matteo, S. (1987). The effect of job stress and job interdependency on menstrual cycle length, regularity and synchrony. *Psychoneuroendocrinology, 12,* 467–476. **191**

Matteo, S. (1988). The effect of gender-schematic processing on decisions about sex-inapprpriate sport behavior. *Sex Roles, 18,* 41–58. **49**

Matteson, D. R. (1991). Attempting to change sex role attitudes in adolescents: Explorations of reverse effects. *Adolescence, 26,* 885–898. **294**

Matthews, W. S. (1981). Sex-role perception, portrayal, and preference in the fantasy play of young children. *Sex Roles, 7,* 979–988. **295**

Mauldin, T., & Meeks, C. B. (1990). Sex differences in children's time use. *Sex Roles, 22,* 537–554. **307**

Maxson, S. C. (1990). The evolution of the mammalian Y chromosome. *Behavior Genetics, 20,* 109–126. **97, 117**

Maxson, S. C., & Roubertoux, P. (1990). The mammalian Y chromosome. *Behaviaor Genetics, 20,* 105–108. **98, 117**

Maxson, W. S. (1988). Progesterone: Biologic effects and evaluation of therapy for PMS. In L. H. Gise (Ed.), *The premenstrual syndromes.* New York: Churchill Livingstone. **195**

Mayer, M., & Rosen, F. (1977). Interaction of glucocorticoids and androgens in skeletal muscle. *Metabolism, 26,* 927–961. **202**

Maynard Smith, J. (1974). The theory of games and the evolution of animal conflicts. *Journal of Theoretical Biology, 47,* 209–221. **60**

_____. (1978). *The evolution of sex.* London: Cambridge University Press. **215**

_____. (1982). *Evolution and the theory of games.* London: Cambridge University Press. **60**

_____. (1984). Game theory and the evolution of behaviour. *The Behavioral and Brain Sciences, 7,* 95–126. **60**

_____. (1985a). The birth of sociobiology. *New Scientist, 26,* 48–50. **13, 86**

_____. (1985b). Sexual selection, handicaps and true fitness. *Journal of Theoretical Biology, 115,* 1–8. **87**

_____. (1988). *Did Darwin get it right: Essays on games, sex and evolution.* New York: Chapman & Hall. **51, 52, 60, 72, 82, 239, 240**

Mazur, A. (1985). A biosocial model of status in face-to-face primate groups. *Social Forces, 64,* 377–402. **348, 349**

McAdams, D. P. (1989, May). *Identity as narrative.* Paper presented and Midwestern Psychological Association. **231**

McArthur, L. Z., & Friedman, S. A. (1980). Illusory correlation in impression formation: Variations in the shared distinctiveness effect as a function of the distinctive person's age, race, and sex. *Journal of Personality and Social Psychology, 39,* 615–624. **287**

McCandless, B. R., Bush, C., & Carden, A. I. (1976). Reinforcing contingencies for sex-role behaviors in preschool children. *Contemporary Educational Psychology, 1,* 241–246. **311, 315**

McCarthy, R. A., & Warrington, E. K. (1988). Evidence for modality-specific meaning systems in the brain. *Nature, 334,* 428–430. **266**

McCauley, C., Stitt, S. L., & Segal, M. (1980). Stereotyping: From prejudice to prediction. *Psychological Bulletin, 87,* 195–208. **266, 277**

McCauley, E., Kay, T., Ito, J., & Treder, R. (1987). The Turner syndrome: Cognitive deficits, affective discrimination, and behavior problems. *Child Development, 58,* 464–473. **114**

McCauley, E., Sybert, V. P., & Ehrhardt, A. A. (1986). Psychosocial adjustment of adult women with Turner syndrome. *Clinical Genetics, 29,* 284–290. **114**

McClintock, M. K. (1971). Menstrual synchrony and suppression.

Nature, 260, 244–245. **190**

McConaghy, N. (1987). A learning approach. In J. Geer II & W. T. O'Donohue (Eds.), *Theories of human sexuality.* New York: Plenum. **389**

McCrae, R. R., & Costa, P. T., Jr. (1988a). Recalled parent-child relations and adult personality. *Journal of Personality, 56,* 417–434. **233**

_____. (1988b). Do parental influences matter? A reply to Halverson. *Journal of Personality, 56,* 445–449. **233**

McEwen, B. S. (1988). Basic research perspective: Ovarian hormone influence on brain neurochemical functions. In L. H. Gise, N. G. Kase, & R. L. Berkowitz (Eds.), *The premenstrual syndromes.* New York: Churchill Livingstone. **139**

_____. (1991a). Non-genomic and genomic effects of steroids on neural activity. *Trends in Physiological Sciences, 12,* 141–147. **124, 136, 139**

_____. (1991b). Steroid hormones are multifunctiontional messengers to the brain. *Trends in Endocrinology & Metabolism, 2,* 62–67. **124, 125, 136, 139**

McFarlane, J., Martin, C. L., & Williams, T. M. (1988). Women versus men and menstrual versus other cycles. *Psychology of Women Quarterly, 12,* 201–223. **190**

McGill, T. E., & Manning, A. (1976). Genotype and retention of the ejaculatory reflex in castrated male mice. *Animal Behaviour, 24,* 507–518. **147**

McGinnis, M. Y., & Dreifuss, R. M. (1989). Evidence for a role of testosterone-androgen receptor interactions in mediating masculine sexual behavior in male rats. *Endocrinology, 124,* 618–626. **142**

McGlone, J. (1980). Sex differences in human brain asymmetry: A critical survey. *Behavioral and Brain Sciences, 3,* 215–263. **400**

_____. (1981). Sexual variation in behaviour during spatial and verbal tasks. *Canadian Journal of Psychology, 35,* 277–282. **392**

McGrew, W. C. (1979). Evolutionary implications of sex differences in chimpanzee predation and tool use. In D. A. Hamburg & E. R. McCown (Eds.), *The great apes.* Menlo Park, CA: Benjamin/ Cummings. **245, 248**

McGue, M., & Bouchard, T. J., Jr. (1989). Genetic and environmental determinants of information processing and special mental abilities: A twin analysis. In R. J. Sternberg (Ed.), *Advances in the psychology of human intelligence* (Vol. 5). New York: Erlbaum. **396**

McGuffin, P., Katz, R., Aldrich, J.,

& Bebbington, P. (1988). The Camberwell Collaborative Depression Study: II. Investigation of family members. *British Journal of Psychiatry, 152*, 766–774. **364**

McGuffin, P., Katz, R., & Bebbington, P. (1987). Hazard, heredity and depression. A family study. *Journal of Psychiatric Research, 21*, 365–375. **364**

McGuinness, D. (1981). Auditory and motor aspects of language development in males and females. In A. Ansara, N. Geschwind, A. Galaburda, M. Albert, & N. Gartrell (Eds.), *Sex differences in dyslexia*. Towson, MD: Orton Dyslexia Society. **373**

_____. (1985). Sensorimotor biases in cognitive development. In R. L. Hall (Ed.), *Male-female differences: A bio-cultural perspective*. New York: Praeger. **372**

_____. (1987). Introduction. In M. A. Baker (Ed.), *Sex differences in human performance*. New York: Wiley & Sons. **42, 43**

McGuinness, D., & Symonds, J. (1977). Sex differences in choice behaviour: The object-person dimension. *Perception, 6*, 691–694. **346**

McGuire, J. (1988). Gender stereotypes of parents with two-year-olds and beliefs about gender differences in behavior. *Sex Roles, 19*, 233–240. **299, 305**

McKee, J. P., & Sherriffs, A. C. (1957). The differential evaluation of males and females. *Journal of Personality, 25*, 356–371. **296**

McKenna, W., & Kessler, S. J. (1977). Experimental design as a source of sex bias in social psychology. *Sex Roles, 3*, 117–128. **39**

McKinney, W. T. (1985). Separation and depression: Biological markers. In M. Reite & T. Field (Eds.), *The psychobiology of attachment and separation*. New York: Academic Press. **365**

McLachlan, R. I., Cohen, N. L., Vale, W. W., Rivier, J. E., Berger, H. G., Bremner, W. J., & Soules, M. R. (1989). The importance of luteinizing hormone in the control of inhibin and progesterone secretion of the human corpus luteum. *Journal of Clinical Endocrinology and Metabolism, 68*, 1078–1085. **145**

McLanahan, S., & Bumpass, L. (1988). Intergenerational consequences of family disruption. *American Journal of Sociology, 94*, 130–152. **223, 299**

McLaren, A. (1990). What makes a man a man? *Nature, 346*, 216–217. **123**

McLaughlin, J. (1975). The doctor shows. *Journal of Communication, 25*, 182–184. **290**

McNeil, T. F. (1986). A prospective study of postpartum psychoses in a high-risk group: I. Clinical characteristics of the current postpartum episodes. *Acta Psychiatrica Scandinavica, 74*, 205–216. **197, 198**

Mead, M. (1939). *Sex and temperament in three primitive societies*. New York: Morrow. **255, 257**

Meador-Woodruff, J. H., Greden, J. G., Grunhaus, L., & Haskett, R. F. (1990). Severity of depression and hypothalamic-pituitary-adrenal axis dysregulation: Identification of contributing factors. *Acta Psychiatrica Scandinavica, 81*, 364–371. **362**

Meck, J. M. (1984). The genetics of the X-Y antigen system and its role in sex determination. *Perspectives in Biology and Medicine, 27*, 560–584. **106**

Mednick, M. T. (1989). On the politics of psychological constructs: Stop the bandwagon, I want to get off. *American Psychologist, 44*, 1118–1123. **10**

Mednick, S. A., Gabrielli, W. F., Jr., & Hutchings, B. (1984). Genetic influences in criminal convictions: Evidence from an adoption cohort. *Science, 224*, 891–894. **358**

Megargee, E. I. (1969). Influence of sex roles on the manifestation of leadership. *Journal of Applied Psychology, 53*, 377–382. **347**

Meikle, A. W., Bishop, D. T., Stringham, J. D., & West, D. W. (1987). Quantitating genetic and nongenetic factors that determine plasma sex steroid variation in normal male twins. *Metabolism, 35*, 1090–1095. **147**

Meikle, A. W., Stanish, W. M., Taylor, N., Edwards, C. Q., & Bishop, C. T. (1982). Familial effects on plasma sex-steroid content in man: Testosterone, estradiol and sex-hormone-binding globulin. *Metabolism, 31*, 6–9. **147**

Meikle, D. B., Tilford, B. L., & Vessey, S. H. (1984). Dominance rank, secondary sex ratio, and reproduction of offspring in polygynous primates. *American Naturalist, 124*, 173–187. **80, 349**

Meiners, M. L., & Sheposh, J. P. (1977). Beauty or brains: Which image for your date? *Personality and Social Psychology Bulletin, 3*, 262–265. **380**

Meisel, R. L., & Pfaff, D. W. (1984). RNA and protein synthesis inhibitors: Effects on sexual behavior in female rats. *Brain Research Bulletin, 12*, 187–193. **136**

Meldrum, D. R., Tataryn, I. V., Frumar, A. M., Erlik, Y., Lu, K. H., & Judd, H. L. (1980). Gonadotropins, estrogens, and adrenal steroids during the menopausal hot

flash. *Journal of Clinical Endocrinology and Metabolism, 50*, 685–689. **200**

Mellon, P. A., Crano, W. D., & Schmitt, N. (1982). An analysis of the role and trait components of sex-based occupational beliefs. *Sex Roles, 8*, 533–542. **278, 331**

Mendlewicz, J., Simon, P., Sevy, S., Charon, F., Brocas, H., Legros, S., & Vassart, G. (1987). Polymorphic DNA marker on X chromosome and manic depression. *Lancet, 1*, No. 8544, May 30, 1230–1232. **110**

Menzel, E. W., & Jung, C. (1982). Marmosets (Saguinus fascicollis): Are learning sets learned? *Science, 217*, 750–752. **214**

Menzies, K. D., Drysdale, D. B., & Waite, P. M. E. (1982). Effects of prenatal progesterone on the development of pyramidal cells in rat cerebral cortex. *Experimental Neurology, 77*, 654–667. **137, 157**

Messick, D. M., & Mackie, D. M. (1989). Intergroup relations. *Annual Review of Psychology, 40*, 45–81. **266, 269, 275**

Meyer, G., Ferres-Torres, R., & Mas, M. (1978). The effects of puberty and castration on hippocampal dendritic spines of mice. A Golgi study. *Brain Research, 155*, 108–112. **228, 369, 397**

Myer, W. J., Migeon, B. R., & Migeon, C. J. (1975). Locus on human X chromosome for dihydrotestosterone receptor and androgen insensitivity. *Proceedings of the National Academy of Sciences, USA, 72*, 1469–1472. **107**

Meyer-Bahlburg, H. F. L. (1984). Psychendocrine research on sexual orientation. Current status and future options. *Progress in Brain Reserch, 61*, 375–398. **388**

Meyer-Bahlburg, H. F. L., & Ehrhardt, A. A. (1982). Prenatal sex hormones and human aggression: A review, and new data on progestogen effects. *Aggressive Behavior, 8*, 39–62. **370**

Meyer-Bahlburg, H. F. L., Ehrhardt, A. A., Endicott, J., Veridiano, N. P., Whitehead, D., & Vann, F. H. (1985). Depression in adults with a history of prenatal DES exposure. *Psychopharmacology Bulletin, 21*, 686–689. **368**

Meyer-Bahlburg, H. F. L., Ehrhardt, A. A., Feldman, J. F., Rosen, L. R., Veridiano, N. P., & Zimmerman, I. (1985). Sexual activity level and sexual functioning in women prenatally exposed to diethylstilbestrol. *Psychosomatic Medicine, 47*, 497–511. **388**

Michael, R. P., Bonsall, R. W., & Rees, H. D. (1987). Sites at which testosterone may act as an estrogen in the brain of the male primate. *Neuroendocrinology, 46*, 511–521. **180**

Michael, R. P., & Rees, H. D. (1982). Autoradiographic localization of 3H-dihydrotestosterone in the preoptic area, hypothalamus, and amygdala of a male rhesus monkey. *Life Sciences, 30*, 2087–2093. **203**

Michael, R. P., Setchell, K. D. R., & Plant, T. M. (1974). Diurnal changes in plasma testosterone and studies on plasma corticosteroids in non-anesthetized male rhesus monkeys (Macaca mulatta). *Journal of Endocrinology, 63*, 325–335. **182**

Michael, R. P., & Zumpe, D. (1978). Potency in male rhesus monkeys: Effects of continously receptive females. *Science, 200*, 451–453. **383**

_____. (1981). Relation between the seasonal changes in aggression, plasma testosterone and the photoperiod in male rhesus monkeys. *Psychoneuroendocrinology, 6*, 145–158. **203**

_____. (1983). Sexual violence in the United States and the role of season. *American Journal of Psychiatry, 140*, 883–886. **196**

Michael, R. P., Zumpe, D., & Bonsall, R. W. (1984). Sexual behavior correlates with the diurnal plasma testosterone range in intact male rhesus monkeys. *Biology of Reproduction, 30*, 652–657. **150, 183**

Michard-Vanheé, C. (1988). Aggressive behavior induced in female mice by an early single injection of testosterone in genotype dependent. *Behavior Genetics, 18*, 1–12. **147**

Michod, R. E. (1982). The theory of kin selection. *Annual Reviews of Ecological Systems, 13*, 23–55. **82**

Miczek, K. A., & Donat, P. (1989). Brain 5-HT systems and inhibition of aggressive behavior. In P. Bevan, A. R. Cools, & T. Archer (Eds.), *Behavioral pharmacology of 5-HT*, pp. 117–145. Hillsdale, NJ: Erlbaum. **351**

Migeon, B. R. (1979). X-chromosome inactivation as a determinant of female phenotype. In H. L. Vallet and I. H. Porter (Eds.), *Genetic mechanisms of sexual development*. New York: Academic Press. **104**

Milinski, M., & Bakker, T. C. M. (1990). Female sticklebacks use male coloration in mate choice and hence avoid parasitized males. *Nature, 344*, 330–333. **87**

Miller, C. L. (1987). Qualitative differences among gender-stereotyped toys: Implications for cognitive and social development in girls and boys. *Sex Roles, 16*, 473–488. **308, 309, 356**

Miller, D. B. (1988). Development of instinctive behavior: An epigenetic and ecological approach. In E. M. Blass (Ed.), *Handbook of behavioral neurobiology: Vol. 9. Developmental psychobiology and behavioral ecology*. New York: Plenum. **20, 156**

Miller, J., Labovitz, S., & Fry, L. (1975). Inequities in the organizational experiences of women and men. *Social Forces, 54*, 365–381. **326**

Miller, M. M., & Reeves, B. (1976). Dramatic TV content and children's sex-role stereotypes. *Journal of Broadcasting, 20*, 35–50. **293**

Miller, P. H. (1989). *Theories of developmental psychology* (2nd edition). New York: W. H. Freeman. **216, 218, 227**

Milner, T. A., & Loy, R. (1982). Hormonal regulation of axonal sprouting in the hippocampus. *Brain Research, 243*, 180–185. **138**

Milton, K. (1981). Distribution patterns of tropical plant foods as an evolutionary stimulus to primate mental development. *American Anthropologist, 83*, 534–548. **215**

Mischel, W. (1966). A social-learning view of sex differences in behavior. In E. E. Maccoby (Ed.), *The development of sex differences*. Stanford: Stanford University Press. **219**

Mischel, W., Shoda, Y., & Peake, P. K. (1988). The nature of adolescent competencies predicted by preschool delay of gratification. *Journal of Personality and Social Psychology, 54*, 687–696. **234**

Mischel, W., Shoda, Y., & Rodriguez, M. L. (1989). Delay of gratification in children. *Science, 244*, 933–938. **234**

Mishell, D. R., Jr., Thorneycroft, I. H., Nagata, Y., Murata, T., & Nakamura, R. M. (1973). Serum gonadotropin and steroid patterns in early human gestation. *American Journal of Obstetrics and Gynecology, 117*, 631–639. **197**

Mitchell, J. E., Baker, L. A., & Jacklin, C. N. (1989). Masculinity and feminiity in twin children: Genetic and environmental factors. *Child Development, 60*, 1475–1485. **358**

Mitton, J. B., & Grant, M. C. (1984). Associations among protein heterozygosity, growth rate, and developmental homeostasis. *Annual Review of Ecological Systems, 15*, 479–499. **75**

Mittwoch, U. (1986). Males, females and hermaphrodites. *Annals of Human Genetics, 50*, 103–121. **106**

_____. (1988). Ethnic differences in testis size: a possible link with the cytogenetics of true hermaphroditism. *Human Reproduction, 3*, 445–449. **106**

_____. (1989). Sex differentiation in mammals and tempo of growth: probabilities vs. switches. *Journal of Theoretical Biology, 137*, 445–455. **106**

_____. (1990). Sex, growth and chance. *Nature, 344*, 389–390. **106**

Miyakawa, M., & Arai, Y. (1987). Synaptic plasticity to estrogen in the lateral septum of the adult male and female rats. *Brain Research, 436*, 184–188. **138, 181**

Miyatake, A., Morimoto, Y., Oishi, T., Hanasaki, N., Sugita, Y., Iijima, S., Teshima, Y., Hishikawa, Y., & Yamamura, Y. (1980). Circadian rhythm of serum testosterone and its relation to sleep: Comparison with the variation in serum luteinizing hormone, prolactin, and cortisol in normal men. *Journal of Clinical Endocrinology and Metabolism, 51*, 1365–1371. **182**

Mizejewski, G. J., Vonnegut, M., & Simon, R. (1980). Neonatal androgenization using antibodies to alpha-fetoprotein. *Brain Research, 188*, 273–277. **158**

Mobbs, C. V., Harlan, R. E., Burrous, M. R., & Pfaff, D. W. (1988). An estradiol-induced protein synthesized in the ventral medial hypothalamus and transported to the midbrain central gray. *Journal of Neuroscience, 8*, 113–118. **136**

Mock, E. J., Kamel, F., Wright, W. W., & Frankel, A. I. (1975). Seasonal rhythm in plasma testosterone and luteinizing hormone of the male laboratory rat. *Science, 256*, 61–63. **203**

Moely, B. E., Skarin, K., & Weil, S. (1979). Sex differences in competition-cooperation behavior of children at two age levels. *Sex Roles, 5*, 329–342. **318**

Moles, J. A. (1977). Standardization and measurement in cultural anthropology: A neglected area. *Current Anthropology, 18*, 235–257. **238, 239**

Molfese, D. L., & Molfese, V. J. (1985). Electrophysiogical indices of auditory discrimination in newborn infants: the bases for predicting later language development? *Infant Behavior and Development, 8*, 197–211. **397**

Molfese, D. L., & Radtke, R. C. (1982). Statistical and methodological issues in "auditory evoked potentials and sex-related differences in brain development." *Brain and Language, 16*, 338–341. **397**

Mollon, J. D., Bowmaker, J. K., & Jacobs, G. H. (1984). Variations of color vision in a New World primate can be explained by polymorphism of retinal photopigments. *Proceedings of the National Academy of Sciences, USA, 222*, 373–399. **105**

Momin, A. R. (1977). Commentary on "Standardization and measurement in cultural anthropology: A neglected area." *Current Anthropology, 18*, 248–249. **240**

Money, J. (1981). Paraphilias: Phyletic origins of erotosexual dysfunction. *International Journal of Mental Health, 10*, 75–109. **169, 383**

_____. (1987). Sin, sickness, or status? Homosexual gender identity and psychoneuroendocrinology. *American Psychologist, 42*, 384–399. **388**

Money, J., & Annecillo, C. (1987). Crucial period effect in psychoendocrinology: Two syndromes, abuse dwarfism and female (CVAH) hermaphroditism. In M. M. Bornstein (Ed.), *Sensitive periods in development*. Hillsdale, N.J: Ehrlbaum. **225**

Money, J., Devore, H., & Norman, B. F. (1986). Gender identity and gender transposition: Longitudinal outcome study of 32 male hermaphrodites assigned as girls. *Journal of Sex & Marital Therapy, 12*, 165–181. **388**

Money, J., & Norman, B. F. (1987). Gender identity and gender transposition: longitudinal outcome study of 24 male hermaphrodites assigned as boys. *Journal of Sex & Marital Therapy, 13*, 75–92. **388**

Mongrain, M., & Zuroff, D. C. (1989). Cognitive vulnerability to depressed affect in dependent and self-critical college women. *Journal of Personality Disorder, 3*, 240–251. **364**

Monk, M. (1987). Epidemiology of suicide. *Epidemiologic Reviews, 9*, 51–69. **366**

Montemayor, M. E., Clark, A. S., Lynn, D. M., & Roy, E. J. (1990). Modulation by norepinephrine of neural responses to estradiol. *Neuroendocrinology, 52*, 473–480. **124**

Montgomery, J. C., Appleby, L., Brincat, M., Versi, E., Tapp, A., Fenwick, P. B. C., & Studd, J. W. W. (1987). Effect of oestrogen and testosterone implants on the psychological disorders in the climacteric. *Lancet*, February 7, 297–298. **201, 368**

Mooradian, A. D., Morley, J. E., & Korenman, S. G. (1987). Biological actions of androgens. *Endocrine Reviews, 8*, 1–28. **152**

Moore, A. J. (1990). The evolution of sexual dimorphism by sexual selection: The separate effects of intrasexual selection and intersexual

selection. *Evolution, 44*, 315–341. **83**

Moore, C. L. (1984). Maternal contributions to the development of masculine sexual behavior in laboratory rats. *Developmental Psychobiology, 17*, 347–356. **276**

_____. (1985). Another psychobiological view of sexual differentiation. *Developmental Review, 5*, 18–55. **17, 154, 386**

Moore, C. L., & Power, K. L. (1986). Prenatal stress affects mother-infant interaction in Norway rats. *Developmental Psychobiology, 19*, 235–245. **17**

Moore, C. L., & Rogers, S. A. (1984). Contribution of self-grooming to onset of puberty in male rats. *Developmental Psychobiology, 17*, 243–253. **17**

Moore, D. P. (1984). Evaluating in-role and out-of-role performers. *Academy of Management Journal, 27*, 603–618. **284**

Moore, K. A., Nord, C. W., & Peterson, J. L. (1989). Nonvoluntary sexual activity among adolescents. *Family Planning Perspectives, 21*, 110–114. **384, 385**

Moore, M. (1978). Discrimination or favoritism? Sex bias in book reviews. *American Psychologist, October*, 936–938. **285**

Moore, M. C. (1991). Application of organization-activation theory to alternative male reproductive strategies: A review. *Hormones and Behavior, 25*, 154–179. **126**

Moore, T. E., & Mae, R. (1987). Who dies and who cries: Death and bereavement in children's literature. *Journal of Communication, 37*, 52–64. **289**

Morawski, J. G. (1985). The measurement of masculinity and femininity: Engendering categorical realities. *Journal of Personality, 53*, 196–223. **10, 13, 42**

Morell, M. A., Twillman, R. K., & Sullaway, M. E. (1989). Would a Type A date another Type A?: Influence of behavior type and personal attributes in the selection of dating partners. *Journal of Applied Social Psychology, 19*, 918–931. **381**

Morgan, M. (1982). Television and adolescents' sex role stereotypes: A longitudinal study. *Journal of Personality and Social Psychology, 43*, 947–955. **293**

Morgan, S. W., & Mausner, B. (1973). Behavioral and fantasied indicators of avoidance of success in men and women. *Journal of Personality, 41*, 457–470. **319**

Morse, C. A. Dennerstein, L., Varnavides, K., & Burrows, G. D. (1988). Menstrual cycle symptoms: Comparison of a non-clinical sample with a patient group. *Journal*

of Affective Disorders, 14, 41–50. **193**

Morse, J. K., Scheff, S. W., & DeKosky, S. T. (1986). Gonadal steroids influence axon sprouting in the hippocampal dentate gyrus: A sexually dimorphic response. *Experimental Neurology, 94*, 649–658. **138**

Morse, S. J., Gruzen, J., & Reis, H. (1976). The "eye of the beholder": A neglected variable in the study of physical attractiveness? *Journal of Personality, 44*, 209–225. **379**

Mos, J., Olivier, B., & van Oorschot, R. (1990). Behavioural and neuropharmacological aspects of maternal aggression in rodents. *Aggressive Behaviour, 16*, 145–163. **351**

Mosher, D. L., & Anderson, R. D. (1986). Macho personality, sexual aggression, and reactions to guided imagery of realistic rape. *Journal of Research in Personality, 20*, 77–94. **386**

Mosher, D. L., & Sirkin, M. (1984). Measuring a macho personality constellation. *Journal of Research in Personality, 18*, 150–163. **386**

Mosley, J. L., & Stan, E. A. (1984). Human sexual dimorphism: Its cost and benefit. In H. W. Reese (Ed.), *Advances in child development and behavior* (Vol. 18), pp. 147–185. . New York: Academic Press. **17**

Moss, H. A., & Susman, E. J. (1980). Longitudinal study of personality development. In O. G. Brim & J. Kagan (Eds.), *Constancy and change in human development*. Boston: Harvard University Press. **357**

Moss, R. L., & Dudley, C. A. (1984). Molecular aspects of the interaction between estrogen and the membrane excitability of hypothalamic nerve cells. *Progress in Brain Research, 61*, 3–22. **152**

Motohashi, T., Wu, C. H., Abdel-Rahman, H. A., Marymore, N., & Mikhail, G. (1979). Estrogen/androgen balance in health and disease. *American Journal of Obstetrics and Gynecology, 135*, 89–95. **197**

Motro, U. (1988). Evolutionarily stable strategies of mutual help between relatives having unequal fertilities. *Journal of Theoretical Biology, 135*, 31–40. **81**

Muehlenhard, C. L., & Cook, S. W. (1988). Men's self-reports of unwanted sexual activity. *Journal of Sex Research, 24*, 58–72. **384, 385**

Mukhopadhyay, C. C., & Higgins, P. J. (1988). Anthropological studies of women's status revisited: 1977–1987. *Annual Review of Anthropology, 17*, 461–495. **261**

Mulder, M. B. (1987). On cultural and reproductive success: Kipsigis evidence. *American Anthropologist, 89*, 617–634. **350**

Muller, R., & Goldberg, S. (1980). Why William doesn't want a doll: Preschoolers' expectations of adult behavior toward girls and boys. *Merrill-Palmer Quarterly of Behavior and Development, 26*, 259–269. **298**

Muoz-Cueto, J. A., Garca-Segura, L., & Ruiz-Marcos, A. (1990). Developmental sex differences and effect of ovariectomy on the number of cortical pyramidal cell dendritic spines. *Brain Research, 515*, 64–68. **157**

Munroe, R. H., Munroe, R. L., & Shimmin, H. S. (1984). Children's work in four cultures: Determinants and consequences. *American Anthropologist, 86*, 369–379. **253, 255**

Munroe, R. L., & Munroe, R. H. (1971). Effect of environmental experience on spatial ability in an east African society. *Journal of Social Psychology, 83*, 15–22. **253**

Murdock, G. P., & Provost, C. (1973). Factors in the division of labor by sex: A cross-cultural analysis. *Ethology, 12*, 203–225. **262**

Murphy, M. R. (1980). Sexual preferences of male hamsters: Importance of preweaning and adult experience, vaginal secretion, and olfactory or vomeronasal sensation. *Behavioral and Neural Biology, 30*, 323–340. **87**

Murray, J. P., & Kippax, S. (1979). From the early window to the late night show: International trends in the study of television's impact on children and adults. *Advances in Experimental Social Psychology*. New York: Academic Press. **291**

Musey, V. C., Collins, D. C., Brogan, D. R., Santos, V. R., Mysey, P. I., Martino-Saltzman, D., & Preedy, J. R. K. (1987). Long term effects of a first pregnancy on the hormonal environment: Estrogens and androgens. *Journal of Clinical Endocrinology and Metabolism, 64*, 111–118. **127**

Mussen, P. (1987). Longitudinal study of the life span. In N. Eisenberg (Ed.), *Contemporary topics in developmental psychology*. New York: Wiley. **232, 233**

Myers, A. M., & Gonda, G. (1982a). Utility of the masculinity-femininity construct: Comparison of traitional and androgyny approaches. *Journal of Personality and Social Psychology, 43*, 514–522. **12, 13, 49, 50**

_____ . (1982b). Empirical validation of the Bem Sex-Role Inventory. *Journal of Personality and Social Psychology, 43*, 304–318. **44, 47**

Myers, F. R. (1988). Critical trends in the study of hunter-gatherers. *Annual Review of Anthropology, 17*, 261–282. **239**

Myers, J. K., & Weissman, M. M. (1980). Use of a self-report symptom scale to detect depression in a commuity sample. *American Journal of Psychiatry, 137*, 1081–1084. **360**

Myers, R. H., Goldman, D., Bird, E. D., Sax, D. S., Merril, C. R., Schjoenfeld, M., & Wolf, P. A. (1983). Maternal transmission in Huntington's disease. *Lancet*, January 29, 208–210. **103**

Nabekura, J., Oomura, Y., Minami, T., Mizuno, Y., & Fukuda, A. (1986). Mechanism of the rapid effect of 17-estradiol on medial amygdala neurons. *Science, 233*, 226–228. **136, 152**

Naftolin, F., & MacLusky, N. (1984). Aromatization hypothesis revisited. In M. Serio, M. Motta, M. Zanisi, & L. Martini (Eds.), *Sexual differentiation: Basic and clinical aspects*. New York: Raven Press. **156**

Nanko, S. (1983). A case of Klinefelter's syndrome with high intelligence level. *Japanese Journal of Human Genetics, 28*, 221–222. **114**

Nanko, S., Saito, S., & Makino, M. (1979). X and Y chromatin survey among 1,581 Japanese juvenile delinquents. *Japanese Journal of Human Genetics, 24*, 21–25. **115, 116**

Nash, S. C. (1975). The relationship among sex-role stereotyping, sex-role preference, and the sex difference in spatial visualization. *Sex Roles 1*, 15–25. **282**

Neel, J. V. (1984). Human evolution: Many small steps, but not punctated equilibria. *Perspectives in Biology and Medicine, 28*, 75–103. **65**

Nei, M. (1988). Relative role of mutation and selection in the maintenance of genetic variability. *Philosophical Transactions of the Royal Society of London. Series B, 319*, 615–629. **57, 64**

Neitz, J., & Jacobs, G. H. (1986). Polymorphism of the long-wave-length cone in normal human color vision. *Nature, 323*, 623–625. **105**

Nelson, D. A., & Marler, P. (1989). Categorical perception of a natural stimulus continuum: birdsong. *Science, 244*, 976–978. **266**

Nelson, P. G., Yu, C., Fields, R. D., & Neale, E. A. (1989). Synaptic connections in vitro: Modulation of number and efficacy by electrical activity. *Science, 244*, 585–587. **225**

Neri, G., Gurrieri, F., Gal, A., &

Lubs, H. A. (1991). XLMR genes: Update 1990. *American Journal of Medical Genetics, 38*, 186–189. **121, 123**

Nerlove, S. B., Munroe, R. H., & Munroe, R. L. (1971). Effect of environmental experience on spatial ability: A replication. *Journal of Social Psychology, 84*, 3–10. **253**

Neve, R. L., & Bear, M. F. (1989). Visual experience regulates gene expression in the developing striate cortex. *Proceedings of the National Academy of Sciences, USA, 86*, 4781–4784. **208, 225**

Nevid, J. S. (1984). Sex differences in factors of romantic attraction. *Sex Roles, 11*, 401–412. **381**

Nevo, B. (1977). Personality differences between kibbutz born and city born adults. *Journal of Psychology, 96*, 303–308. **258**

Newcombe, N., Bandura, M. M., & Taylor, D. G. (1983). Sex differences in spatial ability and spatial activities. *Sex Roles, 9*, 377–386. **391**

Newmann, J. P. (1987, September). Gender differences in vulnerability to depression. *Social Science Review*, 446–468. **366**

Nicolson, N. A. (1987). Infants, mothers, and other females. In B. Smuts, D. L. Cheney, R. M. Seyfarth, R. W. Wrangham, & T. T. Struhsaker (Eds.), *Primate societies*. Chicago: University of Chicago Press. **221**

Nielsen, J., Homma, A., Christiansen, F., & Rasmussen, K. (1977). Women with tetra-X (48,XXXX). *Heriditas, 85*, 151–156. **123**

Nielsen, J., Pelsen, B., & Sorensen, K. (1988). Follow-up of 30 Klinefelter males treated with testosterone. *Clinical Genetics, 33*, 262–269. **115**

Nielsen, J. M. (1990). *Sex and gender in society: Perspectives on stratification, 2nd edition*. Prospect Heights, IL: Waveland Press. **16, 264**

Nielsen, J., & Stradiot, M. (1987). Transcultural study of Turner's syndrome. *Clinical Genetics, 32*, 260–270. **114**

Nieuwenhuijsen, K., Lammers, J. J. C., Neef, K. J. de, & Slob, A. K. (1985). Reproduction and social rank in female stumptail macaques (Macaca arctoides). *International Journal of Primatology, 6*, 77–99. **349**

Nieva, V. F., & Gutek, B. A. (1980). Sex effects on evaluation. *Academy of Management Review, 5*, 267–276. **282, 330**

Nishida, T. (1987). Local traditions and cultural transmission. In B. B. Smuts, D. L. Cheney, R. M. Seyfarth, R. W. Wrangham, & T. T. Struhsaker (Eds.), *Primate societies*. Chicago: University of

Chicago Press. **248**

Nishizuka, M., & Arai, Y. (1982). Synapse formation in response to estrogen in the medial amygdala developing in the eye. *Proceedings of the National Academy of Sciences, 79,* 7024–7026. **138**

Noë, R., & Sluijter, A. A. (1990). Reproductive tactics of male savanna baboons. *Behaviour, 113,* 117–170. **336, 350**

Noel, B., Duport, J. P., Revil, D., Dussuyer, I., & Quack, B. (1974). The XYY syndrome: Reality or myth? *Clinical Genetics, 5,* 387–394. **115**

Nolen, S. B. (1988). Reasons for studying: Motivational orientations and study strategies. *Cognition and Instruction, 5,* 269–287. **232**

Nolen-Hoeksema, S. (1987). Sex differences in unipolar depression: Evidence and theory. *Psychological Bulletin, 101,* 259–282. **366**

Noonan, M., & Axelrod, S. (1989a). The stability and intertest consonance of lateral postural-motor biases in rats: Results and implications. *Behavioral and Neural Biology, 52,* 386–405. **396**

_____. (1989b). Behavioral biases and left-right response differentiation in the rat. *Behavioral and Neural Biology, 52,* 406–410. **396**

Nordeen, E. J., & Nordeen, K. W. (1990). Neurogenesis and sensitive periods in avian song learning. *Trends in Neurosciences, 13,* 31–36. **142**

Nordeen, E. J., Nordeen, K. W., & Arnold, A. P. (1987). Sexual differentiation of androgen accumulation within the zebra finch brain through selective cell loss and addition. *Journal of Comparative Neurology, 259,* 393–399. **142**

Nordeen, E. J., & Yahr, P. (1983). A regional analysis of estrogen binding to hypothalamic cell nuclei in relation to masculinization and feminization. *Journal of Neuroscience, 3,* 933–941. **138**

Nordeen, K. W., & Nordeen, E. J. (1988). Projection neurons within a vocal motor pathway are born during song learning in zebra finches. *Nature, 334,* 149–181. **142**

Nordeen, K. W., Nordeen, E. J., & Arnold, A. P. (1986). Estrogen establishes sex differences in androgen accumulation in zebra finch brain. *Journal of Neuroscience, 6,* 734–738. **142**

_____. (1987). Estrogen accumulation in zebra finch song control nuclei: Implications for sexual differentiation and adult activation of song behavior. *Journal of Neurobiology, 18,* 569–582. **137**

Norman, R. D. (1974). Sex differences in preferences for sex of children:

A replication after 20 years. *Journal of Psychology, 88,* 229–239. **282**

Norman, R. L., & Spies, H. G. (1986). Cyclic ovarian function in a male macaque: Additional evidence for a lack of sexual differentiation in the physiological mechanisms that regulate the cyclic release of gonadotropins in primates. *Endocrinology, 118,* 2608–2610. **145**

Nott, P. N. (1982). Psychiatric illness following childbirth in Southampton: A case register study. *Psychological Medicine, 12,* 557–561. **197**

Nottebohm, F. (1980). Testosterone triggers growth of brain vocal control nuclei in adult female canaries. *Brain Research, 189,* 429–436. **142**

_____. (1985). Neuronal replacement in adulthood. *Annals of the New York Academy of Sciences, 457,* 143–162. **142**

_____. (1989, February). From bird song to neurogenesis. *Scientific American,* 74–79. **142**

_____. (1991). Reassessing the mechanisms and origins of vocal learning in birds. *Trends in Neurosciences, 14,* 206–211. **142**

Nottebohm, F., & Arnold, A. P. (1976). Sexual dimorphism in vocal control areas of the songbird brain. *Science, 194,* 211–213. **142**

Nottebohm, F., Nottebohm, M. E., & Crane, L. (1986). Developmental and seasonal changes in canary song and their relation to changes in the anatomy of song-control nuclei. *Behavioral and Neural Biology, 46,* 445–471. **142**

Nowakowski, R. S. (1987). Basic concepts of CNS development. *Child Development, 58,* 568–595. **152, 224**

Nunney, L. (1985). Group selection, altruism, and structured–deme models. *The American Naturalist, 126,* 212-230. **82**

Nussbaum, R. L., & Ledbetter, D. H. (1986). Fragile X syndrome: A unique mutation in man. *Annual Review of Genetics, 20,* 109–145. **121, 123**

Nyborg, H. (1983). Spatial ability in men and women: review and new theory. *Advances in Behaviour Research and Therapy, 5,* 89–140. **398**

_____. (1987). Individual differences or different individuals? That is the question. *Behavioral and Brain Sciences, 10,* 34–35. **50**

Nyquist, L., Slivken, K., Spence, J. T., & Helmreich, R. L. (1985). Household responsibilities in middle-class couples: The contribution of demographic and personality variables. *Sex Roles, 12,* 15–34. **305, 306, 307**

Nyquist, L. V., & Spence, J. T. (1986). Effects of dispositional dominance and sex role expectations on leader-

ship behaviors. *Journal of Personality and Social Psychology, 50,* 97–93. **347**

Oakley, A. (1985). Social support in pregnancy: The 'soft' way to increase birthweight? *Social Science and Medicine, 21,* 1259–1268. **148**

Ober, C., Elias, S., O'Brien, E., Kostyu, D. D., Hauck, W. W., & Bombard, A. (1988). HLA sharing and fertility in Hutterite couples: Evidence for prenatal selection against compatible fetuses. *American Journal of Reproductive Immunology and Microbiology, 18,* 111–115. **74**

Oberlé, I., Rousseau, F., Heitz, D., Kretz, C., Devys, D., Hanauer, A., Bou, J., Bertheas, M. F., & Mandel, J. L. (1991). Instability of a 550-base pair DNA segment and abnormal methylation in fragile X syndrome. *Science, 252,* 1097–1102. **121**

O'Brien, M., & Huston, A. C. (1985). Development of sex-typed play behavior in toddlers. *Developmental Psychology, 21,* 866–871. **307, 308**

O'Brien, S. J., Roelke, M. E., Marker, L., Newman, A., Winkler, C. A., Meltzer, D., Colly, L., Evermann, J. F., Bush, M., & Wildt, D. E. (1985). Genetic basis for species vulnerability in the cheetah. *Science, 227,* 1428–1434. **72, 75**

O'Brien, S. J., Wildt, D. E., Goldman, D., Merril, C. R., & Bush, M. (1983). The cheetah is depauperate in genetic variation. *Science, 221,* 459–462. **57, 72, 75**

O'Carroll, R., & Bancroft, J. (1984). Testosterone therapy for low sexual interest and erectile dysfunction in men: A controlled study. *British Journal of Psychiatry, 145,* 146–151. **151**

O'Connor, P. A. (1982). Multidimensional ratings of adult occupations. *Psychological Reports, 50,* 747–754. **325, 331**

O'Donald, P. (1980). Sexual selection by female choice in a monogamous bird: Darwin's theory corroborated. *Heredity, 45,* 201–217. **88**

Ogle, T. F., & Kitay, J. I. (1977). Ovarian and adrenal steroids during pregnancy and the oestrous cycle in the rat. *Journal of Endocrinology, 74,* 89–98. **178, 197**

Oh, S. (1987). Remarried men and remarried women: How are they different? *Journal of Divorce, 9,* 107–113. **380**

O'Hara, M. W. (1986). Social support, life events, and depression during pregnancy and the puerperium. *Archives of General Psychiatry, 43,* 569–573. **197**

O'Hara, M. W., Rehm, L. P., & Campbell, S. B. (1983). Postpartum depression: A role for social network and life stress variables. *Journal of Nervous and Mental Disease, 171*, 336–341. **198**

O'Heron, C. A., & Orlofsky, J. L. (1990). Stereotypic and nonstereotyic sex role trait and behavior orientations, gender identity, and psychological adjustment. *Journal of Personality and Social Psychology, 58*, 134–143. **35, 44, 49**

Ojemann, G. A. (1991). Cortical organization of language. *Journal of Neuroscience, 11*, 2281–2287. **166**

Ojemann, G., Ojemann, J., Lettich, E., & Berger, M. (1989). Cortical language localization in left, dominant hemisphere: An electrical stimulation mapping investigation in 117 patients. *Journal of Neurosurgery, 71*, 316–326. **166, 173**

Olian, J. D., Schwab, D. P., & Haberfeld, Y. (1988). The impact of applicant gender compared to qualifications on hiring recommendations: A meta-analysis of experimental studies. *Organizational Behavior and Human Decision Processes, 41*, 180–195. **282**

Oliver, J. M., & Simmons, M. E. (1985). Affective disorders and depression as measured by the diagnostic interview schedule and the Beck Depression Inventory in an unselected adult population. *Journal of Clinical Psychology, 41*, 469–477. **360**

Olivier, B., & Mos, J. (1988). Serotonin, serenics and aggressive behavior in animals. In J. A. Swinkels & W. Blijleven (Eds.), *Depression, anxiety and aggression: Factors that influence the course,* pp. 133–165. Amsterdam: Medidact Medical Didactic Systems. **351**

Olmos, G., Auilera, P., Tranque, P., Naftolin, F., & Garcia-Segura, L. M. (1987). Estrogen-induced synaptic remodelling in adult rat brain is accompanied by the reorganization of neuronal membranes. *Brain Research, 425*, 57–64. **127**

Olmos, G., Naftolin, F., Perez, J., Tranque, P. A., & Garcia-Segura, L. M. (1989). Synaptic remodeling in the rat arcuate nucleus during the estrous cycle. *Neuroscience, 32*, 663–667. **127, 138**

Olsen, K. L., & Whalen, R. E. (1984). Dihydrotestosterone activates male mating behavior in castrated King-Holtzman rats. *Hormones and Behavior, 18*, 380–392. **142**

Olson, J. E., Frieze, I. H., & Detlefsen, G. (1990). Having it all? Combining work and family in a male and a female profession. *Sex Roles, 23*, 515–534. **331**

Olweus, D. (1980a). The consistency issue in personality psychology revisitedwith special reference to aggression. *British Journal of Social and Clinical Psychology, 19*, 377–390. **356, 357**

————. (1980b). Testosterone, aggression, physical and personality dimensions in normal adolescent males. *Psychosomatic Medicine, 42*, 253–269. **356, 357**

O'Malley, B. W., Schwartz, R. J., & Schrader, W. T. (1976). A review of regulation of gene expression by steroid hormone receptors. *Journal of Steroid Biochemistry, 7*, 1151–1159. **136**

Omark, D. R. (1980). The unwelt and cognitive develoment. In D. R. Omark, F. F. Strayer, & D. G. Freedman (Eds.), *An ethological view of human conflict and social interaction.* New York: Garland STPM Press. **348**

Omark, D. R., & Edelman, M. S. (1975). A comparison of status hierarchies in young children: An ethological approach. *Social Science Information, 14*, 87–107. **316, 348**

Oomura, Y., Minami, T., & Nabekura, J. (1986). Effect of estradiol on the amygdala and ventromedial hypothalamic neurons. *Abstracts of the Society for Neuroscience, 12*, #363.6. **136, 152**

Oppenheim, R. W. (1981). Neuronal cell death and some related regressive phenomena during neurogenesis: A selective historical review and progress report. In W. M. Cowan (Ed.), *Studies in developmental neurobiology.* New York: Oxford University Press. **152**

Orlofsky, J. L. (1981). Relationship between sex role attitudes and personality traits and Sex Role Behavior Scale-1: A new measure of masculine and feminine role behaviors and interests. *Journal of Personality and Social Psychology, 40*, 927–940. **45, 48**

Orlofsky, J. L., Cohen, R. S., & Ramsden, M. W. (1985). Relationship between sex-role attitudes and personality traits and the Revised Sex-Role Behavior Scale. *Sex Roles, 12*, 377–392. **45, 270**

Orlofsky, J. L., Ramsden, M. W., & Cohen, R. S. (1982). Development of the Revised Sex Role Behavior Scale. *Journal of Personality Assessment, 46*, 632–638. **45, 48**

Ortner, S. B. (1974). Is female to male as nature is to culture? In M. Z. Rosaldo & L. Lamphere (Eds.), *Woman, culture, and society.* Stanford: Stanford University Press. **260**

Ortner, S. B., & Whitehead, H. (1981). Introduction: Accounting for sexual meanings. In S. B. Ortner & H. Whitehead (Eds.), *Sexual meanings: The cultural construction of gender and sexuality.* Cambridge: Cambridge University Press. **260**

Osherson, D. N., & Smith, E. E. (1981). On the adequacy of prototype theory as a theory of concepts. *Cognition, 9*, 35–58. **266, 268**

Ostfeld, R. S. (1985). Limiting resources and territoriality in microtine rodents. *American Naturalist, 126*, 1–15. **242**

————. (1986). Territoriality and mating system of California voles. *Journal of Animal Ecology, 55*, 691–706. **242**

Otto, M. W., Yeo, R. A., & Dougher, M. J. (1987). Right hemisphere involvement in depression: Toward a neuropsychological theory of negative affective experiences. *Biological Psychiatry, 22*, 1201–1215. **369**

Overpeck, J. G., Colson, S. H., Hohmann, J. R., Applestine, M. S., & Reilly, J. F. (1978). Concentrations of circulating steroids in normal prepubertal and adult male and female humans, chimpanzees, rhesus monkeys, rats, mice, and hamsters: A literature survey. *Journal of Toxicology and Environmental Health, 4*, 785–803. **178**

Owen, D. R. (1979). Psychological studies in XYY men. In H. L. Vallet & I. H. Porter (Eds.), *Genetic mechanisms of sexual development.* New York: Academic Press. **113, 114**

Ozer, D. J. (1987). Personality, intelligence, and spatial visualization: Correlates of mental rotations test performance. *Journal of Personality and Social Psychology, 53*, 129–134. **374, 394**

Paganini-Hill, A., Ross, R. K., & Henderson, R. B. (1988). Postmenopausal oestrogen treatment and stroke: A prospective study. *British Medical Journal, 297*, 519–522. **203**

Page, D. C., Brown, L. G., & de la Chapelle, A. (1987). Exchange of terminal portions of X- and Y-chromosomal short arms in human XX males. *Nature, 328*, 437–440. **106**

Page, D. C., Fisher, E. M. C., McGillivray, B., & Brown, L. G. (1990). Additional deletion in sex-determining region of human Y chromosome resolves paradox of X,t(Y;22) female. *Nature, 346*, 279–281. **123**

Page, D. C., Harper, M. E., Love, J., & Botstein, D. (1984). Occurrence of a transposition from the X-chromosome long arm to the Y-chromosome short arm during human evolution. *Nature, 311*, 119–123. **101**

Pagel, M. D., & Harvey, P. H. (1988). How mammals produce large-brained offspring. *Evolution, 42*, 948–957. **82**

Pak, R. C. K., Tsim, K. W. K., & Cheng, C. H. K. (1984). Pubertal gonadal hormones in modulating the testosterone dependency of hepatic aryl hydrocarbon hydroxylase in female rats. *Pharmacology, 29*, 121–127. **152**

———. (1985). The role of neonatal and pubertal gonadal hormones in regulating the sex dependence of the hepatic microsomal testosterone 5-reductase activity in the rat. *Journal of Endocrinology, 106*, 71–79. **152**

Palmer, J. D., Udry, J. R., & Morris, N. M. (1982). Diurnal and weekly, but no lunar rhythms in human copulation. *Human Biology, 54*, 111–121. **183**

Parikh, I., Rajenedran, K. G., Su, J.-L., Lopez, T., & Sar, M. (1987). Are estrogen receptors cytoplasmic or nuclear? Some immunocytochemical and biochemical studies. *Journal of Steroid Biochemistry, 27*, 1–3. **133, 135**

Park, B., & Hastie, R. (1987). Perception of variability in category development: Instance- versus abstraction-based stereotypes. *Journal of Personality and Social Psychology, 53*, 621–635. **288**

Park, B., & Rothbart, M. (1982). Perception of out-group homogeneity and levels of social categorization: Memory for the subordinate attributes in in-group and out-group members. *Journal of Personality and Social Psychology, 42*, 1051–1068. **269**

Parke, R. D., & Slaby, R. G. (1983). The development of aggression. In E. M. Hetherington (Ed.), *Handbook of child psychology. Vol. IV. Socialization, personality, and social development.* (Series ed.), . P. H. Mussen. New York: Wiley. **234, 356**

Parker, G. (1979). Parental characteristics in relation to depressive disorders. *British Journal of Psychiatry, 134*, 138–147. **364**

———. (1981). Parental reports of depressives: An investigation of several explanations. *Journal of Affective Disorders, 3*, 131–140. **367**

Parker, G. A., & Macnair, M. R. (1979). Models of parent-offspring conflict. IV. Suppression: Evolutionary retaliation by the parent. *Animal Behaviour, 27*, 1210–1235. **221**

Parker, L. N., & Lifrak, E. T. (1981). Adrenal and testicular androgen levels are correlated. *Hormones and Metabolic Research, 13*, 653–654. **147**

Parker, S. T. (1984). Playing for keeps: An evolutionary perspective on human games. In P. K. Smith (Ed.), *Play in animals and humans.* New York: Basil Blackwell. **316, 318**

Parkhouse, B. L., & Williams, J. M. (1986). Differential effects of sex and status on evaluation of coaching ability. *Research Quarterly for Exercise and Sport, 57*, 53–59. **283**

Parlee, M. B. (1982a). Changes in moods and activation levels during the menstrual cycle in experimental naive subjects. *Psychology of Women Quarterly, 7*, 119–131. **192**

———. (1982b). The psychology of the menstrual cycle: Biological and psychological perspectives. In R. C. Friedman (Ed.), *Behavior and the menstrual cycle.* New York: Marcel Dekker, Inc. **176, 193**

———. (1983). Menstrual rhythms in sensory processes: A review of fluctuations in vision, olfaction, audition, taste, and touch. *Psychological Bulletin, 93*, 539–548. **398**

Parsons, J. E., Kaczala, C. M., & Meece, J. L. (1982). Socialization of achievement altitudes and beliefs: Classroom influences. *Child Development, 53*, 322–339. **312**

Parsons, J. E., Meece, J. L., Adler, T. F., & Kaczala, C. M. (1982). Sex differences in attributions and learned helplessness. *Sex Roles, 8*, 421–432. **333**

Parsons, J. E., & Ruble, D. N. (1977). The development of achievement-related expectancies. *Child Development, 48*, 1075–1079. **333**

Pattison, P., & Grieve, N. (1984). Do spatial skills contribute to sex differences in different types of mathematical problems? *Journal of Educational Psychology, 76*, 678–689. **373**

Pau, K.-Y. F., Gliessman, P. M., Hess, D. L., & Spies, H. G. (1988). Effects of estrogen on hypothalamic gonadotropin-releasing hormone release in castrated male rhesus macaques. *Brain Research, 459*, 70–75. **145**

Paul, A., & Kuester, J. (1987). Sex ratio adjustment in a seasonally breeding primate species: Evidence from the Barbary macaque population at Affenbrg Salem. *Ethology, 74*, 117–132. **80**

Paulhus, D. L. (1984). Two-component models of socially desirable responding. *Journal of Personality and Social Psychology, 46*, 598–609. **280**

Paulson, J. D., Keller, D. W., Wiest, W. G., & Warren, J. C. (1977). Free testosterone concentration in serum: Elevation in the hallmark of hirsutism. *American Journal of Obstetrics and Gynecology, 128*, 851–857. **190**

Pazy, A. (1986). The persistence of pro-male bias despite identical information regarding causes of success. *Organizational Behavior and Human Decision Processes, 38*, 366–377. **282**

Pearlstein, T. B., Frank E., Rivera-Tovar, A., Thoft, J. S., Jacobs, E., & Mieczkowski, T. A. (1990). Prevalence of axis I and axis II disorders in women with late luteal phase dysphoric disorder. *Journal of Affective Disorders, 20*, 129–134. **193, 198**

Pearson, J. L., & Ferguson, L. R. (1989). Gender differences in patterns of spatial ability, environmental cognition, and math and English achievement in late adolescence. *Adolescence, 24*, 421–431. **374, 377, 391**

Pearson, J. L., & Ialongo, N. S. (1986). The relationship between spatial ability and environmental knowledge. *Journal of Environmental Psychology, 6*, 299–304. **377**

Peck, J. R., & Feldman, M. W. (1988). Kin selection and the evolution of monogamy. *Science, 240*, 1672–1674. **88**

Pedhazur, E. J., & Tetenbaum, T. J. (1979). Bem Sex Role Inventory: A theoretical and methodological critique. *Journal of Personality and Social Psychology, 37*, 996–1016. **47**

Pellegrini, A. D. (1986). *Rough-and-tumble play: Developmental and educational significance.* Paper published by the Institute for Behavioral Research, University of Georgia, Athens. **316**

Pellegrini, A. D., & Perlmutter, J. C. (1989). Classroom contextual effects on children's play. *Developmental Psychology, 25*, 289–296. **302, 308, 314**

Pellegrini, R. J., Hicks, R. A., & Meyers-Winton, S. (1979). Situational affective arousal and heterosexual attraction: Some effects of success, failure, and physical attractiveness. *Psychological Record, 29*, 453–462. **378**

Pemberton, J. M., Albon, S. D., Guinness, F. E., & Clutton-Brock, T. H. (1991). Countervailing selection in different fitness components in female red deer. *Evolution, 45*, 93–103. **68**

Pennington, B., Puck, M., & Robinson, A. (1980). Language and cognitive development in 47,XXX females followed since birth. *Behavior Genetics, 10*, 31–41. **114**

Pennington, B. F., Heaton, R. K., Karzmark, P., Pendleton, M. G., Lehman, R., & Shucard, D. W. (1985). The neuropsychological phenotype in Turner syndrome. *Cortex, 21*, 391–404. **114**

Peoria Journal Star. (1989). Bachelors gain power in society lacking young brides. February 23, A14. **250**

Peplau, L. A., & Conrad, E. (1989). Beyond nonsexist research: The perils of feminist methods in psychology. *Psychology of Women Quarterly,, 13*, 379–400. **24**

Perachio, A. A., Alexander, M., Marr, L. D., & Collins, D. C. (1977). Diurnal variations of serum testosterone levels in intact and gonadectomized male and female rhesus monkeys. *Steroids, 29*, 21–33. **178, 184**

Perloff, R. M. (1977). Some antecedents of children's sex-role stereotypes. *Psychological Reports, 40*, 463–466. **294**

Perris, C., Maj, M., Perris, M., & Eisemann, M. (1985). Perceived parental rearing behaviour in unipolar and bipolar depressed patients: A verification study in an Italian sample. *Acta Psychiatrica Scandinavica, 72*, 172–175. **367**

Perris, H. (1984a). Life events and personality characteristics in depression. *Acta Psychiatrica Scandinavica, 69*, 350–358. **364**

_____. (1984b). Life events and depression: Part 1. Effect of sex, age and civil status. *Journal of Affective Disorders, 7*, 11–24. **364**

_____. (1984c). Life events and depression: Part 2. Results in diagnostic subgroups, and in relation to the recurrence of depression. *Journal of Affective Disorders, 7*, 25–36. **364**

_____. (1984d). Life events and depression: Part 3. Relation to the severity of the depressive syndrome. *Journal of Affective Disorders, 7*, 37–44. **364**

Perry, D. G., & Bussey, K. (1979). The social learning theory of sex differences: Imitation is alive and well. *Journal of Personality and Social Psychology, 37*, 1699–1712. **230-231**

Perry, D. G., White, A. J., & Perry, L. C. (1984). Does early sex typing result from children's attempts to match their behavior to sex role stereotypes? *Child Development, 55*, 2114–2121. **218, 307**

Pervin, L. A. (1985). Personality: current controversies, issues, and directions. *Annual Review of Psychology, 36*, 83–114. **339**

Peters, S. L., Gray, J. A., & Joseph, M. H. (1991). Pre-weaning non-handling of rats disrupts latent inhibition in males, and results in persisting sex- and area-dependent increases in dopamine and serotonin turnover. *Behavioural Pharmacology, 2*, 215–223. **369**

Peterson, A. C. (1976). Physical androgyny and cognitive functioning in adolescence. *Developmental Psychology, 12*, 524–533. **398**

_____. (1987, September). Those gangly years. *Psychology Today,* 28–34. **322**

Peterson, A. C. (1988). Adolescent development. *Annual Review of Psychology, 39*, 583–607. **228**

Peterson, G. W., Rollins, B. C., Thomas, D. L., & Heaps, L. K. (1982). Social placement of adolescents: Sex-role influences on family decisions regarding the careers of youth. *Journal of Marriage and the Family, 44*, 647–658. **283, 325**

Petrovich, S. B., & Gewirtz, J. L. (1985). The attachment learning process and its relation to cultural and biological evolution: Proximate and ultimate considerations. In M. Reite & T. Field (Eds.), *The psychobiology of attachment and separation.* New York: Academic Press. **365**

Pezaris, E., & Casey, M. B. (1991). Girls who use "masculine" problem-solving strategies on a spatial task: Proposed genetic and environmental factors. *Brain and Cognition, 17*, 1–22. **392**

Pheterson, G. I., Kiesler, S. B., & Goldberg, P. A. (1971). Evaluation of the performance of women as a function of their sex, achievement, and personal history. *Journal of Personality and Social Psychology, 19*, 114–118. **280**

Phillis, J. W., & O'Regan, M. H. (1988). Effects of estradiol on cerebral cortical neurons and their responses to adenosine. *Brain Research Bulletin, 20*, 151–155. **139**

Phoenix, C. H. (1974). Prenatal testosterone in the nonhuman primate and its consequences for behavior. In R. C. Friedman, R. M. Richart, & R. L. Vande Wiele (Eds.), *Sex differences in behavior.* New York: Wiley. **358**

Phoenix, C. H., & Chambers, K. C. (1986). Threshold for behavioral response to testosterone in old castrated male rhesus macaques. *Biology of Reproduction, 35*, 918–926. **387**

Phoenix, C. H., Walther, A. M., Jensen, J. N., & Chambers, K. C. (1989). The effect of human chorionic gonadotropin on serum levels of testosterone, estradiol, and sexual behavior in young and old rhesus males. *Physiology & Behavior, 46*, 647–653. **203**

Pillard, R. C., Poumadere, J., & Carretta, R. A. (1981). Is homosexuality familial? A review, some data, and a suggestion. *Archives of Sexual Behavior, 10*, 465–475. **388, 389**

_____. (1982). A family study of sexual orientation. *Archives of Sexual Behavior, 11*, 511–520. **388, 389**

Pillard, R. C., & Weinrich, J. C. (1986). Evidence of familial nature of male homosexuality. *Archives of General Psychiatry, 43*, 808–812. **388, 389**

Plaznik, A., Kostowski, W., & Archer, T. (1989). Serotonin and depression: Old problems and new data. *Progress in Neuro-Psychopharmacology & Biological Psychiatry, 13*, 623–633. **369**

Pleck, J. H. (1985). *Working wives, working husbands.* Beverly Hills: Sage. **306**

Plomin, R. (1991). Why children in the same family are so different from one another. *Behavioral and Brain Sciences, 14*, 336–338. **234**

Pohl-Apel, G. (1985). The correlation between the degree of brain masculinization and song quality in estradiol treated female zebra finches. *Brain Research, 336*, 381–383. **142**

Pointis, G., Latreille, M.-T., Richard, M. O., D'Athis, P., & Cedard, L. (1987). Effect of natural progesterone treatment during pregnancy on fetal testosterone and sexual behavior of the male offspring in the mouse. *Developmental Pharmacology and Therapeutics, 10*, 385–392. **170**

Polachek, S. (1976). Occupational segregation: An alternative hypothesis. *Journal of Contemporary Business, 5*, 1–12. **331**

_____. (1978). Sex difference in college major. *Industrial and Labor Relations Review, 31*, 498–508. **331**

_____. (1979). Occupational segregation among women: Theory, evidence and a prognosis. In C. Lloyd (Ed.), *Women in the labor market.* New York: Columbia University Press. **331**

_____. (1981). Occupational self-selection: A human capital approach to sex differences in occupational structure. *Review of Economics and Statistics, 58*, 60–69. **331**

Polit, D. F., & LaRocco, S. A. (1980). Social and psychological correlates of menopausal symptoms. *Psychosomatic Medicine, 42*, 335–345. **200**

Polivy, J., & Herman, C. P. (1976). Clinical depression and weight change: A complex relation. *Journal of Abnormal Psychology, 85*, 338–340. **362**

Pollis, C. A. (1988). An assessment of the impacts of feminism on sexual science. *Journal of Sex Research, 25*, 85–105. **12**

Pomerantz, S. M., Goy, R. W., & Roy, M. M. (1986). Expression of male-typical behavior in adult female pseudohermaphroditic rhesus: Comparisons with normal males and neonatally gonadectomized males and females. *Hormones and Behavior, 20,* 483-500. **142, 150**

Pomiankowski, A. (1987). Sexual selection: The handicap principle does work — sometimes. *Proceedings of the Royal Society of London, Series B, 231,* 123-145. **87**

—————. (1989). Choosing parasite-free mates. *Nature, 338,* 115-116. **87**

—————. (1990). How to find the top male. *Nature, 347,* 616-617. **216**

Pontius, A. A. (1989). Color and spatial error in block design in stone-age Acua Indians: Ecological underuse of occipital-parietal system in men and of frontal lobes in women. *Brain and Cognition, 10,* 54-75. **396**

Popiel, E. M., & De Lisi, R. (1984). An examination of spatial ability in relation to factors from the Bem Sex-Role Inventory. *Perceptual and Motor Skills, 59,* 131-136. **391**

Porac, C., Coren, S., & Searleman, A. (1986). Environmental factors in hand preference formation: Evidence from attempts to switch the preferred hand. *Behavior Genetics, 16,* 251-261. **397**

Porter, M. E., Gardner, H. A., DeFeudis, P., & Endler, N. S. (1988). Verbal deficits in Klinefelter (XXY) adults living in the community. *Clinical Genetics, 33,* 246-253. **113**

Post, R. M. (1992). Transduction of psychosocial stress into the neurobiology of recurrent affective disorder. *American Journal of Psychiatry, 149,* 999-1010. **364**

Post-Kammer, P., & Smith, P. L. (1985). Sex differences in career self-efficacy, consideration, and interests of eighth and ninth graders. *Journal of Counseling Psychology, 32,* 551-559. **329**

Powell, G. N. (1987). The effects of sex and gender on recruitment. *Academy of Management Review, 12,* 731-743. **282**

Power, C., & Moynihan, C. (1988). Social class and changes in weight-for-height between childhood and early adulthood. *International Journal of Obesity, 12,* 445-453. **380**

Power, T. G., & Shanks, J. A. (1989). Parents as socializers: Maternal and paternal views. *Journal of Youth and Adolescence, 18,* 203-220. **299**

Powers, K. L. (1979). Sex segregation and the ambivalent directions of sex discrimination law. *Wisconsin Law Review,* 55-124. **278**

Preslock, J. P. (1980). A review of in vitro testicular steroidogenesis in rodents, monkeys and humans. *Journal of Steroid Biochemistry, 13,* 965-975. **156**

Preslock, J. P., & McCann, S. M. (1987). Lesions of the sexually dimorphic nucleus of the preoptic area: Effects upon LH, FSH and prolactin in rats. *Brain Research Bulletin, 18,* 127-134. **162**

Presser, H. B. (1987). Work shifts of full-time dual-earner couples: Patterns and contrasts by sex of spouse. *Demography, 24,* 99-112. **324**

Price, T., Kirkpatrick, M., & Arnold, S. J. (1988). Directional selection and the evolution of breeding date in birds. *Science, 240,* 798-799. **68**

Prince, V. (1985). Sex, gender, and semantics. *Journal of Sex Research, 21,* 92-101. **6**

Pugh, M. D., & Wahrman, R. (1983). Neutralizing sexism in mixed-sex groups: Do women have to be better than men? *American Journal of Sociology, 88,* 746-762. **286**

—————. (1985). Inequality of influence in mixed-sex groups. In J. Berger & M. Zelditch, Jr. (Eds.), *Status, rewards, and influence.* San Francisco: Jossey-Bass. **286**

Purcell, P., & Stewart, L. (1990). Dick and Jane in 1989. *Sex Roles, 22,* 177-186. **289**

Purtilo, D. T., Yang, J. P. S., Allegra, S., DeFloriao, D., Hutt, L. M., Soltani, M., & Vawter, G. (1977). Hermatopathology and pathogenesis of the X-linked recessive lymphoproliferative syndrome. *American Journal of Medicine, 62,* 225-233. **119**

Purvis, K., Calandra, R., & Hansson, V. (1977). Adrenal secretion and plasma CBG levels in the immature male rat: Effects of 5 reduced androgens and antiandrogens. *Journal of Steroid Biochemistry, 8,* 1121-1124. **128**

Pusey, A. E., & Packer, C. (1987a). Dispersal and philopatry. In B. B. Smuts, D. L., Cheney, R. M. Seyfarth, R. W. Wrangham, & T. T. Struhsaker (Eds.), *Primate societies.* Chicago: University of Chicago Press. **242, 243**

—————. (1987b). The evolution of sex-biased dispersal in lions. *Behaviour, 101,* 275-310. **242**

Quackenbush, R. L. (1989). A comparison of androgynous, masculine sex-typed, and undifferentiated males on dimensions of attitudes toward rape. *Journal of Research in Personality, 23,* 318-342. **386**

Quadagno, D. M., Dixon, L. A., Denney, N. W., & Buck, H. W. (1986). Postpartum moods in men and women. *American Journal of*

Obstetrics and Gynecology, 154, 1018-1023. **197**

Quadagno, D. M., Shubeita, H. E., Deck, J., & Francoeur, D. (1981). Influence of male social contacts, exercise and all-female living conditions on the menstrual cycle. *Psychoneuroendocrinology, 6,* 239-244. **190, 191**

Rabson, A. B., Steele, P. E., Garon, C. F., & Martin, M. A. (1983). mRNA transcripts related to full-length endogenous retroviral DNA in human cells. *Nature, 306,* 604-607. **67**

Rachman, S., & Hodgson, R. J. (1968). Experimentally-induced "sexual fetishism:" Replication and development. *Psychological Record, 18,* 25-27. **382**

Ragan, P. V., & McGlashan, T. H. (1986). Childhood parental death and adult psychopathology. *American Journal of Psychiatry, 143,* 153-157. **364**

Rakic, P. (1985a). DNA synthesis and cell division in the adult primate brain. *Annals of the New York Academy of Sciences, 457,* 193-212. **152**

—————. (1985b). Limits of neurogenesis in primates. *Science, 227,* 1054-1055. **152**

—————. (1988). Specification of cerebral cortical areas. *Science, 241,* 170-176. **152**

Rakic, P., Bourgeois, J.-P., Eckenhoff, M. F., Zecevic, N., & Goldman-Rakic, P. S. (1986). Concurrent overproduction of synapses in diverse regions of the primate cerebral cortex. *Science, 232,* 232-235. **225**

Rakic, P., & Riley, K. P. (1983). Overproduction and elimination of retinal axons in the fetal rhesus monkey. *Science, 219,* 1441-1444. **224**

Raleigh, M. J., McGuire, M. T., Brammer, G. L., & Yuwiler, A. (1984). Social and environmental infuences on blood serotonin concentrations in monkeys. *Archives of General Psychiatry, 41,* 405-410. **351**

Ralls, K. (1976). Mammals in which females are larger than males. *Quarterly Review of Biology, 51,* 245-276. **79, 88**

—————. (1977). Sexual dimorphism in mammals: Avian models and unanswered questions. *American Naturalist, 111,* 917-938. **79, 84, 88**

Ralls, K., Brugger, K., & Ballou, J. (1979). Inbreeding and juvenile mortality in small populations of ungulates. *Science, 206,* 1101-1103. **75**

Ramaniah, N. V., & Hoffman, S. C. (1984). Effects of instructions and rating scales on item selection of the BSRI scales. *Journal of Personality Assessment, 48,* 145–152. **44**

Rambo, C. O., & Szego, C. M. (1983). Estrogen action at endometrial membranes: Alterations in luminal surface detectable within seconds. *Journal of Cell Biology, 97,* 679–685. **137**

Ramirez, V. D., & Dluzen, D. (1987). Is progesterone a pre-hormone in the CNS? *Journal of Steroid Biochemistry, 27,* 589–598. **151**

Ramirez, V. D., Feder, H. H., & Sawyer, C. H. (1984). The role of brain catecholamines in the regulation of Lh secretion: A critical inquiry. In L. Martini & W. F. Ganong (Eds.), *Frontiers in neuroendocrinology* (vol. 8). New York: Raven Press. **145**

Ramist, L., & Arbeiter, S. (1986). *Profiles, college-bound seniors, 1985.* College Entrance Examination Board. **373**

Ramsey, C. N., Jr., Abell, T. C., & Baker, L. C. (1986). The relationship between family functioning, life events, family structure, and the outcome of pregnancy. *Journal of Family Practice, 22,* 522–527. **148**

Rand, M. N., & Breedlove, S. M. (1988). Progress report on a hormonally sensitive neuromuscular system. *Psychobiology, 16,* 398–405. **163**

Rasinski, K. A., Crocker, J., & Hastie, R. (1985). Another look at sex stereotypes and social judgments: An analysis of the social perceiver's use of subjective probabilities. *Journal of Personality and Social Psychology, 49,* 317–326. **275**

Rastan, S., Kaufman, M. H., Handyside, A. H., & Lyon, M. F. (1980). X-chromosome inactivation in extra-embryonic membranes of diploid parthenogenetic mouse embryos demonstrated by differential staining. *Nature, 288,* 172–173. **104**

Ratcliffe, S. G. (1981). The effect of chromosome abnormalities on human growth. *British Medical Bulletin, 37,* 291–295. **112**

————. (1982). Speech and learning disorders in children with sex chromosome abnormalities. *Developmental Medicine and Child Neurology, 24,* 80–84. **119**

Ratcliffe, S. G., Bancroft, J., Axworthy, D., & McLaren, W. (1982). Klinefelter's syndrome in adolescence. *Archives of Disease in Childhood, 57,* 6–12. **115**

Ratcliffe, S. G., & Field, M. A. S. (1982). Emotional disorder in XYY children: Four case reports. *Journal of Child Psychology and Psychiatry, 23,* 401–406. **116**

Ratcliffe, S. G., Jenkins, J., & Teague, P. (1990). Cognitive and behavioural development of the 47,XYY child. In D. B. Berch & B. G. Bender (Eds.), *Sex chromsome abnormalities and human behavior: Psychological studies.* Boulder, CO: Westview Press. **116**

Ratcliffe, S. G., Murray, L., & Teague, P. (1986). Edinburgh study of growth and development of children with sex chromosome abnormalities III. *Birth defects: Original Articles Series, 22,* 73–118. **116**

Rauste-von Wright, M., von Wright, J., & Frankenhaeuser, M. (1981). Relationships between sex-related psychological characteristics during adolescence and catecholamine excretion during achievement stress. *Psychophysiology, 18,* 362–370. **322, 332**

Reeb, K. G., Graham, A. V., Zyzanski, S. J., & Kitson, G. C. (1987). Predicting low birthweight and complicated labor in urban black women: A biopsychosocial perspective. *Social Science and Medicine, 25,* 1321–1327. **148**

Rees, H. D., Bonsall, R. W., & Michael, R. P. (1985). Localization of the synthetic progestin 3H-ORG 2058 in neurons of the primate brain: Evidence for the site of action of progestins on behavior. *Journal of Comparative Neurology, 235,* 336–342. **180**

Rees, H. D., & Michael, R. P. (1983). Autoradiographic localization of 3H-dihydrotestosterone in the thalamus and brain stem of a male rhesus monkey. *Neuroendocrinology Letters, 5,* 55–61. **203**

Reinberg, A., & Lagoguey, M. (1978). Circadian and circannual rhythms in sexual activity and plasma hormones (FSH, LH, testosterone) of five human males. *Archives of Sexual Behavior, 7,* 13–30. **196, 203**

Reinberg, A., Lagoguey, M., Cesselin, F., Touitou, Y., Legrand, J.-C., Delassalle, A., Antreassian, J., & Lagoguey, A. (1978). Circadian and circannual rhythms in plasma hormones and other variables of five healthy young human males. *Acta Endocrinologica, 88,* 417–427. **196, 203**

Reinisch, J. M. (1981). Prenatal exposure to synthetic progestins increases potential for aggression in humans. *Science, 21,* 1171–1173. **370**

Reinisch, J. M., & Karow, W. G. (1977). Prenatal exposure to synthetic progestins and estrogens: Effects on human development. *Archives of Sexual Behavior, 6,* 257–288. **370**

Reinisch, J. M., & Sanders, S. A.

(1984). Prenatal gonadal steroidal influences on gender-related behavior. *Progress in Brain Research, 61,* 407–416. **370**

Reinisch, J. M., Ziemba-Davis, M., & Sanders, S. (1991). Hormonal contributions to sexually dimorphic behavioral development in humans. *Psychoneuroendocrinology, 16,* 213–278. **168, 370, 388, 399**

Reisert, I., Engele, J., & Pilgrim, Ch. (1989). Early sexual differentiation of diencephalic dopaminergic neurons of the rat in vitro. *Cell and Tissue Research, 255,* 411–417. **137**

Reisert, I., Han, V., Lieth, E., Toran-Allerand, D., Pilgrim, C., & Lauder, J. (1987). Sex steroids promote neurite growth in mesencephalic tyrosine hydroxylase immunoreactive neurons in vitro. *International Journal of Developmental Neuroscience, 5,* 91–98. **137**

Reiss, A. L., Hagerman, R. J., Vinogradov, S., Abrams, M., & King, R. J. (1988). Psychiatric disability in female carriers of the fragile X chromosome. *Archives of General Psychiatry, 45,* 25–30. **121**

Renner, K. J., Smits, A. W., Quadagno, D. M., & Hough, J. C. (1984). Suppression of sexual behavior and localization of [3H] puromycin after intracranial injection in the rat. *Physiology & Behavior, 33,* 411–414. **136**

Repetti, R. L. (1984). Determinants of children's sex stereotyping: Parental sex-role traits and television viewing. *Personality and Social Psychology Bulletin, 10,* 457–468. **293**

Rescorla, R. A. (1987). A Pavlovian analysis of goal-directed behavior. *American Psychologist, 42,* 119–129. **213**

————. (1988). Pavlovian conditioning: It's not what you think it is. *American Psychologist, 43,* 151–160. **212**

Reske-Nielsen, E., Christensen, A.-L., & Nielsen, J. (1982). A neuropathological and neuropsychological study of Turner's syndrome. *Cortex, 18,* 181–190. **114**

Resko, J. A., Buhl, A. E., & Phoenix, C. H. (1987). Treatment of pregnant rhesus macaques with testosterone propionate: observations on its fate in the fetus. *Biology of Reproduction, 37,* 1185–1191. **168**

Resnick, S. M., Berenbaum, S. A., Gotesman, I. I., & Bouchard, T. J., Jr. (1986). Early hormonal influences on cognitive functioning in congenital adrenal hyperplasia. *Developmental Psychology, 22,* 191–198. **399**

Restak, R. M. (1979). *The brain: The last frontier.* New York: Warner Books. **5**

Rhees, R. W., Shryne, J. E., & Gorski, R. A. (1990a). Onset of the hormone-sensitive perinatal period for sexual differentiation of the sexually dimorphic nucleus of the preoptic area in female rats. *Journal of Neurobiology, 21*, 781–786. **163**

_____. (1990b). Termination of the hormone-sensitive period for differentiation of the sexually dimorphic nucleus of the preoptic area in male and female rats. *Developmental Brain Research, 52*, 17–23. **163**

Rheingold, H. L., & Cook, K. V. (1975). The contents of boys' and girls' rooms as an index of parents' behavior. *Child Development, 46*, 459–463. **308**

Rhine, R. J., Cox, R. L., & Costello, M. B. (1989). A twenty-year study of long-term and temporary dominance relations among stumptailed macaques (Macaca arctoides). *American Journal of Primatology, 19*, 69–82. **79**

Rhine, R. J., Wasser, S. K., & Norton, G. W. (1988). Eight-year study of social and ecological correlates of mortality among immature baboons of Mikumi National Park, Tanzania. *American Journal of Primatology, 16*, 199–212. **80**

Rhodewalt, F., & Agustsdottir, S. (1986). Effects of self-presentation on the phenomenal self. *Journal of Personality and Social Psychology, 50*, 47–55. **279**

Rice, J., Reich, T., Andreasen, N. C., Lavori, P. W., Endicott, J., Clayton, P. J., Keller, M. B., Hirschfeld, R. M. A., & Klerman, G. L. (1984). Sex-related differences in depression: Familial evidence. *Journal of Affective Disorders, 71*, 199–210. **103, 363**

Rice, W. R. (1988). Heritable variation in fitness as a prerequisite for adaptive female choice: The effect of mutation-selection balance. *Evolution, 42*, 817–820. **86, 87**

Rich, C. L., Ricketts, J. E., Fowler, R. C., & Young, D. (1988). Some differences between men and women who commit suicide. *American Journal of Psychiatry, 145*, 718–722. **366**

Rich, D. A., & McKeever, W. F. (1990). An investigation of immune system disorder as a "marker" for anomalous dominance. *Brain and Cognition, 12*, 55–72. **398**

Richards, M. H., & Larson, R. (1989). The life space and socialization of the self: Sex differences in the young adolescent. *Journal of Youth and Adolescence, 18*, 617–626 **297**

Richardson, J. T. E. (1991). The menstrual cycle and student learning. *Journal of Higher Education, 62*, 317–340. **176**

Richardson, S. J., Senikas, V., & Nelson, J. F. (1987). Follicular depletion during the menopausal transition: Evidence for accelerated loss and ultimate exhaustion. *Journal of Clinical Endocrinology and Metabolism, 65*, 1231–1237. **198**

Richert, A., & Hoyenga, K. I. (1982, May). *Measurement of individual differences in sex-role stereotyping.* Paper presented at the meeting of the Midwestern Psychological Association, Minneapolis. **277**

_____. (1986, May). *Measurement of individual differences in sex role stereotyping: Validational evidence for a new approach.* Paper presented at the meeting of the Midwestern Psychological Association, Chicago. **277**

Richter, C. P. (1968). Periodic phenomena in man and animals: Their relation to neuroendocrine mechanisms (a monthly or nearly monthly cycle). In R. P. Michael (Ed.), *Endocrinology and human behavior.* New York: Oxford University Press. **195**

Ridley, R. M., Frith, C. D., Crow, T. J., & Conneally, P. M. (1988). Anticipation in Huntington's disease is inherited through the male line but may originate in the female. *Journal of Medical Genetics, 25*, 589–595. **103**

Riis, B., Thomsen, K., & Christiansen, C. (1987). Does calcium supplementation prevent postmenopuasal bone loss? A double-blind, controlled clinical study. *New England Journal of Medicine, 316*, 173–177. **200**

Riley, D., & Cochran, M. (1987). Children's relationships with nonparental adults: Sex-specific connections to early school success. *Sex Roles, 17*, 637–656. **300**

Rips, L. J., Shoben, E. J., & Smith, E. E. (1973). Semantic distance and the verification of semantic relations. *Journal of Verbal Learning and Verbal Behavior, 12*, 1–20. **266**

Risch, N., Baron, M., & Mendlewicz, J. (1986). Assessing the role of X-linked inheritance in bipolar-related major affective disorder. *Journal of Psychiatric Research, 20*, 275–288. **110**

Rivera-Tovar, A. D., & Frank, E. (1990). Late luteal phase dysphoric disorder in young women. *American Journal of Psychiatry, 147*, 1634–1636. **191**

Rivier, C., Rivier, J., & Vale, W. (1986). Inhibin-mediated feedback control of follicle-stimulating hormone secretion in the female rat. *Science, 234*, 205–208. **145**

Robert, M. (1990). Sex-typing of the water-level task: There is more than meets the eye. *International Journal of Psychology, 25*, 475–490. **394**

Robert, M., & Tanguay, M. (1990). Perception and representation of the Euclidean coordinates in mature and elderly men and women. *Experimental Aging Research, 16*, 123–131. **374**

Roberts, L. (1988). Zeroing in on the sex switch. *Science, 239*, 21–23. **106**

Roberts, T.-A., & Nolen-Hoeksema, S. (1989). Sex differences in reactions to evaluative feedback. *Sex Roles, 21*, 725–748. **365**

Robinson, C. C., & Morris, J. T. (1986). The gender-stereotyped nature of Christmas toys received by 36-, 48-, and 60-month-old children: A comparison between nonrequested vs. requested toys. *Sex Roles, 15*, 21–32. **307**

Robinson, G. E., & Stewart, D. E. (1986). Postpartum psychiatric disorders. *Canadian Medical Association Journal, 134*, 31–37. **197, 198**

Robinson, J. P. (1988, December). Who's doing the housework? *American Demographics*, 24–28, 63. **304, 307**

Robinson, R. G., Lipsey, J. R., Bolla-Wilson, K., Bolduc, P. L., Pearlson, G. C., Rao, K., & Price, T. R. (1985). Mood disorders in left-handed stroke patients. *American Journal of Psychiatry, 142*, 1424–1429. **369**

Rockett, I. R. H., & Smith, G. S. (1989). Homicide, suicide, motor vehicle crash, and fall mortality: United States' experience in comparative perspective. *American Journal of Public Health, 79*, 1396–1400. **356**

Rodin, M. J. (1987). Who is memorable to whom: A study of cognitive disregard. *Social Cognition, 5*, 144–165. **274**

Rodriguez-Sierra, J. F., & Clough, R. W. (1987). Sexual dimorphism in the synaptogenic effect of estradiol in prepuberal female rats. *Synapse, 1*, 258–264. **181**

Rodriguez-Sierra, J. F., Hagley, M. T., & Hendricks, S. E. (1986). Anxiolytic effects of progesterone are sexually dimorphic. *Life Sciences, 38*, 1841–1845. **139**

Rodriguez-Sierra, J. F., Howard, J. L., Pollard, G. T., & Hendricks, S. E. (1984). Effect of ovarian hormones on conflict behavior. *Psychoneuroendocrinology, 9*, 293–300. **139**

Roenneberg, T., & Aschoff, J. (1990a). Annual rhythm of human reproduction: I. Biology, sociology, or both? *Journal of Biological Rhythms, 5*, 195–216. **196**

_____. (1990b). Annual rhythm

of human reproduction: II. Environmental correlations. *Journal of Biological Rhythms, 5*, 217–239. **196**

Roffi, J., Chami, F., Corbier, P., & Edwards, D. A. (1987). Testicular hormones during the first few hours after birth augment the tendency of adult male rats to mount receptive females. *Physiology & Behavior, 39*, 625–628. **150, 160**

Roffwarg, H. P., Sachar, E. J., Halpern, F., & Hellman, L. (1982). Plasma testosterone during sleep: Relationship to sleep stage variables. *Psychosomatic Medicine, 44*, 73–84. **182**

Rohde, P., Lewinsohn, P. M., Tilson, M., & Seeley, J. (1990). Dimensionality of coping and its relation to depression. *Journal of Personality and Social Psychology, 58*, 499–511. **360, 361, 364, 365**

Romano, G. J., Mobbs, C. V., Howells, R. D., & Pfaff, D. W. (1989). Estrogen regulation of proenkephalin gene expression in the ventromedial hypothalamus of the rat: Temporal qualities and synergism with progesterone. *Molecular Brain Research, 5*, 51–58. **139**

Romano, G. J., Harlan, R. E., Shivers, B. D., Howell, R. D., & Pfaff, D. W. (1988). Estrogen increases proenkephalin messenger ribonucleic acid levels in the ventromedial hypothalamus of the rat. *Molecular Endocrinology, 2*, 1320–1328. **139**

Romano, G. J., Krust, A., & Pfaff, D. W. (1989). Expression and estrogen regulation of progesterone receptor mRNA in neurons of the mediaobasal hypothalamus: An in situ hybridization study. *Molecular Endocrinology, 3*, 1295–1300. **136**

Romano, G. J., Mobbs, C. V., Lauber, A., Howells, R. D., & Pfaff, D. W. (1990). Differential regulation of proenkephalin gene expression by estrogen in the ventromedial hypothalamus of male and female rats: Implications for the molecular basis of a sexually differentiated behavior. *Brain Research, 536*, 63–68. **136**

Romero, M. (1985). A comparison between strategies used on prisoners of war and battered wives. *Sex Roles, 13*, 537–548. **353**

Romney, A. K. (1965). Variations in household structure as determinants of sex-typed behavior. In F. A. Beach (Ed.), *Sex and behavior.* New York: Wiley. **356**

Ronkainen, H. R. A., Pakarinen, A. J., & Kauppila, A. J. I. (1986). Adrenocortical function of female endurance runners and joggers. *Medicine and Science in Sports and*

Exercise, 18, 385–389. **196**

Roopnarine, J. L. (1984). Sex-typed socialization in mixed-age preschool classrooms. *Child Development, 55*, 1078–1084. **316**

Rosaldo, M. Z. (1974). Women, culture, and society: A theoretical overview. In M. Z. Rosaldo & L. Lamphere (Eds.), *Woman, culture, and society.* Stanford: Stanford University Press. **259, 260**

_____. (1980). The use and abuse of anthropology: Reflections on feminism and cross-cultural understanding. *Signs: Journal of Women in Culture and Society, 5*, 389–417. **260, 261**

Rosch, E. (1975a). Reply to Loftus. *Journal of Experimental Psychology: General, 104*, 241–243. **266**

_____. (1975b). Cognitive representations of semantic categories. *Journal of Experimental Psychology: General, 104*, 192–233. **266**

Rosch, E., & Mervis, C. B. (1975). Family resemblances: Studies in the internal structure of categories. *Cognitive Psychology, 7*, 573–605. **266, 268**

Rose, J. D. (1986). Functional reconfiguration of midbrain neurons by ovarian steroids in behaving hamsters. *Physiology & Behavior, 37*, 633–647. **181**

Rose, R. J. (1988). Genetic and environmental variance in content dimensions of the MMPI. *Journal of Personality and Social Psychology, 55*, 302–311. **234**

Rosen, G. C., Sherman, G. F., Mehler, C., Emsbo, K., & Galaburda, A. M. (1989). The effect of developmental neuropathology on neocortical asymmetry in New Zealand black mice. *International Journal of Neuroscience, 45*, 247–254. **374**

Rosen, L. N., Moghadam, L. Z., & Endicott, J. (1988). Psychosocial correlates of premenstrual dysphoric subtypes. *Acta Psychiatrica Scandinavica, 77*, 446–453. **193**

Rosenberger, L. M., & Strube, M. J. (1986). The influence of Type A and B behavior patterns on the perceived quality of dating relationships. *Journal of Applied Social Psychology, 16*, 277–286. **381**

Rosenblatt, H., Dyrenfurth, I., Ferin, M., & vande Wiele, R. L. (1980). Food intake and the menstrual cycle in rhesus monkeys. *Physiology & Behavior, 24*, 447–449. **189**

Rosenkrantz, P., Vogel, S., Bee, H., Broverman, I., & Broverman, D. M. (1968). Sex-role stereotypes and self-concepts in college students. *Journal of Consulting and Clinical Psychology, 32*, 287–295. **45**

Rosenthal, N. E., Genhart, M.,

Jacobsen, F. M., Skwerer, R. G., & Wehr, T. A. (1987). Disturbances of appetite and weight regulation in seasonal affective disorder. *Annals of the New York Academy of Sciences, 499*, 216–230. **361**

Rosenthal, N. E., Genhart, M., Sack, D. A., Skwerer, R. G., & Wehr, T. A. (1987). Seasonal affective disorder and its relevance for the understanding and treatment of bulimia. In J. I. Hudson & H. Pope (Eds.), *The psychobiology of bulimia.* New York: American Psychiatric Press. **361**

Rosenthal, N. E., Sack, D. A., Gillin, J. C., Lewy, A. J., Goodwin, F. K., Davenport, Y., Mueller, P. S., Newsome, D. A., & Wehr, T. A. (1984). Seasonal affective disorder. *Archives of General Psychiatry, 41*, 72–80. **361**

Rosenthal, R. (1963). On the social psychology of the psychological experiment: The experimenter's hypothesis as an unintended determinant of experimental results. *American Scientists, 51*, 268–283. **41**

_____. (1966). *Experimenter effects in behavioral research.* New York: Appleton-Century-Crofts. **41**

_____. (1984). *Meta-analytic procedures for social science research.* Newbury Park: Sage. **37**

Rosenthal, R., & Rubin, D. B. (1982). Further meta-analytic procedures for assessing cognitive gender differences. *Journal of Educational Psychology, 74*, 708–712. **37, 372, 273, 389**

Rosner, M. (1967). Women in the kibbutz: Changing status and concepts. *Asian and African Studies, 3*, 35–68. **239, 258**

Rosner, W. (1990). The functions of corticosteroid-binding globulin and sex hormone-binding globulin: Recent advances. *Endocrine Reviews, 11*, 80–91. **136, 158, 178**

Ross, C. E., & Mirowsky, J. (1984). Components of depressed mood in married men and women. *American Journal of Epidemiology, 119*, 997–1004. **363**

_____. (1988). Child care and emotional adjustment to wives' employment. *Journal of Health and Social Behavior, 29*, 127–138. **328**

Ross, H., & Taylor, H. (1989). Do boys prefer daddy or his physical style of play? *Sex Roles, 20*, 23–34. **302**

Ross, M. (1989). Relation of implicit theories to the construction of personal histories. *Psychological Review, 96*, 341–357. **231**

Ross, M. H. (1986). Female political

participation: A cross-cultural explanation. *American Anthropologist, 88*, 843–858. **255**

Rossi, A. S., & Rossi, P. E. (1980). Body time and social time: Mood patterns by menstrual cycle phase and day of week. In J. E. Parsons (Ed.), *The psychobiology of sex differences and sex roles*. New York: McGraw-Hill. **190**

Rothbart, M., & John, O. P. (1985). Social categorization and behavioral episodes: A cognitive analysis of the effects of intergroup contact. *Journal of Social Issues, 41*, 81–104. **276**

Rothfeld, J. M., Harlan, R. E., Shivers, B. D., & Pfaff, D. W. (1986). Reversible disruption of lordosis via midbrain infusions of procaine and tetrodotoxin. *Pharmacology, Biochemistry and Behavior, 25*, 857–863. **136**

Rotter, J. I., Wong, F. L., Lifrak, E. T., & Parker, L. N. (1985). A genetic component to the variation of dehydroepiandrosterone sulfate. *Metabolism, 34*, 731–736. **147**

Rouyer, F., Simmler, M.-C., Johnsson, C., Vergnaud, G., Cooke, H. J., & Weissenbach, J. (1986). A gradient of sex linkage in the pseudoautosomal region of the human sex chromosomes. *Nature, 319*, 291–295. **101**

Rowe, D. C. (1982). Sources of variability in sex-linked personality attributes: A twin study. *Developmental Psychology, 18*, 431–434. **297, 358**

Rowe, D., Rodgers, J. L., Meseck-Bushey, S., & St. John, C. (1989). Sexual behavior and nonsexual deviance: A sibling study of their relationship. *Developmental Psychology, 25*, 61–69. **374**

Rowell, T. E. (1970). Baboon menstrual cycles affected by social environment. *Journal of Reproductive Fertility, 21*, 133–141. **191**

Roy, A. (1981). Risk factors and depression in Canadian women. *Journal of Affective Disorders, 3*, 65–70. **364**

Roy, E. J., Lynn, D. M., & Clark, A. S. (1985). Inhibition of sexual receptivity by anesthesia during estrogen priming. *Brain Research, 337*, 163–166. **124**

Roy-Byrne, P. P., Post, R. M., Uhde, T. W., Porcu, T., & Davis, D. (1985). The longitudinal course of recurrent affective illness: Life chart data from research patients at the NIMH. *Acta Psychiatrica Scandinavica, 71*, 3–34. **362**

Rubinow, D. R., Hoban, C., Grover, G. N., Galloway, D. S., Roy-Byrne, P., Andersen, R., & Merriam, G. R. (1988). Changes in plasma hormones across the menstrual cycle in patients with menstrually related mood disorder and in control subjects. *American Journal of Obstetrics and Gynecology, 158*, 5–11. **195**

Rubinow, D. R., Roy-Byrne, P., Hoban, M. C., Gold, P. W., & Post, R. M. (1984). Prospective assessment of menstrually related mood disorders. *American Journal of Psychiatry, 141*, 684–686. **192**

Ruble, D. N. (1977). Premenstrual symptoms: A reinterpretation. *Science, 197*, 291–292. **192**

Ruble, D. N., Brooks-Gunn, J., & Clarke, A. (1980). Research on menstrual-related psychological changes: Alternative perspectives. In J. E. Parsons (Eds.), *The psychobiology of sex differences and sex roles*. New York: McGraw-Hill. **193**

Ruble, D. N., & Stangor, C. (1986). Stalking the elusive schema: Insights from the developmental and social-psychological analysis of gender schemas. *Social Cognition, 4*, 227–261. **274, 291**

Ruggiero, J. A., & Weston, L. C. (1988). Work involvement among college-educated women: A methodological extension. *Sex Roles, 19*, 491–508. **329**

Rumenik, D. K., Capasso, D. R., & Hendrick, C. (1977). Experimenter sex effects in behavioral research. *Psychological Bulletin, 54*, 852–857. **39**

Rushton, J. P. (1979). Effects of prosocial television and film material on the behavior of viewers. In L Berkowitz (Ed.), *Advances in Experimental Social Psychology*. New York: Academic Press. **291**

—————. (1985). Differential K theory: The sociobiology of individual and group differences. *Personality and Individual Differences, 6*, 441–452. **376**

Rushton, J. P., Fulker, D. W., Neale, M. C., Nias, D. K. B., & Eysenck, H. J. (1986). Altruism and aggression: The heritability of individual differences. *Journal of Personality and Social Psychology, 50*, 1192–1198. **358**

Russell, M. A., & Sines, J. O. (1978). Further evidence that M-F is bipolar and multidimensional. *Journal of Clinical Psychology, 34*, 643–649. **48**

Russell, M. J., Switz, G. M., & Thompson, K. (1980). Olfactory influences on the human menstrual cycle. *Pharmacology, Biochemistry & Behavior, 13*, 737–738. **191**

Russo, N. F., Olmedo, E. L., Stapp, J., & Fulcher, R. (1981). Women and minorities in psychology. *American Psychologist, 36*, 1315–1363. **325**

Rutter, M., & Garmezy, N. (1983). Developmental psychopathology. In E. M. Hetherington (Ed.), *Socialization, personality, and social development. Handbook of child psychology,* vol. 4, (Series ed. P. H. Mussen). New York: Wiley **228, 234**

Ryckman, D. B., & Peckham, P. D. (1987). Gender differences in attributions for success and failure. *Journal of Early Adolescence, 7,* 47–63. **321**

Sabers, D., Cushing, K., & Sabers, D. (1987). Sex differences in reading and mathematics achievement for middle school students. *Journal of Early Adolescence, 7,* 117–128. **373**

Sachs, B. D., & Thomas, D. A. (1985). Differential effects of perinatal androgen treatment on sexually dimorphic characteristics in rats. *Physiology & Behavior, 34,* 735–742. **150, 151**

Sack, D. A., Rosenthal, N. E., Parry, B. L., & Wehr, T. A. (1987). Biological rhythms in psychiatry. In H. Y. Meltzer (Ed), *Psychopharmacology: The third generation of progress*. New York: Raven Press. **191, 193**

Sadalla, E. K., Kenrick, D. T., & Vershure, B. (1987). Dominance and heterosexual attraction. *Journal of Personality and Social Psychology, 52,* 730–738. **379**

Sadker, M., & Sadker, D. (1985). Sexism in the schoolroom of the '80s. *Psychology Today, 19,* 54–57. **312**

Saksena, S. K., & Lau, I. F. (1979). Variations in serum androgens, estrogens, progestins, gonadotropins and prolactin levels in male rats from prepubertal to advanced age. *Experimental Aging Research, 5,* 179–194. **178**

Sakuma, Y., & Pfaff, D. W. (1980). Convergent effects of lordosis-relevant somatosensory and hypothlamic influences on central gray cells in the rat mesencephalon. *Experimental Neurology, 70,* 269–281. **181**

Salaman, D. F., & Birkett, S. (1974). Androgen-induced sexual differentiation of the brain is blocked by inhibitors of DNA and RNA synthesis. *Nature, 247,* 109–112. **136**

Salbenblatt, J. A., Bender, B. G., Puck, M. H., Robinson, A., & Webber, M. L. (1981). Development of eight pubertal males with 47,XXY karyotype. *Clinical Genetics, 20,* 141–146. **115**

Salceda, V. M., & Anderson, W. W. (1988). Rare male mating advantage in a natural population of Drosophila pseudoobscura. *Proceedings of the National Academy of Sciences, USA, 85,* 9870–9874. **68**

Samama, B., & Aron, Cl. (1989). Changes in estrogen receptors in the mediobasal hypothalamus mediate the facilitory effects exerted by the male's olfactory cues and progesterone on feminine behavior in the male rat. *Journal of Steroid Biochemistry, 32*, 525–529. **136**

Sampson, E. (1977). Psychology and the American ideal. *Journal of Personality and Social Psychology, 35*, 767–782. **12**

Sanders, B., & Soares, M. P. (1986). Sexual maturation and spatial ability in college students. *Developmental Psychology, 22*, 199–203. **391**

Sanders, B., Soares, M. P., & D'Aquila, J. M. (1982). The sex difference on one test of spatial visualization: A nontrivial difference. *Child Development, 53*, 1106–1110. **391**

Sanders, K. M., & Harper, L. V. (1976). Free-play fantasy behavior in preschool children: Relations among gender, age, season, and location. *Child Development, 47*, 1182–1185. **316**

Sansom, B. (1978). Sex, age, and social control in mobs of the Darwin hinterland. In J. S. La Fontaine (Ed.), *Sex and age and principles of social differentiation*. New York: Academic Press. **250**

Santos, M., Tarrio, R., Zapata, C., & Alvarez, G. (1986). Sexual selection on chromosomal polymorphism in Drosophila subobscura. *Heredity, 57*, 161–169. **68**

Sapienza, C. (1990). Parental imprinting of genes. *Scientific American, 263*, 52–60. **102, 103**

Sapienza, C., Peterson, A. C., Rossant, J., & Balling, R. (1987). Degree of methylation of transgenes is dependent on gamete of origin. *Nature, 328*, 251–154. **102, 103**

Sapolsky, R. M. (1987). Stress, social status, and reproductive physiology in free-living baboons. In D. Crews (Ed.), *Psychobiology of reproductive behavior: An evolutionary perspective*. Englewood Cliffs, NJ: Prentice Hall. **348**

_____. (1989). Hypercortisolism among socially subordinate wild baboons originates at the CNS level. *Archives of General Psychiatry, 46*, 1047–1051. **348**

Sapolsky, R. M., & Mott, G. E. (1987). Social subordinance in wild baboons is associated with suppressed high density lipoprotein-cholesterol concentrations: The possible role of chronic social stress. *Endocrinology, 121*, 1605–1610. **348**

Sapolsky, R. M,, & Ray, J. C. (1989).

Styles of dominance and their endocrine correlates among wild olive baboons (Papio anubis). *American Journal of Primatology, 18*, 1–13. **348**

Sarrel, P. M., & Masters, W. H. (1982). Sexual molestation of men by women. *Archives of Sexual Behavior, 11*, 117–131. **384, 385**

Sarrieau, A., Mitchell, J. B., Lal, S., Olivier, A., Quirion, R., & Meaney, M. J. (1990). Androgen binding sites in human temporal cortex. *Neuroendocrinology, 51*, 713–716. **180**

Saunders, D. G. (1987, July). *A typology of men who batter their wives: Three types derived from cluster analysis*. Paper presented at Third National Conference for Family Violence Researchers, Univeristy of New Hampshire. **353**

_____. (1988). Wife abuse, husband abuse, or mutual combat? A feminist perspective on the empirical findings. In K. Yllo & M. Bograd (Eds.), *Feminist perspectives on wife abuse*. Beverly Hills: Sage. **352**

Savin-Williams, R. C. (1976). An ethological study of dominance formation and maintenance in a group of human adolescents. *Child Development, 47*, 972–979. **348**

_____. (1977). Dominance in a human adolescent group. *Animal Behaviour, 25*, 400–406. **316**

_____. (1979). Dominance hierarchies in groups of early adolescents. *Child Development, 50*, 923–935. **316, 348**

_____. (1980a). Dominance and submission among early adolescent boys. In D. R. Omark, F. F. Strayer, & D. G. Freedman (Eds.), *An ethological view of human conflict and social interaction*. New York: Garland STPM Press. **348**

_____. (1980b). Dominance hierarchies in groups of middle to late adolescent males. *Journal of Youth and Adolescence, 9*, 75–85. **348**

Savin-Williams, R. C., & Weisfeld, G. E. (1989). An ethological perspective on adolescence. In G. R. Adams, R. Montemayor, & T. P. Gullotta (Eds.), *Biology of adolescent behavior and deveopment*. Newbury Park: Sage. **177, 228**

Schaap, T. (1989). The role of recombination in the evolvement of the fragile X mutation. *Human Genetics, 82*, 79–81. **122**

Schachter, S. C., Ransil, B. J., & Geschwind, N. (1987). Associations of handedness with hair color and learning disabilities. *Neuropsychologia, 25*, 269–276. **172**

Schantz, T. von, Göransson, Andersson, G., Fröberg, I., Grahn, M.,

Helgée, A., & Wittzell, H. (1989). Female choice selects for a viability-based male trait in pheasants. *Nature, 337*, 166–169. **86**

Schiavi, R. C., Theilgaard, A., Owen, D. R., & White, D. (1984). Sex chromosome anomalies, hormones, and aggressivity. *Archives of General Psychiatry, 41*, 93–99. **115, 116**

Schiess, M. C., Jolës, M., & Shinnick-Gallagher, P. (1988). Estrogen priming affects active membrane properties of medial amygadala neurons. *Brain Research, 440*, 380–385. **152**

Schildkraut, J. M., Hulka, B. S., & Wilkinson, W. E. (1990). Oral contraceptives and breast cancer: A case-control study with hospital and community controls. *Obstetrics & Gynecology, 76*, 395–402. **201**

Schlegel, A. (1983). Commentary on "The North American berdache." *Current Anthropology, 24*, 462–463. **258**

Schlegel, A., & Barry, H., III. (1986). The cultural consequences of female contribution to subsistence. *American Anthropologist, 88*, 142–150. **252, 254, 261**

Schmidt, J. B., & Spona, J. (1985). The levels of androgen in serum in female acne patients. *Endocrinologia Experimentalis, 19*, 17–23. **190**

Schnatz, P. T. (1985). Neuroendocrinology and the ovulation cycle—Advances and review. *Advances in Psychosomatic Medicine, 12*, 4–24. **177, 186, 187**

Schöpf, J., Bryois, C., Jonquière, M., & Scharfetter, C. (1985). A family heredity study of post-partum "psychoses." *European Archives of Psychiatry and Neurological Sciences, 235*, 164–170. **197, 198**

Schotzinger, R. J., & Landis, S. C. (1988). Cholinergic phenotype developed by noradrenergic sympathetic neurons after innervation of a novel cholinergic target in vivo. *Nature, 335*, 637–639. **139**

Schuckit, M. A. (1986). Genetic and clinical implications of alcoholism and affective disorder. *American Journal of Psychiatry, 143*, 140–147. **361**

Schüle, R., Muller, M., Kaltschmidt, C., & Renkawitz, R. (1988). Many transcription factors interact synergistically with steroid receptors. *Science, 242*, 1418–1420. **136**

Schumacher, M., Legros, J. J., & Balthazart, J. (1987). Steroid hormones, behavior and sexual dimorphism in animals and men: The nature-nurture controversy. *Experimental and Clinical Endocrinology, 90*, 129–156. **386**

Schuman, M., Gitlin, M. J., & Fairbanks, L. (1987). Sweets, chocolate, and atypical depressive traits. *Journal of Nervous and Mental Disease, 175,* 491–495. **12**

Schwartz, L. A., & Markham, W. T. (1985). Sex stereotyping in children's toy advertisements. *Sex Roles, 12,* 157–170. **289**

Schwartz, S. (1991). Women and depression: A Durkheimian perspective. *Social Science and Medicine, 32,* 127–140. **350**

Schwegler, H., Crusio, W. E., & Brust, I. (1990). Hippocampal mossy fibers and radial-maze learning in the mouse: A correlation with spatial working memory but not with non-spatial reference memory. *Neuroscience, 34,* 293–298. **397**

Searcy, W. A., & Yasukawa, K. (1983). Sexual selection and red-winged blackbirds. *American Scientist, 71,* 166–174. **84, 86**

Sears, D. O. (1986). College sophomores in the laboratory: Influences of a narrow data base on social psychology's view of human nature. *Journal of Personality and Social Psychology, 51,* 515–530. **40**

Seavey, C. A., Katz, P. A., & Zalk, S. R. (1975). Baby X: The effect of gender labels on adult responses to infants. *Sex Roles, 1,* 103–110. **281**

Seccombe, K. (1986). The effects of occupational conditions upon the division of household labor: An application of Kohn's theory. *Journal of Marriage and the Family, 48,* 839–848. **306**

Secord, P. F. (1983). Imbalanced sex ratios: The social consequences. *Personality and Social Psychology Bulletin, 9,* 525–543. **376**

Seegal, R. F. (1985). Lumbar cerebrospinal fluid homovanillic acid concentrations are higher in female than male non-human primates. *Brain Reserach, 334,* 375–379. **351, 369**

Segal, Z. V., Shaw, B. F., & Vella, D. D. (1989). Life stress and depression: A test of the congruency hypothesis for life event content and depressive subtype. *Canadian Journal of Behavioural Science, 21,* 389–400. **364**

Seger, J., & Hamilton, W. D. (1988). Parasites and sex. In R. F. Michod & B. R. Levin (Eds.), *The evolution of sex: an examination of current ideas.* Sunderland, MA: Sinauer Associates. **72**

Seiler, L. H. (1973). The 22-item scale used in field studies of mental illness: A question of method, a question of substance, and a question of theory. *Journal of Health and Social Behavior, 14,* 252–264. **360**

Seligman, M. E. P. (1975). *Helplessness: On depression, development and death.* San Francisco: W. H. Freeman. **212, 213**

———. (1988). Boomer blues. *Psychology Today, 22,* 50–52. **366, 367**

Selvin, S., & Garfinkel, J. (1976). Paternal age, maternal age and birth order and the risk of fetal loss. *Human Biology, 48,* 223–230. **111**

Selzer, M. L., Paluszny, M., & Carroll, R. (1978). A comparison of depression and physical illness in men and women. *American Journal of Psychiatry, 135,* 1368–1370. **363**

Semrud-Clikeman, M., & Hynd, G. W. (1990). Right hemispheric dysfunction in nonverbal learning disabilities: Social, academic, and adaptive functioning in adults and children. *Psychological Bulletin, 107,* 196–209. **374**

Sengelaub, D. R., & Arnold, A. P. (1986). Development and loss of early projections in a sexually dimorphic rat spinal nucleus. *Journal of Neuroscience, 6,* 1613–1620. **163**

Sengelaub, D. R., Jordon, C. L., Kurz, E. M., & Arnold, A. P. (1989). Hormonal control of neuron number in sexually dimorphic spinal nuclei of the rat: II. Development of the spinal nucleus of the bulbocavernosus in androgen-insensitive (Tfm) rats. *Journal of Comparative Neurology, 280,* 630–636. **163**

Sengelaub, D. R., Nordeen, E. J., Nordeen, K. W., & Arnold, A. P. (1989). Hormonal control of neuron number in sexually dimorphic spinal nuclei of the rat: III. Differential effects of the androgen dihydrotestosterone. *Journal of Comparative Neurology, 280,* 637–644. **163**

Serbin, L. A., Connor, J. M., Burchardt, C. J., & Citron, C. C. (1979). Effects of peer presence on sex-typing of children's play behavior. *Journal of Experimental Child Psychology, 27,* 303–309. **314**

Serbin, L. A., O'Leary, K. D., Kent, R. N., & Tonick, I. J. (1973). A comparison of teacher response to the preacademic and problem behavior of boys and girls. *Child Development, 44,* 796–804. **311**

Serbin, L. A., & Sprafkin, C. (1986). The salience of gender and the process of sex typing in three- to seven-year-old children. *Child Development, 57,* 1188–1199. **314**

Serbin, L. A., Zelkowitz, P., Doyle, A. B., Gold, D., & Wheaton, B. (1990). The socialization of sex-differentiated skills and academic

performance: A mediational model. *Sex Roles, 23,* 613–628. **307, 308, 395**

Seress, L. (1985). Postnatal neurogenesis in the rat hypothalamus. *Developmental Brain Research, 22,* 156–160. **152**

Shakin, M., Shakin, D., & Sternglanz, S. H. (1985). Infant clothing: Sex labeling for strangers. *Sex Roles, 12,* 955–964. **298**

Shapiro, S. S. (1988). Treatment of dysmenorrhoea and premenstrual syndrome with non-steroidal anti-inflammatory drugs. *Drugs, 36,* 475–490. **195**

Sharp, P. J., & Hayman, D. L. (1988). An examination of the role of chiasma frequency in the genetic system of marsupials. *Heredity, 60,* 77–85. **100**

Shatz, C. J., & Stryker, M. P. (1988). Prenatal tetrodotoxin infusion blocks segregation of retinogeniculate afferents. *Science, 242,* 87–90. **139**

Sheridan, P. J. (1983). Androgen receptors in the brain: What are we measuring? *Endocrine Reviews, 4,* 171–178. **203**

Sheridan, P. J., & Weaker, F. J. (1982). Androgen receptor systems in the brain stem of the primate. *Brain Research, 235,* 225–232. **203**

Sherif, C. W. (1982). Needed concepts in the study of gender identity. *Psychology of Women Quarterly, 6,* 375–398. **9, 41**

Sherman, G. F., Galaburda, A. M., & Geschwind, N. (1985). Cortical anomalies in brains of New Zealand mice: A neuropathologic model of dyslexia. *Proceedings of the National Academy of Sciences, USA, 82,* 8072–8074. **172**

Sherman, J. (1978). *Sex-related cognitive differences.* Springfield, IL: Thomas. **18**

———. (1980). Mathematics, spatial visualization, and related factors: Changes in girls and boys, grades 8-11. *Journal of Educational Psychology, 72,* 476–482. **373**

Sherrifs, A. C., & McKee, J. P. (1957). Qualitative aspects of beliefs about men and women. *Journal of Personality, 25,* 451–464. **296**

Sherry, D. F., & Schachter, D. L. (1987). The evolution of multiple memory systems. *Psychological Review, 94,* 439–454. **213, 214**

Sherwin, B. B. (1988a). A comparative analysis of the role of androgen in human male and female sexual behavior: Behavioral specificity, critical thresholds, and sensitivity. *Psychobiology, 16,* 416–425. **201, 387**

———. (1988b). Affective changes with estrogen and androgen replacement therapy in surgically menopausal women. *Journal of Affective Disorders, 14*, 177–187. **201**

_____. (1988c). Estrogen and/or androgen replacement therapy and cognitive functioning in surgically menopausal women. *Psychoneuroendocrinology, 13*, 345–357. **201**

Sherwin, B. B., & Gelfand, M. M. (1985). Sex steroids and affect in the surgical menopause: A double-blind, cross-over study. *Psychoneuroendocrinology, 10*, 325–335. **201**

Sherwood, J. J., & Nataupsky, M. (1968). Predicting the conclusions of Negro-white intelligence research from biographical characteristics of the investigator. *Journal of Personality and Social Psychology, 8*, 53–58. **41**

Shields, S. A. (1985). Functionalism, Darwinianism, and the psychology of women: A study in social myth. In J. H. Williams (Ed.), *Psychology of women: Selected readings*. New York: Norton. (Original work published 1975) **13**

_____. (1987). The variability hypothesis: the history of a biological model of sex differences in intelligence. In S. Harding & J. F. O'Barr (Eds.), *Sex and scientific inquiry*. Chicago: University of Chicago Press. (Original work published 1982) **35**

Shinar, E. H. (1975). Sexual stereotypes of occupations. *Journal of Vocational Behavior, 7*, 99–111. **326**

Shiroishi, T., Hanzawa, N., Sagai, T., Ishiura, M., Gojobori, T., Steinmetz, M., & Moriwaki, K. (1990). Recombinational hotspot specific to female meiosis in the mouse major histocompatibility complex. *Immunogenetics, 31*, 79–88. **100, 102**

Shivers, B. D., Harlan, R. E., Parker, C. R., Jr., & Moss, R. L. (1980). Sequential inhibitory effect of progesterone on lordotic responsiveness in rats: Time course, estrogenic nullification, and actinomycin-D insensitivity. *Biology of Reproduction, 23*, 963–973. **136**

Short, R., England, N., Bridson, W. E., & Bowden, D. M. (1990). Ovarian cyclicity, hormones, and behavior as markers of aging in female pigtailed macaques (Macaca nemestrina). *Journal of Gerontology: Biological Sciences, 44*, B131–B138. **198**

Short, R. V. (1979). Sexual selection and its component parts, somatic and genital selection, as illustrated by man and the great apes. In J. S. Rosenblatt, R. A. Hinde, C. Beer, &M. -C. Bushel (Eds.), *Advances in the Study of Behavior*. New York: Academic Press. **88**

Shucard, D. W., Shucard, J. L., Campos, J. J., & Salamy, J. G. (1982). Some issues pertaining to auditory evoked potentials and sex-related differences in brain development. *Brain and Language, 16*, 342–347. **397**

Shucard, J. L., Shucard, D. W., Cummins, K. R., & Campos, J. J. (1981). Auditory evoked potentials and sex-related differences in brain development. *Brain and Language, 13*, 91–102. **397**

Shute, V. J., Pellegrino, J. W., Hubert, L., & Reynolds, R. W. (1983). The relationship between androgen levels and human spatial abilities. *Bulletin of the Psychonomic Society, 21*, 465–468. **398**

Sibbald, J. R., Sirett, N. E., & Hubbard, J. I. (1987). The influence of the estrous cycle, persistent estrus, ovariectomy and estrogen replacement, on the numbers and frequency of spontaneously active neurons in slices of the rat preoptic region in vitro. *Neuroscience Letters, 76*, 323–328. **152, 183**

Sibisi, C. D. T. (1990). Sex differences in the age of onset of bipolar affective illness. *British Journal of Psychiatry, 156*, 842–845. **363**

Siegal, M. (1987). Are sons and daughters treated more differently by fathers than by mothers? *Developmental Review, 7*, 183–209. **299, 300, 302**

Siegel, J. M., Sorenson, S. B., Golding, J. M., Burnam, M. A., & Stein, J. A. (1989). Resistance to sexual assault: Who resists and what happens? *American Journal of Public Health, 79*, 27–31. **384, 385**

Sigall, H., & Landy, D. (1973). Radiating beauty: Effects of having a physically attractive partner on person perception. *Journal of Personality and Social Psychology, 28*, 218–224. **380**

Sigelman, L., Milward, H. B., & Shepard, J. M. (1982). The salary differential between male and female administrators: Equal pay for equal work? *Academy of Management Journal, 25*, 664–671. **322**

Signorella, M. L., & Frieze, I. H. (1989). Gender schemas in college students. *Psychology: A Journal of Human Behavior, 26*, 16–23. **47, 49**

Signorella, M. L., & Jamison, W. (1986). Masculinity, femininity, androgyny, and cognitive performance: A meta-analysis. *Psychological Bulletin, 100*, 207–228. **394**

Signorella, M. L., Vegega, M. E., & Mitchell, M. E. (1981). Subject selection and analysis for sex–related differences: 1968–1970 and 1975–1977. *American Psychologist, 36*, 988–990. **39**

Silk, J. B. (1983). Local resource competition and facultative adjustment of sex ratios in relation to competitive abilities. *American Naturalist, 121*, 56–66. **80, 349**

Silver, J., Rabson, A., Bryan, T., Willey, R., & Martin, M. A. (1987). Human retroviral sequences on the Y chromosome. *Molecular and Cellular Biology, 7*, 1559–1562. **117**

Silverblatt, I. (1988). Women in states. *Annual Review of Anthropology, 17*, 427–460. **240, 261**

Silverman, M. A. (1981). Cognitive development and female psychology. *Journal of the American Psychoanalytic Association, 29*, 581–605. **216**

Silverstein, B., & Perlick, D. (1991). Gender differences in depression: Historical changes. *Acta Psychiatrica Scandinavica, 84*, 327–331. **368**

Simerly, R. B. (1989). Hormonal control of the development and regulation of tyrosine hydroxylase expression within a sexually dimorphic population of dopaminergic cells in the hypothalamus. *Molecular Brain Research, 6*, 297–310. **139**

Simmons, R. G., Blyth, D. A., & McKinney, K. L. (1983). The social and psychological effects of puberty on white females. In J. Brooks-Gunn & A. C. Peterson (Eds.), *Girls at puberty: Biosocial and psychosocial perspectives*. New York: Plenum. **374**

Simmons, R. G., Blyth, D. A., Van Cleave, E. F., & Bush, D. M. (1979). Entry into early adolescence: The impact of school structure, puberty, and early dating on self-esteem. *American Sociological Review, 44*, 948–967. **228**

Simmons, R. G., & Rosenberg, F. (1975). Sex, sex roles, and self-image. *Journal of Young and Adolescence, 4*, 229–258. **282**

Simon, H. A. (1990). A mechanism for social selection and successful altruism. *Science, 250*, 1665–1668. **82, 250**

Simon, N. G., Gandelman, R., & Gray, J. L. (1984). Endocrine induction of intermale aggression in mice: A comparison of hormonal regimens and their relationship to naturally occurring behavior. *Physiology & Behavior, 33*, 379–383. **358**

Simon, N. G., & Whalen, R. E. (1987). Sexual differentiation of androgen-sensitive and estrogen-sensitive regulatory systems for aggressive behavior. *Hormones and Behavior, 21*, 493–500. **146, 358**

Simpson, E., Chandler, P., Goulmy, E., Disteche, C. M., Ferguson-Smith, M. A., & Page, D. A.

(1987). Separation of the genetic loci for the H-Y antigen and for testis determination on human Y chromosome. *Nature, 326,* 876–878. **106**

Simpson, S., McCarrey, M., & Edwards, H. P. (1987). Relationship of supervisors' sex-role stereotypes to performance evaluation of male and female subordinates in nontraditional jobs. *Canadian Journal of Administrative Science, 4,* 15–30. **285**

Sims, K. B., de la chapelle, A., Norio, R., Sankila, E.-M., Hsu, Y.-P. P., Rinehart, W. B., Corey, T. J., Ozelius, L. Powell, J. E., Bruns, G., Gusella, J. F., Murphy, D. L., & Breakefield, X. O. (1989). Monoamine oxidase deficiency in males with an X chromosome deletion. *Neuron, 2,* 1069–1076. **119**

Sinclair, A. H., Berta, P., Palmer, M. S. Hawkins, J. R., Griffiths, B. L., Smith, M. J., Foster, J. W., Frischauf, A.-M., Lovell-Badge, R., & Goodfellow, P. N. (1990). A gene from the human sex-determining region encodes a protein with homology to a conserved DNA-binding motif. *Nature, 346,* 240–244. **123**

Sines, J. O., & Russell, M. A. (1978). The BSRI M, F, and androgyny scores are bipolar. *Journal of Clinical Psychology, 34,* 53–56. **48**

Singer, B. (1984). Conceptualizing sexual arousal and attraction. *Journal of Sex Research, 20,* 230–240. **383**

Singer, J. M., & Stake, J. E. (1986). Mathematics and self-esteem: Implications for women's career choice. *Psychology of Women Quarterly, 10,* 339–352. **330**

Sinnott, J. D., Block, M. R., Grambs, J. D., Gaddy, C. D., & Davidson, J. L. (1980). *Sex roles in mature adults: Antecedents and correlates.* Technical Report NIA-80-1. **44**

Sirevaag, A. M., Black, J. E., & Greenough, W. T. (1991). Astrocyte hypertrophy in the dentate gyrus of young male rats reflects variation of individual stress rather than group environmental complexity manipulations. *Experimental Neurology, 111,* 74–79. **14**

Skrypnek, B. J., & Synder, M. (1982). On the self-perpetuating nature of stereotypes about women and men. *Journal of Experimental Social Psychology, 18,* 277–291. **41, 274**

Slatkin, M. (1984) Ecological causes of sexual dimorphism. *Evolution, 38,* 622–630. **90**

Slevin, K. F., & Wingrove, C. R. (1983). Similarities and differences among three generations of women in attitudes toward the female role in contemporary society. *Sex Roles, 9,* 609–624. **273**

Sluyser, M., Rijkers, A. W. M., De Goeij, C. C. J., Parker, M., & Hilkens, J. (1988). Assignment of estradiol receptor gene to mouse chromosome 10. *Journal of Steroid Biochemistry, 31,* 757–761. **100**

Small, A. C., Erdwins, C., & Gross, R. B. (1979). A comparison of the Bem Sex-Role Inventory and the Heilbrum Masculinity and Femininity Scales. *Journal of Personality Assessment, 43,* 393–395. **46**

Small, M. F., & Hrdy, S. B. (1986). Secondary sex ratios by maternal rank, parity, and age in captive rhesus macaques (Macaca mulatta). *American Journal of Primatology, 11,* 359-365. **80**

Smals, A. G. H., Kloppenborg, P. W. C., & Benraad, Th. J. (1976). Circannual cycle in plasma testosterone levels in man. *Journal of Clinical Endocrinology and Metabolism, 42,* 979–982.

Smeaton, G., & Byrne, D. (1987). The effects of R-rated violence and erotica, individual differences, and victim characteristics on acquaintance rate proclivity. *Journal of Research in Personality, 21,* 171–184. **386**

Smith, D. G., & Smith, S. (1988). Parental rank and reproductive success of natal rhesus males. *Animal Behaviour, 36,* 554–562. **349**

Smith, E. A. (1983). Anthropological applications of optimal foraging theory: A critical review. *Current Anthropology, 24,* 625–651. **215**

Smith, J. (1984). The paradox of women's poverty: Wage-earning women and economic transformation. *Signs: Journal of Women in Culture and Society, 10,* 291–310. **324**

Smith, J. E., Waldorf, V. A., & Trembath, D. L. (1990). "Single white male looking for thin, very attractive. . . ." *Sex Roles, 23,* 675–687. **379**

Smith, K. D., Rodriguez-Rigau, L. J., Tcholakian, R. K., & Steinberger, E. (1979). The relation between plasma testosterone levels and the lengths of phases of the menstrual cycle. *Fertility and Sterility, 32,* 403–407. **190**

Smith, P. A., & Midlarsky, E. (1985). Empirically derived conceptions of femaleness and maleness: A current view. *Sex Roles, 12,* 313–328. **47, 50, 271**

Smith, S. L., & Sauder, C. (1969). Food cravings, depression, and premenstrual problems. *Psychosomatic Medicine, 31,* 281–287. **189**

Smith, S. S. (1989). Estrogen administration increases neuronal responses to excitatory amino acids as a long-term effect. *Brain Research, 503,* 354–357. **137, 139**

Smith, S. S., Waterhouse, B. D., Chapin, J. K., & Woodward, D. J. (1987). Progesterone alters GABA and glutamate responsiveness: A possible mechanism for its anxiolytic action. *Brain Research, 400,* 353–359. **139**

Smith, S. S., Waterhouse, B. D., & Woodward, D. J. (1987a). Sex steroid effects on extrahypothalamic CNS. I. Estrogen augments neuronal responsiveness to iontophoretically applied glutamate in the cerebellum. *Brain Research, 422,* 40–51. **137, 139**

————. (1987b). Sex steroid effects on extrahypothalamic CNS. II. Progesterone, alone and in combination with estrogen, modulates cerebellar responses to amino acid neurotransmitters. *Brain Research, 422,* 52–62. **137, 139**

Smith, S. S., Woodward, D. J., & Chapin, J. K. (1989). Sex steroids modulate motor-correlated increases in cerebellar discharge. *Brain Research, 476,* 307–316. **181**

Smolensky, M. H., Reinberg, A., Bicakova-Rocher, A., & Sanford, J. (1981). Chronoepidemiological search for circannual changes in the sexual activity of human males. *Chronobiologia, 8,* 217–230. **196**

Snarey, J., & Son, L. (1986). Sex-identity development among kibbutz-born males: A test of the Whiting hypothesis. *Ethos, 14,* 99–119. **258**

Snow, C. (1987). Relevance of the notion of a critical period to language acquisition. In M. M. Bornstein (Ed.), *Sensitive periods in development.* Hillsdale, N.J: Ehrlbaum. **225**

Snyder, M. (1984). When belief creates reality. *Advances in Experimental Social Psychology, 18,* 247–305. **41, 274**

Snyder, M., & Ickes, W. (1985). Personality and social behavior. In G. Lindzey & E. Aronson (Eds.), *Handbook of social psychology* (Vol. 2). New York: Random House. **208**

Snyder, M., Simpson, J. A., & Gangestad, S. (1986). Personality and sexual relations. *Journal of Personality and Social Psychology, 51,* 181–190. **384**

Snyder, M., & Swann, W. B., Jr. (1978). Behavioral confirmation in social interaction: From social perception to social reality. *Journal of Experimental Social Psychology, 14,* 148–162. **274**

Sobal, J. (1984). Marriage, obesity and dieting. *Marriage & Family Review, 7,* 115–140. **380**

Södersten, P., & Eneroth, P. (1981). Serum levels of oestradiol-17β and progesterone in relation to sexual receptivity in intact and ovariectomized rats. *Journal of Endocrinology, 89,* 45–54. **178, 183**

Södersten, P., Eneroth, P., & Ekberg, P.-H. (1980). Episodic fluctuations in concentrations of androgen in serum of male rats: possible relationship to sexual behavior. *Journal of Endocrinology, 87,* 463–471. **183**

Södersten, P., Eneroth, P., Hansson, T., Mode, A., Johansson, D., Näslund, B., Liang, T., & Gustafsson, J.-Å. (1986). Activation of sexual behaviour in castrated rats: The role of oestradiol. *Journal of Endocrinology, 111,* 455–462. **146**

Sollenberger, M. J., Carlsen, E. C., Johnson, M. L., Veldhuis, J. D., & Evans, W. S. (1990). Specific physiological regulation of luteinizing hormone secretory events throughout the human menstrual cycle: New insights into the pulsatile mode of gonadotropin release. *Journal of Neuroendocrinology, 2,* 845–852. **150**

Solomon, L., Minton, J., Calano, L., Raber, R., & Rapoport-Taylor, B. (1985). Being female and liking it: An empirical study. *Academic Psychology Bulletin, 7,* 241–252. **282**

Solter, D. (1988). Differential imprinting and expression of maternal and paternal genomes. *Annual Review of Genetics, 22,* 127–146. **102, 103**

Sommer, B. (1973). The effect of menstruation on cognitive and perceptual-motor behavior: A review. *Psychosomatic Medicine, 35,* 515–534. **190**

Sorensen, K., Nielsen, K., Froland, A., & Johnsen, S. G. (1979). Psychiatric examination of all eight adult males with the karyotype 46,XX diagnosed in Denmark till 1976. *Acta Psychiatrica Scandinavica, 59,* 153–163. **114**

Sorensen, K., Nielsen, J., Jacobsen, P., & Rolle, T. (1978). The 48,XXYY syndrome. *Journal of Mental Deficiency Research, 22,* 197–205. **113**

South, S. J., Markham, W. T., Bonjean, C. M., & Corder, J. (1987). Sex differences in support for organizational advancement. *Work and Occupations, 14,* 261–285. **330**

Spalt, L. (1980). Hysteria and antisocial personality: A single disorder? *Journal of Nervous and Mental Disease, 168,* 456–464. **362**

Sparrow, D., Bosse, R., & Rowe, J. W. (1980). The influence of age, alcohol consumption, and body build on gonadal function in men. *Journal of Clinical Endocrinology and Metabolism, 51,* 508–512. **199**

Spelsberg, T. C., Rories, C., Rejman, J. J., Goldberger, A., Fink, K., Lau, C. K., Colvard, D.S., & Wiseman, G. (1989). Steroid action on gene expression: Possible roles of regulatory genes and nuclear acceptor sites. *Biology of Reproduction, 40,* 54–69. **152**

Spence, J. T. (1979). Traits, roles and the concept of androgyny. In J. E. Gullahorn (Ed.), *Psychology and women: In transition.* Washington, DC: V. H. Winston & Sons. **45**

_____. (1985). Gender identity and its implications for the concepts of masculinity and femininity. In T. B. Sonderegger (Ed.), *Nebraska symposium on motivation, 1984 (Vol. 32): Psychology and gender.* Lincoln: University of Nebraska Press. **45, 47, 48**

_____. (1991). Do the BSRI and PAQ measure the same or different concepts? *Psychology of Women Quarterly, 15,* 141–165. **41, 45, 46, 48, 49, 271**

Spence, J. T., & Helmreich, R. L. (1979). The many faces of androgyny: A reply to Locksley and Colten. *Journal of Personality and Social Psychology, 37,* 1032–1046. **45**

_____. (1980). Masculine instrumentality and feminine expressiveness: Their relationships with sex role attitudes and behaviors. *Psychology of Women Quarterly, 5,* 147–163. **9, 45, 276**

_____. (1983). Achievement-related motives and behavior. In J. T. Spence (Ed.), *Achievement and achievement motives.* San Francisco: W. H. Freeman. **318, 320, 331**

Spence, J. T., Helmreich, R. L., & Holahan, C. K. (1979). Negative and positive components of psychological masculinity and femininity and their relationships to self-reports of neurotic and acting out behaviors. *Journal of Personality and Social Psychology, 37,* 1673–1682. **45, 48**

Spence, J. T., Helmreich, R. L., & Pred, R. S. (1987). Impatience versus achievement strivings in the Type A pattern: Differential effects on students' health and academic achievement. *Journal of Applied Psychology, 72,* 522–528. **320**

Spence, J. T., Helmreich, R., & Stapp, J. (1974). The Personal Attributes Questionnaire: A measure of sex role stereotypes and masculinity-femini nity. *Journal Supplement Abstract Service Catalog of Selected Documents in Psychology, 4,* 42 (No. 617). **42, 45**

_____. (1975). Ratings of self and peers on sex role attributes and their relation to self-esteem and conceptions of masculinity and femininity. *Journal of Personality and Social Psychology, 32,* 29–30. **45, 47**

Spence, J. T., & Sawin, L. L. (1985). Images of masculinity and fen ininity: A reconceptualization. In V. E. O'Leary, R. K. Unger, & B. S. Wallston (Eds.), *Women, gender, and social psychology.* Hillsdale, NJ: Erlbaum. **45, 47, 50**

Spiro, M. (1956). *Kibbutz: Venture in utopia.* New York: Schocken Books. **258**

Spranger, S. A., Fahrenbach, W. H., Bethea, C. L. (1991). Steroid acion on estrogen and progestin receptors in monkey pituitary cell cultures. *Endocrinology, 128,* 1907–1917. **136**

Spreadbury, C. L., & Reeves, J. B. (1983). Emotional responses of men and women when labeled nonintelligent and unattractive by various reference groups. *Sociological Spectrum, 3,* 223–235. **284**

Sprecher, S. (1989). The importance to males and females of physical attractiveness, earning potential, and expressiveness in initial attraction. *Sex Roles, 21,* 591–608. **379**

Squire, L. R. (1986). Mechanisms of memory. *Science, 232,* 1612–1619. **208**

Stake, J. E. (1979). The ability/performance dimension of self-esteem: Implications for women's achievement behavior. *Psychology of Women Quarterly, 3,* 365–377. **333**

_____. (1990). Exploring attributions in natural settings: Gender and self-esteem effects. *Journal of Research in Personality, 24,* 468–486. **366**

Stake, J. E., & Granger, C. R. (1978). Same-sex and opposite-sex teacher model influences on science career commitment among high school students. *Journal of Educational Psychology, 70,* 180–186. **329**

Stamps, J. A. (1991). Why evolutionary issues are reviving interest in proximate behavioral mechanisms. *American Zoologist, 31,* 338–348. **98, 220**

Stanhope, R., & Brook, C. G. D. (1988). An evaluation of hormonal changes at puberty in man. *Journal of Endocrinology, 116,* 301–305. **177**

Stanley, H. F., Borthwick, N. M., & Fink, G. (1986). Brain protein changes during development and sexual differentiation in the rat. *Brain Research, 370,* 215–222. **138**

Stanley, H. F., & Fink, G. (1986). Synthesis of specific brain proteins is influenced by testosterone at mRNA level in the neonatal rat. *Brain Research, 370,* 223–231. **138**

Stanley, S. C., Hunt, J. G., & Hunt, L. L. (1986). The relative deprivation of husbands in dual-earner households. *Journal of Family Issues, 7,* 3-20. **300**

Stavenhagen, J. B., & Robins, D. M. (1988). An ancient provirus has imposed androgen regulation on the adjacent mouse sex–limited protein gene. *Cell, 55,* 247-254. **100**

Stead, B. A., & Zinkham, G. M. (1986). Service priority in department stores: The effects of customer gender and dress. *Sex Roles, 15,* 601-612. **285**

Stearns, S. C. (1987a). Why sex evolved and the differences it makes. In S. C. Stearns (Ed.), *The evolution of sex and its consequences.* Boston: Birkhauser. **70, 71, 72**

————. (1987b). The selection-arena hypothesis. In S. C. Stearns (Ed.), *The evolution of sex and its consequences.* Boston: Birkhauser. **70, 71, 74**

Steele, P. E., Rabson, A. B., Bryan, T., & Martin, M. A. (1984). Distinctive termini characterize two families of human endogenous retroviral sequences. *Science, 225,* 943-947. **67**

Steger, R. W., & Peluso, J. J. (1987). Sex hormones in the aging female. *Endocrinology and Metabolism Clinics, 16,* 1027-1043. **198**

Steil, J. M., & Weltman, K. (1991). Marital inequality: The importance of resources, personal attributes, and social norms on career valuing and the allocation of domestic responsibilities. *Sex Roles, 24,* 161-180. **359**

Steinberg, L. (1989). Pubertal maturation and parent-adolescent distance: An evolutionary perspective. In G. R. Adams, R. Montemayor, & T. P. Gullotta (Eds.), *Biology of adolescent behavior and development.* Newbury Park, CA: Sage. **228**

Steinberger, E., Smith, K. D., Tcholakian, R. K., & Rodriguez-Rigau, L. J. (1979). Testosterone levels in female partners of infertile couples: Relationship between androgen levels in the woman, the male factor, and the incidence of pregnancy. *American Journal of Obstetrics and Gynecology, 133,* 133-138. **190**

Steingart, R. M. (& 18 others). (1991). Sex differences in the management of coronary artery disease. *New England Journal of Medicine, 325,* 226-230. **283**

Steinman, D. L., Wincze, J. P., Sakheim, Barlow, D. H., & Mavissakalian, M. (1981). A comparison of male and female patterns of sexual arousal. *Archives of Sexual Behavior, 10,* 529-547. **383**

Steinmetz, S. K. (1980). Women and violence: Victims and perpetrators. *American Journal of Psychotherapy, 34,* 334-350. **352**

Stemp, P. S., Turner, R. J., & Noh, S. (1986). Psychological distress in the postpartum period: The significance of social support. *Journal of Marriage and the Family, 48,* 271-277. **197**

Stericker, A., & LeVesconte, S. (1982). Effect of brief training on sex-related differences in visual-spatial skill. *Journal of Personality and Social Psychology, 43,* 1018-1029. **391**

Stern, M., & Karraker, K. H. (1989). Sex stereotyping of infants: A review of gender labeling studies. *Sex Roles, 20,* 501-522. **281, 315**

Sternberg, R. J. (1986). A triangular theory of love. *Psychological Review, 93,* 119-135. **378**

Sternberg, R. J., & Barnes, M. L. (1985). Real and ideal others in a romantic relationships: Is four a crowd? *Journal of Personality and Social Psychology, 49,* 1386-1608. **382**

Stevenson, M. R., & Black, K. N. (1988). Paternal absence and sex-role development: A meta-analysis. *Child Development, 59,* 793-814. **223**

Stewart, A. (1986). Where next for mammalian male-specific (H-Y) antigen(s)? *Trends in Genetics, 2,* 273-274. **106**

Stewart, A. J. (1980). Personality and situation in the prediction of women's life patterns. *Psychology of Women Quarterly, 5,* 195-206. **331**

Stewart, A. J., & Lykes, M. B. (1985). Conceptualizing gender in personality theory and research. *Journal of Personality, 53,* 93-101. **11**

Stillion, J. M., & McDowell, E. E. (1991). Examining suicide from a life span perspective. *Death Studies, 15,* 327-354. **363**

Stipek, D. J., & Hoffman, J. M. (1980). Children's achievement-related expectancies as a function of academic performance histories and sex. *Journal of Educational Psychology, 72,* 861-865. **322**

Stockard, J., Van de Kragt, A. J. C., & Dodge, P. J. (1988). Gender roles and behavior in social dilemmas: Are there sex differences in cooperation and in its justification? *Social Psychology Quarterly, 51,* 154-163. **319**

Stone, E. A. (1983). Adaptation to stress and brain noradrenergic receptors. *Neuroscience & Biobehavioral Reviews, 7,* 503-509. **362**

Stoneman, Z., Brody, G. H., &

MacKinnon, C. (1984). Naturalistic observations of children's activities and roles while playing with their siblings and friends. *Child Development, 55,* 617-627. **294, 316**

Stoppard, J. M., & Kalin, R. (1978). Can gender stereotypes and sex-role conceptualizations be distinguished? *British Journal of Social and Clinical Psychology, 17,* 211-217. **44, 270**

Storms, M. D. (1979). Sex role identity and its relationships to sex role attributes and sex role stereotypes. *Journal of Personality and Social Psychology, 37,* 1779-1789. **44, 48**

————. (1981). A theory of erotic orientation development. *Psychological Review, 88,* 340-353. **388**

Stott, D. (1971). The child's hazards in utero. In J. G. Howells (Ed.), *Modern perspectives in international child psychiatry.* New York: Bruner-Mazel. **148, 149**

Strähle, U., Boshart, M., Klock, G., Stewart, F., & Schütz, G. (1989). Glucocorticoid- and progesterone-specific effects are determined by differential expression of the respective hormone receptors. *Nature, 339,* 629-632. **107**

Strange, C. C., & Rea, J. S. (1983). Career choice considerations and sex role self-concept of male and female undergraduates in nontraditional majors. *Journal of Vocational Behavior, 23,* 219-226. **327, 328**

Straus, M. (1980). Victims and aggressors in marital violence. *American Behavioral Scientist, 23,* 681-704. **352, 353**

Straus, M. A. (1986). Domestic violence and homicide antecedents. *Bulletin of the New York Academy of Medicine, 62,* 446-465. **352, 353**

Straus, M. A., & Gelles, R. J. (1986). Societal change and change in family violence from 1975 to 1985 as revealed by two national surveys. *Journal of Marriage and the Family, 48,* 465-479. **352, 353**

Straus, M. A., Gelles, R., & Steinmetz, S. (1980). *Behind closed doors.* New York: Doubleday. **357**

Strayer, F. F., & Noel, J. M. (1986). The prosocial and antisocial functions of preschool aggression: An ethological study of triadic conflict among young children. In C. Zahn-Waxler, M. Cummings, & R. Iannotti (Eds.), *Altruism and aggression.* New York: Cambridge University Press. **349**

Stribley, J. A., French, J. A., & Inglett, B. J. (1987). Mating patterns in the golden lion tarmarin (Leontopithecus rosalia): Continuous receptivity and concealed estrus. *Folia Primatologia, 49,* 137-150. **186**

Strum, S. C. (1975). Primate predation: Interim report on the development of a tradition in a troop of olive baboons. *Science, 187*, 755–757. **237, 245**

Stumpf, W. E., & Sar, M. (1978). Anatomical distribution of estrogen, androgen, progestin, corticosteroid and thyroid hormone target sites in the brain of mammals: Phylogeny and ontogeny. *American Zoologist, 18*, 435–445. **180, 203**

Stunkard, A. J., Fernstrom, M. H., Price, R. A., Frank, E., & Kupfer, K. (1990). Direction of weight change in recurrent depression: Consistency across episodes. *Archives of General Psychiatry, 47*, 857–860. **363**

Sugarman, D. B., & Hotaling, G. T. (1989). Violent men in intimate relationships: An analysis of risk markers. *Journal of Applied Social Psychology, 19*, 1034–1048. **353**

Sullivan, G. L., & O'Connor, P. J. (1988). Women's role portrayals in magazine advertising: 1958–1983. *Sex Roles, 18*, 181–188. **289**

Sullivan, J. L., Bryon, K. S., Brewster, F. E., & Purtilo, D. T. (1980). Deficient natural killer cell activity in X-linked lymphoproliferative syndrome. *Science, 210*, 543–545. **119**

Sundet, K. (1988). Sex differences in severity and type of aphasia. *Scandinavian Journal of Psychology, 29*, 168–179. **400**

Surtees, P. G., Miller, P. McC., Ingham, J. G., Kreitman, N. B., Rennie, D., & Sashidharan, S. P. (1986). Life events and the onset of affective disorder: A longitudinal general population study. *Journal of Affective Disorders, 10*, 37–50. **364**

Sutherland, G. R. (1985). The enigma of the fragile X chromosome. *Trends in Genetics, 1*, 108–112. **121**

Svare, B. (1988). Genotype modulates the aggression-promoting quality of progesterone in pregnant mice. *Hormones and Behavior, 22*, 90–99. **147**

Svare, B., & Mann, M. (1981). Infanticide: Genetic, developmental and hormonal influences in mice. *Physiology & Behavior, 27*, 921–927. **146**

Swaab, D. F., & Fliers, E. (1985). A sexually dimorphic nucleus in the human brain. *Science, 228*, 1112–1115. **162, 165**

Swaab, D. F., & Hofman, M. A. (1988). Sexual differentiation of the human hypothalamus: Ontogeny of the sexually dimorphic nucleus of the preoptic area. *Developmental Brain Research, 44*, 314–318. **162, 165, 167**

Swain, J. L., Stewart, T. A., & Leder, P. (1987). Parental legacy determines methylation and expression of an autosomal transgene: A molecular mechanism for parental imprinting. *Cell, 50*, 719–727. **102, 103**

Swann, A. C., Secunda, S. K., Stokes, P. E., Croughan, J., Davis, J. M., Koslow, S. H., & Maas, J. W. (1990). Stress, depression, and mania: Relationship between perceived role of stressful events and clinical and biochemical characteristics. *Acta Psychiatrica Scandinavica, 81*, 389–397. **364, 369**

Swanson, H. H. (1990). Sex differences in behavioral consequences of defeat in the rat are not organized by testosterone during early development. *Aggressive Behavior, 16*, 341–344. **358**

Swim, J., Borgida, E., Maruyama, G., & Myers, D. G. (1989). Joan McKay versus John McKay: Do gender stereotypes bias evaluations? *Psychological Bulletin, 105*, 409–425. **281**

Symons, D. (1979). *The evolution of human sexuality.* New York: Oxford University Press. **2, 371, 379, 383, 384**

_____. (1980). Précis of The evolution of human sexuality. *Behavioral and Brain Sciences, 3*, 171–214. **384**

_____. (1987). An evolutionary approach: Can Darwin's view of life shed light on human sexuality? In J. H. Geer & W. T. O'Donohue (Eds.), *Theory of human sexuality.* New York: Plenum. **379**

_____. (1989). A critique of Darwinian anthropology. *Ethology and Sociobiology, 10*, 131–144. **20, 60**

Sytema, S. (1991). Social indicators and psychiatric admission rates: A case-register study in the Netherlands. *Psychological Medicine, 21*, 177–184. **362**

Sztaba, T. I., & Colwill, N. L. (1988). Secretarial and management students: Attitudes, attributes, and career choice considerations. *Sex Roles, 19*, 651–666. **327, 328, 329**

Takahashi, L. K. (1990). Hormonal regulation of sociosexual behavior in female mammals. *Neuroscience & Biobehavioral Reviews, 14*, 403–413. **150**

Takeda, H., Suzuki, M., Lasnitzki, I., & Mizuno, T. (1987). Visualization of X-chromosome inactivation mosaicism of Tfm gene in XTfm/X¢ heterozygous female mice. *Journal of Endocrinology, 114*, 125–129. **107**

Tambs, K. (1989). No evidence for X linkage in rod-and-frame test (RFT) scores: An answer to Thomas. *Behavior Genetics, 19*, 469–471. **391**

Tanaka, T., & Nei, M. (1989). Positive Darwinian selection observed at the variable-region genes of immunoglobulins. *Molecular Biology and Evolution, 6*, 447–459. **59, 74**

Tanner, J. M. (1981). Postnatal growth of gonads and genital tracts, and development of secondary sex characteristics. In C. R. Austin & R. G. Edwards (Eds.), *Mechanisms of sex differentiation in animals and man.* New York: Academic Press. **229**

Tapasak, R. C. (1990). Diferences in expectancy-attribution patterns of cognitive components in male and female math performance. *Contemporary Educational Psychology, 15*, 284–298. **322**

Tapley, S. M., & Bryden, M. P. (1977). An investigation of sex differences in spatial ability: Mental rotation of three-dimensional objects. *Canadian Journal of Psychology, 31*, 122–130. **391, 392**

Tartellin, M. F., & Gorski, R. A. (1988). Postnatal influence of diethylstilbestrol on the differentiation of the sexually dimorphic nucleus in the rat is as effective as perinatal treatment. *Brain Research, 456*, 271–274. **163**

Taub, J. M., & Berger, R. J. (1974). Diurnal variations in mood as asserted by self-report and verbal content analysis. *Journal of Psychiatric Research, 10*, 83–88. **183**

Tauber, M. A. (1979a). Sex differences in parent-child interaction styles during a free-play session. *Child Development, 50*, 981–988. **302**

_____. (1979b). Parental socialization techniques and sex differences in children's play. *Child Development, 50*, 225–234. **302, 308, 316**

Tax, S. (1988). Pride and puzzlement: A retro-introspective record of 60 years of anthropology. *Annual Review of Anthropology, 17*, 1–21. **239**

Taylor, G. T., Bardgett, M., & Weiss, J. (1990). Behaviour and physiology of castrated rats with different episodic schedules of testosterone restoration. *Hormones and Metabolic Research, 22*, 57–59. **150**

Taylor, G. T., Weiss, J., & Rupich, R. (1985). Suprathreshold manipulations of testosterone and reproductive functioning in gonadally intact sexually experienced and inexperienced male rats. *Physiology & Behavior, 35*, 735–739. **151**

Taylor, M. A., & Abrams, R. (1981). Gender differences in bipolar affective disorder. *Journal of Affective Disorders, 3*, 261–277. **362**

Taylor, M. E., & Hall, J. A. (1982). Psychological androgyny: Theories, methods, and conclusions. *Psychological Bulletin, 92*, 347–366. **48**

Taylor, S. E., & Brown, J. D. (1988). Illusion and well-being: A social psychological perspective on mental health. *Psychological Bulletin, 103*, 193–210. **366, 370**

Taylor, S. E., & Falcone, H.-T. (1982). Cognitive bases of stereotyping: The relationship between categorization and prejudice. *Personality and Social Psychology Bulletin, 8*, 426–432. **279**

Taylor, S. E., & Lobel, M. (1989). Social comparison activity under threat: Downward evaluation and upward contacts. *Psychological Review, 96*, 569–575. **326**

Taylor, W. N., & Black, A. B. (1987). Pervasive anabolic steroid use among health club athletes. *Annals of Sports Medicine, 3*, 155–159. **202**

Teglasi, H. (1981). Children's choices of and value judgments about sex-typed toys and occupations. *Journal of Vocational Behavior, 18*, 184–195. **294, 325**

Teleki, G. (1973). The omnivorous chimpanzee. *Scientific American, 228*, 32-42. **245**

Tennant, F., Black, D. L., & Voy, R. O. (1988). Anabolic steroid dependence with opioid-type features. *New England Journal of Medicine, 319*, 578. **202**

Tennen, H., & Herzberger, S. (1987). Depression, self–esteem, and the absence of self-protective attributional biases. *Journal of Personality and Social Psychology, 52*, 72–80. **366**

Tennes, K., Puck, M., Bryant, K., Frandenburg, W., & Robinson, A. (1975). A developmental study of girls with trisomy X. *American Journal of Human Genetics, 27*, 71–80. **114**

Tetenbaum, T. J., & Pearson, J. (1989). The voices in children's literature: The impact of gender on the moral decisions of storybook characters. *Sex Roles, 20*, 381–395. **289**

Tétreau, B., & Traham, M. (1988). Sexual identification and the maturing vocational interests of pre-adolescent girls. *Applied Psychology: An International Review, 37*, 165–181. **329**

Teyler, T. J., Vardaris, R. M., Lewis, D., & Rawitch, A. B. (1980). Gonadal steroids: Effects on excitability of hippocampal pyramidal cells. *Science, 209*, 1017–1019. **152**

Theilgaard, A. (1972). Cognitive style and gender role in persons with sex chromosome aberrations. *Danish Medical Bulletin, 19*, 276–286. **113**

_____. (1986). Psychologic study of XY and XXY men. In S. Ratcliff & N. Paul (Eds.), *Perspective studies of children with sex chromosome aneuploidy* (pp. 277–292). New York: Alan Liss,. **115, 116**

_____. (1990). Men with sex chromsome aberrationsas subjects and human beings. In D. B. Berch & B. G. Bender (Eds.), *Sex chromosome abnormalities and human behavior: Psychological studies* (pp. 145–160). Boulder, CO: Westview Press,. **115, 116**

Thierry, B., Steru, L., Chermat, R., & Simon, P. (1984). Searching-waiting strategy: A condidate for an evolutionary model of depression? *Behavioral and Neural Biology, 41*, 180–189. **365**

Thiessen, D., & Ross, M. (1990). The use of a sociobiological questionnaire (SQ) for the assessment of sexual dimorphism. *Behavior Genetics, 20*, 297–305. **379**

Thiessen, D. D., & Gregg, B. (1980). Human assortative mating. *Ethology and Sociobiology, 1*, 111–140. **380, 381**

Thoma, S. J. (1986). Estimating gender differences in the comprehension and preference of moral issues. *Developmental Review, 6*, 165–180. **218**

Thompson, L. A., Detterman, D. K., & Plomin, R. (1991). Associations between cognitive abilities and scholastic achievement: Genetic overlap but environmental differences. *Psychological Science, 2*, 158–165. **336**

Thompson, S. K. (1975). Gender labels and early sex role development. *Child Development, 46*, 339–347. **314**

Thorne, B. (1986). Girls and boys together but mostly apart: Gender arrangements in elementary schools. In W. W. Hartup & Z. Rubin (Eds.), *Relationships and development*. Hillsdale, NJ: Erlbaum. **303, 313, 315**

Thornhill, R., & Thornhill, N. W. (1983). Human rape: An evolutionary analysis. *Ethology and Sociobiology, 4*, 137–173. **376, 384**

Tietze, K. J., & Smith, M. C. (1990). More on sex and racial bias in pharmaceutical advertisements. *New England Journal of Medicine, 320*, 1534. **289**

Tiger, L. (1987). Alienated from the meanings of reproduction? In J. M. Reinisch, L. A. Rosenblum, & S. A. Sanders (Eds), *Masculinity/femininity: Basic perspectives*. New York: Oxford University Press. **258**

Tipping, L. M., & Farmer, H. S. (1991). A home-career conflict measure: Career couseling implications. *Measurement and Evaluation in Counseling and Development, 24* 111–118. **327, 331**

Tizard, B., Philps, J., & Lewis, I. (1976). Play in pre-school centers—I. Play measures and their relation to age, sex and I.Q. *Journal of Child Psychology and Psychiatry, 17*, 251–264. **316**

Tobet, S. A., Zahniser, D. J., & Baum, M. J. (1986). Sexual dimorphism in the preoptic/anterior hypothalamic area of ferrets: Effects of adult exposure to sex steroids. *Brain Research, 364*, 249–257. **163**

Tobin, J., Wassertheil-Smoller, S., Wexler, J. P., Steingart, R. M., Budner, N., Lense, L., & Wachspress, J. (1987). Sex bias in considering coronary bypass surgery. *Annals of Internal Medicine, 107*, 19–25. **283**

Tolman, E. C. (1948). Cognitive maps in rats and men. *Psychological Review, 55*, 189–208. **212**

Tomelleri, R., & Grunewald, K. K. (1987). Menstrual cycle and food cravings in young college women. *Journal of the American Dietetic Associations, 87*, 311–315. **189**

Tomlinson, I. P. M. (1988). Diploid models of the handicap principle. *Heredity, 60*, 283–293. **87**

Tonegawa, S. (1985). The molecules of the immune system. *Scientific American, 253*, 122–131. **73**

Tooby, J., & Cosmides, L. (1989). Evolutionary psychology and the generation of culture, Part I. Theoretical considerations. *Ethology and Sociobiology, 10*, 29–49. **60, 214, 250**

Top, T. J. (1991). Sex bias in the evaluation of performance in the scientific, artistic, and literary professions: A review. *Sex Roles, 24*, 73–106. **281**

Toran-Allerand, C. D. (1980). Sex steroids and the development of the newborn mouse hypothalamus and preoptic area in vitro. II. Morphological correlates and hormonal specificity. *Brain Research, 189*, 413–427. **137, 157, 174**

_____. (1984). On the genesis of sexual differentiation of the central nervous system: Morphogenetic consequences of steroidal exposure and possible role of -fetoprotein. *Progress in Brain Research, 61*, 63–98. **137, 157, 158, 174**

Toran-Allerand, C. D., Ellis, L. & Pfenninger, K. H. (1988). Estrogen and insulin synergism in neurite growth enhancement in vitro: Mediation of steroid effects by interactions with growth factors? *Developmental Brain Research, 41*, 87–100. **137**

Toren, N., & Kraus, V. (1987). The effects of minority size on women's position in academia. *Social Forces,*

65, 1090–1100. **330**

Touitou, Y., Carayon, A., Reinberg, A., Bogdan, A., & Beck, H. (1983). Differences in the seasonal rhythmicity of plasma prolactin in elderly human subjects: Detection in women but not in men. *Journal of Endocrinology, 96*, 65–71. **196**

Towle, A. C., & Sze, P. Y. (1983). Steroid binding to synaptic plasma membrane: Differential binding of glucocorticoids and gonadal steroids. *Journal of Steroid Biochemistry, 18*, 135–143. **136**

Tracy, D. M. (1987). Toys, spatial ability, and science and mathematics achievement: Are they related? *Sex Roles, 17*, 115–138. **307, 308, 393**

Traindis, H. C. (1989). The self and social behavior in differing cultural contexts. *Psychological Review, 96*, 506–520. **239, 346**

Trapnell, P. D., & Wiggins, J. S. (1990). Extension of the interpersonal adjective scales to include the big five dimensions of personality. *Journal of Personality and Social Psychology, 59*, 781–790. **339**

Treiman, D. J., & Roos, P. A. (1983). Sex and earnings in industrial society: A nine-nation comparison. *American Journal of Sociology, 89*, 612–650. **322**

Trigg, L. J., & Perlman, D. (1976). Social influences on women's pursuit of a nontraditional career. *Psychology of Women Quarterly, 1*, 138–150. **329**

Trivers, R. (1971). The evolution of reciprocal altruism. *Quarterly Review of Biology, 46*, 35–57. **80, 82**

————. (1972). Parental investment and sexual selection. In B. Campbell (Ed.), *Sexual selection and the descent of man, 1871–1971*. Chicago: Aldine. **77, 82, 86**

————. (1974). Parent-offspring conflict. *American Zoologist, 14*, 249–264. **77, 221**

————. (1988). Sex differences in rates of recombination and sexual selection. In R. E. Michod & B. R. Levin (Eds.), *The evolution of sex: An examination of current ideas*. Sunderland, MA: Sinauer Associates. **100, 101, 102**

Trivers, R. L., & Willard, D. E. (1973). Natural selection of parental ability to vary the sex ratio of offspring. *Science, 179*, 90–92. **62, 79**

Troup, G. A., Bradshaw, J. L., & Nettleton, N. C. (1983). The lateralization of arithmetic and number processing: a review. *International Journal of Neuroscience, 19*, 231–242. **397**

Tsim, K. W. K., Pak, R. C. K., & Cheng, C. H. K. (1985). Prolactin receptor in rat liver: Sex difference in estrogenic stimulation and imprinting of the responsiveness to estrogen by neonatal androgen in male rats. *Molecular and Cellular Endocrinology, 40*, 99–105. **152**

Tsonis, C. G., Messinis, I. E., Templeton, A. A., McNeilly, A. S., & Baird, D. T. (1988). Gonadotropic stimulation of inhibin secretion by the human ovary during the follicular and early luteal phase of the cycle. *Journal of Clinical Endocrinology and Metabolism, 66*, 915–921. **145**

Tsuang, M. T. (1974). Sex chromatin anomaly in Chinese females: Psychiatric characteristics of XXX. *British Journal of Psychiatry, 124*, 299–305. **114**

Tulving, E., & Schachter, D. L. (1990). Priming and human memory. *Science, 247*, 301–306. **208, 214**

Turke, P. W. (1988). Helpers at the nest: Childcare networks on Ifaluk. In L. Betzig, M. B. Mulder, & P. Turke (Eds.), *Human reproductive behaviour*. Cambridge: Cambridge University Press. **146, 244**

Turkenburg, J. L., Swaab, D. F., Endert, E., Louwerse, A. L., & van de Poll, N. E. (1988). Effects of lesions of the sexually dimorphic nucleus on sexual behavior of testosterone-treated female Wistar rats. *Brain Research Bulletin, 21*, 215–224. **162**

Turkkan, J. S. (1989). Classical conditioning: The new hegemony. *Behavioral and Brain Sciences, 12*, 121–179. **209, 213**

Turner, R. J., & Avison, W. R. (1989). Gender and depression: Assessing exposure and vulnerability to life events in a chronically strained population. *Journal of Nervous and Mental Disease, 177*, 443–455. **365**

Uchibori, M., & Kawashima, S. (1985a). Stimulation of neuronal process growth by estradiol-17 in dissociated cells from fetal rat hypothalamus-preoptic area. *Zoological Science, 2*, 381–388. **137**

————. (1985b). Effects of sex steroids on the growth of neuronal processes in neonatal rat hypothalamus-preoptic area and cerebral cortex in primary culture. *International Journal of Developmental Neuroscience, 3*, 169–176. **137**

Udry, J. R., & Morris, N. M. (1978). Relative contribution of male and female age to the frequency of marital intercourse. *Social Biology, 25*, 128–134. **383**

Unenoyama, M. K. (1988). On the evolution of genetic incompatibility systems: Incompatibility as a mechanism for the regulation of outcrossing distance. In R. E. Michod, & B. R. Levin (Eds.), *The evolution of sex: An examination of current ideas*. Sunderland, MA: Sinauer Associates. **74**

Unger, R. K. (1979). Toward a redefinition of sex and gender. *American Psychologist, 34*, 1085–1094. **17**

————. (1981). Sex as a social reality: Field and laboratory research. *Psychology of Women Quarterly, 5*, 645–653. **33**

————. (1983). Toward the looking glass: No wonderland yet! (The reciprocal relationship between methodology and models of reality). *Psychology of Women Quarterly, 8*, 9–32. **10, 41, 45**

Unger, R. K., & Denmark, F. L. (Eds.) (1975). *Women: Dependent or independent variable?* New York: Psychological Dimensions. **12**

U.S. Department of Labor. (1983). *Time of change: 1983 handbook on women workers*. Office of the Secretary, Women's Bureau, Bulletin 298. **322**

Utian, W. H. (1987). Overview on menopause. *American Journal of Obstetrics and Gynecology, 156*, 1280–1283. **200**

Vadász, C., Baker, H., Fink, S. J., & Reis, D. J. (1985). Genetic effects and sexual dimorphism in tyrosine hydroxylase activity in two mouse strains and their reciprocal F1 hybrids. *Journal of Neurogenetics, 2*, 219–230. **147**

Vale, J. R., Ray, D., & Vale, C. A. (1972). The interaction of genotype and exogenous neonatal androgen: Agonistic behavior in female mice. *Behavioral Biology, 7*, 321–324. **147**

————. (1973). The interaction of genotype and exogenous neonatal androgen and estrogen: Sex behavior in female mice. *Developmental Psychobiology, 6*, 319–327. **147**

van Abeelen, J. H. F., Janssens, C. J. J. G., Crusio, W. E., & Lemmens, W. A. J. G. (1989). Y-chromosomal effects on discrimination learning and hippocampal asymmetry in mice. *Behavior Genetics, 19*, 543–549. **397**

Van de Kar, L. D. (1989). Neuroendocrine aspects of the serotonergic hypothesis of depression. *Neuroscience & Biobehavioral Reviews, 13*, 237–246. **369**

Van den Bergh, B. R. H., Mulder, E. J. H., Visser, G. H. A., Poelmann-Weesjes, G., Bekedam, D. J., & Prechtl, H. F. R. (1989). The effect of (induced) maternal emotions on fetal behaviour: A controlled study. *Early Human Development, 19*, 9–19. **148**

Vandenberg, S. G. (1972). Assortative mating, or who marries whom?

Behavior Genetics, 2, 127–157. **380**

van de Poll, N. E., Smeets, J., van Oyen, H. G., & van der Zwan, S. M. (1982). Behavioral consequences of agonistic experience in rats: Sex differences and the effects of testosterone. *Journal of Comparative and Physiological Psychology, 96,* 893–903. **358**

Vanderstichele, H., Eechaute, W., Lacroix, E., & Leusen, I. (1987). Influence of neonatal androgenization on the testicular steroidogenesis in the adult rat. *Journal of Steroid Biochemistry, 28,* 421–427. **127**

Vanfossen, B. E. (1981). Sex differences in the mental health effects of spouse support and equity. *Journal of Health and Social Beahvior, 22,* 130–143. **365**

van Huizen, F., Romijn, H. J., & Corner, M. A. (1987). Indications for a critical period for synapse elimination in developing rat cerebral cortex cultures. *Developmental Brain Research, 31,* 1–6. **225**

Vannicelli, M., & Nash, L. (1984). Effect of sex bias on women's studies on alcoholism. *Alcoholism: Clinical and Experimental Research, 8,* 334–336. **39**

Van Schaik, C. P., Netto, W. J., Van Amerongen, A. J. J., & Westland, H. (1989). Social rank and sex ratio of captive long-tailed macaque females (Macaca fascicularis). *American Journal of Primatology, 19,* 147–161. **80**

Van Strien, J. W., & Bouma, A. (1990). Mental rotation of laterally presented random shapes in males and females. *Brain and Cognition, 12,* 297–303. **393**

Varma, S. K., & Bloch, E. (1987). Effects of prenatal administration of mestranol and two progestins on testosterone synthesis and reproductive tract development in male rats. *Acta Endocrinologica, 116,* 193–199. **127**

Varrela, J., Alvesalo, L., & Vinkka, H. (1984). Body size and shape in 46,XY females with complete testicular feminization. *Annals of Human Biology, 11,* 291–301. **113**

Vathy, I., & Etgen, A. M. (1989). Hormonal activation of female sexual behavior is accompanied by hypothalamic norepinephrine release. *Journal of Neuroendocrinology, 1,* 383–388. **14**

Veevers, J. E. (1988). The "real" marriage squeeze: Mate selection, mortality, and the mating gradient. *Sociological Perspectives, 31,* 169–189. **376**

Veith, J. L., Buck, M., Getzlaf, S., Van Dalfsen, P., & Slade, S. (1983). Exposure to men influences the occurrence of ovulation in women. *Physiology & Behavior, 31,* 313–315. **190**

Ventanas, J., Lopez, C., Garcia, C., & Lopez, A. (1986). Effect of testosterone on protein synthesis in the hypothalamus of newborn female rat. *Neuroendocrinology Letters, 8,* 53–56. **138**

Vermeulen, A. (1983). Androgen secretion after age 50 in both sexes. *Hormone Research, 18,* 37–42. **199**

Veroff, J. (1969). Social comparison and the development of achievement motivation. In C. P. Smith (Ed.), *Achievement-related motives in children.* New York: Russell Sage Foundation. **321, 333**

Vessey, M. P., Fairweather, D. V. I., Norman-Smith, B., & Buckley, J. (1983). A randomized double-blind controlled trial of the value of stilboestrol therapy in pregnancy: Long-term follow-up of mothers and their offspring. *British Journal of Obstetrics and Gynaecology, 90,* 1007–1017. **170, 368**

Vessey, S. H., & Meikle, D. B. (1987). Factors affecting social behavior and reproductive success of male rhesus monkeys. *International Journal of Primatology, 8,* 281–292. **349**

Vetter, B. M. (1981). Women scientists and engineers: Trends in participation. *Science, 214,* 1313–1321. **324**

————. (1989, September 1). Minorities gain, but white women lose ground. *The AAAS Observer* (No. 7), 10. **324**

Viglietti-Panzica, C., Panzica, G. C., Fiori, M. G., Calcagni, M., Anselmetti, G. C., & Balthazart, J. (1986). A sexually dimorphic nucleus in the quail preoptic area. *Neuroscience Letters, 64,* 129–134. **162**

Viney, W (1989). The cyclops and the twelve-eyed toad: William James and the unity-disunity problem in psychology. *American Psychologist, 44,* 1261–1265. **24**

Virkkunen, M., DeJong, J., Goodwin, F. K., & Linnoila, M. (1989). Relationship of psychobiological variables to recidivism in violent offenders and impulsive fire setters: A follow-up study. *Archives of General Psychiatry, 46,* 600–603. **351**

Virkkunen, M., & Linnoila, M. (1990). Serotonin in early onset, male alcoholics with violent behaviour. *Annals of Medicine, 22,* 327–331. **351**

Vittek, J., L'Hommedieu, D. G., Gordon, G. G., Rappaport, S. C., & Southren, A. L. (1985). Direct radioimmunoassay (RIA) of salivary testosterone: Correlation with free and total testosterone. *Life Sciences, 37,* 711–716. **178**

Vomachka, A. J. (1987). Neonatal steroid exposure increases in vitro aromatization ability of peripubertal hamster ovaries. *Biology of Reproduction, 36,* 314–319. **127**

Vomachka, A. J., & Lisk, R. D. (1986). Androgen and estradiol levels in plasma and amniotic fluid of late gestational male and female hamsters: Uterine position effects. *Hormones and Behavior, 20,* 181–193. **147**

vom Saal, F. S., & Finch, C. E. (1988). Reproductive senescence: Phenomena and mechanisms in mammals and selected vertebrates. In E. Knobil & J. Neill et al., (Eds.), *The physiology of reproduction.* New York: Raven Press. **125, 126, 130, 150, 151, 171, 178, 197, 198, 199, 200, 203**

vom Saal, F. S., Quadagno, D. M., Even, M. D., Keisler, L. W., Keisler, D. H., & Khan, S. (1990). Paradoxical effects of maternal stress and fetal steroids and postnatal reproductive traits in female mice from different intrauterine positions. *Biology of Reproduction, 43,* 751–761. **148**

von Baeyer, C. L., Sherk, D. L., & Zanna, M. P. (1981). Impression management in the job interview: When the female applicant meets the male (chauvinist) interviewer. *Journal of Personality and Social Psychology Bulletin, 7,* 44–51. **9**

von Knorring, A.-L., Cloninger, C. R., Bohman, M., & Sigvardsson, S. (1983). An adoption study of depressive disorders and substance abuse. *Archives of General Psychiatry, 40,* 943–950. **367**

Voyer, D., & Bryden, M. P. (1990). Gender, level of spatial ability, and lateralization of mental rotation. *Brain and Cognition, 13,* 18–29. **392**

Vredenburg, K., Krames, L., & Flett, G. L. (1986). Sex differences in the clinical expression of depression. *Sex Roles, 14,* 37–50. **363**

Waber, D. P. (1979). Neuropsychological aspects of Turner's syndrome. *Developmental Medicine and Child Neurology, 21,* 58–70. **114**

Wade, M. J., & Pruett-Jones, S. G. (1990). Female copying increases the variance in male mating success. *Proceedings of the National Academy of Science, USA, 87,* 5749–5743. **216**

Wagner, C. K., Kinsley, C., & Svare, B. (1986). Mice: Postpartum aggression is elevated following prenatal progesterone exposure. *Hormones and Behavior, 20,* 212–221. **358**

Wagner, D. G., Ford, R. S., & Ford, T. W. (1986). Can gender inequalities be reduced? *American*

Sociological Review, 51, 47–61. **286**

Wake, D. B., & Larson, A. (1987). Multidimensional analysis of an evolving lineage. *Science, 238*, 42–48. **224**

Waldrop, M. F., & Halverson, C. F., Jr. (1975). Intensive and extensive peer behavior: Longitudinal and cross-sectional analysis. *Child Development, 46*, 19–26. **314, 316**

Walicke, P. A., Campenot, R. B., & Patterson, P. H. (1977). Determination of transmitter function by neuronal activity. *Proceedings of the National Academy of Sciences, 74*, 5767–5771. **139**

Walker, L. (1984). Sex differences in the development of moral reasoning: A review. *Child Development, 55*, 677–691. **218**

Walker, L. E. A. (1989). Psychology and violence against women. *American Psychologist, 44*, 695–702. **352**

Wallston, B. S., & Grady, K. E. (1985). Integrating the feminist critique and the crisis in social psychology: Another look at research methods. In V. E. O'Leary, R. K. Unger, & B. S. Wallston (Eds.), *Women, gender, and social psychology*. Hillsdale, NJ: Ehrlbaum. **50**

Wallston, B. S., & O'Leary, V. E. (1981). Sex makes a difference: Differential perceptions of women and men. *Review of Personality and Social Psychology, 2*, 9–41. **274, 284**

Walters, J. R., & Seyfarth, R. M. (1987). Conflict and cooperation. In B. B. Smuts, D. L. Cheney, R. M. Seyfarth, R. W. Wrangham, & T. T. Struhsaker (Eds.), *Primate societies*. Chicago: University of Chicago Press. **250**

Walters, M. R. (1985). Steroid hormone receptors and the nucleus. *Endocrine Reviews, 6*, 512–543. **133, 135**

Ward, P. I. (1988). Sexual dichromatism and parasitism in British and Irish freshwater fish. *Animal Behaviour, 36*, 1210–1215. **87**

Ward, W. D., & Jungbluth, J. E. (1980). Sex differences in classroom achievement as a function of participation in monitoring and reinforcement. *Journal of Psychology, 106*, 253–258. **318**

Wareham, K. A., Lyon, M. F., Glenister, P. H., & Williams, E. D. (1987). Age related reactivation of an X-linked gene. *Nature, 327*, 725–727. **105**

Warlick, J. L. (1985). Why is poverty after 65 a woman's problem? *Gerontologist, 40*, 751–757. **283**

Warrington, E. K., & McCarthy, R. A. (1987). Categories of knowledge: Further fractionations and an attempted integration. *Brain, 110*, 1273–1296. **266**

Warrington, E. K., & Shallice, T. (1984). Category specific semantic impairments. *Brain, 107*, 829–854. **266**

Wasser, S. K., & Barash, D. P. (1983). Reproductive suppression among female mammals: Implications for biomedicine and sexual selection theory. *Quarterly Review of Biology, 58*, 513–538. **349**

Watson, D., Clark, L. A., & Carey, G. (1988). Positive and negative affectivity and their relation to anxiety and depressive disorders. *Journal of Abnormal Psychology, 97*, 346–353. **365**

Watson, R. E., Jr., Hoffman, G. E., & Wiegand, S. J. (1986). Sexually dimorphic opioid distribution in the preoptic area: Manipulation by gonadal steroids. *Brain Research, 398*, 157–163. **162**

Weatherhead, P. J., & Robertson, R. J. (1979). Offspring quality and the polygyny threshold: "The sexy son hypothesis." *American Naturalist, 113*, 201–208. **86**

Wee, B. E. F., Weaver, D. R., & Clemens, L. G. (1988). Hormonal restoration of masculine sexual behavior in long-term castrated B6D2F1 mice. *Physiology & Behavior, 42*, 77–82. **147**

Wegner, D. M. (1990, May). *You can't always think what you want: Problems in the suppression of unwanted thoughts*. Paper presented at Midwestern Psychological Association Convention, Chicago. **366**

Weigel, R. M. (1985). Demographic factors affecting assertive and defensive behavior in preschool children: An ethological study. *Aggressive Behavior, 11*, 27–40. **356**

Weinberg, R. S., & Jackson, A. (1979). Competition and extrinsic rewards: Effect on intrinsic motivation and attribution. *Research Quarterly, 50*, 494–502. **319**

Weinberg, R. S., & Ragan, J. (1979). Effects of competition, success/failure, and sex on intrinsic motivation. *Research Quarterly, 50*, 503–510. **319**

Weinraub, M., Clemens, L. P., Sockloff, A., Ethridge, T., Gracely, E., & Myers, B. (1984). The development of sex role stereotypes in the third year: Relationships to gender labeling, gender identity, sex-typed toy preference, and family characteristics. *Child Development, 55*, 1493–1503. **294, 302, 307**

Weisfeld, C. C., Weisfeld, G. E., & Callaghan, J. W. (1982). Female inhibition in mixed-sex competition among young adolescents. *Ethology and Sociobiology, 3*, 29–42. **319**

Weisfeld, G. E. (1980). Social dom-inance and human motivation. In D. R. Omark, F. F. Strayer, & D. G. Freedman (Eds.), *An ethological view of human conflict and social interaction*. New York: Garland STPM Press. **348**

Weisfeld, G. E., & Berger, J. M. (1983). Some features of human adolescence viewed in evolutionary perspective. *Human Development, 26*, 121–133. **377**

Weisfeld, G. E., Omark, D. R., & Cronin, C. L. (1980). A longitudinal and cross-sectional study of dominance in boys. In D. R. Omark, F. F. Strayer, & D. G. Freedman (Eds.), *An ethological view of human conflict and social interaction*. New York: Garland STPM Press. **349**

Weisfeld, G. E., & Weisfeld, C. C. (1984). An observational study of social evaluation: An application of the dominance hierarchy model. *Journal of Genetic Psychology, 145*, 89–99. **348**

Weisheit, R. A. (1984). Women and crime: Issues and perspectives. *Sex Roles, 11*, 567–579. **352**

Weisman, C. S., Teitelbaum, M. A., Nathanson, C. A., Chase, G. A., King, T. M., & Levine, D. M. (1986). Sex differences in the practice patterns of recently trained obstetrician-gynecologists. *Obstetrics & Gynecology, 67*, 776–782. **324**

Weisner, T. S., & Gallimore, R. (1977). My brother's keeper: Child and sibling caretaking. *Current Anthropology, 18*, 169–190. **253**

Weissenbach, J., Levilliers, J., Petit, C., Rouyer, F., & Simmler, J.-C. (1987). Normal and abnormal interchanges between the human X and Y chromosomes. *Development, 101, Supplement*, 67–74. **101**

Weissenburger, J., Rush, A. J., Giles, D. E., & Stunkard, A. J., (1986). Weight change in depression. *Psychiatry Research, 17*, 275–283. **363**

Weissman, M. M. (1974). Epidemiology of suicide attempts, 1960 to 1971. *Archives of General Psychiatry, 30*, 737–746. **366**

⸺. (1987). Advances in psychiatric epidemiology: Rates and risks for major depression. *American Journal of Public Health, 77*, 445–451. **366**

Weissman, M. M., Gammon, G. D., John, K., Merikangas, K. R., Warner, V., Prusoff, B. A., & Sholomskas, D. (1987). Children of depressed parents: Increased pathology and early onset of major depression. *Archives of General Psychiatry, 44*, 847–853. **363**

Weissman, M. M., & Myers, J. K. (1978). Affective disorders in a US urban community: The use of research diagnostic criteria in an epidemiological survey. *Archives of General Psychiatry, 35*, 1304–1311. **368**

Weisz, J., & Ward, I. L. (1980). Plasma testosterone and progesterone titers of pregnant rats, their male and female fetuses, and neonatal offspring. *Endocrinology, 106*, 306–316. **158**

Weitzman, N., Birns, B., & Friend, R. (1985). Traditional and nontraditional mothers' communication with their daughters and sons. *Child Development, 56*, 894–898. **301**

Weitzman, L. J., Eifler, D., Hokada, E., & Ross, C. (1972). Sex-role socialization in picture books for preschool children. *American Journal of Sociology, 77*, 1125–1150. **288**

Weizenbaum, F., Benson, B., Solomon, L., & Brehony, K. (1980). Relationship among reproductive variables, sucrose taste reactivity and feeding behavior in humans. *Physiology & Behavior, 24*, 1053–1056. **189**

Weizenbaum, F. A., Adler, N. T., & Ganjam, V. K. (1979). Serum testosterone concentrations in the pregnant rat. *Journal of Steroid Biochemistry, 10*, 71–74. **158, 197**

Welch, M. R. (1978). Socialization anxiety and patterns of economic subsistence. *Journal of Social Psychology, 105*, 33–36. **254**

Welch, M. R., & Page, B. M. (1981). Sex differences in childhood socialization patterns in African societies. *Sex Roles, 7*, 1163–1173. **254**

Welner, A., Marten, S., Wochnick, E., Davis, M. A., Fishman, R., & Clayton, P. J. (1979). Psychiatric disorders among professional women. *Archives of General Psychiatry, 36*, 169–173. **368**

Wender, P. H., Kety, S. S., Rosenthal, D., Schulsinger, F., Ortmann, J., & Lunde, I. (1986). Psychiatric disorders in the biological and adoptive families of adopted individuals with affective disorders. *Archives of General Psychiatry, 43*, 923–929. **367**

Wentzel, K. R. (1989). Adolescent classroom goals, standards for performance, and academic achievement: An interactionist perspective. *Journal of Educational Psychology, 81*, 131–142. **321**

Werner, D. (1984). Child care and influence among the Medranoti of central Brazil. *Sex Roles, 10*, 395–404. **262**

West, M. J., King, A. P., & Arberg, A. A. (1988). The inheritance of niches: The role of ecological legacies in ontogeny. In E. M. Blass (Ed.), *Handbook of behavioral neurobiology. Vol. 9, Developmental psychobiology and behavioral ecology.* New York: Plenum. **16**

West, M. M., & Konner, M. J. (1976). The role of the father: An anthropological perspective. In M. E. Lamb (Ed.), *The role of the father in child development.* New York: Plenum Press. **252**

Westendorp, F., Brink, K. L., Roberson, M. K., & Ortiz, I. E. (1986). Variables which differentiate placement of adolescents into juvenile justice or mental health systems. *Adolescence, 21*, 23–37. **283**

Westfahl, P. K., Stadelman, H. L., Horton, L. E., & Resko, J. A. (1984). Experimental induction of estradiol positive feedback in intact male monkeys: Absence of inhibition of physiologic concentrations of testosterone. *Biology of Reproduction, 31*, 856–862. **145**

Westphal, U. (1986). *Steroid-protein interactions II.* New York: Springer-Verlag. **158**

Whalen, R. E., & Olsen, K. L. (1978). Chromatin binding of estradiol in the hypothalamus and cortex of male and female rats. *Brain Research, 152*, 121–131. **136, 138**

Wheeler, A. G., Baird, D. T., Land, R. B., & Scaramuzzi, R. J. (1977). Genetic variation in the secretion of oestrogen in the ewe. *Journal of Endocrinology, 75*, 337–338. **147**

Whitam, F. L. (1983). Culturally invariable properties of male homosexuality: Tentative conclusions from cross-cultural research. *Archives of Sexual Beahvior, 12*, 207–226. **389**

Whitam, F. L., & Zent, M. (1984). A cross-cultural assessment of early cross-gender behavior and familial factors in male homosexuality. *Archives of Sexual Behavior, 13*, 427–439. **389**

White, G. M. (1980). Conceptual universals in interpersonal language. *American Anthropologist, 82*, 759–781. **339, 341**

White, L. K., & Brinkerhoff, D. B. (1981). The sexual division of labor: Evidence from childhood. *Social Forces, 60*, 170–181. **307**

White, M. C., De Sanctis, G., & Crino, M. D. (1981). Achievement, self-confidence, personality traits, and leadership ability: A review of literature on sex differences. *Psychological Reports, 48*, 547–569. **321**

White, S. H. (1965). Evidence for a hierarchical arrangement of learning processes. In L. P. Lipsitt & C. C. Spiker (Ed.), *Advances in child development and behavior* (Vol. 2). New York: Academic Press. **227**

Whitehead, H. (1981). The bow and the burden strap: A new look at institutionalized homosexuality in native North America. In S. B. Ortner & H. Whitehead (Eds.), *Sexual meanings: The cultural construction of gender and sexuality.* Cambridge: Cambridge University Press. **258**

Whiting, B., & Edwards, C. P. (1973). A cross-cultural analysis of sex differences in the behavior of children aged three through 11. *Journal of Social Psychology, 91*, 171–188. **255**
_____. (1988). *Children of different worlds.* Cambridge, MA: Harvard University Press. **237, 240, 250, 251, 252, 255, 337, 347**

Whiting, B. B. (1965). Sex identity conflict and physical violence: A comparative study. *American Anthropologist, 67*, 123–140. **259**

Whitley, B. E., Jr. (1983). Sex role orientation and self-esteem: A critical meta-analytic review. *Journal of Personality and Social Psychology, 44*, 765–778. **49**

Whitten, P. L. (1983). Diet and dominance among female vervet monkeys (Cercopithecus aethiops). *American Journal of Primatology, 5*, 139–159. **349**

Whitten, P. L. (1987). Infants and adult males. In B. B. Smuts, D. L. Cheney, R. M. Seyfarth, R. W. Wrangham, & T. T. Struhsaker (Eds.), *Primate societies.* Chicago: University of Chicago Press. **221, 252**

Widiger, T. A., & Settle, S. A. (1987). Broverman et al. revisited: An artifactual sex bias. *Journal of Personality and Social Psychology, 53*, 463–469. **281, 296**

Widnall, S. E. (1988). AAAS presidential lecture: Voices from the pipeline. *Science, 241*, 1740–1745. **319, 321**

Widom, C. S. (1989a). The cycle of violence. *Science, 244*, 160–166. **350, 356**
_____. (1989b). Does violence beget violence? A critical examination of the literature. *Psychological Bulletin, 106*, 3–28. **350, 356**

Wiggins, J. S. (1979). A psychological taxonomy of trait-descriptive terms: The interpersonal domain. *Journal of Personality and Social Psychology, 37*, 395–412. **339**
_____. (1982). Circumplex models of interpersonal behavior in clinical psychology. In P. C. Kendall & J. N. Butcher (Eds.), *Handbook of research methods in clinical psychology*, (pp. 183–221). New York: Wiley. **350**

Wiggins, J. S., & Broughton, R. (1985). The interpersonal circle: A structural model for the integration of personality research. In R.

Hogan & W. H. Jones (Eds.), *Perspectives in personality* (Vol. 1). Greenwich, CN: JAI Press. **339**

Wiggins, J. S., & Holzmuller, A. (1978). Psychological androgyny and interpersonal behavior. *Journal of Consulting and Clinical Psychology, 46*, 40–52. **339, 340**

————. (1981). Further evidence on androgyny and interpersonal flexibility. *Journal of Research in Personality, 15*, 67–80. **339, 340**

Wiggins, J. S., Phillips, N., & Trapnell, P. (1989). Circular reasoning about interpersonal behavior: Evidence concerning some untested assumptions underlying diagnostic classification. *Journal of Personality and Social Psychology, 56*, 296–305. **339, 350**

Wilder, G. Z., & Powell, K. (1989). Sex differences in test performances: A survey of the literature. *College Board Report, No. 89-3.* **372, 391**

Wildt, D. E., Bush, M., Goodrowe, K. L., Packer, C., Pusey, A. E., Brown, J. L., Joslin, P., & O'Brien, S. J. (1987). Reproductive and genetic consequences of founding isolated lion populations. *Nature, 329*, 328–331. **75**

Wildt, D. E., Panko, W. B., Chakraborty, P. K., & Seager, S. W. J. (1979). Relationship of serum estrone, estradiol-17 and progesterone to LH, sexual behavior and time of ovulation in the bitch. *Biology of Reproduction, 20*, 648–658. **183**

Wilkinson, L. C., Lindow, J., & Chiang, C.-P. (1985). Sex differences and sex segregation in students' small-group communication. In L. C. Wilkinson & C. B. Marrett (Eds.), *Gender-related differences in the classroom.* New York: Academic Press. **314**

Willerman, L., Schultz, R., Rutledge, J. N., & Bigler, E. D. (1991). In vivo brain size and intelligence. *Intelligence, 15*, 223–228. **166**

Williams, C. L. (1987). A reevaluation of the concept of separable periods of organizational and activational actions of estrogens in development of brain and behavior. *Annals of the New York Academy of Science, 474*, 282–292. **125, 150**

Williams, C. L., Barnett, A. M., & Meck, W. H. (1990). Organizational effects of early gonadal secretions on sexual differentiation in spatial memory. *Behavioral Neuroscience, 104*, 84–97. **396**

Williams, C. L., & Blaustein, J. D. (1988). Steroids induce hypothalamic progestin receptors and facilitate female sexual behavior in neonatal rats. *Brain Research, 449*, 403–407. **125, 127**

Williams, G. C. (1988). Retrospect on sex and kindred topics. In R. E. Michod, & B. R. Levin (Eds.), *The evolution of sex: An examination of current ideas.* Sunderland, MA: Sinauer Associates. **64**

Williams, J. E., & Best, D. L. (1982). *Measuring sex stereotypes: A thirty-nation study.* Beverly Hills: Sage. **259, 272**

————. (1990). *Sex and the psyche: Gender roles and self-concepts viewed cross-culturally.* Beverly Hills: Sage. **259, 341**

Williams, J. E., Giles, H., Edwards, J. R., Best, D. L., & Daws, J. T. (1977). Sex-trait stereotypes in England, Ireland and the United States. *British Journal of Social and Clinical Psychology, 16*, 303–309. **272**

Williams, K., Goodman, M., & Green, R. (1985). Parent-child factors in gender role socialization in girls. *Journal of the American Academy of Child Psychiatry, 26*, 720–731. **303**

Williamson, N. E. (1976). Sex preferences, sex control, and the status of women. *Signs: Journal of Women in Culture and Society, 1*, 847–862. **282**

Willis, S. L., & Schaie, K. W. (1988). Gender differences in spatial ability in old age: Longitudinal and intervention findings. *Sex Roles, 18*, 189–204. **374, 395**

Wilson, M. I., & Daly, M. (1985). Competitiveness, risk taking, and violence: The young male syndrome. *Ethology and Sociobiology, 6*, 59–73. **301, 351**

Wilson, M. I., Daly, M., & Weghorst, S. J. (1980). Household composition and the risk of child abuse and neglect. *Journal of Biosocial Science, 12*, 333–340. **222, 301**

————. Differential maltreatment of girls and boys. *Victomology: An International Journal, 6*, 249–261. **301**

Wilson, M. P. (1987). Making a difference—Women, medicine, and the twenty-first century. *Yale Journal of Biology and Medicine, 60*, 273–288. **324**

Wilson, W. E., & Agrawal, A. K. (1979). Brain regional levels of neurotransmitter amines as neurochemical correlates of sex-specific ontogenesis in the rat. *Developmental Neuroscience, 2*, 195–200. **157**

Windsor, R., & Dumitru, D. (1989). Prevalence of anabolic steroid use by male and female adolescents. *Medicine and Science in Sports and Exercise, 21*, 494–497. **202**

Wingo, P. A., Layde, P. M., Lee, N. C., Rubin, G., & Ory, H. W. (1987). The risk of breast cancer in postmenopausal women who have

used estrogen replacement therapy. *Journal of the American Medical Association, 257*, 209–2215. **203**

Winokur, G. (1973). Depression in the menopause. *American Journal of Psychiatry, 130*, 92–93. **368**

Winpisinger, K. A., Hopkins, R. S., Indian, R. W., & Hostetler, J. R. (1991). Risk factors for childhood homicides in Ohio: A birth certificate-based case-control study. *American Journal of Public Health, 81*, 1052–1054. **354**

Wise, P. M., Weiland, N. G., Scarbrough, K., Sortino, M. A., Cohen, I. R., & Larson, G. H. (1989). Changing hypothalamopituitary function: Its role in aging of the female reproductive system. *Hormone Research, 31*, 39–44. **198**

Witcher, J. A., & Clemens, L. G. (1987). A prenatal source for defeminization of female rats is the maternal ovary. *Hormones and Behavior, 21*, 36–43. **158**

Witelson, S. F. (1991). Sex differences in neuroanatomical changes with aging. *New England Journal of Medicine, 325*, 211–212. **166**

Witkin, H. A., & Goodenough, D. R. (1977). Field dependence and interpersonal behavior. *Psychological Bulletin, 84*, 661–689. **394**

Witkin, H. A., Goodenough, D. R., & Karp, S. A. (1967). Stability of cognitive styles from childhood to young adulthood. *Journal of Personality and Social Psychology, 7*, 291–300. **374**

Witkin, H. A., Mednick, S. A., Schulsinger, F., Bakkestrm, E., Christiansen, K. O., Goodenough, D. R., Hirschhorn, K., Lundsteen, C., Owen, D. R., Philip, J., Rubin, D. B., & Stocking, M. (1976). Criminality in XYY and XXY men. *Science, 193*, 547–555. **114**

Wolfe, D. A. (1985). Child-abusive parents: An empirical review and analysis. *Psychological Bulletin, 97*, 562–482. **254**

Wolff, N. (1988). Women and the equity of the social security program. *Journal of Aging Studies, 2*, 357–377. **283**

Wong, C.-C., Dhler, K.-D., Geerlings, H., & von zur Mühlen, A. (1983). Influence of age, strain and season on circadian periodicity of pituitary, gonadal and adrenal hormones in the serum of male laboratory rats. *Hormone Research, 17*, 202–215. **182**

Wood, J. H. (1982). Neuroendocrinology of cerebrospinal fluid: Peptides, steroids, and other hormones. *Neurosurgery, 11*, 293–305. **178**

Wood, R. (1976). Sex differences in mathematics attainment at GCE

Ordinary Level. *Educational Studies, 2*, 141–160. **373**

Wood, R. I., Ebling, F. J. P., I'Anson, H., Bucholtz, D. C., Yellon, S. M., & Foster, D. L. (1991). Prenatal androgens time neuroendocrine sexual maturation. *Endocrinology, 128*, 2457–2468. **16**

Wood, W. (1987). Meta-analytic review of sex differences in group performance. *Psychological Bulletin, 102*, 53–71. **343**

Wood, W., & Karten, S. J. (1986). Sex differences in interaction style as a product of perceived sex differences in competence. *Journal of Personality and Social Psychology, 50*, 341–347. **286**

Wood, W., Polek, D., & Aiken, C. (1985). Sex differences in group task performance. *Journal of Personality and Social Psychology, 48*, 63–71. **286**

Wood, W., Rhodes, N., & Whelan, M. (1989). Sex differences in positive well-being: A consideration of emotional style and marital status. *Psychological Bulletin, 106*, 249–264. **365**

Woodruff, R. A., Jr., Robins, L. N., Winokur, G., & Reich, T. (1971). Manic depressive illness and social achievement. *Acta Psychiatrica Scandinavica, 47*, 237–249. **367**

Worell, J. (1978). Sex roles and psychological well-being: Perspectives on methodology. *Journal of Consulting and Clinical Psychology, 46*, 777–791. **24**

———. (1988). Women's satisfaction in close relationships. *Clinical Psychology Review, 8*, 477–498. **346**

Wrangham, R. W. (1980). An ecological model of female-bonded primate groups. *Behaviour, 75*, 262–300. **241, 243, 245**

———. (1987). Evolution of social structure. In B. B. Smuts, D. L., Cheney, R. M. Seyfarth, R. W. Wrangham, & T. T. Struhsaker (Eds.), *Primate societies*. Chicago: University of Chicago Press. **241, 243**

Wright, R. M. (1988). Anthropological presuppositions of indigenous advocacy. *Annual Review of Anthropology, 17*, 365–390. **239**

Wrigley, J. M., & Graves, J. A. M. (1988). Sex chromosome homology and incomplete, tissue-specific X-inactivation suggest that monotremes represent an intermediate stage of mammalian sex chromosome evolution. *Journal of Heredity, 79*, 115–118. **104**

Wu, H. M. H., Holmes, W. G., Medina, S. R., & Sackett, G. P. (1980). Kin preference in infant Macaca nemestrina. *Nature, 285*, 225–227. **83**

Wurtman, J. J. (1990). Carbohydrate craving: Relationship between carbohydrate intake and disorders of mood. *Drugs, 39* (Suppl. 3), 49–52. **189**

Wuttke, W., Arnold, P., Becker, D., Creutzfeldt, O., Langenstein, S., & Tirsch, W. (1975). Circulating hormones, EEG, and performance in psychological tests of women with and without oral contraceptives. *Psychoneuroendocrinology, 1*, 141–151. **190, 201**

Wyer, R. S., Jr., Bodenhausen, G. V., & Srull, T. K. (1984). The cognitive representation of persons and groups and its effect on recall and recognition memory. *Journal of Experimental Social Psychology, 20*, 445–469. **288**

Wyer, R. S., Jr., & Gordon, S. E. (1982). The recall of information about persons and groups. *Journal of Experimental Social Psychology, 18*, 128–164. **288**

Wylie, A. (1991). Gender theory and the archaeological record: Why is there no archeology of gender? In J. M. Gero & M. W. Conkey (Eds.), *Engendering archaelology: Women and prehistory*. Cambridge, MA: Basil Blackwell. **25, 26, 237**

Wynn, R. L., & Fletcher, C. (1987). Sex role development and early educational experiences. In D. B. Carter (Ed.), *Current conceptions of sex roles and sex typing*. New York: Praeger. **301, 314**

Wyss, D., DeLozier, C. D., Daniell, J., & Engel, E. (1982). Structural anomalies of the X chromosome: Personal observation and review of non-mosaic cases. *Clinical Genetics, 21*, 145–159. **113**

Yahr, P. (1988). Sexual differentiation of behavior in the context of developmental psychobiology. In E. M. Blass (Ed.), *Handbook of behavioral neurobiology. Vol. 9. Developmental psychobiology and behavioral ecology*. New York: Plenum Press. **150, 386**

Yalom, I. D., Green, R., & Fisk, N. (1973). Prenatal exposure to female hormones: Effect on psychosexual development in boys. *Archives of General Psychiatry, 28*, 554–561. **170**

Yamamoto, M., Fujimori, R., Ito, T., Kamimura, K., & Watanabe, G. (1975). Chromosome studies in 500 induced abortions. *Humangenetik, 29*, 9–14. **111**

Yamazaki, K., Beauchamp, G. K., Bard, J., & Boyse, E. A. (1990). Chemosensory identity and the Y chromosome. *Behavior Genetics, 20*, 157–165. **117**

Yamazaki, K., Beauchamp, G. K., Kupniewski, D., Bard, J., Thomas, L., & Boyse, E. A. (1988). Familial imprinting determines H-2 selective mating preferences. *Science, 240*, 1331–1332. **74, 87**

Yamazaki, K., Boyse, E. A., Mike, V., Thaler, H. T., Mathieson, B. J., Abbott, J., Boyse, J., Zayas, Z. A., & Thomas, L. (1976). Control of mating preferences in mice by genes in the major histocompatibility complex. *Journal of Experimental Medicine, 144*, 1324–1335. **74**

Yogev, S. (1981). Do professional women have egalitarian marital relationships? *Journal of Marriage and the Family, 43*, 865–871. **304**

Young, J. K., Fleming, M. W., & Matsumoto, D. E. (1986). Sex behavior and the sexually dimorphic hypothalamic nucleus in male Zucker rats. *Physiology & Behavior, 36*, 881–886. **162**

Young, M. A., Scheftner, W. A., Fawcett, J., & Klerman, G. L. (1990). Gender differences in the clinical features of unipolar major depressive disorder. *Journal of Nervous and Mental Disease, 178*, 200–203. **363**

Young, S. N., & Ervin, F. R. (1984). Cerebrospinal fluid measurements suggest precursor availability and sex are involved in the control of biogenic amine metabolism in a primate. *Journal of Neurochemistry, 42*, 1570–1573. **351, 369**

Young, S. N., Smith, S. E., Pihl, R. O., & Ervin, F. R. (1985). Tryptophan depletion causes a rapid lowering of mood in normal males. *Psychopharmacology, 87*, 173–177. **369**

Yu, L., Nguyen, H., Le, H., Bloem, L. J., Kozak, C. A., Hoffman, B. J., Snutch, T. P., Lester, H. A., Davidson, N., & Lbbert, H. (1991). The mouse 5-HT$_{1C}$ receptor contains eight hydrophic domains and is X-linked. *Molecular Brain Research, 11*, 143–149. **369**

Yu, W.-H. A. (1988). Sex difference in neuronal loss induced by axotomy in the rat brain stem motor nuclei. *Experimental Neurology, 102*, 230–235. **138**

Yunis, J. J., & Soreng, A. L. (1984). Constitutive fragile sites and cancer. *Science, 226*, 1199–1204. **75**

Zahavi, A. (1975). Mate-selection—A selection for a handicap. *Journal of Theoretical Biology, 53*, 205–214. **86**

Zahner, G. E. P., & Murphy, J. M. (1989). Loss in childhood: Anxiety in adulthood. *Comprehensive Psychiatry, 30*, 553–563. **364**

Zamble, E., Hadad, G. M., Mitchell, J. B., & Cutmore, T. R. H. (1985). Pavlovian conditioning of sexual arousal: First- and second-order effects. *Journal of Experimental*

Psychology: Animal Behavior Processes, 11, 598–610. **382**

Zammuner, V. L. (1987). Children's sex-role stereotypes: A cross-cultural analysis. In P. Shaver & C. Hendrick (Eds.), *Sex and gender.* Beverly Hills: Sage. **394**

Zanna, M. P., & Pack, S. J. (1975). On the self-fulfilling nature of apparent sex differences in behavior. *Journal of Experimental Social Psychology, 11,* 583–591. **9**

Zemach, T., & Cohen, A. A. (1986). Perception of gender equality on television and in social reality. *Journal of Broadcasting & Electronic Media, 30,* 427–444. **293**

Zhuchenko, A. A., Korol, A. B., Visir, I. Yu., Bocharnikova, N. I., & Zamorzayeva, I. A. (1988). Sex differences for recombination frequency in tomato and arabidopsis. *Genetika, 24,* 1593–1601. **100, 101**

Zielinski, J. J. (1978). Depressive symptomatology: Deviation from a personal norm. *Journal of Community Psychology, 6,* 163–167. **363**

Zimmer, L. (1988). Tokenism and women in the workplace: The limits of gender-neutral theory. *Social Problems, 35,* 64–77. **330**

Zuckerman, D. M. (1980). Self-esteem, personal traits, and college women's life goals. *Journal of Vocational Behavior, 17,* 310–319. **327**

_____. (1989). Stress, self-esteem, and mental health: How does gender make a difference? *Sex Roles, 20,* 429–444. **363**

Zuckerman, D. M., Singer, D. G., & Singer, J. L. (1980). Children's television viewing, racial and sex-role attitudes. *Journal of Applied Social Psychology, 10,* 281–294. **293, 294**

Zuckerman, M., Kuhlman, D. M., & Camac, C. (1988). What lies beyond E and N? Factor analyses of scales believed to measure basic dimensions of personality. *Journal of Personality and Social Psychology, 54,* 96–107. **339**

Zuliani, U., Bernardini, B., Catapano, A., Campana, M., Cerioli, G., & Spattini, M. (1988). Effects of anabolic steroids, testosterone, and HGH on blood lipids and echocardiographic parameters in body builders. *International Journal of Sports Medicine, 10,* 62–66. **202**

Zumoff, B., Miller, L., Levit, C. D., Miller, E. H., Heinz, U., Kalin, M., Denman, H., Jandorek, R., & Rosenfeld, R. S. (1990). The effect of smoking on serum progesterone, estradiol, and luteinizing hormone levels over a menstrual cycle in normal women. *Steroids, 55,* 507–511. **178**

Zumpe, D., & Michael, R. P. (1985). Effects of ovarian hormones on the behavior of captive Macaca fascicularis. *American Journal of Primatology, 8,* 167–181. **387**

_____. (1987). Relation between the dominance rank of female rhesus monkeys and their access to males. *American Journal of Primatology, 13,* 155–169. **349**

INDEX

A

Accommodation, 266
Acetycholine, 181
Ache, 246–247
Achievement motivation, 293, 321, 345
Act frequency research, 339, 347, 354
ACTH. See Adrenocorticotropic hormone
Action potentials, 131–132
Activational hormone effects, 125. See also Perinatal hormones, effects on the brain; Postpubertal hormones, effects on the brain
Active avoidance, 211
Active correlation between child and developmental environment, 234
Activity level, sex differences in, 342
Adapted traits, definition of, 59–60
Adenosine, 139
Adrenal cortex, 128, 152, 178. See also Adrenal gland
Adrenal gland, 128
and circadian rhythms, 182
and perinatal development, 156
Adrenocorticotropic hormone, 143, 152
Adrenogenital syndrome, 169, 399
Adult orientation, 320. See also Peer group
Affective disorder, 176. See also Bipolar disorder; Depression
and menopause, 202
and the premenstrual syndrome, 193–194
AFP. See Alpha-fetoprotein
Agentic, 296
Aggression. See also Homicides
and coping strategies, 365

development of, 347, 350, 356–357
effect of perinatal hormones on, 170, 358, 359
effect of postpubertal hormones on, 192, 196, 201–202, 357–359
and egoistic dominance, 336, 346, 350
genetics of, 358
hostile, 357
and hunting, 245
indirect, 357
and IQ, 357
longitudinal changes in, 357
and mass media, 291–293
measurement of, 338, 351
and paternal absence, 259, 356
of people with sex chromosome anomalies, 113–116
and pubertal maturation rate, 336
and serotonin, 350–351
sex differences in, 337–338, 341–342, 348, 351–356
sex differences in reinforcement for, 301, 311, 315–317, 356
and sex typing, 301–302
and social stratifiction, 254
and stereotypes in children, 294
and toys, 308, 309–310, 356
and Wiggins's cirumplex model, 340, 341, 350
Aging, effects of on the brain, 166, 224–225
Agta, 237, 247
AIDS, 69, 383, 400
Aka, 252–253
Alcoholism, 361
Allele, definition of, 57
Allergies, 173–174
Allocentric, 346–347
Alloparents, 241, 244, 253

Alpha bias, 26
Alpha-fetoprotein, 158, 160
Altruism, 358
Alzheimer's disease, 17, 181
Amygdala, 133, 134, 179, 180
Anabolic steroids, 202
Androgen insensitivity syndrome, 5, 107–108, 153, 168–169, 388
Androgen receptor:
descriptions of, 107–108, 146
effects on development, 155–156
sex differences in perinatal levels of, 160–161, 162
sex differences in postpubertal levels of, 179–180
Androgens, 7. See also Testosterone
Androgyny, 10. See also Bem Sex Role Inventory; Personal Attributes Questionnaire
definition of, 22, 43–44
effects of, 48–49
Androstenedione, 177, 178, 183
Angelman syndrome, 103
Annual cycles, 196
Anovulatory cycle, 188
Anterior commissure, 165
Anterior hypothalamus, 133, 134
Anthropology and sex differences, 237–264
Antigens, 73–74
Antisocial behavior:
and serotonin, 351
and testosterone levels, 176, 359
Anxiety, 139, 170, 193
Aphasia, 398, 400
Arapesh, 258
Aromatization, 146
hypothesis, 156–158, 159, 163, 179
Aromatizing enzyme, 141, 160–161, 179–180

Arthritis, 173
Assimilation, 266
Association cortex, 161
Assortive mating, 375
Attachment, 222
Attitudes:
  defined, 213
  learning of, 213
Attributions, 231
Australian Aborigines, 250
Autism, 121
Automous learning behaviors,
  313
Autosomes, 53
Axon, 130

B
Bandura, A., 205, 219–220,
  231, 232
Barr body, 104
Basic-level categories, 268
Bem Sex Role Inventory, 30,
  42, 45–49, 270, 271,
  327–328, 340–341, 394
Berdarches, 258, 259
Beta bias, 26
Bias, sources of. *See also*
  Biological bias
  in measuring gender dif-
    ferences, 38–41
  of sex linkage research,
    116–117
Bilineal, 243
Biogenic amines, 180–181. *See
  also* Dopamine;
  Norepinephrine; Serotonin
Biological bias:
  definition of, 11
  misuses of, 12–19
Biological determinism:
  and culture, 16
  definition of, 11
  description of, 18–19
  problems with, 13
Bipolar disorder, 368. *See also*
  Manic-depressive disorder
Birth control pill, 201–202
Birth order, 171
Block Design Test, 389, 395

Bound hormone, definition of,
  133
Boyd and Richerson gene-
  culture co-evolution
  theory, 216, 249–250
Brain development, 224–225
Brain organization of people
  with sex chromosome
  anomalies, 113–114
Brain size as related to IQ,
  166
BSRI. *See* Bem Sex Role
  Inventory

C
Career orientation, 169,
  331–332, 359
Castration anxiety. *See* Freud, S.
Categorical versus continuous
  variables, 28
Caudate, 133, 134
Cell body, 130
Cellular growth, effects of sex
  hormones on, 137–138
Cerebellum, 137, 139
Child abuse, 301, 354–355,
  356–357
Chimpanzees, 243, 244, 245,
  248, 348–349
Chores. *See* Gendered
  environments
Circadian cycles, 182–183,
  184–185
Classical conditioning,
  209–210, 211–213
Closed mazes, 396
Cognitive developmental
  theory. *See* Kohlberg, L.
Collectivism, 346
Color vision, 105
Communal, 296
Competition:
  cross-cultural research, 255
  for mates, 376
  and peer versus adult
    orientation
  sex differences in, 345–346
  sex differences in reactions
    to, 318–320

and social comparison,
  320–322
Competitiveness, 318. *See also*
  Competition
Conditioned helplessness, 213
Conformity, 343–344, 345
Consistency mechanism. *See*
  Kohlberg, L.
Continuous variables. *See*
  Categorical versus con-
  tinuous variables
Controlling mother, 251
Coolidge Effect, 383
Cooperation:
  evolution of, 82, 249–250
  sex differences in, 318, 319,
    343–344, 345
Coping strategies, 365–366
Corpus callosum, 164–167,
  396–397
Cortical organization. *See also*
  Lateralization
  sex differences in, 142–146,
    161–167, 1676, 172–174,
    180–181
Corticotropin releasing factor,
  143
Cortisol, 128, 143, 182, 196, 362
Costs of sex, 69–70
Couvade syndrome, 198
Covariance, concept of, 37–38
CRF. *See* Corticotropin releas-
  ing factor
Critical/sensitive period con-
  tinuum, 126–127
Cross-cultural research and sex
  differences, 250–264
Cross-cultural variations in
  stereotypes, 271–272
Crossovers, 65, 66, 99–102,
  117, 121
Cultural units, 249–249
Cytosolic receptors, 160

D
DAT space task, 391, 395
Decision/commitment, 378
Defeminizing effects of hor-
  mones, 128

Delay of gratification, 234. *See also* Impulse control
Demasculinizing effects of hormones, 128
Dendrites, 131
Deoxyribonucleic acid, 53–59, 133–136
Dependent variable, 28
Depression:
    and cognitions, 231, 366–367
    and coping strategies, 365–366
    and creativity, 337, 367–368
    and cultural roles, 366
    definition of, 360
    development of, 350
    effect of menstrual cycle on, 190, 191–195
    effect of perinatal hormones on, 170, 368
    effect of postpubertal hormones on, 368
    and emotional reactivity, 365
    genetics of, 367–368
    during ingestion of anabolic steroids, 202
    during ingestion of the birth control pill, 201–202
    during menopause, 201–202, 368
    postpartum depression, 197–198
    and prosocial dominance, 336, 338, 350
    and puberty, 228
    and serotonin, 350–351, 362–363, 369
    sex differences in, 360–362
    and stress, 362–365
    and Wiggins's circumplex, 350
Depressive realism, 366, 370
Depressogenic cognitions, 366–367
DES. *See* Diethylstilbestrol
Determinism, 25
Developmental process theorists, 205–206, 216–219, 232

Diagnostic information in stereotypes, 275
Diethylstilbestrol, 164, 170, 368, 388
Differentiation stereotypes, 270–271. *See also* Identification stereotypes
Diffuse status characteristic, 282, 286
Dihydrotestosterone:
    masculinizing and defeminizing effects of, 140–151, 386
    and perinatal development, 155–160, 168–169, 171–172
Diploid, 53, 70
Discrimination learning, 210
Dispersal, 242–243
DNA. *See also* Deoxyribonucleic acid
    repair theories of sex, 70–71
Docility, 250
Dominance. *See also* Egoistic dominance; Prosocial dominance
    among children, 314, 316–317
    cross-cultural research, 255
    hierarchies, 62–63, 335, 336, 348–349
    and reproductive success, 336, 349–350
    sex differences in, 345, 346–350, 359–360
    and spatial scores, 394
Dominant gene or trait, 58, 99
Dopamine, 137, 152, 181, 226
Dosage compensation, 105
Dosage effects of hormones. *See* Nonlinear effects of hormones
Drug abuse, 176
Dyscalculia, 374

E
Egoistic dominance:
    defined, 335–336, 337–338
    sex differences in, 341–350
Egoistic training, 251

Electra complex, 217
Electrical activity of neurons:
    descriptions of, 131–133
    effects of hormones on, 136–137, 138–140
Embedded Figures Task, 389, 390, 391, 393, 394
Emotional reactivity, 365
Empathy, 344, 345
Endorphins, 136, 152
Enzyme, definition of, 55
Epigenetic development, 20–21, 140, 146–147
Epistasis, 57
Epistemology of gender knowledge, 5–23
ESS. *See* Evolutionarily Stable Strategy
Estradiol. *See* Estrogen
Estrogen:
    and age, 198–199
    and aggression, 358–359
    effects on electrical activity of nerve cells, 138–139
    as a general growth hormone, 157–158
    genetics of sensitivity to, 146, 147
    masculinizing and defeminizing effects of, 140–151
    and perinatal development, 155–160, 171–172
    and positive feedback, 143–146
    sex differences in perinatal levels of, 160
    sex differences in postpubertal levels of, 177–203
    and sexual activities, 396–397
    and spatial scores, 396, 398
    sources of, 156, 178
Estrogen receptors:
    description of, 135
    and perinatal development, 157
    sex differences in perinatal levels of, 160–161
    sex differences in postpubertal levels of, 179–180

Estrone, 178
Estrous cycles, 183–184
Ethnographic record, 238
Evolutionarily Stable Strategy,
    60–61, 68
Evolutionary mechanisms,
    definition of, 60
Evolutionary selection
    pressures. *See also* Natural
    selection; Sexual selection
    defined, 52
    described, 59–69, 68–69
Evolutionary theory:
    of aggression and
        dominance, 336, 351–356
    of cooperation, 249–250
    of culture, 240–250
    of depression, 365, 367–368
    description of, 2–3
    of learning, 213–216, 249
    of the menstrual cycle,
        184–186
    negative reactions to, 13
    of parental care, 220–223
    of reproductive strategies,
        375–378
    of sex, 51–77
    of sex differences, 76–96,
        99–100
    of sexual reproduction,
        51–75. *See also* DNA,
        repair theories of sex; Red
        Queen theory of sex;
        Tangled Bank theory of
        sex
    of social behaviors, 240–250
    of spatial abilities, 375–378
Expectancies in learning,
    212–213
Experimenter bias, 41
Experimenter gender, 39, 342,
    343, 344, 394
Expressive traits:
    defined, 45
    occupational socialization
        and, 327–328
    and the premenstrual syn-
        drome, 192
    sex differences in, 341–346, 358

in stereotypes, 271
Expressivity, 109
External genitals, development
    of, 155–155
Extinction, 209, 211
Extroversion, 340, 345

F

47, XXY, 112–117
5-alpha-reductase deficiencies,
    168–169
Family history studies, 108–110
Fat, as a source of hormones,
    178, 199, 201
Father absence, 222–223, 259,
    299–300, 356, 376, 395
Fear of success, 10, 345
Female choice:
    developmental experiences,
        87
    genetics of, 87–87
Female kin groups:
    among primates, 243
    evolution of, 241–242,
        244–245
Feminine sexual behaviors:
    age changes in, 199
    defined, 159
    effect of perinatal hormones
        on, 159–160, 386, 387
    and estrous cycle, 183
    Freudian theory of, 217
"Feminine voice" in moral
    development, 10–11
Feminist research, 3, 12–13,
    25–27, 238
Feminizing effects of hor-
    mones, 128
Fetal development, 8
File drawer problem, 40
Follicle stimulating hormone,
    143–146. *See also*
    Gonadotropic hormones
Follicles, 186–187
Follicular stage, 187, 190
Food intake and the menstrual
    cycle, 189
Fragile X, 121–123
Free hormone, defined, 133

Frequency-dependent selection,
    68–69
Freud, S., 14, 205, 216–218
Frontal cortex, 165, 225, 226
FSH. *See* Follicle stimulating
    hormone
Functional analyses of cross-
    cultural data, 262–263
Fuzzy sets, 266–268

G

GABA, 139
Gametes, defined, 64
Gametogenesis, 186, 188
Gender constancy, 219, 233
Gender definitions, 6–8
Gender of experimenter. *See*
    Experimenter gender
Gender flexibility and stereo-
    types, 291
Gender identity, 8–9, 153,
    168–169, 216–220, 229
Gender of rearing, 8
Gender schema, 30, 48
Gender stereotypes. *See*
    Stereotypes
Gender-related differences,
    definition of, 1, 6. *See*
    also Sex differences
Gender-related traits. *See* Sex
    differences
Gender-role identity, 8–9,
    216–220
Gendered environments:
    adults' chores, 255–256,
        303–307
    and aggression, 356–357
    children's chores, 253, 307
    definition of, 8, 206
    and depression, 362–365
    distance from home, 253,
        255
    home, 298–308, 309
    introduction to, 297–298
    school, 308–317
    and sexual responses,
        382–383
    socialization pressures,
        254–255

and spatial performances, 393–396
  toys, 289, 290, 294–295, 307–308, 309–310, 356, 393, 395
  work, 322–332
Gendered inheritance, 97–98
Gene frequencies as part of evolutionary theory, 52
Gene frequency, 59
Gene-culture co-evolution, 248–250
Genetic load, 70
Genetic probes, 110–111
Genetic variability, causes of, 64–69
Genetics:
  of aggression, 358
  of depression, 367–368
  and development, 234
  versus environment, 15–16, 17–18
  of female choice, 86–87
  of gender, 105–117
  of homosexuality, 388–389
  of hormone sensitivity, 146, 147
  of individual differences in hormone levels, 147
  of pubertal timing, 375
  of sex differences, 97–103
  of spatial performances, 396
Genomic functions of sex hormones:
  defined, 130
  described, 133–136, 193
Genomic imprinting. See Parental imprinting
Genotype, 56–59
Geschwind's hypothesis, 172–174
Glutamate, 139
GnRH. See Gonadotropic releasing hormone
Goldberg paradigm of research, 280–281
Gonadotropic hormones, 177–178, 186–189, 398
Gonadotropic releasing hor-

mone, 143, 144, 150
Gonads, 7, 154–155
Good genes theories, 86–87, 375

H
H-Y antigen, 106
Handedness:
  and perinatal hormones, 172–174
  and spatial performances, 397
Handicapping theories, 86–87
Haploid, 65, 75
Helping, sex differences in, 345
Hermaphrodites, 69, 107
Heterogametic, 98
Heterosis, 58–59, 74
Heterozygosity, 57–59, 68–69, 74, 75, 98–100, 121, 248
Highly achieving females, 191, 322, 367–368
Hippocampus, 133, 134, 139, 152, 179, 225, 397
Homicides. See also Aggression
  cross-cultural differences in rates of, 356
  and egoistic dominance, 336
  and intermale conflicts, 355–356
  and kinship relationships, 352–353
  sex differences in, 350–356
Homosexuality:
  animal models of, 387–388
  genes and gemily environments, 388–389
  mating preferences of, 380
  and perinatal hormones, 388
  and sexuality activity, 380, 384
Homozygous, 57–59, 73, 98–100, 248
Honest advertising model, 87
Horizontal associations in categories, 268
Hormone cycles, 181–196
Hormone effects. See also the individual hormones;

Perinatal hormones; Post-pubertal hormones
  on cellular growth, 137–138
  on electrical activity of neurons, 136–137, 138–140
  on organs other than the brain, 127–128
Hormone levels:
  effect of experience on, 149
  genetics of, 146, 147
Hormone receptors, 107. See also the individual hormone receptors
Hormone sensitivity, defined, 128
Hormone synthesizing enzymes, 107
Hot flashes, 20–201
Hotspots in the genome, 100
Human chorionic gonadotropin, 188
Human evolution, 91. See also Evolutionary theory
Human perinatal hormone syndromes, 167–170. See also Perinatal hormones
Humanistic paradigm in anthropology, 239–240
Hunter-gatherer theory, 237, 243–247
Hunting among females, 245–247
Huntington's disease, 17, 103
Hybrid vigor, 58–59
Hypergamy, 347, 376
Hypergyny, 254
Hypothalamus, 133, 134, 143–146, 386. See also Anterior hypothalamus; Preoptic area; Sexually dimorphic nucleus of the preoptic area, Ventromedial area of the hypothalamus

I
Identification stereotypes, 270–271. See also Differentiation stereotypes

Idiocentric, 346–347
Idiographic research, 26
Illiteracy, 262
Illusory correlation and
    stereotypes, 287
Immune disorders, 173–174
Immune system, 172–173
Impression management, 280
Impulse control, 115–116
Inclusive fitness, 81–82
Income, 322–324, 360
Independent assortment, 65–66
Independent variable, 27–29
Individual differences in
    stereotyping, 276–278
Individual variables, 21–22
Individualism, 346
Infanticide, 146, 221–222,
    337–338, 354–355
Influenceability. *See*
    Conformity
Ingroup membership and
    stereotypes, 287–288
Instrumental traits:
    defined, 45
    and occupational socializa-
        tion, 327–328
    and the premenstrual syn-
        drome, 192
    sex differences in, 341–346,
        358
    in stereotypes, 271
Intergroup theories of
    stereotype acquisition,
    286, 259–263
Interindividual studies of hor-
    mone effects, 129
Internal sexual accessory
    organs, development of,
    155–156
Internal validity, 32–34, 167
Interpersonal theories of
    stereotype acquisition,
    286–294
Intimacy, 378
Intraindividual studies of hor-
    mone effects, 129
Intrapersonal theories of
    stereotype acquisition,

286, 276–278
Intrauterine position, 148
Introversion. *See* Extroversion
IQ:
    and aggression, 357
    and brain size, 166
    and pubertal timing, 336
    stability over age, 234

J
Job segregation:
    amount of, 324–325
    effects on income, 322–323
    reasons for, 325–332

K
K selection strategies, 91–92,
    376
Karyotype, definition of, 53
Kernel of truth idea of
    stereotypes, 287–288
Kin aiding, defined, 81
Kin selection, defined, 82
Klinefelter males:
    description of, 112–117
    development of, 375
    sexual activity in, 387
Kohlberg, L., 14, 205,
    218–219, 229, 231, 232,
    236

L
Labeling mechanism. *See*
    Kohlberg, L.
Late Luteal Phase Dysphoric
    or Affective Disorder. *See*
    Premenstrual syndrome
Lateralization:
    of cortical androgen recep-
        tors, 161, 162
    defined, 113
    Geschwind's theory of,
        172–174
    and perinatal hormones,
        172–174
    and spatial performances,
        396–398
Leadership, 343, 341–345
Learning. *See also* Classical

conditioning; Modeling;
    Observational learning;
    Operant conditioning
    defined, 208
Level of reversibility, 126. *See
    also* Biological deter-
    minism
LH. *See* Luteinizing hormone
Life-history strategies, 220
Limbic system, 133, 134, 152,
    161, 179–180, 351. *See
    also* Amygdala, Caudate,
    Hippocampus, Septum
Linkage analysis, 109–111
Locus of control, 345
Longitudinal research, 232–235,
    273–274, 293, 298, 300,
    302–303, 308, 316, 317,
    331, 350, 357, 374, 394
    definition of, 29, 232
Lordosis, 133, 159, 386–387
Luteal phase, 188, 190
Luteinizing hormone, 143–146.
    See also Gonadotropic
    hormones

M
Major gene effect, defined, 57
Major histocompatibility
    complex:
    and Red Queen theory,
        73–74
    and sexual choice, 74
Manic-depressive disorder, 103,
    109, 110–111
MAO. *See* Monoamine oxidase
Marxist analyses of cross-
    cultural data, 263
Masculine sexual behaviors:
    age changes in, 199–200
    and anabolic steroids, 202
    annual cycles of, 196
    circadian rhythms of,
        182–183
    defined, 158–159
    effect of perinatal hormones
        on, 158–160, 386–388
    effect of postpubertal hor-
        mones on, 180, 386–388

and the sexually dimorphic nucleus of the preoptic area, 161

and the spinal nucleus of the bulbocaverosus muscle, 163

Masculinizing effects of hormones, 128

Mass media and stereotypes, 288–290, 291–293

Massa intermedia, 165

Mastery values, 318

Mate guarding, 78, 355

Maternal chromosomes, 53

Maternal effects, 220–221

Maternal employment, 300–301

Maternal inheritance, 98, 220

Maternal selection, 220–221, 233

Mathematical tasks:

anatomy of, 297–398

correlations with spatial tasks, 373–374, 391

sex differences in, 373, 400

Mating system:

defined, 78, 87–88

and homicides, 351

and hormone dosage effects, 151

and the menstrual cycle, 186

Matrilineal, 241–242, 243

Matrilinines, 82

Matrilocal, 243, 264

Mead, M., 10, 238, 257–258

Mechanisms of evolution. *See also* Gene frequencies as part of evolutionary theory; Natural selection; Sexual selection

definition of, 2

proximate, 2

Megargee paradigm, 347

Meiosis, 65–66, 69–70, 74, 100–102, 104, 121

Membrane, of a cell, 130

Membrane potential, 131

Memory:

as affected by stereotypes, 274–275

changes with age in, 227–228

defined, 208

Menarche, 177. *See also* Timing of puberty

Menopause, 198–201, 368

Menstrual cycle, 149, 176, 184–195, 398, 399

Menstrual phase, defined, 189

Menstruation, cultural beliefs and, 260, 264

Mental disorders, 17. *See also* Anxiety; Bipolar disorder; Depression; Manic-depressive disorder; Schizophrenia

Mental rotation factor, 389–391

Messenger RNA. *See* Ribonucleic acid

Meta-analytic studies:

of cognitive skills, 372–373, 389–391

definition of, 36–37

of personality traits, 342–345

of play preferences and the development of spatial skills, 393

of prejudice studies, 281–282

Meta-theory, 21

MHC. *See* Major histocompatibility complex

Micropredators. *See* Viruses

Mitochondria, 97–98

Mitosis, 65

Modeling:

descriptions of, 214, 219, 220, 229–231

evolution of, 249

and gendered environments, 297, 298–299, 300–301, 303–307

and occupational socialization, 329

Monoamine oxidase, 119, 180–181

Monogamy, 77, 87–88, 250, 251, 375, 377

Monosomy X. *See* Turner's syndrome

Monthly hormone cycles in males, 195–196

Moods:

and anabolic steroids, 202

and emotional reactivity, 365

mood changes during the birth control pill, 201–202

mood changes during menopause, 200–201

and neonatal hormones, 171

and postpubertal hormones, 183, 190, 191–195

during pregnancy, 197

Moral development, 217

Moral mechanism. *See* Kohlberg, L.

Mosaics, genetic, 104–105

Muellerian inhibiting hormone, 154–155

Mundugumor, 258

Mutant genes, 57–59

Mutations, 64–64, 117

N

Natural language categories, 265, 266, 269

Natural selection, 76, 77–83

Nature versus nurture, 14–16

Negative feedback, 143, 144, 187–189

Neocortex, effect of hormones on, 153–154, 157, 161, 165–166, 179–180

Neolocal, 243

Neurons, 130

Niche, 60, 71

Node of Ranvier, 131, 132

Nomothetic research, 25

Nonadditive genetic effects, 57

Nongenomic functions of sex hormones:

defined, 130

described, 136–137

Nonlinear effects of hormones, 140, 150–151

Nonspecific hormone effects, 137

Nonverbal sensitivity, 344, 345

Norepinephrine, 139, 181

Nuicleotide, 53, 75

O

Obesity, 36, 375, 378–382
Observational learning, 211–212, 213, 216, 249. *See also* Modeling
Oedipal complex, 216–217
Oncogenes, 100
Onuf's nucleus, 163, 165
Open mazes, 396
Open-ended scales of gender stereotypes, 270
Operant conditioning. *See also* Gendered environments descriptions of, 210–211, 212 evolution of, 249
Operational definition, 29
Optimal foraging theory, 215
Organizational hormone effects, 125. *See also* Perinatal hormones; Postpubertal hormones
Orgasm, 363
Osteoporosis, 200, 201
Outgroup membership and stereotypes, 287
Overdominance, 75
Ovulation, 143–146, 186–190, 198–199
Ovulatory phase, 187

P

Panic attack, 192
PAQ. *See* Personal Attributes Questionnaire
Parent-offspring conflict, 221–222, 228, 354
Parental behaviors. *See also* Gendered environments and sex differences, 232–234, 356–357, 395 and stereotypes, 294, 299 types of, 250–253, 299–301
Parental imprinting, 102–103, 121–122
Parental investment, 77–80, 91–92, 221–222, 228, 303–307

Parthenogenes, 69
Parthenogenic, 64
Passion, 378
Passive avoidance, 211
Passive correlation between child and developmental environment, 234
Paternal absence. *See* Father absence
Paternal behaviors, 251–253, 301–302
Paternal chromosomes, 53
Paternal investment, 79. *See also* Parental investment
Pathological assumptions, 11–19, 191
Patrician, 246
Patrilineal, 243
Patrilocal, 243, 264
Peer group: interactions among, 313–317 orientation toward across cultures, 255 peer orientation versus adult orientation, 320
Penetrance, 109
Performance, defined, 208
Perinatal hormones: and aggression, 358, 359 and depression, 368 effects on the brain, 142–146 sex differences in, 153–174
Perinatal period, 96
Personal Attributes Questionnaire, 42, 45–49, 259, 270, 271, 327–328, 340, 394
Personality. *See also* Wiggins's circumplex model of personality concept of, 338–339 cross-cultural research in, 256–259, 341 measurement of, 339–341 meta-analytic studies of, 341–346 sex differences in, 339–346
Phenotype, 56–59
Pheromones, 186, 190–191
Pituitary, 133, 134, 143–146

Pituitary stock, 143
Pleiotropism, 57
POA. *See* Preoptic area
Polar bodies, 65–66
Political activities, 255–256
Polyandry, 88
Polygamy, 78, 87–88
Polygyny, 78, 87–88, 355, 376–378
Positive feedback, 143–146, 162, 187–189
Postmoderism, 26–27
Postpubertal hormones: and aggression, 358–360 and depression, 368 effects on the brain, 124–152 sex differences in, 176–203
Prader-Willi syndrome, 103
Preference for males, 282
Pregnancy, 127, 138, 197–198, 368
Prejudice, 278–286, 326, 330–331. *See also* Stereotypes
Premenstrual phase, 189, 191–195
Premenstrual syndrome, 191–195
Prenatal stress, 148–149
Preoptic area, 133, 134, 183–184, 145, 159–160, 386
Preoptic-anterior hypothalamic area, 165, 179–180
Preponderance of evidence criterion, 18
Prestige mechanism. *See* Kohlberg, L.
Primates: effects of hormones on sexual behaviors of, 142, 150–151 mating systems, 87–88 ovulation in, 143–146, 152 positive feedback in, 143–146 puberty in, 150 reproductive roles, 79–80 sex hormones and sexual behaviors, 387

Principles of hormone effects, 140–151

Progesterone:
and aggression, 358, 359
and depression, 369
effects on electrical activity of nerve cells, 139
genetics of sensitivity to, 146, 147
and perinatal development, 156–157, 175
sex differences in perinatal levels of, 160
sex differences in postpubertal levels of, 177–203
sources of, 156, 178

Progesterone receptor, 136–137
Progestins. See Progesterone
Prolactin, 141, 177, 196, 197

Prosocial dominance:
defined, 335–336, 337–338
sex differences in, 339–350

Prosocial training, 251
Prostaglandins, 177
Prototypical, 266, 268
Proximate cause, 2, 17, 60
Pseudoautosomal region, 101–102, 106, 111, 118, 120

Psychoanalytic theory. See Freud, S.

Pubertal timing, 228. See also Timing of puberty

Puberty:
biology of, 155–156, 177, 228
effects of, 18

R

r selection strategies, 91–92, 376
Radioimmunoassay procedures, 178, 203
Range of variation, 38
Rape, 384–386
Rating scales of gender stereotypes, 270
Reactive correlation between child and developmental environment, 234

Recessive, 58, 98
Reciprocal altruism. See Cooperation

Recombination. See also Crossovers; Independent assortment
costs of, 69
defined, 65–66
effects of, 68
and linkage analysis, 109–110
sex differences in, 99–102

Red deer, 79, 90
Red Queen theory of sex, 71–74

Reducing enzyme:
definition of, 141
perinatal levels of, 160–161, 168
postpubertal levels of, 179–180

Reinforcement. See also Gendered environments; Operant conditioning
effectiveness of across age-gender groups, 315–316, 317

Relative reality, 274
Releasing factors, 143
Reliability, 32–34
Reproductive roles, 76–80, 89. See also Reproductive strategies
Reproductive senescence, 198

Reproductive strategies:
among humans, 376, 378–382, 384
and prenatal stress, 148

Retardation:
in chromosome anomalies, 113–114
X linkage of, 119–123

Reticular activating system, 133, 134
Retroviruses, 66
Reversibility continuum, 125–126
RFT. See Rod and Frame Test
Ribonucleic acid, 53, 55, 136, 138

Ribosomal RNA. See Ribonucleic acid
Ribosomes, 55, 75
RNA. See Ribonucleic acid
Rod and Frame Test, 389, 391, 394
Roles, sociological definitions of, 9
Rough-and-tumble play, 167, 301–302, 314, 315, 316–317, 347

S

S-M. See Shepherd-Meltzer Mental Rotations Test
Same-sex preference among children, 313–315
Schizophrenia, 114, 198, 234, 235, 236
Scientific paradigm in anthropology, 239–240
SDN-POA. See Sexually dimorphic nucleus of the preoptic area
Seasonal affective disorder, 361
Selection environment, 59
Self-deception, 280
Self-disclosure, 345
Self-esteem, 48–49, 345
Self-medicators, 12
Sensitive/critical period, definition of, 150
Septum, 133, 134, 181
Serotonin, 119, 181, 350–351, 362, 369
Sex chromosomes, 53. See also X chromosome; Y chromosome
abnormalities of, 111–117

Sex differences. See also Gendered environments; the individual traits and characteristics
in academic achievements, 321–322
in aggression, 351–356
in the brain, 142–146, 154, 161–167, 180–181. See also the specific brain areas

Sex differences *(Cont.)*
  in brain development, 225
  in cognitive task perfor-
    mances, 372–374, 389–391
  in depression, 360–362
  in dominance, 346–351
  evolution of, 51–75
  in evolutionary selection
    pressures, 76–96
  Freud, 217–218
  in genetics, 97–123
  in income, 322–324
  in jobs, 324–325
  Kohlberg, 219
  measurement of, 24–41
  in perinatal hormone levels,
    160–167, 171
  in personality, 339–346
  in postpubertal hormone
    levels, 176–203
  in recombination frequen-
    cies, 100–102
  in reproductive roles, 77–83
  in sexual activities, 378–386
  in sexual selection pressures,
    83–88
  in social comparison,
    320–321
Sex hormone-binding globulin,
  158, 160, 174, 199
Sex hormones. *See also* the
  specific hormone
  definition of, 6
Sex ratios, 62, 79–80, 90
Sex roles. *See also* Bem Sex
  Role Inventory; Personal
  Attributes Questionnaire
  biology of, 16, 43
  bipolar, 42, 47–48
  as cultural, 16
  definition of, 41
  measurement of, 41–49
  scales, types of, 45
  unipolar, 43
  validity of scales, 45–49
  variability across cultures,
    257–258
Sex typing, 232, 233
Sex-atypical children, 294,

302–303, 315–316
Sex-biased dispersal. *See*
  Dispersal
Sex-determining genes, 105–107
Sex-limited genes:
  definition of, 99
  evolution of, 99–100
Sex-linked gene effects. *See*
  also X-linked genes; Y-
  linked genes
  on brain anatomy, 140
  defined, 98
  evolution of, 99–100
Sex-typed people, 43, 49–49
Sexual behavior. *See also*
  Feminine sexual behaviors;
  Homosexuality; Masculine
  sexual behaviors
  and age, 199–200
  evolution of, 375–378
  and hormones and, 386–387
  human mating preferences,
    378–382
  and the menstrual cycle, 190
  and pubertal maturation
    rate, 336
  sex differences in, 371,
    378–386, 382–384, 385
  unwanted sex, 384–385. *See*
  also Rape
Sexual dimorphism. *See also*
  Sex differences
  and evolution, 84–86
  and mating systems, 88
Sexual harassment, 330
Sexual prejudice. *See* Prejudice
Sexual selection, 76
  and choice, 84, 86–87
  and competition, 83–84
  and crossover frequency, 102
  and human mate
    preferences, 374, 375–376,
    378–382
  and sexual dimorphism, 86
  types of, 83
Sexual stereotypes. *See also*
  Stereotypes
  definitions of, 9
  effects of, 10

Sexually dimorphic nucleus of
  the preoptic area, 133,
  148, 150, 154, 158
  development of sex dif-
    ferences in, 161–163, 164,
    227
Sexually dimorphic species,
  evolution of, 89–91
Sexy son theory, 86
Shared infrequency and
  stereotypes. *See* Illusory
  correlation and stereotypes
SHBG. *See* Sex hormone-
  binding globulin
Shepherd-Meltzer Mental Rota-
  tions Test, 389, 391, 392,
  394
Shyness, 235. *See also* Timidity
Sickle cell anemia, 248
Sissies. *See* Sex-atypical
  children
SNB. *See* Spinal nucleus of the
  bulbocaverosus muscle
Sociable mother, 251
Social categories, 265–269. *See*
  also Stereotypes
Social comparison processes
  sex differences in, 320–321
Social desirability, 40
  of stereotypes, 271
  tendencies, 280
Social influence, 342–343, 345
Social leadership, 343, 346
Social support, 374–365
Social traits, evolution of,
  80–83, 89–90
Social-cognitive theory. *See*
  Bandura, A.
Socialization of occupational
  strivings, 325, 327–330
Socialization theorists,
  205–206, 219–220, 232
Sociopathy, 234
Song control nuclei in birds'
  brains, 142–143
Spatial ability:
  anatomy of, 396–398
  and brain lateralization,
    396–398

correlations with other tasks, 373–374, 391
cross-cultural studies of, 395–396
definitions of, 371, 389–390
and dominance, 394
evolution of, 375–378
and hormones, 398–400
and mental rotations, 392–393
and perinatal hormone levels, 168, 170, 172
and pubertal timing, 336, 374–375, 377–378
in rodents, 3767–377, 396
sex differences in, 389–391
situational covariates of, 393–396
strategies for solving, 392–393
tasks, types of, 389–391
in Turner's syndrome, 114
Spatial perception factor, 389–391
Spatial skills. *See* Spatial ability
Spatial visualization factor, 389–391, 393
Spinal nucleus of the bulbo-caverosus muscle, 161–163
Status. *See also* Egoistic dominance
cultural, 336, 359–360, 360, 367–368
of women, 238, 240, 255, 259–263, 286, 322–332. *See also* Prejudice
Stereotypes:
changes over time, 272–274
changing, 274–276, 293–294
in children, 290–295
contents of, 269–274
development of, 286–295
effects of disconfirming examples, 275–276
effects on memory processes, 274–275
and gender categories, 266–277

individual differences in, 276–277
maintenance of, 274–276
in mass media, 288–290
methods of studying, 269–271
as prejudice, 277–286
and sex roles, 43, 44–45, 46–48
social desirability of, 272
types of, 269–271
variations in across cultures, 271–272
Stereotypy, 276–278
Strange Situation, 222
Stratification, 254
Strength, 171–172
Stress:
adaptation to, 362
effects on brain development, 225
effects on the menstrual cycle, 191, 192
prenatal, 17
sex differences in stress responses, 362–363
and social support, 364–365
Stria terminalis, 165
Structural versus functional continuum, 126
STS gene, 104, 119
Suicide, 365–366
Super-ego, 217. *See also* Moral development
Suprachiasmatic nucleus, 165
SXD gene. *See* Sex-determining genes
Synapse:
functions of, 132–133
types of, 131
Synaptic potentials, 132–133
Systematic variables, 21–22
Systemic lupus erythematosus, 173, 175

T
Talking platypus phenomenon, 280–281
Tamoxifen, 157–158

Tangled Bank theory of sex, 71
Task leadership, 343, 346
Taste aversion, 248–249
Tchambuli, 258
TDF. *See* Testes-determining factor
Teachers' behaviors, 308–313, 317. *See also* Gendered environments
Techniques of studying hormone effects, 128–130
Temporal cortex, 165
Territoriality, 242, 264
Testes-determining factor, 106
Testicular feminizing mutation, 164. *See also* Androgen insensitivity syndrome
Testosterone:
and age, 198–199
and aggression, 358–360
circadian cycles of, 182–183, 184–185
and depression, 368, 369
and dominance. *See* Aggression, effect of perinatal hormones on, effect of postpubertal hormones on
genetics of sensitivity to, 146, 147
and perinatal development, 155–160
and perinatal development of humans, 168–174
masculinizing and defeminizing effects of, 140–151
sex differences in perinatal levels of, 160, 171
sex differences in postpubertal levels of, 177–203
and sexual activities, 386–388
situational determinants of, 149
sources of, 154–156, 178
and spatial performances, 398–399
Tetraploid, 75
Theories of sex. *See* DNA, repair theories of sex; Red

Queen theory of sex; Tangled Bank theory of sex

Theory, definition of, 19

Three continua of hormone effects. *See also* Critical/sensitive period continuum; Reversibility continuum; Structural versus functional continuum

Timidity, 171, 359

Timing effects of hormones, 140, 149–150

Timing of puberty:
 and aggression, 336, 374
 covariates of, 374–375
 genetic control of, 376
 and homosexuality, 388, 389
 mechanisms of, 375
 and sexual behaviors, 336, 374
 and spatial scores, 374

Tomboys. *See* Sex-atypical children

Toys. *See* Gendered environments

Training mother, 251

Transfer RNA. *See* Ribonucleic acid

Transmitter substances, 132. *See also* Acetylcholine; Adenosine; Dopamine; Endorphins; GABA; Glutamate; Norepine-phrine; Scrotonin

X linkage of, 119

Transsexuals, 227, 229

Trial and error learning, 249. *See also* Operant conditioning

Trivers, R., 77–80

Turner's syndrome, 97, 112–117, 155, 398

Type A characteristics, 381

Typical versus ideal gender stereotypes, 270

U

Ultimate cause, 60

Undifferentiated people, 43

Unipolar disorder, 368. *See also* Depression

V

Validity:
 definition of, 32–34
 of hormone studies, 129–130
 sex differences in, 35–36
 of sex-role scales, 45–49

Variability:
 in biological factors, 16–17
 calculation of, 50
 sex differences in, 35

Variable, 50. *See also* Dependent variable; Independent variable

Ventromedial area of the hypothalamus, 133, 134, 145, 159, 181, 386

Verbal stimulation, sex dif-

ferences in, 301

Verbal tasks, sex differences in, 372–373, 391, 397–398

Vertical associations in categories, 268

Vesicles, 132

Viruses, 66–67, 72–74

Visual cortex, 225, 226

VMH. *See* ventromedial area of the hypothalamus

W

Wife abuse, 352–353, 356

Wiggins's curcumplex model of personality, 339–341, 346, 350

Wolffian structures, 154–155, 156

Work values, 318

Wrangham's theory of social structures, 241–243

X

X chromosome, 95, 97–98

X-inactivation, 103–105

X-linkage, 369

X-linked genes, 98–101, 107–108, 108–111, 119–123

X-linked motor dystrophy, 119

Y

Y chromosome, 70, 95, 97–98

Y-linked genes, 98–101, 105–107, 117–119

Yanomano, 239